KB087307

만점 적중

수능
듣기

모의고사
35회

만점 적중 수능 듣기 모의고사 35회

지은이 소원석, 김문철, 황선용, 강형만
       전길수, 최은영, 육상태, 장정근
펴낸이 임상진
펴낸곳 (주)넥서스

출판신고 1992년 4월 3일 제311-2002-2호 ⑥
10880 경기도 파주시 지목로 5
Tel (02)330-5500 Fax (02)330-5555

ISBN 979-11-5752-670-3 53740

출판사의 허락 없이 내용의 일부를
인용하거나 발췌하는 것을 금합니다.

가격은 뒤표지에 있습니다.
잘못 만들어진 책은 구입처에서 바꾸어 드립니다.

www.nexusEDU.kr
NEXUS Edu는 넥서스의 초·중·고 학습물 전문 브랜드입니다.

만점 적중

수능
영어영역
듣기평가 대비

수능
듣기
모의고사
35회

소원석·김문철·황선용·강형만
전길수·최은영·육상태·장정근

NEXUS Edu

이 책의 구성

듣기 모의고사 35회

- 각 회당 17문항, 총 35회의 수능 듣기 대비 모의고사로 구성하였습니다.
- 평가원 출제 방침에 맞춰 최신 수능 듣기 출제 경향과 문제 유형을 철저하게 반영하였습니다.
- 각 회에 삽입된 QR 코드를 활용하여 언제 어디서든 MP3를 듣고 학습할 수 있습니다.

DICTATION

- 듣기 능력 향상을 위한 DICTATION(받아쓰기) 코너입니다.
- 문제 풀이만 하는 학습에서 벗어나 능동적인 듣기 학습을 위해 빈칸을 받아 적고 완성합니다.
- 반복하여 들으면서 핵심 어휘와 주요 표현들을 따라 말하는 Shadowing 학습을 할 수 있습니다.

정답 및 해설

- 각 회당 정답, 해석, 해설, 어휘, Dictation 정답이 수록되어 있습니다.
- 정확한 해석과 상세한 해설을 제시하여 문제를 쉽게 이해하고 복습하도록 구성하였습니다.
- 문제를 푸는 데 필요한 중요한 어휘 및 표현들이 알맞게 정리되어 있습니다.

듣기 MP3 & 휴대용 어휘 암기 리스트
www.nexusbook.com에서 무료 다운로드

- 본 책의 듣기 대본 MP3 파일 제공
- 수능 듣기 빈출 표현 완전 정복을 위한 휴대용 어휘 암기 리스트 제공

목차

1번부터 17번까지는 듣고 답하는 문제입니다. 1번부터 15번까지는 한 번만 들려주고, 16번부터 17번까지는 두 번 들려줍니다. 방송을 잘 듣고 답을 하시기 바랍니다.

01 대화를 듣고, 여자의 마지막 말에 대한 남자의 응답으로 가장 적절한 것을 고르시오.

① I'm glad you enjoyed it.
② I know where the bathroom is.
③ Come for dinner again any time.
④ I can't wait! My mouth is watering!
⑤ You're too kind. It was nothing really.

02 대화를 듣고, 남자의 마지막 말에 대한 여자의 응답으로 가장 적절한 것을 고르시오.

① What time should I be there?
② Why did you move to the new place?
③ I'm so busy that I don't have the time.
④ I'll give you some information about the party.
⑤ I'd better go to the restaurant first right before the party.

03 다음을 듣고, 남자가 하는 말의 목적으로 가장 적절한 것을 고르시오.

① 내일 날씨를 알려 주려고
② 견학 시 준비물을 전달하려고
③ 견학 시 주의 사항을 전달하려고
④ 견학이 연기되었음을 알려 주려고
⑤ 정상 수업이 취소되었음을 알려 주려고

04 대화를 듣고, 여자의 의견으로 가장 적절한 것을 고르시오.

① 삼각대 없이 찍은 야경치고는 멋지다.
② 신혼여행에서 남는 것은 사진밖에 없다.
③ 야경을 찍을 때 삼각대가 꼭 필요한 것은 아니다.
④ 신혼여행에 제대로 된 삼각대를 가져갔어야 한다.
⑤ 사진보다 중요한 것은 마음속으로 기억하는 것이다.

05 대화를 듣고, 두 사람의 관계를 가장 잘 나타낸 것을 고르시오.

① teacher - student
② father - daughter
③ driver - passenger
④ photographer - model
⑤ film director - actress

06 대화를 듣고, 그림에서 대화의 내용과 일치하지 않는 것을 고르시오.

07 대화를 듣고, 여자가 남자를 위해 할 일로 가장 적절한 것을 고르시오.

① 그림 그리기
② 점심 준비하기
③ 보고서 제출하기
④ 보고서 타이프 치기
⑤ 과학 실험 도와주기

08 대화를 듣고, 남자의 기분이 좋지 않은 이유를 고르시오.

① 기말고사를 잘 못 봐서
② 보고서 기한을 몰라서
③ 영문학 보고서 성적이 나빠서
④ 학급 친구가 도움을 주지 않아서
⑤ 교수님이 자신을 오해하고 있어서

09 대화를 듣고, 여자가 지불해야 할 금액을 고르시오. [3점]

① $27　　　② $45　　　③ $72

④ $75　　　⑤ $80

10 대화를 듣고, 태풍 샌디에 관해 두 사람이 언급하지 <u>않은</u> 것을 고르시오.

① 미국 내 피해 범위
② 태풍 대비 방법
③ 폭풍 해일이 뉴욕을 강타한 시점
④ 뉴욕의 피해 상황
⑤ 심각한 피해 지역

11 giant panda에 대한 다음 내용을 듣고, 일치하지 <u>않는</u> 것을 고르시오. [3점]

① 눈, 귀, 몸에 전반적으로 검은 반점이 있다.
② 원래 중국 중서부와 남서부가 서식지이다.
③ 대나무 이외에 다른 것은 먹지 않는다.
④ 인공적인 개발 등에 의해 원래 살던 터전을 빼앗겼다.
⑤ 너무 게을러서 번식이 쉽지 않다.

12 다음 표를 보면서 대화를 듣고, 두 사람이 보기로 한 영화의 시작 시간을 고르시오.

NEXUS CINEMA

Madagascar 4	Die Hard 7	Spiderman 5
13:00	15:00	14:00
15:30	② 17:30	16:30
① 18:00	③ 20:00	④ 19:00
20:30		⑤ 21:30

13 대화를 듣고, 여자의 마지막 말에 대한 남자의 응답으로 가장 적절한 것을 고르시오.

Man : _____

① There's one in the overhead rack.
② That's above your duty-free limit.
③ Please go to the boarding gate right now.
④ Your reservation is automatically confirmed.
⑤ OK. I will pay the 10% deposit by credit card.

14 대화를 듣고, 남자의 마지막 말에 대한 여자의 응답으로 가장 적절한 것을 고르시오. [3점]

Woman : _____

① I'm sorry. I've got a prior engagement.
② Thanks. I'll be there within half an hour.
③ Not to worry. We'll reschedule for another time.
④ I totally forgot we had an appointment yesterday.
⑤ Could I make an appointment for tomorrow morning?

15 다음 상황 설명을 듣고, Grace가 Will에게 할 말로 가장 적절한 것을 고르시오.

Grace : Will, _____

① please eat something.
② will you lend me some money?
③ will you help me do my homework?
④ will you join the Alpine Club with me?
⑤ please teach me how to play computer games.

[16-17] 다음을 듣고, 물음에 답하시오.

16 남자가 하는 말의 목적으로 가장 적절한 것은?

① to warn young people of alopecia
② to discuss the danger of alopecia
③ to suggest the way of growing hair
④ to advise the way of maintaining your healthy hair
⑤ to give some information about what causes alopecia

17 alopecia의 원인으로 언급되지 <u>않은</u> 것은?

① 스트레스
② 강제적으로 머리 잡아당기기
③ 지속적인 머리 땋기
④ 뜨거운 헤어 아이론으로 머리 다듬기
⑤ 철분 결핍

DICTATION(받아쓰기) 코너입니다.
녹음의 내용을 잘 듣고, 빈칸에 알맞은 말을 쓰시기 바랍니다.

01

W I'm making spaghetti. I hope you like it.
M Mmm... It smells really good. I'm all _____.
W It'll be ready in 10 minutes.
M _____

02

M Lisa, I was wondering if you have time this Saturday.
W Yes, I'm free this Saturday.
M Good! I'm going to _____.
   Could you come with your husband?
W _____

03

M Hello, everyone. This is about the field trip scheduled for tomorrow. _____, we are expecting heavy rainfall with severe thunderstorms tomorrow morning. The faculty members have decided to delay the field trip until next Friday. Please _____ this amended announcement and do not prepare for the field trip tomorrow. Repeat! Tomorrow's field trip is postponed to next Friday due to expected bad weather. Students should come to school normally. Even if the weather is fine tomorrow, regular classes will be continued. Thank you for listening.

04

W Where did you take those pictures?
M I took them on my honeymoon in France.
W Yeah, I can see that. You look really happy in the pictures.
M They are _____, though.
W A little bit. But they are not so bad.
M I should have checked my tripod before the honeymoon. It was broken while taking pictures at night.
W The night scene still looks fantastic.
M Thanks. It was really terrific. I feel awful that I couldn't _____ well.
W You remember the scene in your mind, though. That's the point!

05

M Hey, Beth, what is the matter with you?
W Sorry, sir.
M This is your third mistake. Did you _____ correctly?
W Yes, I did. I don't know why I keep forgetting. Maybe I need more sleep.
M Why? How many hours did you sleep yesterday?
W I slept only three hours. My schedule was quite tight.
M Everybody, listen. We will resume this scene after a thirty-minute break.
W Thank you, sir.
M Please, _____. You are the main character. Without your smooth speech, we can't make a good film.
W I'm very sorry. I will do my best not to make a mistake again.

06

(Telephone rings.)

W Hello, Sam. It's Amanda.

M Hey, Amanda. What's up?

W I'm wondering about the costume party you had yesterday _____. How many kids came to the party?

M About 12. It was hectic but fun.

W Wow. My kids and I should have been there. What did your kids wear?

M Well, Tom was Superman, so he _____ and a large "S" on his chest.

W How about your daughter?

M She adores Snow White these days. So she had a red ribbon in her hair.

W Did she wear a typical blue and yellow dress for Snow White?

M Of course! But she _____ for Snow White. She was so excited and walking around barefoot.

W How cute!

07

M Lynn, could you do me a favor?

W Sure, what is it?

M I have two things that I have to finish before tomorrow morning. One is my paper for science class, and the other is drawing a painting for art class.

W Oh, you have _____. So, what are you going to do?

M I've finished writing my paper by hand, but I have no time to type it up.

W So you want me to type your paper for you?

M No, I want you to draw a picture for me. I know you are a much better artist than I am.

W Oh, no. I don't think that's a good idea. You'd better draw the painting yourself. I will do the other work for you.

M You're right. I'll _____ later.

08

W James, are you doing all right? You don't look so well today.

M You are right. I'm _____ today.

W Why? What's gotten into you?

M I got an "F" on my final report in English literature.

W Really? You studied English literature a lot. I thought there _____ about getting an "A" in it.

M I thought so, too. But I handed in my paper too late. Professor Kim didn't accept it.

W Professor Kim is very strict about deadlines. Why didn't you hand it in on time?

M I thought I had my paper in my bag. But when I was about to hand it in, I realized that I had left it on my desk at home.

W Why didn't you _____ Professor Kim to accept your paper although it was late?

M I tried, but he said there could be no exceptions to the rule.

W Wow. I'm sorry to hear it!

09

M Hello. How may I help you, ma'am?

W I'm _____ for my husband.

M Do you have any particular shirt in mind?

W I want a dress shirt that will go well with his black suit.

M Here is a blue dress shirt. Blue dress shirts are in vogue. They are $30 each.

W _____. I'll take it. How about pink? Do you have it?

M Sure, here it is. You will like this color.

W God, this Indian pink is really great. How much is it?

M It's $50.

W That's quite pricey, but I will take it, too. I have a 10% discount coupon. Can I _____?

M Sure, but only for the pink one and not the blue one.

W Okay. I got it.

M Do you want it gift-wrapped?

W Yes, please.

10

M Hi, I'm Mike from ABC Newspaper.

W _____ to meet you. I'll explain Hurricane Sandy today. Any questions?

M Thank you. First of all, please tell me about the affected places in the USA.

W Sandy affected at least 24 states from Florida to Maine and west to Michigan and Wisconsin.

M Which parts were severely damaged?

W New Jersey and New York.

M When did its storm surge hit New York City?

W It hit there on October 29.

M Please _____ about damage to New York City.

W Sandy flooded streets, tunnels, and subway lines, and cut power in and around the city.

11

W Have you ever heard of giant pandas? You can easily _____ because they have large, distinctive black patches around their eyes, over their ears, and across their body. They are native to central-western and south-western China. Farming, deforestation, and other development led the giant pandas to be driven out of the lowland areas where they once lived. They mostly eat bamboo. In the wild, they often eat eggs or insects for protein. Meanwhile, the giant pandas _____, similar to sloths. So it's uncommon for them to breed.

12

M I'm really bored, Jenny. _____ go to a movie?

W Sounds good. What's playing at the NEXUS Cinema?

M It has *Madagascar 4*, *Die Hard 7*, and *Spiderman 5*.

W Well, what do you want to see?

M I don't like animated series. So, let's forget *Madagascar 4*.

W OK. I don't like animations, either. Then, what do you want to see between *Die Hard 7* and *Spiderman 5*? I heard that *Spiderman 5* is very interesting.

M The Spiderman series uses too many computer graphics. So, it doesn't look so real.

W Do you want to see *Die Hard 7*?

M Yes, the Die Hard series has _____. And Bruce Willis is still pretty cool.

W OK. Let's go and see *Die Hard 7*. It's already 6. Then, we have only one choice.

M That's right.

13

M Hi, I'd like to make a reservation for the May 4th flight to New York.

W I'm sorry, but that flight _____.

M What about the day before, May 3rd?

W That flight is still open. It leaves at 1:40 pm, and you must be at the airport at least two hours before the scheduled departure time.

M All right. I will take that flight.

W Which class would you like? Economy, business, or first class?

M Business class, please. How do I _____?

W We need a 10% deposit now and the balance no later than two weeks before the departure date.

M _____

14

(Telephone rings.)

M Hello. How may I help you?

W Good morning, Dr. Hong. Could I make an appointment for today?

M Let me see. Would 5:50 this afternoon be OK?

W Couldn't you make it _____? My son has developed a strange rash on his face.

M Sorry, but I'm fully booked this afternoon.

W Please help me. It's an emergency.

M Then, how about bringing your son to see my colleague, Dr. Baldwin?

W So, could I come in now?

M _____ while I check with him. (pause) Yes, everything is clear. He'll see your son as soon as you arrive.

W _____

15

W Grace and Will are twins at the same high school. Grace is a very _____ person, but Will is not. Most of the time, Will plays computer games at home. Playing computer games is not just a hobby in his free time. He shows the tendency to get addicted to it. He is up at night playing games and barely eats at home. As a result, his health is declining rapidly. Also, he doesn't do well in school. Their parents worry a lot about their son. So, they talk about the problem to his teachers and school counselor. They come to a conclusion that what Will most needs is to go out with his friends and _____.
They think his sister Grace will be greatly helpful to him and ask her for help. In this situation, what would Grace most likely say to Will?

Grace Will, _____

16-17

M Let's talk about alopecia today. Have you ever heard of this term, alopecia? This term might be a bit unfamiliar to you, but it means _____ from your head and body. It is natural for you to lose your hair while getting older. However, if you start seriously losing hair in your twenties or thirties, you would get stressed a lot. Then, what causes alopecia? First of all, when you _____, you can lose your hair. Hairstyling routines such as tight ponytails or braids are known to cause irreversible hair loss. This is called traction alopecia. Alopecia can also be caused by hot hair irons. Sometimes, iron deficiency _____ alopecia.

1번부터 17번까지는 듣고 답하는 문제입니다. 1번부터 15번까지는 한 번만 들려주고, 16번부터 17번까지는 두 번 들려줍니다. 방송을 잘 듣고 답을 하시기 바랍니다.

01 대화를 듣고, 여자의 마지막 말에 대한 남자의 응답으로 가장 적절한 것을 고르시오.

① Can I borrow your report?
② I have another report to finish.
③ Because I don't know her very well.
④ I don't think it's possible. She is very strict.
⑤ I don't want to extend the length of my report.

02 대화를 듣고, 남자의 마지막 말에 대한 여자의 응답으로 가장 적절한 것을 고르시오.

① I have no idea who Emily is.
② I cannot agree with you more.
③ Yes. She has a good sense in fashion.
④ Transferring to a new school can be a challenge.
⑤ I have known her since I was in elementary school.

03 다음을 듣고, 남자가 하는 말의 주제로 가장 적절한 것을 고르시오.

① 논술의 필요성
② 전문적인 작가의 삶
③ 올바른 문법의 중요성
④ 성공적인 논술을 위한 절차
⑤ 논술 전 심층적인 연구의 필요성

04 대화를 듣고, 여자의 의견으로 가장 적절한 것을 고르시오.

① 지나친 수면은 사람을 둔하게 만든다.
② 시험 전날에는 충분한 수면을 취해야 한다.
③ 평상시와 똑같은 생체리듬을 유지해야 한다.
④ 시험 전에는 영양가 있는 음식을 먹어야 한다.
⑤ 잘 못하는 과목을 시험 전날 공부하는 것이 좋다.

05 대화를 듣고, 두 사람의 관계를 가장 잘 나타낸 것을 고르시오.

① teacher − student
② car dealer − customer
③ police officer − driver
④ driving test supervisor − driving testee
⑤ auto insurance agent − insurance buyer

06 대화를 듣고, 그림에서 대화의 내용과 일치하지 <u>않는</u> 것을 고르시오.

07 대화를 듣고, 남자가 여자에게 부탁한 일로 가장 적절한 것을 고르시오.

① 지원 대학 선별하기
② 유학 경험 수기 써 주기
③ 유학 안내 책자 구해주기
④ 대학 지원 추천서 써 주기
⑤ 대학 입시 설명회 참석하기

08 대화를 듣고, 남자가 실망한 이유를 고르시오.

① 축구 대회에서 졌기 때문에
② 골프 경기가 취소되었기 때문에
③ 일기예보가 맞지 않았기 때문에
④ 체육대회가 연기될 수 있기 때문에
⑤ 다른 행사 때문에 체육대회에 참여할 수 없기 때문에

09 대화를 듣고, 남자가 지불할 금액을 고르시오. [3점]

① $25   ② $30   ③ $50

④ $55   ⑤ $60

10 대화를 듣고, 남자가 구입할 물건으로 언급되지 않은 것을 고르시오.

① 휴지   ② 과일   ③ 넥타이

④ 와이셔츠   ⑤ 지갑

11 sneeze에 관한 다음 내용을 듣고, 일치하지 않는 것을 고르시오.

① 기침과 재채기는 비슷한 이유로 발생한다.

② 재채기는 참으면 세균이 몸 안으로 더 깊이 들어갈 수 있다.

③ 재채기를 참으면 고막에 손상을 줄 수도 있다.

④ 코끝을 꼬집으면 재채기가 멈추기도 한다.

⑤ 기침과 재채기는 참을 수 있다.

12 다음 표를 보면서 대화를 듣고, 두 사람이 탈 놀이기구를 고르시오.

	Attraction	Height Restriction	Thrill Scale 1 (low)→5 (high)	Type
①	Cliff Hanger	150cm	5	extreme thrill ride, drop tower
②	Haunted House	110cm	3	dark ride with many ghosts * Do not enter if you have a heart condition.
③	Transformer	none	2	4D-theatrical presentation with moving seats
④	The Big Flush	130cm	3	water ride
⑤	Carousel	none	1	family ride

13 대화를 듣고, 남자의 마지막 말에 대한 여자의 응답으로 가장 적절한 것을 고르시오.

Woman : _____

① Yes. Now everybody speaks English.

② Sure. We speak English all day. That's my secret.

③ I think that he's still having difficulty living here.

④ Sometimes. But he has greatly improved his English.

⑤ Yes. Fortunately I got a teaching position at a college.

14 대화를 듣고, 여자의 마지막 말에 대한 남자의 응답으로 가장 적절한 것을 고르시오. [3점]

Man : _____

① In that case, you'd better give him up.

② Then, you are not supposed to ask him out.

③ Yeah, it is always difficult to find Mr. Right.

④ Then, what are you waiting for? You should approach him first.

⑤ You should consider his character first before you ask him out.

15 다음 상황 설명을 듣고, Brian이 Andy에게 할 말로 가장 적절한 것을 고르시오. [3점]

Brian : Andy! _____

① Shoot the ball.

② Intercept his pass.

③ Grab the rebound.

④ Throw the ball over here.

⑤ Block the ball right there.

[16-17] 다음을 듣고, 물음에 답하시오.

16 여자가 하는 말의 목적으로 가장 적절한 것은?

① 도서관 운영시간을 공지하려고

② 시간제 일자리 추천을 의뢰하려고

③ 시의 독서 장려 프로그램을 소개하려고

④ 시간제 일자리 지원 방법을 안내하려고

⑤ 도서관 개관 행사에 자원봉사자를 모집하려고

17 Calgary Library에 관한 내용과 일치하지 않는 것은?

① 저녁 6시에 문을 닫는다.

② 초등학생만 이용 가능한 초등학생 전용 도서관이다.

③ 초등학생 대상의 방과 후 수업 프로그램을 운영할 것이다.

④ 프로그램 도우미 고등학생에게 시간당 $9를 지급한다.

⑤ 주말에도 프로그램에 참여 가능한 도우미를 구하고 있다.

DICTATION(받아쓰기) 코너입니다.
녹음의 내용을 잘 듣고, 빈칸에 알맞은 말을 쓰시기 바랍니다.

01

W Did you finish your report?

M Not yet. I have a long way to go. I'm afraid I can't finish it by tomorrow.

W Why don't you visit Professor Lee and _____ _____?

M _____

02

M What do you think of the new student?

W Are you talking about Emily who _____ _____ last week?

M Yeah, she certainly has passion and enthusiasm for everything she does, doesn't she?

W _____

03

M Do you want to make your essay be more professional? Then follow these steps, and you will find that your next formal writing project could be your best. First, _____ and then do in-depth research. Research is necessary not only for the development of your arguments, but also for creating an original piece of writing. Second, after profound research, write the first draft with an objective tone. Then, bring your first draft to your teacher or peers and get it edited. Third, after revising your drafts several times, proofread your final draft. Remember _____ because your final version of paper should be error-free in terms of grammar and structure.

04

M I'll take a university entrance exam tomorrow.

W Right. Tomorrow is the big day. You must be very nervous.

M Yeah, actually I'm afraid that I cannot answer all of the questions within the limited time.

W Don't worry. You can do it. You _____ _____ tonight. Taking a good rest is really important.

M But I don't think it's possible. I think I'm too nervous to go to sleep.

W No, you shouldn't do that. Some people say you have to sleep as usual, but I don't agree with that.

M Why?

W If you don't sleep enough, _____ after eating lunch.

M Really? Actually, I was planning to study history, which I'm poor at.

W Sleep will improve your memory, so just go to bed now.

05

M Are you Ms. Kim?

W Yes, I am. And you are...?

M James White. I'll be with you _____.

W Oh, hi, Mr. White. Now, what am I supposed to do?

M All you have to do is get in the insured vehicle with me and go around the neighborhood.

W Sounds like it's very simple.

M While you're driving, I'll check to see if you follow _____.

W I see. I'm very nervous.

M After you finish driving, I'll decide whether you pass or fail. Now, are you ready?

W Yes, I am. I hope I can pass this time.

M Now, let's get in the car and begin.

06

W Mr. Kim, which one is your daughter, Mary?

M She's over there, doing some exercise.

W Exercise? Oh, she's jump roping with her friends in the middle of the playground, isn't she?

M No, she is _____ in front of the net.

W Oh, I see. Her friend will receive the ball on the opposite side.

M Right. Ms. Lee, where are your boys?

W My boys are over there on the basketball court.

M There are a few kids there. Which ones are your sons?

W One is holding a basketball right now, and the other is _____. He just dunked.

M Wow, he is a very good player. You must be proud of him.

W Yes, indeed. Thank you.

07

M Mrs. Song, could I talk to you for a minute?

W Sure. _____ here.

M Thanks. It's warm and quiet here.

W Yes, it is. So, what can I do for you?

M Well, I'm going to apply for college in the United States.

W Really? _____ are you interested in?

M I'm thinking about some state universities in the midwest.

W Interesting! I studied at Colorado State University, which is located there.

M Then you might give me some information about the colleges in that area.

W Sure. Climate, transportation, campus, tuition, or whatever.

M Thanks. And I wonder if you could write a letter of recommendation for me.

W Of course. It would be my pleasure. You were _____ _____.

08

W What's up?

M According to this schedule, our sports event _____ _____ next Saturday.

W Yeah. Are you looking forward to it?

M Sure, I am. You know I like sports a lot. Next Saturday will be "my day."

W What sports do you like most?

M I like golf and skiing most, but what _____ __ is soccer.

W Sounds like you're an all-around sportsman.

M Everybody says that.

W But the event might be postponed or cancelled, because it will possibly rain next Saturday.

M Really? That's bad news for me. That's discouraging.

W Don't give up too soon. You know, the weather forecast is _____.

09

W Hello, this is ABC Courier Service. May I help you?

M Yes. I'd like to use your courier service now.

W Sure. What is your location?

M I'm in Fort Collins, and I'm going to _____ _____ to Boulder and Greenville.

W What kind of things are they?

M Actually, they're two packs of documents, one for Boulder and the other for Greenville.

W All right. It will be $25 for Boulder and $30 for Greenville.

M What? I don't understand why the delivery to Greenville is more expensive.

W The distance to Greenville is farther than to Boulder.

M No, it's _____ from here, Fort Collins.

W Oh, I'm sorry. Maybe I'm mistaken. I'll make the cost $25 for each.

M Thanks. My name is Pete Baker, and my cell phone number is 970-292-0688.

10

M I'm going to A-Mart now. Do you need me to buy anything for you?

W Well, I think we've _____.

M Toilet paper. Okay, anything else?

W And I'd like to eat some fruit.

M Sure. Several kinds of fruits are in season now.

W But what are you going to A-Mart for?

M Oh, I'm going to _____ for Ted. His birthday is tomorrow.

W Ted? Who's Ted?

M Don't you remember? He's one of the colleagues who helped me a lot with my project.

W I remember him. So, what are you going to buy for him?

M I'm thinking of a tie and a dress shirt. He likes to dress formally.

W I see. Don't forget to _____.

11

M Do you think whether it is bad for you to _____ _____ or not? Let's find out. The cause of sneezing is similar to that of coughing. Sneezing is one of the body's ways of getting rid of our things that ought not to be there such as viruses and dust. If you hold a sneeze, it can also cause _____ _____ to build up in your head and can drive germs deep into the sinuses or ear canals, causing infections. That pressure can damage delicate eardrums. Of course, there are times when it's impolite or embarrassing to let out a loud "Achoo!" At such times, _____ the top of your nose at the first tingle of an oncoming sneeze. This will help you stop it. Coughing cannot be held back but sneezing can be.

12

M Wow, we're finally here.

W Look, there are so many rides, and I can't choose which one we should go on first. How about you?

M They all look exciting and fun to me. How about starting with Transformer?

W I _____ because of carsickness. I think the 4D screen and moving seats will make me feel dizzier. So, I would rather start with Haunted House. What do you think?

M Haunted House is a scary ride. I'm afraid of ghosts. I cannot stand those rides.

W Okay, then why don't we ride Cliff Hanger?

M I want to save that ride for the last. And the carousel _____.

W I got it. I know what you want to ride. Let's go. The clock is ticking.

13

M Ms. Jeon, you speak English like a native.

W Thank you _____.

M What is your secret?

W As a matter of fact, I lived abroad for a long time.

M Really! How long did you live in a foreign country?

W Well, I lived in the States for about ten years. Particularly, I _____ in America.

M Wow, no wonder you speak English fluently!

W In addition, I got married to a Canadian, a native speaker of English.

M It couldn't be better. So, do you talk to your husband in English?

W _____

14

M Sarah, what are you so obsessed with?

W Oh, Paul. I am _____.

M About what? Tell me. What are friends for?

W Well, there's this guy on the campus who I think is my type.

M So you finally found your Mr. Right!

W Yeah, I think so. I want to _____ on a date, but I'm not sure if he will like me or not.

M What is his character like? Is he an extrovert or introvert?

W Why do you ask me such a question?

M Because guys are apt to be attracted by a lady who has an opposite tendency. For example, a guy who is outgoing like me is fascinated by a quiet woman, and a quiet guy is attracted by a woman who makes the first move.

W Oh, is it? I think he is _____ of person from you.

M _____

15

M Brian and Andy are close friends. Particularly, they _____. So they often have a game with other friends. However, Brian finds that Andy always makes his own plays. When he needs to pass the ball, he won't do it, trying to _____. That annoys Brian. Now they are having a basketball game at lunchtime. Again Andy dribbles and tries to shoot the ball, not passing it to Brian. However, Brian is _____ to shoot. In this situation, what would Brian most likely say to Andy?

Brian Andy! _____

16-17

(Beep)

W Hello, Principal Skinner! This is Andrea Kim, chief librarian of Calgary Public Library. I couldn't reach you, so I am _____. As we start a new after-school program, "How to Write a Fairy Tale" for elementary school kids, we are looking for high school students who _____. The students will take care of various activities such as assisting kids with general questions, tutoring for basic writing skills, and arranging stuff after every class. Salary is $9 per hour, and working schedule will be negotiated, but weekend hours could be included. If you know any qualified students for the position, please _____ by 6 pm, which is the closing time of our library. Thank you.

1번부터 17번까지는 듣고 답하는 문제입니다. 1번부터 15번까지는 한 번만 들려주고, 16번부터 17번까지는 두 번 들려줍니다. 방송을 잘 듣고 답을 하시기 바랍니다.

01 대화를 듣고, 여자의 마지막 말에 대한 남자의 응답으로 가장 적절한 것을 고르시오.

① Are you going up?
② No! I'm late. I have to hurry up.
③ Well, it'll take about 40 minutes.
④ Sorry, it's a secret between you and me.
⑤ You don't have to thank me. It's my job.

02 대화를 듣고, 남자의 마지막 말에 대한 여자의 응답으로 가장 적절한 것을 고르시오.

① What do you need?
② No, I'm not ready. Let's delay our trip.
③ Me, too. It will be very interesting to play at the beach.
④ Oh, that's OK. We can buy those on the way to the beach.
⑤ Okay, what about drinks? We don't want to be thirsty, do we?

03 다음을 듣고, 남자가 하는 말의 목적으로 가장 적절한 것을 고르시오.

① 여름 방학 계획을 물어보려고
② 여름 활동 프로그램을 홍보하려고
③ 여름 활동 프로그램의 효과에 대해 논의하려고
④ 여름 활동 프로그램의 장점과 단점을 알려주려고
⑤ 여름 활동 프로그램에 참가할 수 있는 자격 요건을 알려주려고

04 대화를 듣고 여자의 의견으로 가장 적절한 것을 고르시오.

① 늘 새로운 요리를 시도해 보는 것이 좋다.
② 요리를 할 때에는 옆에서 도와주어야 한다.
③ 음식이 완성되기 전에 맛보는 것은 바람직하지 않다.
④ 양파, 마늘, 고추를 많이 사용하는 것이 좋다.
⑤ 음식을 만들 때에는 좋은 재료로 정성껏 만들어야 한다.

05 대화를 듣고, 두 사람의 관계를 가장 잘 나타낸 것을 고르시오.

① customer - teller
② guest - hotel staff
③ customer - cashier
④ employer - employee
⑤ resident - security guard

06 대화를 듣고, 그림에서 대화의 내용과 일치하지 <u>않는</u> 것을 고르시오.

07 대화를 듣고, 남자가 할 일로 가장 적절한 것을 고르시오.

① 벌금을 내기
② 회의에 참석하기
③ 은행에 가기
④ GPS 사러 가기
⑤ 경찰서에 가기

08 대화를 듣고, 여자가 점원이 추천한 물건을 사기로 한 이유를 고르시오.

① 무늬가 산뜻해서
② 할인 행사를 하고 있어서
③ 이불과 무난하게 어울릴 것 같아서
④ 집에 있는 이불과 사이즈가 딱 맞아서
⑤ 제일 최근에 나온 신상품이라 세련되어서

09 대화를 듣고, 남자가 지불해야 할 금액을 고르시오. [3점]

① $800   ② $900   ③ $1,000

④ $1,200   ⑤ $1,400

10 다음 대화를 듣고, 남자가 사야 할 물건이 <u>아닌</u> 것을 고르시오.

① 정장   ② 신발   ③ 와이셔츠

④ 서류가방   ⑤ 넥타이

11 dream에 관한 다음 내용을 듣고, 일치하지 <u>않는</u> 것을 고르시오. [3점]

① 정신 질환을 겪는 사람을 제외한 모든 사람이 꿈을 꾼다.
② 꿈을 꾸지 않는 것이 아니라 기억하지 못하는 것이다.
③ 가끔 실제로 보지 못하는 얼굴을 보기도 한다.
④ 꿈에서는 부정적인 감정을 더 많이 경험한다.
⑤ 남자가 여자보다 공격적인 감정을 더 많이 느낀다.

12 다음 자료를 보면서 대화를 듣고, 남자가 중고차를 구입하러 갈 곳을 고르시오.

Used Car Price Search Results
Make: GM / Model: BM 5 / Class: Deluxe

	Shop	Price	Mileage (km)	Option	Year
①	SM Encar	$3,000	29,000	-	2011
②	Bobae Dream	$2,800	26,000	Airbag	2009
③	Car for You	$2,500	28,000	ABS	2008
④	Car PR	$2,200	50,000	ABS	2008
⑤	Car Mart	$2,000	60,000	Airbag	2007

13 대화를 듣고, 남자의 마지막 말에 대한 여자의 응답으로 가장 적절한 것을 고르시오. [3점]

Woman : _____

① Don't touch my tooth.
② You are such a brave man.
③ I promise. Open your mouth.
④ Will I need to take time off work?
⑤ Why do I have so many cavities?

14 대화를 듣고, 여자의 마지막 말에 대한 남자의 응답으로 가장 적절한 것을 고르시오.

Man : _____

① Thank you, I can't wait.
② It's none of your business.
③ Don't worry. We have enough time.
④ I'm sorry. I've got a prior engagement.
⑤ Thanks. I'll be at Yongpyong by 11 o'clock tomorrow.

15 다음 상황 설명을 듣고, Michael이 아버지에게 할 말로 가장 적절한 것을 고르시오.

Michael : Dad, _____

① I'm not a very good person.
② I won't wash your car. Don't ask me.
③ the assignment was very easy to handle.
④ I'm sorry. Please forgive me for what I did.
⑤ I was not really busy. Why didn't you ask me?

[16-17] 다음을 듣고, 물음에 답하시오.

16 남자가 하는 말의 목적으로 가장 적절한 것은?

① to suggest a new way of life
② to inform people about diabetes
③ to tell how to prevent adult obesity
④ to advise how to deal with childhood obesity
⑤ to give some information about childhood obesity

17 childhood obesity에 관해서 본문에서 언급되지 <u>않은</u> 것은?

① 5세 이하 420만 명의 어린이가 비만이다.
② 대부분 비만인 어린이는 부유한 나라에 살고 있다.
③ 비만인 아이들은 성인이 되어서도 비만인 경향이 있다.
④ 비만인 아이들은 당뇨와 심장혈관 질환에 걸릴 확률이 더 많다.
⑤ 건강하지 않은 음식과 운동 부족이 원인 중 하나이다.

DICTATION(받아쓰기) 코너입니다.
녹음의 내용을 잘 듣고, 빈칸에 알맞은 말을 쓰시기 바랍니다.

01

W Excuse me, what happened?

M This elevator _____. Why don't you take the stairs?

W Thank you for telling me. How long will it take to fix it?

M _____

02

M Hi, Julie! How about _____ with me today?

W Beach? Sounds great! What do I have to bring?

M Swimsuits, sunglasses, a cap, and sunscreen. I think that's all.

W _____

03

M Do you have a special plan on this summer vacation? If you don't, please pay attention to this. We provide you with summer activity programs. The programs will _____ for you to have a wonderful experience during the summer. You can learn and experience through challenging academic and social activities. The activities include swimming, tennis, team sports, creative writing, performing arts, computer technology, and visual arts. All the activities are designed to satisfy students from different age groups. We also _____ leading a wide variety of challenging and fun activities.

04

M Hey, something smells good. What are you cooking?

W I'm making omelets. I hope you like them.

M You cooked the same thing the other day, didn't you?

W This is a new recipe.

M Can I try a bit now? I promise not to eat too much.

W Only if _____ that frying pan over there, and then wait. It's still not cooked properly.

M Okay. Wow, what has this sauce got in it?

W A little bit of this and that. I fried some onions and garlic together with olive oil, then ground in some red pepper, and left it to cook.

M Red pepper? It doesn't seem to match with omelets.

W It's _____ the same dish, isn't it?

05

M How much do I owe you?

W Your total comes to $49.

M Here is $50. Well then, could you _____ to my apartment?

W Sorry, sir. We only deliver for orders above $50.

M If that's the case, I will add this battery. Then, how much would the total be?

W The battery is $1.50. The total would then come to $50.50. We can now deliver to your apartment.

M When can I receive this? I won't be home for an hour.

W We will make the delivery an hour from now. Please write your address and phone number down. Here is the receipt.

M Thank you.

W _____.

06

(Telephone rings.)

W Hello, Bill.

M Hello, Grace. Are you coming home? We're waiting for you.

W I'm sorry I'm almost there. Is there anything I have to buy for Mom's birthday party?

M No, I think I prepared almost everything. You just need to come home as soon as possible. I bought a birthday present and a cake, and put them on the table.

W Then, did you buy a bouquet, too?

M No, I didn't. But I don't think we need it. She ____ _____.

W Then, how about a birthday card?

M Oh, a birthday card. Our little sister made a birthday card for her.

W Really? How does it look? Please tell me.

M It has "Happy Birthday" at the top decorated with ribbons. And below the phrase, there's a beautiful cake _____. I put the card next to the present.

W Wow. She will definitely like it.

07

M Oh, God! This is ridiculous.

W Honey, what's wrong with you?

M I _____ again.

W Oh, no! Not again. When did you speed?

M Do you remember the other day? I was really in a rush to get to the morning conference in time. I guess that's when I did it.

W Are you talking about last Monday? So, how much is the fine?

M It's $100. This is the fourth time. With the money we have paid in fines, we could have bought a GPS.

W It might be better for us to _____ speeding tickets.

M You are right.

W So, are you going to the bank to get money for the fine now?

M No. I will go to Electro Mart to get a GPS. You know about GPS better than me. Could you come along now?

W Sure.

08

M How may I help you, ma'am?

W I'm looking for a bed sheet to _____.

M What size is the blanket?

W Single bed-sized.

M Does it have any patterns?

W No, it doesn't. It is a plain white blanket.

M In that case, I think a striped bed sheet will go well with your blanket.

W You mean that striped bed sheet? Well, why do you think so?

M Solid white blankets are too plain. That striped bed sheet will give it some visual contrast.

W But I don't like any patterns personally.

M Maybe this will change your mind. _____ _____ two such striped bed sheets for the price of one.

W That sounds like a good opportunity. I will take it.

09

M I want to rent a car for our family trip.

W How many days do you want to rent it?

M Six days. My whole family totals seven. So I need a big car.

W If that's the case, you should rent a minivan. It can hold up to eight people, _____.

M That's good. I will get a minivan. How much is it?

W The total charge including insurance is $200 per day. Do you _____?

M Yes, please. And I have a one-day rent-free coupon. Can I use it?

W Sure. May I have your driver's license?

M OK. Here it is.

10

W Michael, I'd be happy to buy you something _____ _____. What do you want me to buy?

M Thanks, Mom. I really appreciate it. Can I have anything that I need?

W Sure, it'd be a present from me and your father. Just name it.

M First of all, I need a suit and a pair of shoes.

W Yes, you don't have a decent suit yet. What else do you need?

M A dress shirt and a tie are necessary.

W OK. But _____. That is also a must.

M Uncle Bill promised to give me a briefcase.

11

W Except people with psychological disorders, everyone dreams. Sometimes you say, "I didn't dream at all last night." But it's not true. In that case, you don't remember your dream. In your dreams, you sometimes see faces you've never seen _____ ___. However, that's not true, either. You've seen lots of faces throughout your lives, and your brain utilizes them during your dreams. And mostly in your dreams, you experience negative emotions rather than positive ones. Related to this, women generally have _____ in their dreams than men.

12

M Honey, our car is very old. Don't you think we should _____?

W I agree with you. I noticed strange noises and leaking oil. I think it's time to do that.

M OK. Let's check the prices of used cars on the Internet. I heard the BM 5 model of GM is quite good.

W Right, BM 5 has a good reputation among drivers. What's the price?

M There are five search results.

W What is your first priority in choosing a car?

M Its mileage should be under 30,000 kilometers.

W Then, we have three choices. What's next in importance? Options or year?

M For me, options are not important. _____ was made is more important.

W Among three choices, SM Encar has the longest mileage. Would it be OK for you? And the price is also the highest.

M It's OK for me, since that's the newest. I _____. I've saved some money for this.

W OK. Let's go to see that car.

13

W Why are you bleeding?

M I've broken my front tooth. I'm _____.

W Sit down and open your mouth. I'll see if I can fix that for you. How did it happen?

M I was playing ball with my friend and fell down. When I got up, my tooth was broken.

W Your gums are _____. I don't think I can save the tooth.

M Well, what are you going to do?

W I have to pull it out.

M Will that hurt a lot?

W No, you won't feel a thing. I will give you an anesthetic.

M I'm afraid of needles. Please treat me gently.

W _____

14

W Peter, what are you doing tomorrow?

M Oh, Angela. I'm doing _____ . Why do you ask?

W I plan to go to Yongpyong tomorrow. Do you want to come along?

M Yongpyong in autumn? But we can't go skiing in autumn.

W Don't worry. There are many things to enjoy at Yongpyong. We could ride a mountain lift.

M Really?

W Yeah. And we could _____ . It would be exciting.

M That sounds interesting. OK. So, what time shall we meet?

W How about 10 in the morning?

M I will be back from my swimming lesson around 10. So 11 would be better.

W Then, I will pick you up at 11 o'clock.

M _____

15

W Michael is a college student. One week ago, Professor Kim gave a big assignment to the students. Michael had to _____ by Friday afternoon. Today is Friday, but he hasn't finished half of his assignment yet. In the morning, his father asked Michael to wash his car with him. But Michael slammed the door, saying he _____ . His father got really angry about his attitude, but he didn't say anything to him since he looked so busy. After Michael handed in his assignment, he _____ _____ toward his father. He really regrets having been so ill-mannered. In this situation, what would Michael most likely say to his father?

Michael Dad, _____

16-17

M Today, I'd like to talk about _____ . It's one of the most serious health problems these days. In 2012, research shows that more than 42 million children under the age of five are obese. Unfortunately, about 35 million of them are living in developing countries. Obese children tend to _____ _____ even when they become adults. What is more serious is that they tend to have more diabetes and cardiovascular diseases when they are young. So what are the causes? There are many factors causing obesity. The main ones are _____ containing a lot of fat and sugars, and low levels of physical activity.

04^회 듣기 모의고사

1번부터 17번까지는 듣고 답하는 문제입니다. 1번부터 15번까지는 한 번만 들려주고, 16번부터 17번까지는 두 번 들려줍니다. 방송을 잘 듣고 답을 하시기 바랍니다.

01 대화를 듣고, 남자의 마지막 말에 대한 여자의 응답으로 가장 적절한 것을 고르시오.

① I've never been fired from a job before.
② I can help you prepare for the interview.
③ ABC Mart is a shopping mall in western Seoul.
④ Successful people manage their time very well.
⑤ They said they would make a decision by next Monday.

02 대화를 듣고, 여자의 마지막 말에 대한 남자의 응답으로 가장 적절한 것을 고르시오.

① It's not as hard as it looks.
② I know you're doing your best.
③ I don't even know how to dance.
④ I'd like to enter the dance contest.
⑤ Embarrassing someone is not kind at all.

03 다음을 듣고, 여자가 하는 말의 목적으로 가장 적절한 것을 고르시오.

① 대중교통 이용을 권장하려고
② 환경 보호 기금을 안내하려고
③ 자동차 보험 상품을 소개하려고
④ 대기 오염의 심각성을 경고하려고
⑤ 무공해 자동차 개발을 촉구하려고

04 대화를 듣고, 여자의 의견으로 가장 적절한 것을 고르시오.

① 외식을 하자.
② 배달 음식을 주문해서 먹자.
③ 집에서 음식을 만들어 먹자.
④ 남자가 요리를 도와야 한다.
⑤ 차를 사기 위해 돈을 모아야 한다.

05 대화를 듣고, 두 사람의 관계를 가장 잘 나타낸 것을 고르시오.

① 학생회 임원 – 교장
② 시의원 – 자선 사업가
③ 신문 기자 – 환경 운동가
④ 면접관 – 경찰관 지원자
⑤ 방송 진행자 – 시장 후보자

06 대화를 듣고, 완성된 방에서 대화의 내용과 일치하지 <u>않는</u> 것을 고르시오.

07 대화를 듣고, 남자가 여자에게 부탁한 일로 가장 적절한 것을 고르시오.

① 짐 들어 주기
② 자리 바꿔 주기
③ 비행기 표 예매하기
④ 비행기 표 취소하기
⑤ 휴대용 컴퓨터 빌려 주기

08 대화를 듣고, 남자가 영어를 공부하는 주된 이유를 고르시오.

① 해외에서 살려고
② 해외 유학을 가려고
③ 국제 무역업을 하려고
④ 해외여행을 다니려고
⑤ 원하는 직업을 얻으려고

09 대화를 듣고, 여자가 거스름돈으로 받은 금액을 고르시오. [3점]

① $10   ② $12   ③ $20
④ $28   ⑤ $30

10 대화를 듣고, 여자가 구입할 MP3 플레이어에 관해 두 사람이 언급하지 <u>않은</u> 것을 고르시오.

① 음악 사이트와의 호환성
② 음악 저장 용량
③ 음악 재생 가능 시간
④ 충전에 걸리는 시간
⑤ 제품 보증 기간

11 platypus에 관한 다음 내용을 듣고, 일치하지 <u>않는</u> 것을 고르시오. [3점]

① 호주 동부에 서식한다.
② 알을 낳는 포유류이다.
③ 특이한 생김새를 가지고 있다.
④ 독이 있지만 통증을 유발하지는 않는다.
⑤ 동전의 도안으로 사용되었다.

12 다음 방송 일정표를 보면서 대화를 듣고, 두 사람이 선택한 채널을 고르시오.

TV Guide

	9 :00	9:30	10:00	10:30
① Channel 6	Bad Boys (reality show)		Lions in the Wild (documentary)	
② Channel 7	Mission Impossible (movie)			
③ Channel 9	Major League Baseball (Yankees vs. Red Sox)			
④ Channel 11	NBA Basketball (Magic vs. Bulls)			
⑤ Channel 13	Prime Time News		Saturday Night Live (talk show)	

13 대화를 듣고, 여자의 마지막 말에 대한 남자의 응답으로 가장 적절한 것을 고르시오.

Man : _____

① It's really hard to tell the truth.
② The dream has become a reality.
③ Sounds like you need a vacation.
④ Thank you very much for the flowers.
⑤ You have no choice but to find some work.

14 대화를 듣고, 남자의 마지막 말에 대한 여자의 응답으로 가장 적절한 것을 고르시오. [3점]

Woman : _____

① So don't drive crazily. Drive with patience.
② You should have seen the stop sign at the corner.
③ I'm sorry. But I don't think baseball is dangerous.
④ You are wrong. So far my car hasn't had any problems.
⑤ That's a pity. Otherwise you could report him to the police.

15 다음 상황 설명을 듣고, Karen이 Jack에게 할 말로 가장 적절한 것을 고르시오.

Karen : Jack! _____

① Are you through with your newspaper?
② Don't take it so seriously. I was just joking.
③ Come on, don't be afraid of making mistakes.
④ I got my report card, and I'm not happy with it.
⑤ You should have asked before you threw them away!

[16-17] 다음을 듣고, 물음에 답하시오.

16 남자가 하는 말의 목적으로 가장 적절한 것은?

① to warn students of bad learning style
② to suggest best learning style for students
③ to advise students on selecting school programs
④ to emphasize importance of knowing your unique learning style
⑤ to explain how brain works most efficiently to learn new information

17 학습 방식에 관해 언급되지 <u>않은</u> 것은?

① 지능에 따라 적합한 학습 방식이 있다.
② 새로운 정보의 효율적 습득과 관련이 있다.
③ 태어날 때부터 지니고 있다.
④ 사람에 따라 좋은 학습 방식이 다를 수 있다.
⑤ 적합한 학습 방식의 선택이 좋은 성적을 낳는다.

DICTATION(받아쓰기) 코너입니다.
녹음의 내용을 잘 듣고, 빈칸에 알맞은 말을 쓰시기 바랍니다.

01

M Hi, Alice. I heard you're looking for a new job. Have you made any progress?

W Yes. I _____ for a store manager position at ABC Mart the day before yesterday.

M Oh, how did it go?

W _____

02

W You seem to be a great dancer. I wish I were good at dancing.

M Would you like to dance? I can teach you.

W You just _____, don't you?

M _____

03

W Hello, everyone! Today, I'm here to talk about _____ _____. Cars do more harm than good. First and foremost, cars are responsible for the deaths of 20,000 people a year and leave more than 300,000 people seriously injured. Secondly, on air pollution grounds alone, the car is a major threat to our health. And then there's the issue of traffic jams. Finally, we need to think about the effect cars are having on our environment. There is no doubt that _____ of life. The solution to these problems is simple. What we should do is use public transportation and our legs more often—for our own sakes.

04

M Honey, what's for dinner today?

W I'm planning to make tomato spaghetti.

M Oh, I already had it for lunch at work.

W Did you? Then I will make fried rice instead.

M Let's eat out tonight. We've not been eating out lately.

W That's true. But I _____. Look! It's raining outside.

M Well, then how about ordering pizza?

W I think we have to live on a tight budget for a while. Did you forget that we bought a new car last month?

M I just wanted to let you have some rest because you looked tired today. OK, I will prepare dinner. How about beef steak?

W Thank you so much. But we have to _____ _____ in the fridge. I think fried rice is better.

M You're right. Then wait on the couch and watch TV.

05

W Today's first guest is Tomas Henderson, a former principal at Boston University. Welcome to the program, Mr. Henderson.

M Thanks. I'm very glad to be here.

W Please tell our audience what made you _____ _____.

M Well, as you know, I've spent my whole life in Boston, and I'd like to give something back to the city and its citizens.

W What's your plan to _____ to live?

M First of all, I'm going to make sure our environment doesn't get any worse.

W Won't that cost a lot?

M My plan is for city authorities and companies in Boston to start a business together and make some profit. We can use that money to protect the environment. In addition, we will probably offer more jobs.

W What about the crime problem here?

M I'm going to spend more money on the police force. Boston's going to be much safer if I'm elected.

06

W Well, here's your new office.

M Wow, this is nice.

W Right, your desk and chair are over by the window, and, of course, your computer and telephone.

M OK.

W You also have a bookcase and a filing cabinet next to the door.

M Oh, good. I'll be _____ over from the old office on Monday.

W I'm glad you mentioned that. We'll put in a few things that aren't here over the weekend. You'll have a couch and a table for entertaining clients. Where do you want to put them?

M I think they would look best along the wall, opposite the bookcase and the filing cabinet.

W I agree with you. Well, how about _____ _____ above the couch?

M That's a good idea.

W We'll also put a flowerpot in the corner, opposite the door, just to liven the place up a bit.

M Thank you very much.

W You're welcome. See you on Monday.

07

M Excuse me, is this your seat? Do you like a window seat?

W No, actually I _____, but there were none left when I bought a ticket.

M Really? Then, would you mind changing seats with my wife? Her seat is an aisle seat.

W Oh, you and your wife got separate seats?

M Unfortunately, the plane is slightly overbooked. So, I didn't have a choice. So, do you mind?

W Actually, it's better for me. _____.

M Thanks to you, my wife and I can sit together.

W No problem. Let me just get my bag and my laptop. Would you please hold this bag for a moment?

M Of course, thanks again.

08

M What's your main reason for studying English?

W I want to get a better job, and for the kind of employment I want, English is an important qualification.

M What kind of job do you want to qualify for?

W Well, I love to travel abroad, and I have a master's degree in economics. So I'd like to _____ _____. But for that, I need to speak English more fluently.

M I see. I think your English sounds really good already.

W Thanks. I think your English is wonderful, too. Why are you studying it?

M Oh, I have lots of reasons. The most important one is my girlfriend. She's American, and we're planning to live in America _____.

W Then you'll need English for everything, won't you?

M I guess so.

W That sounds exciting. You'll have a whole new life!

09

W Would you tell me where the sweaters are?

M Sure, they're on the right, along the wall. May I help you find something?

W I'd like to get a sweater. It's for my boyfriend who is about your size.

M Well, in that case, you'll need a medium. How about this one?

W That's perfect. Could you _____ for a young woman?

M We have a variety of locally made items. How about some jewelry?

W Oh, this necklace is nice. How much is it?

M It's on sale for $50.

W OK. _____ and the necklace.

M That will be $80 plus 10% tax.

W Here's a $100 bill.

M Thank you. Here's your change.

10

M How may I help you?

W I'd like to buy an MP3 player.

M We _____, as you can see.

W Wow, I really don't know where to begin.

M Well, how about this one? It plays music in a lot of different file formats and is compatible with most of the major music download sites. It comes with an FM tuner, a built-in battery charger, and high quality headphones.

W What about its storage capacity and recharge time?

M It has 20 gigabytes of memory and can hold about 5,000 songs. You get about 12 hours of music playback on one charge and it _____ _____. It has a wide color screen, too.

W I think this is what I've been looking for. I'll take it.

11

M Have you heard of platypuses? The platypus is _ _____ which is only found in eastern Australia. The unusual appearance of this egg-laying, duck-billed, beaver-tailed, otter-footed animal baffled European naturalists when they first encountered it. It is _____ mammals. The male platypus has a spur on the hind foot that delivers a venom capable of causing severe pain to humans. The unique features of the platypus make it an important subject in the study of evolutionary biology and an iconic symbol of Australia. It has appeared as _____ and is featured on the reverse of the Australian 20 cent coin. Until the early 20th century, it was hunted for its fur, but it is now protected.

12

W What do you want to watch on TV tonight? There is a reality show at 9:00 on channel 6.

M You know I hate reality shows. I mean, they always show people doing stupid things like eating raw meat.

W Then, how about watching _____ _____ in the wild?

M Personally, I'd like to watch something with more suspense.

W Well. Here's something. Do you want to watch a rerun of *Mission Impossible*?

M I've seen it a million times.

W Hmm, let's see. Oh, how about this? On channel 13 at 10:00, there's a talk show.

M I'm not that interested in gossip about celebrities. I think I'm going to bed.

W OK. Oh, there's _____.

M Really? Then, I'll stay up and keep you company.

W I knew you would change your mind.

13

M What's wrong with you? You look very tired.

W Life is so much the same every day. Sometimes I want to quit my job and just do nothing!

M That would _____, but then what? Is that really your objective in life: to do nothing?

W I don't think so. But, I often dream about living on a small island and not having to work so hard.

M You don't have to live on an island. But having enough leisure time is very important. You must learn to balance work and play.

W I guess you're right. I thought _____ _____ in my life was to study and work.

M Well, we have to try to have time to "stop and smell the roses" as they say.

W I must be working too hard, without any leisure time.

M _____

14

W   Why are you looking so upset?

M   I was waiting for my wife _____ when a truck drew up behind me.

W   Did the truck driver do anything unpleasant?

M   Yes, he made big scratches on the side of my car trying to squeeze past.

W   So, what did you do?

M   I got out of the car to talk to him. Well, _____ _____, he also got out, holding a baseball bat!

W   Oh, my goodness! What did he do with it?

M   He swung it several times, saying nothing. Then, he marched off.

W   _____ his license plate number?

M   No, I was too terrified to do anything.

W   _____

15

W   Karen has to submit a research report on mass media to her professor by next Monday. She collected lots of old newspapers and magazines to write the report and _____. Now, she thinks there is no time to delay writing the report and makes up her mind to start on it. But, to her surprise, the newspapers and the magazines she gathered ___ _____. They are nowhere to be found. It is almost impossible for her to finish the report on time without them. After a moment, she finds out her younger brother, Jack, _____ mistaking them for paper trash. In this situation, what would Karen most likely say to Jack?

Karen   Jack! _____

16-17

M   Hello, students. Here's some advice about studying. Are you _____ in class? You may want to be aware of your unique learning style. Your learning style is the way you prefer to learn. It doesn't have anything to do with how intelligent you are or what skills you have. It has to do with _____ to learn new information. Your learning style has been with you since you were born. There's no such thing as a "good" learning style or a "bad" learning style. Success comes with many different learning styles. We all have our own particular way of learning new information. The important thing is to be aware of ___ _____. If you understand how your brain best learns, you have a better chance of studying in a way that will pay off when it's time to take that dreaded exam.

05회 듣기 모의고사

1번부터 17번까지는 듣고 답하는 문제입니다. 1번부터 15번까지는
한 번만 들려주고, 16번부터 17번까지는 두 번 들려줍니다. 방송을
잘 듣고 답을 하시기 바랍니다.

01 대화를 듣고, 남자의 마지막 말에 대한 여자의 응답으로 가장 적절한
것을 고르시오.

① I work for a computer company.
② I'm sorry, but your card is expired.
③ In that case, we can't give you a loan.
④ OK. Here's your new savings account.
⑤ I'm very cautious about borrowing money.

02 대화를 듣고, 여자의 마지막 말에 대한 남자의 응답으로 가장 적절한
것을 고르시오.

① You're right. I think I should do that.
② Good idea. I won't answer the phone.
③ You must be kidding! I'm serious now.
④ Don't you know? His cell phone's broken.
⑤ Don't be so hard on yourself. It'll be all right.

03 다음을 듣고, 여자가 하는 말의 목적으로 가장 적절한 것을 고르시오.

① 학교 이전을 반대하려고
② 기념식 일정을 안내하려고
③ 최신 유행을 홍보하려고
④ 교복의 필요성을 알리려고
⑤ 선거 참여를 호소하려고

04 대화를 듣고, 여자의 의견으로 가장 적절한 것을 고르시오.

① TV를 시청하면서 식사를 하지 말아야 한다.
② 컴퓨터 게임을 통해 학습량을 늘려야 한다.
③ 비만 예방을 위해 실내 활동을 줄여야 한다.
④ 운동 관련 컴퓨터 프로그램을 이용해야 한다.
⑤ 학교에서 컴퓨터 교육 시기를 앞당겨야 한다.

05 대화를 듣고, 두 사람이 하는 말의 주제로 가장 적절한 것을 고르시오.

① 영화 관람 태도
② 영화 제작 과정
③ 필름 현상 방법
④ 배우 섭외 조건
⑤ 영화 음악 선정

06 대화를 듣고, 그림에서 대화의 내용과 일치하지 <u>않는</u> 것을 고르시오.

07 대화를 듣고, 남자가 여자를 위해 할 일로 가장 적절한 것을 고르시오.

① 마중 가기
② 이사 도와주기
③ 버스표 예매하기
④ 방송 녹화하기
⑤ 발표 준비 도와주기

08 대화를 듣고, 여자가 물건이 있는 위치를 잘 아는 이유를 고르시오.

① 상점 주인이어서
② 자주 오는 곳이어서
③ 방금 산 물건이어서
④ 전에 일한 적이 있어서
⑤ 직접 설계한 건물이어서

09 대화를 듣고, 여자가 지불해야 할 금액을 고르시오. [3점]

① $1.40   ② $1.50   ③ $2.00

④ $2.40   ⑤ $3.00

10 대화를 듣고, 남자가 빌릴 수 있는 차에 해당하지 <u>않는</u> 것을 고르시오.

① black SUV
② black station wagon
③ white sedan
④ gray van
⑤ white station wagon

11 Internship Program에 관한 다음 내용을 듣고, 일치하지 <u>않는</u> 것을 고르시오.

① 교실 밖 환경에서의 학습 경험을 제공한다.
② 평균 3.0 학점 이상의 전공자가 지원 가능하다.
③ 보통 학기 당 매주 8시간에서 12시간이 필요하다.
④ 인턴 생활은 감독관에 의해 정기적으로 보고된다.
⑤ 최종 성적은 마지막 날 보는 시험에 의해 결정된다.

12 다음 영화 상영표를 보면서 대화를 듣고, 두 사람이 보기로 한 영화의 시작 시간을 고르시오.

Grand Cinema

World War Z	Transformer 4	Flight
10:00	10:20	10:30
① 12:30	12:30	④ 12:40
	② 14:40	⑤ 16:10
	③ 16:50	

13 대화를 듣고, 여자의 마지막 말에 대한 남자의 응답으로 가장 적절한 것을 고르시오. [3점]

Man : _____

① No. I told you I can't swim.
② I usually go sailing when I'm free.
③ Actually, scuba diving is my hobby.
④ Yeah, I know a man good at water sports.
⑤ There is a good place for wind surfing here.

14 대화를 듣고, 남자의 마지막 말에 대한 여자의 응답으로 가장 적절한 것을 고르시오.

Woman : _____

① You're welcome. Anytime.
② Then, I'd better tell her to hurry up.
③ Do you know why she can't join us?
④ I'll pick up your dress from the cleaners.
⑤ We are fortunate in arriving here on time.

15 다음 상황 설명을 듣고, Jennifer가 John에게 할 말로 가장 적절한 것을 고르시오.

Jennifer : _____

① Cheer up! You can do it.
② You'll get a chance someday.
③ Sure. I'll lend you some money.
④ Don't worry. My lips are sealed.
⑤ I won't fire you once and for all.

[16-17] 다음을 듣고, 물음에 답하시오.

16 여자가 하는 말의 주제로 가장 적절한 것은?

① 현대 학교의 의미
② 체중 조절의 필요성
③ 체육 수업의 중요성
④ 운동을 통한 학습 유형
⑤ 체육 수업을 위한 활동

17 physical exercise의 이점으로 언급되지 <u>않은</u> 것은? [3점]

① 건강 증진   ② 활력 제공
③ 체중 감량   ④ 흥미 유발
⑤ 정서적 안정감

DICTATION(받아쓰기) 코너입니다.
녹음의 내용을 잘 듣고, 빈칸에 알맞은 말을 쓰시기 바랍니다.

01

M Good afternoon. Can I help you, ma'am?

W Yes. How do I _____?

M May I ask what you do for a living?

W _____

02

W David, you seem to have a problem. What's wrong?

M I've been dialing John's number, but he never answers my phone call.

W Well, why don't you leave him a message? Though he doesn't pick up the phone, he can _____ _____, I think.

M _____

03

W Hello, fellow students. I am here to say that I think we should have uniforms at Jefferson Memorial High School. I would like to _____ for this at the next school board meeting. Everyone will benefit from a switch to uniforms. We can save the extra money we spend on the latest style of clothes. Furthermore, if we are wearing the same thing, we will all feel a sense of unity. I'm holding an informal meeting after school this Tuesday in the library. I hope to see you all there.

04

W Did you know that many countries are facing a serious childhood obesity problem?

M No, I didn't. What is the biggest cause?

W It may be that most of the children want to _____ _____ on the computer rather than go outside to play with their friends.

M Right. Children these days play computer games a lot.

W According to statistics, primary school students play computer games for _____ every day.

M That many?

W Yes. As well as this, they usually spend a lot of time watching TV while they are eating something.

M It means they have less chance to exercise and more chance to get fat, doesn't it?

W Yes. In conclusion, childhood obesity is caused by too _____. I think they should enjoy outdoor activities more often.

05

W Welcome to my studio. I'm Melanie.

M Hi, I'm Alex. Nice to meet you. I'm here to learn how to make films. I think making a film takes a long time.

W Yeah. Films take a long time to make. They go through _____.

M What's the first stage?

W We edit the movie script.

M Then, do you start filming?

W No. We have to _____ and choose where to film the movie. That's the pre-production stage.

M Is that when you build cool sets like these?

W No, we build the movie sets during the production stage. And we film the scenes.

M I see. What is the last stage?

W We _____ and find music for the soundtrack.

M Oh, I didn't know so much work goes into making movies. Thank you for explaining it to me!

06

W Oh, look at this round table. It has _____ _____ on it.

M Yeah. They are pictures of my family.

W Is the picture in the _____ your wedding picture?

M Right. The picture next to it is my first son.

W You mean the one in the frame with a stork on it?

M Yes. The picture on the left is my second son.

W He is holding a milk bottle in his mouth. He's so cute.

M And this is the picture of my whole family.

W The frame _____ around it is so beautiful.

M Really? Thank you.

07

(Telephone rings.)

M Hello.

W Honey, how's the new _____ going?

M It's almost finished. When are you going to come back home?

W I'm afraid I have to work late today. You know I have an important presentation tomorrow.

M Right. I'm so worried that you've been working late every day.

W Thank you for _____.

M Shall I go out to meet you at the bus stop?

W No, you don't need to. By the way, are you going to watch *People are Funny* on TV tonight?

M Of course I am.

W Then, can you _____ so that I can watch it later?

M No problem.

08

M Oh, look who's here! Aren't you Mrs. Smith?

W Oh, Mr. James. _____? I think you don't live around here.

M Actually, it's not long since I moved here.

W I see. Then we are neighbors now.

M You're right. Nice to meet you.

W Me, too. By the way, It seems you have a hard time _____.

M Yeah, right. I'm looking for a hanger and a tap, but I can't find them.

W Hangers are in the section 2, and taps are in section 5.

M Oh, how do you know about that so well?

W I worked here last year.

M I see. Thank you for the information.

W You're welcome. _____.

09

M How can I help you?

W I would like to buy some doughnuts and cookies for my son.

M These doughnuts are fresh and sweet.

W Wow, they _____! How much are they?

M They are seventy cents each.

W Okay. How about these coconut balls?

M They are fifteen cents each, but $1 for ten.

W Good. Could you give me two doughnuts and ten coconut balls?

M Sure. Anything else?

W That's all. Can you _____ for me?

M Of course. No problem.

10

W Good morning, sir. How can I help you?

M I'm interested in _____ .

W Which one would you like?

M Well, I'm travelling with my family so it would be a family car.

W How about this black SUV?

M Oh, no. I _____ that's big enough. I need a large car.

W What about the black station wagon? It's just perfect for a family.

M No, I don't like that color, and I'd prefer a sedan. I'll take that white sedan over there.

W Sorry, but that car has been booked. How about the _____ ?

M The van looks cool, but it's too big. Then, can I go with the white station wagon?

W Sure. Would you fill out the form?

11

W Good morning, students! I'm happy to introduce our new Internship Program. The program is designed to _____ in settings outside the classroom. For students who have completed most of their course work, internships offer work experience in "real-world situations." Students who apply to be interns must be business majors with a 3.0 grade point average or over. The time spent by the intern usually involves from 8 to 12 hours of work per week for the semester. Periodic reports of the intern's work are made by the supervisor. Final grades _____ _____ .

12

W Greg, do you have any plans this Saturday?

M Not particularly. How about you?

W I'm thinking about _____ .

M Sounds good. What's playing at the Grand Cinema?

W I'm not sure. Let's find out on the Internet.

M Okay. Let me see. There are *World War Z*, *Transformer 4*, and *Flight*.

W Let's watch *World War Z*.

M I've already seen that movie. And I have an _____ at 1 o'clock.

W How about *Transformer 4*? They say it is a real spectacle.

M Well, let's watch *Flight*. I'm dying to see Denzel Washington.

W Okay, _____ .

13

W Excuse me. This is a nice boat.

M Thanks for _____ . But it's my friend's boat.

W I see. By the way, I'm from the Water Sports Research Center.

M So?

W Can I ask you some questions about _____ ?

M Sure.

W What's your name?

M Alan Parker.

W Okay. Do you do water sports other than sailing?

M I sometimes _____ .

W Oh, good. Anything else?

M _____

14

M Are you ready?

W Grace is still in her room.

M She _____ . We don't have enough time.

W What time does the movie begin?

M It _____ .

W What's the time now?

M About seven.

W There's no hurry. It only takes ten minutes to get there by car.

M I know, but Grace can take hours to _____ .

W _____

15

M John is working as a part-timer at a convenient store in order to _____ to buy a gift for his mother's birthday. His mother doesn't know about it. If she knew that John was working as a part-timer, she wouldn't be happy. While working at a convenient store after school as usual, Jennifer, John's sister, enters the store and _____ John working as a clerk. John tells her the whole story and wants Jennifer not to tell their mother. Jennifer also thinks that she must keep _____ . In this situation, what would Jennifer most likely say to John?

Jennifer _____

16-17

W Physical exercise is very important in students' growth. Therefore, it is natural that schools should promote _____ of both mind and body of the students. Physical exercise is also important in helping to keep students healthy. Nowadays, many people live sedentary lives. Physical exercise during school will give energy to students and allow them __ _____ . In a sense, daily physical exercise will help fat children lose some weight because even those who despise exercise would have to be physically active for a given time. The most important thing is that students must _____ . In this aspect, physical exercise class will be the time when students can enjoy themselves.

1번부터 17번까지는 듣고 답하는 문제입니다. 1번부터 15번까지는
한 번만 들려주고, 16번부터 17번까지는 두 번 들려줍니다. 방송을
잘 듣고 답을 하시기 바랍니다.

01 대화를 듣고, 남자의 마지막 말에 대한 여자의 응답으로 가장 적절한
것을 고르시오.

① No, I'm given one month's leave of absence.
② Of course. That's the job I've been looking for.
③ Yes. I've been trying to find another job for
her.
④ Exactly. I have a hard time getting a new
worker.
⑤ I won't move for the time being. I'll live with
her.

02 대화를 듣고, 여자의 마지막 말에 대한 남자의 응답으로 가장 적절한
것을 고르시오.

① Not yet. I still need more time to dry it.
② Sure. I think I'm going to take it to the laundry.
③ Right. Actually, it makes your shirt fashionable.
④ Oh, I should have been careful to avoid the
stain.
⑤ Really? I should have checked when I picked it
up.

03 다음을 듣고, 여자가 하는 말의 목적으로 가장 적절한 것을 고르시오.

① 투표를 장려하려고   ② 당선을 축하하려고
③ 상품을 광고하려고   ④ 기금을 모금하려고
⑤ 공로를 치하하려고

04 대화를 듣고, 여자의 의견으로 가장 적절한 것을 고르시오.

① 무분별한 충동구매를 하지 마라.
② 만일의 경우를 대비해서 저축하라.
③ 수입과 소비에 대한 계획을 세워라.
④ 불우이웃돕기 성금 모금에 동참하라.
⑤ 삶의 목표를 돈을 버는 데 두지 마라.

05 대화를 듣고, 두 사람이 하는 말의 주제로 가장 적절한 것을 고르시오.

① 애완견 키우기의 어려움
② 동물 보호 교육의 필요성
③ 유기견의 실태와 보호 방법
④ 선물로서의 애완견의 의미
⑤ 애완용 동물의 교육적 가치

06 대화를 듣고, 그림에서 대화의 내용과 일치하지 <u>않는</u> 것을 고르시오.

07 대화를 듣고, 남자가 여자에게 부탁한 일을 고르시오.

① 아들 데려오기
② 감기약 사 오기
③ 소포 대신 받아 주기
④ 우체국에서 소포 부치기
⑤ 스포츠 센터에 함께 가기

08 대화를 듣고, 여자가 서점에 가는 이유를 고르시오.

① 책을 반환하려고
② 과제를 조사하려고
③ 행사에 참여하려고
④ 직장 상사를 만나려고
⑤ 신간 도서를 구입하려고

09 대화를 듣고, 여자가 지불한 금액을 고르시오. [3점]

① $9   ② $16   ③ $28

④ $30   ⑤ $37

10 대화를 듣고, Sagrada Familia에 관해 언급되지 <u>않은</u> 것을 고르시오.

① 위치   ② 설립 시기   ③ 설계자

④ 용도   ⑤ 완공 연도

11 Parsons Summer Intensive Courses에 관한 다음 내용을 듣고, 일치하지 <u>않는</u> 것을 고르시오. [3점]

① 지역 화가와 디자이너가 강의에 참여한다.
② 학생들은 미술 도구를 준비해야 한다.
③ 필요한 물품 목록은 개강 후 게시판에 공지된다.
④ 6월 1일부터 등록이 시작된다.
⑤ 웹 사이트에 보다 더 자세한 정보가 실려 있다.

12 다음 표를 보면서 대화를 듣고, 순위가 <u>잘못된</u> 것을 고르시오.

What's the best movie?

	Rank	Movie	Total Gross (million)
①	1	Titanic	$601
②	2	Star Wars	$461
③	3	E.T.	$435
④	4	The Lion King	$431
⑤	5	Jurassic Park	$404

13 대화를 듣고, 남자의 마지막 말에 대한 여자의 응답으로 가장 적절한 것을 고르시오. [3점]

Woman : _____

① Right. The Australians are very kind.
② I hope you enjoy your trip to Australia.
③ Yes, studying with you was of help to me.
④ A little, but one year is not enough I think.
⑤ Sure. I'll help you to improve your English.

14 대화를 듣고, 여자의 마지막 말에 대한 남자의 응답으로 가장 적절한 것을 고르시오.

Man : _____

① I'm sorry to hear that.
② You are so lucky to do it!
③ OK, I'll ask him tomorrow.
④ Never. Don't worry about it.
⑤ Cheer up! You can do it next time.

15 다음 상황 설명을 듣고, Cindy가 Sally의 어머니에게 할 말로 가장 적절한 것을 고르시오.

Cindy : _____

① Yes, please. I would love to stay.
② Can I stay here for dinner tonight?
③ Sorry, but I'm not good at cooking.
④ Why don't you stay for dinner tonight?
⑤ Thanks, but I have to be home for dinner tonight.

[16-17] 다음을 듣고, 물음에 답하시오.

16 여자가 하는 말의 목적으로 가장 적절한 것은?

① 종이의 제작 방식을 설명하려고
② 종이 부족에 대한 해결책을 제시하려고
③ 무분별한 종이 사용 자제를 촉구하려고
④ 종이 공예 대중화의 필요성을 강조하려고
⑤ 종이 사용을 통한 환경 보호 방법을 알려 주려고

17 종이의 활용 방법으로 언급되지 <u>않은</u> 것은?

① 물건 포장   ② 노트
③ 도시락 가방   ④ 벽지
⑤ 휴지통 보조

DICTATION(받아쓰기) 코너입니다.
녹음의 내용을 잘 듣고, 빈칸에 알맞은 말을 쓰시기 바랍니다.

01

M Rian, did your grandmother's heart operation come out well?

W Yes. But I still have to nurse her _____.

M What would you do with your job? Will you quit working?

W _____

02

W Honey, did you pick up my T-shirt from the laundry?

M Sure. I put it in the drawer in your room.

W Oh, look at this! There still _____ here.

M _____

03

W Ladies and gentlemen, it gives me great pleasure _____ to praise a member of our town. John Baxter has been a pillar of the community for as long as I can recall. As the past mayor, he served the community well. As a citizen, he has always been at the forefront of _____. I'm sure I don't need to say anything more about his achievements, as you all know him well. So, John, please come forward and accept this as a _____ for your contribution to our town.

04

W Do you have some savings?

M No, not yet. Why do you ask?

W I think you spend _____.

M I know, but I think I can save money later.

W I don't think so. It is important to save up for a rainy day.

M What do you mean by "for a rainy day"?

W If an accident suddenly happens, you may suffer ____ _____ such as hospital bills.

M But things like that hardly happen.

W You may suddenly lose your job and experience a temporary loss of income.

M You're right. I'll save money for _____.

05

M Mom, my friend Eric got a new puppy.

W Where did he get it?

M His mom bought it as his birthday present. Can I get a dog, too?

W Roy, dogs need to be cared for properly. They are not toys.

M What do you mean?

W They need food, water, exercise, a _____ _____, and love.

M I didn't know that they need lots of things like that.

W And that's not the only things you need to do.

M What are the others?

W What about homework? You might get too busy with the dog.

M I see. It is _____.

W Right.

06

M Susan, what's that?

W It's our family tree. I made it yesterday for my homework. Do you want to see it?

M Let me see. The two people _____ are your grandparents, right?

W Yeah. Isn't the mustache of my grandpa so cool?

M Yes, it's so nice. And I bet your grandma likes to wear a hat.

W Exactly. She always wears a hat. The man next to my grandma is my dad.

M Then, the woman next to your grandpa is your mom, right? They all _____.

W You're right. And below them are pictures of me and my sisters.

M I know the girl in the middle is you, but who is your youngest sister? Your two sisters look similar.

W The girl with _____ is my youngest sister.

M I see. Your family looks very happy.

07

(Cell phone rings.)

W Oh, Michael. How are you?

M Oh, hello, Rebecca. I'm good. How's your cold?

W I'm still suffering from it. I don't know why it is ___ _____.

M I'm sorry to hear that. By the way, could you do me a favor?

W What is it?

M I just got a text message from a mailman. He said he would arrive at my home in two hours with a parcel.

W So? You mean you're going to be out then?

M Exactly. Actually, I have to go and _____ from the sports center.

W So, you want me to take your parcel instead of you?

M Yes. Could you do it?

W Of course, I could. What are _____?

08

W Whose call is it, honey?

M It's from my boss. He asked me to _____.

W Oh, my! How bad he is to have you work during the holiday!

M I can't help it because I can only do the work in the office.

W I see. Then, I'll go to the bookstore.

M To buy a book?

W No. Actually, it's going to _____, "Meeting with an Author" this afternoon.

M I see. Then, can you buy me a book named *What Is Justice*?

W Sure. I've wanted to read it, too. By the way, when do you think you will finish?

M I'm not sure. I'll call you later.

09

M Hey, Judy, where have you just been?

W I found a great clothes store _____.

M Really? Let's have a look at what you got.

W OK. I bought three of these dresses for $6 each.

M That's crazy! Then, did you buy a pair of jeans?

W No. They're only $7 a pair, but all of the jeans in my size _____.

M It's a pity! Oh, what did these four blouses cost you?

W Would you believe it? Only $3 each.

M Really? I have to go there. Do they have men's clothes?

W Sorry, the store is _____.

10

M It's hard to believe I'm here in Barcelona.

W This is one of _____ in Spain.

M It's even more fantastic than I imagined.

W Do you know much about the Sagrada Familia?

M Not really. When was it designed?

W Around the beginning of the last century designed by Antoni Gaudi.

M And what was it _____ for?

W It was built as a cathedral.

M It's definitely impressive.

W That's for sure! And it's still unfinished.

M Really? Say, you know a lot about this place.

W Well, it's because I'm interested _____.

M Lucky me! I have a great guide like you.

11

W Hello. I'd like to inform you about Parsons Summer Intensive Courses. These courses are taught by _____ and by many New York-based artists and designers. Students must prepare their own art supplies. A list of required and _____ is distributed by the instructor for each course. Registration for Parsons Summer Intensive Courses begins on June 1st. _____ _____ is advised. Visit our website, www. parsonssummerintensivecourses.com, for more details.

12

M Look at the box office records of old movies.

W Sounds interesting! Which film _____ number one?

M *Titanic*.

W *Titanic*? Personally, I don't like romance movies.

M Then, what kind of movies do you like?

W I like _____ such as *Jurassic Park* and *Star Wars*.

M Oh, *Star Wars* is ranked second, but *Jurassic Park* is not included among the top five movies.

W Then, which film is ranked third?

M The third is *E.T.*, and *The Lion King* is following ___ _____.

W *The Lion King* is fourth? It's unbelievable.

13

W It's been a year since we studied together in this college.

M Yeah. Time has _____. It's almost time for me to leave Korea.

W What do you mean?

M I came here to study only for a year. I'm going back to Australia next week.

W Really? It's _____. I didn't know you were planning to stay here for only one year. You know what?

M What?

W Actually, I was in Australia for a year last year, too.

M Really? What were you doing there?

W I was _____ my English.

M Do you think it helped?

W _____

14

W Who's this tall guy _____ in the picture?

M That's John.

W Do you know him well? I mean, do you have a close relationship with him?

M Our relationship is not really close, but he is one of my coworkers.

W He looks so nice. Would you _____?

M You have a boyfriend, don't you?

W I broke up with him a long time ago. So, yes or no?

M I'm sure he has a girlfriend.

W You _____.

M _____

15

W Sally invited her school friend Cindy over to her home after school. The two girls are playing happily in Sally's room. Meanwhile, Sally's mother is _____, spaghetti, in the kitchen. Later, Sally's mother asks Cindy if she _____ for a spaghetti dinner. Cindy is tempted but remembers that her grandparents will be visiting tonight, and her mother _____ for dinner. In this situation, what would Cindy most likely say to Sally's mother?

Cindy _____

16-17

W Hello, everyone. Today, I'd like to talk about paper. Do you think we have enough paper? No, we don't. Then, what is the solution _____? It is to reuse paper. First, newspapers have many uses after they are read. Old newspaper sheets _____ or fill a box when mailing things. They can be used to cover the floor when painting or cleaning. In addition, one-side printed paper has many uses. The most obvious use is to print things out on the other side of the paper. _____ also make good notepaper for shopping lists or anything. Finally, paper bags from the grocery store can be reused, too; they can be used for groceries again, and they can also carry lunches or line wastebaskets. _____ before it's thrown away is a simple way to conserve paper.

07^회 듣기 모의고사

1번부터 17번까지는 듣고 답하는 문제입니다. 1번부터 15번까지는
한 번만 들려주고, 16번부터 17번까지는 두 번 들려줍니다. 방송을
잘 듣고 답을 하시기 바랍니다.

01 대화를 듣고, 여자의 마지막 말에 대한 남자의 응답으로 가장 적절한
것을 고르시오.

① I'm sure you will be a great actress.
② Thank you for your words of comfort.
③ Come on! Have confidence in yourself.
④ I see. I hope you can do better next time.
⑤ Really? Then, I'll apologize to him right now.

02 대화를 듣고, 남자의 마지막 말에 대한 여자의 응답으로 가장 적절한
것을 고르시오.

① I mean she's been trying to keep her word.
② You know, he is the man I've been looking for.
③ In fact, she seemed worried about her wedding.
④ To my relief, she broke up with him last
  month.
⑤ Surprisingly, she announced her marriage to us.

03 다음을 듣고, 여자가 하는 말의 목적으로 가장 적절한 것을 고르시오.

① to give information about the area
② to explain the lives of useful animals
③ to describe what to do if bitten by animals
④ to teach protection from dangerous animals
⑤ to warn the group about the hazards of snakes

04 대화를 듣고, 남자의 의견으로 가장 적절한 것을 고르시오.

① 걷기는 좋은 운동이다.
② 운동은 매일 해야 한다.
③ 준비 운동은 매우 중요하다.
④ 아침에는 가벼운 산책이 좋다.
⑤ 생활 속에서도 찾을 수 있는 운동이 많다.

05 대화를 듣고, 두 사람의 관계를 가장 잘 나타낸 것을 고르시오.

① doctor – patient
② captain – passenger
③ TV anchor – audience
④ pilot – flight attendant
⑤ travel agent – customer

06 대화를 듣고, 그림에서 대화의 내용과 일치하지 않는 것을 고르시오.

07 대화를 듣고, 여자가 남자에게 부탁한 일을 고르시오.

① 옷 다려주기
② 식당 예약하기
③ 아이 돌봐주기
④ 귀걸이 가져오기
⑤ 침대 옮겨주기

08 대화를 듣고, 남자가 여자를 부른 이유를 고르시오.

① 제품 홍보를 맡기려고
② 사업 계획을 문의하려고
③ 몽골 여행을 제의하려고
④ 손님 배웅을 부탁하려고
⑤ 통역할 사람이 필요해서

09 대화를 듣고, 여자가 지불해야 할 총 금액을 고르시오. [3점]

① $20.00 ② $23.50 ③ $26.00
④ $28.50 ⑤ $30.00

10 대화를 듣고, 여자에 관해 언급되지 <u>않은</u> 것을 고르시오.

① 이름 ② 주소 ③ 수강 강좌
④ 학과 ⑤ 휴가 기간

11 Brazil nuts에 관한 다음 내용을 듣고, 일치하지 <u>않는</u> 것을 고르시오. [3점]

① 아마존 정글에서 자란다.
② 초승달 모양이다.
③ 암 예방에 좋다.
④ 지방이 적고 냄새가 없다.
⑤ 껍질이 단단해서 깨기가 어렵다.

12 다음 표를 보면서 대화를 듣고, 두 사람이 이용할 기차의 운행편을 고르시오. [3점]

	Train No.	Departure	Arrival
①	London 815	8:15	11:15
②	London 900	9:00	12:00
③	London 1030	10:30	1:30
④	London 1100	11:00	2:00
⑤	London 1140	11:40	2:40

13 대화를 듣고, 여자의 마지막 말에 대한 남자의 응답으로 가장 적절한 것을 고르시오.

Man : _____

① Put on your soccer boots.
② Arrange for transportation.
③ Check the time of the game.
④ Take a good hat and sunscreen.
⑤ Practice your goal kicking before the match.

14 대화를 듣고, 남자의 마지막 말에 대한 여자의 응답으로 가장 적절한 것을 고르시오.

Woman : _____

① It's been nice meeting you.
② No. I'll come back later today.
③ That's a good idea. Thank you!
④ Would you really? That's so kind of you.
⑤ No. I'll see if he'll be in tomorrow afternoon.

15 다음 상황 설명을 듣고, John이 의뢰인에게 할 말로 가장 적절한 것을 고르시오.

John : _____

① Good. See you tomorrow.
② That'll be fine. See you then.
③ I'm sorry I'll be late. I overslept.
④ Sorry, I'm in a hurry. Can you call back?
⑤ I'm sorry, but there is a family emergency.

[16-17] 다음을 듣고, 물음에 답하시오.

16 여자가 전화를 건 목적으로 가장 적절한 것은?

① 패션쇼에 관한 정보를 문의하려고
② 세계 의류 박람회 개최를 홍보하려고
③ 새로 개점한 상점의 위치를 물으려고
④ 패션모델 선발 대회에 대해 안내하려고
⑤ 패션 잡지 출판에 관해 상담을 받으려고

17 여자가 궁금해 하는 것으로 언급되지 <u>않은</u> 것은?

① 모델 ② 장소
③ 옷의 종류 ④ 입장료
⑤ 입장권 구매처

07회 | DICTATION

DICTATION(받아쓰기) 코너입니다.
녹음의 내용을 잘 듣고, 빈칸에 알맞은 말을 쓰시기 바랍니다.

01

W How was your performance?

M I was _____ because I couldn't remember the words.

W Think nothing of it. It could happen to anyone.

M _____

02

M Erica is the most beautiful bride that I have ever seen. Don't you think so?

W Yeah, right. _____ that she looks happy.

M What do you mean?

W _____

03

W Now, folks, I'd like to move on to warn you _____ _____ you may encounter during the climbing and how to deal with them. The most common hazard is the bull ant which you can see frequently. They deliver a nasty bite. The best way to avoid them is _ _____ on your legs. Now, the other hazard is a snake encounter. In such a situation, _____ and move away slowly without any fast movement.

04

M Kathy, you look so tired.

W I think it's because I just _____ in the office.

M Why don't you get some exercise?

W What kind of exercise do you prefer?

M I usually do walking.

W Is walking good as an exercise?

M Sure. Walking for more than 40 minutes a day is _____ than any other exercise.

W Really? I didn't know that.

M Besides, a regular walking routine can _____ _____.

W I see. I think I'd better begin walking in the park near my house from now on.

M Great.

05

M Good afternoon, ma'am. Is everything satisfactory?

W Yes. But can I ask you how long it will _____ Southport?

M Well, normally it takes 13 hours, but it might take 15 hours this time.

W Is that because of the bad weather?

M Yes, the seas will _____.

W I see. Will it be a rough ride?

M Probably. But don't worry. My crew and I are very experienced.

W I'm relieved to hear that.

M If you need anything during the voyage, just ask me or _____.

W Thank you!

06

W Honey, could you bring the rectangular-shaped pot to the bathroom? It needs watering.

M Yes, but there are two _____ in the living room.

W Oh, you're right. I mean the one between the window and the TV.

M I found it now.

W Could you help me with one more thing, honey?

M Go ahead. What's that?

W Put this plant label in one of the pots.

M Which pot do you mean? Do you mean the round-shaped pot on _____?

W No. Do you see the pot which is a little swollen in the middle?

M Yeah. Is that the pot I have to put this label in?

W No. The pot next to it.

M Oh, I see. What you mean is _____, right?

W You said it!

07

M Aren't you ready yet?

W No, dear. I've just finished _____. Now I have to do my makeup.

M Oh, we will be late for the appointment.

W I can't go without my makeup.

M Well, we are meeting in the restaurant at 7.

W I know, I know. But I have been busy taking care of the kids all afternoon.

M All right. Just _____.

W John? Where are my earrings?

M How would I know? They're your earrings.

W Oh, I remember now. They're in the drawer. Can you go to the bedroom and _____?

M Sure.

08

M Have a seat, please.

W Thanks. Why did you call me?

M I heard you speak good Mongolian.

W I lived there for ten years. When I was 7 years old, I went there with my parents.

M I see. _____, then?

W Sure, sir. What is it?

M I have an important meeting with a Mongolian buyer. He is very interested in _____.

W Good for you!

M Of course. But the problem is that I need a person who can interpret for us.

W I see what you mean. What should I do now, then?

M The buyer will arrive at the airport this afternoon. Can you go to the airport with me?

W _____. I'm happy to be helpful to you.

09

M How may I help you?

W I would like to buy some fruit. How much are the apples?

M 10 for $5.

W I'll take _____.

M OK. What else?

W Those tangerines look nice. How much?

M They're cheap now. Only $4 per kilogram.

W I'll have _____ then.

M Very good. How about tomatoes? Only $2.50 a kilo.

W I don't need any tomatoes. But I like the grapes.

M They're $5.50 a kilo.

W OK. I'll _____.

M Anything else?

W No thanks.

10

(Telephone rings.)

M Hello. Foreign Student Advisor's office of Kensington University. Can I help you?

W It's Susan Parker here. I'd like to make _____ _____ .

M Tell me your student number, please.

W It's H for Harry 5712.

M H5712. Okay. What's your address, Susan?

W I live at 10th Avenue, Tamworth.

M What course are you taking?

W I'm in the English writing class.

M Who's your professor this term?

W Mrs. Green.

M When do you want to take leave?

W I'd like to be away _____ .

M Okay. I've got that.

11

W Have you eaten Brazil nuts? Brazil nuts come from a giant tree that grows in the Amazon jungle. Shaped like a crescent, Brazil nuts aren't technically a nut but _____ . Brazil nuts are an exceptional food source of the mineral considered to be cancer-fighting. Like other nuts, they also _____ , fiber, and vitamin E. And they are a good source of fats which lend them a rich taste and flavor. Brazil nuts can be a tough nut to crack if you buy them unshelled. You can _____ by boiling them first.

12

M Are we going to London tomorrow morning?

W Yes. We _____ at 2:30 pm.

M Okay. Then, let's take the 11 o'clock train. You know we'll need to allow about 30 minutes to get from the station in London to the meeting.

W I know. But do you mind leaving a bit earlier? I also want to do some shopping in London before the meeting. That'll take less than 2 hours.

M Hmm, OK. It seems that we should go _____ _____ then.

W But I don't want to go that early. I think we'd better leave two hours earlier.

M Then, we'll need to catch this one.

W Yes. That seems like the best option. It'll allow me just enough time _____ and then get to the meeting on time.

13

M What are your plans for the weekend?

W _____ dinner with my friends on Saturday night.

M Then, do you want to do something together on Saturday afternoon? The weather is going to be sunny.

W Yeah. What do you have in mind?

M I want to spend some time out in the sun. How about _____ ?

W Great idea. When is it on?

M It starts at 3 pm. I'll pick you up around 2.

W Should I _____ ?

M _____

14

W Excuse me, is Mr. Barnes available? I'm one of his students.

M I'm sorry, Mr. Barnes is not in the office today.

W Well, I need some _____.

M I'm sure if you come back tomorrow, he will be there.

W That won't do because the assignment is _____ _____.

M Oh, dear.

W If I don't get help today, I cannot _____.

M Hmm. Why don't you try sending him an email? He might be able to answer your questions on-line.

W _____

15

W John has a very important meeting early in the morning with a client. However, his alarm clock _____ him up, and he gets up late. When he wakes, he is shocked to discover that the meeting starts in only 30 minutes. There is no way he will be able to make it. He decides to _____. Before calling, he tries to decide whether to tell a lie and say there is a family emergency or tell the truth. Finally he decides to _____ and calls his client. When the client answers the phone, what would John most likely say to the client?

John _____

16-17

(Telephone rings.)

M Good afternoon, Fashion Fad. May I help you?

W Yes. I'm a fashion model trainee and interested in your fashion show. Can you _____ about the fashion show next Saturday?

M Certainly. How can I help you?

W I'd like to know what kind of clothing you're modeling.

M We're going to _____ for men and women.

W Oh, that should be good. Can you tell me where it is held?

M At the Tanglin Mall.

W OK, and how much are the tickets?

M Tickets are $12 each.

W Available where? At the door?

M Yes, or you can buy them at any of our stores.

W I see. And can you tell me _____?

M At 7 pm. It should run until about 9 pm.

W 7 to 9. OK. Thanks for your help.

08회 | 듣기 모의고사

1번부터 17번까지는 듣고 답하는 문제입니다. 1번부터 15번까지는 한 번만 들려주고, 16번부터 17번까지는 두 번 들려줍니다. 방송을 잘 듣고 답을 하시기 바랍니다.

01 대화를 듣고, 남자의 마지막 말에 대한 여자의 응답으로 가장 적절한 것을 고르시오.

① I'm in a hurry now. I want to go first.
② I'm tired now. Can you leave me alone?
③ Sorry about that. I'm a stranger here, too.
④ Why don't we go out to see the sights now?
⑤ Actually, I've wanted to visit the National Art Gallery.

02 대화를 듣고, 여자의 마지막 말에 대한 남자의 응답으로 가장 적절한 것을 고르시오.

① Sorry, I've never thought of it.
② Hurry up. He'll arrive here soon.
③ Okay. Let's call a taxi right now.
④ Thank you! That's very kind of you.
⑤ How stupid I am! I think I'll be late.

03 다음을 듣고, 여자가 하는 말의 주제로 가장 적절한 것을 고르시오.

① 부단한 노력의 필요성
② 행복과 만족의 차이점
③ 행복의 변하지 않는 속성
④ 성공을 쫓는 다양한 이유들
⑤ 고통이 성장에 미치는 영향

04 대화를 듣고, 여자의 의견으로 가장 적절한 것을 고르시오.

① 하루 8잔의 물을 섭취하는 것이 좋다.
② 물이 아니어도 수분을 섭취할 수 있는 음식이 있다.
③ 물을 많이 섭취하는 것이 건강에 좋다.
④ 물 이외의 음식은 갈증 해소에 방해가 된다.
⑤ 체중 감량을 위해서는 수분 조절이 필요하다.

05 대화를 듣고, 두 사람의 관계를 가장 잘 나타낸 것을 고르시오.

① host – guest
② realtor – client
③ novelist – reader
④ librarian – student
⑤ police officer – witness

06 대화를 듣고, 그림에서 내용과 일치하지 <u>않는</u> 것을 고르시오.

07 대화를 듣고, 남자가 여자에게 부탁한 일로 가장 적절한 것을 고르시오.

① 주말 영화표 예매하기
② 영화 동호회에 가입하기
③ 영화 포스터 구해 주기
④ 콘서트 일정 확인하기
⑤ 영화배우 신상 파악해 주기

08 대화를 듣고, 여자가 서점에 들른 이유를 고르시오.

① 친구를 만나러
② 문학 숙제를 하러
③ 생일 선물을 사러
④ 신간 소설책을 사러
⑤ 과학 잡지를 구독하러

09 대화를 듣고, 여자가 지불해야 할 금액을 고르시오. [3점]

① $95   ② $105   ③ $110

④ $115   ⑤ $125

10 대화를 듣고, 여자가 할 일로 언급되지 <u>않은</u> 것을 고르시오.

① 결혼식장 예약하기
② 비행기 표 예매하기
③ Smith에게 전화 걸기
④ 판매 보고서 복사하기
⑤ 서명할 서류 가져오기

11 bamboo에 관한 다음 내용을 듣고, 일치하지 <u>않는</u> 것을 고르시오. [3점]

① 따뜻한 지역에 분포되어 있는 빨리 자라는 식물이다.
② 중국인들은 장수에 대한 상징으로 여긴다.
③ 적도 기후에서는 집을 짓는 재료로 사용된다.
④ 1880년대 중반 이후 낚싯대로의 사용이 늘었다.
⑤ 음식을 요리하는 데 사용되기도 한다.

12 다음 TV 편성표를 보면서 대화를 듣고, 두 사람이 지금 볼 TV 채널을 고르시오.

TV schedule

	① CH1	② CH2	③ CH3	④ CH4	⑤ CH5
5:00 5:30				Neighbors	CSI
6:00 6:30	Local View	70s Show	CSI	News	Movie: Jurassic Park 2
	News	Wheel of Fortune	CSI	News	Movie: Jurassic Park 2
7:00	CSI	News and Weather	Just a Minute	60 Minutes	Movie: Jurassic Park 2
7:30 8:00	CSI	News and Weather	News	60 Minutes	
8:30	Jo Show	News and Weather	Soccer		

13 대화를 듣고, 여자의 마지막 말에 대한 남자의 응답으로 가장 적절한 것을 고르시오.

Man : _____

① I don't know anything about it.
② A book is always a good present.
③ I can lend you whatever you want.
④ Okay. These 25 red roses are for you!
⑤ Don't worry. It's between you and me.

14 대화를 듣고, 남자의 마지막 말에 대한 여자의 응답으로 가장 적절한 것을 고르시오. [3점]

Woman : _____

① Thank you for finding it.
② I wear it over my shoulder.
③ Sorry. There's not a bag like that.
④ Wait a minute. Let me check it out.
⑤ It's a leather bag with a few pockets.

15 다음 상황 설명을 듣고, Tommy가 선생님에게 할 말로 가장 적절한 것을 고르시오.

Tommy : Ma'am, _____

① why do we have to take a test?
② how many papers do you need?
③ I don't know where your desk is.
④ we didn't get any notice about a test.
⑤ There are not enough hand-outs on your desk.

[16-17] 다음을 듣고, 물음에 답하시오.

16 여자가 하는 말의 목적으로 가장 적절한 것은?

① 실종 어린이 실태를 보고하려고
② 미아를 찾기 위한 안내를 하려고
③ 미아 찾기 홍보 대사를 소개하려고
④ 실종 어린이 신고자에게 감사하려고
⑤ 미아 찾기 캠페인 참여를 요청하려고

17 Jacob의 외모로 가장 적절한 것은?

① tall and fat
② short and fat
③ tall and thin
④ short and thin
⑤ short and muscular

DICTATION(받아쓰기) 코너입니다.
녹음의 내용을 잘 듣고, 빈칸에 알맞은 말을 쓰시기 바랍니다.

01

M Wow! There are so many places to visit here.
W You're right. A famous temple, _____, the National Art Gallery, you name it.
M Where do you want to go first?
W _____

02

W Are you all ready for your trip? Your plane leaves in just a few hours.
M Yes. I think so. Sorry, but can you call a taxi for me? I have _____ to carry on.
W You don't need to. I'll go to the airport to see you off.
M _____

03

W We can't grow without going through pain. Think about _____. You push your biceps or your triceps to the point of exhaustion. It's difficult, and even painful in the short term, but the _____ is that you get stronger, which is satisfying. It's the same process that occurs in getting better at anything, whether it's learning an instrument, playing a sport, or _____ a difficult concept.

04

M Do you know we need to drink eight glasses of water each day?
W Yes, I do.
M Then, do you drink _____ every day?
W No, I think I don't need to.
M Why? They say we should drink a lot of water to have a healthy life.
W Actually, it's a misbelief.
M What do you mean by that?
W I mean it's okay to _____ even if not water.
M You mean we can drink beverages or eat fruit?
W Exactly. Fruit and vegetables are more than 90 percent water. So _____ if you fail to drink eight glasses of water a day.

05

M Welcome to the show, Barbara.
W Thank you.
M It says here you're _____. Is that correct?
W Yes. I work for the Public Library.
M Do you read a lot?
W Quite a lot, yes.
M What are your favorite subjects?
W I read _____. I like science fiction, too.
M And your husband's name is David. Is he here with you?
W Yes, he's here.
M Where is he? Is David in the audience? Oh, there he is. Let's _____ for Barbara and David!

06

W What are you doing, Thomas?

M I'm drawing my dream house. It's homework for art class.

W Can I see it? Oh, it seems that you've _____ .

M Yeah. I was drawing the last part, a bent tree in the left side of the yard.

W I see. The yard has a badminton court in it.

M You know, I like to play badminton very much. What do you think of the tower in the small pond?

W It looks like the Eiffel Tower. And the pond which _____ is unique.

M Actually, I like maple tree leaves in autumn.

W Do you want to live in a castle? The house looks like a castle.

M Yes, I want to build _____ if possible.

07

W Oh, Bruce! What are you doing now?

M I'm arranging old movie posters.

W Wow! You've _____ .

M Right. Watching movies and collecting their posters is my favorite hobby.

W Oh, you're a fan of Audrey Hepburn.

M Yes. I collected all the posters of the films she starred in except *Roman Holiday*.

W You know what? My brother used to be a movie maniac and liked to collect posters like you.

M You mean he's not movie mania anymore?

W Yeah. So he is giving the posters to those _____ .

M Do you think he'll give it to me if he has the poster I want?

W Yes, I do.

M Then, can you ask him if he has it?

W Sure, I can. No problem. What are _____ ?

08

M Hi, Dorothy. You are here to buy books?

W Yes. How about you? Oh, it seems that you bought a book already.

M Yes. It's a novel needed to do the homework for _____ .

W I see. Then, did you buy all the books you need?

M No, I still need to buy a few new science magazines. What books do you want to get?

W Actually, I'm going to give a book to my sister for ___ _____ . But I haven't decided on what book to buy.

M What kind of genre does your sister like to read?

W She likes to read biographies, but I'm still thinking of whose biography to choose.

M How about Steve Jobs? It's so popular these days.

W Oh, that book! Okay, I think I'd better buy it. Thank you for your advice.

M Think _____ . By the way, what are you going to do after buying books? Let's have lunch together in the fast food restaurant.

W That sounds like a good idea.

09

W We still have a lot to buy, Tom. We can only afford to pay $25 for a lamp.

M All right. We'll buy a cheaper one then.

W Is there anything you _____ ?

M There's this one for $20 or the smaller one for $15.

W I like the square shape of the smaller one. It'll fit neatly onto my desk.

M And it's the cheapest. Okay, we'll buy that one.

W Good, now we need to _____ .

M I'd like to get a portable phone. You know, a cordless one.

W I think it's a good idea.

M How about this one? $90.

W Oh, it's expensive.

M It's only $20 more than the _____ .

W Okay, take that one.

10

M Jennifer, can you call Mr. Smith?

W Sure. What shall I tell him, then?

M Please, tell him I want to _____.

W Okay, sir. But why?

M I have to go to my sister's wedding on that day.

W Oh, I see. I heard your sister lives in London. Did you _____ ?

M Not yet. Could you possibly book it?

W No problem. Oh, there are a few papers waiting for your signature.

M Okay. Bring them, please. Also, I want you to _____ of our sales report.

W All right, sir.

11

W Bamboo is the fastest-growing plant primarily distributed in _____. It is a Chinese symbol of long life, while in India it is a symbol of friendship. In tropical climates, it is used in _____, as well as for fences, bridges, or walking sticks, etc. Bamboo has been the traditional material used to make fishing rods, but since the invention of fiberglass in the mid-1800s, its use in fishing rods has declined rapidly. The _____ in its stalks is often used to cook food in many Asian cultures.

12

M Let's watch TV tonight. Which channel do you want to watch?

W Well, I want to watch CSI and the News. What's _____ ?

M CSI is on three channels. Take your pick.

W What time is it now?

M It's 5:40.

W 5:40? Then this channel is out.

M Now, that _____.

W Hmm. I prefer the shorter News. 30 minutes of News is better. Also, I'd like to see CSI after the News rather than before.

M Right! So, let's watch this channel.

W OK. Looks like we have time to make dinner before the news.

M Does that mean you are _____ ?

W All right. But only if you wash up.

13

(Doorbell rings.)

W Who's there? Who is it?

M It's Karl.

W Karl? (opens the door) What's up?

M I just _____ to say happy birthday.

W Karl, you do know my birthday is tomorrow, right?

M I know. I got the invitation to your birthday party, but I have to go on a business trip tomorrow.

W Oh, that's not good. Then, you can't come to my birthday party?

M Yeah, that's why I chose to stop by today. I also brought a present for you. _____ ?

W I don't know. A book or gloves?

M No.

W Come on, tell me right now.

M _____

14

(Telephone rings.)

M Lost and Found. How can I help you?

W Yes, I'm ringing because I _____ yesterday.

M I see. Well, we received 38 bags yesterday. What color is it, and what's it made of?

W It's black, and it's made of leather.

M I've got _____ here. Can you give me some more information?

W Yes. It's got a zip in front and a long strip.

M Has it got any pockets in front?

W No, but there's a pocket on the side for a mobile phone.

M Okay, how big is it?

W _____

15

M Jenny is an English teacher. She gives the hand-outs to the students. They contain a list of vocabulary words. After a while, Tommy stands up and says there aren't _____. Jenny thinks she counted the number of papers accurately. But it is true that the papers _____. Jenny decides to let Tommy get some papers at her desk. She asks Tommy to go to her desk and get some papers. But Tommy doesn't know _____. In this situation, what would Tommy most likely say to his teacher?

Tommy Ma'am, _____

16-17

W Thank you for visiting our Lakeview Shopping Mall. We are looking for a 10-year-old boy named Jacob Burk. His father says he was last seen at around 12:30 pm, when he left the store _____ at Ben & Jerry's, Jacob's favorite ice cream store. When Jacob was last seen, he was carrying two shopping bags with the items _____ in them. And he was wearing a red T-shirt and blue jeans. Jacob is tall, about 130cm. He is slim and has a square face. If you have any information about Jacob or know where he is, please contact his parents urgently. You can phone or _____. The phone number is 281-455-5964. Thank you.

09^회 | 듣기 모의고사

1번부터 17번까지는 듣고 답하는 문제입니다. 1번부터 15번까지는
한 번만 들려주고, 16번부터 17번까지는 두 번 들려줍니다. 방송을
잘 듣고 답을 하시기 바랍니다.

01 대화를 듣고, 남자의 마지막 말에 대한 여자의 응답으로 가장 적절한
것을 고르시오.

① No, it's a waste of money.
② Sure, I will keep that in mind.
③ No, I like action movies better.
④ Yes, he is my favorite movie star.
⑤ Yes, there is one I don't want to miss.

02 대화를 듣고, 여자의 마지막 말에 대한 남자의 응답으로 가장 적절한
것을 고르시오.

① Time flies like an arrow.
② He did nothing wrong in this case.
③ It will be the same for a few years.
④ I'd like to invite you to our house.
⑤ He has been ill for the past month.

03 다음을 듣고, 남자가 하는 말의 목적으로 가장 적절한 것을 고르시오.

① 전기 절약을 호소하려고
② 꾸준한 운동을 권장하려고
③ 현대 사회의 조급함을 지적하려고
④ 효율적인 시간 관리를 강조하려고
⑤ 엘리베이터 안전 수칙을 안내하려고

04 대화를 듣고, 여자의 의견으로 가장 적절한 것을 고르시오.

① 자전거 전용 도로를 늘려야 한다.
② 일찍 일어나는 습관은 건강에 좋다.
③ 지하철을 더 청결하게 관리해야 한다.
④ 자전거 안전 장비를 잘 갖추어야 한다.
⑤ 출근할 때 지하철을 이용하는 것이 좋다.

05 대화를 듣고, 두 사람의 관계로 가장 적절한 것을 고르시오.

① policeman – driver
② father – daughter
③ repairman – customer
④ teacher – student
⑤ doctor – patient

06 대화를 듣고, 그림에서 대화의 내용과 일치하지 <u>않는</u> 것을 고르시오.

07 대화를 듣고, 남자가 여자에게 부탁한 일을 고르시오.

① 표 사 주기
② 표 바꿔 주기
③ 가방 맡아 주기
④ 음료수 사 주기
⑤ 휴대 전화 빌려 주기

08 대화를 듣고, 여자가 걱정하는 이유를 고르시오.

① 출석률이 좋지 않아서
② 실험실에서 사고를 쳐서
③ 기말고사를 못보고 놓쳐서
④ 과제물을 제출하지 못해서
⑤ 졸업 필수 과목에 낙제할 것 같아서

09 대화를 듣고, 남자가 거스름돈으로 받은 금액을 고르시오. [3점]

① $10   ② $12   ③ $14

④ $16   ⑤ $18

10 대화를 듣고, 남자의 하루 일과에서 시간을 알 수 <u>없는</u> 것을 고르시오.

① 기상 시간   ② 출근 시간   ③ 퇴근 시간

④ 저녁 식사 시간   ⑤ 취침 시간

11 East Ocean Restaurant에 관한 다음 내용을 듣고, 일치하지 <u>않</u>는 것을 고르시오.

① 차이나타운의 중심에 위치해 있다.
② 전통 요리와 현대식 요리를 모두 제공한다.
③ 각 테이블에 호출기가 달려있다.
④ 아이들과 함께 외식하기에 좋은 곳이다.
⑤ 각종 모임을 위한 방이 준비되어 있다.

12 다음 표를 보면서 대화를 듣고, 두 사람이 선택한 여행 상품을 고르시오.

Korea Package Tours

	Locations	Duration (days)	Price (per person)
①	Seoul	2	$280
②	Jeju Island	3	$530
③	Eastern Korea	4	$870
④	Western Korea	5	$1,050
⑤	Western Korea + Jeju Island	7	$1,500

13 대화를 듣고, 여자의 마지막 말에 대한 남자의 응답으로 가장 적절한 것을 고르시오. [3점]

Man : _____

① What makes her work so hard?
② I'm sick and tired of this boring job.
③ I hope she recovers from her illness.
④ She should go to the hospital right away.
⑤ If that's the case, then we shouldn't hold her back.

14 대화를 듣고, 남자의 마지막 말에 대한 여자의 응답으로 가장 적절한 것을 고르시오.

Woman : _____

① I don't know what to think.
② Of course. You will be fine.
③ You don't have to do it now.
④ Don't worry. That's not your fault.
⑤ Let's decide after asking your father.

15 다음 상황 설명을 듣고, Jason이 Brian에게 할 말로 가장 적절한 것을 고르시오.

Jason : Brian! _____
① Drive carefully.
② It's none of your business.
③ Well, honesty is the best policy.
④ There is nothing you can do about it.
⑤ Cheer up! You can do better next time.

[16-17] 다음을 듣고, 물음에 답하시오.

16 남자가 하는 말의 목적으로 가장 적절한 것은? [3점]

① To suggest good food for children
② To show how to select good cereal
③ To emphasize the importance of breakfast
④ To encourage people to eat breakfast at home
⑤ To inform about the best time to eat breakfast for children

17 남자가 하는 말과 일치하지 <u>않는</u> 것은?

① 아침 식사는 기억력 향상에 도움이 된다.
② 최근에서야 영양 성분이 학생들의 기억력에 미치는 영향이 연구되었다.
③ 연구에 참여한 학생 집단 중 한 집단에게만 아침 식사가 제공되었다.
④ 아침 식사를 하는 장소가 기억력에 영향을 미친다.
⑤ 아침 식사를 늦게 하는 편이 기억력에 더 좋을 수도 있다.

DICTATION(받아쓰기) 코너입니다.
녹음의 내용을 잘 듣고, 빈칸에 알맞은 말을 쓰시기 바랍니다.

01

M Would you like to go to a movie or a concert?

W I'd like to go to the movies.

M Do you have _____?

W _____

02

W How's everyone in your family? I haven't seen them for years.

M You're right. It's _____. Everybody's doing fine except my dad.

W What's wrong with him?

M _____

03

M Time has become a scarce commodity. Everyone wants more of it. The refrain, "If only I had more time," echoes around offices and homes all over the world. Hastiness is becoming _____ of the modern society. People are working longer and longer hours and struggling to fit more and more into every day. Symptoms include jabbing the "close" button on elevator doors to save the two to four seconds required for that to happen on its own and being unable to do one thing at a time because people are always on the phone anywhere and anytime. More and more of us are putting ourselves on the running machine of constant activities, taking on an increasingly heavy workload, and _____ to ask why.

04

W Peter, you missed the staff meeting again. What happened today?

M I'm sorry I am late. I was caught in traffic for an hour.

W How far do you drive?

M It's only a half-hour drive _____ _____. So I'm considering riding my bicycle to work.

W But I think it sounds too risky. There is no bike lane from your home to here, is there?

M That's right. Then what should I do?

W Why don't you get up a little early?

M I'd love to. But I am not a morning person. I couldn't easily wake up in the morning.

W If that's the case, _____?

M It is too crowded and dirty.

W But it's punctual anyway. I think _____ _____ in the morning.

M I can't agree with you more. I think I have no other choice. Thanks for your advice.

05

M Switch your engine off, please.

W Yes, sir. Would you tell me why you have _____?

M Because you just drove through a red light.

W But the yellow light was on when I drove through, Officer.

M It was most definitely on red when you drove through. I have photographic evidence of that. May I please see _____?

W I'm sorry. I don't have it on me. Honestly, I forgot it back at the house. But I have the insurance policy with me. Here it is.

M Please wait here. I'll come back in a moment.

06

(Telephone rings.)

M Hello, this is Chris. _____ how the decoration for the Christmas special room is going.

W It's going well. I put up a big Christmas tree in front of the window.

M Well done. Guests will love it. Did you also place an armchair?

W Yes, it is on the left side of the tree.

M What about champagne?

W I put a bottle of champagne and two glasses on the round table as you ordered.

M Did you get a snowman doll? I think kids will like it very much.

W Yes, I managed to find one and _____.

M Is there anything you've added for final touches?

W I placed a big gift box under the tree.

M Excellent! One more thing, don't forget to take a picture of the room and upload it to our hotel's website.

W Don't worry. I already did so.

07

M Excuse me. Are you _____ for the concert tickets?

W Yes.

M Can you do me a favor?

W Sure. What is it?

M Can you keep an eye on my bag, please? Nature's calling.

W Sure. Will it be long? The line is moving fast.

M No. I just want to use the bathroom. I guess I drank too much soda.

W Go ahead. _____.

08

M Mary, you look worried. What's wrong with you?

W I think I'm going to fail my biology class.

M Why do you say that?

W Well, _____ on my final exam.

M Have you attended class regularly and handed in all your assignments?

W Yes, I have no problems with my attendance and assignments.

M Hmm. What about lab?

W I don't go very often. I have a lot on my mind these days.

M How about _____?

W I can't. I need this class to graduate next year. What do you think I should do?

M Talk to the professor and explain your situation.

09

M I'd like to send this package to London _____. How much will it cost?

W $55, sir. Oh, I'm afraid it is overweight. You must pay an extra charge.

M No problem. How much is the extra charge?

W $15. So your total comes to $70.

M I want _____ just in case. How much is the insurance?

W It's 20% of the total.

M Good. Here is $100.

W Thank you. Here is the change and the receipt.

10

W So, what's your usual day like? You always seem so busy.

M Well, I usually get up around 5 am and _____ _____ until 6.

W Why do you get up so early?

M Well, I have to leave home at twenty to seven so I can catch a bus at 7. It takes me about twenty minutes to walk to the bus stop from my house.

W And what time do you get to work?

M My bus takes about an hour to get there, but it stops right in front of my office.

W That's nice. And what time do you _____ ?

M Around 5 o'clock. Then, we eat dinner around 6:30, and my wife and I play with the kids until 8.

11

M In the heart of Sydney's Chinatown is the award-winning East Ocean Restaurant. Enjoy traditional and modern Chinese cuisine at one place. Choose from a unique menu of _____ including more than 100 varieties of our famous dim sum served twice a day. Each table is equipped with a server call button so your servers are always there when you need them. A wide variety of fine wine and beer is also available. Private rooms for _____ _____ are ready. East Ocean is available to guests 19 and older only. For reservations, call 9212-4189.

12

W What are you looking at, Tim?

M I'm _____ for our summer vacation to Korea.

W Let me see. Which do you think is best?

M I think the seven-day tour of Western Korea plus Jeju Island is the best. We can travel from top to bottom of Korea.

W Hmm. You may be right, but it is way over our budget. Besides, we won't be able to have any time to take a rest at home after our travel if we take that tour.

M That's right. I completely forgot. How about the Seoul or Jeju Island tour?

W I don't want to be in a big city like Seoul for my vacation. It must _____ . And I've been to Jeju Island before. I'd like to try new locations this time.

M I see. They are also a little short for our vacation anyway. Then, we have one choice left.

W Why is it that? There are two choices left.

M The same reason as yours. I've traveled Eastern Korea before. It's just _____ , but I think it won't be a problem.

W Yeah, we can afford it. OK, let's call them and find out more about it.

13

M Do you happen to know where Amy is? I can't find her anywhere.

W She _____ .

M Please, tell me the truth. I know she's job-hunting.

W Yes, but she doesn't want anyone to know.

M Why does she want to quit?

W I think she is just looking for a better job.

M She may think _____ , but she has a great job here.

W But her heart isn't in our company any longer.

M _____

14

W You look worried. Why?

M I _____ of the Student Council, Mom.

W That's great news. What's the problem?

M I'm not sure I've got enough qualifications or experience to do that.

W You'd better _____.

M But I don't really think I'm good enough.

W If the students didn't think you were good enough, they wouldn't have chosen you.

M Do you really think so?

W _____

15

W Jason's friend, Brian, started taking driving lessons two weeks ago. He was confident that he could drive a car without any help. A few days ago, he drove his mother's car without permission. However, he made _____ while parking the car. That night, she noticed the scratches and became very angry. She asked him if he knew anything about it. But Brian told her that he had nothing to do with it. _____ and not knowing what to do, Brian asks Jason for advice. In this situation, what would Jason most likely say to Brian?

Jason : Brian! _____

16-17

M Pediatricians and nutritionists often stress how important it is for students to eat a good breakfast. But the exact benefits of a morning meal may depend in part on _____. Only recently have researchers begun investigating how nutrition affects students' memory and learning. A team of pediatricians and psychologists reports a study in which students took memory tests and were divided into three groups. One group of students was put on a daily at-school breakfast of corn flakes and milk, another group of students skipped breakfast, and the other group of students ate breakfast at home. After two weeks on these diets, all of the students were re-tested. The results showed that _____ _____ enjoyed a significantly higher level of memory performance than students who skipped breakfast. No surprise there. But kids who ate at home two hours before the memory tests also scored lower than the students who ate cereal at school 30 minutes before the tests. This suggests that when kids eat breakfast determines _____ _____. Filling their cereal bowl several hours before school begins, the team concluded, may offer students less of a benefit than a meal consumed a half hour before classes begin.

10회 듣기 모의고사

1번부터 17번까지는 듣고 답하는 문제입니다. 1번부터 15번까지는 한 번만 들려주고, 16번부터 17번까지는 두 번 들려줍니다. 방송을 잘 듣고 답을 하시기 바랍니다.

01 대화를 듣고, 여자의 마지막 말에 대한 남자의 응답으로 가장 적절한 것을 고르시오.

① Sure, who is it for?
② Go ahead. I'll wait for you.
③ Why not? Let's listen together.
④ Let's go to the cafe on the next corner.
⑤ I'm sorry we don't carry Jason Mraz CDs.

02 대화를 듣고, 남자의 마지막 말에 대한 여자의 응답으로 가장 적절한 것을 고르시오.

① Where did you hear that?
② I'm really sorry to hear that.
③ Fortunately, I'm satisfied with my job.
④ I have a good relationship with my manager.
⑤ Why not? I already told my manager about that.

03 다음을 듣고, 남자가 하는 말의 목적으로 가장 적절한 것을 고르시오.

① 새로운 비행기를 홍보하기 위해
② 비행기를 갈아타야 함을 알리기 위해
③ 비행기 탑승 시 유의 사항 안내를 위해
④ 기체 고장으로 인한 회항을 알리기 위해
⑤ 연결 비행편으로 갈아타는 방법을 설명하기 위해

04 대화를 듣고, 여자의 의견으로 가장 적절한 것을 고르시오.

① 물건 구매 전에 계획을 잘 세워야 한다.
② 식품을 대량으로 구매하는 것은 낭비이다.
③ 공동 구매로 산 물품은 반품하기가 어렵다.
④ 대량으로 구매하면 물건을 저렴하게 살 수 있다.
⑤ 유통 기간이 긴 물건은 대량으로 구매하는 것이 좋다.

05 대화를 듣고, 두 사람이 하는 말의 주제로 가장 적절한 것을 고르시오.

① 관광객 유치 방법
② 외국인 관광객의 증가
③ 나라별 관광객들의 특성
④ 무분별한 관광지 개발의 문제점
⑤ 외국인에게 추천할 만한 관광 명소

06 대화를 듣고, 그림에서 대화의 내용과 일치하지 <u>않는</u> 것을 고르시오.

07 대화를 듣고, 여자가 할 일로 가장 적절한 것을 고르시오.

① 세차하기
② 병원에 가기
③ 배터리 교체하기
④ 정비소에 가기
⑤ 긴급 출동 서비스에 전화하기

08 대화를 듣고, 여자가 스승의 날에 메시지를 보내는 이유로 가장 적절한 것을 고르시오.

① 편지보다는 메시지가 간편해서
② 선생님을 직접 찾아뵐 수 없어서
③ 스승의 날 선물을 보낼 수 없어서
④ 친구가 메시지를 보낸다기에 같이 보내기 위해서
⑤ 찾아뵙고 메시지도 보내면 선생님이 좋아하실 것 같아서

09 대화를 듣고, 남자가 지불해야 할 금액을 고르시오. [3점]

① $20　　　② $40　　　③ $50

④ $70　　　⑤ $100

10 대화를 듣고, 여자의 통증에 관해 두 사람이 언급하지 <u>않은</u> 것을 고르시오.

① 통증 부위　　　② 통증 지속 기간

③ 통증 관리법　　　④ 통증 부위의 병력

⑤ 현재 복용하는 약

11 yoga에 관한 다음 내용을 듣고, 일치하지 <u>않는</u> 것을 고르시오. [3점]

① 요가는 고대 인도에서 유래되었다.

② 요가의 목적은 심신을 조절하는 것이다.

③ 요가를 하면 밝고, 긍정적인 성격을 가질 수 있다.

④ 요가를 통해 근육을 발달시킬 수 있다.

⑤ 요가는 숙련된 강사를 만나는 것이 중요하다.

12 다음 광고지를 보면서 대화를 듣고, 대화의 내용과 일치하지 <u>않는</u> 것을 고르시오.

TIRE-STATION

size 215/54/15R

	Brand	Price per tire	Special Offer	Manufacturer's Origin
①	Hangil	$120	-	Korea
②	Komho	$120	-	Korea
③	Brightstone	$180	20% discount	Indonesia
④	Panolli	$180	20% discount	India
⑤	Michilen	$200	buy four, get one free	USA

13 대화를 듣고, 여자의 마지막 말에 대한 남자의 응답으로 가장 적절한 것을 고르시오.

Man : _____

① There's always next year for us.

② That movie was very interesting.

③ The food in New Zealand is terrible.

④ It will take about twelve hours by bus.

⑤ Yes, I really want to go to America next year.

14 대화를 듣고, 남자의 마지막 말에 대한 여자의 응답으로 가장 적절한 것을 고르시오. [3점]

Woman : _____

① You should go right now.

② Okay, you convinced me.

③ I'd love to do this again, too.

④ Your parents are so strict about time.

⑤ I know driving is a good way of saving time.

15 다음 상황 설명을 듣고, Owen의 선생님이 Owen에게 할 말로 가장 적절한 것을 고르시오.

Owen's teacher : Owen, _____

① you have to study more.

② you don't look so good.

③ basketball is not for you.

④ don't be late for school again.

⑤ our team won the game thanks to you.

[16-17] 다음을 듣고, 물음에 답하시오.

16 여자가 하는 말의 목적으로 가장 적절한 것은?

① to advise people on their health

② to warn people of serious depression

③ to explain the symptoms of depression

④ to promote a new medicine for depression

⑤ to give tips on how to deal with depression

17 우울증을 앓는 사람의 증상으로 언급된 것이 <u>아닌</u> 것은?

① 전에는 좋아했던 일에 흥미를 잃는다.

② 어떤 일에 집중하는 것이 힘들다.

③ 어떤 일을 결정하는 것에 어려움을 느낀다.

④ 사람들을 잘 알아보지 못한다.

⑤ 자살을 시도하기도 한다.

01

W Hey, Bill. What are you listening to?

M Hi. I'm listening to *I'm Yours* by Jason Mraz. _____ ___, what brings you here?

W I'm here to buy a CD for a present. Will you help me?

M _____

02

M I'm thinking about moving to another job.

W Why is that? Are you under great pressure?

M Yes. I always _____ my manager.

W _____

03

M Good morning, ladies and gentlemen, this is the captain speaking. We are very sorry to inform you that we are currently experiencing _____ _____ right now. Please exit the plane and wait at the terminal. Our Air Asia staff at the gate will guide you to a connecting flight. We are very _____ _____ this may have caused you. Thank you, and have a good day.

04

W Are we _____?

M Yes. I have a shopping list.

W Can I see it? Wow, that's a lot to buy. Do we really need all of these things?

M Not all of them are for us. Some of them are for my sister.

W Oh, your sister, Cindy, asked you to buy some stuff.

M Yes. Since we're going to the wholesale store, I asked her if she needs anything.

W Honey, did you check this list? I think we just need a small amount of bread. If we buy bread there, we cannot eat it all _____.

M But it's very cheap if we buy there. Even though we buy bread in the retail store, we buy a much smaller amount of bread at the same price.

W But I think _____.

M Don't worry. We'll eat it all.

05

W Wow, I love this place!

M Yeah, Myoung-dong is one of my favorite places in Seoul.

W Look at those Japanese people all over the place.

M I know. I heard Myoung-dong is _____ _____.

W I can see that. Here we can enjoy various goodies for the mouth, shopping, and street performing. Actually, one of my friends from Germany is coming next week. Do you have another place to recommend?

M How about Gyeongbokgung? You can see the changing of the guards ceremony.

W Good! My friend's really into Korean history.

M I'll lend you _____ in Korea. Check it out.

W Thanks a lot.

M My pleasure. Have a great time with your friend!

06

W Did you watch the talk show on TV last night?

M Are you talking about *Hidden Songs*?

W Yes, that's the one. So, did you watch?

M No, I missed it. Tell me about the show in detail. Who is on it?

W I can't call up the name of the band. There are _____ _____.

M How do they look?

W Both of the women wear a hat and a white suit.

M And the guys?

W The guys are wearing sunglasses and a black suit. Does this ring a bell?

M Does one of the guys _____?

W Right, he was playing the drums. And both women were singing, and the other guys were playing the guitar.

M I think I know who they are. The two guys have short hair and the women are slim and have long straight hair, right?

W Right. I guess you know.

07

M Hello. Are you okay? Is there anything I can do to help you?

W Yes, Officer. My car won't start. I don't know why.

M Well, there could be something wrong with the battery.

W Oh, what should I do?

M Ma'am, have you _____?

W Yes, I have.

M Then, it might be better for you to call the emergency service of your insurance company. I guess they could come here to help you in about 30 minutes.

W Oh, I didn't know about that service. Thank you for telling me.

M You're welcome. I will be in the patrol car until the serviceman comes to help you. Please _____ _____ right now and get in your car. It's very cold outside.

W Thank you for your kindness.

M You don't have to thank me at all. It's my job to help people.

08

M Jenny, do you know what tomorrow is?

W I just know tomorrow is Wednesday. Is it a special day?

M Yes, tomorrow is "Teacher's Day."

W Oh, time flies. It has been more than three months since we _____.

M Yes, right. I really want to see Mr. Park from our high school. He really took care of our class. So I will go and see him tomorrow with flowers.

W Yes, I really _____ during our high school days.

M No doubt about it. So, do you want to come along?

W I want to, but I have an important prior appointment with Professor Kim.

M Then, why don't you send him a message? Maybe he would be happy to see your message.

W Oh, you are right. I will do that. Please give him ____ _____.

09

M Hi, good afternoon!

W Good afternoon. How can I help you?

M I'd like to send two parcels.

W Where do you want to send them?

M Paris. What is the rate to send a parcel to Paris?

W Well, that _____ and the service. What's inside these parcels?

M One has foodstuffs, and the other has books.

W Let me check the weight of each parcel. (pause) The foodstuffs weigh 6kg and books 9kg. Each parcel is under 10kg, so you can send those for the same charge. _____, the regular service charge would be $20, and the express service charge would be $50.

M I will send the foodstuffs by express service and the books by regular service.

W OK, I got it.

10

M Good morning. What brings you in?

W Good morning. I _____ in my lower back.

M How long has your back been bothering you?

W I've been having pain there for about two weeks.

M Do you have any history of back problems?

W No, this is the first time. So I _____ this is happening.

M Are you taking any medicine at the moment?

W No, just aspirin from time to time to kill the pain.

M OK. Let's _____ at your back. Please lie on your face on the bed.

W OK, Dr. Davis.

11

M Have you tried yoga? Yoga originated in ancient India. The purpose of yoga is to free oneself and to control one's body and spirit _____. By practicing yoga, you can have a balanced, bright, and positive character. Furthermore, your muscles will become relaxed by massaging your whole body. Are you still just staying in your house like a couch potato, doing nothing in particular? Please get up and _____. One thing you should remember! When you start yoga, it's very important to work with skilled instructors. We are offering an unbelievable chance to experience yoga with skilled instructors and at special prices. If you are interested, _____ at 777-YOGA. They can correct your pose while you're practicing.

12

M Honey, I think it is time for us to change the tires. Don't you think so?

W Yes, I noticed all four tires have already worn out. Have you _____ by any chance?

M I already checked them at Tire-Station. Look at this leaflet.

W The prices of Hangil and Komho are _____. Both are $120 per tire.

M Yes, they offer the cheapest prices. But I heard some noise when I drove on them before.

W Then, why don't we use Brightstone or Panolli? Their prices per tire are the same. Besides, they are offering a 20% discount.

M Their tires are made in Indonesia. _____ about their quality.

W Then, why don't we try Michilen tires? Their price per tire is $200, but we can get one free if we buy four. Besides, they are made in the USA. I think it's a good deal for us.

M OK. Let's do that.

13

W It's finally summer vacation!

M Yes, it is. Are you _____ during the summer vacation?

W Yes, I plan to take a trip to New Zealand.

M Really? Have you ever been there?

W Yes, this is my second time. I went there last year _____. Have you been there?

M No, but I want to go sometime.

W Why don't you join me?

M You know, I have to take the summer course.

W Right. By the way, do you know anything good about New Zealand?

M You know that the movie *Lord of the Rings* was filmed there, don't you? I heard the scenery there is fantastic.

W Yes, I'm sure it is. I'm really sorry that we can't go together.

M _____

14

W I have to be going now. It's _____ .

M Must you go so soon? We still have so much to discuss about our science project.

W I want to stay longer, but my parents will worry about me if I'm out too late.

M You can call your parents. Please, _____ .

W It's a school day tomorrow, and we both have to get up early. So I'll be saying goodbye now.

M OK. I'll give you a ride, since it's a half-hour to your house on foot.

W That's very thoughtful of you. Thanks a lot.

M If I drive you home, you can _____ , right? So how about staying thirty minutes longer?

W _____

15

M Owen was not good at studying, and his teacher was very concerned about him. His teacher called him to talk about his problem. _____ , his teacher came to know that he was good at playing basketball. Owen's teacher helped him join the basketball team at school. He practiced a lot and finally became a key player. He _____ play in a game against a rival team. In the fourth quarter, he made a three-point shot at the final second. That allowed his team to win at the buzzer. Also, his teacher was there. After the game, what would Owen's teacher most likely say to him?

Owen's teacher Owen, _____

16-17

W Have you ever been deeply depressed? When you are depressed, you may feel sad, anxious, worried, _____ . A depressed mood doesn't necessarily mean a mental disorder. A normal person can be depressed, too. However, when you're depressed for a long period, it can have a negative effect both on mental and physical health. In terms of mental health, depressed people _____ in what they liked. Also, they have difficulties in concentrating, making decisions, or remembering details. In severe cases, they may attempt suicide. In terms of physical health, depressed people lose their appetite or eat too much. They also find it difficult to sleep, or they sleep too much. They _____ , aches, and pains. Indigestion is one of the common problems among depressed people.

11^회 | 듣기 모의고사

1번부터 17번까지는 듣고 답하는 문제입니다. 1번부터 15번까지는 한 번만 들려주고, 16번부터 17번까지는 두 번 들려줍니다. 방송을 잘 듣고 답을 하시기 바랍니다.

01 대화를 듣고, 남자의 마지막 말에 대한 여자의 응답으로 가장 적절한 것을 고르시오.

① I'll take care of it for you.
② Yes, I had all kinds of trouble.
③ Come to me if you are ever in any difficulty.
④ You know what they say. Easy come, easy go.
⑤ Let's plant trees and flowers for a better future.

02 대화를 듣고, 여자의 마지막 말에 대한 남자의 응답으로 가장 적절한 것을 고르시오.

① I don't like the color of that dress.
② I think you drink too much coffee.
③ I'm telling you this is nobody's fault.
④ I'll call you right away when it's ready.
⑤ I also have an appointment this Sunday.

03 다음을 듣고, 여자가 하는 말의 목적으로 가장 적절한 것을 고르시오.

① 매장의 이전을 알리려고
② 새로운 메뉴를 알리려고
③ 새로운 매장의 개점을 알리려고
④ 배달 서비스를 시작한다는 사실을 알리려고
⑤ 음식의 신선함을 유지하는 방법을 알리려고

04 대화를 듣고, 여자의 의견으로 가장 적절한 것을 고르시오.

① 정상까지 올라가야 한다.
② 바로 산을 내려가야 한다.
③ 응급 구조를 요청해야 한다.
④ 귀가 시에 버스를 타고 가야 한다.
⑤ 등산 시에 충분한 장비와 음식을 준비해야 한다.

05 대화를 듣고, 두 사람의 관계를 가장 잘 나타낸 것을 고르시오.

① boss – secretary
② publisher – writer
③ professor – student
④ travel agent – customer
⑤ interviewer – job applicant

06 대화를 듣고, 그림에서 대화의 내용과 일치하지 <u>않는</u> 것을 고르시오.

07 대화를 듣고, 여자가 남자를 위해 할 일로 가장 적절한 것을 고르시오.

① to pay for dinner
② to get musical tickets
③ to book a riverboat tour
④ to reserve museum tickets
⑤ to cancel a flight reservation

08 대화를 듣고, 남자가 기뻐하는 이유를 고르시오.

① 아내와 화해해서
② 직장에서 승진해서
③ 아내의 병이 회복되어서
④ 아내에게 생일 선물을 받아서
⑤ 직장 상사에게 칭찬을 받아서

09 대화를 듣고, 남자가 지불해야 할 금액을 고르시오. [3점]

① $20   ② $26   ③ $30
④ $36   ⑤ $40

10 다음을 듣고, 방송 내용에 관해 언급하지 <u>않은</u> 것을 고르시오.

① 한국 자동차 수출 감소
② 한국의 평균 출산율 감소
③ 패스트푸드로 인한 비만 인구 증가
④ 5년간 흡연자 수 5퍼센트 감소
⑤ 서울에서 국제 불꽃놀이 축제 개최

11 James Cook에 관한 다음 내용을 듣고, 일치하지 <u>않는</u> 것을 고르시오.

① 영국의 탐험가였다.
② 지구와 태양간의 거리를 측정하고자 했다.
③ 호주 북부를 지도에 담았다.
④ 마지막 탐험은 항로를 찾기 위한 것이었다.
⑤ 원주민에게 인질로 잡혔다가 풀려났다.

12 다음 표를 보면서 대화를 듣고, 여자가 담당할 반을 고르시오.

Blue Ocean Swimming School
<Morning Classes>

	Level	Time
①	Beginner	6:00 ~ 6:50
②	Intermediate	7:00 ~ 7:50
③	Beginner	8:00 ~ 8:50
④	Intermediate	9:00 ~ 9:50
⑤	Beginner	10:00 ~ 10:50

13 대화를 듣고, 여자의 마지막 말에 대한 남자의 응답으로 가장 적절한 것을 고르시오. [3점]

Man : _____

① Biology is my favorite subject.
② I think watching baseball is boring.
③ I don't know how to fix a computer.
④ I want to, but they're always occupied.
⑤ You are welcome to any book in my library.

14 대화를 듣고, 남자의 마지막 말에 대한 여자의 응답으로 가장 적절한 것을 고르시오.

Woman : _____

① Would you like a cup of coffee?
② Try to use the computer less often.
③ I'm not interested in computer games.
④ How about taking one or two aspirins?
⑤ Why don't you come over to my office?

15 다음 상황 설명을 듣고, Frank가 할머니에게 할 말로 가장 적절한 것을 고르시오.

Frank : Grandma, _____

① you need to get your rest.
② age is only a state of mind.
③ I'm really sorry to hear that.
④ why don't you save some money?
⑤ you have a memory like a computer.

[16-17] 다음을 듣고, 물음에 답하시오.

16 Care Alert을 시작한 것은 누구인가?

① children   ② volunteers
③ the police   ④ kidnap victims
⑤ television stations

17 Care Alert에 대해 언급되지 <u>않은</u> 것은? [3점]

① 사건을 대중들에게 알리는 것이 목적이다.
② 방송국에 사건 정보를 제공한다.
③ 자신의 아이를 납치하는 사건은 다루지 않는다.
④ 아이를 학대하는 부모를 신고한다.
⑤ 아이들의 생명을 구할 것으로 기대된다.

DICTATION(받아쓰기) 코너입니다.
녹음의 내용을 잘 듣고, 빈칸에 알맞은 말을 쓰시기 바랍니다.

01

M Growing plants was _____ I thought.

W I know what you mean. They need constant care and attention.

M You're right. Was it _____, too?

W _____

02

W Could you _____ on my dress? I spilt coffee on it.

M Hmm, I'm not 100% sure, but I'll try my best.

W When can I _____? I need that dress this Sunday.

M _____

03

W Hello, everyone. Here is good news for you. Red Hat Chicken now has _____ to serve you. Customers in the old downtown area can find us at our original location on Eastern Boulevard across from Woodfield Mall. Customers in the new downtown area can come and see us at our new location on Madison Avenue next door to the Metropolitan Department Store. But _____ _____ you choose, you'll be sure to enjoy Red Hat Chicken's home-style fried chicken, biscuits, French fries, and more. As you know, we don't offer delivery service as other chicken chains do. Instead, we guarantee freshness, because when it comes to truly delicious fried chicken, freshness matters.

04

M What a wonderful view! It's so nice to be climbing this mountain.

W I agree. But I think we'd better go down right away. My legs hurt.

M Come on. The peak is only an hour away. Let's make it to the top.

W Don't you notice _____?

M That's not a problem. We have flashlights and enough food.

W The night climbing could be very dangerous. We might have to call emergency rescue.

M I understand. We've already used up lots of energy. And people say _____ than ascending.

W Right. Besides, we should take the train schedule home into account.

M Oh, I almost forgot. Thanks for reminding me.

W You're welcome. Sorry to disappoint you.

M There's always next time. Let's hurry.

05

M Miss Parker, I just have a few more questions.

W What would you like to know?

M As you know, there's a lot of computer work _____ _____. How fast do you type?

W About 70 words a minute.

M OK. Well, it's not a requirement, but once we publish our studies, we often give presentations of our findings throughout the country. Do you have any experience in public speaking?

W Well, yes. _____ last year to the professors at my college.

M Great. And, of course, we'd offer you a company car when you travel.

W Good, that would save me some money.

M Right. Now, do you have any questions?

W Yes. How much international travel would there be?

M Just a few days a month, but you wouldn't be expected to travel on holidays.

06

W Hi, David. What are you looking at?

M Hi, Anna. It's a _____ . The kids in the picture are my nephew and niece.

W Let me see. They are living in America, aren't they?

M How did you know? I don't remember I told you about them before.

W It's not a big deal. I just guessed it from the star-striped banner in front of the light house over there.

M I see.

W How cute, _____ waiting for fish to bait!

M Look. Their dog seems to be sitting and waiting for fish, too. Don't you think it really looks like a painting?

W Yes, I agree. I'd love to visit there.

M You can! I'm going to visit them next month. They will _____ if you can come with me.

W Really? I'll check my schedule and let you know.

07

W When are you going back home, Ted?

M I've _____ on a flight to New York this Saturday.

W So you have only two days left here in London. I think you must want to do something tomorrow. Have you been to any museums yet?

M Yes. I've already been to several museums here.

W Then, what about an evening riverboat tour?

M Actually, I've already gone twice this week.

W What do you want to do?

M Well, I haven't been to the theater in a long time.

W Oh, OK. I hear there's a terrific musical at the Prince Edward Theater.

M Great! How can _____ ?

W Don't worry about the tickets. I'll take care of them.

M Thank you. Then I'll treat you to dinner.

08

W Why do you look so serious?

M _____ with my wife.

W What's the matter? Oh... Please don't tell me you forgot her birthday again.

M Yeah, she's really hurt.

W Hmm. I hope this news can make her feel better.

M What is it?

W Don't you know? You got promoted! I just heard about it from your boss.

M Really? I can't believe it. It would be a wonderful gift for her.

W Even though it is a little bit late.

M You're right. _____ that I have become a manager now.

09

W Good evening, sir. Which movie would you like to see?

M *Toy Story 4*, please.

W How many tickets do you need?

M I need tickets for two adults and two children. How much would that be?

W It _____ . What time do you want?

M 8:20, please.

W Then it would be $10 per adult and $5 per child.

M I see. Could I get a discount with this credit card?

W Oh, that's our membership credit card. You can _____ _____ for up to two people.

M That's good. Here's my credit card.

W Please sign here. Here's your receipt. Is there anything else I can help you with?

M No, thank you.

W Four tickets for *Toy Story 4*. Two adults and two children. Here you are.

10

(news music)

M Hello. I'm Tom Brown. This is Korea Today. Here are today's headlines:
- Korean car exports to North America and Western Europe are declining.
- The average birthrate in Korea is decreasing each year.
- A recent study in Korea warns that _____ _____ can harm children's health.
- The number of smokers in Korea has fallen by five percentage points over the past five years.
- The International Fireworks Festival will be held in Seoul.

I'll be back in a minute. _____. You are watching Korea Today.

(news music)

11

W James Cook was _____ and astronomer who went on many expeditions to the Pacific Ocean, Antarctic, Arctic, and around the world. On his first journey, he sailed to Tahiti in order to observe Venus as it passed between the Earth and the Sun in order to try to determine the distance between the Earth and the Sun. During this expedition, he also mapped northern Australia. Cook's second expedition took him to Antarctica and to Easter Island. Cook's last expedition was a search for the Northwest Passage across North America to Asia. Cook was killed by a mob on Feb. 14, 1779, on the Sandwich Islands. At that time, he was trying to _____ to get the natives to return a sailboat they had stolen.

12

M Nice to meet you. I'm the director of the Blue Ocean Swimming School. What can I do for you?

W I'm applying for the job listed in the newspaper. How many instructors will you be hiring?

M Two, maybe three. I need people to teach _____ _____ classes in the morning. Can you teach both levels?

W No, I can't teach intermediate level, but I can teach beginners.

M I see. How long have you been teaching swimming?

W This will be my second year teaching.

M Good. I think _____. Your first class will start at 6 o'clock in the morning. And the second class...

W Wait a minute! 6 in the morning? I can't arrive here before 8:30. I live about forty kilometers away.

M If that's the case, you will have only one class to teach. Would it be OK for you?

W That's all right. It's better than doing nothing.

13

(Telephone rings.)

W Hello, Mike? This is Anne.

M Hi, Anne. What's up?

W Well, I'm _____ for a history exam.

M Are you at home?

W Yes, I usually study at the library, but I thought I might get more work done at home.

M So, are you studying hard?

W No, not really. In fact, I'm watching a baseball game right now. What about you? What are you doing now?

M I'm writing out my biology report on paper.

W On paper? Don't you have a computer at home?

M Well, I do, but _____. So, for now, I can't use it.

W Many students often use the computers at the library. How come you don't use them?

M _____

14

W Hi, Ken. What seems to be the problem?

M Well, I'm _____ .

W Have you tried taking aspirins?

M Yes, but it just gives me an upset stomach.

W You'd better not take any more aspirins, then. Do you drink a lot of coffee?

M Yes. About five or six cups a day.

W Oh! That's a lot of caffeine! Try drinking water, instead. When do you get these headaches?

M Generally when I'm at the office.

W How long do you use your computer each day?

M For about 8 to 10 hours. I couldn't live _____

_____ .

W _____

15

M Frank calls his grandmother who retired three months ago and asks how she is doing these days. She says she is doing fine and has been very busy since she retired. She says she _____ and takes an advanced computer course. She also says she takes yoga in the evening, and sometimes when she can't sleep, she stays up late and surfs the Internet. Listening to her, Frank comes to think that she is _____ , considering her age—even though she says she is healthy. In this situation, what would Frank most likely say to his grandmother?

Frank Grandma, _____

16-17

W Sometimes children are kidnapped. It is important that kidnapped children be found and brought home as soon as possible. _____ about a kidnapping, the sooner it might be able to help. Some volunteers decided to start a program that would alert the public about kidnappings right away. This program is called "Care Alert." The Care Alert program gives television and radio stations important information about a recently kidnapped child. These stations will then tell the public what happened in hopes that someone might be able to help. Anyone who may have seen something about the kidnapping could then call the police. Sometimes one parent of a child kidnaps his or her own child. These kidnappings are not used in the Care Alert program. The Care Alert program is only used when a stranger has taken a child. When a child is kidnapped, he or she is in a lot of danger. It is expected that this new Care Alert program will _____ .

12 회 | 듣기 모의고사

1번부터 17번까지는 듣고 답하는 문제입니다. 1번부터 15번까지는 한 번만 들려주고, 16번부터 17번까지는 두 번 들려줍니다. 방송을 잘 듣고 답을 하시기 바랍니다.

01 대화를 듣고, 여자의 마지막 말에 대한 남자의 응답으로 가장 적절한 것을 고르시오.

① I have to finish it by this Friday.
② Okay. As soon as I am done with it.
③ I don't feel like watching a movie tonight.
④ I will be available probably on the weekend.
⑤ Finishing the report is my priority at this moment.

02 대화를 듣고, 남자의 마지막 말에 대한 여자의 응답으로 가장 적절한 것을 고르시오.

① There is no parking fee.
② You can take the subway.
③ The convention center is not open yet.
④ You are not supposed to leave your car here.
⑤ There is a pretty cheap public parking lot on 5th Avenue.

03 다음을 듣고, 남자가 하는 말의 주제로 가장 적절한 것을 고르시오.

① 자연재해의 위험성
② 홍수에 대처하는 상황별 방법
③ 갑자기 시동이 꺼진 차를 살리는 방법
④ 응급 상황 발생 시 침착한 대처의 중요성
⑤ 라디오나 텔레비전을 통한 최신 정보 취득의 필요성

04 대화를 듣고, 여자의 의견으로 가장 적절한 것을 고르시오.

① 낚시를 하면서 떠들면 안 된다.
② 물고기를 잡기 위해 기다리는 시간은 매우 지루하다.
③ 낚시를 하면서 물고기를 잡는 순간이 가장 즐겁다.
④ 물고기를 잡는 것보다 그 과정을 즐기는 것이 낚시의 묘미다.
⑤ 낚시하는 사람들은 물고기를 잡는 것보다 사람들과 즐기는 것을 더 좋아한다.

05 대화를 듣고, 두 사람의 관계를 가장 잘 나타낸 것을 고르시오.

① model – sponsor
② photographer – client
③ businessman – client
④ photographer – model
⑤ movie director – actress

06 대화를 듣고, 그림에서 대화의 내용과 일치하지 않는 것을 고르시오.

07 대화를 듣고, 두 사람이 할 일로 가장 적절한 것을 고르시오.

① to go to the party
② to take a makeup class
③ to visit Brenda's uncle's house
④ to take care of Brenda's cousins
⑤ to go to the Reading Club meeting

08 대화를 듣고, 남자가 병문안을 갈 수 없는 이유를 고르시오.

① 여름휴가로 하와이를 가야 해서
② 차가 고장 나서 이용할 수 없어서
③ 자동차 사고로 두 다리를 깁스해서
④ 공항에 아버지를 태우러 가야 해서
⑤ 월요일까지 마쳐야 하는 숙제가 있어서

09 대화를 듣고, 여자가 지불할 금액을 고르시오. [3점]

① $160   ② $170   ③ $180
④ $190   ⑤ $200

10 대화를 듣고, 남자가 어제 한 일로 언급되지 않은 것을 고르시오.

① 무대 장치 설치
② 댄스 경연 대회 참가
③ 방송제 사회 보기
④ 선생님께 꽃 달아 드리기
⑤ 행사 장소 청소

11 olive에 관한 다음 내용을 듣고, 일치하지 않는 것을 고르시오. [3점]

① 그리스와 이탈리아 음식에 주로 사용된다.
② 열매, 나무, 잎이 유용해서 버릴 것이 거의 없다.
③ 어떤 기후에서도 잘 자란다.
④ 열매를 수확하기가 어렵지는 않다.
⑤ 두 해에 걸쳐 열매를 맺는 경우는 드물다.

12 다음 표를 보면서 대화를 듣고, 대화의 내용과 일치하지 않는 것을 고르시오.

	Activities	Body Part Affected (workout area)	Kcal (per hour)
①	dusting	shoulders, chest	180
②	vacuuming	back, arms	240
③	shopping for clothes	legs, chest, back, shoulders	240
④	window washing	chest, legs	260
⑤	pushing a child on a swing	chest, hips, legs	290

13 대화를 듣고, 남자의 마지막 말에 대한 여자의 응답으로 가장 적절한 것을 고르시오. [3점]

Woman : _____

① We need to learn more about music therapy.
② Because therapy may be divided into several types.
③ I would say that not all kinds of music work for us.
④ Music has been popular among doctors for a long time.
⑤ In fact, I'm thinking of studying it in graduate school.

14 대화를 듣고, 여자의 마지막 말에 대한 남자의 응답으로 가장 적절한 것을 고르시오.

Man : _____

① I guess you should go on a diet, too.
② Why do you think vegetarian food is healthy?
③ Maybe I should consider changing my diet, too.
④ You know, having an inactive lifestyle is bad for you.
⑤ You should've eaten more meat in your young days.

15 다음 상황 설명을 듣고, 민수가 김 선생님에게 할 말로 가장 적절한 것을 고르시오.

Minsu : Ms. Kim, _____

① could you write a speech manuscript for me?
② would you help me with my English pronunciation?
③ would you proofread my English speech manuscript?
④ I'd like to participate in the English speech contest.
⑤ what should I do to improve my speaking ability?

[16-17] 다음을 듣고, 물음에 답하시오.

16 여자가 하는 말의 목적으로 가장 적절한 것은?

① 연설의 중요성을 강조하려고
② 좋은 연설가의 자질들을 설명하려고
③ 수업 일정이 바뀌었음을 공지하려고
④ 좋은 학점을 얻기 위한 비결을 알려주려고
⑤ 수업에 관한 전반적인 사항들을 안내하려고

17 public speaking 수업에 관한 내용과 일치하지 않는 것은?

① 수업은 매주 화요일과 목요일 오후에 진행된다.
② 출석 점수는 학점에 영향을 미치지 않는다.
③ 대중 연설은 학점의 50 퍼센트를 차지한다.
④ 첫 수업의 내용은 좋은 연설가들의 특징에 관한 것이다.
⑤ 학생들은 좋은 연설가가 되기 위한 기초적인 기술을 공부할 것이다.

01

W Jimmy, how about _____ for a movie? I've got two movie tickets.

M Sorry. I am really busy. I have to write a report.

W You do? When is it due?

M _____.

02

M Excuse me, could you show me the way to the convention center?

W It's that building on the right, but _____ there is no parking spot there.

M Then, do you happen to know where I can leave my car for a few hours?

W _____.

03

M In this world of drastic weather changes, _____ _____ for any kind of natural disasters. Especially with the coming of monsoon season, you should keep in mind what to do when a true emergency such as floods comes up _____. Firstly, when you are inside your house, turn on the radio or television to get the latest information. Get your emergency supplies, and if you are told to leave, do so immediately. Secondly, if you are outside, climb to high ground or a building and wait patiently to be rescued. Lastly, if you are in a car and it stalls, _____ and climb to higher ground. Many deaths have been caused by attempts to move stalled vehicles.

04

W Mr. Baker, as I said, I _____.

M Don't worry. I'll teach you everything about it. Just do as I tell you.

W By the way, be rather quiet here. People don't talk to each other.

M I know. If it's noisy, fish will feel someone is here, and they will go and hide.

W I guess so.

M Maybe to you, people who are here _____ and look like they do nothing but sitting. But when you catch a fish, you cannot say how happy you are at the moment.

W Oh, no, no, I don't think they look bored. They look like they enjoy fishing and nature. I mean their faces look very peaceful and happy. Looking at their faces, I think the real pleasure of fishing is waiting and enjoying the time.

M You're right. And after fishing, you can _____ _____ which you caught and share with other people.

W I think fishing is a really good leisure activity.

05

W Can I see the pictures _____?

M Sure. Come here and look at them.

W I think this picture looks pretty good. My face looks natural.

M I agree, but in this picture, we cannot clearly see the clothes. Maybe the background is too dark.

W Yeah, maybe so.

M You know we are not the one who picks the pictures. _____ the pictures. So, the products must appear vividly in this picture.

W Then, how can we do that?

M Let's try using light and a reflecting plate. _____ bright pictures.

W Okay, I got it. And I'll try to pose so as not to hide the products.

06

W Look, there's _____ at the end of the crossing.

M Yeah, I see the construction sign.

W There are some paving stones.

M Maybe they will change the paving stones. But they haven't started construction yet.

W Right. Nobody's there. Then, what shall we do? Our destination is _____.

M Just ignore the sign and pass through between the stones.

W I don't think that's a good idea. Even though nobody is working there now, it still looks dangerous.

M You're right. Oh, there's another sign. It says "Use Other Side."

W The other sidewalk _____ _____. There are many trees along the road. Let's get going. The light is green.

07

M Brenda, why didn't you come to the Reading Club meeting last Friday?

W I went to my uncle's house and took care of my little cousins.

M Why? Was your aunt busy?

W Yeah, nowadays _____ at the local college.

M Then, are you going to look after your cousins every Friday?

W No. Actually, it was a sort of makeup lesson because her professor was not able to come to class last week.

M I see. Oh, wait! Today is Thursday, right?

W Right. What's the matter?

M _____ have a meeting for the Reading Club this evening.

W Why?

M Most of the club members said they are going to the party this Friday, so it was moved up one day. I think I have to go there now. Can you come?

W I can't miss it today. Let's hurry up!

08

W Hey, Jason. Long time no see. Where have you been?

M I went to Hawaii for summer vacation.

W Oh, did you? You must have had a wonderful time. By the way, did you hear that Tim _____?

M No, that is news to me. What happened?

W He got hit by a car, and both of his legs are in a cast. I am planning to _____ this Friday night. You want to come along?

M I really want to, but my dad comes back from his business trip on Friday night. I need to pick him up at the airport.

W Why don't you ask your mom for a favor?

M Her car broke down, and it is _____.

W How about your brother?

M He said his homework is due next Monday.

W I see. Have fun with your family, then.

09

W May I help you?

M Yes, I want to buy a pair of blue jeans.

W You've come just _____. We are giving 20% off most of our blue jean brands.

M Great. How much is this one?

W It is one of the most popular items. Since its list price is $100, you can have it for $90.

M Didn't you say that you would give me 20% off?

W Yes, but it is a brand-new product, and you can ___ _____ of the price.

M I see.

W But if you buy more than two pairs, you can have an additional 5% off.

M Really? Then, it would be 15% of the total.

W Yes, that's right.

M All right. I'll purchase two pairs of brand-new blue jeans.

10

W How was your school festival?

M Oh, it was fantastic. It was a very busy day for me.

W Why is that?

M It's because I participated in _____.

W Tell me what you did.

M First of all, I helped set the stage because I was the MC of the broadcasting festival.

W Wonderful. I'm sure _____.

M And I entered the dance contest as Jane's partner.

W Did you win a prize?

M No, unfortunately. But it was a good experience.

W Did you have some event for your teachers, like giving them flowers?

M No. This was an annual school festival, not a Teachers' Day event.

W I see. What else did you do?

M Well, after the festival finished, _____ with other club members.

W Wow, what a busy day for you!

11

M Olive trees are very useful. We make food using olives and also get oil from these. Especially, olives _____ in Greek and Italian food. We plant and grow olive trees for olive oil, fine wood, olive leaves, and olive fruit. Almost every part of the olive tree is put to use. The olive trees grow well _____, but they are weak to frost and long-continued rains. However, it is not difficult to get the crop from olive trees. Sometimes we can _____ gatherings of fruit, but they seldom bear well two years in succession. Olives are famous for healthy food, too.

12

W Look at this table. The chart shows how many calories are consumed by daily activities and which body part they use.

M Oh, interesting. I can consume 180 Kcal per hour by dusting.

W Yeah. It's because dusting works on your shoulders and chest. Also vacuuming, working on the back and arms, consumes 240 Kcal per hour.

M Shopping for clothes works on legs, chest, back, and shoulders, consuming the same number of calories.

W Right. What is the activity _____ _____?

M It's pushing a child on a swing or window washing, both of which consume 290 Kcal per hour.

W I see. Since I have no child, window washing is the one I can choose to consume the most calories.

M Yes. Window washing _____ your chest, shoulders, back, and legs.

13

W Have you ever heard of music therapy?

M Of course, I have. But I don't know exactly what it is.

W Well, _____, it's a method to treat physical illnesses through music.

M How does it work?

W Listening to music drops stress hormones and improves our immune system.

M Interesting!

W So, if you listen to good music, you'll feel relaxed and _____ and tension.

M I agree. Listening to music is a way of relieving my stress.

W Absolutely. In that way, music helps us treat our own bodies.

M By the way, what made you bring up music therapy suddenly?

W _____

14

M Julie, I didn't know you are a vegetarian.

W I am. Actually I _____ since I was fifteen.

M Really? What made you change?

W When I was in elementary school, I was a couch potato who did not like exercising and lived an inactive life. As a result, I _____ and decided to follow a vegetarian diet.

M Did you? What kind of change did you feel most after you became a vegetarian?

W Well, I lost almost 20 pounds after I changed my eating habits.

M Any mental changes?

W I felt revitalized, rejuvenated, and above all I came to _____ in myself.

M Wow, it is worth trying.

W Yes, and I'll never go back to eating meat.

M _____

15

M Minsu plans to participate in the English speech contest promoted by his local community. He _____ _____ his own speech manuscript first. So he worked on a speech manuscript for a couple of days and finally finished it. However, he's not confident of it. It _____ in vocabulary, grammar, or sentence structure. He thinks that he needs somebody to read it in order to find any mistakes in it. So he's going to ask Ms. Kim, his English teacher, to do that. In this situation, what would Minsu most likely say to Ms. Kim?

Minsu Ms. Kim, _____

16-17

W Welcome, all who _____ public speech class. Before we begin our first lesson, I'd like to briefly talk about this course. We are going to meet every Tuesday and Thursday from 2 pm to 4 pm. In this course, we will generally study basic skills and techniques to become a good speaker. Speaking of the evaluation, participation and attendance _____ _____ of the grade, and your final exam is 40 percent of the total grade. The other 50 percent will be evaluated based on your public speech. My office is on the third floor of this building, so if you have any questions or need any help, don't hesitate to come and see me during my office hours. Okay, let's start _____ "Characteristics of Excellent Speakers."

13^회 | 듣기 모의고사

1번부터 17번까지는 듣고 답하는 문제입니다. 1번부터 15번까지는 한 번만 들려주고, 16번부터 17번까지는 두 번 들려줍니다. 방송을 잘 듣고 답을 하시기 바랍니다.

01 대화를 듣고, 여자의 마지막 말에 대한 남자의 응답으로 가장 적절한 것을 고르시오.

① Sorry. You dialed the wrong number.
② You have a double bedroom booked for next Friday.
③ There are no rooms available for the next weekend.
④ You must have forgotten your confirmation number.
⑤ If you don't have a reservation number, I can't help you.

02 대화를 듣고, 남자의 마지막 말에 대한 여자의 응답으로 가장 적절한 것을 고르시오.

① Oh, here, please.
② I am not ready to order yet.
③ No, thanks. I have already ordered.
④ Wow, you can make a Caramel Macchiato?
⑤ Sounds delicious. I will have two, please.

03 다음을 듣고, 남자가 하는 말의 주제로 가장 적절한 것을 고르시오.

① 규칙적인 생활의 중요성
② 규칙적인 운동의 중요성
③ 만성 피로를 느끼는 이유
④ 숙면을 취하기 위한 방법
⑤ 카페인이 건강에 미치는 영향

04 대화를 듣고, 여자의 의견으로 가장 적절한 것을 고르시오.

① 규칙적인 생활은 질병 치료에 도움이 된다.
② 어지러움을 느끼면 바로 병원에 가야 한다.
③ 체중이 갑자기 증가하면 당뇨병 검사를 해야 한다.
④ 체중 감량 시에는 식이요법과 운동을 병행해야 한다.
⑤ 건강을 위해 두 달 동안 체중을 10kg 감량해야 한다.

05 대화를 듣고, 두 사람의 관계를 가장 잘 나타낸 것을 고르시오.

① travel agent – traveler
② store clerk – customer
③ taxi driver – passenger
④ customs officer – tourist
⑤ taxi driver – parking attendant

06 대화를 듣고, 그림에서 대화의 내용과 일치하지 않는 것을 고르시오.

07 대화를 듣고, 두 사람이 할 일로 가장 적절한 것을 고르시오.

① to go to the movies
② to write a term paper
③ to go to the rental shop
④ to apologize to a friend
⑤ to prepare for a quiz tomorrow

08 대화를 듣고, 여자가 남자를 돕지 못하는 이유를 고르시오.

① 끝마쳐야 할 숙제가 있어서
② 오늘 저녁 가족 모임이 있어서
③ 다음 주에 있을 세미나를 준비해야 해서
④ 추천서를 받기 위해 교수님을 만나야 해서
⑤ 오늘 밤 자정까지 숙제를 이메일로 보내야 해서

09 대화를 듣고, 여자가 선물 값으로 지불할 금액을 고르시오. [3점]

① $20   ② $25   ③ $35
④ $45   ⑤ $50

10 대화를 듣고, 면접자에 대해 언급되지 <u>않은</u> 것을 고르시오.

① 전공   ② 경력   ③ 해외 체류 경험
④ 가족 관계   ⑤ 성격

11 방송을 듣고, 일치하지 <u>않는</u> 것을 고르시오.

① Kim은 수영 400미터 자유형에서 자신의 기록을 단축하였다.
② Kim은 현재 세계 기록을 보유하고 있다.
③ Yoon은 국제 피겨 스케이팅 대회에서 3위를 차지하였다.
④ Lee는 유타에서 열린 세계 빙상 대회에서 3위를 하였다.
⑤ Lee는 남자 1,000m 경기에서 한국 신기록을 세웠다.

12 다음 표를 보면서 대화를 듣고, 일치하지 <u>않는</u> 것을 고르시오. [3점]

		18	20	25	30	35	40	45	50	55	60	65 and up
①	blood pressure	every 2 years										
②	cholesterol			every 5 years								
③	cancer						yearly					
④	blood sugar								every 3 years			
⑤	eye disease									every 1~2 years		

13 대화를 듣고, 남자의 마지막 말에 대한 여자의 응답으로 가장 적절한 것을 고르시오.

Woman : _____

① Sure, they'll pay you for the last project.
② The information on your account is confidential.
③ No, your recording might be necessary just in case.
④ I'm not sure. Why don't you go to the bank right now?
⑤ You need to know your account number, resident registration number, and password.

14 대화를 듣고, 여자의 마지막 말에 대한 남자의 응답으로 가장 적절한 것을 고르시오. [3점]

Man : _____

① I believe it'll give you confidence.
② You don't have to worry about side effects.
③ Well, you'd better give it a second thought.
④ Well, I wish I could have double eyelid surgery, too.
⑤ Then, how about getting nose surgery while you are at it?

15 다음 상황 설명을 듣고, Peter의 어머니가 Peter에게 할 말로 가장 적절한 것을 고르시오.

Peter's mother : Peter, _____

① I'd like you to be a school teacher.
② you did a good job. Congratulations!
③ I don't think you can be a civil servant.
④ never give up. You're going to make it.
⑤ what would you do if you failed again?

[16-17] 다음을 듣고, 물음에 답하시오.

16 남자가 하는 말의 목적으로 가장 적절한 것은?

① to warn students of cleanliness
② to introduce dormitory policies
③ to announce how to pay for dormitory fees
④ to notify students how to enter the dormitory
⑤ to warn students of dangers of drinking in the dorm

17 Nation High School Campus Housing에 관한 내용과 일치하지 <u>않는</u> 것은?

① 주중 통금 시간은 밤 11시까지이다.
② 어떤 상황에서도 술을 소지하는 것은 금지된다.
③ 주말에는 모든 학생들이 퇴실해야 한다.
④ 통금 시간이 지나 기숙사에 들어오면 알람이 울린다.
⑤ 방의 청결 상태 확인을 위해 학생의 방을 검열할 수 있다.

DICTATION(받아쓰기) 코너입니다.
녹음의 내용을 잘 듣고, 빈칸에 알맞은 말을 쓰시기 바랍니다.

01

W Hello, I would like to _____ for next week.
M Okay. Do you have your reservation number?
W Sure. It is 109453.
M _____ .

02

M Hello, _____ order your drinks now?
W Can you tell me what's in a Caramel Macchiato?
M It is a mix of espresso, milk, and caramel syrup.
W _____ .

03

M Are you feeling tired lately? Can't you sleep every night? Consider several tips for your better life. First, _____ . Go to bed and wake up at the same time every day even on weekends and holidays. Sticking to a set sleep schedule creates the body clock, and it actually leads you to better sleep. Second, make your bedroom more sleep-friendly. _____ all disturbances that interfere with your sleep and keep the temperature of your room slightly cool with adequate ventilation. Above all, the key to getting good sleep is to eat right and get regular exercise. The importance of cutting down on caffeine and avoiding alcohol before bed _____ _____ enough.

04

W Are you on a diet?
M Yes, I am. I'm so worried about my weight.
W Well, as you know, _____ of many diseases.
M I agree. I barely lost 10kg over the last two months, and I'm planning to lose another 10.
W Wow, it sounds like hard work. So, what do you do to lose weight?
M First of all, I try to eat less, and I exercise regularly.
W Very good. It's important to eat healthily and exercise as well.
M Yeah, but I'm rather worried about _____ _____ . I feel a little dizzy these days.
W You should be careful not to lose your health.

05

M Are you going somewhere abroad?
W Actually, I'm going back to my country.
M Oh, I see. How long have you been away?
W For three years.
M That's _____ . You must miss your family.
W Yeah, indeed. I'm excited about seeing them again.
M Here we are. This is JFK International Airport.
W How much do _____ ?
M $15.
W Here is a twenty-dollar bill. Keep the change.
M Oh, it's too much.
W No. _____ , please. I insist.
M Well, thanks a lot.

06

W This is the new apartment we'll move into.

M Wow, this apartment is all furnished. And the wallpaper looks new, too.

W Do you like the wallpaper with horizontal lines?

M I prefer _____, but the horizontal lines are okay. We don't need to change it. By the way, I like the round table.

W Me, too. There's no corner, so it's safer for our kids. Oh, the chairs are just right. Four of them.

M Honey, do you think we need to buy a TV set?

W I think it's just fine without a television. It's also good for the kids.

M But I think it'll be perfect, if there's a TV in the middle of the wall. I _____ and watch TV.

W Oh, that looks pretty comfortable. It's good that we don't have to buy a new couch.

07

M Let's go to the theater. *Taken 2* is now playing.

W I'd love to, but I can't.

M Why not?

W I have a quiz tomorrow. I _____ when you came in.

M Oh, come on! It's just a quiz.

W No. It takes up quite a big portion of my grade.

M I also have a term paper due tomorrow. But I can't wait to see that movie. We'll be home early. Let's go.

W Sorry, but I don't think I can make it this time. Why don't you ask Steve instead?

M Oh, you didn't know that? We are not on speaking terms. We _____ while we were playing basketball.

W You did? Why don't you apologize to him first?

M Not a chance! I'd rather rent a DVD and stay home.

W Okay. In that case, I will _____ for you. Let's go to the DVD shop.

08

M Kelly, are you busy tonight?

W Well, what's up?

M I finished my essay homework, and I need to _____ _____.

W I am sorry. I am supposed to meet Professor Linda Baker tonight.

M I really need your help. Is there any chance you can put off your appointment with her?

W Sorry again. I need a letter of recommendation from her _____ next semester.

M Is Professor Baker the only person you can ask such a favor?

W Yeah, Professor Kim told me he is busy preparing for the seminar next week. Why don't you ask Steve?

M He said he _____ tonight.

W I can help you tomorrow if it is all right.

M I have to email this homework to my teacher by midnight tonight.

09

M What are you going to buy for your brother's birthday present?

W I haven't decided yet. Would you recommend something for him?

M Sure. What price range did you _____?

W My budget is approximately $50.

M This necktie looks nice, and its price is reasonable. What do you say?

W How much is it?

M It's $35.

W I think it's a little expensive. Hey, this one looks pretty good, but it's only $25.

M All right. You made a good choice. But I don't think it is _____. I mean I'd like to add another item as a present, something like a dress shirt.

W A dress shirt?

M Yes. This dress shirt costs only $20.

W All right. It seems to go well with the necktie. I'll buy both of them.

10

W Would you introduce yourself to us?

M Yes. My name is Kim Jiho, and I live in Seoul with my family.

W Can you speak Chinese?

M Yes, I lived in Beijing for three years, and I also _____ at the university.

W Do you have any job experience?

M Yes, I worked as an editor at *The China Daily*. I believe my experience as a reporter will benefit this great broadcasting company.

W Sure, that'll help. Lastly, do you have anything to tell us?

M If you choose me, you'll not regret it. I'm a very _____, so if there are any news items, I'll run to anywhere, anytime. Thank you very much.

11

(news music)

M This is today's YBC Sports News. Here are the current headlines:

• Kim finished the 400m freestyle in 3 minutes, 30 seconds, a full 4 seconds quicker than his previous year Swimming Championship record of 3 minutes, 34 seconds. It's also _____. Now, he is a world-record holder.

• Korea's Yoon, who's 17 years old, skated to victory in the third round of the International Figure Skating Union Grand Prix in China on Saturday.

• South Korea's Lee skated to third place Sunday with a new South Korean national record. He _____ of 1 minute, 7.7 seconds in the men's 1,000m in the World Speed Skating Championship in Utah.

That's all for now. I'll be back in a few minutes.

(news music)

12

W Look, this seems like a very useful table.

M Yeah. After age 18, you should _____ _____ every two years.

W Keep reading, will you?

M Yes. After 20, you should be checked for cholesterol every five years.

W It's because cholesterol might cause high blood pressure.

M And if you are over 35 years old, you need to get tests to detect cancer every other year.

W Yeah. Cancer is _____ for death among Koreans.

M Also, you'd better check your blood sugar every three years if you are over 45 years old.

W Right. Diabetes is one of the main reasons for death, too.

M After 50, you need to check whether you have eye trouble every one or two years.

W Can you remember all that?

M No. But I see that _____ requires a lot of effort.

W I agree with you.

13

M Ms. Kim, have you been paid for your last project?

W I'm not sure. I haven't checked my bank account.

M Our project manager said that we would be paid today.

W It might be delayed _____. I heard that he didn't get final approval from management.

M I wish I could confirm my pay.

W Why don't you call the bank? The automatic answering machine will tell you about your balance.

M Really? Please tell me how to do that.

W First, call your bank and do whatever the recording says.

M Is that all that I'm supposed to do _____ I want?

W _____

14

M   Why have you been looking at yourself in the mirror so long?

W   I am _____ double eyelid surgery.

M   Why? Your eyes look OK.

W   I always wish my eyes were a little larger and prettier.

M   But you know what? Guys are sometimes attracted by a woman's natural appearance rather than a surgically altered one.

W   Do you think so?

M   Yeah, besides I heard a lot of side effects follow plastic surgery.

W   I know, but it'll give me more confidence, and I'll feel better about myself.

M   It might be true, but I firmly believe the sum of _____ outweighs that of the positive effects.

W   I don't know. Having attractive eyes is my top priority anyway.

M   _____

15

W   Peter _____ last year. Although he wanted to get a job right after graduation, he couldn't because the job market was very competitive. Since then, he's been preparing for civil service exams. But _____ are still slim. The competition for open positions reached almost 100:1. Peter is very discouraged. So, Peter's mother wants to encourage him _____. In this situation, what would she most likely say to him?

Peter's mother   Peter, _____

16-17

M   Welcome all new residents at Nation High School Campus Housing! Before you guys start dormitory life here, housing staff wants you to _____ about several important policies. First, dormitory curfew is at 11:00 pm Monday through Friday and 12:00 am on weekends. Hall doors are locked, and the alarm is set at this time, so be sure to come in the dorm on time. Second, while we _____ a student's personal privacy, the housing staff has the right to enter a student's room to check up cleanliness and general maintenance. Lastly, the possession or consumption of alcohol at the dormitory _____ _____. If you have any questions, please call the Housing Department. Thank you.

1번부터 17번까지는 듣고 답하는 문제입니다. 1번부터 15번까지는 한 번만 들려주고, 16번부터 17번까지는 두 번 들려줍니다. 방송을 잘 듣고 답을 하시기 바랍니다.

01 대화를 듣고, 남자의 마지막 말에 대한 여자의 응답으로 가장 적절한 것을 고르시오.

① I enjoyed talking with her.
② She is the only one that I can trust.
③ I can't face her after what I've done to her.
④ I guess I'm going to complain to the manager.
⑤ She changed her mind and promised me not to do so.

02 대화를 듣고, 여자의 마지막 말에 대한 남자의 응답으로 가장 적절한 것을 고르시오.

① He lives in Sydney now.
② There is nothing I can tell.
③ He lives in an old apartment.
④ Anyplace will be fine with me.
⑤ Australia is famous for its wildlife.

03 다음을 듣고, 남자가 하는 말의 목적으로 가장 적절한 것을 고르시오.

① 신간 도서를 홍보하려고
② 신입 직원을 환영하려고
③ 오늘의 연설자를 소개하려고
④ 우수 인재를 회사에 추천하려고
⑤ 새로 부임한 관리자에 대한 정보를 제공하려고

04 대화를 듣고, 여자의 의견으로 가장 적절한 것을 고르시오.

① 청소원을 더 늘려야 한다.
② 쓰레기통을 더 설치해야 한다.
③ 해변에 경찰서를 설치해야 한다.
④ 쓰레기 투기에 벌금을 물려야 한다.
⑤ 해변에서 음식을 먹지 못하도록 해야 한다.

05 대화를 듣고, 두 사람의 관계를 가장 잘 나타낸 것을 고르시오.

① judge – lawyer
② prosecutor – suspect
③ police officer – reporter
④ police officer – victim
⑤ repairperson – landlord

06 대화를 듣고, 그림에서 대화의 내용과 일치하지 <u>않는</u> 것을 고르시오.

07 대화를 듣고, 남자가 여자를 위해 한 일을 고르시오.

① 가방 가져다주기
② 보고서 제출해 주기
③ 펜과 종이 빌려 주기
④ 자습실 위치 가르쳐 주기
⑤ 휴대용 저장 장치 빌려 주기

08 대화를 듣고, 여자가 약속에 늦은 이유를 고르시오.

① 버스가 고장 나서
② 점심 식사를 준비하느라
③ 엘리베이터가 고장 나서
④ 자명종이 울리지 않아서
⑤ 헤어드라이어가 고장 나서

09 대화를 듣고, 여자가 지불할 금액을 고르시오. [3점]

① $150   ② $165   ③ $175

④ $185   ⑤ $195

10 대화를 듣고, 여자의 한국 방문에 대해 두 사람이 이야기하지 <u>않은</u> 것을 고르시오.

① 방문 목적   ② 체류 기간

③ 체류 장소   ④ 소지품

⑤ 이전 방문 경험

11 No Escape에 관한 다음 내용을 듣고, 일치하지 <u>않는</u> 것을 고르시오. [3점]

① 액션 영화이다.

② 여름에 개봉할 예정이다.

③ 사랑 이야기가 포함되어 있다.

④ 남자 주인공은 FBI요원이다.

⑤ 범죄 조직과의 대결을 다루고 있다.

12 대화를 듣고, 다음 안내 표지판에 <u>잘못</u> 표기된 것을 고르시오.

The National Museum

Hours	① Monday through Saturday: 9:00 am ~ 6:00 pm Sunday: Closed
Admission Fee	Adults: $15 Children: $5 ② Senior citizens / Students: $8 (Picture ID Required)
* Note	③ The East Wing is under construction.
* Caution	④ No Flash Photography No Food & Drinks ⑤ No Readmission without ID

13 대화를 듣고, 여자의 마지막 말에 대한 남자의 응답으로 가장 적절한 것을 고르시오. [3점]

Man : _____

① I'm not interested in economics.

② I'd like to retire at an early age.

③ I'm in big trouble with my parents.

④ I broke up with my girlfriend last month.

⑤ I'm broke, and I have to pay off my student loan.

14 대화를 듣고, 남자의 마지막 말에 대한 여자의 응답으로 가장 적절한 것을 고르시오.

Woman : _____

① Then I'll treat you to dinner.

② Where did you get the tickets?

③ I can't find your report anywhere.

④ Cats are really incredible animals.

⑤ Tickets for the concert were sold out.

15 다음 상황 설명을 듣고, 선생님이 Mary에게 할 말로 가장 적절한 것을 고르시오.

Mary's teacher : _____

① You don't need to be so upset.

② Getting enough sleep is important.

③ I'm sorry, but there is no second chance.

④ Your schoolwork shows much improvement.

⑤ You need to pay more attention to the teacher.

[16-17] 다음을 듣고, 물음에 답하시오.

16 여자가 하는 말의 목적으로 가장 적절한 것은?

① to raise money for poor students

② to advise students not to skip their meals

③ to introduce a program that helps kids be well-fed

④ to encourage children to use the free school meals program

⑤ to urge the city government to start a free school meals program

17 Free School Meals 프로그램에 관한 내용으로 언급되지 <u>않은</u> 것은?

① 아이들에게 아침과 점심 식사를 제공한다.

② 18세 미만의 아이들을 대상으로 한다.

③ 일부 학교에서는 아직 시행되지 않는다.

④ 방학 기간에는 저소득층 학생들을 대상으로 한다.

⑤ 소득에 관계없이 모든 아이들을 대상으로 한다.

14회 DICTATION

01

M Why don't you _____ with your roommate?

W I tried, but it didn't work. She keeps on making loud noises at midnight. She really _____.

M I think you should do something. What do you plan to do about it?

W _____

02

W I'd really love to visit Australia. Have you ever been there?

M No, not yet. But I _____ my brother there soon.

W Really? Which part of the country does he live in?

M _____

03

M Good evening, everyone. _____ today's speaker, Brian Berkley, author of this year's best seller *Making People Work for You*. Before he became a successful writer, Mr. Berkley worked for more than fifteen years on Wall Street as the Chief Executive Officer of BCA Manhattan Bank. He has also written dozens of articles on investing and personal finance for a number of popular magazines and professional journals. _____ _____ to Mr. Brian Berkley.

04

M Sally, look at the beach! There is trash all over it.

W You're right. I can't find anywhere to sit down and rest.

M Look at those plastic cups, candy wrappers, beer bottles, and ice cream sticks. It seems that nobody cleans here.

W No, _____. I saw dozens of cleaners cleaning the beach early in the morning.

M Did you? So, what do you think the matter is?

W I think there are too many litterbugs.

M How about installing more trash cans?

W That would be only temporarily effective. Too many vendors are roaming around the beach area. I think no food but water should be allowed on the beach.

M That's quite harsh. Do you think it is possible?

W _____ if there is a security group of hired people or volunteers making sure it is imposed and being followed.

M Yeah, something must be done decisively to change this situation.

05

M I understand you had a theft tonight. _____ ___ what happened?

W Yes, of course. I was sleeping, and I heard a loud noise in the living room.

M And what did you do?

W I got up and went downstairs very quietly. Then I saw a man going out of the window.

M Can you describe the suspect?

W Sure. He had _____. I couldn't see his face well, but he was wearing a white shirt.

M Did he run away with anything?

W Well, it was very strange.

M What do you mean?

W _____ the refrigerator and took away all the food!

06

W Honey, have you finished setting the table? The guests are coming in about half an hour.

M I know. But I almost forgot _____ properly.

W It's not that complicated. Start by setting out dinner plates. Then, place the forks directly to the left of the plate. The fork for salad, I mean the short one, should be furthest from the plate.

M Where should the napkin go?

W It should go to the left of the forks.

M Like you always did. What about glasses?

W Place glasses for water and wine slightly above and to the right of the dinner plate. Then, what's left?

M Dinner knife and spoons.

W Put the dinner knife directly to the right of the plate, with _____.

M What should I place next to the knife? The short spoon or the long one?

W The short one is a tea spoon. It goes right next to the knife.

M I see. I'll do some final touches myself.

07

M What's the matter with you? You look worried.

W I can't believe it! I _____ at home!

M What? You're kidding!

W No, and I've got a lot of work to do today.

M Don't you have _____?

W No. I've got to be in class in twenty minutes. Do you have a pen and some paper I could use?

M I'm sorry, I don't. But you can get them in the study room in the library.

W That's a good idea. Oh, what about an extra USB flash drive? I have to write a biology report this afternoon.

M Let me see. Yeah. Here you go.

W Thanks! You're a life saver. I'll give it back this Saturday.

M _____ one. If you fail to submit your report again, Mr. Anderson will get mad at you.

W That's right.

08

W Hi, Bill! Sorry, I'm late.

M What kept you, Maggie? No, wait, don't tell me. _____ _____. Your alarm didn't go off.

W No, that's not what happened.

M Let me see. The elevator went out of order or your hair dryer didn't work, like last time.

W Come on. What's the matter? I said I was sorry.

M I know, but this happens all the time. I have to always wait for you.

W But _____! There is always a reason!

M I know, I know. So, what was the reason this time?

W The bus broke down, and I had to walk.

M Hmm... Never be late anymore. Anyway, let's have something for lunch. I'm starving.

09

M Hi. How can I help you?

W I'd like to rent a car.

M Take a look at this catalog, please. We have compact, mid-size, and full-size cars available. How about this compact car?

W I think the compact car is _____.

M How many people are with you?

W There are five people, including me.

M In that case, I recommend this full-size car. The daily rate is $70.

W That's a little expensive. I'd prefer the mid-size car. How about this blue one?

M Wow! You have an eye for cars. It'd cost you $50 a day. How long would you need it?

W For three days. Do you _____?

M Yes, we do. Our complete insurance package would be only $15 extra for three days.

W That sounds good. I'll take it. Here is my credit card.

10

M What is the purpose of your visit?

W I'm here to _____ for the first part of my trip, and then I plan on touring Seoul.

M Where will you be staying?

W I'll be staying at the Nexus Hotel downtown.

M And what do you have in your luggage?

W Just my personal belongings. Clothes, a few books, and a laptop computer.

M OK. Everything's fine. By the way, _____ ____ to this country?

W Well, yes and no. Actually, I was born here when my parents were working in Seoul many years ago, but this is my first trip back since then.

M Well, enjoy your trip.

W Thanks.

11

W If you want great action for the _____, *No Escape* is the ticket. Fernando Valenta looks fantastic as he kicks, punches, shoots, and blasts his way across the screen. This must be one of the few action movies in history to rank _____. The guys can glory in Valenta's bloody rampages while the women look at the gorgeous Spaniard and sigh. The plot concerns FBI agent Valenta's attempts to bring down a high-profile drug gang. That means _____ before an explosive showdown with the gang's truly evil boss. *No Escape* is a great escape from the daily grind and a terrific summer movie. Don't miss it.

12

W Could you tell me the hours of operation for the museum?

M It's open from 9 am to 6 pm, Monday through Saturday. It's closed on Sunday.

W Thanks. Do you know if I'm allowed to use my flash to take photos in the museum?

M You can take pictures, but _____ _____. Food and drinks are prohibited, too.

W Do you know if all of the exhibits are open to the public today?

M The East Wing is under construction, but the rest of the galleries are open.

W Thanks a lot. How much is admission?

M It's $15 for adults, $5 for children, and $8 for senior citizens and students with picture IDs.

W If I leave after I pay, _____?

M Yes. But you'd have to show your ticket. Anything else?

W No. Thank you so much.

13

M So, what are you going to do _____?

W Well, I've saved some money, and I think I'd really like to travel.

M Lucky you. That sounds exciting!

W Yeah. Then I plan to get a job and my own apartment.

M You're not going to _____?

W No, I don't want to depend on my parents—not after I start to work.

M I know what you mean. I envy you.

W What about you? Do you have any plans yet?

M I'm going to get a job, too. But I'll live with my parents.

W Why have you decided to do so?

M _____

14

W What are you doing tonight? Would you like to go out?

M Oh, sorry, I can't. I'm going to _____ . I have to finish this report.

W Well, how about tomorrow night? Are you doing anything then?

M No, I'm not. What are you planning to do?

W I'm going to see a musical. You know I love musicals very much.

M What's the title?

W It's the world-famous musical *Cats*. Would you like to come?

M Sure, I'd love to! But _____ this time. It's my turn.

W _____

15

W One day, Mary woke up at 7:30 because the battery in her alarm clock had died. Usually she catches the bus at 7:45 to get to school in time for her first class, but just as she got to the bus stop, she saw the bus leaving. The next bus didn't come until 8:00, so she was _____ . The worst part was that her teacher gave the class a quiz at the beginning of class, but she missed it because she was late. Her teacher got annoyed and told her to come to his office. In his office, she told him what happened in the morning and sincerely apologized, asking him to let her _____ _____ the next day. In this situation, what would Mary's teacher most likely say to Mary?

Mary's teacher _____

16-17

W Do you know how many children are sent to school with empty stomachs? More than two thousand kids are suffering in our city alone. It must be hard for them to concentrate and study when they are hungry. Fortunately, the city government has started the "Free School Meals" program to make sure they are well-fed. Anyone under 18 years of age can get a free breakfast and lunch. It is, however, _____ _____ yet. Parents can call their school to ask when their kids can get these free meals. Children can now get breakfast and lunch during their vacations, too. In the past, the meals were only served during the school year. Many families are very happy to get this extra help for their children. Students of low-income families used to have to sign up for the free-meal program, but now _____ . The city government spends more than $5 million a year on this free food program. It is very important for children to be well-fed. Bodies and minds work better when they are well-nourished. Thanks to this program, many children are getting the food they need all year long.

15^회 | 듣기 모의고사

1번부터 17번까지는 듣고 답하는 문제입니다. 1번부터 15번까지는 한 번만 들려주고, 16번부터 17번까지는 두 번 들려줍니다. 방송을 잘 듣고 답을 하시기 바랍니다.

01 대화를 듣고, 남자의 마지막 말에 대한 여자의 응답으로 가장 적절한 것을 고르시오.

① I knew we were late.
② I don't want to go trick or treating.
③ It took me almost an hour to go to the party.
④ I couldn't decide on my Halloween costume.
⑤ Halloween is a traditional holiday in America.

02 대화를 듣고, 여자의 마지막 말에 대한 남자의 응답으로 가장 적절한 것을 고르시오.

① Yeah, against Australia.
② I am really proud of our national team.
③ The World Cup is held every four years.
④ Right. I think it was an important match for us.
⑤ Yeah. The head is an important body part in soccer.

03 다음을 듣고, 남자가 하는 말의 주제로 가장 적절한 것을 고르시오.

① 보트 탑승 시 유의점
② 성공적인 소개팅을 위한 비결
③ 사회생활에서의 에티켓의 중요성
④ 연인 관계에 있어 고려해야 할 사항
⑤ 비언어적 요소가 대화에 미치는 영향

04 대화를 듣고, 여자의 의견으로 가장 적절한 것을 고르시오.

① 금요일 밤에는 교통 체증이 심하다.
② 약속 시간에 늦는 것은 무례한 행동이다.
③ 약속 시간보다 일찍 가는 것은 시간 낭비이다.
④ 미리 계획하여 시간을 효율적으로 사용해야 한다.
⑤ 회의 시작 전에 자료를 다시 읽어 보는 것이 많은 도움이 된다.

05 대화를 듣고, 두 사람의 관계를 가장 잘 나타낸 것을 고르시오.

① realtor – tenant
② mover – customer
③ professor – student
④ accountant – taxpayer
⑤ housing director – student

06 대화를 듣고, 그림에서 대화의 내용과 일치하지 <u>않는</u> 것을 고르시오.

07 대화를 듣고, 남자가 여자에게 부탁한 일로 가장 적절한 것을 고르시오.

① 저녁 식사 준비
② 대학원 원서 접수
③ 대학원 원서 작성
④ 시험 날 교통편 제공
⑤ 대학원 입시 정보 입수

08 대화를 듣고, 여자가 파티에 참석할 수 <u>없는</u> 이유를 고르시오.

① 파티에 초대 받지 못해서
② 시험공부 때문에 피곤해서
③ 어머니의 심부름을 해야 해서
④ 오늘 저녁에 야간 근무를 해야 해서
⑤ 내일까지 마감인 보고서를 작성해야 해서

09 대화를 듣고, 남자가 수업한 총 시간 수와 출제한 문항 수를 고르시오. [3점]

① 25시간, 60문항   ② 50시간, 70문항

③ 75시간, 80문항   ④ 75시간, 100문항

⑤ 100시간, 100문항

10 대화를 듣고, ABC 고등학교의 내년도 변동 사항이 <u>아닌</u> 것을 고르시오.

① 오전 7시 반에 1교시가 시작된다.

② 교복이 새로 바뀐다.

③ 학생회실이 지하로 옮겨진다.

④ 학생회 예산이 삭감된다.

⑤ 등록금이 인상된다.

11 감기에 관한 다음 내용을 듣고, 일치하지 <u>않는</u> 것을 고르시오. [3점]

① 예방하는 방법 중 하나는 입과 얼굴을 만지지 않는 것이다.

② 손을 씻는 것은 바이러스 입자를 제거해 준다.

③ 항균성 비누는 감기에 효과가 뛰어나다.

④ 일반 감기는 다양한 종류의 바이러스 때문에 생긴다.

⑤ 바이러스의 성공적인 면역은 불가능하다.

12 다음 표를 보면서 대화를 듣고, 일치하지 <u>않는</u> 내용을 고르시오.

Commercial Marks		
①	@ : at	the abbreviation for the phrase at the rate of
②	% : percent	the symbol used to indicate a percentage
③	# : number	the symbol used to indicate number
④	© : copyrighted	the symbol for copyright
⑤	R : registered trademark	the symbol used to indicate that the mark has been registered

13 대화를 듣고, 여자의 마지막 말에 대한 남자의 응답으로 가장 적절한 것을 고르시오. [3점]

Man : _____

① I think that dry-cleaning is the only way to do it.

② Let's open the windows and let the bad air out.

③ Hang it outside for a few hours. One day will be enough.

④ Sorry, I cannot smell anything because my nose is stuffy.

⑤ You'd better get some laundry dry-cleaned as soon as possible.

14 대화를 듣고, 남자의 마지막 말에 대한 여자의 응답으로 가장 적절한 것을 고르시오.

Woman : _____

① Don't worry, Dad. It will live.

② I can't believe it will die soon.

③ Oh, too much is sometimes bad.

④ I think the rich soil is better for the plant.

⑤ You should have paid more attention to it, Dad.

15 다음 상황 설명을 듣고, Sarah가 Brady에게 할 말로 가장 적절한 것을 고르시오.

Sarah : Brady, _____

① even a worm will turn.

② the early bird catches the worm.

③ birds of a feather flock together.

④ out of the frying pan into the fire.

⑤ a bad workman always blames his tools.

[16-17] 다음을 듣고 물음에 답하시오.

16 여자가 하는 말의 목적으로 가장 적절한 것은?

① 비행기내 면세용품 구입을 안내하려고

② 비행기가 비상 착륙하게 되었음을 알리려고

③ 비행기 탑승 게이트가 변경되었음을 공지하려고

④ 비행 도중 응급 상황 발생 시 대처 방법을 안내하려고

⑤ 기상 악화로 비행기 탑승 시간이 지연되었음을 공지하려고

17 방송 내용과 일치하지 <u>않는</u> 것은?

① 승객은 디트로이트 메트로폴리탄 공항 내에 있어야 한다.

② 뉴욕에서 출발하여 인천으로 향하는 비행기이다.

③ 현재 디트로이트 상공 35,000피트를 운항 중이다.

④ 모든 짐은 머리 위 선반에 넣어야 한다.

⑤ 기상 악화로 디트로이트 메트로폴리탄 공항에 비상 착륙할 것이다.

DICTATION(받아쓰기) 코너입니다.
녹음의 내용을 잘 듣고, 빈칸에 알맞은 말을 쓰시기 바랍니다.

01

M Come on, Jenny! Hurry up! We are going to be late for the Halloween party.

W Sorry, _____. I am almost dressed.

M What took you so long?

W _____

02

W Steve, where are you _____?

M I am going to the World Cup Stadium to watch a soccer match.

W Oh, our national team has a preliminary game tonight, right?

M _____

03

M Are you truly looking forward _____ _____ with whom you want to spend the rest of your life? Here are the most important Do's and Don'ts on blind dating. First, remember that a small amount of manners goes a long way. Holding a door open and _____ for your date are basic manners. Also, show your interest to your partner with intimate body gestures and cordial replies to her questions. Second, do not show up late and be punctual. And when you meet your date, do not bore her by talking endlessly about yourself. _____ ___ sometimes and let your partner have a chance to talk about herself, too.

04

M We've got to go now.

W It's too early. We still have two hours before the meeting.

M We have to _____. There is always heavy traffic on Friday night.

W I know, but do you think it's too early to get going?

M I don't think so.

W But if there is no traffic, then we have to wait for almost one and half hours. Don't you think it's a waste of time?

M Absolutely not. If you get there early, while we're waiting, we _____ to read the document again. We can use our extra time very efficiently.

W But it usually take us thirty minutes to get there. We need only thirty minutes to read it again.

M Then, think about it this way. If we get stuck in heavy traffic, we cannot get there on time or we will make them wait for us for a long time. You know it's _____ _____ for a meeting.

W Believe me. We'll not be late.

05

M Excuse me. Are you in charge here?

W Yes. How can I help you?

M Well, I _____ yesterday.

W What is it about?

M I'm living in Graduate Tower B now, but it says that I should move out of it before next Friday.

W What is your name?

M Kevin Hong.

W Kevin Hong. Right. You've got to move out before May 7.

M Why is that?

W As you know, this semester has almost finished, and we need _____.

M I see. Then, where am I supposed to move to?

W Well, you may get a place at an apartment off-campus or apply for another place in our dormitory.

M Hmm. I need some _____. When should I give you an answer?

W The sooner, the better.

06

W Wow, there are a lot of cars on this side of the road.

M We are late for the concert. We must hurry to find a parking space.

W The other road is empty. We can park there.

M No, we can't. There is a no-parking zone.

W Then, let's _____ . Oh, there's a garage.

M We can't park there, either. There's a sign of "Parking Full" in front of the door.

W But it's strange. I see one spot is empty.

M Right. I saw it, too. Let's _____ who is next to the door.

W I hope we can park there.

07

M Jane, did you do as I asked?

W Yes. Successfully.

M Thank you for your help.

W Oh, it's nothing, though I had some difficulty.

M What?

W You _____ in the application form for graduate school.

M Oh, didn't I? So, what did you do?

W Since I knew you majored in English literature in college, I marked it on your application form myself.

M Thanks. I didn't know that information was left out.

W There was no problem on the application form except for that.

M Good. Thanks to your help, I could apply for graduate school.

W If you pass the exam, you'll have to _____ .

M Of course I will.

08

M Wow, the mid-term exam is finally over. How was the test?

W It was all right. But I _____ now.

M Cheer up! James is going to throw a party tonight at his place. Don't you remember?

W Wait, you are right. It totally slipped my mind.

M How can you forget about it? So, you cannot come to the party tonight?

W I am afraid not. I _____ my grandparents' place to bring them groceries.

M I really wanted to have fun with you.

W Usually my mom does it, but she's working the night shift tonight, so she asked me to do it.

M Why don't you ask your brother instead?

W He said he would _____ a term paper due tomorrow.

M Gee. Next time, then!

09

W Mr. Kim, how was your summer vacation?

M Well, I had a hectic summer.

W Oh, why?

M Among other things, I had to teach _____ ___ for three weeks.

W Five hours per day for three weeks? Was it Monday through Friday?

M Yes. Also, _____ from one of my colleagues, I had to make listening and reading comprehension questions.

W How many?

M At first, he said it would be 60 questions, but the number increased again and again. 70 questions, 80 questions... And finally I worked on 100 questions.

W Wow, that was such a huge amount of work! But I'm sure you _____ .

M Of course. Without payment, I wouldn't have done it.

W You are right. No wonder your work is rewarding.

10

M Mom, I'm worried about next year's school life changes.

W Tell me more about the changes.

M Most of all, first period is scheduled to begin at 7:30 am.

W I think that might be _____ .

M Yeah. I'm not confident going to school so early. Also, our school uniform will be changed next year.

W Really?

M Yes. They've already decided on a new school uniform, based on a survey of students and teachers.

W Then, I've _____ about the expense of your new uniform. What else?

M The student union office is going to move into the basement.

W You don't like the basement?

M Of course not. What's worse, the budget for the union _____ next year.

W Gosh. When it rains, it pours.

11

W The best way _____ is to avoid close contact with existing sufferers, to wash hands thoroughly and regularly, and to avoid touching one's mouth and face. Anti-bacterial soaps _____ on the cold virus; it is the mechanical action of hand washing that removes virus particles. The common cold is caused by a large variety of viruses, which alter structure quite frequently _____, resulting in constantly changing virus types. Thus, successful immunization is not possible.

12

W Ryan, I need your help.

M What is it?

W Would you explain _____ for me?

M Sure. The first symbol reads "at." It is commercially used as the abbreviation for the phrase "at the rate of."

W I see. I'm familiar with the second mark, "%." It indicates a percentage, doesn't it?

M Of course, it's a common symbol. And the third one can be used to mean "number."

W Oh, _____ "number." I see. And I've seen the fourth one many times in my textbooks. It means "copyrighted."

M Exactly. It's the symbol for copyright.

W But I'm not sure about the last one. What does "R" mean?

M Well, in the United States some films are rated R to show that children under 17 years old are _____ _____ if an adult is with them.

W Thanks for your help.

13

W Excuse me. My husband got this jacket dry-cleaned yesterday.

M Yeah, I remember the jacket. Something's wrong with it?

W He says it _____ .

M That can't be. It was definitely dry-cleaned.

W Did you do it yourself?

M No. Actually my assistant did it.

W Then, how could you be so sure about it? My husband says that it smelled all day, and he couldn't stand it.

M You should understand that if you had _____ _____ or something for a long time, a smell might not disappear even with dry cleaning.

W Then, what should I do in order to remove the smell?

M _____

14

W Dad, could you take a look at this flower I planted?

M Oh, it doesn't look good. What's wrong with it?

W I _____ . I took really good care of it. I even fed it with nutritional supplement.

M Then, there must be a problem with watering. How often did you water it?

W Every three or four days, I guess.

M Well, that's the problem. This kind needs watering _____ at most.

W Really? Why?

M Because it is a kind of drought-tolerant plant which thrives in poor soil conditions. If you water it too much, the soil becomes too rich for the plant to live.

W Oh, I understand. So, do you think it will live ___ _____ often?

M It depends. Let's wait and see.

W _____

15

M Brady and Sarah are coworkers teaching at the same high school. Actually, they are also close friends and neighbors. Usually, Brady comes to school early in the morning. He is _____ . But Brady is surprised to find that Sarah is much more diligent. Sarah says that it is her habit to come to school at 6:30 am. Gosh! 6:30 am! Brady thinks to himself, "_____ _____ does she get up?", "What on earth does she do at school at 6:30 am?" Now, Brady asks Sarah why she _____ in the morning. In this situation, what would Sarah most likely say to Brady?

Sarah Brady, _____

16-17

W Attention passengers! This is the head stewardess speaking. Our Boeing 747 from New York to Incheon International Airport is currently flying _____ 35,000 feet over the city of Detroit. However, because of heavy thunderstorms and wind strength, we cannot move forward any farther and have no choice _____ at Detroit Metropolitan Airport. Make sure your seat belt is securely fastened, and all luggage is put underneath the seat in front of you while we make a landing. The local time in Detroit is 3:30 pm, and the temperature is 70°F. We want all passengers to stay in Detroit Metropolitan Airport until a further announcement is made. We will take off again _____ . We will do our best to minimize passengers' discomfort. Thank you.

16회 듣기 모의고사

1번부터 17번까지는 듣고 답하는 문제입니다. 1번부터 15번까지는 한 번만 들려주고, 16번부터 17번까지는 두 번 들려줍니다. 방송을 잘 듣고 답을 하시기 바랍니다.

01 대화를 듣고, 남자의 마지막 말에 대한 여자의 응답으로 가장 적절한 것을 고르시오.

① Of course! I can lend it to you.
② I didn't know it ended so soon.
③ Don't tell me! I'm almost done.
④ I'd like to tell him myself someday.
⑤ Please tell me the title of the novel.

02 대화를 듣고, 여자의 마지막 말에 대한 남자의 응답으로 가장 적절한 것을 고르시오.

① I hope her father gets better soon.
② Do you know when he will be back?
③ I don't understand why he did it to her.
④ Oh, no! You mean Mr. Gordon is gone?
⑤ You bet. This is the third time this month.

03 다음을 듣고, 남자가 하는 말의 목적으로 가장 적절한 것을 고르시오.

① 헌혈의 장점을 설명하려고
② 헌혈의 안전성을 홍보하려고
③ 헌혈 운동에 참여를 촉구하려고
④ 헌혈 시 주의 사항을 안내하려고
⑤ 혈액 부족 문제의 심각성을 알리려고

04 대화를 듣고, 여자의 의견으로 가장 적절한 것을 고르시오.

① 복권 구입 매수를 제한해야 한다.
② 복권 당첨 금액을 대폭 낮춰야 한다.
③ 복권의 종류를 다양화할 필요가 있다.
④ 복권 구입으로 이익을 얻을 수는 없다.
⑤ 복권을 통해 얻는 수익은 부당한 것이다.

05 대화를 듣고, 두 사람의 관계를 가장 잘 나타낸 것을 고르시오.

① clerk – shopper
② nurse – patient
③ teller – customer
④ ticket agent – traveler
⑤ repairman – customer

06 대화를 듣고, 그림에서 대화의 내용과 일치하지 <u>않는</u> 것을 고르시오.

07 대화를 듣고, 여자가 할 일로 가장 적절한 것을 고르시오.

① 소설 읽기
② 전화 걸기
③ 전화 수리하기
④ 아파트 청소하기
⑤ 자동응답기 구입하기

08 대화를 듣고, 여자가 전화를 건 이유를 고르시오.

① 엘리베이터 안에 갇혀서
② 사나운 개의 공격을 받아서
③ 괴한들이 집에 침입하려고 해서
④ 부상자의 긴급 이송이 필요해서
⑤ 화재가 발생했는데 대피하지 못해서

09 대화를 듣고, 여자가 지불할 금액을 고르시오. [3점]

① $80   ② $96   ③ $104
④ $128   ⑤ $144

10 대화를 듣고, 공연에 관해 두 사람이 언급한 것을 고르시오.

① 공연이 열린 장소
② 입장권의 할인 가격
③ 함께 공연을 보러 간 사람
④ 다음 공연이 시작되는 시각
⑤ 입장권 구매를 위해 기다린 시간

11 대화를 듣고, 일치하지 <u>않는</u> 것을 고르시오.

① 남자는 이미 오페라 입장권을 예약해 놓은 상태이다.
② 여자는 할 일이 많아 오늘 오페라를 관람할 수 없다.
③ 여자는 오페라 관람을 다음 주로 미루고 싶어 한다.
④ 남자는 오페라 입장권을 다시 예약하려고 할 것이다.
⑤ 여자는 오페라를 보는 날 남자에게 저녁을 대접할 것이다.

12 다음 일정표를 보면서 대화를 듣고, 두 사람의 대화 내용과 일치하지 <u>않는</u> 것을 고르시오.

San Francisco Events

	Date	Event & Location
①	Thu., Mar 1st	Magic show Berkeley Theatre
②	Sat., Mar 3rd	Flea Market Golden Gate Park
③	Tue., Mar 6th	Japanese Print Exhibition Museum of Modern Art
④	Thu., Mar 8th	Independent Film Festival Fort Mason Center
⑤	Fri., Mar 9th	Romeo and Juliet Lincoln Center

13 대화를 듣고, 여자의 마지막 말에 대한 남자의 응답으로 가장 적절한 것을 고르시오. [3점]

Man : _____

① Don't worry. I'll give you a ride home.
② Because you don't have your receipt now.
③ Only if the product has some major defects.
④ You can take a bus or a subway downtown.
⑤ We'll send a delivery person to collect the shoes.

14 대화를 듣고, 남자의 마지막 말에 대한 여자의 응답으로 가장 적절한 것을 고르시오.

Woman : _____

① Thanks. I'll have a look at it tomorrow.
② You don't have to. I've already checked it.
③ Sure. I'll have a housewarming party soon.
④ There'll be four or five people including you.
⑤ I want to move into the apartment by next week.

15 다음 상황 설명을 듣고, Susan이 부모님에게 할 말로 가장 적절한 것을 고르시오.

Susan : _____

① Mom, I'm home. I want to eat something.
② Did you hear that sound? Let's call the police.
③ I was scared to death. Why didn't you call me?
④ Where is my brother? I miss him very much, too.
⑤ Why didn't you wake me up? I'm late for school.

[16-17] 다음을 듣고, 물음에 답하시오.

16 여자가 하는 말의 목적으로 가장 적절한 것은?

① to advise about making friends online
② to promote online language learning
③ to warn about private information leakage
④ to advertise a new social network service
⑤ to educate people about how to deal with voice phishing

17 주의해야 할 점으로 언급되지 <u>않은</u> 것은? [3점]

① 혼자 만나지 말 것
② 주소를 밝히지 말 것
③ 공공장소에서 만날 것
④ 실명을 사용하지 말 것
⑤ 재학 중인 학교를 확인할 것

01

M Oh, you're reading John Grisham's new novel! _____?

W So far so great. I can't _____ of it. Have you read it?

M Yes. In fact, I just finished it. The ending is perfect.

W _____

02

W Did you hear about Annie? _____.

M No, I didn't. What happened to her?

W Her father _____ last night. Annie must be devastated.

M _____

03

M During the month of July, we will be conducting a blood drive. The city blood-mobile will _____ _____. During the first week of July, the blood mobile will be at the Hill Top Shopping Center. From July 12th until the 22nd, you can donate blood in front of the Metropolitan Cineplex. _____ _____, the blood mobile will be stationed in front of the Civic Center Plaza on State Street. The hours will be from 10 am to 5 pm. Juice and cookies _____ all participants. As you know, blood donations drop during summer months, so we'd really appreciate your support.

04

M Honey, you'll never believe this!

W What? What happened?

M _____!

W Are you serious? That's incredible!

M I know! This is the first time I've ever won something.

W Well, how much did you win?

M I won a hundred dollars!

W A hundred dollars? Do you know _____ _____ lottery tickets so far?

M I'm not sure but maybe about two thousand.

W Don't you think it's unprofitable? I would stop buying lottery tickets _____.

05

W How can I help you?

M I want to _____.

W OK. Can I have your account number, please?

M 381335.

W Your balance is $201.

M OK. And I asked my father to _____. I'd like to know if it's arrived.

W I'm sorry, but your account doesn't show any recent deposits.

M Oh, no. I need to pay my rent tomorrow. What do you think I ought to do?

W Well, we're having some computer problems today. So, why don't you _____? Or you can come back. We're open until 5:00 pm.

M OK, thanks.

W You're welcome.

06

M I brought some photos of my family with me. _____ _____ to you.

W Let me see. Oh, what a nice family!

M These are my grandparents. We had a party for my grandfather's birthday last month.

W I can tell he's 70 years old from the candles. But he _____ .

M You're right. This girl in the middle is my younger sister, Carol.

W Is this dog a golden retriever?

M Yes, his name is Clarence. He always sits in the front whenever we take a picture.

W He's so cute. Is that your parents _____ ?

M Yeah, and that's me, before I got my hair cut short. We were having a ski trip in the Alps.

W I didn't know you can snowboard.

M It was the first time that I _____ . So I tumbled and rolled quite a lot.

07

M Melissa, what's going on? _____ . Can you stand still for a minute?

W No, I can't. I'm trying to get up the nerve to leave a message on someone's answering machine.

M Are you _____ ?

W I freeze up and get tongue-tied, and I don't really know why. I just don't like talking into machines.

M Do you want me to do it for you?

W Thanks, but I think I should do this on my own.

M How about _____ and then reading it into the recording?

W That's a good idea. OK. "Hi, this is Melissa. I'm calling about the apartment for rent..."

M Do you want me to leave while you make your call?

W Don't be silly. Just have a seat and _____ ! All right, now I'm ready. Here I go!

08

(Telephone rings.)

M 911 Emergency Services.

W Help! Please, help me!

M Calm down and tell me exactly what problem you're having.

W There are _____ between the 15th and 16th floors.

M Do you know the name of the building?

W Yes, I'm calling from the Glass Tower on East Avenue.

M Did you _____ ?

W Yeah, but it didn't work. And I'm really allergic to dogs. I might have a lot of trouble breathing.

M Don't worry. Just try to keep as far away from the dog as you can.

W You've got to get us out of here now!

M I've already _____ and an ambulance. Listen, don't try to open the door.

W OK. Oh, please hurry.

09

M Could I help you with anything?

W Yes, I'm looking for a pair of roller blades.

M Is there a particular style you're looking for?

W I'd like a pair with metal frames. And _____ _____ .

M How about these navy ones? You can try these on.

W They fit perfectly. What's the price? I saw that these are on sale.

M That's right. They were originally $80, but with a 20% discount, they come to $64.

W _____ .

M If you buy these, we'll give you a second pair for half off, not 20% off.

W That's great! I'll buy two pairs.

10

W Jeff, how was the concert?

M I didn't get in.

W You're kidding! I thought you stood in line for many hours.

M I did, but the tickets were sold out before I got to the front. It was awful. I _____.

W Standing?

M Well, I did sit down for a while. I killed time by listening to music and sleeping.

W Sleeping? Did you have a sleeping bag?

M Yes. Luckily, I had just bought a really good one that was on sale for only $35.

W I guess you're not going to _____.

M Of course, I will! Tickets will go on sale on Saturday at 10 am, and I'm planning to be there on Friday morning.

W You're crazy! _____.

11

W Steve! You know, we _____ this evening?

M You're not going to say you can't come, are you? I've already reserved our seats.

W Well, I've got so much work to do that I have to work until eight o'clock.

M Oh, Susie! You know how much I've been looking forward to this opera.

W Sorry, but I can't help it. _____?

M Really? When will be convenient for you?

W Shall we try next Thursday? That might be better.

M OK. There must be some tickets left. I'm going to check right now.

W Sorry for this. _____, I'll buy you some snacks today. What do you want to eat?

M I'd like some doughnuts. Thanks.

12

M Are there _____?

W Yes. I was thinking of going to one of them.

M Could you recommend any one in particular?

W There is going to be a magic show on March 1st.

M Interesting. _____?

W At Berkeley Theatre. There is also a flea market opening on the first Saturday of the month at Golden Gate Park.

M How about art exhibitions or movies?

W Yeah, there is a Japanese print exhibit at the Museum of Modern Art on the 6th. Also, the Independent Film Festival at Fort Mason Center opens the next day.

M _____ Japanese art.

W You might like this, though: *Romeo and Juliet* at Lincoln Theater on Friday, the 9th.

M Sounds great. Would you like to go together?

W Sure.

13

(Telephone rings.)

M Steven's Shoes. How may I help you?

W Hi, I bought a pair of shoes through your website, and _____.

M What is it?

W The ribbon on one of the shoes came off as soon as I put them on.

M Oh, it _____. I'm sorry about that. We will exchange it for another pair.

W Actually, I want a full refund.

M Would you reconsider? You know that was a real bargain.

W No, I want you to give me a refund.

M OK. We're going to _____ right away.

W Thanks. Then how can I return them?

M _____

14

M _____, Tracy?

W Almost. Thanks for asking.

M So, what is your apartment like?

W It's a studio with a separate kitchen.

M Where is it located?

W It is in the Riverside area, near my work.

M Good for you. So, _____
_____?

W It's very cozy with a good interior design, and it has a big swimming pool.

M It sounds like it's perfect for you. _____
_____ so I can take a look.

W _____

15

M It's Saturday night, and Susan is alone in the house because _____
for the weekend. Susan has just fallen asleep while reading a book in her bed. It's a little past midnight, and she wakes up _____
_____. She hears somebody walk around quietly. She wants to call the police, but she's too frightened to make a sound. _____
_____, she hears footsteps on the stairs. Then the door to her bedroom opens slowly. It's her mother and father. They have come back ahead of schedule. In this situation, what would Susan most likely say to her parents?

Susan _____

16-17

W Text chatting and instant messaging are quickly becoming _____
_____. These forms of communication allow people to share information and to learn foreign languages and world cultures in almost real time. In addition, _____
with others from different countries. However, you have to be careful and considerate when finding friends on the Internet because you don't know who the person is at the other end. When chatting online, always use a nickname and _____
_____ such as your age, your location, your real name, and the name of your school. _____
_____,
but if you would like to do so, make sure it is in a public place and go with a friend or a family member. Finally, call the police if you feel you are in danger. Chatting with others online may be not only enjoyable but educational if you are careful when doing so.

1번부터 17번까지는 듣고 답하는 문제입니다. 1번부터 15번까지는 한 번만 들려주고, 16번부터 17번까지는 두 번 들려줍니다. 방송을 잘 듣고 답을 하시기 바랍니다.

01 대화를 듣고, 남자의 마지막 말에 대한 여자의 응답으로 가장 적절한 것을 고르시오.

① I took a few novels with me.
② I don't have friends living there.
③ It's perfect for a family vacation.
④ I went with my husband and in-laws.
⑤ It went on raining with thunder and lightning.

02 대화를 듣고, 여자의 마지막 말에 대한 남자의 응답으로 가장 적절한 것을 고르시오.

① Come on, it looks good on her.
② I don't know when she came back.
③ Then, why don't you lend it to her?
④ Now I know why you want to buy it.
⑤ Yes, she spends too much on her clothes.

03 다음을 듣고, 여자가 하는 말의 목적으로 가장 적절한 것을 고르시오.

① 동아리 활동을 홍보하려고
② 수강신청 방법을 안내하려고
③ 학교 대표 선수를 선발하려고
④ 교내 체육 시설을 소개하려고
⑤ 종목별 운동 방법을 설명하려고

04 다음을 듣고, 남자가 하는 말의 주제로 가장 적절한 것을 고르시오.

① 안전사고 예방 방법
② 긴급 전화 통화 요령
③ 위기 대처 교육 일정
④ 구조 요청 접수 절차
⑤ 장난 전화 처벌 방안

05 대화를 듣고, 남자의 의견으로 가장 적절한 것을 고르시오.

① 계산대의 개수를 더 늘려야 한다.
② 표지판의 크기를 더 확대해야 한다.
③ 직원의 서비스 교육을 강화해야 한다.
④ 소량 전용 계산대임을 알려줘야 한다.
⑤ 신용카드 영수증 제시를 요구해야 한다.

06 대화를 듣고, 그림에서 대화의 내용과 일치하지 <u>않는</u> 것을 고르시오.

07 대화를 듣고, 남자가 여자를 위해 할 일로 가장 적절한 것을 고르시오.

① 상품 추가 발송
② 재고 상품 회수
③ 주문 상품 교환
④ 음반 주문 취소
⑤ 대금 입금 확인

08 대화를 듣고, 남자가 기뻐하는 이유를 고르시오.

① 연극 대회에서 입상하게 되어서
② 잃어버린 연극 대본을 찾게 되어서
③ 연극 대본 제출 마감 날짜가 연기되어서
④ 연극 연습을 더 많이 할 수 있게 되어서
⑤ 영화배우로부터 연기 지도를 받게 되어서

09 대화를 듣고, 여자가 지불해야 할 금액을 고르시오. [3점]

① $350   ② $400   ③ $450
④ $500   ⑤ $550

10 대화를 듣고, SUV에 관해 두 사람이 언급하지 <u>않은</u> 것을 고르시오.

① 가격   ② 안전성
③ 승차 인원   ④ 연료 효율
⑤ 적재 능력

11 juju에 관한 다음 내용을 듣고, 일치하지 <u>않는</u> 것을 고르시오.

① 서아프리카에서 발생한 음악 중의 하나이다.
② 나이지리아 전통 음악에 그 바탕을 두고 있다.
③ 북, 기타, 건반 악기를 함께 사용하여 연주한다.
④ 1920년대에 시작되어 지금은 거의 사라졌다.
⑤ 공연 중에 관객이 연주자에 지폐를 던진다.

12 다음 신청서를 보면서 대화를 듣고, 두 사람의 대화 내용과 일치하지 <u>않는</u> 것을 고르시오.

PARKING PERMIT APPLICATION			
① Name	Steve	Carlson	
	Last	First	Middle Initial
② Address	3251 Washington Street		
	Phone: 555-0103		
③ Car	Ford	Explorer	2003
	Make	Model	Year
④ License Plate	AWJ	130	
⑤ □ Fall Semester	Amount enclosed		
□ Spring Semester	: $ 210.00		
☑ All Year			

13 대화를 듣고, 남자의 마지막 말에 대한 여자의 응답으로 가장 적절한 것을 고르시오.

Woman : _____

① What do you want to do now?
② I'm sorry, but I didn't mean it.
③ Then let's make it this Saturday.
④ I'm glad that you changed your mind.
⑤ How about playing a video game instead?

14 대화를 듣고, 여자의 마지막 말에 대한 남자의 응답으로 가장 적절한 것을 고르시오. [3점]

Man : _____

① We should also try not to use plastic bags.
② That's good. And how's the transportation?
③ OK, let's roll up our sleeves and get to work.
④ What are we going to do with all these bottles?
⑤ That's not enough to dispose of all the garbage.

15 다음 상황 설명을 듣고, Peter가 Betty에게 할 말로 가장 적절한 것을 고르시오.

Peter : _____

① I know a good TV repairman.
② Let's go to the ball park someday.
③ Can you introduce me to that lady?
④ Would you tell me the time, please?
⑤ Would you mind if I turned on the TV?

[16-17] 다음을 듣고, 물음에 답하시오.

16 여자가 하는 말의 목적으로 가장 적절한 것은? [3점]

① to advertise a new public school
② to attract investors to a new business
③ to appeal to voters for their support
④ to praise a politician for his achievement
⑤ to criticize the policies of the government

17 담화의 내용에 언급되지 <u>않은</u> 것은?

① 공립 학교 신설   ② 택지 개발
③ 녹지 조성   ④ 도심 인구 집중 해소
⑤ 경전철 건설

DICTATION(받아쓰기) 코너입니다.
녹음의 내용을 잘 듣고, 빈칸에 알맞은 말을 쓰시기 바랍니다.

01

M Wow! You look very healthy. Where did you get that suntan?

W I just got back from vacation in Florida. It was really nice to _____.

M Who did you go with?

W _____

02

W Daniel! Look at Lisa. _____.

M I wouldn't say that. It looks just fine to me.

W Are you kidding? Don't you think it's behind the times? _____.

M _____

03

W Good morning, everyone. I'm Jenny Stewart, ___ _____. At this university, all of our sports facilities are in the northeast corner of the campus. We have six multipurpose athletic fields, used for football, soccer, rugby, or baseball. We also have four basketball courts and two swimming pools, one indoors and one outdoors. We also have a brand-new fitness center with all of the exercise equipment that _____ and stay in that way. We want to help you build up strong bones and muscles. I'll be happy to answer any of your questions now.

04

M _____.
It's important for everyone to be ready in case of an emergency. The phone number for reporting emergencies is 911, but are you ready to make that call for help? _____, _____. Try not to panic. First, explain the problem. Next, say where the problem is and who you are. A wrong address will mean that the emergency help will take longer to get there. Give the name of the person or people who need the emergency help. Answer other questions. _____ until you are sure they have all the information.

05

M Hey, Carol, look at that guy.

W You mean the man with the full basket? What does he think he's doing?

M I don't know, but _____.

W You have to watch out. I heard about someone who started a fight when he was told _____ ___.

M But the line is only for customers with 5 items or less.

W Yeah, you're right. But you have to be careful when you deal with strangers. They might get angry.

M He might not have seen the sign. We could just go over to him and tell him in a nice way.

W _____?

M He will leave the counter before the manager arrives.

W Well, then, let's see what the cashier does when it's his turn.

M If he didn't see the sign, it's really not fair to make him go back and _____. I'll go and talk to him.

06

W OK, we start by _____
_____ plate. I mean the bigger one.

M All right. Now what?

W You need to set the water glass. It goes above the plate and a little to the right.

M Like this?

W Exactly. Now, this little plate here is for bread. Put it _____.

M All right. What's next?

W Silverware. Take this knife and put it to the right of the dinner plate. Then put the spoon to the right of the knife.

M Like this?

W Good. Now, to the left of the plate, first put this big fork. That's the dinner fork. And _____
_____. It's for salads. Well done!

M Thanks, Mrs. Riley. You've been a great help!

07

(Telephone rings.)

M Hello, Benson Software Customer Services.

W Hi, this is Judy Williams from Lakeside Supermarket. I'm calling about the CD-ROMs you sent last week.

M Oh, Ms. Williams. Is there any problem with them?

W I'm afraid _____.

M Oh, dear. I'm sorry about that. How many did you receive?

W We received fifty, but we ordered a hundred and fifty.

M Just a moment, I'll check your order. According to our records, you seem to have ordered fifty.

W Oh, really? Perhaps there's been a mistake. I'm sure we ordered a hundred and fifty.

M Ms. Williams. _____.
We'll get the extra hundred to you as soon as possible.

W Thanks very much. Sorry to trouble you.

M No problem.

08

W Hi, Robert! How's your script going?

M Oh, Laura, hi. I have some problems with that. _____
_____.

W Don't you think we need a surprise ending? It would be rather dull without it.

M Yeah, but I don't have enough time to make up a nice ending.

W When is the deadline to submit our entry?

M Wednesday. We're supposed to _____
and the script to Mr. Crawford.

W I think we can't help our situation. (incoming text message signal) You've got a message. Who is it from?

M Mr. Crawford. Look! We're lucky.

W Let me see. _____
_____ to Friday. Now we have two more days.

M I guess it's a sign that we will win the drama contest.

W I hope so.

09

M Good afternoon. Can I help you?

W I need to buy a digital camcorder.

M You came to the right place. We _____
_____, and we are actually having a 20% off sale right now.

W Great. I'm looking for a camcorder with a quality zoom lens.

M How about this one?

W Hmm, it looks good, but I want _____
_____.

M Then, how about this one?

W It's $500. This is the price before discount, isn't it?

M Yes, but we only offer 10% off on that model. It's one of the latest.

W It's a bit expensive, but I like it. OK, I'll take this.

10

W Hey, Nick! _____ .

M OK. What kind of a car would you like to buy?

W Maybe a mid-sized sedan or an SUV. I can't make up my mind.

M I would recommend an SUV because it's more practical. I mean, you can _____ when you travel.

W I hear the fuel efficiency of an SUV is very low compared to that of a sedan.

M It's true, but it's because SUVs are _____ . And you also have to consider safety factors.

W You mean SUVs are safer than sedans?

M Yes. They usually have stronger bodies and _____ _____ .

W But SUVs are more expensive than sedans. I'm on a tight budget.

M Then, how about _____ ? One of my friends is a used car dealer. I think he can give you a good deal.

W Oh, really? That would be great!

M I'll tell him to get in touch with you.

11

M Good evening, and thank you for coming. This evening, I'm going to give a short introduction to music from the African continent. There are various styles of music _____ Western Africa. One example I'd like you to hear is juju. Juju _____ _____ , but instead of being played only on drums, guitars and keyboards are also used. Juju started out in the 1920s and is still popular today, _____ _____ such as King Sunny Adé. Juju is a Yoruba word meaning "throwing" or "something being thrown," and in performance, audiences commonly shower juju musicians with paper money.

12

M Hi, _____ . Is the parking lot nine available?

W Yes, it is. What's your name, please?

M Steve Carlson.

W And your address and phone number?

M 3251 Washington Street, 555-0103.

W OK. What's the year and make of your car?

M Two thousand three, Ford Explorer.

W _____ ?

M AWJ 130.

W OK. That'll be $210 for the semester or $420 for the year.

M I just need it _____ .

W All right. Send in your payment, and we'll send you a permit.

M Great. Thank you very much.

13

W Hi, Frank. How are you doing?

M I'm OK, but busy.

W Can you make time to go to a movie this afternoon?

M I wish I could, but I have a lot of homework.

W Come on, _____ . You're always studying! You're going to turn into a robot before you know it.

M Well, I still have a lot to do. Don't you have work to do?

W I did, but I got it over with. Listen, it's my birthday.

M Really? I didn't know! Happy birthday!

W Thanks. I wanted to celebrate it with you.

M Well, _____ , how can I refuse? You talked me into it.

W _____

14

W Hold it, Dave! What in the world are you doing?

M What are you talking about?

W Don't you recycle? How can you throw glass away?

M Take it easy, Cathy. _____ _____ in my town.

W I'm sorry. It's just that I've been doing some research on pollution, and I've found out that _____ _____ places to put our garbage.

M I do care about the environment, too. I just want to clean up.

W Listen, why don't we go through the bags and take the bottles out? I'll take them home and recycle them.

M Are you sure it's no trouble?

W No problem at all. We've _____. They pick up newspapers, bottles, and cans once a week in my neighborhood.

M _____

15

W   Peter and Betty have been _____ for almost ten years. Last month, Betty moved into a new apartment, and today she's having a housewarming party. Peter is attending the party, and now he's talking with some people in the living room. But _____ and looks at his watch often. Peter is a great fan of baseball, and today his favorite team is playing a big game. It's now being broadcast, but the TV set is off. _____ _____. In this situation, what would Peter most likely say to Betty?

Peter _____

16-17

W Ladies and gentlemen, _____ _____ in Congress, there are several things I will do to ensure that your needs are met every day. First of all, I plan on proposing a new law that will invest more tax money in our schools. New funding would be used to hire good teachers and _____ _____. Second, I'm proposing a downtown area revitalization project. It will promote new businesses, new residential areas, and new green areas to _____. And third, I am proposing the construction of a light rail train system, to be built over the next decade, to meet the growing demands of our citizens. I'm not a career politician who has lost touch _____ _____. My work as a business owner has given me a unique perspective on the pains and challenges you face. If elected, I promise to make sure your issues and concerns are fully addressed at the local and national level. Thank you.

1번부터 17번까지는 듣고 답하는 문제입니다. 1번부터 15번까지는 한 번만 들려주고, 16번부터 17번까지는 두 번 들려줍니다. 방송을 잘 듣고 답을 하시기 바랍니다.

01 대화를 듣고, 남자의 마지막 말에 대한 여자의 응답으로 가장 적절한 것을 고르시오.

① Don't be cruel to yourself.
② I think you're exaggerating.
③ I can't tell a goose from a duck.
④ You need to drink something cold.
⑤ The number of polar bears is decreasing.

02 대화를 듣고, 여자의 마지막 말에 대한 남자의 응답으로 가장 적절한 것을 고르시오.

① Then I'll take both of them.
② Thanks. I'll keep that in mind.
③ Great. I've brought my receipt.
④ Really? Let me think some more.
⑤ I don't understand why you do it.

03 다음을 듣고, 여자가 하는 말의 주제로 가장 적절한 것을 고르시오.

① 건전한 이성 교제의 장점
② 논쟁에서 승리하는 방법
③ 효과적인 토론 진행 방법
④ 문화에 따른 예절의 차이
⑤ 데이트할 때의 대화 요령

04 대화를 듣고, 여자의 의견으로 가장 적절한 것을 고르시오.

① 강아지의 청력이 많이 손실되었다.
② 강아지를 하루 동안 입원시켜야 한다.
③ 애완동물은 반려자의 역할을 할 수 있다.
④ 애완동물에게는 예방접종이 꼭 필요하다.
⑤ 강아지에게 적당한 양의 먹이를 주어야 한다.

05 대화를 듣고, 두 사람의 관계를 가장 잘 나타낸 것을 고르시오.

① doctor – patient
② landlord – tenant
③ plumber – housewife
④ car mechanic – driver
⑤ consumer – telemarketer

06 대화를 듣고, 완성된 표지에서 대화의 내용과 일치하지 <u>않는</u> 것을 고르시오.

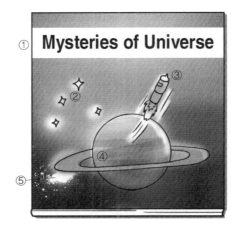

07 대화를 듣고, 여자가 남자에게 부탁한 일로 가장 적절한 것을 고르시오.

① 전화로 깨워 주기
② 생일 선물 구입하기
③ 공항에 마중 나오기
④ 비행기 예약 취소하기
⑤ 비행기 출발 시각 알아보기

08 대화를 듣고, 여자가 고마워하는 이유를 고르시오.

① 잃어버린 물건을 찾아주어서
② 고장이 난 TV를 수리해 주어서
③ 이삿짐 옮기는 것을 도와주어서
④ 부모님 집의 위치를 알려 주어서
⑤ 옆집에 사는 이웃을 소개해 주어서

09 대화를 듣고, 남자가 지불해야 할 입장권의 금액을 고르시오. [3점]

① $20   ② $22   ③ $25

④ $30   ⑤ $32

10 대화를 듣고, 남자가 할 일로 여자가 언급하지 <u>않은</u> 것을 고르시오.

① 세차

② 마당 청소

③ 쓰레기 내놓기

④ 야구 유니폼 세탁하기

⑤ 저녁 식사 시간 지키기

11 Sun Bear에 관한 다음 내용을 듣고, 일치하지 <u>않는</u> 것을 고르시오. [3점]

① 동남아시아 열대 우림에서 주로 서식한다.

② 키가 4피트로 곰 중에서 가장 작다.

③ 수컷이 암컷보다 조금 더 크다.

④ 저지대 기후에서 살아 털이 짧다.

⑤ 가슴 부위를 제외하고 모두 검은 색이다.

12 다음 표를 보면서 대화를 듣고, <u>잘못</u> 표시된 것을 고르시오.

INTERVIEWER'S CHECKLIST Check all items that apply:		
①	job application for √ full-time position ___ part-time position	
②	availability √ mornings √ afternoons ___ weekends	
③	highest education level completed ___ elementary school √ college ___ high school ___ graduate school	
④	qualifications √ enjoys working with people ___ good telephone skills ___ enjoys working alone ___ good writing skills	
⑤	skills and interests √ foreign languages ___ familiar with office machines ___ other ( )	

13 대화를 듣고, 여자의 마지막 말에 대한 남자의 응답으로 가장 적절한 것을 고르시오.

Man : _____

① Let's ask him where we are.

② It can be fun to sleep in a tent.

③ Then we'd better not buy an RV.

④ We'll see the real thing in a minute.

⑤ I regret camping out in this weather.

14 대화를 듣고, 남자의 마지막 말에 대한 여자의 응답으로 가장 적절한 것을 고르시오. [3점]

Woman : _____

① All we can do now is watch and wait.

② You'd better find another job quickly.

③ Why don't we go on vacation together?

④ I guess it's time to change our door lock.

⑤ We should be more careful not to overeat.

15 다음 상황 설명을 듣고, Steve가 점원에게 할 말로 가장 적절한 것을 고르시오.

Steve : _____

① Hi, have you seen my wife shopping here?

② Hello. Could you help me choose some apples?

③ Sorry, do you know where I can wash my hands?

④ Excuse me. Could I shop for another ten minutes?

⑤ Would you tell me what the announcement was about?

[16-17] 다음을 듣고, 물음에 답하시오.

16 남자가 하는 말의 쟁점으로 가장 적절한 것은?

① the influence of fast food on health

② the reason why fast food is popular

③ the prospect of food service industry

④ the bad effects of American fast food

⑤ the origin of multinational corporations

17 두 사람이 하는 말의 내용과 일치하지 <u>않는</u> 것은?

① 남자는 맥도날드의 해외 매출이 증가할 것으로 예상한다.

② 남자는 미국 기업 때문에 자국의 문화가 파괴된다고 생각한다.

③ 여자는 패스트푸드 업체가 현지화 전략으로 성공했다고 생각한다.

④ 여자는 패스트푸드 식당이 결국 모두 문을 닫을 것으로 판단한다.

⑤ 여자는 패스트푸드 식당이 가족적인 분위기를 제공한다고 생각한다.

DICTATION(받아쓰기) 코너입니다.
녹음의 내용을 잘 듣고, 빈칸에 알맞은 말을 쓰시기 바랍니다.

01

M Cindy! The office is like a refrigerator.

W No, it's not! To me, it's just perfect. _____.

M Yeah, if you're a polar bear. Look at me. Even ___ _____!

W _____

02

W Is there anything else you would like to buy?

M No, thank you. _____.

W Okay. (pause) Here you go. And when you want an exchange or a refund, _____ within a week. Don't forget to bring your receipt.

M _____

03

W Welcome to Etiquette with Catherine. I'm Catherine Jones, and tonight I will talk about dating etiquette. You should _____. When your date says something interesting, respond. You can say, "Oh, really?" or just "Uh-huh," but say something. _____ about yourself. Your date will want to know you, but don't tell him or her every little detail about your life. Definitely don't talk about your ex-boyfriend or ex-girlfriend. And _____ controversial topics like religion or politics. You may _____ talking about music and movies. That will give you an idea about shared values.

04

W So, what seems to be the problem?

M Max was awake all night long. And this morning, he wouldn't eat anything. Look, he can't _____ his right ear.

W It sounds like something is wrong. Will you hold him so I can take his temperature? Yes, he does have a fever.

M I feel sorry for him. Look at his sad eyes.

W He'll be better by tomorrow. These pills will _____ _____ his infection quickly.

M What infection?

W He has an ear infection. You can pick him up tomorrow.

M What do you mean?

W I mean I'd like to keep him here overnight.

M But I live alone. I need him _____.

W It's only for one night.

M One night is a long time. I hope he can go home with me.

05

(Telephone rings.)

M Hello?

W Is this Mr. Smith?

M Yes, speaking.

W Hi, Mr. Smith. It's Janet Anderson in Apartment 2B.

M Hi, Mrs. Anderson. What's the matter?

W I'm calling because the heater stopped working. I woke up this morning, and _____. My husband and I have terrible colds now.

M Oh, I'm sorry to hear that. I'll _____.

W Today?

M Yes, of course. It will be sometime before noon.

W Great. Thank you so much. Bye.

06

W James! I want some _____ a book cover.

M Is this the title of the book? *Mysteries of Universe*?

W Yes, this book is about space. I'm going to put a planet in the center. A planet in the shape of _____ _____ .

M You mean the planet that looks like Saturn?

W Yes. And a rocket will go toward the planet, like this.

M I think a rocket leaving the planet would be better.

W Hmm... You're right. How about putting some bright stars beyond the planet?

M Or maybe a galaxy would _____ . You know, numerous stars and planets in mysterious colors.

W I don't think so. It would make the design too complicated. I'll just go with a few distant stars.

M Where are you going to place the title? I guess it would look good above the background picture.

W I think so, too. Well... That's it. _____ _____ . Thank you.

07

(Telephone rings.)

M Hello?

W Hi, Bruce. This is Pam.

M Oh, Pam! Where are you now?

W I'm still in Detroit. _____ .

M Do you know when the plane will be leaving?

W I guess not for another hour at least.

M That means you won't arrive here until midnight.

W Yeah. And that's why I'm calling. Would it be a lot of trouble for you _____ ?

M Of course not. Just call me right before you take off.

W Thanks, I will. By the way, I bought a nice present for you. It's a...

M Don't tell me. I'm going to _____ .

W OK. See you later.

08

M Hi, I'm Sam Brown. _____ for almost ten years. My parents live next to me.

W Nice to meet you. I'm Rachel Johnson.

M Are you the new owner of this house?

W Yes. This is my first house. I'm very excited.

M Congratulations! I saw you trying to lift that TV. I came to help you.

W Oh, thank you. _____ .

M It's nothing. Should I take this end?

W Yeah. Let's do it on three. One, two, three.

M Oooh, it's heavy. I hope this is the only TV you have.

W Yes, it is. OK. _____ right here.

M Shall we bring in something else?

W No, I can do the rest. The TV was the hardest thing to deal with. Thank you very much.

09

(Telephone rings.)

W Hi, this is Sherry speaking. Can I help you?

M Yes, I want two tickets for the show on August 4th.

W Just a second, please. Yes, _____ .

M Is there a special price for students?

W Yes, student tickets are $10.

M OK, that's good.

W All right, two student tickets at $10 each. There is also a service charge of $1 per ticket. _____ _____ pay for your tickets?

M Can you hold them for me for 10 minutes? I'm just a block away from you.

W I can do that. And if you pick up the tickets at the box office, _____ . May I have your name and phone number, please?

M Yes. Travis Johnson. 310-555-0176.

W OK. Remember to bring your student ID with you for the student price.

M Thank you very much. Bye-bye.

10

W   Johnny, are you going anywhere this afternoon?

M   Why? Do you want me to get you anything, Mom?

W   No. I just wonder if you could help me _____.

M   I wish I could. But I'm supposed to go to baseball practice. I said I would be there. How about doing it tomorrow?

W   OK. But could you wash the car _____?

M   I heard that it'll rain all day tomorrow. I promise I'll do it this weekend.

W   You always make promises but never keep them.

M   Mom, it's nothing like that. I just forget what I said.

W   OK, OK. You _____ on your way out, can't you?

M   Sure, no problem. Is there anything else I can do for you, Mom?

W   Just be careful not to get your clothes dirty. And don't be late for dinner.

M   I'll try. See you later.

11

W   The Sun Bear is a bear found primarily in the tropical rain forests of Southeast Asia. The Sun Bear stands _____, and it is the smallest member in the bear family. Males tend to be slightly larger than females. Unlike other bears, the Sun Bear's fur is short and smooth. This is probably _____ it inhabits. Black fur covers most of its body, except the chest where there is a pale yellow marking _____ a horseshoe. This distinct marking gives the sun bear its name. Similar colored fur can be found around the mouth and the eyes.

12

W   I'm looking for a summer job.

M   _____ working full-time?

W   Yes, I am.

M   Can you work on weekends?

W   No. I go to church every Sunday, and I also have to study on weekends.

M   OK. Where do you go to school?

W   I go to George Washington University.

M   _____?

W   Next June.

M   Do you have any special skills or interests?

W   Well, I enjoy working with others, and I know how to speak Spanish.

M   I see. OK, Miss Nelson. _____ you as soon as we can.

13

W   Look! There's the campground. Mrs. Simpson wrote her campsite number _____. I have it somewhere... Oh! Here it is.

M   Hmm... Can you imagine Mr. and Mrs. Simpson sleeping in a tent? They must be seventy years old!

W   Oh, no! The Simpsons _____. They don't sleep in a tent. They sleep in their own bed.

M   Their own bed? How can they do that?

W   The Simpsons travel in a motor home. It is called "RV."

M   You mean _____?

W   Yes. It probably has a bedroom, a bathroom, a kitchen, a washer, a dryer, and so on.

M   _____. I've never been inside an RV.

W   Neither have I.

M   _____

14

M _____? I just came home from the store.

W Oh, I'm so glad to see you. I was afraid you were trapped in your apartment. Where are your kids?

M They're at the zoo with my wife.

W Oh, good. You're all safe!

M When did the fire start?

W _____ around 11:30. The building manager told us to leave the building.

M Do you know how it started?

W No. Some people think it started in the Harrisons' apartment. _____.

M This is awful! What should we do?

W _____

15

M It's a Friday evening, and Steve is shopping in a grocery store. He's buying some groceries for a picnic tomorrow. Holding the shopping list his wife gave him, he _____ between the aisles. It's a little difficult for him to find the items he needs. He wishes his wife were with him now. Then, while selecting apples, he hears through the speakers the announcement that _____. After checking his shopping list, he estimates that he needs at least twenty more minutes. When Steve sees _____, what would he most likely say to him?

Steve _____

16-17

M There are few countries in the world today that do not have American fast-food restaurants. McDonald's has been especially successful. There are more than 8,000 McDonald's restaurants in about 100 countries. In fact, 59 percent of McDonald's profits _____ outside the United States. And this amount is likely to increase. Each country has its own kind of foods. These foods are disappearing, and our diets are being Americanized. In my opinion, American businesses like McDonald's are destroying our cultures. _____!

W There are many reasons for the success of fast-food chains like McDonald's. First of all, they _____. For instance, McDonald's sells wine in France, vegetarian burgers in India, and a salmon sandwich in Norway. Other factors contributing to fast-food success abroad are cleanness, a family atmosphere, and efficient service. _____ that American fast food is destroying other cultures. No one is making anyone buy hamburgers. If people refuse to eat fast food, then all the fast-food restaurants will close.

1번부터 17번까지는 듣고 답하는 문제입니다. 1번부터 15번까지는 한 번만 들려주고, 16번부터 17번까지는 두 번 들려줍니다. 방송을 잘 듣고 답을 하시기 바랍니다.

01 대화를 듣고, 남자의 마지막 말에 대한 여자의 응답으로 가장 적절한 것을 고르시오.

① Then, what do we get for Father?
② That would be nice. She'll like that.
③ I already bought some flowers for her.
④ Can you afford such an expensive gift?
⑤ They look beautiful, but I don't know her size.

02 대화를 듣고, 여자의 마지막 말에 대한 남자의 응답으로 가장 적절한 것을 고르시오.

① Give me a break! It must be fake.
② Now you know how to shop online.
③ Sorry, but I'm out of budget myself.
④ Thanks. This is exactly what I wanted.
⑤ This is my final offer. Take it or leave it.

03 다음을 듣고, 남자가 하는 말의 주제로 가장 적절한 것을 고르시오.

① 교통사고 신고 요령
② 차량 절도 예방법
③ 자동차 정비의 중요성
④ 안전운전 교육의 필요성
⑤ 도시의 범죄 발생 증가

04 대화를 듣고, 여자의 의견으로 가장 적절한 것을 고르시오.

① 작은 개가 큰 개보다 더 시끄럽다.
② 개는 고양이보다 돌보기가 더 쉽다.
③ 애완동물로 고양이보다 개가 더 좋다.
④ 개는 매일 한 번씩 산책을 시켜야 한다.
⑤ 애완동물을 기르려면 책임감이 필요하다.

05 대화를 듣고, 두 사람의 관계를 가장 잘 나타낸 것을 고르시오.

① defendant – judge
② inhabitant – janitor
③ shopper – firefighter
④ moviegoer – ticket agent
⑤ driver – police officer

06 대화를 듣고, 그림에서 대화의 내용과 일치하지 <u>않는</u> 것을 고르시오.

07 대화를 듣고, 남자가 여자에게 부탁한 일로 가장 적절한 것을 고르시오.

① 신청서 우송하기
② 지원서 접수하기
③ 증명서 발급하기
④ 문제지 복사하기
⑤ 주소지 변경하기

08 대화를 듣고, 남자가 걱정하는 이유를 고르시오.

① 친구가 다쳐서
② 교통신호를 위반해서
③ 교통사고에 연루되어서
④ 회의에 참석하지 않아서
⑤ 파티 분위기를 망쳐 놓아서

09 대화를 듣고, 여자가 지불할 금액을 고르시오. [3점]

① $120   ② $150   ③ $160
④ $180   ⑤ $200

10 다음을 듣고, 시드니의 관광지로 언급되지 <u>않은</u> 것을 고르시오.

① 항구   ② 동물원
③ 수족관   ④ 수산시장
⑤ 오페라 하우스

11 Tough Guy & Girl Challenge에 관한 다음 내용을 듣고, 일치하지 <u>않는</u> 것을 고르시오.

① 13세 이상이 되어야 참가할 수 있다.
② 참가자는 늪, 그물 등의 장애물을 통과해야 한다.
③ 거리에 따라 두 부문으로 나누어진다.
④ 10명 이상의 단체에게는 참가비가 할인된다.
⑤ 참가자에게 운동모자를 무료로 제공한다.

12 다음 시간표를 보면서 대화를 듣고, 여자가 출근 시 이용할 버스 번호를 고르시오.

Bus Schedule

No.	approximate frequency in minutes				
	Rush Hour	Day	Night	Sat.	Sun.
① 12	5	10	12	12	12
② 25	6	15	25	15	15
③ 63	12	15	30	30	30
④ 124	7	10	15	15	15
⑤ 150	5	10	15	15	20

13 대화를 듣고, 남자의 마지막 말에 대한 여자의 응답으로 가장 적절한 것을 고르시오. [3점]

Woman : _____

① It's $850! How do you want to pay?
② It takes about 12 hours. It's so boring.
③ I get $5 an hour working at a restaurant.
④ Yeah, most things are rather expensive there.
⑤ I'm not sure but that's too much money for me.

14 대화를 듣고, 여자의 마지막 말에 대한 남자의 응답으로 가장 적절한 것을 고르시오.

Man : _____

① Don't you think that's too much?
② What do you do at that late hour?
③ I prefer to study in the early morning.
④ I can't concentrate for more than an hour.
⑤ No wonder you think nine hours is too much.

15 다음 상황 설명을 듣고, Susan이 동료에게 할 말로 가장 적절한 것을 고르시오. [3점]

Susan : _____

① I'm not good at Italian yet.
② I just can't wait another day.
③ I'll pay for the tickets this time.
④ I'd like to go to an opera instead.
⑤ I have another engagement that day.

[16-17] 다음을 듣고, 물음에 답하시오.

16 여자가 하는 말의 목적으로 가장 적절한 것은?

① to advertise a specific MP3 player
② to stress the importance of listening
③ to warn against the illegal use of MP3 files
④ to ask for the improvement of media players
⑤ to inform about a way of foreign language learning

17 MP3 플레이어의 기능으로 언급된 것은?

① 파일 변환   ② 음성 녹음
③ 라디오 청취   ④ 텍스트 저장
⑤ 동영상 재생

DICTATION(받아쓰기) 코너입니다.
녹음의 내용을 잘 듣고, 빈칸에 알맞은 말을 쓰시기 바랍니다.

01

M Good morning. May I help you?

W I'd like to get some flowers for Mother's Day.

M How about _____ in a pretty vase?

W _____

02

W I'm _____ of all time.

M Oh no, not again. What did you get this time?

W I was walking down the street, and I saw a guy selling top-brand handbags for $100. I bargained with him, and he gave one to me _____.

M _____

03

M Good afternoon. I'm Officer Mike Brown. It's true that there's been very little violent crime in this area, especially compared to other parts of the city, but the number of car thefts _____. I'm not here to try to scare you. What I really want to do is to give you some simple advice that will make your cars safer. First, if you have a garage, _____, not for your billiard table. The most important thing is, if you have valuables in the car, hide them in the trunk. Don't leave them out on the seat, _____!

04

M Hey, Amy. You have a pet dog, don't you?

W Yes. Why?

M _____.

W What's it about?

M My mother promised to buy me a pet. But I can't decide between a dog and a cat.

W If I were you, I would get a dog. Dogs are friendlier than cats.

M I know, but dogs are noisier than cats, especially little dogs.

W _____ how you take care of them. And you can also take dogs wherever you go.

M OK. I'm convinced. Then, do you know where I can get a good dog?

W Sure. If you want, _____.

M Really? Thanks for your help. Let's go there right now.

05

M Wait, wait! That's my car!

W Oh, is it? Then I won't need a tow truck.

M No! I'll move it right away!

W Good. It's illegal _____.

M I know, but there wasn't anywhere else to park. I was only gone for a minute.

W I see. Here's your ticket.

M You're going to give me a ticket?

W That's right. _____.

M But just for a minute!

W Every minute is important when firefighters need water.

M OK. I understand.

06

M Linda, have you decided on our wedding cake?

W No, not yet. It's difficult to _____. Why don't we discuss it together?

M OK. I think it should be quite tall so that all the guests can see it. How about a three-layer cake?

W David, our table will be there on the podium, so a two-layer will be enough.

M Yeah, right. How many candles are we going to have?

W Well, let's have two. One for you, and one for me.

M I guess _____ because now we are one, a husband and wife.

W That's great. It'll be a lovely sight to see us blowing out a candle together. What about decoration?

M A heart with roses would look beautiful. _____?

W It's too plain. I'd like something more unique. A heart and a bride and groom figure would look better.

M OK. And what do you want to be written on the side of the cake?

W Let's make it short. How about "Love Forever"?

M It's good. It'll be a wonderful wedding cake. _____.

07

M Could you help me, please? My name is John Davis. _____ at this school.

W Oh, hi. I remember you. How are you?

M Fine, thanks.

W What can I help you with?

M I want to _____ for the TOEFL test.

W You mean the international TOEFL IBT? Let's see. They used to be here on this shelf. It looks like they're all gone.

M Really? Not even one is left?

W I'm sorry. You'll have to wait until more come in next week.

M _____ one when they come in?

W No problem. What's your address?

M I live at 1223 East Park Avenue. Thank you.

08

M Julie, I'm so worried.

W What is it?

M Well, you know the party I went to last night?

W Yeah. You should have gone to a meeting, but you went to the party instead, right?

M Yeah. Anyway, _____ with Nick. He was driving pretty fast. When he was passing a truck, he hit a street sign.

W Did you stop?

M Well, I know _____, but Nick said it was all right.

W Oh, great! Not stopping after an accident is breaking the law.

M Yeah, I know.

W Why don't you call the police now?

M But Nick will _____. I don't know what to do.

09

M May I help you?

W Yes. I'm interested in looking at some pillows.

M We carry a number of different kinds. _____.

W Do you have any goose down pillows in flowered patterns?

M Yes, we do. How about these?

W Oh, lovely. I'll buy them. How much are they?

M The price tag reads $50 each, but _____. So you can get a 20% discount.

W Oh, that's a great deal. Then, I want four of them.

M You're lucky, ma'am. We're also having a 3 plus 1 sale. If you buy 3, _____.

W I'm glad that I stopped in here today.

10

W If you come to Sydney, you'll really enjoy it. Sydney Harbor is absolutely beautiful, and it's the largest in the world. You can choose from _____ ____. If you really want to see some local animals, you should come to Taronga Zoo. There are all kinds of unique Australian animals, including kangaroos and koalas. In the Sydney Aquarium, more than 150 meters of _____ the underwater exhibits. You can see fish and sharks swimming around and above you. The Sydney Fish Market is a really great spot to enjoy some quality local seafood _____. Market staff members are used to visitors and are friendly and helpful.

11

M If you've got power and endurance, then Tough Guy & Girl Challenge is for you. This unique off-road running event on August 14th _____ _____ competitors who are 13 years of age and older. Challenge yourself on a course that includes swamp crossings, a spider's web net climb, mud slides, and a rope bridge. You can run, walk, or climb through a variety of natural and man-made obstacles. There are two courses, a 12-kilometer full course, and a 6-kilometer half course. An individual entry fee is $10, and groups of 20 or more _____. Every participant will get a free sports cap. Grab your family or friends and come for a truly amazing experience.

12

W Excuse me. I haven't used this route before. Could you tell me how often this bus comes by here?

M Let's see. On weekdays, during the day, it runs by here _____.

W Do you happen to know how often it comes during rush hour? I'm going to start taking the bus to work.

M Good for you! But I'm sorry I don't know how often it comes then.

W I guess it comes more often than it would _____ _____.

M Maybe you're right.

W And what about on weekends?

M It's the same schedule for Saturdays and Sundays, and at night every fifteen minutes. You know, you can get a schedule downtown at the bus station.

W Oh, great. I'll get it. Thanks for your help.

M _____.

13

M Are you from around here?

W No. I'm from Seoul, Korea.

M Really? That's interesting. Seoul's the capital of Korea, isn't it?

W Yes, that's right.

M Are you going home for New Year's?

W Are you kidding? Seoul's _____!

M That's no problem. There are a lot of flights to Seoul from this city.

W Yeah, but you left out one important thing.

M What's that?

W The airfare! I'm a student, and _____ here.

M So, how much is it to Seoul?

W _____

14

W How many hours a night do you sleep?

M Usually nine or ten.

W Wow! That's a lot!

M I don't think so. I think people need _____ _____.

W Maybe you're right, but I read that eight hours is normal for most people.

M Perhaps that's the average, but don't you think that everyone is different?

W I'm not sure. Eight hours _____.

M How many hours do you sleep?

W Usually five or six.

M _____

15

M Susan just started working at a company. One day _____ and asked her to go to an opera with him. Susan had never been to an opera and she didn't like it, either. But she didn't want to seem rude. So she went to the opera, but it was all in Italian and really boring. After that, Susan _____ in the office. But a few days later, _____, and he invited her to go to another opera. In this situation, what would she most likely say to him?

Susan _____

16-17

W Today, I'd like to talk about MP3 players. These media players offer users the ability to listen to MP3 audio files and other formats anywhere anytime. So _____ for foreign language students like you? First of all, reading materials from textbooks can be digitalized from an audio CD, converted to MP3 audio files, and then uploaded to a media player. Then, you can listen to the media files as you _____ from the class textbook. Furthermore, many MP3 audio players have a recording feature that will allow you to record your voice. One practical use of such a feature is to keep a digital voice journal. That is, you can keep weekly recordings of your life events much like you would in a traditional diary. _____, you can go back weeks, months, or years later to hear evidence of your progress in language learning.

20^회 듣기 모의고사

1번부터 17번까지는 듣고 답하는 문제입니다. 1번부터 15번까지는 한 번만 들려주고, 16번부터 17번까지는 두 번 들려줍니다. 방송을 잘 듣고 답을 하시기 바랍니다.

01 대화를 듣고, 여자의 마지막 말에 대한 남자의 응답으로 가장 적절한 것을 고르시오.

① I should have studied harder.
② That's too bad for Bulls fans.
③ I hope he's not seriously injured.
④ Sounds like I missed a good game.
⑤ It was good to watch the game with you.

02 대화를 듣고, 남자의 마지막 말에 대한 여자의 응답으로 가장 적절한 것을 고르시오.

① I think I left my purse at your store.
② I don't know. I'll tell you when I find it.
③ It's the wrong size. Can you exchange it?
④ I can't find the shirt that I wanted to buy.
⑤ The CD is not readable. Can I get a refund?

03 다음을 듣고, 남자가 하는 말의 목적으로 가장 적절한 것을 고르시오.

① 신축 아파트를 광고하려고
② 원하는 아파트를 설명하려고
③ 신설 버스 노선을 안내하려고
④ 임대 주택 입주자를 모집하려고
⑤ 새로운 취미 활동을 소개하려고

04 대화를 듣고, 여자의 의견으로 가장 적절한 것을 고르시오.

① 과도한 음주는 건강에 매우 해롭다.
② 체중을 줄여야 부상을 예방할 수 있다.
③ 사우나에서 근육을 풀어주는 것이 좋다.
④ 규칙적인 운동으로 근육을 강화해야 한다.
⑤ 가끔씩 친구들과 어울리는 것이 필요하다.

05 대화를 듣고, 두 사람이 하는 말의 주제로 가장 적절한 것을 고르시오.

① 대도시 생활의 지루함
② 대도시의 교통 체증 문제
③ 지하철 이용 시 불편한 점
④ 차량 증가에 따른 대기 오염
⑤ 유가 인상으로 인한 연료비 부담

06 대화를 듣고, 그림에서 남자가 열쇠를 찾은 곳을 고르시오.

07 대화를 듣고, 여자가 할 일로 가장 적절한 것을 고르시오.

① 카드 대금 입금하기
② 재학증명서 발급 받기
③ 운전면허증 신청하기
④ 연극 예매권 구입하기
⑤ 현금 인출 카드 재발급 받기

08 대화를 듣고, 남자가 금연을 결심한 이유를 고르시오.

① 운동하는 데 지장이 많아서
② 최근에 건강이 매우 악화되어서
③ 담뱃값으로 지출되는 돈이 아까워서
④ 자녀들에게 교육적으로 좋지 않아서
⑤ 다른 사람들이 담배 피우는 것을 싫어해서

09 대화를 듣고, 여자가 하루에 달리는 거리와 소요 시간을 고르시오. [3점]

① 2 miles, 14 minutes
② 2 miles, 18 minutes
③ 3 miles, 18 minutes
④ 3 miles, 21 minutes
⑤ 3 miles, 24 minutes

10 대화를 듣고, 현재 시장의 업적으로 언급되지 <u>않은</u> 것을 고르시오.

① 세금 인하　　② 범죄율 감소
③ 깨끗한 거리　　④ 노숙자 수 감소
⑤ 실업자 수 감소

11 Mexican walking fish에 관한 다음 내용을 듣고, 일치하지 <u>않는</u> 것을 고르시오. [3점]

① 사람들이 애완동물로 물속에서 키운다.
② 멕시코시티 근처의 호수가 서식지이다.
③ 다리가 네 개이고 30센티미터까지 자란다.
④ 스스로 만든 독을 이용하여 먹이를 잡는다.
⑤ 다리가 잘려도 기능이 완전한 새 다리가 생긴다.

12 다음 일정표를 보면서 대화를 듣고, 남자가 진료 받을 요일을 고르시오.

	SUN	MON	① TUE	② WED	③ THU	④ FRI	⑤ SAT
am			10:30 Central Station			10:00 Susan	9:00 Brian
pm				5:30 Central Station	3:30 sales meeting		

13 대화를 듣고, 여자의 마지막 말에 대한 남자의 응답으로 가장 적절한 것을 고르시오. [3점]

Man : _____

① No problem. I have plenty of time.
② Thanks a lot. I'm relieved to hear that.
③ Then, I'd like to change my destination.
④ That's OK. I'm not going to change my plans.
⑤ That doesn't make sense. I have my receipt here.

14 대화를 듣고, 남자의 마지막 말에 대한 여자의 응답으로 가장 적절한 것을 고르시오.

Woman : _____

① Anybody can make a mistake sometimes.
② I should get one of these for my computer.
③ You sound as if you were a native speaker.
④ I want my computer to be fixed by tomorrow.
⑤ I'm sorry, but I did my best to make it perfect.

15 다음 상황 설명을 듣고, Jane이 뒤에 있는 사람에게 할 말로 가장 적절한 것을 고르시오.

Jane : _____

① This counter is for credit card holders only.
② Please go ahead. I'm waiting for my husband.
③ Excuse me. Have you seen my kids around here?
④ Sorry, but would you mind saving my place in line?
⑤ Thank you for telling me your recipe for steak sauce.

[16-17] 다음을 듣고, 물음에 답하시오.

16 여자가 하는 말의 목적으로 가장 적절한 것은?

① to promote communication using email
② to instruct on choosing an email account
③ to announce the latest Internet technology
④ to give tips on how to write efficient email
⑤ to warn against the harm caused by junk mail

17 생산성을 위해 고려해야 할 사항으로 언급된 것은?

① 이메일 계정의 수명
② 개인 정보 유출의 가능성
③ 스팸 메일을 걸러내는 기능
④ 체계적인 주소록 관리 기능
⑤ 대용량 파일의 첨부 가능 여부

DICTATION(받아쓰기) 코너입니다.
녹음의 내용을 잘 듣고, 빈칸에 알맞은 말을 쓰시기 바랍니다.

01

W Did you watch the basketball game last night?

M No. I wanted to, but I had to study. Who won?

W The Chicago Bulls. They were losing by two points with three seconds left in the game, and Jordan _____ _____ to win the game.

M _____

02

(Telephone rings.)

M Urban Outfitters. What can I do for you?

W Hi! I bought a shirt the other day online. And _____ _____.

M Can you tell me what's wrong with it?

W _____

03

M _____ from Detroit. I don't know anyone in this city yet, but the people at work are very friendly. I work downtown and don't have a car yet. So, I'd really like to find a place that has a bus line that _____. Even though I'm single, I would like two bedrooms, but I can only pay $600 a month. Since I'm new in this city I don't have any furniture, so _____. I won't need a very big kitchen because I don't really like to cook. But I must have a bathtub.

04

W We're going to have a drink after work tonight. Would you like to come with us?

M Thanks, Mary. I'd love to, but _____!

W Why? What happened?

M You know, I was working out at the gym yesterday, and I think _____.

W Oh, you poor thing. What are you going to do for it?

M Nothing, really.

W You know, you should check to see whether your gym has one of those saunas.

M Well, yeah, I think they do, but I've never used it.

W You should try it.

M Is it for losing weight? And I wouldn't like the heat in there.

W It's rather hot, but it'll really _____.

05

W This is the one of the reasons I hate working in a big city.

M I know. Every day, it's the same thing.

W This is terrible! We may be here all night! I hope we don't _____.

M Don't worry about that. I think there's enough.

W Let's turn on the radio. Maybe there's some good music.

M Sorry, the radio's not working.

W I think I'll take the subway tomorrow. _____ up all the way home, but it will take much less time.

M I envy you. There's no subway station near my house. So I would have to _____.

W Oh, the signal has changed to green. But look! Nobody's moving!

M Take it easy! I just hope there's no big accident ahead.

06

W Hurry! We're late!

M Wait. I don't have my keys.

W You _____ the coffee table, don't you?

M Yeah. But they are not there now.

W Did you look under the sofa? You might have kicked them away.

M Maybe. Nope. I can't see them.

W They're not on the desk. _____, either.

M Oh, now I remember. After I unlocked the door, I put them in my pocket. Do you know where my raincoat is?

W Yes. I saw it in the closet.

M OK. Just a second. _____. Let's go.

07

W Peter, are you going downtown today?

M Yes. Why?

W Could you give me a ride? _____.

M Where do you need to go exactly?

W I have to go to the bank. Could you drop me off at the corner of King Boulevard and Second Avenue?

M King and Second? Sure. I know where that is. But why are you going to the bank? _____ the ATM on campus?

W Because my cash card isn't working. I've got to get a new one. So, what are you going to do downtown?

M I'm going to the courthouse. I've got to pay a ticket.

W No kidding! I have to pay a ticket, too. _____ last week.

M But you don't drive.

W I know. I got a ticket for jaywalking. I didn't know it was illegal to _____ even in the campus!

08

M I've decided I've got to stop smoking.

W Oh, Jerry, I'm really happy. You know smoking is so dangerous for your health. Just weeks after you stop, you'll feel a big difference.

M But I'm a little afraid that I might _____. They say that you eat a lot more because of nerves when you stop smoking.

W Don't worry about that. It's just what people say.

M Are you sure?

W Listen, just get involved in some exercise program, and it will help you relax. I didn't gain any weight when I stopped smoking.

M That's true. You didn't seem to have much trouble at all.

W Well, it was not easy, but I did it because I wanted to _____ and live to be old enough to see my grandchildren grow up.

M In fact, I'm not worried about my health at all. I'm as healthy as a horse.

W Then _____ quit smoking?

M I can't stand nonsmokers asking me to leave the room.

09

M Have you always been a jogger?

W Oh, no. I never used to do any exercise.

M Really? Then, when did you start jogging?

W About 5 months ago. I started running a mile a day. I hated it in the beginning. But after a few weeks, I started feeling great. Now I'm running 2 miles more.

M _____?

W Every day. How about you? Do you get any exercise?

M I used to. But now I can never find the time. So, how fast do you run?

W I was very slow at first. _____ 14 minutes to run a mile.

M What about now?

W _____ and running 3 miles a day. But I want to run 3 miles in less than 18 minutes.

10

W Are you voting for Anderson for mayor again?

M I haven't really made up my mind yet. I'm not 100 percent happy with the job that Anderson has done.

W I have to say the streets are really a lot cleaner than they were _____ .

M I know. I admit I'm much happier about the way the city looks. But don't forget that it was the tax increase that helped to clean up the city.

W What about crime? The crime rate is lower than before.

M Yeah, you've got to _____ there.

W And he has done some impressive work with his homelessness campaign.

M It's true that his redevelopment project has reduced the number of homeless people.

W And the number of the unemployed has also decreased.

M That tempts me the most to vote for him again, but I'm going to wait for next Sunday's debate before _____ _____ for certain.

11

W There are many strange little pets, but few creatures are more peculiar than the Mexican walking fish. Their native habitat is the lakes near Mexico City. Though they live in water, they are not actually fish. Like frogs, they are amphibians. They have a long, slimy body _____ 30 centimeters, and they have four legs. But their curious appearance is not the only unusual feature. They make poison and _____ _____ , so they become an undesirable meal for any would-be predator. They also have amazing powers of regeneration. They can regrow a lost or damaged leg in about eight weeks, and the new leg is _____ the old one.

12

(Telephone rings.)

W Dr. Carter's Office.

M Hi, I'd like to _____ to see Dr. Carter, please.

W Is this your first visit?

M Yes, it is. My name is Jack Wagner.

W OK, Mr. Wagner. How about tomorrow afternoon?

M _____ Wednesday afternoon.

W Then how about Thursday at four o'clock?

M Um... Do you have an opening in the morning?

W Yes. But just on Friday and Saturday.

M I can't wait that long. How late are you open in the evenings?

W If you come before 7, you'll be able to see Dr. Carter.

M I think _____ the day I come back from my trip.

W OK. We'll be waiting for you then. Goodbye.

13

M Hi. I'd like to go to Walt Disney World, so I need information on flights to Florida.

W OK. I think _____ for you to Orlando. Do you want to go first class, business class, or economy?

M Economy, of course. I'd like the lowest fare you can find.

W All right. And that's one-way or round-trip?

M Round-trip. I'd like to leave on Sunday the 12th and return on Saturday the 18th.

W There's a very low fare on Sunday morning. It's only $145, but _____ . You'd have to change planes in Atlanta. There's a direct flight, but the fare on that one is $680.

M That's OK. I'll change planes in Atlanta.

W OK. It departs at 8:15 am on Sunday the 12th and arrives in Orlando at 12:15 pm.

M That sounds good.

W And there's one more thing. It's a special low fare, so _____ .

M _____

14

W Why are you talking to your computer?

M I'm not talking to it. I'm _____ .

W What do you mean?

M It's this great software program. It understands what I'm saying and writes down my words.

W Wow. So you don't have to type at all?

M No, _____ . I'm a slow typist, so this program is a lifesaver.

W Can I try it?

M Sure. First, you have to train the computer to recognize your voice.

W Oh. Why?

M Because everybody's pronunciation is different. If it doesn't know your voice, _____ .

W _____

15

M It's a Friday evening, and Jane is shopping in a supermarket by herself. As usual, the supermarket is crowded with people, and her shopping cart is full of groceries. Now Jane _____

_____ , and she is waiting in a long line at the checkout counter. Then she suddenly realizes that she forgot to buy something. She promised her husband and kids that she would make delicious steaks tomorrow. _____ and get some beef, but she doesn't want to go back to the end of the long line. In this situation, what would Jane most likely say to the person behind her?

Jane _____

16-17

W Email accounts have become popular for international communication because _____ . But how can you find the best email account? First, you have to consider how long the company will exist. If the company has been around for years, then there is more of a chance it will be _____

_____ . Nobody wants to set up an email account with a service that might not be here tomorrow. Next, choose a company that will provide you with an unlimited storage or at least a huge email storage limit. In the past, companies offered mailboxes of just a few hundred megabytes, but now they have extended that limit to no limit because to send pictures or video clips by email, you need quite a lot of storage. Lastly, check to see _____ filtering spam or junk mail. Spam is becoming a serious problem that not only transmits viruses but reduces productivity as well, because _____ review and delete unwanted messages. Taking these steps will allow you to get the best email account possible.

1번부터 17번까지는 듣고 답하는 문제입니다. 1번부터 15번까지는 한 번만 들려주고, 16번부터 17번까지는 두 번 들려줍니다. 방송을 잘 듣고 답을 하시기 바랍니다.

01 대화를 듣고, 남자의 마지막 말에 대한 여자의 응답으로 가장 적절한 것을 고르시오.

① Don't worry. You can work at the center.
② That's all. You'll see the center on your right.
③ It'll take only 5 minutes to go there by subway.
④ Then, you should turn in your membership card.
⑤ Sorry, but I'm not interested in going to the center.

02 대화를 듣고, 여자의 마지막 말에 대한 남자의 응답으로 가장 적절한 것을 고르시오.

① I'm sorry. What's the late fee?
② He didn't have to pay the late fee.
③ Right. I'm a member of your shop.
④ How much did you pay for the DVD?
⑤ It's $1 a day. So you should pay $3 in total.

03 다음을 듣고, 남자가 하는 말의 주제로 가장 적절한 것을 고르시오.

① 유아의 신체 발달 과정
② 성격 장애 아동의 특성
③ 유아 교육의 목적과 방법
④ 유아의 지적 능력 향상 방안
⑤ 자녀 교육 시 유의해야 할 사항

04 대화를 듣고, 여자의 의견으로 가장 적절한 것을 고르시오.

① 과일의 영양소는 껍질에 있다.
② 아침에 과일을 먹으면 건강해진다.
③ 제철 과일이 하우스 과일보다 맛있다.
④ 유기농으로 재배된 과일이 비싼 것은 당연하다.
⑤ 과일에 비타민 C가 많다는 것은 잘못된 사실이다.

05 대화를 듣고, 두 사람의 관계를 가장 잘 나타낸 것을 고르시오.

① doctor – nurse
② husband – wife
③ customer – clerk
④ parent – babysitter
⑤ son-in-law – mother-in-law

06 대화를 듣고, 그림에서 대화의 내용과 일치하지 <u>않는</u> 것을 고르시오.

07 대화를 듣고, 남자가 여자를 위해 할 일로 가장 적절한 것을 고르시오.

① 식당 예약하기
② 포장지 사 오기
③ 해산물 사 오기
④ 케이크 가져오기
⑤ 부모님 모셔 오기

08 대화를 듣고, 남자가 전화를 건 이유를 고르시오.

① 구직 인터뷰 일정을 변경하려고
② 주문한 제품의 배송 여부를 확인하려고
③ 온라인으로 주문한 내역을 취소하려고
④ 고장이 난 캠코더의 수리를 요청하려고
⑤ 배송 받을 주소가 변경되었음을 알리려고

09 대화를 듣고, 남자가 지불할 금액을 고르시오. [3점]

① $26   ② $29   ③ $30
④ $34   ⑤ $35

10 대화를 듣고, 두 사람이 구입할 가구가 아닌 것을 고르시오.

① 침대   ② 소파   ③ 식탁
④ 의자   ⑤ 옷장

11 Volunteering Essay Contest에 관한 다음 내용을 듣고, 일치하지 않는 것을 고르시오. [3점]

① 가장 권위 있는 교내 행사 중 하나이다.
② 개교 20주년 기념일에 개최된다.
③ 참가 자격은 자원봉사 경험의 유무이다.
④ 1등 상품은 최신형 디지털 카메라이다.
⑤ 심사위원은 문학 담당 교사들이다.

12 다음 포스터를 보면서 대화를 듣고, 일치하지 않는 것을 고르시오.

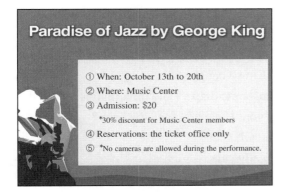

Paradise of Jazz by George King

① When: October 13th to 20th
② Where: Music Center
③ Admission: $20
   *30% discount for Music Center members
④ Reservations: the ticket office only
⑤ *No cameras are allowed during the performance.

13 대화를 듣고, 남자의 마지막 말에 대한 여자의 응답으로 가장 적절한 것을 고르시오.

Woman : _____

① Really? You're so lucky. I envy you.
② Thank you. Then see you next week.
③ I see. You can go on leave tomorrow.
④ Absolutely! In that case, it's not your fault.
⑤ I understand why you like your grandparents.

14 대화를 듣고, 여자의 마지막 말에 대한 남자의 응답으로 가장 적절한 것을 고르시오. [3점]

Man : _____

① Yeah, I have experience looking after babies.
② OK. I'm leaving. Take good care of your sister.
③ Sorry, but I'm going to visit my grandma tonight.
④ Really? Then, you must have misunderstood the homework.
⑤ Don't mention it. Without your help, I couldn't have made it.

15 다음 상황 설명을 듣고, Andrew가 Kate에게 할 말로 가장 적절한 것을 고르시오.

Andrew : _____

① Help yourself. Dinner is on me.
② Sorry, I'm not interested in climbing.
③ Let's go. The summit is just over there.
④ I feel so exhausted. I can't go on anymore.
⑤ Don't worry. I have enough water and snacks.

[16-17] 다음을 듣고, 물음에 답하시오.

16 여자가 하는 말의 목적으로 가장 적절한 것은?

① to demand reconstruction of the parking lot
② to prevent students from driving to the school
③ to invite students to the basketball competition
④ to ask for the construction of a basketball court
⑤ to praise the school's decision to build a parking lot

17 비어 있는 땅에 학교가 만들려고 계획하는 건물로 적절한 것은?

① 식당   ② 주차장
③ 도서관   ④ 학생 회관
⑤ 교수 회관

DICTATION(받아쓰기) 코너입니다.
녹음의 내용을 잘 듣고, 빈칸에 알맞은 말을 쓰시기 바랍니다.

01

M Excuse me, can you _____ the Royal Sports Center?

W Royal Sports Center? Turn left at the corner and go straight two blocks.

M Turn left and go two blocks. Okay, _____. And then?

W _____

02

W Sorry. _____ returning the DVD.

M Then, I'm afraid you'll have to pay a late fee.

W Well, _____?

M _____

03

M All parents want their child to develop not only physically but also intellectually. Good nutrients will help your child develop physically. But how can you _____? Soothing music and massages can benefit your child by encouraging mental development. Reading to your child also fosters mental development. In fact, ____ _____ will help your child develop intellectually.

04

M Good morning, Jane. Are you okay? You worked overtime last night—almost until 11 o'clock.

W Sure, no problem. I'm just as fit as usual.

M Wow, great! I think you really stay healthy. Is there _____?

W Sure. My health secret is to eat fruit in the morning.

M Well, I heard that fruit is good for our body.

W You know, eating fruit can give you a lot of vitamin C and strengthen the immune system.

M _____? I didn't know that.

W What's even better is that fruit has a lot of dietary fiber. You know dietary fiber can reduce cholesterol level, don't you?

M Yeah, I know. Now I understand why you said your health secret is fruit.

W Remember, the more fruit you eat in the morning, the healthier you'll be.

05

W Congratulations! Finally you've become a dad.

M Yeah, I'm so happy.

W Here are some diapers and milk bottles for the baby.

M Thank you. Have you seen the baby?

W Not yet. Oh, I'm _____.

M He is really cute.

W Who does he look like? You or Angela?

M Angela said the baby just looks like me.

W Then, he must be very smart.

M I hope so.

W By the way, what about Angela? _____?

M Yes, she's OK now. She's waiting for you. Let's go to see her.

06

M Honey, did you see the picture that Sally drew at school?

W No, not yet. Let me have a look at the picture my lovely daughter drew.

M Here it is. I think Sally _____.

W Yeah, look at the sunflowers on the right and the bird flying over the sky. It's really good.

M Right. What do you think of this cloud? It's just like _____.

W It's so cute. How clever Sally is!

M I think Sally also drew the apple tree in the middle quite well.

W That's right. What score would you give her painting, if you were a teacher?

M 100! It's really good. What about you, honey?

W Well, 90 or so. If Sally _____ ___, I would have given her 100, too.

M Well, I think the picture is perfect the way it is now, without a rainbow.

07

W Don't forget that tomorrow is my mother's birthday.

M Don't worry! I already _____ at the seafood restaurant on White Street.

W Good. Thank you, honey.

M What about a birthday present? Have you bought anything?

W Yes, I have. I bought this brooch set. What do you think about it?

M Oh, it's beautiful. Your mother is sure to be pleased.

W I hope so.

M By the way, it'll look better if it's gift-wrapped.

W Do you think so? But we don't have any wrapping paper left.

M Don't worry. I'll go and _____ ____ right now.

W Thank you. Go to Anderson Mart. It's nearest to us.

08

(Telephone rings.)

W Green Shopping Mall. Customer Service. _____ ____?

M I ordered a camcorder on your website ten days ago.

W Are there any problems with your order?

M A big problem. I haven't received it yet.

W Really? _____. May I have your name?

M My name is Daniel Redford.

W Wait a minute, please. You live at Pacific Apartments on Sudder Street, don't you?

M Yeah, that's right.

W I'm sorry. We _____ to the delivery department. There must have been a computer malfunction.

M What? I can't understand.

W I'm so sorry about that.

09

W Hi, may I help you?

M Yes, please. _____ a birthday present for my seven-year-old daughter.

W Then, what about this princess doll? It's very popular.

M Oh, it's cute. How much is it?

W It is $30, but we're offering a 20% discount today.

M That's good. All right, I'll take it.

W Thank you.

M _____, please?

W Sure. Ah, and your daughter would be more pleased if you bought this clothing set, too. It's just $5.

M OK. I'll buy it, too.

10

M Jennifer, why don't we buy some furniture for our new apartment this afternoon?

W _____. Let's go to the Star Furniture Store. They're selling good furniture at a good price.

M Okay. Before we go, let's think about what to buy.

W Good. Most of all, we have to buy a bed and a sofa.

M I think we should buy a dinner table and chairs, too.

W _____ my sister already bought a marble table for us? We don't need to buy one.

M That's good. Then we only have to buy chairs.

W Right. Ah, we also need to buy a closet. The one ___ _____. I'd like to buy one with a more modern and unique style.

M Okay. There are lots of things we have to buy.

11

M _____ about the Volunteering Essay Contest, which is one of the most prestigious school events. The contest is held _____ the school's 20th foundation day. It will be held on October first, which is just a week before the anniversary day. Only students who have experienced volunteer activity can _____. The first prize winner will receive a brand-new digital camera. The essay should be between 1,500 words and 2,000 words, and literature teachers will be reading and evaluating the participants' essays as usual. I hope many of you will take part in the contest and _____ ____.

12

W Did you know that George King is having some concerts in our town?

M George King? Oh, he is my favorite jazz musician. When? Where?

W In October, from 13th to 20th, at the Music Center.

M I have a Music Center membership card. So, _____ _____ on any performance.

W Good. Then, you can save $6 because the admission is $20.

M _____. Can I do that online?

W Sure!

M I'll take a lot of photos of him during the performance.

W I think you won't be able to do that.

M Why?

W The poster says that people will _____ _____ during the performance.

13

M Excuse me? May I come in?

W Yes, please. The door is open.

M Hi, Mrs. Brown. May I talk to you for a minute?

W Sure, what is it, Jack?

M _____ tomorrow?

W Why? Is there any special reason for that?

M My grandparents from Denver are visiting me tomorrow. They said they will take the subway, but I think I'd better pick them up at the airport.

W Okay, I understand. What time are _____ ____?

M They will arrive at 2 o'clock.

W _____

14

M Lucy, do you remember what you have to do while I visit your grandma?

W Yes, Dad.

M OK, _____ . What should you do if your sister cries?

W Change her diaper or give her some milk.

M Right. And if _____ ?

W Take her in my arms.

M Good. And don't forget to _____ in the living room.

W Don't worry. I won't forget it.

M How about your homework? Have you finished it yet?

W Sure, I have already finished it.

M _____

15

W Andrew, who likes outdoor activities, is climbing Mt. Rainier with his friend Kate. _____, they have been climbing more than 9 hours, and they're almost at the summit. Kate feels tired, and she wants to take a break. Noticing that Kate is exhausted, Andrew suggests _____ . They sit, drink water, and have some snacks. About twenty minutes later, Andrew thinks they should start climbing again __ _____ before the sun sets. In this situation, what would Andrew most likely to say to Kate?

Andrew _____

16-17

W Hi, _____ today. I'm Gina Jackson, a 2nd year student majoring in economics. I'm here to talk about how to use the vacant land next to the student union building. I heard that the school is planning to build a parking lot on this area. This decision _____ . The area should be developed for the improvement of students' school life by building a basketball court. Many students have complained that there's not enough space to work out or to do exercise. If the school decides to build the court, _____ a solution to this problem. Do you remember last year when the school built the professors' restaurant, instead of a fitness center? I'm worried that the same thing will happen to us this year. I'd like to ask the school: why they don't listen to students' suggestions? _____ that the vacant land should be developed for students.

1번부터 17번까지는 듣고 답하는 문제입니다. 1번부터 15번까지는 한 번만 들려주고, 16번부터 17번까지는 두 번 들려줍니다. 방송을 잘 듣고 답을 하시기 바랍니다.

01 대화를 듣고, 남자의 마지막 말에 대한 여자의 응답으로 가장 적절한 것을 고르시오.

① Okay, I'll get you the newest version.
② Help me. I think I lost my digital camera.
③ Don't worry, I'll borrow it from my friend.
④ I don't know how to use this digital camera.
⑤ Congratulations! This is a birthday present for you.

02 대화를 듣고, 여자의 마지막 말에 대한 남자의 응답으로 가장 적절한 것을 고르시오.

① If I were you, I would fly to Seattle.
② Absolutely! Seattle is a good place to visit.
③ Friday? Okay, let's see a movie together that day.
④ Sounds good. When did you return from the trip?
⑤ We have tickets on that day. What time will you fly?

03 다음을 듣고, 여자가 하는 말의 목적으로 가장 적절한 것을 고르시오.

① 신간 서적을 광고하려고
② 특강의 연사를 소개하려고
③ 약물 남용 방지를 촉구하려고
④ 강의 시간표의 변경을 알리려고
⑤ 신축 병원의 개설을 축하하려고

04 대화를 듣고, 남자의 의견으로 가장 적절한 것을 고르시오.

① MP3 플레이어는 용량이 클수록 좋다.
② 인터넷 쇼핑몰을 통해 돈을 벌기는 쉽지 않다.
③ 전자제품은 매장에 직접 가서 사는 것이 바람직하다.
④ www.everything.com은 쇼핑하기에 좋은 사이트이다.
⑤ 쇼핑 사이트마다 제품 가격이 다른 것은 이해되지 않는다.

05 대화를 듣고, 두 사람의 관계를 가장 잘 나타낸 것을 고르시오.

① dentist – patient
② husband – wife
③ father – daughter
④ teacher – student
⑤ baker – customer

06 대화를 듣고, 그림에서 남자가 성적표를 숨긴 곳을 고르시오.

07 대화를 듣고, 여자가 남자를 위해 할 일로 가장 적절한 것을 고르시오.

① 항공권 구입하기   ② 인도 돈으로 환전하기
③ 기념품 사다 주기   ④ 동계 침낭 빌려 주기
⑤ 점심 식사 사 주기

08 대화를 듣고, 여자가 전화를 건 이유를 고르시오.

① 방송국 견학을 요청하려고
② 잃어버린 애완견을 찾으려고
③ 구직 인터뷰 날짜를 정하려고
④ 사업을 함께 하자고 제안하려고
⑤ 아파트 임대에 대해 문의하려고

09 대화를 듣고, 여자가 지불할 금액을 고르시오. [3점]

① $35   ② $30   ③ $28

④ $20   ⑤ $15

10 대화를 듣고, 두 사람이 potluck dinner에서 먹게 될 음식이 <u>아닌</u> 것을 고르시오.

① 칠면조   ② 피자   ③ 쿠키

④ 초콜릿 케이크   ⑤ 샐러드

11 Short Movie Clip Contest에 관한 다음 내용을 듣고, 일치하지 <u>않</u>는 것을 고르시오.

① 학교 축제의 일부로 개최된다.
② 재학생이면 누구나 참여할 수 있다.
③ 동영상의 내용은 학교생활이어야 한다.
④ 동영상의 길이는 5~7분 이내이다.
⑤ 심사위원은 영화 클럽 회원들이다.

12 다음 호텔 숙박표를 보면서 대화를 듣고, 두 사람이 투숙하게 될 방으로 가장 적절한 것을 고르시오.

Hillside Hotel

	Room Type	View	Price	Internet Access
	Superior	Ocean	$110	O
①	Superior	Mountain	$80	O
②	Deluxe	City	$60	X
③	Deluxe	Ocean	$130	O
④	Deluxe	Mountain	$90	O
⑤	Grand Deluxe	City	$170	O
	VIP	Ocean	$200	X

13 대화를 듣고, 남자의 마지막 말에 대한 여자의 응답으로 가장 적절한 것을 고르시오.

Woman : _____

① Let me see. I'll take this convertible.
② I'm afraid I don't have a driver's license yet.
③ If I were you, I would stop at the gas station.
④ Thank you. Your car is next to the front door.
⑤ Really? I live in an apartment on Oxford Street, too.

14 대화를 듣고, 여자의 마지막 말에 대한 남자의 응답으로 가장 적절한 것을 고르시오. [3점]

Man : _____

① Excuse me, where is the Lost and Found?
② When do you think you lost your wallet?
③ I see. Wait a minute, please. I'll go and check.
④ How much is the hand bag on the second shelf?
⑤ Thank you. Thanks to you, I've found my hand bag.

15 다음 상황 설명을 듣고, Ron이 판매원에게 할 말로 가장 적절한 것을 고르시오.

Ron : _____

① Could you show me something cheaper?
② I'm looking for earrings, not a necklace.
③ Excuse me, where is the accessories store?
④ This one is good. I'll take it. How much is it?
⑤ I'd like to get a refund on this necklace. Here is my receipt.

[16-17] 다음을 듣고, 물음에 답하시오.

16 여자가 하는 말의 주제로 가장 적절한 것은?

① how people ate garlic first
② side effects of eating garlic
③ nutritional values of raw garlic
④ various ways of using raw garlic
⑤ why garlic has such a strong taste and aroma

17 Orange Hall에서 사람들이 할 일로 가장 적절한 것은? [3점]

① 건강 검진 받기   ② 마늘빵 만들기
③ 요리기구 준비하기   ④ 마늘 요리 시식하기
⑤ 마늘에 대해 토론하기

DICTATION(받아쓰기) 코너입니다.
녹음의 내용을 잘 듣고, 빈칸에 알맞은 말을 쓰시기 바랍니다.

01

M Mom, don't forget that next Friday is my birthday.

W Sure! _____ my lovely son's birthday? Is there anything you would like as a birthday present?

M A digital camera. I really want to get a digital camera.

W _____

02

W Hi, I'd like to _____ to Seattle for this Wednesday.

M Wait a minute, please. I'm sorry, but _____ ____.

W I'm sorry to hear that. How about Friday?

M _____

03

W Many people have excess stress that affects their health, happiness, and other areas of their lives. In fact, it's been estimated that more than 90% of health problems that _____ are stress-related! But if you change your lifestyle just a little bit, the stress you feel decreases considerably. Dr. Rey is here tonight to teach us _____ our everyday stress. Dr. Rey is both a psychology professor and the author of the bestseller, *Happy Virus to All of You.* Please welcome him _____ _____.

04

M Look! I bought a new MP3 player.

W When did you buy it? The design is so cool.

M It has a 16 gigabyte memory chip. Why don't you buy one, too?

W _____?

M Don't be surprised. I only paid $50 for it.

W Just $50? Really? Where did you buy it?

M www.everything.com. Have you ever visited the shopping site?

W No, I haven't. Do they sell MP3 players _____?

M Yeah. They sell all kinds of electronics such as MP3 players, digital cameras, and mobile phones at quite low prices _____.

W Really? All right, I'll visit that website.

M I'm sure you won't regret it. It's a really good website.

05

M Are you OK? _____.

W I have a toothache.

M Really? I think it's because you don't brush your teeth regularly.

W Maybe. _____, I won't forget to do it after each meal.

M And try to stop eating chocolate and candy. You eat too much of that junk.

W Okay. I'll try.

M Either your mother or I will _____ when she comes home.

W When is she coming?

M She just called to say that she would be here ____ minutes.

W I wish my teeth didn't hurt so much.

06

W Peter, come here. There is something _____ _____.

M Okay, what is it?

W Your homeroom teacher told me that he gave you the report card.

M Did he? I'm sorry, Mom. I didn't want to disappoint you.

W So, _____? Is it still in your bag?

M No, it isn't. I hid it in my room.

W Did you? Where? Actually, I checked the drawers of your desk and closet.

M Well, I put it under the pillow.

W Really? _____. I just searched for it under the bed.

M Mom, I'm really sorry. Next time, I'll study harder.

W Okay. Anyway, bring your report card to me right now.

M Okay, Mom. Wait a minute, please.

07

W David, how's your preparation for the trip to India going?

M _____. Yesterday, I finally got the airline ticket.

W Have you exchanged dollars for rupees?

M No. I heard that _____ in India.

W Yeah, that's true. My friend who visited India last month said the same thing.

M If you go with me, the trip will be more exciting.

W You know, I have to work. Anyway, don't forget to _____ for me.

M All right. By the way, do you have a winter sleeping bag?

W Yes, I do.

M Then, can I borrow it? I only have a summer one.

W OK, I'll bring it to you tomorrow.

08

(Telephone rings.)

M Hello?

W May I speak to Robert Kim?

M Speaking.

W Hi, my name is Cathy Johnson. I saw your ad about renting an apartment. _____?

M Sure. Are you a student or a businessperson?

W I'm working for a local broadcasting company.

M I see. Do you have any pets? In fact, _____ in the apartment.

W Don't worry about that. I don't have any pets.

M Good. Why don't you come and _____ the apartment first before you decide?

W Okay, can I visit you this evening after work? It'll be around 7.

09

(Telephone rings.)

M Little King Grocery. How can I help you?

W I'd like to buy some vegetables. Could you _____?

M Sure. What kinds of vegetables do you want?

W Cabbages, carrots, and tomatoes. How much are the cabbages and the carrots?

M $2 per cabbage head and $1 per kilogram of carrots.

W Then, can _____ and three kilograms of carrots?

M Sure. And how many tomatoes do you want? They are $3 per kilogram.

W 5 kilograms, please. That's all.

M I see. _____, please?

W I live at 14 Green Street.

M All right, we'll deliver them to you in 30 minutes.

10

M Did you hear that there will be a potluck dinner at Sally's house?

W A potluck dinner? What is that?

M Well, a potluck dinner is a meal where everyone who is invited brings something to eat.

W Sounds great! Then _____?

M Sally told me she will cook a turkey, and Jane will bake some pizza.

W Then, why don't we bring some cookies?

M Since Chris will bring a chocolate cake, _____ _____.

W Okay, let's make some salad. If we bring some salad, the dinner will be perfect.

M _____. Honey, what about adding some fruit in the salad?

W Good idea! I'll make sure to put enough fruit in it.

11

M Hi, students. Today, _____ the annual Short Movie Clip Contest. The contest, as usual, will be held as a part of the school festival. Anyone who attends our school can participate in the contest. The content of the movie clip should be about your school life—for example, club activities. The length of the movie clip should be between five and seven minutes. Unlike last year, when the judges were movie club students, this year 12 teachers who love movies _____. First prize is a brand-new video camera. For more information, please visit the school website.

12

W Sam, have you decided which hotel we'll stay at during our honeymoon?

M What do you think about the Hillside Hotel? It is a five-star hotel.

W That's good. Then _____ right now.

M But the problem is its price. The cheapest room with an ocean view is $110 a day.

W That's too expensive. _____ more than $100 a day.

M Then we have to give up the ocean view.

W No problem. But I'd like a room where I can have access to the Internet.

M Then we have two choices left. _____ _____?

W Well, I think the Deluxe would be better.

M All right, I'll reserve the room right now.

13

M Excuse me?

W How can I help you?

M Last night, I reserved a car _____.

W May I have your name and address?

M My name is Allen Kim, and I live at 87 Oxford Street.

W Wait a second, please. Ah, you reserved a convertible car for a day. Am I right?

M Yeah, that's right.

W It's $80 for a day including insurance. How would you like to pay?

M _____. Here is $80.

W _____

14

W Excuse me, _____ . Could you help me find it?

M When did you lose it?

W This afternoon, around 3 o'clock.

M Do you know the number of the train you were on?

W I'm sorry, but I don't. But it was the one going to Milford. And I got off at City Hall Station.

M I see. Could you describe your bag to me?

W It's square-shaped, white, and _____ .

M Was your ID card or driver's license inside the bag?

W No. My mobile phone and some books were inside.

M _____

15

W Ron, who is _____ , has a girlfriend. His girlfriend, Andrea, works at the same school. Now, Ron is in an accessories store to buy Andrea a present because tomorrow is her birthday. Ron _____ buying her a necklace. What the salesperson recommends doesn't appeal to Ron. So the salesperson shows him a different necklace. This time, Ron likes it. _____ _____ . In this situation, what would Ron most likely say to the salesperson?

Ron _____

16-17

W As we know well, garlic is famous for its strong taste and aroma. Garlic _____ around the world for cooking, and we believe that food containing garlic is good for our health. However, _____ , "There are two sides to the same coin," garlic also has some negative influences on your body. Garlic is very strong, so eating too much could produce problems such as irritation of, or even damage to, the digestive system. Also there are some people who are allergic to garlic. If they eat garlic, _____ _____ such as skin rashes or headaches. Garlic could potentially promote blood thinning, so it's best to avoid eating garlic before surgery. Please ____ _____ . Okay, that's all. After the break, you'll have time to make garlic bread on your own at Orange Hall. Everything is perfectly prepared from cooking equipment to flour. Please have some rest and go to the hall.

23회 듣기 모의고사

1번부터 17번까지는 듣고 답하는 문제입니다. 1번부터 15번까지는 한 번만 들려주고, 16번부터 17번까지는 두 번 들려줍니다. 방송을 잘 듣고 답을 하시기 바랍니다.

01 대화를 듣고, 남자의 마지막 말에 대한 여자의 응답으로 가장 적절한 것을 고르시오.

① Sure! All women like jewelry.
② Could you refund this gold necklace?
③ Sorry, I can't attend the birthday party.
④ Your wife should have worked with you.
⑤ Okay, I'll buy this necklace. How much is it?

02 대화를 듣고, 여자의 마지막 말에 대한 남자의 응답으로 가장 적절한 것을 고르시오.

① I'm not interested in soccer.
② Yeah, I'd like to visit Brazil.
③ I don't think I can go with you.
④ Sure! England is richer than Brazil.
⑤ I think so, too. Brazil is sure to win!

03 다음을 듣고, 남자가 하는 말의 목적으로 가장 적절한 것을 고르시오.

① 분실물을 찾아 갈 것을 안내하려고
② 교복을 입고 등교할 것을 촉구하려고
③ 부실한 사물함 관리에 대해 항의하려고
④ 개인 사물함을 비워 줄 것을 요청하려고
⑤ 교복 물려주기 운동에 동참을 권유하려고

04 대화를 듣고, 여자가 하는 말의 주제로 가장 적절한 것을 고르시오.

① 새집 증후군의 원인
② 친환경 건축 자재 구별법
③ 실내 공기를 정화하는 요령
④ 아파트 생활의 다양한 장점
⑤ 새 아파트 입주 시 주의 사항

05 대화를 듣고, 두 사람의 관계를 가장 잘 나타낸 것을 고르시오.

① doctor – patient
② doctor – nurse
③ coach – trainer
④ coach – nurse
⑤ reporter – player

06 대화를 듣고, 그림에서 대화의 내용과 일치하지 않는 것을 고르시오.

07 대화를 듣고, 남자가 여자에게 부탁한 일로 가장 적절한 것을 고르시오.

① 출장을 대신 가 줄 것
② 서울에 관한 책을 사 줄 것
③ 애완견을 돌보아 줄 것
④ 휴대용 컴퓨터를 빌려 줄 것
⑤ 모니터를 수리해 줄 것

08 대화를 듣고, 남자가 전화를 건 이유로 가장 적절한 것을 고르시오.

① 주문 내역을 취소하려고
② 가죽 제품을 수선하려고
③ 주소 변경을 알려 주려고
④ 상품의 교환을 문의하려고
⑤ 불량 상품에 대해 항의하려고

09 대화를 듣고, 남자가 지불해야 할 금액을 고르시오. [3점]

① $70   ② $85   ③ $115
④ $120   ⑤ $135

10 대화를 듣고, 여자가 좋아하는 과일로 언급되지 <u>않은</u> 것을 고르시오.

① 사과   ② 포도   ③ 수박
④ 딸기   ⑤ 바나나

11 Strawberry Festival에 관한 다음 내용을 듣고, 일치하지 <u>않는</u> 것을 고르시오. [3점]

① 가장 인기 있는 축제 중 하나이다.
② 총 10일간 계속된다.
③ 500명이 넘는 농부들이 참가한다.
④ 입장료는 5달러이다.
⑤ 방문객에 의해 '올해의 딸기'가 결정된다.

12 다음 표를 보면서 대화를 듣고, 여자가 구입할 내비게이션을 고르시오.

	Name	Company	Size of Monitor	Price	DMB
①	Naviking	Bixco	7"	$330	O
②	FreeRoad	Bixco	7"	$300	X
	Insight	Apple	5"	$250	X
③	Seven	Apple	7"	$350	O
	TooTan	Cambridge	5"	$250	O
④	WideTank	Cambridge	7"	$280	O
⑤	RoadNavi	Cambridge	7"	$250	X

13 대화를 듣고, 남자의 마지막 말에 대한 여자의 응답으로 가장 적절한 것을 고르시오.

Woman : _____

① Don't worry about it. My ankle is OK.
② Yeah, the Lakers are the most popular team.
③ Sure! I'm really looking forward to the game.
④ But the team I'm rooting for is the LA Lakers.
⑤ Right. I should have made a reservation earlier.

14 대화를 듣고, 여자의 마지막 말에 대한 남자의 응답으로 가장 적절한 것을 고르시오.

Man : _____

① My pleasure. Anything else for me to do?
② Hurry up. Otherwise, we'll miss the concert.
③ Well, I'm not interested in going to the party.
④ It doesn't matter. If you like it, it's OK with me.
⑤ Which do you want to have for dinner, meat or seafood?

15 다음 상황 설명을 듣고, Robert가 Jessica에게 할 말로 가장 적절한 것을 고르시오.

Robert : _____

① I'm hungry. Do we have anything to eat?
② The grapes look good. I'll buy 5 kilograms.
③ I'd like to sell the vineyard. What about you?
④ Thanks to you, we have good grapes this year.
⑤ In fact, I like grape jam more than any other jam.

[16-17] 다음을 듣고, 물음에 답하시오.

16 여자가 하는 말의 요지로 가장 적절한 것은? [3점]

① Many drops make a shower.
② Don't judge a book by its cover.
③ A bad workman always blames his tools.
④ Don't count your chickens before they are hatched.
⑤ Never put off until tomorrow what you can do today.

17 Rainbow Hall에서 할 일로 가장 적절한 것은?

① 자신의 꿈에 대해 발표하기
② 강사에게 개인적으로 질문하기
③ 올해 이루고 싶은 목표 작성하기
④ 회의 형식에 맞게 좌석 정리하기
⑤ 삶의 만족도에 관한 설문조사 참여하기

DICTATION(받아쓰기) 코너입니다.
녹음의 내용을 잘 듣고, 빈칸에 알맞은 말을 쓰시기 바랍니다.

01

M This Friday is my wife's birthday. _____ is a good present for her?

W How about jewelry? A gold necklace would be good.

M A gold necklace? Do you really think my wife would like it?

W _____

02

W At last, the World Cup final between Brazil and England _____ this evening.

M Yeah. Who do you think will be the world champion?

W Of course, Brazil. No country can defeat Brazil. What do you think?

M _____

03

M Good morning! Please pay attention. _____ _____ that a new set of lockers will be delivered this afternoon. Workers will come to the school tomorrow, take away the old lockers, and install new ones. So I want all students _____ before leaving the school today. You can put your personal belongings such as textbooks or school uniforms in the main hall of the student building. But don't forget to write your names on each item. _____ _____.

04

M What do you think of my new apartment?

W _____. The view from the living room is wonderful.

M That's the reason I decided to rent this one.

W But don't you think the air inside is not that fresh?

M It's because it's newly built. _____, it'll improve.

W Why don't you put some plants in the living room? It will help to improve the quality of the air inside.

M That's a good idea.

W It's also effective to open all the windows for at least 30 minutes twice a day.

M Yeah, I know that.

W If you installed an electronic air cleaners or a purifier, that would be _____.

05

(Knock on the door.)

M Come in.

W Hi, here is the videotape you mentioned.

M Good. _____, we have to watch this tape over and over. The players, too.

W I see, Mr. Dega.

M So, do you think Laura can play in the final?

W I think so. She said to me that she has no more pain in her knee.

M Great! What about Jessica? Jessica _____ her slump.

W Well, I'll try to talk to her about it.

M I trust you. It's up to you whether Jessica can play in the final or not.

W By the way, what is our strategy for the final?

M You know, _____. That's my strategy.

06

W Patrick, look at this picture. It's our picture of about five years ago.

M That's right. We looked really young then.

W Look at your curly hair in the picture. You look so funny.

M But back then, that hairstyle was very popular. What about your big glasses? _____.

W I agree with you. Oh, you didn't wear glasses then.

M Right. My eyesight was not bad enough to wear glasses then.

W But you know, _____ with glasses than before without glasses.

M Thank you. Lucy, the headband you are wearing in this picture is the one I bought you for your birthday present, isn't it?

W That's right. These heart-shaped earrings were also a gift from you.

M Yeah, I remember that you were so happy about my presents.

07

(Telephone rings.)

W Hello? May speaking.

M Hi, May. This is Ralph. How are you?

W Hi, Ralph! I'm fine. How have you been? I heard you were going on a business trip to Seoul.

M Yes. _____. May, could I ask you a favor?

W Sure. Do you want me to take care of your pet while you're in Seoul?

M No. My cousin will do that. May, could I borrow your laptop computer?

W What about yours? You bought a new one a month ago.

M _____ right now, so I can't bring it with me.

W Ah, I see. OK. I'll bring it to work tomorrow for you.

M Thank you, May. You're always _____.

08

(Telephone rings.)

W Hi, Sun & Moon Shopping. May I help you?

M Yes, please. I ordered a leather jacket through your website last week.

W Is there any problem with your order?

M Well, _____.

W Why do you want to cancel your order?

M My wife bought the exact same thing yesterday.

W I see. _____ and address, please?

M My name is Lee Thomson, and I live in Victoria Apartments, 708 Wellington Avenue.

W Wait a second, please. All right, your order has been canceled.

M Thank you.

09

M Excuse me, I'd like to take a Korean grammar course. _____.

W We have two courses. One is a normal course, which costs $70, and the other is an intensive course, which costs $120.

M What's the difference between the two?

W The normal course _____. And the intensive course is every day. I think the intensive course is better.

M All right, I'll take the intensive course. Also, do I have to buy a textbook?

W Yes. That's $15.

M I see. I'll take the book, too. _____ ____?

W Yes, you can. May I have your credit card, please?

M Here you are.

W Thank you. Please sign here.

10

M I'm full. The dinner was really good.

W I'm full, too, but I still want some dessert. How about you?

M Me, too. Let's have some watermelons and bananas. You like them, right?

W Yeah, I like them because they are very juicy and sweet. You know, _____ "fruit killer" when I was young.

M Fruit killer? Sounds funny. What else do you like to eat, except watermelons and bananas?

W Strawberries and apples. I really like to drink strawberry juice, and I used to eat apples in the morning.

M I know you like almost all kinds of fruit, but I don't think I've seen you eat grapes so far.

W You're right. Last summer, _____ after eating some grapes. After that, I don't eat them anymore.

M Oh, really? I didn't know that.

W Well, we should _____, especially during the summer.

11

W Okay, let's go to the Strawberry Festival, one of the most popular festivals in Florida. The festival is going to start on March 1st and end on March 10th. _____ _____ Rainbow Green Park. More than 500 strawberry farmers will attend the festival and they will show their tasty strawberries during the festival. The entrance is free _____, and visitors can buy 1 kilogram of strawberries for only $5, which is half the price of the markets on the street. Visitors also _____ "the strawberry of the year," which means the most delicious strawberry. The farmer who grows "the strawberry of the year" will receive a $1,000 cash prize.

12

M Ann, _____?

W Well, I want to buy a navigation system. But it's not easy to choose a good one.

M I think you need one with at least a seven-inch monitor.

W You're right.

M Why don't you buy a FreeRoad?

W Its reputation is not so good. Also, I'd like to buy one with a DMB function.

M What is the most _____?

W $300.

M Then, what about this one made by Cambridge?

W Yeah, _____. OK, I'll order it.

13

M At last, the final between the LA Lakers and the Chicago Bulls will be held tonight.

W Right. The game will be really exciting.

M Which team do you think will win this year?

W Of course, the LA Lakers.

M But the Chicago Bulls will _____. Their defense is the strongest in the league.

W I know. But the Lakers have Kobe Bryant. He is the best shooter _____.

M Will Kobe play in the game? As far as I know, he hasn't fully recovered from his ankle injury yet.

W That's not true. The coach said _____ _____, and he will play in the game.

M If that's true, the Lakers are more likely to win the game.

W _____

14

W Oh, It's already 5 o'clock. Hurry up. People will arrive soon.

M Don't worry. Everything is almost ready for the housewarming party.

W Did you _____?

M Yes, I did. I also set up the table, and the barbecue grill is ready to be fired up.

W Good. I just finished cleaning inside the house.

M How about the food?

W I bought some meat and vegetables yesterday.

M Then I'll bring the meat and the vegetables to the backyard, so _____.

W Really? Thank you, honey. You're so sweet.

M _____

15

M Robert has a small vineyard and _____ _____. He grows grapes with his wife, Jessica. They work hard every day of the year. At last, it's time for them to pick the grapes. While looking at _____, Robert is sure that they will earn a lot of profit this year. Robert is very pleased. He thinks that it's all because of Jessica's hard work. _____ to Jessica. In this situation, what would Robert most likely say to Jessica?

Robert _____

16-17

W _____ a final question. Do you want to be successful in your life? Absolutely, yes! There is no one who does not want to be successful in life, but in practice there are only a few who are really successful. Why is this? It's because many people ___ _____ they should do today until tomorrow. Once, I decided I would begin preparing for the monthly examination on Monday. However, when Monday came, I decided to start on Tuesday. On Tuesday, I decided to wait until Wednesday. In the end, I didn't prepare and failed the exam. _____ ___, I would never put off anything important until the next day. Okay, that's all. After lunch break, you'll go to Rainbow Hall on the second floor, and there you'll have some time to write down some goals that you want to accomplish this year. _____. Enjoy your lunch, please.

24^회 | 듣기 모의고사

1번부터 17번까지는 듣고 답하는 문제입니다. 1번부터 15번까지는 한 번만 들려주고, 16번부터 17번까지는 두 번 들려줍니다. 방송을 잘 듣고 답을 하시기 바랍니다.

01 대화를 듣고, 여자의 마지막 말에 대한 남자의 응답으로 가장 적절한 것을 고르시오.

① I lost my sandals yesterday.
② Really? Thank you very much.
③ $30. It's a really good bargain.
④ If you pay $2, I'll repair the sandals.
⑤ Okay, I'll buy this pair of pink sandals.

02 대화를 듣고, 남자의 마지막 말에 대한 여자의 응답으로 가장 적절한 것을 고르시오.

① Okay, I'll install this program.
② I got it. I'll buy this laptop computer.
③ Well, I spilled coffee onto the keyboard.
④ Sure, you can use my notebook computer.
⑤ A laptop computer is much more convenient to use.

03 대화를 듣고, 여자가 하는 말의 목적으로 가장 적절한 것을 고르시오.

① 차량 광택제를 광고하려고
② 자동차의 정비 불량을 항의하려고
③ 효과적인 차량 정비법을 알려주려고
④ 차량 정비 회사의 직원을 모집하려고
⑤ 안전 관리를 교육할 연사를 소개하려고

04 대화를 듣고, 여자가 하는 말의 주제로 가장 적절한 것을 고르시오.

① 구직 인터뷰를 잘하는 요령
② 직장 선택 시 주의 사항
③ 꾸준한 자기 계발의 중요성
④ 고속 승진의 부정적 효과
⑤ 직장 동료와 친해지는 비결

05 대화를 듣고, 두 사람의 관계를 가장 잘 나타낸 것을 고르시오.

① 휴대 전화 상점 주인 – 고객
② 분실물 센터 직원 – 지갑 분실자
③ 경찰 – 소매치기 피해자
④ 신문사 기자 – 지갑 디자이너
⑤ 쇼핑 몰 관리인 – 옷 가게 점원

06 대화를 듣고, 남자가 소개 받기로 한 여자를 고르시오.

07 대화를 듣고, 여자가 남자에게 부탁한 일을 고르시오.

① 정부의 지원을 받아 올 것
② 공장 부지를 알아봐 줄 것
③ 해고 예정자를 선발해 줄 것
④ 은행 융자에 대해 문의할 것
⑤ 신제품의 디자인을 맡아 줄 것

08 대화를 듣고, 두 사람이 다음 휴게소에 들르려는 이유로 가장 적절한 것을 고르시오.

① 잠시 휴식을 취하려고
② 먹을 음식을 구입하려고
③ 자동차에 기름을 넣으려고
④ 자동차 타이어를 점검하려고
⑤ 뉴욕에 있는 친구에게 전화하려고

09 대화를 듣고, 여자가 지불할 금액을 고르시오. [3점]

① $50   ② $60   ③ $70

④ $80   ⑤ $90

10 대화를 듣고, 남자가 방문할 도시가 <u>아닌</u> 곳을 고르시오.

① 부산   ② 마산   ③ 광주

④ 서울   ⑤ 대전

11 Tom Jones에 관한 다음 내용을 듣고, 일치하지 <u>않는</u> 것을 고르시오. [3점]

① 20세기 중반에 태어났다.
② 주로 단편 소설을 저술했다.
③ 대학에서 야구부 활동을 했다.
④ 베트남 전쟁에 참전했다.
⑤ 현재 영화배우로 활동 중이다.

12 다음 구인 광고 포스터를 보면서 대화를 듣고, 두 사람의 대화 내용과 일치하지 <u>않는</u> 것을 고르시오.

Little Indian Pizza looking for a deliver person		
Age	①	21 years old or order
Qualification	②	motor cycle driver's license
Working Hours	③	5 to 10 pm (7 days a week)
Payment	④	– trainee period (first 2 months) : $8 per hour
	⑤	– full-time worker : $12 per hour
Phone		523–2279

13 대화를 듣고, 여자의 마지막 말에 대한 남자의 응답으로 가장 적절한 것을 고르시오.

Man : _____

① Good. Then, I'll reserve two tickets.
② Me, too. It was worse than I expected.
③ Let's watch an opera instead of a musical.
④ Students with ID cards can get a 50% discount.
⑤ I'm sorry but I'd like a refund on these tickets.

14 대화를 듣고, 남자의 마지막 말에 대한 여자의 응답으로 가장 적절한 것을 고르시오. [3점]

Woman : _____

① Not at all. Thanks for your help.
② But I can't speak Chinese fluently.
③ Thank you. Please fill out this form.
④ Here is your change. Enjoy your class.
⑤ Then, I'd like to take a summer course.

15 다음 상황 설명을 듣고, Cindy가 점원에게 할 말로 가장 적절한 것을 고르시오.

Cindy : _____

① May I see your receipt, please?
② Oh, this blouse really suits you.
③ Could I have a day off tomorrow?
④ I see. How much more do I have to pay?
⑤ Could I ask you when you opened the laundry?

[16-17] 다음을 듣고, 물음에 답하시오.

16 대화가 이루어지는 장소로 가장 적절한 곳은?

① 병원   ② 배
③ 카메라 수리점   ④ 식당
⑤ 항구

17 대화가 끝난 직후, 남자가 할 일로 가장 적절한 것은?

① 두통약 복용하기
② 샌드위치 만들기
③ 카메라 가지고 오기
④ 점심 식사 준비하기
⑤ 오렌지 주스 사 오기

01

W I think this pair of pink sandals _____.

M I think so, too. If you buy this one, you'll have no regret.

W Okay, _____. How much is it?

M _____

02

M Hi, how can I help you?

W My notebook computer suddenly _____.

M I see. Did something happen to the computer?

W _____

03

W Ladies and gentlemen, let me introduce you to the most efficient car polish on the market today. I'm talking about the Car Protector—the only polish that not only _____ but also removes dirt. Buy a package of Car Protector today, and you will get one set of brushes absolutely free! Hurry! _____ only until October 31st. Get your Car Protector now!

04

W Your job interview is this Friday, isn't it?

M Yeah, that's right. I'm a little bit nervous. As you know, this is my first job interview.

W Well, _____ for the interview. If not, the interviewers will have a bad impression of you.

M Of course, I should.

W Your clothes can play an important role, too. I think a gray-colored suit will be better than any other color.

M Okay, thank you for the tip.

W Ah, there's one more very important thing _____ _____.

M What is it? Tell me.

W It's about your answers to the questions. If they ask too a difficult question for you to answer, you'd better say "Sorry, I don't know about that."

M You mean, _____, right?

W Yeah, that's right.

05

M Good evening! How can I help you?

W I came here two hours ago to buy a mobile phone.

M So...

W _____ I got home, I realized I didn't have my wallet.

M Do you think you lost your wallet here?

W Yes, I think so. I think I left it at one of the stores I visited. Before coming here, I went to the mobile phone store. They told me I'd better go and ask ____ _____.

M Okay, I see. Some women's wallets were left here today. Could you describe your wallet, please?

W It's a square one with a heart print on it.

M I think we have that.

W Really?

M Wait a moment, please. _____.

06

W Oh, Eric! _____.

M How can I miss your birthday party, Sally?

W Well, I think it's not because of my birthday party that you came tonight, but rather _____

_____.

M Ha ha! So, who is Gina?

W Can you see three women standing near the window?

M Yeah. Is the girl with a long hair Gina?

W No. She is Anica. Gina _____ and is wearing a short skirt.

M You mean the girl with the big earrings?

W Yes, that's right. What do you think of her?

M Oh, she looks very cute. I like her.

07

W Albert, we are in a very difficult financial situation. We have to start saving.

M I think so, too. What do you think about _____

_____?

W That's not a good idea.

M Then, what about moving our factory to a rural area?

W That's what I had in mind. Then, we could get support from the government.

M That's right.

W Do you think we could _____, too?

M Well, I'm not sure.

W Albert, can you go to ABC Bank to inquire about it?

M I'll go there right away.

W By the way, when will the new product go on the market?

M _____.

08

M Jenny, how much longer before we reach New York?

W Two more hours. You know it's a long way.

M Yeah. But we would have been there already if we had taken a plane.

W You're right. But _____.

M Anyway, let's stop at the next service area.

W Why?

M I'm hungry. You know, I haven't eaten anything since one o'clock.

W Okay. I'll buy some sandwiches and drinks for you.

M Thank you. Look! The sign says the next service area is just 10km away.

W Yeah. How about gas? Do we have to _____ now?

M No. We have enough gas.

09

W Hi, I'd like to buy a tennis racket.

M Do you have _____?

W Do you have one made by Teran?

M Yes, we do. We have two kinds of rackets by Teran. One is $50, and the other is $70.

W Which one is lighter?

M The second one is lighter. Usually, the more expensive the racket, _____.

W I see. I'll take the lighter one. Also, do you have headbands and wristbands?

M Yes. A headband is $10, and a wristband is $5. They are also made by Teran.

W Then I'll buy one headband and two wristbands. How much do _____?

M Wait a second, please. Let me add them up.

10

M Sara, finally I'm going to Korea next Friday.

W Wow, I envy you. Which city will you go to first in Korea?

M Busan! _____ and enjoy the beach there.

W I once visited Busan, too. It's such a beautiful city. What is your next destination?

M I'll visit Masan and Ulsan near Busan.

W Masan and Ulsan? Well, I don't think I've heard about these cities.

M Maybe because they're not as big as Busan. After the cities, I'll go to Gwangjoo.

W How about Daejeon or Seoul, the capital of Korea?

M Seoul is my final destination. But I don't have any plan to visit Daejeon.

W Why? I heard Daejeon is also a good place to travel.

M I know, but _____ Daejeon twice so far.

11

W Tom Jones, born on January 26, 1945, is an American writer, _____. Jones was raised in Aurora, Illinois and attended the University of Hawaii, where he played catcher on the school baseball team. Jones joined the army after _____ _____ and fought in the Vietnam War. His experience in the war influenced his writing. His first book, published in 1993, was a short story collection. The stories _____ of pain and death. Recently, he has written screenplays.

12

W Ken, come here. _____.

M Where? Oh, Little Indian Pizza is looking for a delivery person.

W You have a motorcycle driver's license, don't you?

M Yes, I got it last year.

W Then, why don't you _____? You are over 21.

M But I don't think the salary is good.

W $8 per hour during the training period is good compared to other part-time jobs.

M But the salary of a full time worker is not high enough. It's only $10 per hour.

W Remember that you can't have everything in life.

M _____. But I don't feel like applying for that job.

13

W Kevin, have you seen the poster for the opera *My Life* on the school board?

M No. Tell me about it.

W The opera will be performed at the Royal Culture Center from the first to the end of next month.

M How much are the tickets?

W They are $20, but students _____.

M Oh, we'd only have to pay $10. Good. Let's go to see it together.

W _____. But I think we have to reserve the tickets. This opera is very popular.

M Can we make reservations through the Internet?

W Sure, we can.

M Then, do you know the website _____ _____?

W It's www.ticketforyou.com.

M _____

14

W Hi, may I help you?

M Yes, please. ＿＿＿＿＿＿ a Chinese conversation class.

W Have you ever taken a Chinese conversation class before?

M No, it's my first time.

W Then, ＿＿＿＿＿＿＿＿＿＿. The tuition is $70 including the two textbooks.

M I heard that there was a 20% discount for students. I'm a college student.

W Sorry, the discount is only during summer and winter vacations.

M Really? I didn't know that.

W But it's our policy.

M I see. Here is $70.

W ＿＿＿＿＿＿＿＿＿＿＿＿＿＿＿

15

W Cindy is ＿＿＿＿＿＿. She has three blouses and two suits that need to be cleaned. She asks the clerk how much the dry cleaning is and ＿＿＿ ＿＿＿＿＿＿. The clerk says that it's $3 per blouse and $5 per suit, and it'll take two days. Cindy is wondering if she can get her clothes by this evening. The clerk says that if she ＿＿＿ ＿＿＿＿＿, her clothes will be ready by then. Cindy wants to have her clothes back as early as possible. In this situation, what would Cindy most likely say to the clerk?

Cindy ＿＿＿＿＿＿＿＿＿＿＿＿＿＿

16-17

M Wow, the wind is so cool!

W Yeah, right. How is your headache? Is it better than before?

M I think so. Thanks to the nice wind, I feel better.

W ＿＿＿＿＿＿! Actually, I was very worried.

M Don't worry about me anymore. I'm okay now. Look! There are seagulls flying over there.

W Oh, they're really beautiful. I'd like to take a picture of them.

M Then let me ＿＿＿＿＿＿＿＿ from the cabin. Just wait a little while.

W Will you? Thank you. Ah, don't you feel hungry now?

M Well... a little bit. As you know, I haven't eaten anything since this morning, because of my headache.

W Right. I'll buy some sandwiches at the snack bar downstairs ＿＿＿＿＿＿＿＿.

M Okay. Please buy an orange juice for me, too.

25^회 듣기 모의고사

1번부터 17번까지는 듣고 답하는 문제입니다. 1번부터 15번까지는 한 번만 들려주고, 16번부터 17번까지는 두 번 들려줍니다. 방송을 잘 듣고 답을 하시기 바랍니다.

01 대화를 듣고, 여자의 마지막 말에 대한 남자의 응답으로 가장 적절한 것을 고르시오.

① I'm sure I can buy this computer.
② I think it's more convenient to use.
③ Sure, you can borrow my notebook.
④ A notebook computer breaks down easily.
⑤ I have a strong preference for a notebook computer.

02 대화를 듣고, 남자의 마지막 말에 대한 여자의 응답으로 가장 적절한 것을 고르시오.

① Your movie is really great.
② It's $24 in total. Enjoy the movie.
③ Sorry, I can't see you this evening.
④ I'll lend you the rest of the money.
⑤ Thank you for inviting me to this movie.

03 다음을 듣고, 여자가 하는 말의 목적으로 가장 적절한 것을 고르시오.

① 캥거루의 사육법을 알려주려고
② 동물원 증축 자금을 모금하려고
③ 동물원의 신규 직원을 채용하려고
④ 새로 개장한 동물원을 홍보하려고
⑤ 동물 보호 운동의 동참을 촉구하려고

04 다음을 듣고, 남자가 하는 말의 주제로 가장 적절한 것을 고르시오.

① 자전거 통근의 장점
② 자전거의 발달 과정
③ 좋은 자전거의 구별법
④ 자전거 전용 도로의 필요성
⑤ 고장이 난 자전거의 수리 요령

05 대화를 듣고, 두 사람의 관계를 가장 잘 나타낸 것을 고르시오.

① realtor – customer
② landlord – tenant
③ husband – wife
④ teacher – parent
⑤ librarian – student

06 대화를 듣고, 여자가 생각하는 우승 후보를 고르시오.

07 대화를 듣고, 남자가 여자에게 부탁한 일로 가장 적절한 것을 고르시오.

① 체중계를 사다 줄 것
② 마라톤화를 빌려 줄 것
③ 함께 쇼핑 몰에 가 줄 것
④ 저녁 식사를 준비해 줄 것
⑤ 도서관 자리를 잡아 줄 것

08 대화를 듣고, 남자가 마지막에 말한 "I'll be able to save some money from now on."의 의미로 가장 적절한 것을 고르시오.

① 휴대 전화를 공동구매를 통해 살 것이다.
② 할인율이 높은 쇼핑몰을 찾아다닐 것이다.
③ 가격 비교 사이트를 통해 물건을 살 것이다.
④ 최신 전자 제품의 구입을 서두르지 않을 것이다.
⑤ 홍보에 현혹되어 충동구매를 하지 않을 것이다.

09 대화를 듣고, 여자가 거스름돈으로 받은 금액을 고르시오. [3점]

① $1   ② $4   ③ $5

④ $6   ⑤ $11

10 대화를 듣고, 여자가 좋아하는 운동으로 언급되지 <u>않은</u> 것을 고르시오.

① 배구   ② 야구   ③ 스케이트

④ 스키   ⑤ 수영

11 Paralympics에 관한 다음 내용을 듣고, 일치하지 <u>않는</u> 것을 고르시오.

① 장애인들이 참가하는 올림픽이다.
② 1회 대회 개최국은 이탈리아다.
③ 올림픽과 같은 해에 개최된다.
④ 출전 선수가 해마다 줄고 있다.
⑤ 2014년 동계 대회 주최국은 러시아이다.

12 다음 광고지를 보면서 대화를 듣고, 대화의 내용과 일치하지 <u>않는</u> 것을 고르시오. [3점]

Item	Price	Note
sleeping bag	① $2 a day	
back pack	② $3 a day	25 liter
	③ $5 a day	45 liter
cooking equipment	$2 a day	
tent	④ $10 a day	
	⑤ *30% discount for more than 7days	

Rent for You

13 대화를 듣고, 여자의 마지막 말에 대한 남자의 응답으로 가장 적절한 것을 고르시오.

Man : _____

① OK. The kids will be very pleased.
② But I'd really like to go to Sydney.
③ Sorry, we can't afford to go on a trip.
④ Have you ever been to Sydney before?
⑤ How much did you spend on your trip?

14 대화를 듣고, 남자의 마지막 말에 대한 여자의 응답으로 가장 적절한 것을 고르시오. [3점]

Woman : _____

① I like this apartment a lot. OK, I'll rent it.
② Then I have to help you. That's what friends are for.
③ I want it, but the painting is too expensive for me.
④ Sorry, but I have to go to an art gallery tomorrow evening.
⑤ If you had visited the gallery, you would have been satisfied.

15 다음 상황 설명을 듣고, Juliet이 Derrik에게 할 말로 가장 적절한 것을 고르시오.

Juliet : _____

① Thank you, Derrick. You're a really good son!
② I forgot to do it. I'll clean the house right now.
③ Oh, I should have helped you find another job.
④ Is it OK to work with you at the department store?
⑤ I've finished washing the dishes. Is there anything else to do?

[16-17] 다음을 듣고, 물음에 답하시오.

16 대화가 이루어지는 장소로 가장 적절한 곳은?

① in a bakery
② in front of a jewelry store
③ in an escalator
④ in front of a flower shop
⑤ in front of a hotel reception desk

17 대화가 끝난 직후에, 남자가 할 일로 가장 적절한 것은?

① 꽃 사러 가기
② 생일 카드 작성하기
③ 꽃 가게 약도 그리기
④ 생일 케이크 사기
⑤ 다이아몬드 클럽 가입하기

DICTATION(받아쓰기) 코너입니다.
녹음의 내용을 잘 듣고, 빈칸에 알맞은 말을 쓰시기 바랍니다.

01

W Which do you think is better, this laptop computer or that desktop computer?

M If I were you, I'd buy this notebook computer.

W Would you? _____ you prefer a notebook computer?

M _____

02

M Excuse me, can I have three tickets for the movie *Silent King*?

W Sure. _____ see the movie?

M 7 o'clock in the evening.

W _____

03

W _____ something exciting to do this weekend? Come to Wild World Zoo. At last, we, Wild World Zoo, have opened our doors! There are more than 200 types of animals waiting for you. Touch and hug wild animals such as koalas or kangaroos. _____.
Seeing animals will also give you exciting moments. There is an aquarium where you can see various types of marine animals. Come and enjoy your weekend at the zoo.

04

M Bicycling, for me, is one of the most pleasant ways to _____. Rather than creating stress, like when I drive, the exercise relieves my stress. Commuting to my office by bike reduces air pollution. It also _____ money on gasoline and vehicle repairs. The biggest benefit for me, _____, is that my bike enables me to use my time more efficiently. I never experience _____ _____ on my way to work.

05

W Bill, _____?

M About this house.

W This house? Why?

M Well, you know, we've been living here for more than five years.

W Yeah, _____. The kids are already going to primary school.

M So I'm thinking about moving to a more spacious house.

W Really? If we did, the kids would be very pleased.

M I think so. Where do you want to move?

W Laymond would be nice. It has a good public library, and its public transportation is convenient.

M OK. _____ in Laymond tomorrow.

06

M Look! The race will start soon.

W Yeah. _____, we will know who the fastest man in the world is.

M So, who do you think will win the race?

W Of course, Tyson Guy.

M Tyson Guy? Who is he?

W Can you see the man _____?

M You mean, the one wearing the necklace?

W No, he's Gerry Cooper. I mean the person right next to Gerry Cooper.

M He is wearing a one-piece uniform. _____.

W I'm sure he will win the race.

07

W Charles, I heard that you were going to run in a marathon.

M Yes. I think I need to do some exercise to lose weight.

W Good decision! To run in a marathon is certainly _____.

M Do you know anything about marathons?

W Didn't you know I belonged to a running club during my high school days?

M Really? Then, could you go with me to the shopping mall this afternoon?

W Why do you want to go to the mall?

M I need to buy a pair of shoes for the marathon. _____ what to buy.

W All right. Let's meet at 4 o'clock in front of the library.

M Okay, _____. I'll treat you to a good dinner.

08

M Oh, it's a brand-new smart phone. When did you buy it?

W Last weekend. I bought it _____.

M Really? How?

W Have you ever heard about cooperative buying?

M Yes, I have. So, how cheap was it?

W I bought it for almost half price.

M That's cool! _____ through cooperative buying?

W No. Just join the website and follow the instructions there. That's all. It's really simple.

M _____ the website address? Actually, I was thinking about changing my phone as well.

W It's www.buytogether.com.

M OK, I'll join the website right now. I'll be able to save some money _____.

09

W I'm looking for a gift for my son. Could you _____?

M What do you think about this game?

W Oh, this game looks exciting.

M Right. _____, this game is the most popular among teens.

W OK, I'll take it. How much is it?

M It's $14. Your son will be very pleased.

W I hope so. Ah, I have a $5 discount coupon. _____?

M Let me see. I'm sorry, you can't. This coupon is for old game CDs. The one you bought is the newest one.

W Well, I see. Here is $20.

M Thank you. _____.

W Ah, do you have a mouse pad? I need one.

M Well, I'll give you one for free. Wait a second, please.

10

M Stella, I heard that you joined the school volleyball club.

W Yeah. Volleyball is my favorite sport.

M How about baseball? Didn't you say _____ _____ baseball?

W Yes, I am. Baseball is another of my favorite sports.

M I think you really like sports, unlike other girls.

W Yeah, right.

M Do you like winter sports, too?

W Sure, I love skating and skiing. They're really exciting sports.

M Wow, _____. What about water sports?

W Um, that's the only thing I don't want to mention. Actually, I don't know _____.

M Really? Oh, I'm surprised that a sports lover like you can't swim.

11

M Have you ever heard about the Paralympics? Paralympics are _____. The first Paralympics were held in Rome, Italy in 1960, and since then every four years it _____ _____ as the Olympic Games. The number of athletes participating in the Summer Paralympics has increased, from about 400 athletes from 23 countries in Rome in 1960 to about 3,800 athletes from 136 countries in Athens in 2004. Sochi in Russia will host the next 2014 Winter Paralympics, whereas the 2016 Summer Paralympics will be in Rio de Janeiro, Brazil.

12

W Excuse me, _____ some camping equipment and a sleeping bag.

M How long will you need that stuff for?

W 10 days.

M The rental fee for a sleeping bag is $2 per day. The rental fee for other camping equipment depends on the item.

W I see. What about backpacks? How much are they per day?

M _____. For a 25-liter one, it's $3 per day. For a 45-liter one, it's double that.

W Then I'd like to rent a 25-liter back pack.

M Anything else?

W I'll also need a tent.

M That's $10 per day, but those who rent _____ _____ get a 30% discount.

W That's good.

13

W Honey, what do you think about _____ with the kids during the Christmas holiday?

M That's just what I had in mind.

W Do you have _____?

M What about Guam? The kids like to swim.

W But we went there last year. I'd like to go to a new place.

M Then, what about Sydney? Sydney _____ _____.

W That's good. But don't you think it'll cost too much?

M I don't think so. According to my friend who has been there, the cost of a trip to Sydney is just a little more expensive than that of Guam.

W Really? In that case, let's go there. Let me tell the kids about it.

M _____

14

M Jenny, tomorrow is our school anniversary. Do you have any special plans?

W Well, _____ go to an art gallery near City Hall in the afternoon.

M Go to an art gallery?

W Yeah, there is an exhibition of Picasso's paintings. ____ _____ Picasso.

M Then, do you have time in the evening?

W Yeah, I'm free then. Why? Do you have any exciting plans?

M _____, could you help me pack my stuff?

W Ah, you're supposed to move to a new apartment on Sunday.

M Right. So I need some help.

W _____

15

W Derrick often helps his mother, Juliet, _____ _____ because Juliet works at a department store. Today, when Derrick comes home after school, he realizes that the living room is very messy. So he decides to _____. He vacuums the carpet, using a vacuum cleaner. When Juliet _____, she is surprised to see the living room so clean. She asks Derrick whether he cleaned the living room or not, and Derrick answers that he did. In this situation, what would Juliet most likely say to Derrick?

Juliet _____

16-17

M Excuse me, _____?

W Yes, please. How can I help you?

M Actually, today is my wife's birthday, so I'd like to buy a birthday cake. Where is a bakery located here?

W It's downstairs just next to the escalator. By the way, do you have a membership card at our hotel?

M Yes, I'm a member of the Diamond Club.

W That's nice. For a member of the Diamond Club, ____ _____.

M Really? That's good. Then I only have to buy a flower. Do you have a flower shop, too?

W Sure, it's just next to the bakery.

M Okay, I'll go and buy some flowers right away.

W Before going, _____ your room number and the time you want to receive a cake. We'll send a cake to your room at that time.

M Good. I'm staying in room 1004. Please send the cake by 7 pm.

W Okay, I got it. I hope you _____ with us.

1번부터 17번까지는 듣고 답하는 문제입니다. 1번부터 15번까지는 한 번만 들려주고, 16번부터 17번까지는 두 번 들려줍니다. 방송을 잘 듣고 답을 하시기 바랍니다.

01 대화를 듣고, 여자의 마지막 말에 대한 남자의 응답으로 가장 적절한 것을 고르시오.

① She's got some pain. Could you do me a favor?
② I don't think it's right for her. Let's wait a little.
③ She avoids talking to her friends. I'm so worried.
④ I haven't. Don't worry. I'll take good care of her.
⑤ Tell her using smart phones is forbidden at school.

02 대화를 듣고, 남자의 마지막 말에 대한 여자의 응답으로 가장 적절한 것을 고르시오.

① I borrowed it from one of my friends.
② You can call the service center right now.
③ Finally, check the virus. It can be infected.
④ Of course. But it seems to have another problem.
⑤ No, I've only finished the report for English class.

03 다음을 듣고, 여자가 하는 말의 주제로 가장 적절한 것을 고르시오.

① 우리 몸이 칼슘을 얻는 방법
② 우리 몸에 칼슘이 필요한 이유
③ 우유 섭취가 건강에 미치는 영향
④ 칼슘 부족이 건강에 미치는 영향
⑤ 칼슘과 함께 섭취해야 하는 영양소

04 대화를 듣고, 남자의 의견으로 가장 적절한 것을 고르시오.

① 마라톤 훈련은 식이요법과 병행되어야 한다.
② 마라톤을 완주한다는 것은 의미 없는 활동이다.
③ 마라톤 완주를 위해서는 철저한 훈련이 우선이다.
④ 마라톤 행사를 위한 자원봉사자 연수가 필요하다.
⑤ 기아에 고통 받는 아이들을 위한 기부가 필요하다.

05 대화를 듣고, 두 사람의 관계를 가장 잘 나타낸 것을 고르시오.

① 의사 – 환자
② 간호사 – 의사
③ 간병인 – 환자
④ 의사 – 환자 보호자
⑤ 요양원 원장 – 요양원 입소자

06 대화를 듣고, 그림에서 대화의 내용과 일치하지 <u>않는</u> 것을 고르시오.

07 대화를 듣고, 여자가 남자를 위해 할 일로 가장 적절한 것을 고르시오.

① 숙제 도와주기　② 선물 배달하기
③ 식사 함께 하기　④ 편지 전달해 주기
⑤ 편지 대신 써 주기

08 대화를 듣고, 여자가 회사를 옮기고 싶어 하는 이유를 고르시오.

① 일이 너무 많아서
② 승진을 하지 못해서
③ 일이 재미가 없어서
④ 동료와 사이가 안 좋아서
⑤ 정기적으로 발표를 해야 해서

09 대화를 듣고, 남자가 지불할 총액을 고르시오. [3점]

① $60   ② $62   ③ $64

④ $66   ⑤ $68

10 대화를 듣고, 두 사람이 언급하지 <u>않은</u> 것을 고르시오.

① 무용 수업의 종류   ② 무용을 하려는 이유
③ 무용 수업 시간   ④ 무용 수강 학생 수
⑤ 무용 강사

11 아이스 링크에 대한 다음 내용을 듣고, 일치하지 <u>않는</u> 것을 고르시오.

① 실외 스케이트장이다.
② 음료수를 즐길 수 있는 카페가 있다.
③ 선물을 살 수 있는 기념품 가게가 있다.
④ 개장과 폐장 시간이 정해져 있다.
⑤ 모든 사람이 무료로 이용할 수 있다.

12 다음 편의시설 사용 안내표를 보면서 대화를 듣고, 남자가 하려고 하는 일을 고르시오. [3점]

Nam Sports Resort

	Utilities	Cost (per person)	Time
①	Swimming Pool	$3	10:00 am ~ 6:00 pm
②	Fitness Center	free	9:00 am ~ 9:00 pm
③	Beach Jogging	free	6:00 am ~ 5:00 pm
	Film Festival	free	7:00 pm ~ midnight
④	Barbecue & Beer (summers only)	$10	9:00 pm ~ midnight
⑤	Sauna (winters only)	$5	11:00 am ~ 8:00 pm
	Karaoke	$5	7:00 pm ~ 11:00 pm

13 대화를 듣고, 남자의 마지막 말에 대한 여자의 응답으로 가장 적절한 것을 고르시오.

Woman : _____

① OK. We are his best friends.
② I know it's his lifetime dream.
③ It would be hard for him to do it.
④ I really like studying math, too.
⑤ Why don't we call his house first?

14 대화를 듣고, 여자의 마지막 말에 대한 남자의 응답으로 가장 적절한 것을 고르시오. [3점]

Man : _____

① That's too bad. I wish you liked your work.
② Oh, you can have another holiday this winter.
③ I must leave now because of my business trip.
④ That was terrible. I should have gone to Jejudo.
⑤ You can put your vacation off until next month.

15 다음 상황 설명을 듣고, Peter가 Edner에게 할 말로 가장 적절한 것을 고르시오.

Peter : Edner, _____

① let's ask Louise. She might help us.
② have you already finished your report?
③ it's all right. There isn't anything to do.
④ Louise told me that she couldn't help us.
⑤ how about studying together to finish it?

[16-17] 다음을 듣고, 물음에 답하시오.

16 남자가 하는 말의 주제로 가장 적절한 것은?

① 학교 실적 홍보
② 장학금 수령 방법
③ 장학금 수여식 안내
④ 교내 장학금의 종류
⑤ 특별 장학금 교부 계획

17 남자의 말과 일치하는 것은?

① Ms. Griffin의 노력으로 SAT성적이 향상되었다.
② Ms. Griffin에게 학생들의 감사패가 전달되었다.
③ Ms. Griffin은 모범 학생에게 장학금을 주었다.
④ 교내 장학금 혜택이 늘어날 예정이다.
⑤ 모든 교내 장학금에는 성적 제한이 있다.

DICTATION(받아쓰기) 코너입니다.
녹음의 내용을 잘 듣고, 빈칸에 알맞은 말을 쓰시기 바랍니다.

01

W Your daughter Kristi _____ at school. How's she at home?

M In fact, she will not say anything at home. She just talks to her friends on her smart phone _____.

W There must be some problems with her. Why don't you meet the school consultant with her?

M _____

02

M What's wrong? I've been waiting for you to give me the report _____.

W Sorry, but my computer doesn't work. I tried to fix it, but I failed.

M Did you have a virus check? The computer could be infected with a virus.

W _____

03

W When people think of calcium, they usually think of milk. However, _____? Actually, milk is not the only calcium source. It is just one of many sources of calcium. Of course, it is true that milk and dairy products are the most convenient sources of calcium for most people, but dark leafy green vegetables can also supply calcium. In addition, vitamin D helps our body absorb calcium. Another way of getting calcium for our body is _____ _____. When the blood levels of calcium drop too low, the body draws calcium from bones. We have to be careful not to let this kind of situation happen too often since this borrowed calcium can't be replaced simply _____.

04

W I will run in a marathon for starving children.

M You mean the one in June?

W Yes. I could finish it in about six hours.

M _____. It sounds so hard.

W No, it doesn't. Running is easy. I jog every morning.

M Come on! Jogging is different from marathons. You need training.

W But I'm already _____. I'll complete it.

M Oh, dear! Then you must start training right away.

W Do I have to run every day for an hour or so?

M Oh, you don't know anything about marathons. _____ _____, let's meet and practice together.

W Thank you. I knew you would say that.

M Shall we meet at 6:00, before dinner?

W That'd be OK. See you then.

05

M Her injury is perfectly healed, but her forgetfulness is getting worse.

W I know. But there's no one _____.

M It's a big problem. If she loses her way, it's hard to find her because of her forgetfulness.

W What can I do now? I have little time to take care of her. I must work.

M How about hiring a live-in nurse?

W I did. But she couldn't handle my mom and left.

M You could use our hospital's senior citizen's ward. If you want, I could give you a recommendation.

W Really? That'd be good. How long could my mother stay there?

M In her case, about six months.

W Could you tell me if her condition gets better?

M _____, I think her outlook is positive.

W Thank you. I'm very relieved.

06

W Look at our house. It's so messy.

M Mom and Dad will arrive soon. I think we need to clean up the house.

W _____. When they see it, they'll be angry at us.

M Yeah. Look what we did. My black socks are on the couch.

W You even left the pizza box and a cola can from last night's dinner on the table.

M _____ who messes up the house. Look at your slacks and T-shirt. They are on the floor. Why don't you hang them on hangers?

W Okay, _____. What about you?

M I'll start with vacuuming the carpet. Would you turn off the TV, so we can concentrate on our cleaning.

W Good idea. You know what is a good thing? At least, we don't have a kitten that bites our socks.

07

M Hi, Cindy. It's Vincent.

W Hi, Vincent. What's up?

M Could you tell me why Angela shouted at me yesterday?

W Oh, Vincent. Maybe Angela misunderstood you.

M But she didn't tell me why. If I have done something wrong to her, _____ to her.

W No, it's not your fault. It's her fault.

M Do you think so? Oh, I can't understand her.

W _____. Maybe she was afraid of talking to you.

M Why? If she apologized to me, I would accept it.

W Really? In fact, she did regret her behavior and asked me to deliver a letter to you.

M _____.

W If you want, I could take the letter to you now.

M How about meeting at Mac's Cafe in an hour?

W OK. See you then.

08

M Hi, Ann. I heard you _____. Congratulations!

W Thank you.

M By the way, is there something wrong? You don't look happy.

W No, nothing. It's just... Suddenly, _____ the work in this company fits me. I want to change my job.

M Really? Why? You did like your job. It may be too much work for you to do after your promotion.

W No, it's not that. If there's too much work, I can talk to my boss and reschedule it or something else. _____, my coworkers will always help me.

M Then, why don't you tell me about your problem? Maybe we can solve the problem together.

W Actually, I have to _____ every Monday in front of all the executives. You know I'm a kind of shy person. I know I have to overcome that, but it's too much for me. It's just that I'm not ready yet.

09

M I'm looking for some presents for my kids.

W How about the teddy bears? They're $30 each. However, if you buy one, you'll get another one free.

M Oh, _____. But my kids already have too many teddy bears.

W Are they girls?

M Yes. One's eight and the other's ten years old.

W Then, how about these dolls? They're made of cotton.

M How much are they?

W Well, _____: $50 each.

M That's too expensive. How much are these puppets?

W Oh, one puppet is $40, but if you buy two, I'll give you 20% off the total price.

M OK. I'll buy two. My daughters will like them.

W I think so, too. _____ for you.

10

M Would you like to have some coffee?

W No, thank you. I've just had some. So, could you ____ _____ about your dancing classes?

M Okay. We have Latin dance, tap dance, Salsa dance, and belly dance classes.

W Wow! There are many kinds of dance classes. ____ _____ pick one.

M Why don't you choose whatever you are interested in? Do you have anything in mind?

W Actually I'm interested in tap dance. Do you think it will help me lose weight?

M Sure, definitely. Is that the reason you want to learn dance?

W _____, yes. Would you show me the time schedule?

M Here you are. We have afternoon classes and evening classes on weekdays and morning classes on Saturdays. There's no class on Sundays.

W How many people are usually in one class?

M It depends on class time, but usually about 10. Can I ask how you learned about this place?

W _____. By the way, how much is the course fee? I hope it's not too expensive.

11

W The most enchanting ice rink is set in Kew Gardens, and _____ to experience the fun of outdoor skating. With spectacular views and a truly magical atmosphere, skating at Kew has become a "must do" Christmas treat for all. It has a cafe _____ _____ like hot chocolate, so skaters of all ages can warm up after a spin or two on the ice. Also, you can _____ for your friends and family at the souvenir shop. It opens at 10:00 am and closes at 10:00 pm. Every person under 18 can enter free. In addition, adults can enter _____ around: $5 each. Now have the most exciting experience this winter: Kew Gardens!

12

M Wow, we can enjoy many things here.

W Aren't you tired? I'm so tired I can't do anything.

M Come on! If we don't enjoy ourselves now, ____ _____.

W Okay, then. How about going to the sauna?

M But we can use it only in winter.

W That's too bad. Anyway, Peter, _____.

M Then, let's go to the Barbecue & Beer after dinner.

W OK, but now you can do something _____ if you want. It's just 3:00 pm.

M Are you OK?

W Don't worry about me. I'm just tired.

M OK. Then, after some beach running, _____ with you.

W That's a good idea. Go ahead.

13

M It's the start of the new term.

W Yes. There's so much to do.

M Right. By the way, have you seen Dave?

W No, I haven't seen him in _____. I am starting to worry about him.

M Then you haven't heard about him, either. Actually, last semester he told me that he would _____ ____, but I didn't think he would really do so.

W Really? He didn't say anything to me.

M Well, he chose his major because his father wanted him to be a lawyer.

W I know. Then, what major was he really interested in?

M He always wanted to study mathematics.

W Oh, dear. How about advising him as friends?

M _____. But how could we find him now?

W _____

14

M　_____?

W　It was great! I enjoyed myself at the beach with my family.

M　You went to Jejudo, didn't you?

W　No, I went to Sokcho because I only had three days' vacation.

M　Did you take your youngest daughter, Cindy?

W　Of course. She was _____. At the beach, she enjoyed making sand castles.

M　It sounds like you and your family had a great time there.

W　Yes, we did. And I was happy to be with my family all day long.

M　Right! Before you left, you were so busy with your work. I know how you must feel now.

W　Yes. _____ spend more time with my family.

M　_____

15

M　Edner was writing a report for his biology class. However, he couldn't finish it because his Internet access was not good, and he didn't have the right books. So he called his friend, Peter, _____ ____. However, Peter didn't have enough books and couldn't find enough articles on the Internet, either. He was worried about his own report, too. _____, it occurred to Peter that Louise was very interested in biology and had many books on that subject. So Peter thought that both he and Edner could _____ from Louise. In this situation, what would Peter most likely say to Edner?

Peter　Edner, _____

16-17

M　Our School has made a dramatic improvement in SAT scores with Ms. Griffin's perseverance and commitment to our students. Ms. Griffin _____ _____ from the Los Angeles High School Alumni Association as well as $2,000 for her efforts and hard work. She donated the money to the scholarship fund _____. So our school committee made a decision to give a special scholarship to whoever is eligible this month. First of all, the income of parents is most important. _____, the higher the possibility to get the scholarship is. Secondly and lastly, you must have at least a B average grade. Now if you want to be the candidate to get the scholarship, you have to _____ in your classroom. You can visit the student union office for more information. Thank you for listening.

1번부터 17번까지는 듣고 답하는 문제입니다. 1번부터 15번까지는 한 번만 들려주고, 16번부터 17번까지는 두 번 들려줍니다. 방송을 잘 듣고 답을 하시기 바랍니다.

01 대화를 듣고, 남자의 마지막 말에 대한 여자의 응답으로 가장 적절한 것을 고르시오.

① I've only finished writing the introduction.
② How wonderful! You've finished your project.
③ I'm not sure which one you mean. Let me check.
④ Cheer up! You are the best student I've ever known.
⑤ Sounds good! Do you have any ideas to write it?

02 대화를 듣고, 여자의 마지막 말에 대한 남자의 응답으로 가장 적절한 것을 고르시오.

① OK. I'll treat you to dinner if you win the race.
② I'm proud of you. You've completed your race!
③ I'm not sure I've got enough experience to do it.
④ Please wish me luck for the race. I'll do my best.
⑤ I'm afraid that can be an awful experience for me.

03 다음을 듣고, 여자가 하는 말의 주제로 가장 적절한 것을 고르시오.

① 화재 시 비상 탈출구 확보의 중요성
② 정기적 가스 검침의 필요성과 의의
③ 가스 안전사고 방지를 위한 대비책
④ 가스 누출 시 신속한 대처의 중요성
⑤ 가스 사고 시 관련 직원의 응대방법

04 대화를 듣고, 여자의 의견으로 가장 적절한 것을 고르시오.

① 실수로 발생한 손상이지만 배상해야 한다.
② 물에 빠진 전화기는 잘 말리면 사용이 가능하다.
③ 아이의 실수로 인한 손해는 배상할 필요가 없다.
④ 실수로 인해 고장 난 전화기는 배상해 줄 수 없다.
⑤ 아이들이 노는 곳에는 항상 어른이 동행해야 한다.

05 대화를 듣고, 두 사람의 관계를 가장 잘 나타낸 것을 고르시오.

① lawyer – client
② teacher – pupil
③ doctor – patient
④ counselor – customer
⑤ interviewer – interviewee

06 대화를 듣고, 그림에서 대화의 내용과 일치하지 <u>않는</u> 것을 고르시오.

07 대화를 듣고, 남자가 여자를 위해 할 일로 가장 적절한 것을 고르시오.

① 담당 직원 연결해 주기
② 도쿄 여행안내해 주기
③ 여행안내 책자 찾아 주기
④ 도쿄 지하철 정보 알려 주기
⑤ 도쿄에 있는 호텔 예약해 주기

08 대화를 듣고, Mike가 남자의 집에 온 이유를 고르시오.

① 엄마 심부름으로
② 서점에 함께 가려고
③ 빌린 책을 돌려주려고
④ 포장 재료를 갖다 주려고
⑤ 엄마의 스카프를 가져가려고

09 대화를 듣고, 여자가 지불할 총액을 고르시오. [3점]

① $50   ② $51   ③ $52

④ $53   ⑤ $54

10 대화를 듣고, Ashley Jude에 대해 두 사람이 언급하지 않은 것을 고르시오.

① what she is doing at school
② why she joined a badminton game
③ what other boys think of her
④ when she came to notice Josh
⑤ who she is interested in

11 mechanical mouse에 관한 다음 내용을 듣고, 일치하지 않는 것을 고르시오. [3점]

① 두 개의 롤러로 구성되어 있다.
② 표면이 평평하지 않으면 작동되지 않기도 한다.
③ 처음에는 단독 입력 장치로 버튼 없이 사용 되었다.
④ 15년여에 걸친 연구 끝에 만들어진 것이다.
⑤ Macintosh 디자인의 영향으로 인기를 얻게 되었다.

12 다음 표를 보면서 대화를 듣고, 두 사람이 이용할 항공편을 고르시오.

Flight Schedule [Seoul — Tokyo]

	Date	Flight No.	Departure	Arrival
①		KA032	Kimpo 10:00 am	Haneda 11:50 am
②	WED	OA054	Incheon 4:40 pm	Narita 6:30 pm
③		KA073	Kimpo 8:20 pm	Narita 10:10 pm
④	THU	OA045	Incheon 9:00 am	Narita 10:50 am
⑤		KA009	Kimpo 3:30 pm	Haneda 5:20 pm

13 대화를 듣고, 남자의 마지막 말에 대한 여자의 응답으로 가장 적절한 것을 고르시오. [3점]

Woman : _____

① Then, I'd better come back at 6:00.
② Great! How long will you stay here?
③ I'll send it by home delivery service.
④ Oh, it didn't take long. It looks great.
⑤ How about getting it tomorrow morning?

14 대화를 듣고, 여자의 마지막 말에 대한 남자의 응답으로 가장 적절한 것을 고르시오.

Man : _____

① It's so difficult to be a famous person.
② I prefer playing basketball to watching TV.
③ You must have watched the show last night.
④ Sorry, but he didn't tell me anything about it.
⑤ Oh, you should have watched my performance.

15 다음 상황 설명을 듣고, Ralph가 Albert에게 할 말로 가장 적절한 것을 고르시오.

Ralph : _____

① I'm sorry to hear that you missed your date.
② You should have bought perfume for her.
③ Thank you for your advice. I'll buy some flowers for her.
④ Do you know what kind of gift would be good for a girl?
⑤ Could you tell me what kind of clothes I should wear on my date?

[16-17] 다음을 듣고, 물음에 답하시오.

16 여자가 하는 말의 목적으로 가장 적절한 것은?

① 여름학교의 영향력을 강조하려고
② 여름학교 프로그램들을 소개하려고
③ 여름학교 등록 취소 기간을 알리려고
④ 여름학교 활동의 중요성을 강조하려고
⑤ 여름학교 등록 기간 준수를 당부하려고

17 academic program에 대한 내용과 일치하는 것은?

① 모든 학년이 등록할 수 있다.
② 추가된 프로그램에 속한다.
③ 수학과 과학 과목으로 구성되어 있다.
④ 오전에 진행되는 프로그램이다.
⑤ 수준별로 나누어 진행된다.

DICTATION(받아쓰기) 코너입니다.
녹음의 내용을 잘 듣고, 빈칸에 알맞은 말을 쓰시기 바랍니다.

01

M Professor Smith has just given me my first independent project to do.

W Congratulations! He really thinks you are good enough.

M Well, I'm not sure I've _____ to do that for myself.

W _____

02

W I _____ a 1000m swimming race next month.

M You are kidding! You haven't trained seriously. I'm afraid that you'll never finish the course.

W You just wait and see how I finish the race. I've already started training.

M _____

03

W At the beginning of this month, I thought I smelled gas at home, but my husband didn't, so I thought _____. But last week, I smelled gas again when I was watching TV in the living room by myself. I couldn't be sure there was a leak, but I also _____. So I opened up all of the doors and windows immediately and called the gas company. The engineer _____ and confirmed that gas was leaking from the pipe. At that time, I realized that people should call the gas company right away when they suspect a gas leak because it is always better _____.

04

(Telephone rings.)

M Hello, this is Mike Collins.

W Hello, this is Lila's mom. Lila is a friend of your daughter, as you might know.

M Oh, Lila, I know. Now Jenny is playing with her in your house, isn't she?

W Yes, she is. By the way, my daughter, Lila, dropped Jenny's cell phone into the pool _____. Though the kids fished it out and dried it well, it stopped working.

M Oh. Is it still not working?

W No. I'm so sorry. _____ your daughter for the ruined cell phone.

M Thank you, but this happening seems to be abrupt for me.

W I know, but I feel so bad due to my daughter's mistake. It is my responsibility for what she did. It doesn't matter whether it's a mistake or not.

M Okay, can you just give me some time _____?

W Sure, when you make up your mind, please call me. I'm sorry again.

05

W Long time no see, Peter.

M I missed you very much, Jane.

W Finally, you graduated from college. Congratulations!

M Thank you, but I'm a little afraid for my future.

W Why? You are going to law school, aren't you?

M Right. But _____, I'm not sure that is what I really want to do.

W Really? As far as I know, you did everything well. You were a very smart boy. You will be a great man.

M That's encouraging. Did you know I liked your class most?

W Really? You often tried to _____ in my class, but I loved your tricks.

M Oh, I miss those good old days.

W _____. It was fortunate that I had a chance to teach a brilliant student like you.

M Thank you. I'll study hard and be a good lawyer.

06

W Oh, they all look so good.

M Yes, _____ all the pieces of furniture here.

W I understand, but we need a desk, a chair, and a bed most.

M How about the desk with a bookshelf on the left? It looks so practical.

W Sure, it is, but we have enough bookshelves in our room. I don't think we need another bookshelf.

M Then, what about the antique-style desk _____ _____?

W Don't you think the desk is too big for our room? I would prefer a simple and small one.

M Oh, look at that. It might fit in our room. It's simple, small and has many drawers.

W Where? I got it. You mean the desk _____, right? Okay, let's buy that one. What's next? A chair, right?

M What about that white chair next to the stairwell? It seems to match our desk well.

W Yeah, I think so, too. At last, we should buy a bed.

M Look up. There's a sign: "Beds are upstairs."

07

W Well, I'd like to _____ about Tokyo.

M Do you have any plan to go there on your holiday?

W Yes, but I'm not sure.

M If you go, when would you like to leave?

W Maybe in August. Usually I have a holiday in August.

M There are usually many tourists in August, but I recommend a subway tour.

W Would you tell me why?

M The subway system in Tokyo is good. It is easy ___ _____. Besides, it is less expensive than a bus tour.

W I don't like group tours.

M Of course, you can travel alone. If you want, I could give you a brochure about the tour.

W Could I get it right now? _____.

M OK. Wait a moment.

08

M Can I go to the bookstore now?

W It's too late, David. When does the bookstore close?

M It closes at 10:00 o'clock. Don't worry, Mom. I will go with Mike.

W It's 9 o'clock. OK, you can go. Is Mike on the way?

M Actually Mike is already here. _____ on the porch.

W Oh, I just remembered I have to send this scarf to Mike's mother.

M Do you want me to ask Mike to come in now?

W Wait a minute. You don't have to.

M Why? Mike can take it to his mom.

W I haven't _____. David, can you buy a small box to put it in?

M Can I buy it after buying some books?

W Yes, of course. Ah! And some ribbons, too.

M Okay, _____ to buy them.

09

M May I help you?

W Yes. I'm looking for a swimsuit for my daughter.

M How old is she?

W Nine years old. She likes the color pink.

M _____? This is a bikini type.

W It looks good. How much is it?

M It's $40, but you can buy it at 30% off.

W That's great. One more thing, could I look at a pair of goggles? _____.

M What color do you have in mind? We have white, black, or blue.

W I'd prefer white.

M Well, how about this one? It's $25, but there's no discount.

W OK. I'll buy both the swimsuit and the goggles. _____?

10

W Josh, do you know Ashley Jude?

M The cheerleader? Yes, I know her.

W Well, _____, she is interested in you.

M What? How does she know me?

W She noticed you at the badminton game last year.

M Oh, at that time, I won a singles match.

W Yes. You played so well that Ashley became interested in you.

M Wow! _____! She is the most beautiful girl in our school. Every boy likes her.

W Right. Now if you want, you can meet her. She wants to meet you.

M But I'm not tall, I'm not intelligent and I'm...

W Don't be shy. I'm sure you are a nice guy.

M However, I need some _____. Thank you, anyway.

11

M A mechanical mouse is a hand-held device. It consists of two rollers _____ located inside an object like a box. The user can slide it over a flat surface. If the surface is not flat, sometimes _____ _____. When it is rolled across the surface, a cursor moves in a corresponding way on a display screen. Originally, it was part of an input panel with a number of switches. People continually _____ _____ computer communication, and finally this device was made after 15 years of research. It became popular because of the Macintosh design which was commercially successful and technically influential. This device gets its name from its appearance, a small box with a tail-like wire.

12

W Well, we must go to Tokyo next month _____.

M Let's make a reservation for flight tickets beforehand.

W Look. We can book our tickets at this website.

M Really? Great. It'd be easier than going to a travel agency.

W Our meeting will be on Friday, but if we arrive earlier, we can have enough _____.

M Then, how about this flight on Wednesday morning?

W But Kimpo Airport is too far from my house. I prefer Incheon Airport. How about you?

M Either one is okay to me, but since Kimpo Airport is inconvenient to you, let's go to Incheon Airport. Let's see. I take my mother to the hospital every Wednesday afternoon, so after Wednesday evening is fine.

W Then, _____.

M Okay, let's take that one. It's good that we will still have one day to prepare for the meeting.

13

M May I help you?

W Yes. The strap on my bag has torn badly.

M _____. Oh, it's too heavy to lift.

W Yes. I am always overloading the bag.

M It would be better to replace it with a stronger one.

W Do you have a stronger strap than this one?

M Yes, and don't worry about color and quality. How about these? Among them, you can choose.

W There are _____, but I don't think they fit my bag. Oh, this looks the same as the original one.

M Right, that's the same one. If you don't like the others, how about using two straps? That would be stronger.

W That's a good idea. Because of my job, I always overload the bag with papers and books.

M Now, you can _____ after about two hours or you can wait here if you want.

W _____

14

W Did you watch the Hymann Show on TV last night?

M No, I went to play basketball with Peter, and I don't like watching TV.

W Well, _____ .

M What was it? Something special?

W Of course, it was. The interviewer, Hymann, asked Bill Jones some private questions.

M The famous singer, Bill? Is Bill involved in an affair with an actress?

W Yes, he is. Bill _____ and was angry at Hymann.

M On TV? How rude he was!

W That wasn't all. He called him names.

M Maybe he couldn't hide his real emotions at that time. He is a human being like us, too.

W Right. I think so, too, but he should not have behaved like that.

M _____

15

W Ralph is going to have a date with Susan tonight. He decided to give her something special, so he went to the department store. But he couldn't decide what to buy _____ for her. Besides, the things that caught his eye were too expensive. Finally, he just gave up and _____ _____ . At that time, he met his friend, Albert, and it occurred to Ralph that Albert could choose a present better than he could. So, he decided to _____ _____ . In this situation, what would Ralph most likely say to Albert?

Ralph _____

16-17

W Hello, everyone. As you may have been noticed before, our summer school will be open from June 11 through July 6. Now we decided that sports camps will be included. They are for skills improvement and physical fitness. So I'll tell you more precisely about the school with the new programs. The academic program is only for 8th grade students, and meets from 8:15 am to 3:30 pm. Students will be grouped _____ in math, reading, and language arts. The emphasis in this program is on review and strengthening of skills in each of those three academic areas. Our Summer Athletic Programs are for students in grades 6 through 12. The programs include volleyball, basketball, and physical fitness camps. _____ , contact the school homepage. Thank you.

28^회 듣기 모의고사

1번부터 17번까지는 듣고 답하는 문제입니다. 1번부터 15번까지는 한 번만 들려주고, 16번부터 17번까지는 두 번 들려줍니다. 방송을 잘 듣고 답을 하시기 바랍니다.

01 대화를 듣고, 여자의 마지막 말에 대한 남자의 응답으로 가장 적절한 것을 고르시오.

① I don't think it's right for him now.
② You cannot use your smart phone now.
③ Mike teased me about my bad eyesight.
④ Don't worry. I'll take good care of him.
⑤ I'll ask him what happened between you.

02 대화를 듣고, 남자의 마지막 말에 대한 여자의 응답으로 가장 적절한 것을 고르시오.

① I'd like to shorten the length of my pants.
② I'd like to wear the school uniform tightly.
③ Don't worry. I'll be taller in a few months.
④ Let's reform your uniform to fit your body.
⑤ How about buying another one for me, Dad?

03 다음을 듣고, 여자가 하는 말의 목적으로 가장 적절한 것을 고르시오.

① 자원 봉사 활동을 권유하려고
② 건강 검진의 중요성을 알리려고
③ 아픈 직원의 병원비를 모금하려고
④ 우호적인 회사 분위기를 독려하려고
⑤ 복귀 직원의 환영 행사를 공고하려고

04 대화를 듣고, 여자의 의견으로 가장 적절한 것을 고르시오.

① 구입 후 1년이 지난 휴대 전화는 고장이 잦다.
② 계획에 따라 이루어지는 소비는 낭비가 아니다.
③ 돈을 효율적으로 쓰려면 계획을 잘 세워야 한다.
④ 스마트폰을 구입하는 것은 돈을 낭비하는 것이다.
⑤ 청소년 소비에 부모의 지나친 간섭은 독이 될 뿐이다.

05 대화를 듣고, 두 사람의 관계를 가장 잘 나타낸 것을 고르시오.

① engineer – auto designer
② used car dealer – customer
③ clothes shop manager – dress designer
④ parking officer – customer
⑤ bank teller – car owner

06 대화를 듣고, 그림에서 대화의 내용과 일치하지 <u>않는</u> 것을 고르시오.

07 대화를 듣고, 여자가 남자를 위해 할 일로 가장 적절한 것을 고르시오.

① 병원에 데려다 주기
② 병원 예약하기
③ 감기약 사다 주기
④ 잠에서 깨워 주기
⑤ 공책 빌려 오기

08 대화를 듣고, 여자가 Harry를 만나려는 이유를 고르시오.

① to play tennis with him
② to help him get a racket
③ to bring her racket to him
④ to borrow a racket from him
⑤ to lend his racket to a friend

09 대화를 듣고, 남자가 회의를 끝낸 후 집에 도착하는 데 걸린 시간을 고르시오. [3점]

① 30분   ② 1시간   ③ 1시간 30분
④ 2시간   ⑤ 2시간 30분

10 대화를 듣고, 두 사람이 언급하지 <u>않은</u> 것을 고르시오.

① 가게 문 여는 시간   ② 가게 하루 운영 시간
③ 여자의 직업   ④ 오늘의 수입
⑤ 내일의 예상 고객 수

11 Buddy에 관한 다음 내용을 듣고, 일치하지 <u>않는</u> 것을 고르시오. [3점]

① Buddy를 쓰다듬지 말 것
② Buddy를 방해하지 말 것
③ Buddy에게 재주 부리기를 요구하지 말 것
④ 계단을 이용할 때 통행 공간을 확보해 줄 것
⑤ Buddy에게 먹이를 주지 말 것

12 다음 영화 상영표를 보면서 대화를 듣고, 두 사람이 보기로 한 것을 고르시오.

MGV Cinema November 2013

Title	Time		
Pride and Prejudice	① 10:00		② 19:00
Queen Victoria	11:00	③ 15:00	18:00
Next	10:30	15:30	
Disturbia	11:00	④ 16:30	⑤ 19:00

13 대화를 듣고, 남자의 마지막 말에 대한 여자의 응답으로 가장 적절한 것을 고르시오. [3점]

Woman : _____

① Yes, I like him. He is a terrific guy.
② Go ahead. That's what mothers are for.
③ So, you want me to buy it for you, right?
④ Well, you can wash the dishes after dinner.
⑤ Sorry to hear that. You must help your friend.

14 대화를 듣고, 여자의 마지막 말에 대한 남자의 응답으로 가장 적절한 것을 고르시오.

Man : _____

① That's too bad. I really miss him, too.
② I'm sorry that I can't meet Philip now.
③ Now, let's have lunch with Aunt Martha.
④ Oh, I'm looking forward to seeing him soon.
⑤ Uncle Ben and I used to walk around the garden.

15 다음 상황 설명을 듣고, Mary의 아버지가 Mary에게 할 말로 가장 적절한 것을 고르시오.

Mary's father : _____

① Sorry, but you'd better find another person.
② You'd better check their next concert schedule.
③ Sorry. I can't make it because of a business trip.
④ Sorry for disappointing you. I can't go with you.
⑤ We can go to the concert next month. What do you think?

[16-17] 다음을 듣고, 물음에 답하시오.

16 여자가 하는 말의 주제로 가장 적절한 것은?

① 학부모 의견 수렴의 중요성
② 성적 향상을 위한 학습 방법
③ 고등학교 학업 성취도의 의의
④ 유급 방지를 위한 학교의 대책
⑤ 학업 성취를 위한 가정의 역할

17 언급된 통계의 내용으로 가장 적절한 것은?

① 우수한 성적으로 고등학교를 졸업한 학생의 비율
② 고등학교 학업 성취도와 대학교 학업 성취도의 상관 비율
③ 9학년 학생들의 학업 성취도에 따른 고등학교 졸업 비율
④ 높은 학업 성취도를 보인 9학년 학생들의 비율과 그 의미
⑤ 대학 공부를 하는 데 필요한 지식을 고등학교 때 습득한 비율

28회 DICTATION

DICTATION(받아쓰기) 코너입니다.
녹음의 내용을 잘 듣고, 빈칸에 알맞은 말을 쓰시기 바랍니다.

01

W David, _____. Are there any problems with the test results?

M No. It's not that. I just don't want to go to school anymore.

W Oh, dear. Tell me what happened to you at school.

M _____

02

M Sue, your school uniform seems to be too short for you.

W Actually, I feel uncomfortable _____.

M You've grown a lot. When we bought it, you weren't that tall.

W _____

03

W Good afternoon, everyone. I'm your boss, Jessica. ___ _____ good and exciting news for you. You know Jack London in the sales department. Recently he was in the hospital because of a dangerous illness. And you know well _____ the painful surgery. Now, he has returned! He is healthy, and he can work with us again. Without your support and prayers, we would not have seen him again. I'm proud of him, and I'm so happy to be with him. I believe you're like me. So, _____ tonight at 7:00 o'clock. Let's come and congratulate Jack on his recovery. I expect to see all of you tonight. Thank you for listening.

04

W Dad, Grandpa gave me some money as a birthday gift.

M Great! Do you plan to buy anything?

W I would like to buy a new smart phone. The money I already have and plus this money, I think I can buy a new smart phone. Can I?

M _____. Your phone is not old. You bought it a year and half ago.

W But Dad, I really want to have a smart phone. All of my friends have smart phones.

M _____ to use your money.

W I've saved money to buy a smart phone for a year. You know I spend my money according to a strict plan.

M I know. But _____, your phone is still usable. You'd better be careful about spending your money.

W Dad, it is not an impulsive buying and it is not waste of money. I planned it for a year, so please give me a break this time.

M Okay, I'm sure you're not a wasteful person. If you hadn't planned it, I wouldn't let you do it. But you say you planned it for quite a long time, so I'll allow you to make this purchase.

05

M Can I test-drive it?

W Of course. You can try any of our fine vehicles.

M Oh, that's very nice. By the way, these look a little different from what I saw on the Internet.

W Different? As you know, _____.

M But there are some scratches here. Look at this. It is also a little dented. When I saw it on your homepage, it looked perfect.

W Yeah, I agree. The photographs cannot tell you everything, but it still has excellent fuel efficiency. _____, too.

M How much is it?

W $1,000. Whenever you drive the car, you can enjoy a good quality ride.

M I think it's too expensive for me. Can you discount the price a little?

W Then, how about $900? _____.

M OK. I'll take it. Can I use my credit card?

W Yes, of course. You chose the best car here.

06

M Lost and Found, how may I help you?

W I lost my bag around 9 am today. Would you please check to see _____?

M Okay, some people turned in a few bags today.

W Great. My bag is black.

M A black bag? Can you see the black bags on the shelf?

W No, I only see some electronics. Cellphones on the first shelf and cameras on the second shelf.

M Look at _____ carefully. You can see several black bags. Is the black square-shaped one yours?

W No. Mine is not that big. Oh, on the fourth shelf, there's something black. Can I see it?

M Sure, but I don't think it's your bag. It's a black-round hat. Could you describe your bag more in detail?

W Okay, it's small and round with a leather strap.

M Then there's no one matching your description here. _____, I'll call you. I'm sorry that I couldn't help you.

W Thank you very much anyway.

07

W Good morning. _____ the test this Friday?

M Not ready enough. I fell asleep last night.

W But I know you have studied hard. Don't worry. You'll get a good grade.

M No, this time is different. I have a headache, and I can't _____ these days.

W It may be so stressful for you when you take tests.

M I agree. I think I have a test-phobia or something.

W A test-phobia? What are your symptoms? You said you had a headache, and what else?

M I can feel a fever coming on.

W I think you're coming down with a cold. Not because of a test-phobia. You'd better take a pill and some rest.

M Okay, I will _____ and buy some medicine.

W And if you need help for your study, just tell me. I can study with you or lend you my notebook.

M Great. _____ after taking a pill, I want someone to wake me up next to me. So, would you?

W No problem.

08

W What time will our tennis game begin?

M At 11:00. _____. How do you feel?

W Not bad, but I'm nervous.

M Did you bring your tennis racket?

W Oh, dear. I didn't. How terrible! Is there a tennis racket in our school?

M _____. I heard the other team borrowed all the rackets yesterday.

W Then, I must hurry home and get my racket.

M Calm down. I think Harry always brings his tennis racket to school. He plays tennis with the math teacher every afternoon.

W I don't know him well. So, could you find him and ask him to lend me his?

M Oh, look! _____. Wait here. I'll go and talk to him.

W I'll go with you since he is here. You just need to introduce me to him. Overall, _____.

09

W What time is it now?

M It's half past twelve. Sorry. I'm late again.

W You promised to come home early, didn't you?

M Yes, I did. But I had an important meeting.

W But you said it would finish at eight.

M You're right. But we couldn't finish it then.

W I'm so worried about your health. Nowadays, ____ _____.

M Don't worry. I'm trying to take good care of myself. In addition, I like my job a lot.

W I know, but think you're not a teenager. By the way, when did the meeting finish?

M It finished at ten, but _____ on the way home.

W A car accident? Are you OK?

M My car was a little dented, but I was not hurt.

W Oh, _____! Please be careful.

10

M You look awful.

W Yeah, I'm tired. There were so many people in the store today. _____.

M You must have done a lot things. How about drinking some hot tea and chatting?

W Great idea! Today we held a clearance sale, and we opened the store one hour earlier than usual.

M That early? It usually opens at ten. I think that's too early for customers to come.

W I had thought so, too, but it proved that _____ _____. Maybe it was because we advertised on TV all of last month.

M Yeah, maybe.

W I was too busy to take a minute to sit down. I had to help almost 100 people to try on clothes before lunch.

M Wow, that's a lot.

W After lunch, even more people came in. We counted how many customers visited the store and _____ _____ today.

M Since tomorrow is Saturday, you're probably expecting more people to come, right?

W Sure, we're expecting double today's number. The number of customers today was about 300, and the income of today was _____.

11

W I am a physically challenged woman and this is a service dog, Buddy. He is specially trained to help me and goes everywhere with me. Now, I have some suggestions. Please ask me whether it's all right before talking to him or petting him. My dog is working for my safety, not playing with me. Even a moment's inattention on the dog's part can cause me serious injury. Please let my dog do his job without interrupting. And do not ask Buddy to demonstrate his skills. _____, he is there to assist me, not entertain you. Do not give him any food. This can also _____ _____. And lastly, please give us some room so that we can safely negotiate stairs, elevators, aisles and so on. Thank you very much.

12

M Susan, let's go to the movies. Here's the schedule of films at the cinema.

W Okay, _____. I don't like horror movies. Are there any horror movies among them?

M I heard *NEXT* is pretty scary. How about seeing *Pride and Prejudice* at 10?

W I have to _____ in the morning. How about going during the afternoon?

M I can't. I have a piano lesson at 3 and then have to go to the dentist at 5.

W Even so, we can go to the cinema in the evening.

M Right. _____, I don't really prefer romantic movies.

W I got it. Then, since *Pride and Prejudice* is a love story and *Queen Victoria* is, too, we have only one choice left.

M OK. Let's watch that one.

13

M Mom, can I _____?

W Oh, thank you, Dave. Have you done your homework?

M Of course, I have. And I studied math for the final test.

W Great! _____!

M I decided to behave better and study harder.

W You look strange. Is there something you want to tell me?

M No, nothing. I just wanted to be a good boy for you.

W _____ very much. Thank you.

M By the way, Scott's mom bought a new game for him. It's educational.

W No, it's not. That's just a game.

M But the game says it can raise my intelligence level.

W _____

14

W Hi, David. _____?

M I'm fine. You look better, Jane. How are you? And how is family?

W Of course, we're fine. Dad sometimes says how bright and fabulous you are. And Philip is always saying what a great tennis player you are.

M I have missed Uncle Ben, Aunt Martha, and Philip very much.

W They have missed you, too. Mom is _____ _____.

M Oh, is she? Let's go to see her right now.

W Take it easy. You must meet Philip. He is waiting outside in the car.

M Oh, Philip is here? Why didn't he come inside?

W Either he or I have to stay in the car. _____ _____. Let's go.

M _____

15

W The Super Racers _____ this weekend. Mary really likes this group, and she decided to go to the concert with her father because he likes the group, too. So, she asked him if he could go to the concert with her this Saturday. He was glad to hear that, but he said he couldn't _____ this weekend. He knew how much she wanted to go, so he didn't want to disappoint her. He checked the Super Racers' next concert schedule and found out next month they would have another one. In this situation, what would her father most likely say to Mary?

Mary's father _____

16-17

W As a ninth grader, your child is now entering _____ _____ of his or her education. It is important for you, as a parent, to encourage your child throughout these four years to ensure he or she continues on to graduation. _____, only 32% of students who graduated from high school have sufficient knowledge to understand and succeed in college. With your help, your child can excel in 9th grade and go on to high school graduation. A supportive home environment can make a tremendous difference in your child's success in high school. You must carefully _____ at home, showing your concerns for studying. Actually, many high school dropouts said they would have worked harder if their parents had expected more of them. Now _____ your helping your child. Thank you for listening.

29회 | 듣기 모의고사

1번부터 17번까지는 듣고 답하는 문제입니다. 1번부터 15번까지는 한 번만 들려주고, 16번부터 17번까지는 두 번 들려줍니다. 방송을 잘 듣고 답을 하시기 바랍니다.

01 대화를 듣고, 여자의 마지막 말에 대한 남자의 응답으로 가장 적절한 것을 고르시오.

① It took two weeks. It was a great experience.
② Much the same, except I have some big plans.
③ Everyone gets excited during summer vacation.
④ Two weeks, but Mom won't allow me to do that.
⑤ I haven't made a perfect plan for it, but maybe two weeks.

02 대화를 듣고, 남자의 마지막 말에 대한 여자의 응답으로 가장 적절한 것을 고르시오.

① You know I don't like coffee. I prefer Coke.
② I agree with you. I have lived on caffeine, too.
③ Oh, dear, you'd better cut down on drinking it.
④ Don't worry about your health. It's caffeine-free.
⑤ How about taking a break? I'll treat you to coffee.

03 다음을 듣고, 여자가 하는 말의 목적으로 가장 적절한 것을 고르시오.

① 피부 관리법을 알려주려고
② 피부 미용 전문가를 소개하려고
③ 피부에 좋은 음식을 소개하려고
④ 친환경 음식 문화를 장려하려고
⑤ 피부 미용에 좋은 화장품을 홍보하려고

04 다음을 듣고, 남자가 하는 말의 주제로 가장 적절한 것을 고르시오.

① The reason that human viruses could grow
② Some skyscrapers that cause sickness to men
③ Some chemical cleaners that can be a pollutant
④ The importance of air circulation for well-being
⑤ The case that the building itself suffers from a sickness

05 대화를 듣고, 두 사람의 관계를 가장 잘 나타낸 것을 고르시오.

① plumber – tenant
② professor – student
③ hotel manager – customer
④ building owner – architect
⑤ real estate agent – house hunter

06 대화를 듣고, 그림에서 대화의 내용과 일치하지 <u>않는</u> 것을 고르시오.

07 대화를 듣고, 여자가 남자에게 부탁한 일로 가장 적절한 것을 고르시오.

① 음식 만들기
② 집안 청소하기
③ 차고 청소하기
④ 음식 재료 사오기
⑤ 요리법 프린트하기

08 대화를 듣고, 여자가 전화를 하려고 하는 이유를 고르시오.

① to repair the machine
② to change the machine
③ to get lost money back
④ to make a warning sign
⑤ to buy another cup of coffee

09 대화를 듣고, 여자가 가지게 될 동전의 개수를 고르시오. [3점]

① 2개   ② 3개   ③ 4개
④ 6개   ⑤ 10개

10 대화를 듣고, 두 사람이 언급한 사항이 <u>아닌</u> 것을 고르시오.

① Somalia 체류 기간
② Somalia의 상황
③ 의료진 증원의 필요성
④ 봉사활동이 주는 가치
⑤ 여자가 현재 하고 있는 일

11 피아노 경연대회에 관한 다음 내용을 듣고, 일치하지 <u>않는</u> 것을 고르시오.

① 그리스의 한 섬에서 개최된다.
② 매년 개최되는 행사이다.
③ 그리스 사람만을 위한 행사이다.
④ 15세에서 30세까지 참가 가능하다.
⑤ 우승자는 상금을 받는다.

12 다음 여행 안내표를 보면서 대화를 듣고, 두 사람이 선택한 것을 고르시오.

	World	Travel	Agency
①	China (Beijing)	Dec. 19 ~ 24	$650
②	Australia (Sydney)	Dec. 15 ~ 22	$1000
③	Indonesia (Bali)	Dec. 17 ~ 22	$750
④	Indonesia (Bali)	Dec. 13 ~ 20	$850
⑤	Philippines (Boracay)	Dec. 16 ~ 19	$700

13 대화를 듣고, 남자의 마지막 말에 대한 여자의 응답으로 가장 적절한 것을 고르시오.

Woman : _____

① I'm so sorry. It won't happen again.
② No problem. I already asked my mom.
③ Oh, great. I'll be expecting you at 6:00.
④ No. Don't forget your appointment with me.
⑤ How about looking at your vacation schedule?

14 대화를 듣고, 여자의 마지막 말에 대한 남자의 응답으로 가장 적절한 것을 고르시오. [3점]

Man : _____

① Is it? I wonder what it will be.
② Great! But I can't tell you anything.
③ OK. I'm sorry I can't come with you.
④ But I don't know how long it will take.
⑤ Then, how about meeting next Saturday?

15 다음 상황 설명을 듣고, Christine이 직원에게 할 말로 가장 적절한 것을 고르시오. [3점]

Christine : _____

① I'd better give up on this tour. Thanks, anyway.
② I'd rather stay alone though it is more expensive.
③ It's the best chance to have a thrilling experience.
④ Could you give me some advice about traveling to Bhutan?
⑤ How about going to Tibet? Backpacking tours are good there.

[16-17] 다음을 듣고, 물음에 답하시오.

16 여자가 말하고 있는 장소로 가장 적절한 것은?

① 공연장   ② 환영회장
③ 설명회장   ④ 강연 회장
⑤ 환송회장

17 여자에 대한 내용으로 일치하는 것은?

① 자원봉사를 계획하고 수립하는 일을 한다.
② 공항에서 자원봉사자인 Alice를 마중하였다.
③ 친구와 함께 아프리카로 왔다.
④ 자원봉사를 위해 해외 체류 중이다.
⑤ 학교를 짓는 자원봉사를 하고 있다.

DICTATION(받아쓰기) 코너입니다.
녹음의 내용을 잘 듣고, 빈칸에 알맞은 말을 쓰시기 바랍니다.

01

W   Andy, do you have _____?

M   I'll travel around the country in my car. I've already gotten permission from my parents.

W   I envy you so much. How long do you think it will take you to do that?

M   _____

02

M   Let's go and _____. I'm so tired.

W   But you seem to have had many cups of coffee today. How many cups of coffee did you drink today?

M   About 4 or 5. Actually, without coffee, I couldn't live a day.

W   _____

03

W   Hi, everyone. I'm Susan Johnson. _____ _____ a special opportunity. Well, all of you may wonder what kind of opportunity it is. It is a chance to meet the best expert in skincare. This is not a human being but a kind of food. I know you'll be surprised at this news. And don't be disappointed. This food can _____ and help stimulate blood circulation to make you look younger. Look at this food. It looks like a pill, but it is the food that astronauts in outer space eat. Now, _____ to try it. Don't hesitate.

04

M   Have you ever heard about how a building can be sick? Sometimes many people who work or live in the same building get headaches, _____, coughs, and other symptoms without having a specific illness. Also, they do not know where they got their illness. Usually, however, they feel much better when they go outside. This is a classic case of Sick Building Syndrome. Usually, _____ the air circulation within the building. Either old air doesn't leave the building properly or new air is polluted. Also, common chemical cleaners can be a pollutant from outside, which _____. Finally, human or animal viruses can become trapped and grow within the building. The result is that people feel bad.

05

W   _____ the drain?

M   It's clogged with hair, so the water overflowed.

W   How terrible! It's only been two days since I moved here.

M   It's lucky that you discovered this problem early.

W   But it can't be my fault. I guess the people who lived here before didn't clean the bathtub.

M   I guess so. Anyway, the situation _____. This acid can dissolve the hair down there.

W   Oh, it smells very bad.

M   Now you know you must always clean your bathtub after you use it.

W   I see. _____?

M   Well, you have to pay $25 in labor.

W   That's expensive, but I'll pay it. Here you are.

M   Thank you. Call me whenever you have a problem with your drain.

06

M I want to buy a shirt. Look! There are some shirts in the window. _____ ? If there's anything I like, I can go in to buy it.

W Okay, what kind of shirts do you want to buy? How about the first one from the left?

M Well, it has too many flower patterns. It gives me a headache just looking at it.

W You like tidy and simple shirts, don't you?

M Yes. Then, how about the second one? This shirt is white _____ .

W It looks okay, but what do you think of the first one from the right?

M Even though I like simple ones, don't you think that's too simple? There's nothing on it, not even a dot.

W _____ ! Simple but not too simple. I think the third one is just right for you.

M The blue stripes look good. I want to buy it.

W Oh my God! Look at the sign. They are closed. We must come here another time.

07

W Our housewarming party is tomorrow.

M Are we ready for that? I don't think we have prepared much.

W Don't worry. _____ . You just need to clean the house. I'll take care of all of the food and drinks.

M Okay, then, I'll clean the house tomorrow morning. But do you think we have to clean the whole house? I mean not only inside the house but also outside, including the garage.

W The kids cleaned the garage and front and back yards already, so you just need to clean inside the house.

M Great. _____ to help you except for the cleaning?

W No, nothing. The kids and I went to the store this morning and bought all of the ingredients for food. And I printed out recipes and put them on the refrigerator.

M Sounds perfect. Then I'll do what I need to do.

W Thank you, honey. _____ . Our party will be great.

08

M Why are you hitting that vending machine?

W Oh, Robert, I lost another 50 cents in this machine. What a stupid thing it is!

M I'm not surprised. Didn't you know _____ _____ ?

W Yes, I did, but I thought it'd be okay today.

M It ate my money, too. But hitting that machine never works.

W I was so upset. Anyway, how about putting an "Out of Order" sign on it?

M That's a good idea. Otherwise, the same thing will happen to others.

W Then, _____ ? I'll call the company that owns this machine.

M Sure, but do you know the telephone number?

W Yes, I can find it on the front of the machine. I must _____ .

M Oh, forget it. It's nothing.

W No, it's important. Anyway, I'll wait for you here.

M OK. I'll be back soon.

09

M May I help you?

W Yes. I want to change a 10,000 won note.

M Sorry, but this is not a bank.

W I know it isn't. But I need to have some change. Help me, please.

M OK. But _____ , OK?

W I see. Can I have one 5,000 won note and the rest in 1,000 won notes?

M But I don't have enough 1,000's.

W Then, _____ instead.

M OK. How about one 5,000 won note, four 1,000's and the rest in 100 won coins?

W Well, I don't want too many coins. How about some 500 won coins instead of 100's?

M OK then, here you are. _____ .

W That's okay. Thank you very much.

10

M So, _____ in Somalia?

W For about a year. I live here to help poor people.

M Because of conflicts, many people are dying and getting injured in this country.

W You're right. I'm not a doctor, but _____ hurt people.

M Oh, isn't it difficult?

W Yes, but it has some attractions.

M Could you tell me something about them?

W Umm… The people. They are so pure and nice. Every day, I learn many things from them.

M But _____ food shortages and diseases.

W Yes, they are. But they endure most difficulties well.

M They are so great! What is the most rewarding thing to you?

W Well, it is learning the importance of love.

11

M An international piano competition known as "The Muse" will take place in Santorini, one of the most beautiful islands of Greece. _____ in which both tourists and island residents will have a wonderful opportunity to listen to young pianists from the 1st until the 8th of September 2013. The main goal of the competition is to discover and to introduce new talents. _____ pianists aged 15 to 30 years old. The first-prize winner will be awarded $1,000. Everyone involved in the competition, whether they are participants, jury members, organizers, or audience members from around the world, may enjoy a _____ _____.

12

M Alice, when is your holiday?

W It's next month from the 16th to the 23rd.

M My holiday is a little longer than yours. _____ the 15th to the 25th.

W Then, let's look at this trip brochure.

M Well, we can't go to Australia.

W Right. I really wanted to go there _____.

M Then, we can go some other time. How about China?

W Derrick, didn't I just tell you about my holiday? We can't.

M Oh, I forgot. How about the Philippines? We can enjoy scuba diving and golfing there.

W But that trip's too short. Though it's a little expensive, I want to go to Bali.

M OK. Let's go there.

W Oh, I'm really _____.

13

M Wow! Vacation has started.

W You look excited. Do you have any plans for the vacation?

M Well, first of all, I must study, and play...

W Tom, _____ your vacation schedule.

M Mom. Schedules are not important. I'm not a machine.

W I know, Tom. But a good life starts with planning.

M Mom, please. Bill and Peter are waiting for me outside.

W I understand, but...

M I know what you want to say. _____ _____.

W How bright you are! OK. After you play with them, let's make vacation plans.

M OK, Mom. And can I _____ Bill's house tonight?

W _____

14

W Will you join the year-end party?

M Of course I will. I heard it's this Saturday.

W Right. The year is finally over.

M Yeah, _____ . By the way, will you come, too?

W Didn't you know I'm one of the organizers of the party?

M Great! If you organize it, it will be fantastic.

W I'm glad to hear that. _____ .

M By the way, did you plan anything special for the party?

W Actually, we will have a song contest.

M Really? But you will _____ making people sing. I don't think people like to sing in front of a crowd.

W Don't worry. We have a fantastic solution. But it's a secret.

M _____

15

W Christine _____ about Asia and Asian culture. Especially, she wanted to go to a country like Bhutan. But she didn't know about that country at all. So she visited a travel agency _____ about tours to Bhutan. The travel agent said that backpacking tours were not recommended and he suggested that she do a group tour and could choose either sharing a room with a stranger or using a room by herself _____ . She doesn't like the extra charge but wants to have her own room. So she decided not to share a room. In this situation, what would Christine most likely say to the agent?

Christine _____

16-17

W First of all, I appreciate Alice for helping me. Without her quick and decent responses to my letters, I would not have decided to come to this country. And it was Alice who waited for me when I arrived at Nairobi Airport. She was always _____ to answer any questions or resolve my worries. In fact, _____ before coming here, especially being young at age 17 and being a female traveling alone. But I have had the best 5 weeks of my life! I really love working at this orphanage and _____ ___ my volunteering. It is so nice to spend time with children talking and playing together. I will definitely recommend this program to others. Now I'm so sorry that I must leave this country tomorrow. I'll remember you and your kindness forever. Thank you so much for this surprise party. _____ _____ to all my fantastic friends, too.

30^회 듣기 모의고사

1번부터 17번까지는 듣고 답하는 문제입니다. 1번부터 15번까지는 한 번만 들려주고, 16번부터 17번까지는 두 번 들려줍니다. 방송을 잘 듣고 답을 하시기 바랍니다.

01 대화를 듣고, 남자의 마지막 말에 대한 여자의 응답으로 가장 적절한 것을 고르시오.

① I think your choice couldn't be better.
② He shouldn't have given a penalty to you.
③ Can you tell me how to use a smart phone?
④ I'd rather turn off my phone during the class.
⑤ How about checking the Lost and Found center?

02 대화를 듣고, 여자의 마지막 말에 대한 남자의 응답으로 가장 적절한 것을 고르시오.

① I'll do my best to achieve my dream.
② You can make it. Now breathe deeply.
③ To my relief, I didn't make any mistakes.
④ Don't worry. Failure never discouraged me.
⑤ After this course, you can start to write lyrics.

03 다음을 듣고, 여자가 하는 말의 목적으로 가장 적절한 것을 고르시오.

① 동호회 가입을 권유하려고
② 국기의 소중함을 알리려고
③ 깃발의 중요성을 홍보하려고
④ 깃발 만드는 법을 알려주려고
⑤ 교육용 재료 구매를 촉진하려고

04 대화를 듣고, 남자의 의견으로 가장 적절한 것을 고르시오.

① 업무 효율을 높이기 위해 에어컨을 사용해야 한다.
② 공기 청정기를 사용하여 실내공기를 순환해야 한다.
③ 건강을 위해서는 에어컨 사용을 자제하는 것이 좋다.
④ 섭씨 28도 이하에서는 에어컨 작동을 자제해야 한다.
⑤ 너무 차가운 음료수를 마시는 것은 건강에 좋지 않다.

05 대화를 듣고, 두 사람의 관계를 가장 잘 나타낸 것을 고르시오.

① husband – wife
② nurse – doctor
③ teacher – parent
④ grandmother – grandson
⑤ baby sitter – baby's father

06 대화를 듣고, 그림에서 대화의 내용과 일치하지 않는 것을 고르시오.

07 대화를 듣고, 여자가 남자에게 부탁한 일로 가장 적절한 것을 고르시오.

① 저녁 함께 먹기
② 식당 추천해 주기
③ 데이트 주선해 주기
④ 서점에 데려다 주기
⑤ 데이트에 관한 조언해 주기

08 대화를 듣고, 남자가 전화를 걸려고 하는 이유를 고르시오.

① 회의 시간을 늦추려고
② 비행기 표를 바꾸려고
③ 회의 날짜를 바꾸려고
④ 출장 포기 사실을 전하려고
⑤ 어머니를 병세를 알아보려고

09 대화를 듣고, 남자가 지불할 총액을 고르시오. [3점]

① $14 ② $15 ③ $16
④ $17 ⑤ $18

10 대화를 듣고, 두 사람이 대화하고 있는 장소로 적절한 것을 고르시오.

① 사무실 ② 병원 ③ 도서관
④ 연주회장 ⑤ 세미나실

11 Holland Flowers Festival에 관한 다음 내용을 듣고, 일치하지 않는 것을 고르시오. [3점]

① 야외 정원에서 행해지는 행사이다.
② 운동과 관련된 주제가 정해졌다.
③ 2월에 행해지는 행사이다.
④ 오후부터 밤까지 개장한다.
⑤ 전화로 표를 구매할 수 있다.

12 다음 프로그램 표를 보면서 대화를 듣고, 여자가 선택할 강좌를 고르시오.

	MON	TUE	WED	THU	FRI
10:00 ~ 10:50	Jazz Dance	Yoga	Weight Training	Jazz Dance	④ Yoga
11:00 ~ 11:50	Yoga	Weight Training	Jazz Dance ①	Yoga	Jazz Dance
14:00 ~ 15:00	Squash	Swimming	Swimming ②	Swimming	Squash ⑤
17:00 ~ 18:00	Swimming	squash	Squash ③	Aerobics	Swimming

13 대화를 듣고, 남자의 마지막 말에 대한 여자의 응답으로 가장 적절한 것을 고르시오.

Woman : _____

① Well, you should be kinder to me.
② I think you should understand her.
③ Did he? That really makes me happy.
④ Oh, dear, I didn't know he lost his job.
⑤ Anyway, thanks for the wonderful meal.

14 대화를 듣고, 여자의 마지막 말에 대한 남자의 응답으로 가장 적절한 것을 고르시오. [3점]

Man : _____

① Don't worry. It will finish in an hour.
② But I hope you don't regret your choice.
③ How kind you are! I'll accept your offer now.
④ Oh, dear. I'm sorry you can't go to New York.
⑤ No, I won't. I'm happy to be with my wife.

15 다음 상황 설명을 듣고, Patty가 Derreck에게 할 말로 가장 적절한 것을 고르시오.

Patty : _____

① Cheer up. It's time to get back to your job.
② How about going on a trip to take a little rest?
③ I'm glad that you have overcome your difficulty.
④ Hurry up. You'll have another chance to get your wish.
⑤ I bet a car dealer would be the most suitable job for you.

[16-17] 다음을 듣고, 물음에 답하시오.

16 여자의 의견으로 가장 적절한 것은?

① 깨끗한 휴양지를 위한 관련 법령 제정이 시급하다.
② 담배꽁초를 버리지 않도록 적극적 간섭이 필요하다.
③ 담배꽁초를 버리는 일에 법적 제재가 가해져야 한다.
④ 휴양지와 같은 공공장소에서는 흡연을 금지해야 한다.
⑤ 흡연자를 위한 장소를 제공하는 것이 보다 합리적이다.

17 대화 직후 여자가 하게 될 일로 가장 적절한 것은?

① to persuade the man not to follow her
② to clean up the area she was sitting on
③ to organize a campaign for the environment
④ to ask the man to pick up what he threw away
⑤ to go to the young man and ask him not to smoke

DICTATION(받아쓰기) 코너입니다.
녹음의 내용을 잘 듣고, 빈칸에 알맞은 말을 쓰시기 바랍니다.

01

M   Mom, I won't take my cell phone to school anymore.

W   What happened? You're the last person to live without your phone.

M   To tell the truth, _____. My phone rang during the class.

W   _____

02

W   You look so nervous. Cheer up! You can do it well.

M   Thank you, Mom. But I'm afraid I'll forget the lyrics.

W   Don't worry, David. _____. This is only your first audition.

M   _____

03

W   Do you know what your state's flag means? Clubs and organizations also have flags _____. The Olympic flag, for example, features the five Olympic rings representing the coming together of people from five continents for competition. Each flag has a unique purpose and meaning. Now, in our club, you can learn the unique meaning of various flags and _____. Imagine making one for yourself and your family. Wouldn't it be exciting? Of course, children can join us, too. _____!

04

W   Oh, it's too hot. I'll turn on the air conditioner.

M   But it's only under 28° Celsius. We don't need to use the mechanical help.

W   I don't think so. _____ and hot. I can't stand this weather.

M   How about having a cool drink? And I'll open the window for you. It will help you feel better.

W   I can't understand you. The heat like this weather can make us ineffective during work.

M   But it's better for your health to circulate air _____ _____.

W   OK. But I'll turn on the air conditioner when I can't stand it anymore.

M   Thank you for accepting my opinion.

W   You seem _____.

M   No, I'm not. In fact, I am only concerned about your health, not something like saving money.

W   I see. Thanks.

05

W   Andrew, you look tired. Didn't you get a good night's sleep?

M   No. Peter _____ all night yesterday.

W   That's too bad. Did he cry a lot?

M   Yes. He kept crying, and I had to stay with him, soothing and patting him.

W   Oh, dear. But fortunately, he doesn't look sick now.

M   Really? I was worried last night because I thought he cried too much. He is sleeping now. _____!

W   Yes, he is. By the way, when will your wife come back?

M   Next Tuesday. When she comes back, I'll be relieved.

W   I understand. Hurry up, or you'll be late again.

M   It's already 8 o'clock. Please _____ Peter.

W   Don't worry. He is a nice boy, and he seems to like me.

M   Thank you. You remind me of my grandmother. She always _____. Oh, here is your pay for this week. I nearly forgot.

W   Thank you.

06

W What do you think of these?

M Did you draw all of these paintings in this room?

W Yes, of course. _____.

M They're fantastic! Could you explain what this one represents?

W The cup represents our hearts: they can hold many things and thoughts.

M I see. I like that painting next to the big window. That's a very interesting sunflower.

W Do you think so? I respect Van Gogh. So I imitated his painting.

M _____, but a little different. There's only one sunflower, so it shows your originality well.

W Thank you. How about this picture?

M _____. The woman with an umbrella in the rain attracts me.

W And look at this picture. I painted the scenery of Seorak Mountain. I like it very much.

M It's a very nice landscape.

07

M Hello, Monica.

W Hello, Ted. You look so neat and happy. Something good? Going somewhere?

M I _____. I'm going to meet Susan.

W Congratulations! You finally achieved your goal!

M Yes, but it was a little difficult.

W Where will you meet her?

M At Tasha's Garden. I heard it's a very beautiful and romantic place.

W I know the place. I _____, too. It's very nice.

M I'm worried about the date with Susan.

W Don't worry. You can succeed through your uniqueness. By the way, can you give me a ride to the bookstore which is next to the restaurant?

M Of course, I can. _____.

W Thanks a lot. I'm lucky to meet you here.

08

M Gena, I can't go to the meeting this Wednesday.

W Can't you? Why? I don't want to have the meeting without you.

M My mother is too sick, so I must take her to the hospital. I can't just let her go there by herself.

W You're right. But what about your _____ _____? You're going to San Diego on Wednesday evening.

M Did you know about my trip? In fact, I'm afraid I'll have to give it up because of my mother's illness.

W But it's the most important thing in your career. Am I right?

M Yes. It's a good chance _____ in this company, I know.

W How about trying to change the airline tickets?

M Well, it could be too late to do that, but I'll call the airport right now. _____.

W You're welcome. And if you can't get your ticket changed, let's think about another solution for this problem.

09

W Thank you for calling Queen's Pizza. May I help you?

M Yes. I'd like a potato pizza.

W _____?

M How much is the large one?

W $17. But if you order one, you can get an additional medium-sized one free.

M Well, what if I ordered a medium-sized pizza?

W In that case, you'd get spaghetti absolutely free. And the price would be $13.

M Then, I'll have a medium-sized potato pizza.

W How about a cola? A large one would be $2.

M _____ for a bottle of Coke.

W If you have a coupon, you can get a large Coke at 50% off.

M I see. Let me have a large Coke. You can deliver it to me at 137 New York Street.

W Thank you. We'll bring it to you _____.

10

W You're finally here, Bill. I've waited for you _____ _____.

M Sorry for being late. The seminar just finished.

W Anyway, I'm glad to see you again.

M Well, you look better today. _____? Comic books?

W Yes, they are. Aunt Polly brought them to me. They're so much fun.

M Wow! Alice reads comic books! I'm so surprised.

W Without these books, I couldn't stand my boring lives here.

M _____. How about going out? I'll help you.

W OK. But be careful of the others. They don't like noise.

M That woman looks quite sick. How miserable she must be!

W Right. Could you bring me the wheelchair from over there?

M OK.

11

W Welcome to Holland Flowers Festival. This year's Festival is set in the largest indoor flower garden in the world. _____ endlessly among the colorful flowers set in beautiful spring gardens and _____ at the fair. We made this year's Festival theme "TOP SPORT" because cultivating flowers is just as much an achievement as playing a sport _____. It opens at 1:00 pm and closes at 9:00 pm every day. Tickets can be bought online or by calling. From the 20th to the 24th of February, the Holland Flowers Festival will be brimming with ideas, inspiration, and creativity. Don't miss it!

12

M It's a fitness center program. Do you have time to learn anything?

W Yes, but only on Wednesdays and Fridays.

M Then, how about swimming? I know you are a good swimmer.

W I want to learn something I can't already do well.

M How about yoga? I think it would be good for your health.

W I'd like to, but _____ on Friday mornings.

M Then, you could learn jazz dance.

W But, I don't like to dance. Could I learn squash? I don't think I will learn something through weight training.

M Sure, you could. Jane is learning that, too.

W Really? Then, I will do that.

M By the way, you have French lessons on Wednesday evenings, don't you?

W Right, I do. But _____, and I can choose it.

13

M It's a wonderful day for a drive, isn't it?

W Yes. _____, Mike.

M Mom, it's nothing. I really wanted to take a drive with you.

W Wow! A "date" with my son.

M Mom, I know what you think. Don't worry about Andrew.

W Oh, did you know I was worrying?

M Yes, of course. Andrew told me his problems. Besides, _____, too.

W He worries about me? But his behavior toward me is still bad.

M Mom, Andrew knows he has a problem, and he's trying to correct it.

W He was a nice boy when he was young. I really love him as much as you. But he tells me that I always compare him to you.

M _____, Mom. Andrew told me that he would be a good son to you.

W _____

14

W It is my last day in this office.

M What are you talking about? _____?

W No, I'm serious. I quit this job.

M Why? You are one of the executives that the boss believes in firmly.

W I know, but I had to quit. _____.

M Because of your husband, Philip?

W Right. Philip was transferred to Boston, and we decided to move there together.

M Then, have you gotten another job in Boston?

W Yes, but I must begin as a mid-level manager.

M _____.

W But living a happy life together with my husband is the most important thing to me.

M _____

15

M Derreck wanted to quit his job as a car dealer. He _____ the job. In fact, he was interested in teaching, and his major was math education. So, he began looking for a new job. But _____ _____ a new job, so he decided to go back to being a car dealer again. Disappointed, he called his sister, Patty. After hanging up, Patty decided to find a way to help him. Patty asked her husband if he could find a job for Derreck _____.
Patty's husband was an English teacher, and he told her that his school was looking for a math teacher. Now, filled with hope, she called her brother, Derreck. In this situation, what would Patty most likely say to Derreck?

Patty _____

16-17

W I can't believe that I'm in _____ as this. It's wonderful!

M This beach is really famous for its beauty and cleanness.

W Right. I'm sure we can enjoy our vacation fully. Oh my God! Look at the guy.

M Oh, dear. The young man threw his lit cigarette onto the sand. _____!

W Why does he do that? Does he think someone walks behind him to clean up this area?

M He might think the world is his ashtray.

W As you know, I have never been one to deny anyone the right to smoke. But I can't stand that behavior. We have to do something.

M Right. And cigarette butts are not biodegradable.

W I'll go and tell him to pick up his cigarette butt right now.

M Wait a moment! He could be angry at you. In fact, if he is a nice guy, he will not do such a thing again.

W But I think it's my duty to make him do that. _____ _____.

1번부터 17번까지는 듣고 답하는 문제입니다. 1번부터 15번까지는 한 번만 들려주고, 16번부터 17번까지는 두 번 들려줍니다. 방송을 잘 듣고 답을 하시기 바랍니다.

01 대화를 듣고, 여자의 마지막 말에 대한 남자의 응답으로 가장 적절한 것을 고르시오.

① I'd like to get a loan for $500.
② It won't take that long, I guess.
③ No problem. Put it on this scale.
④ I can lend you some if you want.
⑤ Everything that's in this piggy bank.

02 대화를 듣고, 남자의 마지막 말에 대한 여자의 응답으로 가장 적절한 것을 고르시오.

① No, I've never heard about him.
② Yes, I have, but I was so young then.
③ Don't worry. I'm used to driving at night.
④ The night view at Nam San is much nicer.
⑤ Thanks for inviting me, but I'm afraid I can't go.

03 다음을 듣고, 여자가 하는 말의 목적으로 가장 적절한 것을 고르시오.

① TV 프로그램을 홍보하려고
② 방송국에 학생들을 초대하려고
③ 기자가 되는 방법을 설명하려고
④ 뉴스 방송 시청률을 파악하려고
⑤ 뉴스 경연 대회 참가를 독려하려고

04 대화를 듣고, 남자의 의견으로 가장 적절한 것을 고르시오.

① 정기 검진을 매년 받아야 한다.
② 경험은 인생을 풍족하게 해준다.
③ 두려움은 극복해야 할 대상이다.
④ 격언은 인생의 진리를 담고 있다.
⑤ 헌혈은 고귀한 인류애의 실천이다.

05 대화를 듣고, 두 사람의 관계를 가장 잘 나타낸 것을 고르시오.

① teacher – parent
② doctor – patient
③ director – actor
④ reporter – witness
⑤ attendant – customer

06 대화를 듣고, 그림에서 대화의 내용과 일치하지 <u>않는</u> 것을 고르시오.

07 대화를 듣고, 대화 후 남자가 할 일로 가장 적절한 것을 고르시오.

① 생일 선물 사기
② 케이크 구입하기
③ 아내 데리러 가기
④ 비디오 삼각대 설치하기
⑤ 비디오 작동법 설명하기

08 대화를 듣고, 남자가 전화를 건 목적으로 가장 적절한 것을 고르시오.

① 택시를 부르려고
② 불친절에 항의하려고
③ 투자 상담을 받으려고
④ 저축 계좌를 개설하려고
⑤ 휴대 전화를 돌려주려고

09 대화를 듣고, 현재 시각을 고르시오. [3점]

① about 3:30　　　② about 4:00
③ about 4:30　　　④ about 5:00
⑤ about 6:00

10 대화를 듣고, 여자가 권한 것이 <u>아닌</u> 것을 고르시오.

① 연고를 바를 것
② 마사지를 받을 것
③ 앞으로 숙이지 말 것
④ 휴식을 자주 취할 것
⑤ 등 받침대를 사용할 것

11 Sharon Rose에 관한 다음 내용을 듣고, 일치하는 것을 고르시오. [3점]

① 어제 열린 달걀 많이 먹기 대회에서 우승하지 못했다.
② 이번 대회에서 그녀는 자신의 이전 기록을 경신하였다.
③ 이번 대회에서 처음으로 50개 이상의 달걀을 먹어치웠다.
④ 2년 전에 자신의 세계 기록이 깨지는 것을 목격하였다.
⑤ 자신의 기록에 실망하여 앞으로 대회에 나가지 않기로 했다.

12 대화를 듣고, 두 사람이 대여하기로 한 비디오를 고르시오.

① Bed of Roses　　② One Fine Day
③ Spy Game　　　④ Fight Club
⑤ Meet Joe Black

13 대화를 듣고, 남자의 마지막 말에 대한 여자의 응답으로 가장 적절한 것을 고르시오.

Woman : _____

① I'm sorry to keep you waiting.
② Don't forget to bring your receipt.
③ I'll keep that in mind. Thanks a lot.
④ Excuse me? I told you it wasn't my fault.
⑤ I think designs are as important as functions.

14 대화를 듣고, 여자의 마지막 말에 대한 남자의 응답으로 가장 적절한 것을 고르시오. [3점]

Man : _____

① Of course. I do like cold weather.
② Wow, it was a really fantastic concert.
③ Don't you know I am a big hip-hop fan?
④ Let me check the weekend schedule first.
⑤ Really? That's amazing! What's his name?

15 다음 상황 설명을 듣고, Peter가 Sally에게 할 말로 가장 적절한 것을 고르시오.

Peter : _____

① I'm sorry, but I'm full enough.
② It's been years since we last saw each other.
③ I know a cafe around here. Let's go and talk.
④ I wonder if you still have pets, dogs and cats.
⑤ Isn't it difficult to keep all your pets at home?

[16-17] 다음을 듣고, 물음에 답하시오.

16 남자가 하는 말의 목적으로 가장 적절한 것은?

① 박물관 운영 기금을 모금하려고
② 박물관의 교육 효과를 홍보하려고
③ 박물관의 시설 개선을 촉구하려고
④ 박물관 방문시의 주의 사항을 안내하려고
⑤ 박물관에 대한 정부 지원 필요성을 알리려고

17 목적을 달성하지 못할 경우 가장 우려되는 사항으로 남자가 지적한 것은?

① 관광 수입의 감소
② 국가 정체성의 약화
③ 국가 유물의 손상 우려
④ 교육, 문화적 기회의 불균형
⑤ 문화유산에 대한 자긍심 감소

31회 DICTATION

01

W May I help you?

M Yes. I want to _____ in my savings account.

W How much do you want to deposit?

M _____

02

M Look at this view! _____?

W Yeah. This is the greatest night view I've ever seen.

M You have been here before, haven't you?

W _____

03

W The Young Persons News Award is open to all students between 12 and 15 years old. We are looking for your comments, suggestions, analyses, and criticism of all news broadcasts. _____ _____, we want to know how we can make news broadcasts more interesting for young people. Please _____ as entries to the competition. As part of the prizes, you will be given a chance to produce your own news broadcast and to spend a day with news journalists. _____ is December 20th. So send your entries to us.

04

W I am sorry, but _____ this.

M Rachel. We've talked about it several times.

W Yes, yes. But I can't stand the thought of having a needle injection.

M It won't take long. Besides, _____.

W You know I almost fainted in my high school days when I had to take my blood test.

M That's a long time ago.

W I know, but it feels as if it happened yesterday. It's still bothering me a lot.

M That's just a fear, and a fear should be overcome.

W It's not so easy as you say.

M At least you should try. Everybody has their own fears, but _____ them.

W All right, but promise me you're going to be with me through the whole procedure.

M I promise. I'm sure you can do it.

05

W Sorry to have kept you waiting.

M That's okay. At least it's here now.

W We are really busy on Friday evening.

M I understand. I saw _____. Are you okay? You almost dropped your tray.

W I'm okay. Thanks.

M It looks like your job requires careful attention to children since not all parents keep their kids _____ _____.

W Kind of, but I guess that's part of the job.

M Well, I'd never put up with that kind of behavior from my kids, especially in public places like movie theaters, department stores, and hospitals.

W Good for you. Actually, kids need to learn _____ _____. Sorry but enjoy your meal. I have lots of orders to deal with.

M Oh, I'm sorry. I've been keeping you.

06

W Is this the picture you took on the company field day?

M Yes. It came out pretty well, didn't it?

W Yes, it did. Is that you with a towel in your hand in the rear?

M Yes. The picture was taken after the tug-of-war, and I _____ .

W Oh, I see. Who's Sammy? Does he still run to work?

M Yes. He has crew-cut hair. He is sitting in the first row with a wrist band on his right hand.

W _____ . Who's the lady sitting next to you in the office? You said she always calls her boyfriend at work.

M She's Grace. She's sitting in the first row with big square earrings.

W Wow! _____ . Who is Tina, your tennis partner?

M She's standing next to me. She always wears a headband.

W Your boss must be sitting in the middle of the front row with glasses.

M You're right.

07

W Hi, Dad. I'm home. Is Mom home?

M No, she went to the gym.

W Whew! Did you record a birthday message?

M Not yet. By the way, did you get cake and candles?

W Dad, you know _____ . Look at this cake with 42 candles.

M Good! Here's the video camera. Can you get the video tripod from upstairs?

W Okay, Dad. (pause) Here you go. How does the camera work?

M Just press this button and slide the cassette in. _____ you rewind the video cassette to the very beginning.

W Where's the rewind button? Oh, I see it.

M When you want to start recording, press "record." But not now. I need to fix the camera onto the tripod first. _____ .

08

(Telephone rings.)

W Hello. This is First Bank. How may I help you?

M Hello, could you connect me to Susan, please?

W Just a moment. I'm sorry, _____ . Would you like to hold, or should I ask her to call you back?

M Ask her to call me back. My phone number is 734-9925.

W All right. Well, was there any problem with a money transfer?

M No. I don't _____ with your bank.

W Then, wasn't she kind enough to you when she was consulting?

M No, not at all. Actually, I know nothing about Susan, and I can't remember what she looks like. I didn't know she works there.

M Oh, I see. Then can I ask you what it's about?

W Sure. I'm a taxi driver, and she left her cell phone in my taxi, and I found it.

W Oh, _____ . I'll have her call you as soon as possible.

09

(Telephone rings.)

M Hello.

W Hi, Toby. It's Sara. Would you like to come to my house this evening? I have a new computer.

M Really? You finally got it.

W Yes. Come _____ . I really want to play a computer game with you.

M All right. I'll be able to leave in 30 minutes.

W Great! Will you pick up Tim _____ ? He's at home.

M Pick up Tim? Why?

W He's on crutches, but he said he's itching to play computer games.

M All right.

W _____ ?

M It takes about thirty minutes from here to Tim's home by bicycle. And thirty minutes to your house from there.

W Then you will be here around six. I'll prepare dinner so that we can enjoy the whole evening.

M Good idea. See you then.

10

M Excuse me. Can you help me?

W Certainly.

M I wonder if you have anything for backaches.

W This ointment is very good.

M I've used that. It didn't really help. I sit at the computer about ten hours a day. I think that's the problem.

W _____ this back-support cushion? It might help.

M All right. I will give it a try. And are there any special instructions?

W Yes, there are. Try not to lean forward when you work with your computer. And _____ to stretch your muscles.

M Okay. _____ . Thanks.

11

W There was an Egg-eating Contest at the River Place Shopping Mall yesterday. Sharon Rose, a pharmacist, failed in her attempt to become the premier egg eater although she won the contest. It was her second attempt _____ . In a contest two months before, she had succeeded in eating as many as 51 eggs in an hour. This time she ate 53 hard-boiled eggs. But it was three eggs _____ Sam Wilson's world record. Two years before, Sam had managed to down 55 eggs in a contest. Sharon seemed obviously disappointed. But she said she'll challenge the world record again in another contest in two months.

12

M Haven't you decided on a video yet? How about one of these two: *Bed of Roses* and *One Fine Day*?

W No, they are old movies, and Brad Pitt is not in them. Besides, _____ .

M Let me see. *Spy Game*? Does it have to be a Brad Pitt movie?

W You said I could choose, and I want to see something with Brad Pitt.

M _____ Brad Pitt, but I heard that it is a little boring.

W Then what about *Fight Club*?

M No way! That's an action movie. You know I don't like action. Wait a minute. Here's a Brad Pitt movie I haven't seen: *Meet Joe Black*.

W I'm not so sure about that one, but I've heard it's really long. Look! It's two hours and thirty minutes.

M Really? Then we can't watch the whole story. Well, let's decide on what you chose first. I hope it's not too boring.

W It's not. I know Brad Pitt. Let's check it out.

13

W Can I help you, sir?

M Yes, I bought this watch here last week, and I've been having some problems with it.

W What seems to be the trouble?

M Well, the salesperson said it was waterproof, but when I wore it in the swimming pool, _____ _____ .

W Let me see. Oh, yes. We have had some problems with this brand. Would you like me to replace it with a similar model?

M Actually, I'd rather have my money back.

W Of course, you would. We can do that for you. ___ _____ ?

M Yes, here it is

W Thank you.

M You know, I think you should check what you sell more carefully.

W _____

14

W _____ tonight.

M Yeah, it is. But actually, I kind of like cold weather.

W Do you? But I don't like cold weather. By the way, there are a lot of people out in the concert tonight in this weather.

M Yeah, _____ on weekends.

W Do you come here a lot?

M Yeah, I do, actually.

W So you are a big hip-hop fan, right?

M Yeah, I am. Are you?

W Actually, no, but my brother's in the band tonight. ___ _____ to the concert.

M _____

15

M On his way out of a restaurant, Peter _____ _____, Sally. They graduated from the same high school and had lived next door to each other, when Peter finally got married and moved out of the neighborhood. Peter hadn't seen her in ages, so he thought they needed to _____ _____. He wondered if she still had her pets of every kind, and whether her husband still worked abroad. So he _____ her to go to a cafe nearby and talk more about each other over coffee. In this situation, what would Peter most likely say to Sally?

Peter _____

16-17

M Today, let's talk about the situation of our museums. We know museums are expensive to run, with the costs of special exhibitions, maintenance, staff salaries, and so on. Despite all these costs, museums should be _____ because museums preserve and display our artistic, social, scientific and political heritage. They also offer educational opportunities to people of every age. If museums are not funded sufficiently by the government, they _____ charge for entry, and this will inevitably deny many potential visitors access, and especially the poor and those whose educational and cultural opportunities have already been limited _____ their rights to learn. Complete access is essential to provide the freedom of cultural and educational opportunity. The government should _____ that visitors to the museums in Seattle declined by 15% after it started charging for admission.

32^회 듣기 모의고사

1번부터 17번까지는 듣고 답하는 문제입니다. 1번부터 15번까지는 한 번만 들려주고, 16번부터 17번까지는 두 번 들려줍니다. 방송을 잘 듣고 답을 하시기 바랍니다.

01 대화를 듣고, 여자의 마지막 말에 대한 남자의 응답으로 가장 적절한 것을 고르시오.

① I'm flattered. Thanks, anyway.
② Let me try on that dress, please.
③ There is a fitting room over there.
④ You know, actions speak louder than words.
⑤ No, really. You look very beautiful in that dress.

02 대화를 듣고, 남자의 마지막 말에 대한 여자의 응답으로 가장 적절한 것을 고르시오.

① Don't worry. I'll be a good mother.
② I'm eight and a half months pregnant.
③ Well, I didn't want to find out beforehand.
④ Actually, I don't care as long as it's healthy.
⑤ It was horrible. Every morning I felt nauseous.

03 다음을 듣고, 남자가 하는 말의 목적으로 가장 적절한 것을 고르시오.

① 시 발전 후원금의 사용 내역을 알리려고
② 다음 후원회의 개최일과 장소를 공고하려고
③ 후원회 사무실의 변경된 연락처를 공고하려고
④ 시를 홍보할 배너에 새겨 넣을 문양을 설명하려고
⑤ 시의 기념 배너에 후원하는 마지막 기회를 알리려고

04 대화를 듣고, 두 사람이 하는 말의 주제로 가장 적절한 것을 고르시오.

① 남녀공학의 장점
② 스포츠 활동과 성적
③ 남녀 고교생의 성적 차
④ 고교생의 학업 성취도 향상
⑤ 교사가 성적에 미치는 영향

05 대화를 듣고, 두 사람의 관계를 가장 잘 나타낸 것을 고르시오.

① fan – athlete
② player – coach
③ donor – recipient
④ viewer – performer
⑤ reporter – charity collector

06 대화를 듣고, 그림에서 대화의 내용과 일치하지 <u>않는</u> 것을 고르시오.

07 대화를 듣고, 여자가 남자를 위해 할 일로 가장 적절한 것을 고르시오.

① 상장 수령하기
② 신청서 보내주기
③ 비행기 예약하기
④ 여행 일정 조정하기
⑤ 받게 될 상품 알아보기

08 대화를 듣고, 여자가 늦은 이유를 고르시오.

① 택시를 못 잡아서
② 출퇴근 교통 체증 때문에
③ 지하철 운행이 중단되어서
④ 주차할 장소를 찾지 못해서
⑤ 사고 구경에 차량들이 서행해서

09 대화를 듣고, 두 사람이 내일 만나기로 한 시간을 고르시오. [3점]

① 10:00 am   ② 10:30 am   ③ 11:00 am
④ 7:00 pm   ⑤ 7:30 pm

10 대화를 듣고, 좋은 출판업자가 되기 위한 조건으로 남자가 언급하지 않은 것을 고르시오.

① 근면성   ② 참을성   ③ 친화력
④ 집중력   ⑤ 과감성

11 asthma에 관한 다음 내용을 듣고, 일치하지 않는 것을 고르시오. [3점]

① 숨을 쉬는 통로가 좁아져서 생기는 병이다.
② 걸리면 폐에 드나드는 공기의 양이 줄어든다.
③ 어린이들에게 가장 흔한 만성적인 질병이다.
④ 경제적 빈부의 차에 의해 발병되는 경향이 있다.
⑤ 세계적으로 10년마다 평균 50%씩 증가한다.

12 다음 일정표를 보면서 대화를 듣고, 두 사람이 역사 보고서를 위해 만나기로 한 요일을 고르시오.

Weekly Schedule		
	SUN	- to buy presents for parents
①	MON	- to clean the house
②	TUE	
③	WED	- to go grocery shopping - to make dinner
④	THU	- to pick up Uncle
⑤	FRI	- a part-time job
	SAT	

13 대화를 듣고, 여자의 마지막 말에 대한 남자의 응답으로 가장 적절한 것을 고르시오.

Man : _____

① I think I have to ask my boss for days off.
② I'm going to participate in another contest.
③ I guess you and Dad will have a good time there.
④ Don't ask me. It was you who wanted to go there.
⑤ I am going to work for him so he can go to Egypt.

14 대화를 듣고, 남자의 마지막 말에 대한 여자의 응답으로 가장 적절한 것을 고르시오. [3점]

Woman : _____

① Sorry. You got the wrong person.
② Yes, she was suspected of stealing money.
③ I don't think so. She wouldn't commit suicide.
④ Of course. It was filled with suspense and thrills.
⑤ Yes, she was seen arguing with her neighbor last night.

15 다음 상황 설명을 듣고, Dave가 아내에게 할 말로 가장 적절한 것을 고르시오.

Dave : Honey, _____

① don't be surprised. I'll be there tomorrow.
② what kind of present should I get for Sue?
③ it's already been a week since we were here.
④ can you tell her to call me when she wakes up?
⑤ how's the conference going? It's almost over, isn't it?

[16-17] 다음을 듣고, 물음에 답하시오.

16 여자가 하는 말은 무엇에 관한 내용인가?

① In-flight announcement
② Pre-landing announcement
③ Post-landing announcement
④ Pre-departure announcement
⑤ Post-departure announcement

17 여자가 하는 말과 일치하지 않는 것은?

① 비행기의 최종 목적지는 London이다.
② 도착지까지 비행시간은 10시간 30분이 될 것이다.
③ 이륙 전에 모든 전자 제품의 전원을 꺼야 한다.
④ 좌석 등받이와 테이블은 제자리로 해야 한다.
⑤ 안전벨트 사인에 불이 꺼지면 휴대 전화 사용이 가능하다.

DICTATION(받아쓰기) 코너입니다.
녹음의 내용을 잘 듣고, 빈칸에 알맞은 말을 쓰시기 바랍니다.

01

W What do you think of this dress?
M Wow, it looks great! _____!
W Oh, come on. I know you're just saying that.
M _____

02

M You'll be a mother soon. Congratulations!
W Thanks. I can't still believe that I'm going to be a mom.
M You will. _____, a boy or a girl?
W _____

03

M We have announced the last opportunity to sponsor a banner celebrating our town's 200th birthday. With 185 banners installed _____, some individuals have been calling to ask if banners could be still ordered. Yes, we have 15 banners to be installed. You have to _____ by December 31st. The banners will remain up until Dec. 31 next year. The sponsorship fee is $250, and you may include business or family information on the two-sided street banner. _____ by emailing Pazda at pazda@banner.com. For additional information, you may contact Sharon Barker at 759-6188.

04

W What an interesting article it is!
M What is it about?
W It's about high school girls and boys, and their grades.
M _____?
W Girls are getting better grades than boys. And the grade gap between girls and boys is getting bigger.
M I'm a little bit worried about the present situation, but it comes as no surprise. _____ grades, I've never beaten you. By the way, there must be some reasons.
W Some say boys are more interested in sports activities.
M _____. You know, I spend weekends playing football.
W And some say girls are favored by teachers.
M Well, I don't believe it. _____, do you?

05

M _____. A word for the people waiting here.
W Thanks. We're really happy to have made it.
M Great. What was it like riding bicycles across America?
W Well, some of the time it was great, some of the time it was just plain hard work, and some of the time it was really scary.
M Any idea how much money you raised for the Food Aid for Africa campaign?
W _____. About $1 million, we think. That's more than we expected when we decided to collect money while travelling on bicycles.
M That's incredible. Congratulations! What are you going to do now?
W Chuck's going to have _____ immediately, and I'm going to sleep at least two days.
M You must be very tired. Please say something for the _____.
W Thank you for your encouragement and constant support.

06

M What a wonderful day to walk in the park!

W Yes, _____. It's so peaceful.

M That elderly couple on the bench looks very relaxed.

W Yes, they look happy. Two boys are playing baseball next to the tree.

M I envy them. It reminds me of playing Frisbee with my brother. It was real fun.

W Can you see the boy playing with his dog to the other side of the tree?

M Yes, they seem to be _____.

W So do those three girls behind the elderly couple. They are skipping merrily.

M Oh, yes. Look at the baby trying to walk in front of the tree. He is so lovely.

W _____!

M I really like this place. Let's come here often.

W Okay. I'm pleased to be living next to this beautiful park.

07

W How are you doing, Richard?

M Hi, Lynn. I feel great!

W I can see that. _____.

M I have every reason to be happy.

W Do you? What happened to you?

M I just found out that _____ in a contest I entered.

W Really? That's fantastic. So, what did you win?

M I don't know yet. I have to call this number to find out what I won.

W Why don't you do that right away? I'm curious. Maybe we can go to Hawaii on vacation.

M Well, as you can see, I'm too nervous to make the call.

W If so, I'll do that for you. _____.

M Thank you.

08

M Hey! Over here!

W Hi! I'm coming. I'm sorry to have _____.

M That's okay.

W Actually, there was a pile-up accident in the opposite lane on the expressway. Tow trucks, ambulances, and police cars. _____.

M Cars and buses must have driven slowly to see what had happened.

W Exactly. We humans are always curious.

M Yeah. Let me carry your bags. Wow! They are heavier than they look.

W That's why I asked you to pick me up. And I have one more reason to thank you.

M I wonder what it'll be.

W Otherwise, I should take a taxi. You know, the subway stops running after midnight.

M That's it? Forget it. You must be tired. _____ _____.

W All right. Where is your car?

M It's in the parking lot, waiting for its owner.

09

M I just feel like seeing a movie tomorrow. What do you say?

W Yeah. Actually, I've been wanting to see the new Tom Cruise movie.

M Me, too. _____. I'll see when it's playing. Sorry, my connection is a bit slow.

W Okay. Take your time.

M Here it is. It says that there are six shows a day. The first one is at 11 o'clock, and the last one is at 8 o'clock. The 8:00 showing should be all right. How does that sound to you?

W I'm having dinner with my sister, but I'll be able to make it home by about 7.

M Great. _____ at 7:30. Oh, wait a minute. The 8:00 show is all sold out.

W Well, that's just our luck.

M Hey, what about the 11:00 showing? We can have a nice lunch afterwards.

W That sounds like _____.

M Then why don't I pick you up thirty minutes before? It's about 20 minutes to the movie theater from your house.

W All right. See you then.

10

W _____?

M I'm a publisher.

W Really? Being a publisher must be very interesting.

M Well, yes, it can be, although it involves a lot of hard work. That means you have to be diligent.

W I see. What else is needed to be a good publisher?

M You need to _____.

W And I imagine you have to work well in a team.

M Oh, yes. That's certainly true. And you have to be patient as well.

W I am poor at staying patient, especially when I'm dealing with problems!

M It takes a long time to learn _____ problems at work. And above all, you have to be able to concentrate for long periods of time.

W Oh, I'm terrible at that. I just can't concentrate at all.

11

W Asthma is a disorder that causes breathing passages to narrow. This _____ entering and leaving the lungs, causing difficulty in breathing. The World Health Organization (WHO) says that asthma affects about two hundred million people worldwide. It is the most common chronic disease among children. The disease affects people _____ _____ and does not discriminate in terms of social or economic status. Asthma affects not only millions of individuals, but families and economies alike. The yearly economic cost of the disorder is said to be close to $20 billion. The WHO warns that asthma _____ worldwide by an average of fifty percent every ten years.

12

W Rich, where have you been?

M What do you mean?

W I've been trying to contact you _____, but you didn't answer the phone.

M Oh, I had my mobile phone fixed, and I got it back today. So, what's up?

W We need to talk about our group report on history. Can we get together today?

M Not today. Actually, my sister and I've been quite busy preparing for our parents' twentieth wedding anniversary.

W Oh, really? _____?

M We bought presents for our parents and cleaned the house. And today, we have to go grocery shopping and make a nice dinner for them.

W What about tomorrow or the day after tomorrow?

M Tomorrow, I have to pick up my uncle, but ____ _____. I have a part-time job the day after tomorrow.

W Well, tomorrow looks more convenient for you.

13

M Mom, I got two plane tickets to Egypt in a website contest, and I can't decide which friend to take.

W Why don't you take Morris? He's your best friend.

M Sure, but the problem is that the ticket is only good for next month. He is taking his law degree final next month, so he can't go.

W Well, there is always Kevin. You like _____ _____.

M He's been to Egypt twice already. So I don't think he would be interested in going again.

W Why not take Sam? He is always there for you whenever you have a problem.

M I'd love to, but he got a new job, and now it's not possible for him to take a few days off.

W So, _____ do with the tickets?

M _____

14

M So, when do you suppose the victim died?

W Judging by the woman's body temperature, I'd say she was murdered around midnight.

M Do you think this is the room _____ _____ ?

W It appears that she was killed in the kitchen and then dragged into the bedroom.

M Have you been able to _____ yet?

W Looks like she was struck on the head with a heavy object. We found a baseball bat and sent it to the lab to see if it was used in the murder.

M Very good. And who _____ ?

W It was reported by the maid when she came to work this morning at 8:00.

M Do you have any suspects?

W _____

15

M Dave _____ . It's already a week since he left his home. Tomorrow afternoon, after a seven-day conference, Dave will be on a flight to California, where his wife and his daughter, Sue, live. He _____ to ask Sue what she likes to get as a present. And his wife answers. After talking to her for a while, he asks if he can talk to Sue. But his wife says that Sue is sound asleep. Dave _____ his wife what Sue wants to have. In this situation, what would Dave most likely say to his wife?

Dave Honey, _____

16-17

W Good afternoon, ladies and gentlemen. We would like to welcome you on board Han Guk Airlines flight KE 070 _____. This is Ann Jackson, your cabin services manager for this flight. Today's flight time will be 10 hours and 30 minutes following take-off. All personal electronic devices must be switched off for take-off. If you wish to use a device that has a flight safety mode, please make sure you can use it _____ for departure. You may then use your device when the fasten seat belts sign goes out. Before our departure, please make sure to _____ and that your seat back is in the upright position and seat tables are stowed away. The use of portable phones and all electronic devices is prohibited at all times throughout the flight. Your cooperation would be much appreciated. If there is anything we can do for you, please let me or any of _____. We wish you a pleasant flight. Thank you.

33^회 **듣기 모의고사**

1번부터 17번까지는 듣고 답하는 문제입니다. 1번부터 15번까지는 한 번만 들려주고, 16번부터 17번까지는 두 번 들려줍니다. 방송을 잘 듣고 답을 하시기 바랍니다.

01 대화를 듣고, 여자의 마지막 말에 대한 남자의 응답으로 가장 적절한 것을 고르시오.

① Now I remember where I put it.
② Let's keep in touch with each other.
③ Wow, that password is too complicated.
④ You should make it longer and unusual.
⑤ Make sure to keep this between you and me.

02 대화를 듣고, 남자의 마지막 말에 대한 여자의 응답으로 가장 적절한 것을 고르시오.

① The pain will go away in a week.
② I often wear the shirt you gave me.
③ I'm sure it produces no side effects.
④ Every three hours, until the pain stops.
⑤ Don't open it unless you're ready to use it.

03 다음을 듣고, 여자가 하는 말의 목적으로 가장 적절한 것을 고르시오.

① to promote health-related programs in school
② to ask for establishment of vending machines
③ to appreciate making more school programs
④ to praise reduction of school sports programs
⑤ to apologize for not offering much hospitality

04 대화를 듣고, 여자의 의견으로 가장 적절한 것을 고르시오.

① 자동 점등 장치를 설치하여야 한다.
② 친구와의 여행은 관계를 돈독히 해준다.
③ 정기적 배달 구입은 저렴한 소비 형태이다.
④ 범죄 예방을 위한 순찰활동의 강화가 필요하다.
⑤ 집을 장기간 비울 때는 배달을 중지시켜야 한다.

05 대화를 듣고, 두 사람의 관계를 가장 잘 나타낸 것을 고르시오.

① coach – player
② director – agent
③ lawyer – witness
④ policeman – reporter
⑤ customer – hair dresser

06 대화를 듣고, 그림에서 대화의 내용과 일치하지 <u>않는</u> 것을 고르시오.

07 대화를 듣고, 여자가 남자에게 부탁한 일로 가장 적절한 것을 고르시오.

① to let her use his car
② to nail picture frames
③ to spend some time with her
④ to give her a ride to the airport
⑤ to pick her up at the shopping mall

08 대화를 듣고, 남자가 전화를 건 이유를 고르시오.

① 파티에 사용할 꽃을 주문하려고
② 꽃가게의 주소를 물어보려고
③ 주문한 꽃이 배달되지 않아서
④ 꽃 배달원의 불친절을 신고하려고
⑤ 꽃을 배달할 주소를 가르쳐 주려고

09 대화를 듣고, 여자가 지불한 금액을 고르시오. [3점]

① $90   ② $100   ③ $120
④ $130   ⑤ $150

10 대화를 듣고, 남자가 오늘 한 일이 아닌 것을 고르시오.

① 물건 구입하기   ② 담임 면담하기
③ 양복 맡기기   ④ 결혼식 참석하기
⑤ 세탁기 수리 의뢰하기

11 Teddy Bear Museum에 관한 다음 내용을 듣고, 일치하지 않는 것을 고르시오. [3점]

① 2001년 4월에 처음으로 개관하였다.
② 갤러리는 역사관과 예술관으로 나누어져 있다.
③ 음식과 음료를 박물관에 가지고 들어갈 수 없다.
④ 국경일을 제외하고 연중무휴로 개관한다.
⑤ 다양한 기념품을 구입할 수 있는 곳이 있다.

12 다음 공원 안내표를 보면서 대화를 듣고, 두 사람이 지금 관람할 수 있는 것을 고르시오.

Enjoy Yourself at Our Amusement Park

	Attractions	Times (pm)
①	Fashion Show	12:00 ~ 1:00
		3:00 ~ 4:00
②	Bird Show	12:30 ~ 2:00
③	Train Ride	3:30 ~ 3:30
	Snow Festival	4:30 ~ 5:00
④	Moonlight Parade	6:30 ~ 7:00
⑤	Dream in the Sea	7:10 ~ 7:30

13 대화를 듣고, 남자의 마지막 말에 대한 여자의 응답으로 가장 적절한 것을 고르시오.

Woman : _____

① Wait a minute! It won't last long.
② No problem. I will get it done in no time.
③ Well, my laptop computer is still charged.
④ No. It's inconvenient to go without electricity.
⑤ Yeah, I agree. Candlelights can make a romantic atmosphere.

14 대화를 듣고, 여자의 마지막 말에 대한 남자의 응답으로 가장 적절한 것을 고르시오. [3점]

Man : _____

① Yes, I used to wander outside.
② I changed the job a long time ago.
③ I'm really into Latin dance now.
④ Sure. It's really fun to walk pets.
⑤ I still have it. It's such a beautiful house.

15 다음 상황 설명을 듣고, Pena 부인이 경찰관에게 할 말로 가장 적절한 것을 고르시오.

Ms. Pena : _____

① I don't think I opened an account here.
② I haven't seen him since I was at the airport.
③ Sorry, but I have nothing to say at the moment.
④ No. There was no record of withdrawal or transfer.
⑤ Did I do anything wrong? I wasn't speeding, was I?

[16-17] 다음을 듣고, 물음에 답하시오.

16 여자가 전화를 건 목적으로 가장 적절한 것은?

① 현재 시청중인 프로그램을 파악하려고
② TV 시청 습관에 대해 설문 조사를 하려고
③ 자사 프로그램에 대한 만족도를 알아보려고
④ 뉴스 프로그램 평균 시청 시간을 문의하려고
⑤ 중간 광고에 대한 시청자의 반응을 확인하려고

17 여자가 질문한 사항이 아닌 것은?

① 연령   ② 직업
③ 자녀   ④ 선호 프로그램
⑤ 하루 TV 시청 시간

DICTATION(받아쓰기) 코너입니다.
녹음의 내용을 잘 듣고, 빈칸에 알맞은 말을 쓰기기 바랍니다.

01

W I think a hacker _____ my computer files!

M What kind of password do you use?

W I keep my password short and _____.

M _____

02

M I need something for my sunburn.

W _____. It'll help relieve the pain.

M How often do I put this on?

W _____

03

W At a time when sports and other extracurricular activities are being cut from schools, solely _____ _____ is nothing but a temporary measure. I understand how soda helps worsen the problems of obesity and diabetes. But we must not forget that physical education and sports programs, which also prevent obesity and diabetes, are being trimmed from school budgets every year. I _____ _____ to expel vending machines from school. And I suggest that those efforts be extended to highlight the importance of the programs essential for health.

04

W Hi, Jonathan. Is your house okay?

M My house? What do you mean?

W Didn't you hear? The neighborhood is having trouble with some sneaky thieves recently.

M Really? We should be careful. Well, I'll be away from home for a week because _____ with my friends this Friday.

W For a week? That's too long. You should definitely hold the newspaper delivery.

M Thank you for the tip.

W Don't you get milk or anything like that delivered to your house?

M Yes. Milk is delivered every other day.

W _____, too.

M All right. Maybe I'll call the post office and ask them to hold all the mail for a week.

W That's a very important point. If anything is left untouched long enough at your doorstep, your house might be the target of thieves.

M _____.

05

M Sydney, I need three actors.

W If the actors you need are here in town, I'll get them for you right away.

M I'm not looking for big stars, just three regular actors who each _____.

W Three regular actors, huh? Okay. Just tell me what you need.

M First, we need two men. The first one should be young, and the second one should be middle-aged.

W Young and middle-aged. Got it. Can you give me a _____?

M For the first one, we're looking for someone who's average height and build with brown hair.

W And for the second one?

M Short and heavyset with brown hair.

W Okay. The third one must be a woman?

M Yes. She has to be European-American blonde, rather young, tall, and thin.

W All right. _____ right away.

06

M Maybe we'll be late. _____. Where is Mr. Jackson?

W I don't know. Oh, wait, there he is, by the gate speaking to the security guard.

M I wonder _____.

W Where are Jack and Jill?

M I haven't seen them for a while. Didn't Jack say he needed motion sickness tablets for the flight?

W Did he? Oh, they are in the drugstore.

M We don't have much time, and there are many people lining up now. We should line up, too.

W Wait, what about Margaret?

M Oh, I forgot about her. She said she had to send an email to her parents. She and Michael are using the computer over there.

W Let's gather everyone together and _____.

07

W Good afternoon, Eric.

M Hi, Cindy. What brings you here?

W I am here to see you. _____.

M Yes. I just finished nailing some picture frames. What hard work!

W Oh, I see. Listen. _____?

M Just let me hear it first. What is it?

W I've been wondering if I can use your car.

M Use my car? You mean now?

W Yes. I have to pick up my grandma at the airport. She is expected to arrive at 3:30.

M Can you return it by 5:30? I have to drive my mom to the shopping mall.

W Sure. It just _____ to get to the airport.

08

(Telephone rings.)

W Good afternoon, you're through to Flower Station. How may I help you?

M I ordered a bouquet of flowers yesterday, but they haven't arrived yet.

W _____. Do you have an order number?

M Yes, it's FS2315G.

W Oh, Mr. Smith. Let me check with the delivery man. Can you hold for a moment?

M Sure. (pause)

W I've spoken to the delivery man and he tells me that when he got to the address, no one was there.

M Did you get my address right?

W Maybe we didn't get the correct address. I remember the connection was pretty bad yesterday. Can you confirm it for me, please?

M It's 43, 22nd Avenue, New York.

W I'm sorry _____. We have 23rd Avenue on our system.

M That is not acceptable. You should have confirmed the delivery address. What are you going to do to fix this?

W I'm sorry. _____. I'll have the flowers delivered right now.

09

W You did a great job.

M I am really glad you like it.

W Here's a $100 bill. _____. It's for your fine work.

M Excuse me, ma'am?

W Yes? Something wrong?

M I am afraid I don't get what I deserve.

W _____? Isn't it $50 for wallpapering and $40 for painting?

M Yes, that's right. But you forgot about wallpaper.

W Oh, I am sorry. _____! How much is that?

M It is $30.

W I see. Wait a minute! Here's another $30.

10

W Hi, honey.

M So, how was your day? You look a little tired.

W Yeah. I was so busy I didn't have time for lunch. By the way, did you _____?

M Yes, I did. I bought everything on your list.

W Oh, thank you. Did you pick up Ben from school today and talk with his teacher?

M Yes, I did. His teacher said he is doing quite well.

W And did you remember _____ at the dry cleaners today? My sister's wedding is this Saturday, you know.

M Yes, dear, I remembered.

W And did you call the repairman to fix the washer?

M Yes, I did. He'll be here tomorrow morning at 10:00.

W _____! What would I do without you?

11

W Welcome to the Teddy Bear Museum. Here you will find _____ about Teddy Bears. The Teddy Bear Museum opened on April 24, 2001. It contains a history gallery and an art gallery. It also has a gift shop. The Teddy Bear Museum _____ ____ from 9 am to 7 pm, and year round. No food or drinks are allowed to be brought into the museum. Our museum shop, the Teddy Bear Republic, has more than 800 products. There you will find Teddy Bear dolls, Teddy Bear jewelry, T-shirts, cups, and much more. The Teddy Bear Museum is more exciting than ever with "Teddy Bear" entertainment _____.

12

W So, what do you want to do now?

M Let's go and see the Fashion Show.

W We can't. The show started ten minutes ago. Besides, we _____.

M Ah, I really want to see the show.

W Don't worry. We can see it about three hours later.

M Good. What time does the Snow Festival start?

W It starts at 4:30.

M Oh, _____ more than four hours to watch it.

W Right. And we have just one thing to watch now.

M I know. _____. Before that, let's make a reservation for the Fashion Show.

13

(Telephone rings.)

W I'm so glad you called.

M Sorry, honey. I just _____. It was a hard day. You know I'm in charge of a lot of meetings. Are the lights still out?

W Yes, they are. And not just the lights. Everything is out. Do you have any idea how big this blackout is?

M No, but I'm getting online _____ right now. Carla, it looks like the power is out in about five states!

W Does it say when it'll come back on?

M Let's see. It says here that it might _____ until tomorrow.

W Oh, no.

M I'm sorry I am not there with you.

W Me, too. I'm working by candlelight, and it's very romantic.

M Working? Without electricity?

W _____

14

M Sonia? Hi, long time no see.

W Greg? Wow! It's great to see you.

M _____?

W Around three years or so.

M Mmm, _____! So tell me, what have you been up to?

W Same old thing. I'm still teaching Spanish at the same high school.

M And are you still living in that great house at the beach?

W That's _____. So, what's new with you?

M Oh, well, this and that.

W I wonder if you are still swimming and working out at the club.

M _____

15

W Ms. Pena reported that her husband was missing. Her husband disappeared while he was _____ _____ at the airport. Now Ms. Pena is at the police station. One police officer asks her to describe him, his clothes and his job. After hearing that his job is a bank manager, the officer asks if there are any signs of withdrawing or transferring money. After checking his and her accounts, she finds that _____ _____. In this situation, what would Ms. Pena most likely say to the police officer?

Ms. Pena _____

16-17

(Telephone rings.)

M Hello?

W Hello. Is this Mr. Jackson?

M Yes, I'm Peter Jackson.

W Hello, Mr. Jackson. I'm calling from TV29. We are conducting a survey of TV viewing habits in your area. _____? It'll only take a minute.

M Sure, how can I help you?

W Well, first, we'd like to find out the average age of viewers. How old are you and your wife?

M We're both 45.

W Okay. _____?

M Yes. I'm a middle school teacher. And my wife is a journalist.

W And do you have any children?

M Yes, three. But, we don't let them watch TV.

W Well, that brings me to my next question. About how many hours of TV does your family watch each day?

M _____, about an hour and a half a day. My wife and I like to watch the news in the evening.

W Well, Mr. Jackson, thank you very much for your time.

34^회 | 듣기 모의고사

1번부터 17번까지는 듣고 답하는 문제입니다. 1번부터 15번까지는 한 번만 들려주고, 16번부터 17번까지는 두 번 들려줍니다. 방송을 잘 듣고 답을 하시기 바랍니다.

01 대화를 듣고, 여자의 마지막 말에 대한 남자의 응답으로 가장 적절한 것을 고르시오.

① That will be no problem.
② I know where the laundry shop is.
③ It leaks. Can you call the plumber?
④ Be careful. It's heavier than it looks.
⑤ Then let's buy a new washing machine.

02 대화를 듣고, 남자의 마지막 말에 대한 여자의 응답으로 가장 적절한 것을 고르시오.

① I saw you getting off there.
② Then let me take your bag.
③ You forgot to take your cell phone.
④ Oh, thank you. That's very kind of you.
⑤ Don't get me wrong. I'm just tired now.

03 대화를 듣고, 두 사람이 하는 말의 주제로 가장 적절한 것을 고르시오.

① 용돈 인상의 타당성
② 친구 사귀기의 어려움
③ 집안일 공유의 필요성
④ 쓰레기 분리수거의 장점
⑤ 정기적 가족회의의 중요성

04 대화를 듣고, 두 사람의 의견으로 가장 적절한 것을 고르시오.

① 상대방의 입장을 고려해서 행동해야 한다.
② 불편한 점은 이야기를 해서 해결해야 한다.
③ 숙면을 취해야 일의 능률을 제고할 수 있다.
④ 애완동물은 외로울 때 좋은 벗이 될 수 있다.
⑤ 정보의 공유가 단체의 결속력을 강화시킨다.

05 대화를 듣고, 두 사람의 관계를 가장 잘 나타낸 것을 고르시오.

① editor – reporter
② housewife – plumber
③ prosecutor – witness
④ interviewer – applicant
⑤ customer – photographer

06 대화를 듣고, 그림에서 대화의 내용과 일치하지 <u>않는</u> 것을 고르시오.

07 대화를 듣고, 두 사람이 할 일로 가장 적절한 것을 고르시오.

① 일기예보 청취   ② 제설 작업 참여
③ 조기 퇴근 건의   ④ 동료의 병문안
⑤ 연장 근무 신청

08 대화를 듣고, 두 사람이 대화하고 있는 장소로 가장 적절한 곳을 고르시오.

① on the street
② in the classroom
③ in the courtroom
④ at the police station
⑤ at the broadcasting station

09 대화를 듣고, 여자가 지불할 금액을 고르시오. [3점]

① $ 70 ② $ 80 ③ $ 150
④ $160 ⑤ $ 200

10 대화를 듣고, 여자가 남자에게 질문한 것이 <u>아닌</u> 것을 고르시오.

① 자기소개 ② 경력
③ 전공 ④ 적정 보수
⑤ 병력

11 다음 내용을 듣고, 일치하지 <u>않는</u> 것을 고르시오.

① 18~24세는 파티를 최고의 주말 활동이라 생각한다.
② 25~34세는 가족과 함께 쉬는 것을 최고의 주말 활동으로 꼽았다.
③ 18~24세는 휴가지로 해변을 가장 선호한다.
④ 25~34세는 휴가지로 해외를 가장 선호한다.
⑤ 35~44세는 차로 지역 관광지를 둘러보는 것을 즐긴다.

12 대화를 듣고, 두 사람의 의견이 일치하고 있는 그룹이나 음악가를 고르시오. [3점]

① B3 ② Candy Warner
③ Horn of Plenty ④ Tessa Traynor
⑤ The Castaways

13 대화를 듣고, 여자의 마지막 말에 대한 남자의 응답으로 가장 적절한 것을 고르시오.

Man : _____

① Our church has a new pastor.
② I mean, you go to church, don't you?
③ You bet I do! I'm dying to see that show.
④ I've got a pair of tickets for the Saturday show.
⑤ You know what I mean. Promises should be kept.

14 대화를 듣고, 남자의 마지막 말에 대한 여자의 응답으로 가장 적절한 것을 고르시오. [3점]

Woman : _____

① I know you are a good player.
② Sorry, but count me out this time.
③ That can't be an excuse. It's not fair.
④ So tell me if we won the game or not.
⑤ I wish I could be there, but I'm busy then.

15 다음 상황 설명을 듣고, Angela가 노숙자에게 할 말로 가장 적절한 것을 고르시오.

Angela : _____

① tell me what happened to you after that.
② what's it like to live from hand to mouth?
③ do your parents know what you are doing?
④ don't tell me you are satisfied with your life.
⑤ thank you for the interview. It was of great help.

[16-17] 다음을 듣고, 물음에 답하시오.

16 누가 누구에게 한 말인가?

① 교사가 학생에게
② 공무원이 지역 주민에게
③ 교장이 학부모에게
④ 경찰이 목격자에게
⑤ 후보자가 유권자에게

17 제기한 사안에 대한 문제점으로 언급되지 <u>않은</u> 것은?

① 사고의 위험성 ② 인근 주민들의 민원
③ 주변 환경 오염 ④ 위화감 조성
⑤ 관련 규정 위반

DICTATION(받아쓰기) 코너입니다.
녹음의 내용을 잘 듣고, 빈칸에 알맞은 말을 쓰시기 바랍니다.

01

W Honey, can you help me _____?
M Sure. I am always ready to share. What should I do?
W You can clean the kitchen sink. While you are cleaning, I'll _____.
M _____

02

M Excuse me, ma'am. Why don't you take my seat here?
W Oh, that's okay.
M No, really. _____.
W _____

03

M Mom, do you have a minute?
W Certainly. What's on your mind?
M Well, I think _____.
W Why? Don't you think you get enough?
M I thought so, but since I am a high school student now, I need to hang around with my friends more, which costs me extra.
W Is that the only reason?
M It's a pretty good reason, and _____. I do more work around the house these days.
W Like what?
M I shine Dad's shoes once a week and separate garbage, taking it out every Sunday. You know _____ _____ with the dishes.
W Sounds like you have good reasons. I'll discuss it with your father when he comes home.

04

M Good morning, Linda.
W Hi, Henry. Listen, sorry to say this, but... never mind.
M Linda, what is it? Something must be bothering you.
W Well, it's not that serious. It's your dog's dung. I see it quite often when I see Jack off.
M Oh, sorry. I'll try to _____. Thank you for informing me of that. Oh, come to think of it, that new stereo system you bought at the garage sale, remember?
W Yeah?
M You were playing it very late last night and it kept me awake for a couple of hours.
W Really? I'm sorry. I didn't realize that it was that loud.
M It was a bit loud, and it only happened once, but I thought it's better to say.
W Sure. I'm glad _____.
M So am I. We need to work it out any time something comes up.

05

W Are you an electronics expert?
M Expert is a big word.
W _____. Have you worked in electronics for a long time?
M Yes. For about twenty years.
W Can you install miniature microphones?
M Well, it depends on what kind of microphone it is.
W Please answer yes or no.
M Yes, I can.
W Have you met Bob Gibson, editor of *the Daily News*?
M I don't think _____.
W Then can you explain this picture of you and Bob drinking at the bar downtown?
M Well, I didn't know he was Bob Gibson.
W _____, Your Honor.

06

W Jimmy, congratulations! You are finally a father.

M Hi, Mom. You made it in time. We're about to see the baby. Come this way.

W Finally, I get to see my first grandson. Don't tell me who my grandson is.

M All right, Mom. We are here. Look at all these newborn infants.

W Let's see. Oh, they all look alike. _____ _____ aren't my grandson.

M How dare my son sleep in the presence of his grandma?

W Is this crying coming from him?

M No. He's just _____.

W Oh, there are two of them looking at the ceiling: One trying to grab something with hands, and the other... I guess I found him. _____ from the blanket, right?

M Wow! How did you know that, Mom?

W Well, that's the way you were when you were a baby.

07

W Look at the sky.

M Looks like there is a big snowstorm on the way. It's getting pretty dark out there!

W I saw the weather forecast last night. There's a _____.

M Really? Did they say how much snow we're supposed to get?

W 20 centimeters. That's what they said.

M It sounds like it's going to be just like that big snowstorm we had last year. Remember? No one could get to work. Practically, _____ _____.

W I remember that my husband had a back problem after digging his car out.

M Look! It's already starting to snow.

W Hey, why don't we _____ _____ a little earlier today?

M That's a good idea. Maybe that's what he's thinking now. Go ahead.

08

W I can't believe this. You're Jim, aren't you?

M Margo? The girl with pimples all over her face?

W Yeah, it's me. _____.

M Yes, that's what I am doing now.

W I remember that in high school you always wanted to be a lawyer.

M Yeah. I guess it was all those TV shows about lawyers. I started law school but then I realized it just wasn't the right career for me.

W Isn't it a dangerous job? _____ with guns...

M Sometimes I wish it were a little more dangerous. Right now, as you see, all I do is write traffic tickets. It's kind of boring, actually. By the way, is this your car?

W No. You know I'm not the kind of person _____ _____.

09

M Can I help you?

W Yes. I was looking at that sweater in the window.

M You mean the pink and gray one?

W No. I am talking about the blue one.

M Oh, that's the man's sweater.

W That's right. It's for my husband. _____ _____?

M It comes in dark green and pale blue.

W My husband likes both colors. How much does it cost?

M Its original price is $100, but we are offering a 20% discount.

W I'll take a couple of sweaters. I mean _____ _____.

M Really? Then I can give you an additional discount of $10 for the second one.

W Great!

10

W Ah, Mr. Stewart, you're _____ . Would you tell me about yourself?

M Well, when I was a kid, I used to dream of being a pilot. _____ to the airport and watching the planes.

W But you're not a pilot. Why didn't you become a pilot?

M As you see, I wear glasses. I started wearing them when I was fourteen. I am very nearsighted.

W So, what is your major?

M I majored in Electrical Engineering.

W Good, then could you _____ ?

M I'm a mechanic. In fact, I worked for a small company which made radio parts, but the salary was kind of low. I couldn't support my family with it.

W I see. Can I _____ ?

M Sure, I have never gone through any serious illness.

W Okay, then, I have the right job for you. It's an elevator service engineer. How does that sound?

M Sounds great. Thanks a lot.

11

W A survey conducted by *Lifestyle* magazine asked one hundred people between the ages of 18 and 44 to _____ in "Weekends" and "Vacations." The survey shows that as we age, our ideas about "_____" age, too. Those between 18 and 24 rated "_____" as the number one weekend activity, while the 25-to-34 age group said that their favorite way to spend the weekend is hiking or skiing. People between the ages of 35 and 44 said that "_____" is the best way to spend the weekend. In the category of "Vacations," the 18-to-24 set rated "_____" as the best way to spend a vacation, while the 25-to-34 year olds prefer traveling overseas. The last age group said they enjoy short trips by car to local sights.

12

W How's it going, Del?

M Hi, Marcia. I'm fine. Did you watch the music awards last night?

W No. I was too busy. _____ ?

M It was okay but can you believe B3 won Song of the Year? I can't stand that group.

W Hmm. I think B3 is a great group.

M Well, what do you think of Candy Warner? She got the award for Best New Artist.

W I think _____ .

M I can't agree with you. What else? Oh, Best Rock Band went to Horn of Plenty.

W That's great. I really like that group.

M Do you? Well, I don't care about that group.

W I bet Best Dance Album went to Tessa Traynor.

M You guessed it right, but I think Jimmy Rollins should have gotten it. Best Pop Album went to The Castaways.

W You're kidding! They don't deserve an award.

M I _____ .

13

(Telephone rings.)

W Hello?

M Hello, Jessica? It's Rob here.

W Hello, Rob. I'm sorry about the other day. Something urgent happened so _____ .

M That's okay. At least you called me to keep me from standing out in the cold.

W That's comforting! By the way, what's up?

M Well, I just called to find out what you're doing this weekend?

W No plans, really. I was hoping to go to the Glory Hounds concert, but I couldn't get tickets.

M Well, then, _____ .

W What do you mean?

M _____

14

W Hi, Tom. What are you up to?

M Hi, Lin. I'm writing down the schedules of the games tomorrow. There's a volleyball competition for the Under 16 clubs.

W _____?

M There's a list here. Look.

W Steve, Otis, Ali, Tom. Wow! You are also playing. Nick? Nick is not under 16! I went to his birthday party last Saturday. _____ last Saturday.

M So what? He's just 16 and three days.

W No, Tom. If he's 16, he's not under 16.

M Look, Lin. Nick has to play. If he doesn't play, then _____. We haven't got enough players for the team without him.

W _____

15

W Angela is a reporter. She _____ _____. These days, she's been writing a series of articles about homeless men. Today, she interviewed a homeless man living on the street. In the interview, she got to know a great deal about the past of the homeless man. _____, she learned that he had a college degree and that he had once worked for a big company. Curious, she wanted to know ____ _____, living from hand to mouth. In this situation, what would Angela most likely say to the homeless man?

Angela _____

16-17

W Good afternoon. I'm happy to see so many of you coming here. Thank you for taking the time today. I asked you to come here, since we have a very important thing for which _____. Recently, some parents have been driving their children to school, and there have been some problems involved in that. First, it is very dangerous. _____, a lot of students rush to the school. There might be an accident. Second, it causes a lot of complaints from the neighborhood because it blocks the flow of vehicles. Third, it can hurt the feelings of students whose parents have no car or cannot give them a ride. Last but not least, students who turn to their parents for coming to school ____ _____ regarding shoes and the school uniform because they don't need to be outside much. As a person in charge of everything in school, I would really appreciate your cooperation.

1번부터 17번까지는 듣고 답하는 문제입니다. 1번부터 15번까지는 한 번만 들려주고, 16번부터 17번까지는 두 번 들려줍니다. 방송을 잘 듣고 답을 하시기 바랍니다.

01 대화를 듣고, 남자의 마지막 말에 대한 여자의 응답으로 가장 적절한 것을 고르시오.

① You're very considerate.
② Well, I think it's rather bitter.
③ This is for you. Happy birthday.
④ This isn't what I've been looking for.
⑤ You dressed well, but it's not my taste.

02 대화를 듣고, 여자의 마지막 말에 대한 남자의 응답으로 가장 적절한 것을 고르시오.

① The sooner, the better.
② I will follow your advice.
③ My decision turned out to be right.
④ Really? What did you decide to major in?
⑤ Well, I want a job that's more challenging.

03 다음을 듣고, 남자가 하는 말의 목적으로 가장 적절한 것을 고르시오.

① 내선번호를 알리려고
② 부동산 물건을 광고하려고
③ 맞춤식 서비스를 제공하려고
④ 금주의 신간 도서를 안내하려고
⑤ 아파트 분양 광고를 게재하려고

04 대화를 듣고, 두 사람이 하는 말의 주제로 가장 적절한 것을 고르시오.

① 학업 능력 개발
② 대인 관계의 중요성
③ 역할 모델의 필요성
④ 성별에 따른 역할 인식
⑤ 개인별 과제 부여의 원칙

05 대화를 듣고, 두 사람이 대화하고 있는 장소로 가장 적절한 곳을 고르시오.

① at home
② in the car
③ in the elevator
④ in the hospital
⑤ at the parking lot

06 대화를 듣고, 여자가 찾는 할아버지의 군인 시절 모습을 고르시오.

07 대화를 듣고, 대화 후에 여자가 할 일로 가장 적절한 것을 고르시오.

① 남자 친구 만나기
② 부모님 도와드리기
③ 친구 만나러 가기
④ 웨딩드레스 맞추기
⑤ 체중 감량을 위해 운동하기

08 대화를 듣고, 남자가 전화를 건 이유를 고르시오.

① 도서관에서 공부에 집중이 안 되어서
② 공부가 잘 되어가고 있는지 물으려고
③ 손님들이 모두 도착하였는지 확인하려고
④ 도서관 사서의 근무 태만을 하소연하려고
⑤ 집에 두고 온 휴대폰을 꺼달라고 부탁하려고

09 대화를 듣고, 여자가 지불할 금액을 고르시오. [3점]

① $80   ② $85   ③ $89

④ $90   ⑤ $100

10 다음 음성 메모를 듣고, 언급되지 <u>않은</u> 내용을 고르시오.

① 예약 시간   ② 담당 의사

③ 예약 취소 방법   ④ 진료실 위치

⑤ 진료 과목

11 대화를 듣고, 남자가 구매를 추천한 야구 용품이 <u>아닌</u> 것을 고르시오.

① 야구 장갑   ② 야구 방망이

③ 야구공   ④ 야구화

⑤ 야구복

12 다음 표를 보면서 대화를 듣고, <u>잘못된</u> 지역을 고르시오.

Today's National Weather Forecast

region	weather
① Northwest	
② Southeast	
③ South-Central	
④ Northeast	
⑤ Southwest	

13 대화를 듣고, 여자의 마지막 말에 대한 남자의 응답으로 가장 적절한 것을 고르시오.

Man : _____

① Sorry, but I'm not good at cooking.

② I can't miss all that. Okay, I will go!

③ Oh, I forgot to give him an invitation.

④ You must be very proud of your mother.

⑤ I wish I were invited to his birthday party.

14 대화를 듣고, 남자의 마지막 말에 대한 여자의 응답으로 가장 적절한 것을 고르시오. [3점]

Woman : _____

① Maybe it will come after I die.

② I don't believe in those things.

③ Because I really wanted to see it.

④ Well, I'd like to major in astronomy.

⑤ I used to chase shooting stars as a child.

15 다음 상황 설명을 듣고, Andrew가 사장에게 할 말로 가장 적절한 것을 고르시오.

Andrew : _____

① How's your father? Is he feeling better?

② I'd like to invite you to my dad's restaurant.

③ Why don't you take over my dad's restaurant?

④ Can I take a few days off? My dad is in bad health.

⑤ I'm afraid I have to quit. I have to take over my dad's restaurant.

[16-17] 다음을 듣고, 물음에 답하시오.

16 남자가 하는 말의 주제로 가장 적절한 것은?

① 위기의 출판 업계

② 독서 인구의 증가

③ 책 값 인상의 이유

④ 대학 서점의 문제점

⑤ 전자책 시대의 도래

17 Borders에 관한 내용으로 언급되지 <u>않은</u> 것은? [3점]

① 창립 장소   ② 창립 연도

③ 회사 규모   ④ 설립자

⑤ 파산 이유

DICTATION(받아쓰기) 코너입니다.
녹음의 내용을 잘 듣고, 빈칸에 알맞은 말을 쓰시기 바랍니다.

01

M Look what I've got _____ .

W Wow! It looks wonderful. What's that?

M I picked it off my fruit tree in the back yard. Taste it and _____ .

W _____

02

W Hi, Ben. How have you been?

M Good. I'm thinking about _____ .

W That's great! What made you decide to do that?

M _____

03

M Thank you for calling Cornerstone Properties. Here's a look at this week's new property listings. _____ is a stunning beachfront apartment on Lakeshore Avenue. This top-floor apartment has three large bedrooms, each one with its own bathroom. There is also a separate bathroom and a large balcony off the living room. Although the kitchen is small, it includes _____ . This apartment is a must-see. Hurry! It's sure to sell very quickly. To speak to an operator about this property, press one and mention listing number seven-four-one.

04

M Thank you for coming.

W You're welcome. What seems to be the problem with Jimmy?

M Well, I am afraid _____ . I also have some concerns about his study skills.

W Can you give me an example?

M His mathematics abilities are a little weak.

W I know it's not one of his strong points.

M And he's lacking a bit in spelling.

W I see. _____ ?

M That's not a bad idea, but it costs money. Maybe it's enough to sit with him while he does his homework.

W Thank you. I'll _____ .

M Jimmy has a lot of potential, so I hope to see him improve.

W That's very nice of you to say so.

05

W Here, I'll _____ .

M Thanks.

W What are all these papers you've got?

M I've been working on the company's annual report. It takes a lot of time. That's why I'm taking work home with me.

W _____ . Looks like you don't sleep enough.

M Actually, I don't. I've got a lot of work to do. I have to do Bob's work because he's in the hospital.

W Oh, can't some of the other managers help you?

M I've asked them, but they all say they're too busy.

W That's too bad. By the way, is your car parked in the basement garage?

M Yes. I'll _____ .

W All right. I've got to get out of here. Let me know if I can help with anything.

M Thank you for saying that. See you tomorrow.

06

W Grandpa, what is this black-and-white picture?

M It's the picture I took when _____. Guess which one is me.

W Well, all the soldiers are wearing the same hat. And it makes it harder to recognize you.

M Take a close look. Can't you see the lines on the hat?

W Oh, I see. How many lines were there on your hat?

M I was a sergeant. That means _____ _____ on it.

W Let me see. There are three soldiers wearing a four-lined hat. You are kind of tall. I don't think you are the smallest one.

M You're right.

W And you are wearing glasses. That means you are the second man from the right.

M Actually, _____ that I didn't wear glasses then.

07

M Melissa, are you still going out with that guy? What was his name?

W Roger. Yeah. In fact, we're _____ _____.

M Really? It's been three months since you started seeing each other, hasn't it?

W Yes. Three months and five days, _____.

M Wow! Both of you really love each other. How's the preparation going?

W Very smoothly. We're planning it ourselves, but our parents are helping us a lot _____.

M It must be a lot of work. Why don't we go somewhere and talk?

W I wish I could, but I'm on my way _____ _____.

M Sounds nice.

W Now I'm trying to lose weight so that I can look beautiful in it.

M I wish you good luck. Maybe some other time.

08

(Telephone rings.)

W Hello?

M Hi, Mom.

W Hi, Paul. How's your studying going?

M That's why I am calling. Are your friends _____ _____?

W Yes, they are. Why do you ask?

M Well, I can't concentrate where I am. _____.

W What do you mean? Aren't you at the library?

M Yes, but someone's cell phone always seems to be ringing.

W Doesn't the library have a policy about cell phones?

M Yes, there are signs _____ saying to turn off your phone or put it on vibrate mode. But most people don't seem to care.

W Why don't you tell the librarians? I am sure they can do something about it.

M All right. I guess that's _____.

09

M Good morning. What can I do for you?

W Hi. _____. I want to frame them.

M Okay. What kind of frame would you like?

W Well, the heart-shaped frame over there, how much would it be?

M The original price is $10 each, but I will give you 10% off.

W _____? You know I've had five rolls of film developed recently.

M Well, that's why I offer you a 10% discount. How many pictures are you going to frame?

W Ten pictures all together.

M In that case, I'll give you an extra $1 off for each one.

W Now that's _____.

10

W Hello. This is Central Hospital calling. I'm just calling to make sure that you know _____ your daughter on Tuesday, ten thirty in the morning. She is supposed to see Dr. Jennings. His office is _____ of the hospital. Please come to the receptionist's desk ten minutes earlier, and let us know you are here. _____, please let us know at least one hour before. You can contact us by calling 735-9116. Have a wonderful day and see you tomorrow.

11

W You play baseball, don't you, George?

M Yes, I do. _____.

W Where do you buy your baseball equipment?

M There's a good sporting goods store downtown, Mickey's Sports. It has all kinds of athletic equipment, and it has pretty good prices, too.

W Sounds good. My daughter just started playing baseball. She also joined a neighborhood team. What will she need?

M _____?

W No. She just received her uniform. She's only seven. She has a baseball cap, but that's all.

M Well, then she'll need a good glove. And maybe a bat and a ball. Ah, she'll definitely need a pair of good baseball shoes. I guess that's enough.

W You've been a big help. Thanks, George!

12

M Good morning. Here is today's national weather forecast. The Northwest region is currently seeing some low temperatures, and it will be cool and cloudy, _____. Don't forget your umbrella. In the Southeast region, the weather will be very pleasant. It will be generally warm and sunny, with occasional light winds. The forecast for the South-Central region _____ with strong winds developing in the afternoon. Temperatures will drop to around 15 degrees Celsius. If you are going to be in the Northeast region, dress warmly. The weather will be cold and very windy, _____. The Southwest region will see some high temperatures, and there is a possibility of tornadoes in some areas. That's our report for this hour. Have a great day.

13

W Jake, are you invited to Juan's birthday party?

M Yeah. But I'm not sure _____. Are you going?

W Of course! It'll be fabulous. Juan's having a Mexican birthday party this year. He's going to have a pinata. Isn't that cool?

M What's that?

W It's an animal made out of paper, and it's filled with candies. Then it's hung up somewhere high like a tree branch. First, _____.

M Sounds like fun. What do you do after that?

W Then he hits the pinata with a stick. After that, we take turns hitting the pinata.

M I see. And as soon as _____, all the candies come out, right?

W That's right. You'll have fun. It'll be a great chance to meet new people! Besides, I heard Juan's mother is an awesome cook!

M _____

14

W Have you heard of Halley's Comet? It's a comet named after Edmund Halley.

M What about it?

W Do you know _____ every 75 years?

M No, I don't. When was the last time it came?

W In 1986. Even before I was born!

M So that means it will be back in 2061, right?

W Yes. Talking about comets, there's one up there. Look!

M Where? Oh, that's not a comet. That's a shooting star. When you see a shooting star, _____ ____!

W So, what did you wish for?

M It's a secret! My lips are sealed. What about you?

W _____

15

W Andrew works for a small company. He likes his job because it is his first job, and he likes his boss and co-workers. Tonight, Andrew gets a call from his mother. She says that his father, who has owned a restaurant for forty years, _____ __. Andrew hurriedly books a flight to New York and leaves for the airport. On the way to the airport, he looks back on his childhood when his father taught him how to serve customers and set the table. Then he realizes he has to call his boss to _____ ___. He calls, and his boss answers. After exchanging a few words, he thinks it's time to say why he called. In this situation, what would Andrew most likely say to his boss?

Andrew _____

16-17

M Good evening. It's the six o'clock news, and I'm Ted Parker. I'm sorry to say that Borders, once the second largest bookstore in the U.S.A., is now history. Borders _____ yesterday. Borders first opened a bookstore on the University of Michigan campus in 1971. It eventually grew into a company with more than 1,200 bookstores worldwide. It was the second largest bookstore in the U.S.A. But poor management, _____, and a rocky economy made problems for Borders. Today, Borders announced it would close its remaining 399 stores and lay off nearly 11,000 employees. Looking at Borders' failure, the publishing industry is _____ of any forms in the future. Here's what analyst Michael Norris says. "There are going to be fewer people buying books. If people believe that every former Borders buyer is going to turn into an e-book consumer, they believe in the tooth fairy." The publishing industry _____ _____.

만점 적중

★★★★★
수능
영어영역
듣기평가 대비
★★★★★

수능 듣기

모의고사

35회

정답 및 해설

NEXUS Edu

01 ④	02 ①	03 ④	04 ⑤	05 ⑤	06 ③
07 ④	08 ③	09 ④	10 ②	11 ③	12 ③
13 ⑤	14 ②	15 ④	16 ⑤	17 ①	

01 ④

해석 여 스파게티를 만들고 있어요. 당신이 좋아했으면 좋겠어요.

남 음…… 냄새가 정말 좋네요. 전 식사 준비를 마쳤어요.

여 10분 후면 완성될 거예요.

남 <u>못 기다리겠어요! 군침이 돌아요!</u>

해설 여자가 스파게티를 만들고 있고, 남자는 이 음식에 관심을 보인다. 10분 후에 먹을 수 있다고 한 여자의 말에 대해 남자는 빨리 먹고 싶다는 말을 하는 것이 적절할 것이다. ① 맛있었다니 기쁘군요. ② 욕실이 어디인지 알고 있어요. ③ 저녁 먹으러 언제든 다시 오세요. ⑤ 아주 친절하시군요. 정말 아무것도 아니에요.

어휘 water 군침이 돌다

02 ①

해석 남 Lisa, 혹시 이번 토요일에 시간이 될지 궁금해요.

여 네, 이번 토요일은 한가해요.

남 잘됐네요! 집들이를 하려고요. 남편과 함께 올 수 있어요?

여 <u>몇 시까지 가면 될까요?</u>

해설 남자가 토요일에 집들이에 초대를 했으니 몇 시에 가면 되는 지와 같은 집들이 관련 정보를 구체적으로 묻는 것이 적절하다. ② 왜 새로운 곳으로 이사했어요? ③ 너무 바빠서 시간이 없어요. ④ 파티에 대한 정보를 알려 드릴게요. ⑤ 파티 가기 바로 전에 식당에 먼저 가는 게 좋겠어요.

어휘 wonder 궁금해 하다 free 선약이 없는, 한가한 house warming party 집들이

03 ④

해석 남 안녕하세요, 여러분. 내일 견학에 대해서 알려 드립니다. 일기 예보에 따르면, 내일 아침에 심한 뇌우를 동반한 폭우가 예상됩니다. 우리 교직원들은 견학을 다음 주 금요일로 연기하기로 결정했습니다. 이 수정된 발표를 숙지하고 내일 견학 준비를 하지 마십시오. 반복합니다! 내일 견학은 예상되는 기상 악화로 인하여 다음 주 금요일로 연기되었습니다. 학생들은 정상적으로 등교해야 합니다. 내일 날씨가 좋더라도 정상 수업을 진행할 것입니다. 들어 주셔서 감사합니다.

해설 내일 예정된 견학이 악천후로 인하여 다음 주 금요일로 연기되었음을 알려 주는 내용이다.

어휘 field trip 견학 heavy rainfall 폭우 severe 맹렬한 thunderstorm 뇌우(雷雨) faculty 교수진, 교직원 delay 연기하다 take into account ~을 고려하다 amended 수정된 even if 비록 ~일지라도

04 ⑤

해석 여 이 사진들은 어디에서 찍은 거야?

남 프랑스로 신혼여행 가서 찍은 거야.

여 그렇구나, 알겠다. 사진에서 너는 정말 행복해 보여.

남 그런데 사진들이 좀 흐려.

여 조금 그러네. 그래도 나쁘지는 않은 걸.

남 신혼여행 가기 전에 삼각대를 확인했어야 했는데 말이야. 밤에 사진을 찍는데 고장 난 거지.

여 그래도 야경이 환상적이야.

남 고마워. 정말 멋졌어. 소중한 순간을 잘 포착하지 못해서 너무 기분이 안 좋아.

여 그래도 마음속에서 그 장면을 기억하잖아. 그게 중요한 거야!

해설 여자의 마지막 말에서 여자는 사진보다 중요한 것이 마음속으로 기억하는 것이라고 생각하고 있음을 알 수 있다.

어휘 blurry 흐릿한 tripod 삼각대 awful 끔찍한 precious 소중한, 귀중한

05 ⑤

해석 남 이봐요, Beth, 무슨 일 있어요?

여 죄송해요, 감독님.

남 이번이 세 번째 실수예요. 대사를 제대로 외우긴 한 거예요?

여 네, 외웠어요. 왜 계속 잊어버리는지 모르겠어요. 아마도 잠이 좀 더 필요한가 봐요.

남 왜요? 어제 몇 시간이나 잤는데요?

여 겨우 3시간 잤어요. 스케줄이 빡빡했어요.

남 모두들, 잘 들어요. 30분 간 휴식 후에 이 장면을 다시 시작할게요.

여 감사합니다, 감독님.

남 휴식을 좀 취해요. 당신은 주인공이에요. 당신의 매끄러운 대사가 없으면 좋은 영화를 만들 수 없어요.

여 정말 죄송해요. 다시는 실수하지 않도록 최선을 다할게요.

해설 여배우의 대사 실수로 인해서 영화 촬영이 매끄럽게 되지 않고 있는 상황으로, 영화감독인 남자와 배우인 여자 사이의 대화이다.

어휘 memorize 외우다 tight 빡빡한, 조이는 resume 다시 시작하다 take a break 휴식을 취하다 main character 주인공 smooth 매끄러운

06 ③

해석 (전화벨이 울린다.)

여 안녕, Sam. 나 Amanda야.

남 안녕, Amanda. 무슨 일이야?

여 어제 너희 집에서 열린 변장 파티가 궁금해서. 애들은 몇 명이나 왔니?

남 12명쯤. 정신은 없었는데 재미있었어.

여 와. 우리 애들과 나도 갔어야 했는데. 너희 애들은 뭘 입었어?

남 음, Tom은 슈퍼맨이어서 붉은 망토를 입고 가슴에는 커다란 S자를 달았어.

여 네 딸은 뭘 입었어?

남 그 애는 요새 백설 공주를 정말 좋아하거든. 그래서 머리에 빨간 리본을 달았어.

여 백설 공주가 입는 전형적인 파란색과 노란색 드레스를 입었어?

남 물론이지! 그런데 백설 공주가 신는 구두는 깜박했어. 너무 들떠서 맨
  발로 돌아다니지 뭐야.
여 진짜 귀엽다!

해설 남자의 딸은 구두를 신고 있지 않고 맨발로 돌아다녔다고 했으므로 여자아이가
  구두를 신은 것이 일치하지 않는다.

어휘 costume party 변장 파티 hectic 정신이 없는 adore 아주 좋아하다 typical
  전형적인 barefoot 맨발로

07 ④

해석 남 Lynn, 부탁 좀 들어줄래?
  여 물론이지, 뭔데?
  남 내일 아침까지 끝내야 할 일이 두 가지 있어. 하나는 과학 수업을 위한
    보고서이고, 다른 하나는 미술 수업을 위한 그림을 그리는 거야.
  여 오, 너 할 일이 많구나. 그래서 어떻게 할 건데?
  남 내가 손으로 써서 보고서 작성은 끝냈는데, 그걸 타이핑할 시간이 없
    어.
  여 그래서 내가 너 대신 네 보고서를 타이핑해 주길 원하니?
  남 아니, 나 대신 그림을 그려 줬으면 해. 네가 나보다 그림을 더 잘 그리는
    것을 알고 있거든.
  여 오, 안 돼. 그건 좋은 생각이 아냐. 네 그림은 너 스스로 그리는 게 좋을
    것 같아. 다른 일을 해 줄게.
  남 네 말이 맞아. 내가 나중에 점심을 살게.

해설 남자는 내일 아침까지 해야 할 보고서 타이핑하기와 그림 그리기 중 그림 그리기
  를 여자에게 부탁했으나, 여자는 이를 거절하고 다른 일을 도와주겠다고 했으므
  로 "보고서 타입 치기"가 정답임을 알 수 있다.

어휘 paper 보고서 plenty of 많은 by oneself 스스로

08 ③

해석 여 James, 괜찮아? 오늘 안 좋아 보인다.
  남 맞아. 오늘 기분이 안 좋아.
  여 왜? 무슨 일 때문에 그래?
  남 영문학 기말 보고서에서 'F'를 받았어.
  여 정말? 너 영문학 공부 많이 했잖아. 'A'를 받는 게 당연하다고 생각했
    는데.
  남 나도 그렇게 생각했지. 그런데 보고서를 너무 늦게 제출했거든. 김 교
    수님께서 받아 주시지 않더라고.
  여 김 교수님께서는 제출 기한에 대해서는 엄격하시지. 왜 제 시간에 제출
    하지 못했니?
  남 난 내 가방에 보고서가 있다고 생각했어. 그런데 보고서를 제출하려는
    순간 집 책상 위에 두고 온 것을 알았어.
  여 늦었지만 네 보고서를 받아 달라고 김 교수님을 설득해보지 그랬어?
  남 그랬지, 그런데 누구도 규정에서 예외가 될 수는 없대.
  여 아, 그 이야기를 들으니 유감이다.

해설 남자는 보고서 기한을 지키지 못해 보고서에서 'F'를 받아 기분이 좋지 않다.

어휘 in a good mood 기분이 좋은 English literature 영문학 final exam
  기말시험(cf. mid-term exam 중간시험) hand in 제출하다 accept ~을 받아들이
  다 strict 엄격한, 깐깐한 exception 예외

09 ④

해석 남 안녕하세요. 손님, 무엇을 도와드릴까요?
  여 제 남편에게 줄 셔츠를 찾고 있어요.
  남 특별히 생각하신 셔츠가 있으신가요?
  여 남편의 검정색 정장과 잘 어울릴 와이셔츠를 원해요.
  남 여기 파란색 와이셔츠가 있습니다. 파란색 와이셔츠가 유행이에요. 각
    각 30달러씩입니다.
  여 가격이 적당하네요. 이걸로 할게요. 분홍색은 어떤가요? 있나요?
  남 그럼요, 여기 있습니다. 이 색이 맘에 드실 거예요.
  여 어머나, 이 인디안 핑크가 정말 훌륭하군요. 얼마죠?
  남 50달러입니다.
  여 값이 꽤 나가지만 그것도 할게요. 저에게 10% 할인 쿠폰이 있어요. 할
    인 받을 수 있죠?
  남 그럼요. 하지만 분홍 셔츠만 가능하고 파란 셔츠는 안 돼요.
  여 네, 알겠어요.
  남 선물 포장 해드릴까요?
  여 네, 해주세요.

해설 파란 셔츠가 30달러, 분홍 셔츠는 50달러인데 10% 할인 쿠폰이 분홍 셔츠에만
  적용되므로 여자가 지불할 돈은 총 75달러이다.

어휘 dress shirt 와이셔츠 go with ~와 어울리다 in vogue 유행 중인 pricey 값이
  나가는 gift-wrap 선물 포장하다

10 ②

해석 남 안녕하세요, ABC 신문의 Mike입니다.
  여 만나서 반가워요. 오늘은 태풍 샌디에 대해서 설명 드릴게요. 질문 있으신
    가요?
  남 감사합니다. 먼저, 미국 내 피해 지역에 대해 말씀해 주세요.
  여 샌디는 플로리다 주에서 메인 주 그리고 서쪽으로는 미시간 주와 위스
    콘신 주까지 최소한 24개 주에 영향을 줬어요.
  남 어느 지역이 심각하게 피해를 입었나요?
  여 뉴저지와 뉴욕이요.
  남 폭풍 해일은 뉴욕 시를 언제 강타했나요?
  여 10월 29일이었어요.
  남 뉴욕시의 피해 상황에 대해서 좀 더 구체적으로 말씀해 주세요.
  여 거리와 터널, 지하철 선로 등이 물에 잠기고 시 주변의 전기가 끊어졌
    어요.

해설 태풍 피해 지역이나 시점, 피해 상황에 대해서는 언급했으나 태풍 대비 방법에 대
  한 언급은 없다.

어휘 severely 심각하게 storm surge 폭풍 해일 flood ~에 물이 넘치다 cut
  power 전기를 끊다

11 ③

해석 여 대왕판다에 대해서 들어본 적이 있습니까? 대왕판다는 쉽게 알아볼
    수 있는데, 크고 독특한 검은 반점이 눈 주변과 귀를 덮고, 몸체를 가로
    질러 있기 때문입니다. 대왕판다의 서식지는 중국의 중서부와 남서부
    입니다. 농업, 벌채, 그리고 다른 개발로 인해 한때 살았던 저지대에서
    쫓겨나게 되었습니다. 그들은 대부분 대나무를 먹습니다. 야생에서는

단백질을 위해 알이나 곤충들을 가끔 잡아먹기도 합니다. 한편 대왕판다는 나무늘보와 비슷하게 매우 게을러서 번식을 하는 것이 드뭅니다.

해설 단백질 보충을 위해 알이나 곤충을 잡아먹는다고 했으므로 대나무 이외에 다른 것은 먹지 않는다는 것은 일치하지 않는다.

어휘 recognize ~을 보고 곧 알아보다, 인지하다 distinctive 독특한 patch 반점 native 원산의 deforestation 벌채 bamboo 대나무 sloth 나무늘보 breed 번식하다

12 ③

해석 남 정말 따분하다, Jenny. 우리 영화 보러 갈까?
여 좋아. NEXUS Cinema에서 무엇을 상영 중이니?
남 'Madagascar 4', 'Die Hard 7', 'Spiderman 5'가 상영 중이야.
여 그래, 무엇을 보고 싶니?
남 나는 만화 영화류는 좋아하지 않아. 그러니 'Madagascar 4'는 제외하자.
여 좋아. 나도 만화 영화는 안 좋아해. 그렇다면 'Die Hard 7'과 'Spiderman 5' 중에서 무엇을 볼래? 내가 듣기로는 'Spiderman 5'가 정말 재미있대.
남 Spiderman 시리즈는 컴퓨터 그래픽을 너무 많이 사용해. 그래서 진짜 같아 보이지 않아.
여 'Die Hard 7'을 볼래?
남 그래, Die Hard 시리즈는 항상 스릴이 있지. 그리고 Bruce Willis는 여전히 꽤 멋있어.
여 좋아. 'Die Hard 7'을 보러 가자. 벌써 6시네. 그렇다면, 한 가지 선택밖에 없구나.
남 맞아.

해설 남자와 여자는 모두 만화 영화를 좋아하지 않고, 남자는 Spiderman 시리즈가 컴퓨터 그래픽을 너무 많이 사용해 현실감이 떨어지기 때문에 보고 싶어 하지 않는다. 결국 두 사람은 'Die Hard 7'을 보러 가기로 했고, 현재 시간이 6시이므로 8시, 즉 20시에 시작하는 영화를 볼 것이다.

어휘 play (영화가) 상영하다 thrilling 스릴 있는 pretty 상당히, 꽤 cool 멋있는

13 ⑤

해석 남 안녕하세요, 5월 4일 뉴욕행 비행기를 예약하고 싶어요.
여 죄송하지만, 그 항공편은 예약이 다 찼어요.
남 그 전날인 5월 3일은 어떤가요?
여 그 항공편은 아직 자리가 있어요. 오후 1시 40분 출발이고요, 예정된 출발 시간보다 적어도 두 시간 전에는 공항에 오셔야 해요.
남 알겠어요. 그 항공편으로 할게요.
여 이코노미, 비즈니스, 일등석 중 어떤 좌석을 원하세요?
남 비즈니스로 할게요. 계산은 어떻게 해야 하나요?
여 지금 10%의 예약금을 내셔야 하고 나머지는 늦어도 출발 2주전까지 계산하셔야 해요.
남 **알겠습니다. 예약금 10%는 신용카드로 지불할게요.**

해설 비행기 표를 예약하는 상황이며, 지불 시기에 대해 설명했으므로 응답으로 "알겠습니다. 예약 10%는 신용카드로 지불할게요."가 가장 적절하다. ① 머리 위의 선반에 하나 있어요. ② 면세 제한 금액을 초과했어요. ③ 지금 바로 탑승구로 가

세요. ④ 예약이 자동으로 확인됩니다.

어휘 deposit 선수금, 예치금 balance 남은 차액 no later than ~보다 늦지 않게

14 ②

해석 (전화벨이 울린다.)
남 여보세요, 무엇을 도와드릴까요?
여 안녕하세요, 홍 박사님. 오늘 예약을 할 수 있나요?
남 어디 봅시다. 오늘 오후 5시 50분은 괜찮으신가요?
여 조금만 더 일찍 봐 주실 수는 없으신가요? 제 아들 얼굴에 이상한 발진이 생겼거든요.
남 미안합니다만, 오늘 오후는 예약이 다 찼어요.
여 제발 도와주세요. 급해요.
남 그렇다면, 제 동료인 Baldwin 박사에게 아드님을 데려가시는 건 어떠세요?
여 그럼, 지금 가도 될까요?
남 그에게 확인하는 동안 잠시만 기다려주세요. 네, 괜찮습니다. 도착하자마자 아드님을 봐 드릴 겁니다.
여 **감사합니다. 30분 내로 갈게요.**

해설 의사인 남자는 자신의 동료 Baldwin 박사에게 진료 받을 것을 추천하며 그의 스케줄을 확인하고 바로 진료가 가능하다고 했으므로 이에 여자는 곧 진료를 받으러 가겠다고 해야 적절할 것이다. ① 죄송해요. 선약이 있어요. ③ 걱정 마세요. 다음에 다시 일정을 잡을 거예요. ④ 어제 약속이 있었다는 것을 완전히 잊었어요. ⑤ 내일 아침에 예약할 수 있나요?

어휘 develop (병이) 발병하다 rash 발진, 뽀루지 colleague 동료

15 ④

해석 여 Grace와 Will은 같은 고등학교에 다니는 쌍둥이다. Grace는 매우 사교적이고 외향적이지만 Will은 그렇지 않다. 그는 주로 집에서 컴퓨터 게임을 한다. 컴퓨터 게임을 하는 것은 단순히 여가에 하는 취미가 아니다. 그는 게임에 중독된 경향을 보인다. 게임하느라 밤을 꼬박 새고, 집에서는 잘 먹지도 않는다. 결국, 건강도 급격하게 나빠지고 있다. 또한, 학교에서 성적이 좋지 않다. 부모는 아들에 대한 걱정이 크다. 그래서 그들은 학교 선생님과 상담 선생님에게 이 문제에 대해 얘기한다. 그들은 Will이 가장 필요한 것은 또래 친구들과 나가서 놀고 맑은 공기를 마시는 것이라는 결론을 내렸다. 그들은 그의 여자 형제인 Grace가 큰 도움이 될 거라고 생각하고 도움을 요청했다. 이 상황에서, Grace가 Will에게 할 말로 가장 적절한 것은 무엇인가?
Grace Will, **나랑 등산 클럽에 같이 가입할래?**

해설 Grace가 Will에게 친구들과 어울려서 맑은 공기를 마실 수 있는 활동을 제안하는 것이 가장 적절하다. ① 제발 음식 좀 먹어라. ② 나 돈 좀 빌려 줄래? ③ 나 숙제하는 것 좀 도와줄래? ⑤ 컴퓨터 게임하는 것 좀 가르쳐 줘.

어휘 alpine club 산악회 sociable 사교적인 outgoing 외향적인 tendency 경향 addicted ~에 빠져 있는 barely 거의 ~없다 decline 감소하다 rapidly 급격하게

16-17 ⑤, ①

해석 남 오늘은 탈모에 대해서 얘기해 봅시다. 탈모라는 용어에 대해 들어본 적

있나요? 이 용어가 친숙하지 않을 수도 있지만 간단히 말해서 머리나 몸에서 털이 빠지는 것을 의미합니다. 나이가 들면서 탈모가 진행되는 것은 자연스러운 일입니다. 하지만 20, 30대에 탈모가 심각하게 시작된다면 심한 스트레스를 받기도 합니다. 그렇다면 탈모의 원인은 무엇일까요? 먼저 당신의 머리카락을 강제적으로 잡아당기면 머리카락이 빠질 수 있습니다. 특히 평상시에 머리를 심하게 당겨서 묶거나 땋는 것과 같은 머리 모양을 하는 것은 돌이킬 수 없는 머리카락의 손실의 원인으로 알려져 있습니다. 이것을 견인성 탈모증이라고 부릅니다. 고데기로 머리를 하는 것도 탈모를 유발할 수 있습니다. 때때로 철분 결핍이 탈모의 원인이 되기도 합니다.

해설 16 처음에는 탈모의 정의에 대해 간단히 언급하고, 그 이후에는 탈모의 원인에 대해 설명했다.

17 본문에서 탈모가 20, 30대에 급격히 진행될 때 스트레스를 받는다고 언급되었을 뿐 원인으로 언급된 것은 아니다.

어휘 **alopecia** 탈모 **compulsively** 강제적으로 **ponytail** 포니테일(말꼬리 모양으로 묶은 머리) **braid** 땋아 늘인 머리 **irreversible** 돌이킬 수 없는 **traction** 견인, 당기기 **iron deficiency** 철 결핍 **lead to** ~의 원인이 되다

Dictation

01 ready to eat
02 have a housewarming party
03 According to the weather forecast / take into account
04 all blurry / catch the precious moment
05 memorize your lines / take a break
06 at your place / wore a red cape / forgot to put on shoes
07 plenty of work to do / treat you to lunch
08 not in a good mood / would be no doubt / try to persuade
09 looking for a shirt / That's reasonable / get a discount
10 It's a pleasure / tell me in detail
11 recognize the giant pandas / are extremely lazy
12 Why don't we / always been thrilling
13 is fully booked / pay for that
14 a little bit earlier / Hold on a second
15 sociable and outgoing / get some fresh air
16-17 loss of hair / pull your hair compulsively / can lead to

02회 듣기 모의고사
p.12-13

01 ④	02 ②	03 ④	04 ②	05 ④	06 ②
07 ④	08 ④	09 ③	10 ⑤	11 ⑤	12 ④
13 ②	14 ④	15 ④	16 ②	17 ②	

01 ④

해석 여 리포트 끝냈어?
남 아직. 갈 길이 멀어. 내일까지 끝내지 못할 것 같아.
여 이 교수님께 가서 기한 좀 연장해 달라고 부탁해 보는 게 어때?
남 **불가능할 것 같아. 그녀는 아주 엄격해.**

해설 이 교수님을 찾아가서 기한을 연장해 보라고 권유하는 말이므로 "불가능할 것 같아. 그녀는 아주 엄격해."라고 대답하는 것이 가장 적절하다. ① 네 리포트 좀 빌릴 수 있을까? ② 난 끝내야 할 리포트가 하나 더 있어. ③ 왜냐하면 난 그녀를 잘 모르기 때문이야. ⑤ 나는 리포트의 길이를 늘이는 것을 원하지 않아.

어휘 **strict** 엄격한 **extend** 늘리다, 연장하다 **have a long way to go** 갈 길이 멀다 **extension** 기한 연장

02 ②

해석 남 새로 온 전학생 어떻게 생각해?
여 지난주에 우리 반으로 전학 온 Emily 말하는 거야?
남 어. 그 아이는 확실히 하는 일마다 열정과 열의가 있어. 그렇지 않니?
여 **네 말에 전적으로 동감이야.**

해설 전학생이 열정적이라는 말을 하고 난 뒤 그것을 어떻게 생각하는지 물었으므로 "네 말에 전적으로 동감이야."라고 답하는 것이 가장 적절하다. ① 난 Emily가 누구인지 잘 모르겠어. ③ 응. 그녀는 패션 감각이 있어. ④ 새로운 학교로의 전학은 도전일 수 있어. ⑤ 나는 그녀를 초등학교에 다닐 때부터 알아왔어.

어휘 **cannot agree with you more** 전적으로 동의하다 **transfer** 전학하다 **certainly** 분명히 **passion** 열의

03 ④

해석 남 에세이를 더 전문적으로 쓰기를 원하십니까? 그러면 이 절차를 따르십시오. 그러면 당신의 다음 논술 프로젝트가 당신의 최고의 작품이 될 수 있음을 알게 될 것입니다. 우선 당신의 논지를 계획하고 철저한 연구 조사를 하십시오. 연구 조사는 당신의 주장을 내세우기 위해 필요할 뿐 아니라 초안을 작성하는 데 필수적입니다. 둘째, 깊이 있는 연구 조사 후 객관적인 논조를 유지하면서 초고를 작성하세요. 그 다음, 초고를 선생님이나 친구들에게 가져가서 수정해 달라고 하세요. 셋째, 초고를 몇 번 수정한 다음, 최종 원고를 다시 한 번 교정하세요. 교정 작업은 정말 중요하다는 것을 기억해야 하는데, 최종 원고는 문법이나 문장 구조 면에서 오류가 없어야 하기 때문입니다.

해설 전문적인 논술 작성을 위해 글쓴이가 해야 할 일을 차례대로 소개하고 있는 글이다.

어휘 **professional** 전문적인 **argument** 주장, 논지 **in-depth** 철저한, 상세한 **profound** 심도 있는, 깊이 있는 **draft** 원고 **edit** 수정하다 **revise** 수정하다 **proofreading** 교정 **error-free** 실수가 없는 **in terms of** ~의 면에서

04 ②

해석 남 나 내일 대학 입학시험을 봐.
여 그렇구나. 내일이 바로 그날이네. 아주 긴장되겠다.
남 응, 사실 제한 시간 안에 모든 문제에 답을 할 수 없을 것 같아서 두려워.

여 걱정 마. 너는 할 수 있을 거야. 오늘밤에는 일찍 자야 해. 충분히 휴식을 취하는 것은 정말 중요해.

남 하지만 가능할 것 같지 않아. 너무 긴장돼서 잠을 잘 수 없을 것 같아.

여 아냐, 그러면 안 돼. 어떤 사람들은 평상시처럼 잠을 자야 한다고 말하지만, 나는 그것에 동의하지 않아.

남 왜?

여 충분히 잠을 자지 않으면 점심 식사 후에 졸릴 거야.

남 정말? 사실, 나는 역사 공부를 할 계획이었어. 내가 역사를 못하잖아.

여 수면이 너의 기억력을 향상시켜 줄 거야. 그러니까 그만 가서 자도록 해.

해설 여자는 시험 전날에 충분히 휴식을 취해야 하며, 수면이 기억력을 향상시켜 줄 것이라고 말하고 있다.

어휘 limited 제한된 take a rest 휴식을 취하다 be poor at ~을 못하다

05 ④

해석 남 김 씨이신가요?

여 예, 그렇습니다. 당신은…….

남 James White입니다. 제가 오늘 운전 실기 시험을 맡아 할 겁니다.

여 오, 안녕하세요. White 씨. 이제 제가 어떻게 하면 되나요?

남 하셔야 할 일은 저와 함께 보험에 든 차량을 타시고 부근을 도는 것입니다.

여 아주 간단한 일 같은데요.

남 당신이 운전하는 동안, 제가 교통 신호와 규정을 지키는지 점검할 겁니다.

여 알겠습니다. 매우 긴장되네요.

남 운전을 마친 다음 합격, 불합격 여부를 결정하겠습니다. 자, 준비됐나요?

여 예. 이번에는 합격해야 할 텐데요.

남 자, 차에 타고 시작하시죠.

해설 운전 실기 시험의 감독관과 응시자의 대화이다.

어휘 insured 보험에 든 traffic signal 교통 신호 regulation 규정

06 ②

해석 여 김 선생님, 누가 딸 Mary이죠?

남 저기서 운동을 하고 있어요.

여 운동이요? 아, 운동장 한가운데에서 친구들과 줄넘기를 하고 있죠, 그렇죠?

남 아니오. 네트 앞에서 서브 연습을 하고 있어요.

여 아, 알겠어요. 친구가 반대편에서 공을 받을 건가 봐요.

남 맞아요. 이 선생님, 선생님의 아들들은 어디 있어요?

여 저기 농구 코트에 있어요.

남 아이들이 몇 명 있는데, 그 중 누구예요?

여 한 명은 지금 농구공을 들고 있고, 다른 아이는 농구 골대에 매달려 있어요. 방금 덩크슛을 했어요.

남 와, 농구를 잘하네요. 자랑스럽겠어요.

여 네, 정말 그래요. 감사합니다.

해설 배구 네트를 사이에 두고 남자의 딸과 딸의 친구가 공을 주고 받으려 하고 있다고

했는데, 네트 반대편에 사람이 없으므로 대화의 내용과 일치하지 않는다.

어휘 jump rope 줄넘기하다 receive ~을 받다 opposite 반대쪽의, 마주보는 hang on ~에 매달리다 dunk 덩크슛을 하다 indeed 정말로

07 ④

해석 남 송 선생님, 잠시 얘기할 수 있을까요?

여 그래. 여기 앉으렴.

남 고맙습니다. 이곳은 따뜻하고 조용하네요.

여 그렇지. 그래, 무슨 일이니?

남 음, 제가 미국의 대학에 지원하려고 하는데요.

여 그래? 어느 대학에 관심이 있니?

남 중서부 지역의 주립 대학을 생각하고 있어요.

여 그렇구나! 나는 중서부 지역에 있는 콜로라도 주립 대학에서 공부했단다.

남 그러면 그 지역의 대학에 대해서 정보를 좀 주실 수 있겠네요.

여 물론이지. 기후, 교통, 캠퍼스, 등록금, 기타 뭐든지.

남 감사합니다. 그리고 저의 추천서를 써 주실 수 있는지 궁금해요.

여 물론이지. 영광이구나. 너는 나의 가장 훌륭한 학생들 중 하나였잖니.

해설 여자가 남자를 위해 할 일은 대학 지원에 필요한 추천서를 써 주는 일이다.

어휘 apply for 지원하다 tuition 등록금 or whatever 혹은 뭐든지 a letter of recommendation 추천서

08 ④

해석 여 무슨 일이야?

남 이 일정에 따르면, 우리 학교 체육 대회가 다음 토요일에 있을 예정이래.

여 그래. 기다려지니?

남 물론이야. 너도 알다시피 나는 스포츠를 아주 좋아하잖아. 다음 토요일은 '나의 날'이 될 거야.

여 무슨 스포츠를 가장 좋아하니?

남 골프와 스키를 가장 좋아하지만, 내가 정말 잘하는 것은 축구야.

여 너는 만능 스포츠맨 같구나.

남 모두 그렇게 얘기해.

여 하지만 다음 토요일은 비가 올 수도 있어서 행사가 연기되거나 취소될지도 몰라.

남 그래? 나로서는 안 좋은 소식인데. 실망이야.

여 너무 미리 포기하지 마. 알잖아, 일기예보는 자주 틀리니까.

해설 여자가 다음 주 토요일에 비가 올 수도 있어 체육 대회가 연기되거나 취소될지도 모른다고 말하자 남자가 실망이라고 이야기했다.

어휘 look forward to ~ 기대하다 all-around 다재다능한 postpone 연기하다 discouraging 낙담시키는 weather forecast 일기 예보 inaccurate 부정확한

09 ③

해석 여 여보세요. ABC 배달 서비스입니다. 무엇을 도와드릴까요?

남 예. 지금 배달 서비스를 이용하고 싶은데요.

여 예. 위치가 어디시죠?

남 저는 Fort Collins에 있고, Boulder와 Greenville로 배달을 부탁할 거예요.

여 어떤 물건인가요?

남 실은 서류 뭉치 두 개인데, 하나는 Boulder로, 다른 하나는 Greenville로 보낼 겁니다.

여 좋습니다. Boulder는 25달러이고 Greenville은 30달러입니다.

남 어? Greenville이 왜 더 비싼지 잘 이해가 안 되는데요.

여 Greenville까지의 거리가 Boulder 보다 더 멀거든요.

남 아뇨. 여기 Fort Collins에서는 거의 같은 거리인데요.

여 오, 죄송합니다. 제가 착각한 것 같아요. 각각 25달러로 해드릴게요.

남 고맙습니다. 제 이름은 Pete Baker이고, 휴대 전화번호는 970-292-0688입니다.

해설 각각의 배달 장소에 대해 25달러로 정정하였으므로 지불할 금액은 50달러이다.

어휘 **courier service** 배달 서비스 **pack** 꾸러미 **document** 문서 **farther** far(먼, 멀리)의 비교급 **mistaken** 틀린, 착각한

10 ⑤

해석 남 나 지금 A마트에 갈 거예요. 사다 줄 것이 있나요?

여 음, 휴지가 떨어진 것 같아요.

남 휴지. 알겠어요. 다른 건요?

여 그리고 과일이 좀 먹고 싶어요.

남 좋아요. 여러 가지 과일이 지금 제철이죠.

여 근데 A마트에는 왜 가려고 해요?

남 아, Ted를 위해 선물을 사려고요. 내일이 생일이거든요.

여 Ted요? Ted가 누구죠?

남 기억 안 나요? 내가 프로젝트를 할 때 많이 도와줬던 직장 동료 중 한 명이에요.

여 기억나요. 그래서 무엇을 살 거예요?

남 넥타이하고 와이셔츠를 사려고요. 그는 정장을 입는 것을 좋아하거든요.

여 알겠어요. 지갑 가져가는 것 잊지 마세요.

해설 지갑은 남자가 구입할 물건이 아니라 가져가야 할 물건이다.

어휘 **run out of** 다 떨어지다 **toilet paper** 휴지, 화장지 **be in season** 제철이다 **colleague** 동료

11 ⑤

해석 남 당신은 재채기를 참는 것이 나쁘다고 생각하나요, 아니면 그렇지 않다고 생각하나요? 답을 알아보도록 합시다. 재채기의 원인은 기침의 원인과 유사합니다. 재채기는 우리 몸이 바이러스나 먼지 같은 거기 있지 않아야 할 것을 없애는 방법 중 하나입니다. 만약 당신이 재채기를 참으면 빠르고, 강한 압력이 머릿속에서 생성되어서 세균을 코나 귀의 구멍으로 더 깊숙이 밀어 넣어서 감염을 유발할 수 있습니다. 그 압력은 예민한 귀 고막에 손상을 줄 수도 있습니다. 물론 그냥 "에이취!"라고 큰 소리를 내는 것이 예의에 어긋나거나 민망한 순간이 있습니다. 그런 때에는 처음 재채기가 나올 것 같이 찡할 때 코끝을 꼬집어보세요. 이것이 재채기를 멈추는 데 도움이 될 것입니다. 기침은 참을 수 없지만 재채기를 참을 수 있습니다.

해설 재채기는 참을 수 있지만, 기침은 참을 수 없다고 했다.

어휘 **hold back** 참다 **sneeze** 재채기, 재채기하다 **intense** 강렬한 **sinus** 부비강 (두개골 속의 코 안쪽으로 이어지는 구멍) **delicate** 섬세한 **let out** (소리를) 내다 **oncoming** 다가오는

12 ④

해석 남 와, 드디어 우리가 여기에 왔어.

여 봐, 탈 것이 아주 많아서 어떤 걸 먼저 타야 할지 결정을 할 수 없어. 너는?

남 모두 흥미롭고 재미있을 것 같아. Transformer부터 타는 게 어때?

여 멀미를 해서 약간 어지러워. 4D 화면하고 움직이는 의자 때문에 더 어지러울 것 같아. 그래서 난 차라리 Haunted House에 들어가고 싶은데, 어때?

남 Haunted House는 무서운 거잖아. 나는 귀신이 무서워. 그런 건 견딜 수가 없어.

여 알겠어. 그럼 Cliff Hanger를 타는 건?

남 그건 마지막을 위해 남겨 두고 싶어. 그리고 회전목마는 너무 지루하고.

여 이해했어. 네가 무엇을 타고 싶어 하는지 알겠다. 가자. 시간이 가고 있어.

해설 Transformer는 어지럽고, Haunted House는 무섭고, Cliff Hanger는 마지막에 타고 싶고, 회전목마는 지루하다고 했으므로 두 사람이 탈 놀이기구는 The Big Flush이다.

어휘 **carousel** 회전목마 **ride** 놀이기구, 탈 것 **dizzy** 어지러운 **carsickness** 차멀미 **stand** 견디다 **tick** 똑딱거리며 지나가다

13 ②

해석 남 전 선생님. 영어를 원어민처럼 하시네요.

여 칭찬해 주셔서 감사합니다.

남 비결이 무엇인가요?

여 사실은 오랫동안 해외에 살았어요.

남 그랬군요! 외국에 얼마나 오래 사셨나요?

여 음. 미국에서 약 10년 살았어요. 특히, 미국에서 석사 학위를 취득했죠.

남 와, 영어를 유창하게 하시는 게 당연하네요!

여 게다가, 영어 원어민인 캐나다 사람과 결혼했죠.

남 더 좋은 것이 없겠네요. 그러면 남편과 영어로 대화를 하시나요?

여 물론이죠. 하루 종일 영어로 이야기해요. 그게 저의 비결이죠.

해설 남자가 여자에게 남편과 영어로 대화를 하느냐고 질문했으므로 매일 영어로 대화를 한다고 답하는 것이 가장 적절하다. ① 예. 지금은 모두가 영어를 해요. ③ 그는 아직 이곳에서 생활하는 데 어려움을 겪고 있는 것 같아요. ④ 가끔요. 하지만 그의 영어 실력이 크게 향상되었어요. ⑤ 예. 다행히 대학에 강사직을 구했어요.

어휘 **compliment** 칭찬 **as a matter of fact** 사실은 **the States** 미국 **master's degree** 석사 학위

14 ④

해석 남 Sarah, 무엇에 그렇게 몰두하고 있니?

여 오, Paul. 나 망설이고 있어

남 뭘? 말해봐. 친구 좋다는 게 뭐야.

여 음, 캠퍼스에 내 타입인 것 같은 그런 남자가 있어.

남 마침내 네 이상형을 찾았구나!

여 어, 그런 것 같아. 그에게 데이트 신청을 하고 싶은데, 그가 좋아할지 아닐지 잘 모르겠어.

남 그 사람 성격은 어때? 외향적이야? 내성적이야?

여 왜 그런 질문을 하는 거야?

남 왜냐하면 남자들은 반대 성향의 여성에게 끌리는 경향이 있거든. 예를 들면 나처럼 외향적인 사람은 조용한 여성에게 매료되고, 조용한 남자는 먼저 다가오는 여자에게 끌려.

여 오, 그래? 그는 너랑은 완전히 반대 타입의 사람인 것 같아.

남 그럼 무엇을 기다리니? 그에게 먼저 다가가야 해.

해설 조용한 남자는 활발한 여성에게 끌리는 경향이 있으므로 남자는 여자에게 먼저 다가가라고 충고하는 것이 가장 적절할 것이다. ① 그런 경우라면 그 남자를 포기하는 것이 낫겠어. ② 그러면 그에게 먼저 데이트 신청해서는 안 돼. ③ 응, 완벽한 이상형의 남자를 찾는 것은 항상 어려워. ⑤ 그에게 데이트 신청하기 전에 그의 성격을 고려해야 해.

어휘 **Mr. Right** 완벽한 이상형의 남자 **be obsessed with** ~에 몰두되어 있다 **ask out on a date** 데이트 신청을 하다 **extrovert** 외향적인 **introvert** 내성적인 **be apt to** ~하는 경향이 있다 **make the first move** 먼저 행동을 취하다

15 ④

해석 남 Brian과 Andy는 친한 친구이다. 특히 그들은 농구를 좋아한다. 그래서 자주 다른 친구들과 시합을 한다. 하지만, Brian은 Andy가 언제나 자기만의 플레이를 하려고 하는 것을 발견한다. 공을 패스해야 할 때도 하지 않고, 자신이 슛을 하려고 한다. 그것이 Brian을 짜증나게 한다. 지금, 점심시간에 둘은 농구 시합을 하고 있다. 또 Andy는 드리블을 하면서, Brian에게 패스를 하지 않고 슛을 하려고 한다. 하지만, 슛을 하기에는 Brian이 더 좋은 위치에 있다. 이 상황에서, Brian이 Andy에게 할 말로 가장 적절한 것은 무엇인가?

Brian Andy! 이쪽으로 공을 던져.

해설 Brian이 Andy보다 득점하기 유리한 위치에 있으므로 "이쪽으로 공을 던져."라고 말하는 것이 가장 적절하다. ① 슛 해. ② 그의 패스를 가로채. ③ 리바운드를 잡아. ⑤ 바로 거기서 공을 막아.

어휘 **intercept** 가로채다 **shot** (농구의) 슛; 슛을 하다 **annoy** 짜증나게 하다, 괴롭히다 **dribble** 드리블하다

16-17 ②, ②

해석 (삑소리)

여 안녕하세요, Skinner 교장 선생님! Calgary 공공 도서관의 관장 Andrea Kim입니다. 연락이 안 되어서 이렇게 음성 메시지를 남깁니다. 초등학생을 대상으로 '동화 쓰는 방법'이라는 방과 후 프로그램을 새로이 시작함에 따라, 어린이들에게 도움을 줄 수 있는 고등학생을 찾고 있습니다. 학생들은 어린이에게 질문에 대한 답변을 하고, 간단한 쓰기 테크닉을 가르칠 것이며, 매 수업이 끝나고 자료를 정리하는 등의 다양한 활동을 하게 될 것입니다. 급여는 시간당 9달러이며, 일하는 시간은 협의될 것이지만, 주말이 포함될 수도 있습니다. 교장 선생님께서

그 자리에 적합한 학생들을 아신다면 저희 도서관의 폐관 시간인 저녁 6시까지 전화 주십시오. 감사합니다.

해설 16 도서관 총 책임자로서 시간제 일자리에 적합한 고등학생을 추천해 줄 것을 요청하고 있다.

17 도서관에서 초등학생을 대상으로 방과 후 프로그램을 운영한다는 것이지 초등학생만 이용 가능한 초등학생 전용 도서관이라는 언급은 하지 않았다.

어휘 **principal** 교장 **after-school program** 방과 후 프로그램 **tutor** 가르치다 **negotiate** 상의하다, 협의하다 **qualified** 자격을 갖춘

Dictation

01 ask for an extension

02 transferred to our class

03 plan an argument / proofreading is really vital

04 should go to bed early / you will feel sleepy

05 for today's driving test / traffic signals and regulations

06 practicing serves / hanging on the basket

07 Have a seat / Which colleges or universities / one of my best students

08 will be held / I'm really good at / often inaccurate

09 have my things delivered / almost the same distance

10 run out of toilet paper / buy a present / bring your wallet

11 hold back your sneeze / a rapid and intense pressure / try pinching

12 feel a little dizzy / sounds too boring

13 for your compliment / got my master's degree

14 still hesitating / ask him out / a totally different type

15 like to play basketball / make his own shot / in a better position

16-17 leaving a message / can give them a hand / call me back

03회 듣기모의고사
p.18-19

01 ③	02 ⑤	03 ②	04 ①	05 ③	06 ⑤
07 ④	08 ②	09 ③	10 ④	11 ③	12 ①
13 ③	14 ①	15 ④	16 ⑤	17 ②	

01 ③

해석 여 실례합니다. 무슨 일인가요?

남 엘리베이터가 고장 났어요. 계단을 이용하세요.

여 알려주셔서 고마워요. 고치는 데 얼마나 걸릴까요?

남 글쎄요. 40분쯤 걸릴 거예요.

해설 여자가 엘리베이터 고치는 데 걸리는 시간을 물었으므로 남자가 시간과 관련된 대답을 하는 것이 적절하다. ① 올라가시나요? ② 안 돼요! 늦었어요. 서둘러야 해요. ④ 미안해요. 그건 당신과 나 사이에 비밀이에요. ⑤ 고마워하실 필요 없어요. 그건 제 일인걸요.

어휘 out of order 고장이 난 take the stairs 계단을 올라가다 fix 수리하다

02 ⑤

해석 남 안녕, Julie! 오늘 나랑 바닷가에 가는 거 어때?
여 바닷가? 좋아! 뭘 가져갈까?
남 수영복, 선글라스, 모자, 자외선 차단제······. 내 생각엔 이게 전부인 것 같아.
여 **좋아. 음료수는? 목마르길 원하지는 않잖아, 그렇지?**

해설 여자가 말한 준비물 외에도 음료수가 필요하다고 말하는 것이 가장 적절하다. ① 넌 뭐가 필요해? ② 아니, 난 준비가 안 됐어. 여행을 미루자. ③ 나도 그래. 바닷가에서 노는 건 재미있을 거야. ④ 오, 괜찮아. 바닷가 가는 길에 살 수 있잖아.

어휘 sunscreen 자외선 차단제

03 ②

해석 남 여름 방학에 특별한 계획이 있으신가요? 없으시다면, 여기에 주목하세요. 우리는 여름 활동 프로그램을 제공합니다. 이 프로그램은 여름 동안 굉장한 경험을 하도록 도와줄 것입니다. 도전적인 학문적이고 사회적인 활동을 통해 배우고 경험할 수 있습니다. 활동은 수영, 테니스, 팀으로 하는 운동, 창의적인 글쓰기, 공연 예술, 컴퓨터 기술, 시각 예술 등이 포함됩니다. 모든 활동은 다양한 나이 집단의 학생들을 만족시킬 수 있도록 고안되었습니다. 우리는 도전적이고 재미있는 활동을 이끌어 나갈 자격을 갖춘 교사진을 갖추고 있습니다.

해설 여름 활동 프로그램의 수업 종류와 선생님들에 대해 언급하면서 프로그램에 대한 홍보를 하고 있다.

어휘 pay attention to ~에 주목하다 provide sb with sth ~에게 ~을 제공하다 challenging 도전적인 visual arts 시각 예술 be designed to ~하도록 이루어지다(고안되다)

04 ①

해석 남 여보, 냄새가 좋네요. 무엇을 요리하고 있어요?
여 오믈렛을 만들고 있어요. 당신이 좋아했으면 좋겠어요.
남 지난번에 똑같은 음식을 했잖아요, 안 그래요?
여 이번은 새로운 요리법이에요.
남 지금 좀 먹어 봐도 되요? 많이 먹지 않을게요.
여 저기 있는 프라이팬만 나에게 건네 주신다면요, 그리고 기다려요. 요리가 아직 다 안 됐어요.
남 좋아요. 와, 이 소스 안에 도대체 무엇을 넣은 거죠?
여 이것저것 조금씩 넣었어요. 올리브 오일에 양파와 마늘을 같이 넣고 볶은 후에, 빨간 고추를 갈아 넣고 좀 더 익혔어요.
남 빨간 고추라고요? 오믈렛이랑 안 어울릴 것 같은데요.
여 똑같은 음식을 만드는 건 지루하잖아요, 안 그래요?

해설 여자의 마지막 말에서 여자는 음식을 만들 때 늘 새로운 시도를 즐긴다는 것을 알 수 있다.

어휘 omelet 오믈렛 recipe 요리법 hand over 건네주다 garlic 마늘 grind 갈다 leave 놔두다 match with ~와 어울리다

05 ③

해석 남 얼마죠?
여 총 합계가 49달러예요.
남 여기 50달러 있어요. 그런데, 제 아파트까지 배달해 주실 수 있나요?
여 죄송해요, 손님, 50달러 이상만 배달해 드려요.
남 그렇다면, 이 배터리도 추가해 주세요. 그럼 총액이 얼마죠?
여 배터리가 1달러 50센트예요. 총액은 50달러 50센트입니다. 아파트까지 배달해 드릴 수 있겠네요.
남 언제 받을 수 있죠? 한 시간 안에는 제가 집에 없을 건데요.
여 지금부터 한 시간 후에 배달해 드리죠. 주소와 전화번호를 적어 주세요. 여기 영수증 있어요.
남 고맙습니다.
여 천만에요.

해설 물건 값 계산과 배달을 요청하는 대화 내용을 통해 가게에 온 손님과 계산원 간의 대화임을 알 수 있다.

어휘 come to 합계가 ~이다 arrange 준비하다, 마련하다 delivery 배달 total 총액 receipt 영수증

06 ⑤

해석 (전화벨이 울린다.)
여 여보세요, Bill.
남 여보세요, Grace. 집에 오는 중이야? 너를 기다리고 있어.
여 미안해. 거의 다 왔어. 엄마의 생일 파티를 위해 내가 사야 할 것은 없어?
남 없어, 내가 거의 다 준비한 것 같아. 너는 가능한 한 집에 빨리 오기만 하면 돼. 생일 선물과 케이크를 사서 테이블 위에 놓았어.
여 그럼, 꽃다발도 샀어?
남 아니. 그건 사지 않았지만, 필요할 것 같지 않아. 엄마는 꽃 알레르기가 있어.
여 그럼 생일 카드는?
남 아, 생일 카드. 우리 여동생이 엄마를 위해 생일 카드를 만들었어.
여 정말? 어떻게 생겼어? 말해 줘.
남 위에 "Happy Birthday"라고 쓰여 있고, 리본으로 장식되어 있어. 그 아래에는 초와 꽃으로 장식된 케이크가 그려져 있어. 선물 옆에 카드를 놓아두었어.
여 와, 엄마가 분명 좋아할 거야.

해설 엄마가 꽃 알레르기가 있어서 꽃다발은 사지 않았다고 했으므로 꽃다발은 대화의 내용과 일치하지 않는다.

어휘 bouquet 꽃다발 be allergic to ~에 알레르기가 있다 phrase 문구

07 ④

해석 남 오, 맙소사! 이건 말도 안 돼요.
여 여보, 무슨 일 있어요?

남 속도위반 딱지를 또 받았어요.

여 오, 안 되는데. 또요? 언제 과속했어요?

남 지난번 기억해요? 아침 미팅에 맞춰 가려고 정말 서둘렀던 일. 내 추측엔 그때인 거 같아요.

여 지난주 월요일 말하는 거예요? 그래, 벌금이 얼마죠?

남 100달러예요. 이번이 네 번째예요. 우리가 여태껏 낸 벌금이면 GPS 한 개를 살 수도 있었겠어요.

여 다시 속도위반 딱지를 떼이지 않기 위해서 GPS를 사는 것이 더 나을 것 같아요.

남 당신이 맞아요.

여 그래서 지금 벌금 내러 은행에 갈 건가요?

남 아뇨, GPS를 사러 Electro Mart에 갈 거예요. 당신이 GPS에 대해선 나보다 더 잘 알잖아요. 지금 같이 갈 수 있어요?

여 물론이죠.

해설 남자가 과속으로 딱지를 받고 아내와 대화하는 상황으로, 네 번의 벌금을 합하면 딱지를 떼이는 것을 방지할 수 있는 GPS를 살 수 있다고 동의하고 남자는 전자 마트에 가서 GPS를 사겠다고 말하고 있다.

어휘 ridiculous 웃기는, 말도 안 되는 speeding ticket 과속 위반딱지 conference 회의 fine 벌금 GPS(Global Positioning System) 범지구 위성항법시스템 come along 같이 가다

08 ②

해석 남 손님, 어떻게 도와드릴까요?

여 제 이불과 어울릴 침대보를 찾고 있어요.

남 이불 사이즈가 어떻게 되시죠?

여 싱글 사이즈요.

남 무늬가 있나요?

여 아뇨, 없어요. 무늬가 없는 흰색 이불이에요.

남 그런 경우라면, 줄무늬 침대보가 손님의 이불과 잘 어울릴 것 같네요.

여 저 줄무늬 침대보 말인가요? 글쎄요, 왜 그렇게 생각하시죠?

남 무늬가 없는 흰색 이불은 너무 평범해요. 저 줄무늬 침대보가 시각적 대조 효과를 줄 거예요.

여 하지만 개인적으로 어떤 무늬도 좋아하지 않아요.

남 이게 아마 당신의 마음을 바꿀 거예요. 게다가, 저희는 지금 한 개 가격으로 두 개의 싱글 사이즈 줄무늬 침대보를 제공하고 있어요.

여 좋은 기회 같군요. 그걸로 살게요.

해설 무늬가 있는 침대보를 좋아하지 않아서 부정적인 반응을 보였지만, 마지막에 점원이 한 개 가격으로 두 개를 살 수 있다 해서 줄무늬 침대보를 사기로 결정했다.

어휘 bed sheet 침대보 blanket 이불, 담요 pattern 무늬, 양식 plain 평범한, 무늬가 없는 solid 무늬가 없는, 색 변화가 없는 visual contrast 시각적 대조 for the price of one 한 개 가격으로

09 ③

해석 남 가족 여행을 위해서 차를 빌리고 싶어요.

여 며칠 동안 차를 빌리실 거죠?

남 6일이요. 가족은 총 7명입니다. 그래서 큰 차가 필요해요.

여 그렇다면, 미니밴을 하세요. 운전자를 포함해서 8명까지 탈 수 있어요.

남 좋아요. 미니밴으로 하죠. 요금이 얼마죠?

여 보험료가 포함된 총 금액은 하루에 200달러입니다. 보험에 드실 건가요?

남 네, 그래 주세요. 그리고 하루 무료 대여 쿠폰이 있는데. 사용할 수 있죠?

여 그럼요. 면허증 좀 주시겠어요?

남 알겠어요. 여기 있어요.

해설 미니밴을 빌리는 비용은 보험료를 포함하여 하루에 200달러이다. 6일간 빌리는 총 요금은 1,200달러인데, 하루 무료 대여 쿠폰을 사용할 수 있으므로 200달러를 빼면 1,000달러가 정답이 된다.

어휘 rent a car 차를 대여하다 whole 전체의 up to ~까지

10 ④

해석 여 Michael, 너의 첫 출근을 위해 무언가 사 주고 싶어. 무엇을 사 주길 원하니?

남 고마워요, 엄마. 정말 감사해요. 내가 필요한 것은 어떤 것이든 되나요?

여 물론이지, 나와 네 아버지가 너에게 주는 선물이란다. 말만 하렴.

남 우선, 정장 한 벌과 구두 한 켤레가 필요해요.

여 그래, 너는 아직 적당한 정장이 없지. 또 무엇이 필요하니?

남 정장용 셔츠하고 넥타이는 필수죠.

여 알았다. 하지만 너는 서류 가방도 없잖니. 그것 또한 필수인데.

남 Bill 삼촌이 서류 가방을 주기로 하셨어요.

해설 삼촌이 서류 가방을 주기로 했으므로 서류 가방은 살 필요가 없다.

어휘 appreciate ~을 고맙게 생각하다 decent 적당한, 알맞은 necessary 필요한, 없어서는 안 될 briefcase 서류 가방 must 필요한 것

11 ③

해석 여 정신 질환을 앓고 있는 사람을 제외하고 모든 사람은 꿈을 꾼다. 때때로 "난 어젯밤에 꿈 안 꿨어."라고 말하곤 하는데 이것은 사실이 아니다. 이 경우 당신은 꿈을 기억하지 못하는 것뿐이다. 당신은 꿈에서 가끔 현실 세계에서 본 적이 없는 얼굴을 보기도 한다. 하지만 이 역시 사실이 아니다. 당신은 삶 속에서 많은 사람의 얼굴을 보고 당신의 뇌는 꿈을 꾸는 동안 그 얼굴을 활용하는 것이다. 그리고 대부분 당신은 꿈에서 긍정적인 감정보다 부정적인 감정을 경험한다. 이것과 관련해서 여자들은 일반적으로 남자들보다 덜 공격적인 감정을 느낀다.

해설 실제로는 본 얼굴들이지만 기억하지 못하는 것이라고 언급되어 있다.

어휘 psychological disorder 정신 질환 utilize 활용하다 negative 부정적인 positive 긍정적인 aggressive 공격적인

12 ①

해석 남 여보, 우리 차는 너무 오래 되었어요. 차를 새로 사야 한다고 생각하지 않아요?

여 저도 동의해요. 이상한 소리도 나고 기름이 새는 것을 봤어요. 때가 된 것 같아요.

남 좋아요. 인터넷으로 중고차 가격을 확인해 봅시다. GM의 BM 5 모델이 상당히 좋다고 들었어요.

여 맞아요, BM 5가 운전자들 사이에서 평판이 좋아요. 가격은 어때요?

남 5개의 검색 결과가 나왔어요.

여 당신의 자동차를 고르는 첫 번째 조건이 뭐예요?

남 주행 거리가 3만 킬로미터 이하여야 해요.

여 그러면 3가지 선택권이 있어요. 다음은 무엇이 우선이죠? 선택 사양인가요, 아니면 연식인가요?

남 나에게 선택 사양은 중요하지 않아요. 차가 몇 년도에 만들어졌는지가 더 중요해요.

여 3개 선택 중에 SM Encar의 주행 거리가 가장 길어요. 괜찮겠어요? 그리고 가격도 가장 비싸고요.

남 가장 새 것이니 괜찮아요. 난 금전적으로 여유가 있어요. 이것을 위해 돈을 좀 모아 두었어요.

여 좋아요. 그 차를 보러 가요.

해설 남자가 중고차를 고르는 첫 번째 기준이 주행 거리가 3만km 이하이므로 Car PR와 Car Mart는 우선 제외된다. 그 다음으로는 연식인데, SM Encar의 차가 연식이 가장 최근이다. 주행 거리가 남은 세 개 중 가장 길고 가격도 가장 비싸지만 그 차량을 보러 가자고 했으므로 남자는 SM Encar로 중고차를 사러 갈 것이다.

어휘 leak 새다 reputation 평판 mileage 주행거리 option 선택 사항 year 연식 can afford ~할 여유가 있다

13 ③

해석 여 왜 피가 나죠?

남 앞니가 부러졌어요. 통증이 정말 심해요.

여 앉아서 입을 벌려 보세요. 고칠 수 있는지 좀 봅시다. 어쩌다 이렇게 됐죠?

남 친구와 공을 가지고 놀다가 넘어졌어요. 일어나 보니, 이가 부러졌어요.

여 잇몸이 많이 부어있네요. 그 치아는 살릴 수 없겠는데요.

남 그럼, 어떻게 하실 거죠?

여 뽑아야겠어요.

남 많이 아플까요?

여 아뇨, 아무것도 못 느끼실 거예요. 마취를 할 거예요.

남 저는 주사 바늘을 무서워해요. 살살해 주세요.

여 약속해요. 입을 벌리세요.

해설 부러진 이를 뽑아야 하는 상황에서 남자가 주사 바늘을 무서워하니 살살해 달라고 부탁하고 있으므로 남자를 안심시키는 말로 치료를 시작하는 것이 가장 적절하다. ① 내 치아를 건드지 마세요. ② 당신은 정말 용감하신 분이군요. ④ 휴가를 신청해야 할까요? ⑤ 난 왜 이렇게 충치가 많죠?

어휘 bleed 피가 나다 front tooth 앞니 fall down 넘어지다 swell 부풀다 pull out 뽑다 put ~ under an anesthetic ~를 마취시키다

14 ①

해석 여 Peter, 내일 뭐하니?

남 오, Angela. 특별한 건 없는데. 왜 묻는 거야?

여 내일 용평에 갈 계획이야. 같이 갈래?

남 가을에 용평에 간다고? 그런데 가을에는 스키를 탈 수 없잖아.

여 걱정 마. 용평에 가면 즐길 게 많아, 산에 리프트를 타고 올라갈 수 있어.

남 정말이니?

여 그래. 그리고 산악 오토바이도 탈 수 있어. 신 날 거야.

남 재미있겠는데. 알겠어. 그럼 언제 만날까?

여 아침 10시는 어떨까?

남 난 수영 강의에서 10시쯤 돌아올 거야. 그러니 11시가 더 나을 것 같아.

여 좋아. 11시에 너를 데리러 갈게.

남 고마워. 빨리 가고 싶다.

해설 남자는 용평에 가자는 여자의 제안에 동의했고, 여자가 11시에 데리러 간다고 했으므로 "고마워. 빨리 가고 싶다."라고 답하는 것이 가장 적절하다. ② 네가 상관할 일이 아니야. ③ 걱정 마. 우린 시간이 충분해. ④ 미안해. 선약이 있어. ⑤ 고마워, 내일 11시까지 용평에 있을게.

어휘 in particular 특별히 lift (스키장) 리프트

15 ④

해석 여 Michael은 대학생이다. 일주일 전에 김 교수님이 학생들에게 큰 과제물을 내주셨다. Michael은 금요일 오후까지 이 과제물을 제출해야 했다. 오늘은 금요일이지만, 그는 아직 과제물의 반도 끝내지 못했다. 아침에 아버지가 Michael에게 같이 세차를 하자고 말했다. 하지만 Michael은 시간이 없다고 말하면서 문을 꽝 하고 닫았다. 그의 아버지는 그의 태도에 정말로 화가 났지만 그가 정말 바빠 보여서 아무 말도 하지 않았다. Michael은 과제물을 제출하고 나서, 아버지에 대한 그의 잘못된 태도가 기억이 난다. 그는 그렇게 버릇없게 행동한 것에 대해서 정말로 후회한다. 이 상황에서, Michael이 아버지에게 할 말로 가장 적절한 것은 무엇인가?

Michael 아빠, 죄송해요. 제가 했던 일을 용서해 주세요.

해설 Michael은 아버지께 무례하게 행동한 것을 후회하고 용서를 구하려고 하므로 "아빠, 죄송해요. 제가 했던 일을 용서해 주세요."라고 말하는 것이 가장 적절하다. ① 저는 아주 좋은 사람이 아니에요. ② 세차 안 할 거예요. 시키지 마세요. ③ 과제물을 해결하는 건 매우 쉬웠어요. ⑤ 별로 안 바빴어요. 왜 시키지 않으셨어요?

어휘 handle 처리하다, 해결하다 slam the door 문을 꽝 하고 닫다 behavior 행동, 행위 ill-mannered 버릇없는, 예의 없는

16–17 ⑤, ②

해석 오늘은 소아 비만에 대해 얘기하고자 합니다. 이것은 요즘 가장 심각한 건강 문제 중 하나입니다. 2012년에 한 연구는 5세 이하의 어린이 4천2백만 명 이상이 비만이라고 밝혔습니다. 안타깝게도 그 중 3천5백만 명의 어린이가 개발 도상국에 살고 있습니다. 비만 아동은 성인이 되어서도 비만인 경향이 있습니다. 더 심각한 것은 아이들이 어린 나이에 당뇨와 심장 혈관 질환에 걸릴 확률이 더 많다는 것입니다. 그렇다면 원인은 무엇일까요? 비만을 유발하는 다양한 요소가 있습니다. 주요 요소로는 지방과 설탕이 많이 함유된 건강하지 않은 음식을 먹는 것과 낮은 수준의 신체적인 활동이 있습니다.

해설 **16** 5세 이하의 소아 비만 아동의 수와 소아 비만이 주로 나타나는 지역, 관련 질병, 원인 등 전반적으로 소아 비만에 대해 정보를 제공하는 글이다.

17 5세 미만의 비만 아동 중 다수가 개발 도상국에서 살고 있다고 했다.

어휘 **childhood obesity** 소아 비만 **obese** 비만인 **developing country** 개발도상국 **tend to** ~하는 경향이 있다 **diabetes** 당뇨 **cardiovascular** 심장 혈관의

Dictation

01 is out of order
02 going to the beach
03 be a great help / have qualified teachers
04 you hand me / boring to cook
05 arrange for delivery / Don't mention it
06 is allergic to flowers / decorated with candles and flowers
07 got a speeding ticket / buy a GPS to avoid
08 go with my blanket / We are currently offering
09 including the driver / want insurance
10 for your first day at work / you don't have a briefcase
11 in your real life / less aggressive emotions
12 get a new one / What year the car / can afford it
13 in real pain / very swollen
14 nothing in particular / ride mountain bikes
15 hand in this assignment / had no time / remembered his bad behavior
16-17 childhood obesity / stay obese / eating unhealthy food

04회 듣기 모의고사
p.24-25

01 ⑤	02 ①	03 ①	04 ③	05 ⑤	06 ③
07 ②	08 ①	09 ②	10 ⑤	11 ④	12 ③
13 ③	14 ⑤	15 ⑤	16 ④	17 ①	

01 ⑤

해석 남 안녕, Alice. 새 직장을 찾고 있다고 들었어. 진전이 좀 있니?
여 응, 그저께 ABC 마트의 점장 자리 면접을 보았어.
남 오, 어떻게 되었어?
여 **다음 주 월요일까지 결정해서 말해 주겠대.**

해설 남자는 여자가 취업 면접을 보았다는 말을 듣고 그 결과를 묻고 있으므로 가장 적절한 응답은 "다음 주 월요일까지 결정해서 말해 주겠대."이다. ① 전에 한 번도 해고돼 본 적이 없어. ② 면접 준비하는 걸 도와줄게. ③ ABC 마트는 서울의 서쪽에 있는 쇼핑몰이야. ④ 성공한 사람들은 시간 관리를 아주 잘해.

어휘 **fire** 해고하다 **prepare for** ~을 준비하다 **make a decision** 결정하다 **progress** 진보 **the day before yesterday** 그저께

02 ①

해석 여 너는 춤을 정말 잘 추는 것 같아. 나도 춤을 잘 추면 좋을 텐데.
남 같이 출래? 내가 가르쳐 줄 수 있어.
여 나를 망신시키고 싶어서 그러는 거지, 그렇지?
남 **보기보다 어렵지 않아.**

해설 춤추기를 주저하는 여자에게 보기보다 어렵지 않다고 말하는 것이 가장 적절하다. ② 나도 네가 최선을 다하고 있다는 것을 알아. ③ 나는 춤추는 법조차 몰라. ④ 나도 댄스 경연대회에 나가고 싶어. ⑤ 누군가를 난처하게 만드는 것은 전혀 친절한 행동이 아니야.

어휘 **embarrass** 난처하게 하다

03 ①

해석 여 안녕하세요, 여러분! 저는 우리가 자동차를 덜 이용함으로써 우리 자신을 구원할 수 있다는 점에 대해 이야기하기 위해 이 자리에 섰습니다. 자동차는 득보다는 해가 됩니다. 무엇보다 먼저 자동차로 인해 매년 2만 명이 목숨을 잃고, 30만 명 이상이 크게 다치고 있습니다. 둘째로, 대기오염 측면에서만 보아도 자동차는 우리의 건강에 커다란 위협이 됩니다. 게다가 교통 정체도 문제가 됩니다. 끝으로 우리는 자동차가 우리의 환경에 미치는 영향을 생각해 볼 필요가 있습니다. 의심의 여지 없이 자동차는 우리의 삶을 송두리째 파괴하기 시작했습니다. 이러한 문제에 대한 해결책은 간단합니다. 우리가 해야 할 일은 우리 자신을 위해서 대중교통과 우리의 다리를 보다 자주 사용하는 것입니다.

해설 자동차 이용으로 인한 각종 문제를 나열하면서 더 자주 대중교통을 이용하고 걸어 다닐 것을 해결책으로 제시하고 있다.

어휘 **first and foremost** 무엇보다 먼저 **be responsible for** ~에 책임이 있다 **pollution** 오염 **grounds** 근거, 논거 **threat** 위협 **issue** 문제점 **for one's sake** ~를 위하여

04 ③

해석 남 여보, 오늘 저녁은 뭐예요?
여 토마토 스파게티를 만들려고 해요.
남 오, 이미 회사에서 점심으로 먹었어요.
여 그래요? 그럼 대신 볶음밥을 하죠.
남 나가서 먹는 게 어때요? 최근에 나가서 먹은 적이 없잖아요.
여 맞아요. 하지만 나가고 싶은 기분이 아니네요. 봐요! 밖에 비가 오잖아요.
남 음, 그럼 피자를 시키는 건 어때요?
여 당분간은 돈을 아껴서 생활하는 게 좋겠어요. 지난달에 차를 새로 샀던 것을 잊었어요?
남 난 그냥 당신이 오늘 피곤해 보여서 좀 쉬게 해주려고 그랬죠. 좋아요, 저녁은 내가 할게요. 소고기 스테이크 어때요?
여 정말 고마워요. 하지만 냉장고에 있는 많은 채소를 처리해야 해요. 내 생각에는 볶음밥이 더 좋겠어요.
남 그 말이 맞네요. 그럼 소파에서 TV보면서 기다려요.

해설 여자는 지난달에 차를 새로 사서 돈을 아껴야 하고 냉장고에 있는 채소를 처리해야 해서 집에서 음식을 만들어 먹는 것이 좋겠다고 말하고 있다.

어휘 eat out 외식하다 budget 예산 fridge 냉장고 couch 소파

05 ⑤

해석 여 오늘의 첫 번째 손님은 전 보스턴 대학 학장이신 Tomas Henderson 씨입니다. 저희 프로그램에 오신 것을 환영합니다. Henderson 씨.

남 감사합니다. 이 자리에 서게 되어 기쁩니다.

여 시청자 여러분께 왜 시장 선거에 출마하게 되었는지 말씀해 주시죠.

남 음, 아시다시피, 저는 평생을 보스턴에서 살아 왔고, 도시와 시민들에게 뭔가 보답하고 싶습니다.

여 도시를 더 살기 좋은 곳으로 만들기 위한 계획은 무엇인가요?

남 우선, 환경이 더는 나빠지지 않도록 하겠습니다.

여 많은 예산이 들지 않을까요?

남 제 계획은 시 당국과 보스턴에 있는 기업들이 함께 사업을 시작해서 이익을 내는 거예요. 그 돈을 환경을 보호하는 데 사용할 수 있어요. 게다가, 아마 더 많은 일자리도 제공할 거예요.

여 범죄 문제는 어떻게 하실 건가요?

남 더 많은 돈을 경찰력에 투자할 것입니다. 제가 당선되면 Boston은 훨씬 안전한 도시가 될 것입니다.

해설 방송 진행자가 시장 후보에게 시장 선거에 출마한 이유, 도시를 살기 좋은 곳으로 만들기 위한 계획, 범죄 문제에 대한 대책 등을 질문하고 있다.

어휘 principal 교장 audience 청중, 시청자 run for ~에 출마하다 mayor 시장 authorities 당국 make profits 수익을 올리다 elect 선출하다

06 ③

해석 여 여기가 당신의 새 사무실입니다.

남 와, 멋진데요.

여 그렇죠. 당신의 책상과 의자는 저기 창가에 있어요. 그리고 물론 컴퓨터와 전화도 있고요.

남 알겠습니다.

여 문 옆에 나란히 책꽂이와 파일 캐비닛도 있습니다.

남 오, 좋군요. 월요일에 예전 사무실에서 제 물건을 가져올 거예요.

여 그 말을 들으니 반갑군요. 여기에 없는 물건 몇 가지를 주말 동안 들여 놓을 거예요. 고객 접대를 위해서 소파와 탁자를 들여 놓을 거예요. 어디에 두기를 원하세요?

남 제 생각엔 책꽂이와 파일 캐비닛 맞은편에 벽을 따라 두는 것이 가장 좋아 보일 것 같군요.

여 제 생각도 그래요. 음, 소파 위쪽 벽면에 그림을 거는 건 어떨까요?

남 그거 좋은 생각이네요.

여 분위기를 좀 밝게 하기 위해 문 맞은 편 구석에 화분도 하나 놓도록 할게요.

남 정말 고맙습니다.

여 천만에요. 월요일에 뵐게요.

해설 그림은 소파 위쪽 벽에 걸릴 것이므로 창 오른쪽 옆에 걸려 있는 그림은 일치하지 않는다.

어휘 filing cabinet 파일 캐비닛 entertain (손님을) 대접, 환대하다 opposite 맞은편에, 반대편에 liven up 쾌활[활발]하게 하다

07 ②

해석 남 실례합니다. 이 좌석이 당신 자리인가요? 창가 쪽 자리를 좋아하세요?

여 아니오, 사실 전 복도 쪽 자리를 선호하지만 제가 표를 살 때는 자리가 남아 있지 않았어요.

남 정말요? 그럼, 제 아내와 자리를 좀 바꿔 주실 수 있어요? 제 아내는 복도 쪽 자리거든요.

여 오, 아내와 자리가 떨어지셨어요?

남 불행하게도, 비행기가 약간 초과 예약을 받았더군요. 그래서 선택의 여지가 없었어요. 그래서, 바꿔 주실래요?

여 사실, 저한테는 더 좋죠. 바꿔 드릴게요.

남 덕분에 아내와 함께 앉을 수 있겠네요.

여 별말씀을요. 가방과 노트북만 좀 챙길게요. 잠깐 이 가방 좀 들어주시겠어요?

남 물론이죠. 다시 한 번 감사합니다.

해설 남자는 아내와 같이 앉을 수 있도록 여자에게 아내와 자리를 바꿔 달라고 부탁하고 있다.

어휘 window seat 창가 쪽 자리 prefer ~을 선호하다 aisle seat 복도 쪽 자리 separate 떨어진, 분리된 slightly 약간 overbook 정원을 초과해서 예약을 받다

08 ①

해석 남 당신이 영어를 공부하는 주된 이유가 뭔가요?

여 더 나은 직업을 얻고 싶은데, 제가 원하는 직업을 얻으려면 영어가 중요한 자격 요건이거든요.

남 당신이 자격을 갖추고 싶은 직업이 무엇인데요?

여 음, 저는 해외여행을 정말 좋아하는데다가 경제학 석사 학위를 가지고 있어요. 그래서 국제 비즈니스에 종사하고 싶어요. 하지만 그러려면 영어를 더 유창하게 해야 해요.

남 알겠네요. 제 생각엔 당신의 영어는 이미 아주 훌륭한 것 같아요.

여 고마워요. 제 생각엔 당신의 영어야말로 정말 멋져요. 왜 영어를 공부하세요?

남 오, 여러 가지 이유가 있어요. 가장 중요한 이유는 제 여자 친구예요. 그녀는 미국인이고 우리는 결혼 후에 미국에서 살려고 계획 중이거든요.

여 그럼 모든 면에서 영어가 필요하시겠네요, 그렇죠?

남 그럴 거 같아요.

여 그거 흥미로운데요. 완전히 새로운 삶을 사시겠군요!

해설 남자는 미국인 여자 친구와 결혼해서 미국에서 살 계획이기 때문에 영어를 공부하고 있다.

어휘 employment 고용 qualification 자격 요건 qualify for ~의 자격을 얻다 master's degree 석사 학위 fluently 유창하게

09 ②

해석 여 스웨터가 어디에 있는지 말해 주시겠어요?

남 네, 오른편에 벽을 따라서 있습니다. 물건을 찾으시는 것을 도와드릴까요?

여 스웨터를 사려고 해요. 당신 정도 몸집의 남자 친구에게 줄 거예요.

남 음, 그러시다면 중간 사이즈로 하셔야 될 겁니다. 이건 어떠세요?

여 아주 좋아요. 젊은 여자를 위한 선물도 추천해 주시겠어요?

남 저희는 다양한 지역 생산품을 갖추고 있습니다. 장신구류는 어떠세요?

여 오, 이 목걸이가 멋지네요. 얼마죠?

남 세일가로 50달러입니다.

여 좋아요. 이 스웨터와 목걸이를 사도록 할게요.

남 합쳐서 80달러에 10%세금이 추가됩니다.

여 여기 100달러 지폐예요.

남 감사합니다. 잔돈 받으세요.

해설 스웨터와 목걸이가 합쳐서 80달러이고 세금 10%가 추가되므로 총 금액은 88달러이며 여자가 100달러 지폐를 냈으므로 거스름돈은 12달러가 된다.

어휘 a variety of 많은 locally-made item 토산품, 지역 생산품 jewelry 장신구류

10 ⑤

해석 남 무엇을 도와드릴까요?

여 MP3 플레이어를 사려고 해요.

남 보시다시피 저희는 다양한 물건들을 갖추고 있습니다.

여 와, 무엇부터 봐야 할지 모르겠네요.

남 그럼, 이건 어떠세요? 여러 가지 다양한 파일 형식을 재생하고 대부분의 주요 음악 다운로드 사이트와 호환이 돼요. FM 수신기와 내장 배터리 충전기가 달려 있고 좋은 품질의 헤드폰이 제공됩니다.

여 저장 용량과 충전 시간은 어떻게 되나요?

남 20기가바이트의 메모리를 가지고 있고 5,000곡 정도 저장 가능합니다. 한 번 충전에 약 12시간 동안 음악 재생이 되고 대략 3시간에 충전이 완료됩니다. 넓은 컬러 화면도 갖추고 있어요.

여 제가 찾던 물건인 것 같네요. 그걸로 할게요.

해설 제품의 성능에 관한 언급만이 있을 뿐, 보증이나 수리에 대한 내용은 없다.

어휘 selection (선택, 구매 따위를 위한) 전시품, 선택의 대상이 되는 물품 file format 파일 형식 compatible 호환성이 있는 built-in 내장형의 battery charger 충전기 storage capacity 저장 용량

11 ④

해석 남 오리너구리에 대해 들어보셨나요? 오리너구리는 호주 동부에서 유일하게 발견되는 반수생의 포유류입니다. 이 알을 낳고, 오리 같은 부리와 비버 같은 꼬리 그리고 수달 같은 발을 가진 동물의 특이한 생김새는 이 동물을 처음 마주쳤을 때 유럽의 동물학자들을 어리둥절하게 만들었습니다. 이 동물은 몇 안 되는 독을 가진 포유류입니다. 수컷 오리너구리는 뒷발에 사람에게 심한 고통을 줄 수 있는 독을 지닌 발톱을 가지고 있습니다. 오리너구리의 독특한 특징들은 이 동물을 진화 생물학의 중요한 연구 대상이자 호주의 상징물이 되도록 했습니다. 이 동물은 국가적 행사에 마스코트로 등장하며 호주의 20센트 동전의 뒷면에 새겨져 있기도 합니다. 20세기 초반까지는 털을 목적으로 사냥되었지만 지금은 보호받고 있습니다.

해설 수컷 오리너구리의 뒷발에 있는 독은 사람에게 심한 고통을 줄 수 있다.

어휘 platypus 오리너구리 semi-aquatic 반수생의 mammal 포유류 egg-laying 알을 낳는 duck-billed 오리 같은 부리를 가진 beaver-tailed 비버 같은 꼬리가 있는 otter-footed 수달 같은 발을 지닌 baffle 어리둥절하게 하다 naturalist 동물학자, 자연주의자 encounter 마주치다 spur 발톱 hind 뒤쪽의

venom 독 severe 심한 feature 특징, 특색; ~을 특징으로 하다 evolutionary biology 진화 생물학

12 ③

해석 여 오늘 저녁에 TV에서 뭘 보고 싶어? 6번에서 9시에 리얼리티 쇼를 해.

남 내가 리얼리티 쇼를 싫어하는 거 알잖아. 내 말은, 리얼리티 쇼는 항상 사람들이 날고기를 먹는 것 같이 멍청한 행동을 하는 것만 보여 주잖아.

여 그럼, 야생의 사자에 대한 다큐멘터리를 보는 건 어때?

남 나는 좀 더 긴장감 있는 것을 보고 싶어.

여 음, 여기 적당한 게 있어. 'Mission Impossible' 재방영하는 거 볼래?

남 그거 백만 번은 본 것 같아.

여 흠, 어디 보자. 이건 어때? 10시에 13번에서 토크쇼를 한다.

남 유명 인사들에 대한 뜬소문에는 별로 관심 없어. 잠이나 자야겠어.

여 알았어. 오, 야구 경기한다.

남 정말? 그럼 안고 같이 있어 줄게.

여 난 네가 생각을 바꿀 줄 알았어.

해설 여자가 여러 가지 TV 프로그램들을 제안했으나 남자는 별 흥미를 보이지 않다가 야구 중계를 하고 있다는 것을 듣고 같이 보기로 했으므로 두 사람이 선택한 채널은 9번이다.

어휘 raw 날것의 suspense (영화 등의) 지속적인 긴장감, 서스펜스 rerun 재상영, 재방송 gossip 뜬소문 keep ~ company 같이 있다, ~와 동행하다

13 ③

해석 남 무슨 일 있어? 아주 피곤해 보여.

여 인생이 매일매일 똑같아. 때때로 일을 그만두고 아무 것도 안 하고 싶어!

남 몇 주 정도는 그것도 괜찮겠지만 그러고 나면 어떻게 할 건데? 아무 것도 안 하는 게 정말 너의 삶의 목표니?

여 그렇지는 않아. 하지만 가끔은 그렇게 열심히 일할 필요 없이 조그만 섬에서 사는 꿈을 꿔.

남 섬에서 살 필요까지는 없어. 하지만, 충분한 여가를 갖는 것은 아주 중요해. 일과 여가 사이의 균형을 맞추는 방법을 배워야 해.

여 네 말이 맞는 것 같아. 난 내 인생의 목표를 달성하는 유일한 방법은 공부하고 일하는 것 밖에 없다고 생각했어.

남 음, 사람들이 말하는 것처럼 '여유를 갖고 인생을 즐길' 시간을 내려고 노력해야 해.

여 난 분명히 쉬지도 않고 너무 열심히 일하고 있는 것 같아.

남 **넌 휴가가 필요한 것 같구나.**

해설 남자는 여자에게 인생의 목표를 달성하기 위해서는 적당한 휴식과 여가도 필요하다는 말을 하고 있으므로 여자의 마지막 말에 대한 남자의 대답으로 "넌 휴가가 필요한 것 같구나."가 적절하다. ① 사실을 말하는 것은 너무 어려워. ② 꿈이 현실이 되었어. ④ 꽃을 줘서 정말 고마워. ⑤ 넌 일자리를 좀 찾아보는 수밖에 없겠구나.

어휘 tell the truth 사실을 말하다 objective 목표 leisure 여가 stop and smell the roses 여유를 가지고 인생을 즐기다

14 ⑤

해석 여 왜 그렇게 화가 났어요?

남 아내가 은행에서 나오는 것을 기다리고 있었는데 트럭 한 대가 제 뒤에 붙어 섰어요.

여 그 트럭 운전자가 뭔가 불쾌한 일을 했나요?

남 네, 제 차를 억지로 뚫고 나가려고 하다가 제 차 측면을 크게 긁었어요.

여 그래서 어떻게 하셨어요?

남 그 사람한테 말을 하려고 차에서 내렸어요. 그런데 정말 놀랍게도 그도 차에서 내리는데 야구방망이를 들고 있는 거예요!

여 오, 세상에나! 그가 방망이로 뭘 했나요?

남 아무 말 없이 몇 번 휘두르더니 가버렸어요.

여 그 사람의 자동차 번호를 적어 두었어요?

남 아뇨. 너무 겁에 질려서 아무것도 할 수가 없었어요.

여 <u>안됐네요. 그렇지 않았다면 경찰에 신고할 수 있었을 텐데요.</u>

해설 너무 겁이 나서 아무 것도 할 수 없었다고 말하는 남자에게 번호를 적어 두었다면 경찰에 신고할 수 있었을 텐데 안타깝다고 말하는 것이 가장 적절하다. ① 그러니까 난폭하게 운전하지 마. 참을성을 갖고 운전해. ② 너는 코너에서 정지 신호를 봤어야 했어. ③ 미안하지만 나는 야구가 위험하다고 생각하지 않아. ④ 네가 틀렸어. 지금까진 내 차에 어떤 문제도 없어.

어휘 **pity** 유감, 불쌍히 여김 **upset** 화 난, 혼란한, 뒤집힌 **scratch** 할퀸 상처 **squeeze** 억지로 뚫고 나가다; 짜내다 **to one's astonishment** 놀랍게도 **march** 행군하다; 행진 **take down** 적어 놓다 **license plate** (자동차) 번호판 **terrify** 겁나게 하다

15 ⑤

해석 여 Karen은 다음 월요일까지 교수님께 대중 매체에 관한 연구 보고서를 제출해야 한다. 그녀는 보고서를 쓰기 위해서 많은 오래된 신문과 잡지를 모아서 자신의 책상 밑에 두었다. 이제 그녀는 보고서를 쓰는 것을 미룰 시간이 없다고 생각하고 보고서를 쓰기 시작하기로 결심한다. 하지만 놀랍게도 그녀가 모아둔 신문과 잡지가 사라지고 없다. 어디서도 그것을 찾을 수 없다. 그것 없이 그녀가 보고서를 제시간에 쓴다는 것은 거의 불가능하다. 잠시 후, 그녀는 남동생 Jack이 그것을 폐휴지로 착각하고 버렸다는 것을 알게 된다. 이 상황에서 Karen이 Jack에게 할 말로 가장 적절한 것은 무엇인가?

Karen **Jack! 그걸 버리기 전에 내게 물어봤어야지!**

해설 보고서를 쓰기 위한 참고 자료를 쓰레기로 착각하고 마음대로 버린 남동생에게 버리기 전에 물어봤어야 한다고 하는 것이 가장 적절하다. ① 신문 다 읽었니? ② 너무 심각하게 받아들이지 마. 그냥 농담이었어. ③ 괜찮아, 실수하는 걸 두려워하지 마. ④ 성적표를 받았는데 별로 만족스럽지 못해.

어휘 **submit** 제출하다 **mass media** 대중 매체 **delay** 연기하다, 미루다 **make up one's mind** 결심하다 **to one's surprise** 놀랍게도 **throw away** 버리다 **mistake A for B** A를 B로 착각하다

16-17 ④, ①

해석 남 안녕하세요, 학생 여러분. 여러분의 학습에 관한 조언을 좀 드리겠습니다. 수업 중에 새로운 정보를 습득하는 데 어려움을 겪고 있습니까? 여러분은 여러분 고유의 학습 방식에 대해 좀 더 알고 싶을지도 모릅니다. 여러분의 학습 방식은 여러분이 선호하는 학습 방법입니다. 그것은 여러분이 얼마나 머리가 좋은지 또는 어떤 기술을 지니고 있는 지와 아무 상관이 없습니다. 그것은 여러분의 두뇌가 새로운 정보를 습득하기 위해 가장 효율적으로 활동하는 방법과 관련이 있습니다. 여러분의 학습 방식은 여러분이 태어나면서부터 타고나는 것입니다. '좋은' 혹은 '나쁜' 학습 방법이라는 것은 없습니다. 많고 다양한 학습 방식이 성공을 가져다 줄 수 있습니다. 우리 모두는 새로운 정보를 습득하는 자기 자신의 독특한 방법을 가지고 있습니다. 중요한 것은 여러분의 학습 방식의 성향을 아는 것입니다. 여러분이 여러분의 두뇌가 어떻게 가장 잘 학습하는지를 안다면, 여러분은 두려워하던 시험을 치를 때 좋은 결과를 가져다 줄 방법으로 공부하게 될 가망이 높습니다.

해설 16 각자에게 맞는 독특한 정보 습득 방법이 있다고 말하면서 자신의 정보 습득 스타일을 아는 것이 중요하다고 강조하고 있다.

17 개인이 지닌 지능과 학습 방식은 무관하다.

어휘 **do with** ~와 관련이 있다 **efficiently** 효율적으로 **particular** 독특한, 특별한 **be aware of** ~을 알다, 알아차리다 **dreaded** 두려워하던

🎯 Dictation

01 had an interview

02 want to embarrass me

03 saving ourselves by using our cars less / cars are starting to destroy our entire way

04 don't feel like going out / use up lots of vegetables

05 decide to run for mayor / make this city a better place

06 moving my things / hanging a picture on the wall

07 prefer an aisle seat / I'll change it for you

08 work in international business / after we get married

09 also recommend a gift / I'll take the sweater

10 have a large selection / charges up in about three hours

11 a semi-aquatic mammal / one of the few poisonous / a mascot at national events

12 a documentary on the life of lions / a baseball game on

13 be nice for a few weeks / the only way to reach the goals

14 to come out of a bank / to my great astonishment / Did you take down

15 put them under her desk / are missing / threw them away

16-17 having trouble learning new information / how your brain works most efficiently / the nature of your learning style

05회 | 듣기 모의고사

01 ①	02 ①	03 ④	04 ③	05 ②	06 ①
07 ④	08 ④	09 ④	10 ③	11 ⑤	12 ⑤
13 ③	14 ②	15 ④	16 ③	17 ⑤	

01 ①

해석 남 안녕하세요. 도와 드릴까요, 손님?
여 예. 어떻게 하면 대출을 받을 자격이 되나요?
남 직업을 여쭤어 봐도 될까요?
여 컴퓨터 회사에서 일합니다.

해설 남자가 여자에게 무슨 일을 하냐고 물었으므로 자신의 직업에 대해 이야기하는 것이 가장 적절하다. ② 죄송하지만, 카드의 유효 기간이 지났습니다. ③ 그런 경우에는 대출해 드릴 수 없습니다. ④ 좋습니다. 여기 새로운 통장입니다. ⑤ 저는 돈을 빌리는 데 매우 신중합니다.

어휘 work for ~에서 일하다 expire 만기가 되다 in that case 그런 경우에는 loan 대출 saving account 예금 계좌 cautious 신중한 qualify ~할 자격이 있다

02 ①

해석 여 David, 문제가 있어 보여요. 무슨 일이에요?
남 John에게 전화를 걸고 있는데 받지를 않아서요.
여 그럼, 그에게 메시지를 남기지 그래요? 제 생각에 전화는 받지 않아도 메시지는 확인할 수 있을 거예요.
남 당신 말이 맞아요. 그래야겠네요.

해설 John에게 메시지를 남겨 보라는 여자의 조언에 대한 남자의 응답으로 "당신 말이 맞네요. 그래야겠네요."가 가장 적절하다. ② 좋은 생각이에요. 전화를 받지 않을게요. ③ 농담하지 마세요! 저는 지금 심각해요. ④ 모르세요? 그의 휴대 전화가 고장 났어요. ⑤ 너무 자책하지 마세요. 괜찮을 거예요.

어휘 be hard on ~을 심하게 나무라다 leave 남기다 though ~일지라도

03 ④

해석 여 안녕하세요, 동료 학생 여러분. 제가 여기에 선 이유는 Jefferson Memorial 고등학교에서 교복을 입어야 한다고 생각하기 때문입니다. 저는 다음 학생회 회의에서 이것에 대한 여러분의 지지를 모으고 싶습니다. 교복으로 바꾸면 모든 사람들이 혜택을 받을 수 있습니다. 우리는 최신 유행하는 스타일의 옷을 사는 데 쓰는 돈을 절약할 수 있습니다. 게다가 우리가 똑같은 것을 입고 있다면, 우리는 모두 소속감을 느낄 수 있을 것입니다. 저는 이번 주 화요일 방과 후에 도서관에서 비공식 회의를 개최할 것입니다. 거기서 여러분 모두를 뵙기를 바랍니다.

해설 여자는 학생들에게 복장을 교복으로 바꾸면 얻을 수 있는 이점을 설명하고 있다.

어휘 fellow 동료의 support 지지 board meeting 임원 회의 benefit from ~로부터 이익을 얻다 furthermore 더욱이 unity 결속성, 통일성 hold a meeting 회의를 열다 informal 비공식의

04 ③

해석 여 많은 국가가 심각한 소아 비만 문제에 직면해 있다는 것을 알았나요?
남 아뇨, 몰랐어요. 가장 큰 원인이 무엇이죠?
여 대부분의 아이들이 친구들과 밖에 나가서 놀기보다는 집에서 컴퓨터로 게임을 하려는 것이 원인인 것 같아요.
남 맞아요. 요즘 아이들은 컴퓨터 게임을 많이 해요.
여 통계에 의하면, 초등학교 학생들은 적어도 매일 세 시간 동안 컴퓨터 게임을 한다고 하더군요.
남 그렇게나 많이요?
여 그래요. 이것뿐만 아니라, 그들은 보통 뭔가를 먹으면서 TV를 보는 데 많은 시간을 보내요.
남 그건 운동할 기회는 적고 뚱뚱해질 기회는 많다는 것을 의미하겠군요, 그렇죠?
여 네. 결론적으로 소아 비만은 너무 많은 실내 활동 때문에 발생되는 거죠. 저는 아이들이 더 자주 야외 활동을 즐겨야 한다고 생각해요.

해설 여자는 아이들이 좀 더 자주 야외 활동을 해야 한다고 했으므로 여자의 의견은 "비만 예방을 위해 실내 활동을 줄여야 한다."이다.

어휘 childhood obesity 소아 비만 cause 원인 statistics 통계 primary school 초등학교 indoor 실내의

05 ②

해석 여 제 작업실에 오신 것을 환영합니다. 저는 Melanie입니다.
남 안녕하세요, 저는 Alex입니다. 만나서 반가워요. 저는 영화를 어떻게 만드는지 배우려고 이곳에 왔어요. 제 생각에 영화를 만드는 것은 오랜 시간이 걸릴 것 같아요.
여 예. 영화는 제작하는 데 오래 걸려요. 네 단계를 거치지요.
남 첫 번째 단계가 뭔가요?
여 영화 스크립트를 편집해요.
남 그런 다음에는 촬영을 시작하나요?
여 아뇨. 배우를 고용하고 영화를 촬영할 곳을 선택해요. 그것이 제작 이전 단계죠.
남 이런 멋진 세트를 설치하는 것이 그 단계인가요?
여 아뇨, 제작 단계에서 영화 세트를 설치해요. 그리고 장면을 촬영해요.
남 그렇군요! 마지막 단계는 뭔가요?
여 촬영한 필름을 편집하고 영화를 위한 음악을 찾아요.
남 오, 영화를 만드는 데 그렇게 많은 일을 하는지 몰랐어요. 설명해 주셔서 감사합니다!

해설 여자는 자신의 작업실을 방문한 남자에게 영화가 만들어지는 과정을 자세히 설명해 주고 있다.

어휘 go through ~을 거치다 edit 편집하다 soundtrack 영화 음악

06 ①

해석 여 오, 이 둥근 테이블을 보세요. 테이블 위에 사진이 많네요.
남 예. 저희 가족사진이에요.
여 저기 종 모양의 액자 속 사진은 결혼사진인가요?
남 예. 그 옆에 있는 사진은 제 첫째 아들이에요.

여 황새가 새겨진 액자 속의 아이 말인가요?

남 예. 왼쪽에 있는 사진은 제 둘째 아들이에요.

여 입에 우유병을 물고 있는 사진이네요. 참 귀엽군요.

남 그리고 이것은 가족사진이에요.

여 둘레에 장미꽃 무늬가 장식된 액자가 참 예쁘네요.

남 그래요? 고마워요.

해설 왼쪽에 있는 사진의 아기는 우유병을 입에 물고 있다고 했으므로 손가락을 빨고 있는 아이 사진은 대화의 내용과 일치하지 않는다.

어휘 picture frame 액자 stork 황새 pattern 무늬

07 ④

해석 (전화벨이 울린다.)

남 여보세요.

여 여보, 새 가구 배치는 어떻게 되고 있어요?

남 거의 다 끝나가요. 당신은 언제 집에 오나요?

여 오늘 늦게까지 일해야 할 것 같아요. 내일 중요한 발표가 있잖아요.

남 그래요. 매일 그렇게 늦게까지 일해서 너무 걱정이에요.

여 걱정해 줘서 고마워요.

남 버스 정류장까지 마중 나갈까요?

여 아뇨, 그럴 필요는 없어요. 그건 그렇고, 오늘밤 'People are Funny'
라는 TV 프로그램을 볼 거예요?

남 물론 볼 거예요.

여 그러면 나중에 제가 볼 수 있도록 녹화해 줄래요?

남 그럴게요.

해설 여자는 남자에게 나중에 보도록 TV 프로그램을 녹화해 달라고 부탁했고 남자는 흔쾌히 수락했으므로 남자가 여자를 위해 할 일은 '방송 녹화하기'이다.

어휘 arrangement 배열, 배치 concerned 염려하는 record 녹화(녹음)하다, 기록하다

08 ④

해석 남 오, 이게 누구세요? Smith 부인 아닌가요?

여 오, James 씨. 이곳은 어쩐 일이에요? 댁이 이 근처가 아닌 걸로 아는데요.

남 사실, 이곳으로 이사 온 지 얼마 되지 않았어요.

여 그렇군요. 이제 같은 동네에 사는 거네요.

남 맞아요. 만나서 반가워요.

여 저도요. 그건 그렇고, 물건을 찾느라 고생하는 것처럼 보여요.

남 네, 맞아요. 옷걸이와 수도꼭지를 찾고 있는데, 어디 있는지 모르겠네요.

여 옷걸이는 2번 섹션에 있고 수도꼭지는 5번 섹션에 있어요.

남 아니, 어떻게 그렇게 잘 아세요?

여 작년에 여기에서 일했어요.

남 그렇군요. 알려줘서 고마워요.

여 천만에요. 즐거운 쇼핑하세요.

해설 "I worked here last year."를 통하여 여자가 물건이 있는 위치를 잘 아는 이유는 '전에 일한 적이 있어서'라는 것을 알 수 있다.

어휘 Look who's here! 이게 누구예요? neighbor 이웃 stuff 물건 hanger 옷걸이 tap 수도꼭지

09 ④

해석 남 무엇을 도와드릴까요?

여 아들에게 줄 도넛 몇 개와 쿠키를 사려고요.

남 이 도넛은 신선하고 맛이 좋아요.

여 와, 맛있어 보이네요! 얼마인가요?

남 하나에 70센트에요.

여 그렇군요. 이 코코넛 볼은요?

남 하나에 15센트인데, 10개를 사시면 1달러에 드려요.

여 그거 좋군요. 도넛 2개와 코코넛 볼 10개 주실래요?

남 물론이죠. 더 필요한 것 있으세요?

여 없습니다. 그것들을 종이 봉지에 담아 주시겠어요?

남 물론, 그렇게 해드리겠습니다.

해설 여자는 하나에 70센트인 도넛 2개와 10개에 1달러인 코코넛볼 10개를 샀으므로 여자가 지불할 금액은 2.40달러이다.

어휘 delicious 맛 좋은 that's all 그게 전부다

10 ③

해석 여 안녕하세요, 손님. 무엇을 도와드릴까요?

남 차를 한 대 빌리고 싶은데요.

여 어느 것을 원하시나요?

남 글쎄요. 가족과 함께 여행을 하니까 가족용 차여야죠.

여 이 검은색 SUV는 어때요?

남 오, 싫어요. 충분히 큰 것 같지 않아요. 저는 큰 차를 원해요.

여 검은 station wagon은 어때요? 가족용으로 완벽해요.

남 아뇨, 색깔이 마음에 안 들고, sedan이 더 낫네요. 저기 있는 흰색
sedan으로 하겠어요.

여 죄송하지만, 그 차는 이미 예약되었어요. 회색 van은 어때요?

남 그 van은 좋아 보이지만 너무 크네요. 그럼 흰색 station wagon으로
해도 될까요?

여 물론이죠. 이 서류를 작성해 주세요.

해설 흰색 sedan은 이미 예약이 되어 있는 상태이기 때문에 남자가 빌릴 수 없다.

어휘 rent 임대하다 perfect 완벽한 prefer ~을 선호하다 book 예약하다

11 ⑤

해석 여 안녕하세요, 학생 여러분! 새 인턴십 프로그램을 소개하게 되어서 기쁩니다. 이 프로그램은 교실 밖 환경에서의 학습 경험을 제공하기 위하여 계획된 것입니다. 대부분의 정규 학업을 마친 학생들에게 인턴 제도는 '실제 사회생활에서의 업무 경험'을 제공합니다. 인턴에 지원하는 학생들은 평균 학점 3.0 이상의 전공자여야 합니다. 인턴을 하는 데 보내는 시간은 보통 학기당 매주 8시간에서 12시간입니다. 인턴의 업무에 대한 정기 보고서가 감독관에 의해 만들어 집니다. 최종 성적은 이 보고서에 의해 결정됩니다.

해설 최종 성적은 정기적으로 보고되는 보고서에 의해 결정된다고 했으므로 "최종 성적은 마지막 날 보는 시험에 의해 결정된다."는 내용과 일치하지 않는다.

어휘 **setting** 환경 **major** 전공 학생 **involve** 포함하다 **semester** 학기 **periodic** 정기의, 주기적인 **supervisor** 감독자 **determine** ~을 결정하다

12 ⑤

해석 여 Greg, 이번 토요일에 무슨 계획 있니?
남 특별히 없어. 너는?
여 영화를 보러 갈까 생각하고 있어.
남 좋아. Grand 극장에서 무엇을 상영하고 있니?
여 잘 모르겠어. 인터넷으로 찾아보자.
남 좋아. 어디 보자. World War Z, Transformer 4, 그리고 Flight를 하네.
여 World War Z를 보자.
남 그 영화는 이미 봤어. 그리고 1시에 치과 예약을 해놨어.
여 Transformer 4는 어때? 정말 볼 만하다고 그러더라.
남 글쎄, Flight를 보자. Denzel Washington을 보고 싶어서 못 견디겠어.
여 좋아, 정 그렇다면.

해설 남자는 1시에 치과 예약을 해두었고 영화는 'Flight'를 볼 것이므로 16시 10분에 하는 Flight가 정답이다.

어휘 **find out** 찾아보다 **have an appointment** 약속을 하다 **spectacle** 장관, 구경거리 **be dying to** ~하고 싶어서 못 견디다 **insist** 우기다, 고집하다

13 ③

해석 여 실례합니다. 멋진 보트군요.
남 그렇게 말씀해 주셔서 감사합니다. 하지만 이것은 제 친구의 보트예요.
여 그렇군요. 그건 그렇고, 저는 수상 스포츠 연구 센터에서 왔습니다.
남 그런데요?
여 수상 스포츠에 대해 몇 가지 질문을 드려도 될까요?
남 물론이죠.
여 성함이 어떻게 되시나요?
남 Alan Parker입니다.
여 알겠습니다, Alan. 보트 타기 이외에 다른 수상 스포츠도 하시나요?
남 파도타기를 가끔 합니다.
여 오 좋네요. 그 밖에 다른 것은요?
남 사실, 스쿠버 다이빙이 제 취미입니다.

해설 보트 타기를 제외하고 다른 수상 스포츠로 무엇을 즐기는지 묻는 여자의 말에 대한 남자의 응답으로 "사실, 스쿠버 다이빙이 제 취미입니다."가 가장 적절하다. ① 아뇨, 수영할 줄 모른다고 말씀드렸잖아요. ② 시간이 나면 주로 보트를 타러 가요. ④ 예, 저는 수상 스포츠에 능숙한 남자를 알아요. ⑤ 여기에 윈드서핑을 하기에 좋은 장소가 있어요.

어휘 **by the way** 그건 그렇고 **research** 연구 **except** ~을 제외하고 **surfing** 파도타기

14 ②

해석 남 준비 다 됐니?

여 Grace가 아직 방에 있어.
남 그녀는 서둘러야 해. 우린 시간이 별로 없어.
여 영화는 몇 시에 시작해?
남 7시 50분에 시작해.
여 지금 몇 시지?
남 7시쯤 됐어.
여 서두를 필요 없어. 차로 거기에 도착하는 데 10분밖에 안 걸려.
남 나도 알지만 Grace가 준비하는 데 시간이 많이 걸릴 수 있잖아.
여 그럼 그녀에게 서두르라고 말하는 게 좋겠다.

해설 아직 준비가 안 된 Grace에게 영화 시간에 늦지 않기 위해 할 말로 가장 적절한 것은 "그럼 그녀에게 서두르라고 말하는 게 좋겠다."이다. ① 천만에. 언제든지. ③ 그녀가 왜 우리와 함께 갈 수 없는지 아니? ④ 내가 세탁소에서 네 옷을 찾아 올게. ⑤ 제 시간에 여기에 도착하다니 우린 운이 좋구나.

어휘 **rush** 서두르다 **get ready** 준비를 하다

15 ④

해석 남 John은 어머니의 생일 선물을 사기 위한 돈을 벌기 위해 편의점에서 시간제로 일을 하고 있다. 그의 어머니는 이 사실을 모른다. 만일 그녀가 John이 시간제로 일을 한다는 사실을 아신다면 그녀는 기분이 좋지 않을 것이다. 평소처럼 학교가 끝난 후 편의점에서 일하고 있을 때 John의 여동생인 Jennifer가 가게로 들어오고, John이 점원으로 일하고 있는 것을 보고 놀란다. John은 그녀에게 모든 것을 털어 놓았고, 그 이야기를 어머니께 말하지 않기를 원한다. Jennifer 또한 이 사실을 비밀로 해야 한다고 생각한다. 이 상황에서 Jennifer가 John에게 할 말로 가장 적절한 것은 무엇인가?
Jennifer 걱정 마. 난 입이 무거워.

해설 Jennifer가 John에게 할 말은 John이 편의점에서 일하는 것을 비밀로 하겠다는 의미인 "걱정 마. 난 입이 무거워."가 가장 적절하다. ① 힘내! 너는 그것을 할 수 있어. ② 언젠가는 기회가 올 거야. ③ 물론, 네게 돈을 빌려 줄게. ⑤ 이번 한 번만 해고하지 않을 거야.

어휘 **once and for all** 단 한 번만 **sealed** 봉인된 **convenient store** 편의점 **earn** 돈을 벌다 **as usual** 늘 하던 대로 **keep something secret** ~을 비밀로 해두다

16-17 ③, ⑤

해석 여 체육은 학생들의 신체 성장에 매우 중요합니다. 그러므로 학교가 학생들의 몸과 마음 모두의 균형 잡힌 성장을 증진시켜야 한다는 것은 당연한 것입니다. 체육은 또한 학생들의 건강을 유지하는 데 도움을 준다는 면에서 중요합니다. 오늘날, 많은 사람들은 늘 앉아서 생활을 합니다. 체육은 학교에 있는 동안 학생들에게 활력을 줄 것이고 그들을 좀 더 활동적으로 만들 것입니다. 어떤 점에서 보면, 날마다 하는 체육은 운동을 싫어하는 뚱뚱한 아이들도 주어진 시간 동안에는 육체적으로 활동하도록 만들기 때문에 그들이 어느 정도 살을 빼는 데 도움이 될 것입니다. 가장 중요한 것은 학생들이 학교에 있는 동안 재미를 느껴야 한다는 것입니다. 이러한 점에서, 체육 수업은 학생들이 즐거워할 수 있는 시간이 될 것입니다.

해설 16 체육 수업은 학생들의 균형적인 성장에 도움이 되고, 비만인 학생에게 운동을

할 수 있는 기회를 제공해 준다는 내용이므로 여자의 말의 주제로는 "체육 수업의 중요성"이 가장 적절하다.

17 건강 증진, 활력 제공, 뚱뚱한 아이들의 체중 감량, 아이들에게 즐거움을 주는 것은 언급이 되었지만, 정서적 안정감에 대한 언급은 없다.

어휘 **physical exercise** 체육 **promote** 증진시키다, 촉진시키다 **sedentary** 앉아 지내는, 늘 앉아만 있는 **in a sense** 어떤 의미에서는 **somewhat** 어느 정도, 다소 **despise** 몹시 싫어하다, 경멸하다

Dictation

01 qualify for a loan
02 check the message
03 gather your support
04 stay at home to play games / at least three hours / many indoor activities
05 four stages / hire actors / edit the film
06 many picture frames / bell-shaped frame / with a rose pattern
07 furniture arrangement / being concerned / record the program
08 What brings you here / finding stuff / Enjoy your shopping
09 look delicious / put them in a paper bag
10 renting a car / don't think / gray van
11 provide learning experiences / are determined from these reports
12 going to a movie / appointment with the dentist / if you insist
13 saying like that / water sports / go surfing
14 needs to rush / starts at seven fifty / get ready
15 earn money / is surprised to see / this fact a secret
16-17 the balanced growth / to be more active / have fun while in school

06회 듣기 모의고사

p.36-37

01 ①	02 ⑤	03 ⑤	04 ②	05 ①	06 ④
07 ③	08 ③	09 ④	10 ⑤	11 ③	12 ⑤
13 ④	14 ③	15 ⑤	16 ②	17 ④	

01 ①

해석 남 Rian, 할머니 심장 수술은 잘 됐어요?
여 예. 하지만 제가 여전히 당분간 할머니를 간호해 드려야 해요.
남 직장은 어떻게 하고요? 그만두실 건가요?
여 **아뇨, 한 달 간 휴가를 얻었어요.**

해설 할머니를 간호해 드리려면 직장을 그만두어야 하는 거냐고 묻는 남자의 말에 대한 여자의 응답으로 "아뇨, 한 달 간 휴가를 얻었어요."가 가장 적절하다. ② 물론이죠. 그것은 제가 찾고 있던 직업이에요. ③ 예. 저는 그녀를 위해 다른 직업을 찾고 있는 중이에요. ④ 정확해요. 저는 새 직원을 구하는 데 어려움을 겪고 있어요. ⑤ 저는 당분간은 이사하지 않을 거예요. 저는 그녀와 함께 살 거예요.

어휘 **leave of absence** 휴가 허가[기간], 휴직 **for the time being** 당분간 **operation** 수술

02 ⑤

해석 여 여보, 세탁소에서 내 티셔츠를 찾아왔나요?
남 그럼요. 당신 방 서랍에 넣어놨어요.
여 오, 이것 좀 봐요! 여기에 여전히 얼룩이 남아 있어요.
남 **정말요? 찾아올 때 그것을 확인해 봐야 했는데 안 했네요.**

해설 세탁소에서 찾아 온 셔츠에 얼룩이 묻어 있는 것을 안 남자의 응답으로 "정말요? 그것을 찾아올 때 확인해 봐야 했는데 안 했네요."가 가장 적절하다. ① 아직요. 저는 그것을 말릴 시간이 아직 더 필요해요. ② 물론이지요. 그것을 세탁소에 맡겨야 될 것 같아요. ③ 맞아요. 사실 그것은 당신의 셔츠를 더 멋져 보이게 만들어요. ④ 오, 얼룩을 묻히지 않도록 조심해야 했어요.

어휘 **fashionable** 유행하는 **stain** 얼룩 **laundry** 세탁소 **drawer** 서랍

03 ⑤

해석 여 신사 숙녀 여러분. 시장으로서 우리 마을의 훌륭한 시민을 칭찬한다는 것은 제게 큰 기쁨입니다. John Baxter 씨는 제가 기억하는 한 지역 사회의 기둥 역할을 해 오고 있습니다. 전(前) 시장으로서 그는 지역 사회를 위해 잘 봉사했습니다. 시민으로서 그는 항상 긍정적인 변화의 선두에 서 있었습니다. 여러분도 그를 잘 아시다시피, 그의 업적에 대해서는 더 이상 다른 말을 할 필요가 없다고 확신합니다. 그럼, John, 앞으로 나오셔서 우리 마을에 기여한 것에 대한 존경의 표시로 드리는 이것을 받아 주시겠습니까?

해설 여자의 말 마지막 부분에서 John Baxter의 공로를 치하하며 그에게 상을 주려고 하는 말임을 알 수 있다.

어휘 **pillar** 기둥 **as long as** ~하는 한 **recall** 생각해 내다, 상기하다 **at the forefront of** ~의 선두[중심]이 되어 **achievement** 성취, 업적 **as a token of** ~의 표시로 **contribution** 기여, 기부

04 ②

해석 여 당신은 저축을 하나요?
남 아니요, 아직요. 왜 물어보는 거죠?
여 버는 것보다 좀 많이 쓰는 것 같아서요.
남 저도 알아요, 하지만 저축은 나중에 하면 된다고 생각해요.
여 전 그렇게 생각하지 않아요. 만일의 경우에 대비해서 저축하는 것은 중요해요.
남 '만일의 경우'라니요?
여 갑자기 사고가 나면, 병원비와 같은 막대한 지출로 어려움을 겪을 거예요.
남 하지만 그런 일은 거의 일어나지 않아요.
여 갑자기 직업을 잃고 일시적인 수입의 손실을 경험할지도 모르죠.

남 맞아요. 예상치 못할 일에 대비해서 저축을 해야겠네요.

해설 저축하지 않고 돈을 함부로 쓰는 남자에게 여자는 혹시 모를 미래에 대비해서 저축하는 습관을 가지라고 조언하고 있다.

어휘 savings 저축 earn 벌다 for a rainy day 만일의 경우를 대비해서
expenditure 지출, 비용 bill 청구서 temporary 일시적인 loss 상실, 손실
income 수입, 소득 unpredictable 예측하지 못하는

05 ①

해석 남 엄마, 제 친구 Eric이 새 강아지를 얻었어요.
　　여 어디서 얻었는데?
　　남 엄마가 생일 선물로 사주었대요. 저도 강아지를 키워도 되나요?
　　여 Roy, 개는 적절하게 돌봐 주어야 한단다. 그들은 장난감이 아니란다.
　　남 무슨 말씀이세요?
　　여 그들은 음식, 물, 운동, 잠 잘 따뜻한 곳, 그리고 사랑을 필요로 한단다.
　　남 그렇게 많은 것을 필요로 하는지 몰랐어요.
　　여 그리고 그게 다가 아니야.
　　남 뭐가 또 있는데요?
　　여 숙제는 어떡하고? 개가 있으면 너무 바쁠 거야.
　　남 그렇군요. 개를 기르는 것이 쉽지가 않네요.
　　여 그렇단다.

해설 아들이 애완견을 사달라고 하자 엄마는 개를 키우기가 어렵다는 점에 대해 말하고 있고 결국 아들도 그것에 동의하고 있는 내용의 대화이므로 두 사람이 하는 말의 주제는 '애완견 키우기의 어려움'이다.

어휘 present 선물 care 돌보다 properly 적절하게

06 ④

해석 남 Susan, 그것이 뭐니?
　　여 우리 집안 가계도야. 어제 숙제로 만들었어. 볼래?
　　남 어디 보자. 맨 위에 있는 두 분이 조부모님이겠구나, 맞지?
　　여 그래. 할아버지의 콧수염이 멋지지 않니?
　　남 그래, 아주 멋있어. 그리고 할머니는 모자 쓰시는 것을 좋아하시는구나.
　　여 맞아. 늘 모자를 쓰셔. 할머니 옆에 계신 분이 아버지야.
　　남 그럼, 할아버지 옆에 계신 분은 어머니겠네, 맞지? 두 분 다 안경을 쓰셨네.
　　여 맞아. 그리고 아래쪽에는 나와 내 여동생들 사진이야.
　　남 가운데 소녀가 너인 건 알겠는데 누가 네 막내 동생이니? 둘이 비슷하게 생겼어.
　　여 오른쪽에 모자를 쓰고 있는 여자애가 막내 동생이야.
　　남 그렇구나. 너희 가족은 참 행복해 보이는구나.

해설 여자의 어머니는 안경을 쓰고 있다고 했으므로 안경을 쓰고 있지 않은 여자의 어머니가 대화의 내용과 일치하지 않는다.

어휘 family tree 가계도 mustache 콧수염 similar 비슷한

07 ③

해석 (휴대 전화가 울린다.)

　　여 오, Michael. 잘 지내요?
　　남 오, 안녕하세요. Rebecca. 저는 잘 지내요. 감기는 어때요?
　　여 아직도 고생하고 있어요. 왜 아직도 낫지 않는지 모르겠어요.
　　남 유감이네요. 그건 그렇고, 부탁 좀 들어 줄래요?
　　여 뭔데요?
　　남 지금 막 집배원으로부터 문자 메시지를 받았는데, 2시간 후면 소포를 가지고 집에 도착할 거라고 해서요.
　　여 그런데요? 그때 집 밖에 있을 거라는 거예요?
　　남 예. 사실, 스포츠 센터에 있는 아들을 데리러 가야 해요.
　　여 그래서 제가 대신 소포를 받아 주길 원하나요?
　　남 맞아요. 해줄 수 있나요?
　　여 물론이지요, 할 수 있어요. 이웃 좋다는 게 뭐겠어요.

해설 남자의 집에 2시간 후에 소포가 도착할 예정인데 남자는 그 시간에 집에 없을 것이므로 남자가 여자에게 부탁한 일은 '소포 대신 받아 주기'이다.

어휘 suffer from ～로 고생하다 heal 낫다, 치료하다 mailman 집배원 parcel 소포

08 ③

해석 여 여보, 누구에게서 온 전화인가요?
　　남 직장 상사요. 지금 사무실로 들어오라고 하네요.
　　여 오, 이런! 휴일에도 부르다니, 너무하네요!
　　남 회사에서 나만 할 수 있는 일이니 어쩔 수 없어요.
　　여 알겠어요. 그럼 전 서점에나 가야겠네요.
　　남 책을 사려고요?
　　여 아니오. 사실, 오늘 오후에 거기서 '작가와의 만남' 행사가 있어요.
　　남 그렇군요. 그럼 '정의란 무엇인가'라는 책 좀 사다 줄 수 있나요?
　　여 물론이죠. 저도 읽고 싶었어요. 그건 그렇고, 언제 끝날 것 같아요?
　　남 잘 모르겠어요. 나중에 전화할게요.

해설 서점에서 '작가와의 만남' 행사가 있을 예정이라고 했으므로 여자가 서점에 가려는 이유가 '행사에 참여하려고'임을 알 수 있다.

어휘 hold 개최하다 author 작가

09 ④

해석 남 이봐요, Judy, 방금 어디에 갔었어요?
　　여 옷을 싸게 파는 좋은 가게를 발견했어요.
　　남 그래요? 무엇을 샀는지 봅시다.
　　여 좋아요. 드레스 세 벌을 각각 6달러에 샀어요.
　　남 설마요! 그럼, 청바지도 샀어요?
　　여 아뇨, 한 벌에 7달러밖에 안 했는데, 지금 제 사이즈는 다 품절됐어요.
　　남 안됐군요! 오, 이 블라우스 네 벌은 얼마나 주셨어요?
　　여 믿어지세요? 겨우 각각 3달러예요.
　　남 그래요? 저도 거기에 가야겠네요. 남자 옷도 있나요?
　　여 안타깝게도 그 가게는 여성 옷 가게예요.

해설 여자가 지불한 금액은 드레스 18달러($6 X 3 = $18), 블라우스 12달러($3 X 4 = $12)이므로 총 30달러이다.

어휘 bargain price 특가 be sold out 다 팔리다

10 ⑤

해석 남 내가 바르셀로나에 있다니 믿겨지지 않아.
여 여기는 스페인에서 가장 유명한 곳 중 하나야.
남 내가 상상했던 것보다 더 환상적이야.
여 사그라다 파밀리아 성당에 대해 아니?
남 잘 몰라. 언제 세워졌니?
여 지난 세기 초반 경에 Antoni Gaudi에 의해 고안됐어.
남 원래 무슨 용도로 지어졌니?
여 대성당으로 지어졌어.
남 아주 인상적이구나.
여 확실히 그렇지! 그런데 아직 완공은 안 됐어.
남 그러니? 야, 너는 이곳에 대해 아는 것이 많구나.
여 음, 내가 건축에 관심이 있어서 그래.
남 나는 운이 좋구나! 너 같은 훌륭한 가이드가 있으니 말이야.

해설 아직 완공되지 않았다는 언급이 있지만 완공 연도는 언급되지 않았다.

어휘 originally 원래, 최초에 cathedral 대성당 definitely 확실히, 틀림없이
impressive 인상에 남는, 인상적인 unfinished 완성되지 않은 architecture
건축술[학]

11 ③

해석 여 안녕하세요. Parsons Summer Intensive Courses에 대해 정보
를 드리고자 합니다. 이 강의는 우리 교직원과 뉴욕에 근거지를 둔 많
은 화가와 디자이너에 의해 이루어집니다. 학생들은 자신의 미술 용
품을 준비해야 합니다. 필요하거나 추천하는 물품의 목록은 매 강
의 시간에 강사에 의해 배포됩니다. Parsons Summer Intensive
Courses 등록은 6월 1일부터 시작합니다. 일찍 등록하는 것을 권
장합니다. 좀 더 자세한 설명을 원하시면 저희 웹 사이트인 www.
parsonssummerintensivecourses.com을 방문하세요.

해설 필요하거나 추천하는 물건의 목록은 매 강의 시간에 강사에 의해 배포된다고 되
어 있으므로 "필요한 물품 목록은 개강 후 게시판에 공지된다."가 내용과 일치하
지 않는다.

어휘 inform 알려주다 intensive 집중적인 faculty 교직원 supply 물품
distribute 배포하다 instructor 강사 registration 등록

12 ⑤

해석 남 옛 영화의 흥행 순위를 좀 봐.
여 재미있을 것 같구나! 어느 영화가 1위지?
남 'Titanic'이야.
여 'Titanic'이라고? 개인적으로 나는 로맨스 영화는 좋아하지 않아.
남 그럼 어떤 영화를 좋아하니?
여 'Jurassic Park'나 'Star Wars' 같은 공상 과학 영화를 좋아해.
남 오, 'Star Wars'는 2위에 있지만 'Jurassic Park'는 상위 다섯 개의 영
화에는 포함되어 있지 않아.
여 그럼 어느 영화가 3위야?
남 3위는 'E.T.'이고 'The Lion King'이 그 뒤를 잇고 있어.
여 'The Lion King'이 4위라고? 믿기지가 않아.

해설 'Jurassic Park'는 상위 다섯 개의 영화에 포함되어 있지 않다고 했으므로 5위의
'Jurassic Park'는 잘못된 것이다.

어휘 box office 흥행 (수익), 매표소 rank 평가하다, 분류하다 unbelievable 믿을 수
가 없는

13 ④

해석 여 이 대학에서 함께 공부한 지 일 년이 지났어.
남 그래. 시간이 정말 빨리 지나갔어. 내가 한국을 떠날 때가 거의 다 됐네.
여 무슨 말이야?
남 난 여기에 일 년 동안 공부하러 온 거야. 다음 주에 호주로 다시 돌아 갈
거야.
여 그래? 믿기 어렵구나. 나는 네가 여기에 겨우 일 년만 머무를 계획이었
는지 몰랐어. 그런데 그거 아니?
남 뭐?
여 사실 나도 작년에 일 년 동안 호주에 있었어.
남 정말? 거기서 무엇을 했는데?
여 영어 실력을 기르고 있었어.
남 도움이 됐다고 생각하니?
여 약간은, 하지만 일 년은 충분한 시간이 아닌 것 같아.

해설 호주에서 일 년 동안 영어를 공부했다는 여자의 말에 남자가 그것이 도움이
되었느냐고 물었으므로 "약간은, 하지만 일 년은 충분한 시간이 아닌 것 같
아."라고 답하는 것이 가장 적절하다. ① 맞아. 호주 사람들은 매우 친절해.
② 호주에서 즐거운 여행을 하길 바래. ③ 응, 너와 함께 한 공부는 내게 도움이 되
었어. ⑤ 물론, 네 영어 실력을 향상시키도록 도와줘.

어휘 improve 향상시키다 It's almost time ~ 거의 ~할 시간이다 You know
what? 있잖아.

14 ③

해석 여 이 사진에서 네 옆에 있는 키 큰 남자는 누구야?
남 John이야.
여 그를 잘 아니? 내 말은, 친한 사이야?
남 우리 사이는 아주 친한 사이는 아니지만, 그는 나의 회사 동료 중 한 명
이야.
여 정말 멋져 보인다. 나를 그에게 소개시켜 줄래?
남 너 남자 친구 있잖아, 그렇지?
여 오래전에 헤어졌어. 그래서, 해줄 거야, 안 해줄 거야?
남 내가 장담하는데 그는 여자 친구가 있어.
여 혹시 모르잖아.
남 좋아. 내일 물어볼게.

해설 여자가 남자에게 John을 소개시켜 달라는 부탁을 하자 그는 여자 친구가 있을 거
라고 거절했지만 혹시 모르니 소개시켜 달라고 하는 상황에서 남자가 할 말로 가
장 적절한 것은 "좋아. 내일 물어볼게."이다. ① 그거 안됐네. ② 그것을 하다니 넌
운이 좋구나! ④ 전혀. 걱정하지 마. ⑤ 기운 내! 다음에는 할 수 있을 거야.

어휘 coworker 동료 introduce 소개하다 break up with ~와 헤어지다

15 ⑤

해석 여 Sally는 방과 후에 학교 친구인 Cindy를 집에 초대했다. 두 소녀는

Sally의 방에서 재미있게 놀고 있다. 한편, Sally의 어머니는 주방에서 저녁 식사로 스파게티를 요리하고 계신다. 나중에 Sally의 어머니는 Cindy가 스파게티를 먹고 갈 것인지를 묻는다. Cindy는 그러고 싶지만 그녀의 할아버지와 할머니께서 오늘밤 집에 오실 것이며, 어머니가 저녁 식사 때에 맞춰 그녀가 집에 오기를 기다리는 것을 기억한다. 이 상황에서 Cindy가 Sally의 어머니에게 할 말로 가장 적절한 것은 무엇인가?

Cindy **감사합니다만, 오늘 밤 저녁은 집에서 먹어야 해요.**

해설 Cindy는 Sally의 집에서 같이 스파게티를 먹고 싶지만 오늘밤 할머니, 할아버지가 오셔서 함께 저녁을 먹기로 했기 때문에 그럴 수 없다. 따라서 Cindy가 Sally의 어머니에게 할 말은 "감사합니다만, 오늘 밤 저녁은 집에서 먹어야 해요."가 적절하다. ① 네, 이곳에 있는 것이 좋아요. ② 제가 오늘 여기서 저녁 식사를 해도 될까요? ③ 죄송하지만, 저는 요리를 잘 못해요. ④ 오늘 밤에 여기서 저녁을 먹는 게 어때요?

어휘 **meanwhile** 한편 **tempt** 유혹하다 **expect** ~을 기대하다, 예상하다

16-17 ②, ④

해석 안녕하세요, 여러분. 오늘은 종이에 대해 얘기하고자 합니다. 여러분은 종이가 충분하다고 생각하나요? 아뇨, 그렇지 않습니다. 그럼 종이 부족에 대한 해결책은 무엇일까요? 종이를 재사용하는 것입니다. 먼저, 신문은 다 읽은 후에 다시 사용할 수 있는 많은 방법들이 있습니다. 오래된 신문지는 그릇을 싸거나 물건을 우편으로 보낼 때 상자 안을 채우는 용도로 사용될 수 있습니다. 그것들은 페인트칠이나 청소를 할 때 바닥에 덮는 데 사용될 수도 있습니다. 또한, 이면지는 여러 가지로 사용이 가능합니다. 가장 확실한 사용법은 나머지 면에 인쇄를 하는 것입니다. 또한 여러 페이지를 모으면 쇼핑 목록이나 다른 것을 적는 좋은 메모장이 됩니다. 마지막으로 식료품 가게에서 나온 종이봉투 또한 재사용될 수 있는데, 그것들은 다시 식료품을 담는 데 사용될 수 있고 도시락을 넣거나 휴지통 안에 덧댈 수 있습니다. 종이를 버리기 전에 재사용하는 것은 종이를 아끼는 간단한 방법입니다.

해설 16 종이 부족에 대한 해결책으로 종이를 재사용하는 방법을 제시하고 있다.
17 pack dishes에서 물건 포장이, good notepaper에서 노트가, carry lunches or line wastebaskets에서 도시락 가방과 휴지통 보조가 언급되었지만 벽지에 대해서는 언급되어 있지 않다.

어휘 **solution** 해결(책) **shortage** 부족 **reuse** 재사용하다 **obvious** 분명한 **scrap** 조각 **line** ~의 안을 받치다, 안감을 대다 **throw away** 버리다 **conserve** 보존(보호)하다

◎ Dictation

01 for the time being
02 remains a stain
03 as mayor / positive change / token of our respect
04 more money than you earn / large expenditures / unpredictable things
05 warm place to sleep / not easy to raise a dog
06 on the top of the tree / wear glasses / a cap on the right side

07 not yet healed / pick up my son / neighbors for
08 come to work / hold an event
09 with bargain prices / are sold out now / for women only
10 the most famous sites / originally built / in architecture
11 members of our faculty / recommended materials / Early registration
12 is ranked / science fiction movies / just behind it
13 really flown by / hard to believe / trying to improve
14 next to you / introduce me to him / never know
15 cooking dinner / would like to stay / expects her to come home
16-17 to the shortage of paper / can be used to pack dishes / Scraps of pages / Reusing paper

07회 듣기 모의고사
p.42-43

01 ②	02 ③	03 ④	04 ①	05 ②	06 ①
07 ④	08 ⑤	09 ②	10 ④	11 ④	12 ②
13 ④	14 ③	15 ③	16 ①	17 ①	

01 ②

해석 여 공연은 어땠어요?
남 대사를 기억 못해서 너무 당황했어요.
여 신경 쓰지 마세요. 누구에게나 일어날 수 있는 일이에요.
남 **위로해 줘서 고마워요.**

해설 공연 중에 대사를 기억 못해 당황한 남자에게 여자가 위로의 말을 건네주고 있으므로 응답으로 "위로해 줘서 고마워요."가 가장 적절하다. ① 저는 당신이 훌륭한 배우가 될 거라 확신해요. ③ 이봐요! 자신감을 가지세요. ④ 알겠어요. 다음에는 더 잘하길 바라요. ⑤ 그래요? 그럼 지금 당장 그에게 사과할게요.

어휘 **word** 대사 **comfort** 위로 **confidence** 자신감 **embarrassed** 당황한 **Think nothing of it.** 신경 쓰지 마세요.

02 ③

해석 남 Erica는 제가 여태껏 본 신부 중 가장 아름다워요. 그렇게 생각하지 않나요?
여 네, 맞아요. 그녀가 행복해 보여 안심이 되네요.
남 무슨 말씀인가요?
여 **사실, 그녀는 결혼에 대해 걱정하는 것처럼 보였어요.**

해설 신부가 행복해 보여서 다행이라는 여자의 말에 남자가 왜 그런 말을 하냐고 물었으므로 응답으로 "사실, 그녀는 결혼에 대해 걱정하는 것처럼 보였어요."가 가장 적절하다. ① 그녀가 약속을 지키려 노력해왔다는 뜻이에요. ② 당신도 알다시피, 그는 제가 찾고 있던 남자에요. ④ 다행히도, 그녀는 지난달에 그와 헤어졌어요. ⑤ 놀랍게도, 그녀는 우리에게 자신의 결혼을 발표했어요.

03 ④

해석 여 자, 여러분, 저는 이제 여러분이 등산 중에 맞닥뜨릴지도 모르는 두 가지 위험을 경고하고, 그것에 대처하는 방법에 대해서 말씀드리고자 합니다. 가장 흔한 위험은 여러분이 자주 볼 수 있는 불독개미입니다. 그들에게 물리면 몹시 아픕니다. 그들을 피하는 가장 좋은 방법은 다리에 살충제 스프레이를 뿌리는 것입니다. 다음으로, 다른 위험은 뱀을 만나는 것입니다. 그런 상황에서는 침착하시고, 빨리 움직이려고 하지 마시고 천천히 움직이십시오.

해설 등산 중에 맞닥뜨릴 위험 중 위험한 동물 두 종을 소개하고 그 대처법을 설명하고 있다.

어휘 folk 사람들 hazard 위험 encounter ~과 우연히 마주치다 frequently 자주 deliver 가하다, 뿜어내다, 주다 nasty 몹쓸, 위험한 avoid 피하다 insect spray 살충제

04 ①

해석 남 Kathy, 당신 너무 피곤해 보여요.
여 온종일 사무실에서 일만해서 그런 것 같아요.
남 운동을 하는 게 어때요?
여 당신은 무슨 운동을 좋아해요?
남 저는 주로 걷기 운동을 해요.
여 걷는 것이 운동으로 괜찮나요?
남 그럼요. 하루에 40분 이상 걷는 것은 다른 어떤 운동보다도 효과가 좋아요.
여 정말요? 몰랐어요.
남 게다가, 규칙적으로 걷기 운동을 하면 다양한 질병을 예방할 수 있어요.
여 그렇군요. 저도 이제부터 집 근처 공원에서 걷기를 시작해야겠어요.
남 잘 생각하셨어요.

해설 남자는 하루에 40분 이상 걷는 것은 어떤 운동 못지않게 좋다고 말하고 있다.

어휘 exercise 운동; 운동하다 effective 효과적인 prevent 예방하다 a variety of 다양한 illness 질병

05 ②

해석 남 안녕하세요, 부인. 모든 것이 마음에 드시나요?
여 예. 그런데 Southport에 가는 데 얼마나 걸리는지 알 수 있을까요?
남 음, 보통은 13시간 걸리는데 이번에는 15시간이 걸릴 것 같네요.
여 기상 악화 때문인가요?
남 예, 바다 상태가 나빠 좀 느려질 것 같아요.
여 그렇군요. 항해는 힘들까요?
남 아마도요. 하지만 걱정 마세요. 선원들과 저는 능숙하니까요.
여 그렇게 말씀하시니 위안이 되네요.
남 항해 도중에 필요하신 것이 있으시면 저나 선원 중 한 명에게 요청하세요.

여 감사합니다!

해설 "the seas will slow us down a bit", "my crew and I are very experienced", "during the voyage" 등을 통해 두 사람의 관계가 선장과 승객임을 알 수 있다.

어휘 satisfactory 만족스러운 rough 험악한 voyage 항해 assist 돕다

06 ①

해석 여 여보, 직사각형 모양의 화분을 욕실로 갖다 줄래요? 물을 줘야겠어요.
남 그래요. 그런데 거실에는 직사각형 모양의 화분이 두 개 있어요.
여 오, 맞아요. 창문과 TV 사이에 있는 것 말이에요.
남 이제 찾았어요.
여 여보, 하나만 더 도와줄래요?
남 그래요. 뭔데요?
여 이 푯말을 화분 중 하나에 꽂아주세요.
남 어떤 화분 말인가요? 소파 왼쪽 옆의 둥근 모양의 화분 말인가요?
여 아뇨. 가운데가 약간 불룩한 화분 보여요?
남 네. 이 푯말을 꽂을 화분이 그것인가요?
여 아뇨. 그 옆에 있는 화분이에요.
남 오, 알겠어요. 당신이 말하는 화분은 정사각형 모양의 화분이군요, 그렇죠?
여 맞아요!

해설 가운데가 약간 불룩한 화분 옆의 화분은 세모 모양이 아니라 정사각형 모양이다.

어휘 rectangular 직사각형의 pot 화분 water ~에 물을 주다 plant label 화분에 꽂아 놓은 식물의 이름을 쓴 푯말 round 둥근 swollen 부풀어 오른 square 정사각형의

07 ④

해석 남 아직 준비가 안 됐나요?
여 아직요, 여보. 이제 막 옷을 다 다렸어요. 이제 화장을 해야 해요.
남 오, 약속 시간에 늦을 거예요.
여 화장을 하지 않고 갈 수는 없어요.
남 음, 7시에 식당에서 만날 거예요.
여 알아요, 알아요. 하지만 오후 내내 아이들을 돌보느라 바빴어요.
남 알겠어요. 서두르기나 해요.
여 John? 제 귀걸이가 어디 있어요?
남 내가 어떻게 알아요? 당신 귀걸이잖아요.
여 오, 이제 기억이 나네요. 서랍에 있어요. 침실로 가서 가져다줄래요?
남 물론이지요.

해설 여자는 침실에서 귀걸이를 가져다 달라고 부탁했다.

어휘 iron 다림질하다 makeup 화장 appointment 약속 take care of ~을 돌보다 get a move on 서두르다 drawer 서랍

08 ⑤

해석 남 앉으세요.
여 감사합니다. 저를 왜 부르셨나요?
남 당신이 몽골어에 능통하다고 들었어요.

여 거기에서 10년 동안 살았어요. 7세 때 부모님과 함께 그곳에 갔어요.

남 그렇군요. 그럼 부탁 좀 들어 주시겠어요?

여 물론이죠. 뭔데요?

남 몽골인 구매자와의 중요한 회의가 있어요. 그는 우리의 신제품에 관심이 많아요.

여 잘됐군요!

남 물론 그래요. 그렇지만 문제는 우리를 위해 통역해 줄 사람이 필요하다는 거예요.

여 무슨 말씀인지 알겠어요. 그럼 제가 지금 무엇을 해야 하나요?

남 그 구매자가 오늘 오후에 공항에 도착할 거예요. 저와 함께 공항에 가 주실 수 있나요?

여 기꺼이요. 제가 당신께 도움이 되어서 기뻐요.

해설 남자가 여자를 부른 이유는 몽골 바이어와 만날 때 통역할 사람이 필요해서이다.

어휘 **Mongolian** 몽골말, 몽골 사람의 **do somebody a favor** ~의 부탁을 들어주다 **interpret** 통역하다 **My pleasure.** 기꺼이.

09 ②

해석 남 무엇을 도와드릴까요?

여 과일을 좀 사려고요. 이 사과는 얼마인가요?

남 10개에 5달러입니다.

여 20개 주세요.

남 알겠습니다. 그밖에는요?

여 그 귤이 맛있어 보이네요. 얼마인가요?

남 지금은 저렴해요. 킬로 당 4달러 밖에 안 합니다.

여 그럼 귤 2킬로 주세요.

남 좋습니다. 토마토는요? 킬로당 2.5달러밖에 안 해요.

여 토마토는 됐어요. 하지만 포도가 마음에 드네요.

남 킬로당 5.5달러입니다.

여 그렇군요. 1킬로 주세요.

남 그밖에는요?

여 됐어요.

해설 여자가 지불해야 할 총 금액은 사과 값 10달러, 귤 값 8달러, 포도 값 5달러 50센트 이므로 총 23달러 50센트이다.

어휘 **tangerine** 귤

10 ④

해석 (전화벨이 울린다.)

남 여보세요. Kensington 대학 외국인 학생 고문 사무실입니다. 무엇을 도와드릴까요?

여 저는 Susan Parker입니다. 특별 휴가 신청을 하려고요.

남 학생증 번호를 말씀해 주세요.

여 Harry의 H이고 5712입니다.

남 H57120이요. 알겠습니다. 주소는요, Susan?

여 Tamworth 10번가입니다.

남 무슨 강좌를 듣고 있나요?

여 영작문 수업이에요.

남 이번 학기 교수님은 누구신가요?

여 Green 선생님이에요.

남 언제 휴가 가기를 원해세요?

여 5월 31일부터 6월 4일이면 좋겠어요.

남 알겠습니다. 접수했습니다.

해설 Susan이라는 이름, 10th Avenue, Tamworth라는 주소, the English writing class라는 수강 강좌, be away May 31 to June 4라는 휴가 기간이 언급되었지만 학과에 대한 언급은 없다.

어휘 **make a request** 요청하다 **leave** 휴가 **term** 학기

11 ④

해석 여 브라질너트를 먹어 본 적이 있습니까? 브라질너트는 아마존 정글에서 자라는 거대한 나무에서 생산됩니다. 초승달 모양의 브라질너트는 전문적으로 견과류는 아니지만 먹을 수 있는 씨앗입니다. 브라질너트는 항암 작용을 한다고 여겨지는 음식 중에서는 매우 뛰어난 미네랄의 원천입니다. 다른 견과류와 마찬가지로 그것들은 또한 어느 정도의 단백질, 섬유질, 그리고 비타민 E를 제공합니다. 그리고 그것들은 풍부한 맛과 향을 주는 지방의 좋은 원천입니다. 브라질너트는 껍질을 벗기지 않은 상태로 산다면 깨기가 어려울 수가 있습니다. 먼저 그것들을 삶아서 껍질을 부드럽게 할 수 있습니다.

해설 브라질너트는 지방이 많고 맛이 풍부하다고 되어 있으므로 "지방이 적고 냄새가 없다."가 일치하지 않는다.

어휘 **crescent** 초승달 **edible** 먹을 수 있는 **exceptional** 매우 뛰어난, 드문, 예외적인 **fiber** 섬유질 **rich** 풍부한 **flavor** 향 **crack** 깨다 **unshelled** 껍질을 벗기지 않은 **boil** 끓이다

12 ②

해석 남 내일 아침에 London에 가는 거지?

여 응. 오후 2시 30분에 모임이 있어.

남 알았어. 그럼 11시 기차를 타자. 너도 알다시피 London 역에서 모임 장소까지 가는 데 30분 정도는 필요할 거야.

여 알아. 그런데 약간 더 일찍 출발하는 건 어때? 모임 전에 London에서 쇼핑을 하고 싶어. 두 시간 좀 안 걸릴 거야.

남 음, 좋아. 그럼 가능한 한 일찍 떠나야겠네.

여 하지만 그렇게 일찍 떠나고 싶지는 않아. 두 시간만 더 일찍 출발하면 될 것 같아.

남 그럼 이걸 타야겠다.

여 응. 가장 좋은 선택 같아. 쇼핑을 할 충분한 시간을 가질 수 있고 모임에 도 제 시간에 도착하겠어.

해설 모임 시간보다 두 시간 일찍 출발하기로 했으므로 두 사람이 이용할 기차는 9시에 출발하는 것이다.

어휘 **allow** 허용하다 **as early as possible** 가능한 한 일찍 **option** 선택

13 ④

해석 남 주말에 무엇을 할 거니?

여 토요일 밤에 친구들과 저녁 먹는 것 말고는 아직 없어.

남 그럼 토요일 오후에 함께 뭐 좀 할래? 날씨가 좋을 거야.

여 그래. 무엇을 할 생각인데?

남 야외에서 햇빛을 쐬면서 시간을 보내고 싶어. 축구 경기를 관람하는 것은 어때?

여 좋은 생각이다. 언제 하는데?

남 오후 3시에 시작해. 2시쯤에 너를 데리러 갈게.

여 내가 준비해야 할 것이 있니?

남 적당한 모자와 자외선 차단제를 챙겨 와.

해설 오후 3시에 하는 축구 경기를 햇볕이 쬐는 가운데 보러 가기로 한 상황에서 여자가 뭐 준비할 것이 따로 없냐고 물었으므로 응답은 "적당한 모자와 자외선 차단제를 챙겨 와."가 적절하다. ① 축구화를 신어. ② 교통편을 마련해. ③ 경기 시간을 확인해. ⑤ 시합 전에 골 킥 연습을 해.

어휘 arrange ~을 계획하다, 준비하다 sunscreen 자외선 차단제 as yet 아직까지 have in mind 염두에 두다

14 ③

해설 여 실례합니다. Barnes 교수님 계신가요? 저는 교수님의 학생이에요.

남 미안합니다. Barnes 교수님은 오늘은 사무실에 나오시지 않아요.

여 음, 과제를 하는 데 도움이 필요해요.

남 내일 다시 오시면 교수님께서 계실 거예요.

여 과제가 내일 아침까지라 그건 안 돼요.

남 오, 저런.

여 오늘 도움을 받지 못하면 제시간에 과제를 마칠 수가 없어요.

남 음. 이메일을 보내는 것은 어때요? 온라인상으로 당신의 질문에 답변을 해 주실 수 있을 지도 몰라요.

여 좋은 생각이네요. 감사합니다!

해설 교수님께서 자리에 안 계시니 이메일을 써서 문의해 보라는 조언을 해 줄 때의 여자의 답변으로는 "좋은 생각이네요. 감사합니다!"가 적절하다. ① 만나 뵈어서 반가웠습니다. ② 아뇨, 오늘 이따가 다시 올게요. ④ 정말이요? 당신은 정말 친절하시군요. ⑤ 아니오. 교수님께서 내일 오후에 계실지를 확인해 보겠습니다.

어휘 available 만날 시간이 있는 assignment 과제 due ~하기로 되어 있는

15 ③

해설 여 John은 의뢰인과 아침 일찍 아주 중요한 회의가 잡혀 있다. 그런데 알람 소리를 듣지 못하고 늦잠을 잔다. 그는 일어나서 회의가 겨우 30분 후에 시작한다는 것을 알고 놀란다. 그가 시간에 맞춰 도착할 방법은 없다. 그는 의뢰인에게 전화를 걸기로 결심한다. 전화를 걸기 전에 그는 거짓말로 집에 급한 일이 있다고 말할까, 아니면 사실을 말할까를 정하려고 한다. 마침내 그는 사실을 말하기로 결정을 내리고 의뢰인에게 전화를 건다. 의뢰인이 전화를 받을 때 John이 의뢰인에게 할 말로 가장 적절한 것은 무엇인가?

John 죄송하지만 늦을 것 같아요. 늦잠을 잤어요.

해설 거짓말을 할까, 사실을 말할까 고민하다가 결국 사실대로 말하기로 결정을 내렸으므로 John이 할 말은 "죄송하지만 늦을 것 같아요. 늦잠을 잤어요."가 가장 적절하다. ① 좋아요. 내일 봐요. ② 괜찮아요. 그때 봐요. ④ 미안합니다만, 제가 지금 급해서요. 다시 전화 걸어 주실래요? ⑤ 죄송합니다만, 집에 급한 일이 있어서요.

어휘 oversleep 늦잠자다 emergency 응급상황 client 고객 discover 발견하다 make it 제시간에 도착하다

16-17 ①, ①

해설 (전화벨이 울린다.)

남 안녕하세요, Fashion Fad입니다. 무엇을 도와드릴까요?

여 네, 저는 모델 지망생이고, 귀사의 패션쇼에 관심이 많아요. 다음 주 토요일에 열리는 패션쇼에 관한 정보를 얻을 수 있을까요?

남 물론이죠. 무엇을 도와드릴까요?

여 어떤 유형의 옷을 선보이는지 알고 싶어요.

남 저희는 남성 및 여성용 정장에 집중할 예정입니다.

여 오, 좋을 것 같네요. 어디서 열리는지 알려 주시겠어요?

남 Tanglin Mall에서 열립니다.

여 알겠습니다. 그리고 입장료는 얼마죠?

남 일인당 12달러씩입니다.

여 어디서 구입 가능하죠? 출입구에서요?

남 네. 또는 저희 매장 어디에서나 구입할 수 있습니다.

여 알겠습니다. 몇 시에 시작하는지 알려주실 수 있나요?

남 오후 7시요. 오후 9시경까지 계속됩니다.

여 7시에서 9시까지군요. 알겠어요. 도움 감사합니다.

해설 16 여자의 말 "Can you give me some information about the fashion show next Saturday?"로 미루어 보아, 여자가 전화를 건 목적은 '패션쇼에 관한 정보에 관해 문의하려고'임을 알 수 있다.

17 패션쇼 개최에 관한 정보 중에서 모델에 관한 내용은 언급되지 않았다.

어휘 trainee 교육을 받는 사람 fad 일시적 유행 focus on ~에 집중하다 formal dress 정장

🎯 Dictation

01 so embarrassed

02 I'm relieved

03 about two hazards / to apply insect spray / remain calm

04 work all day / more effective / prevent a variety of illnesses

05 take to get to / slow us down a bit / one of the crew to assist

06 rectangular-shaped pots / the left side of the sofa / the square-shaped pot

07 ironing my dress / get a move on / bring them for me

08 Would you do me a favor / our new product / My pleasure

09 20 of those / 2 kilos of tangerines / take one kilo

10 a request for special leave / May 31 to June 4

11 an edible seed / offer some protein / soften the shell

12 have a meeting / as early as possible / to do my shopping

13 None as yet except for / watching the soccer game / prepare anything

14 help with this assignment / due tomorrow morning / finish it in time

15 fails to wake / call his client / tell the truth

16-17 give me some information / focus on formal dress clothes / what time it starts

01 ⑤	02 ④	03 ⑤	04 ②	05 ①	06 ②
07 ③	08 ③	09 ②	10 ①	11 ④	12 ①
13 ④	14 ②	15 ③	16 ②	17 ③	

01 ⑤

해석 남 왜! 이곳에는 들를 곳이 아주 많이 있네요.
여 그래요. 유명한 사찰, 두 곳의 고대 궁궐, 국립 미술관 등등이요.
남 어디를 먼저 가 보고 싶어요?
여 사실, 국립 미술관을 가 보고 싶었어요.

해설 어디에 가고 싶은지 묻는 남자의 말에 대한 여자의 응답으로 "사실, 국립 미술관을 가보고 싶었어요."가 가장 적절하다. ① 저 지금 급해요. 먼저 가고 싶어요. ② 저는 지금 피곤해요. 혼자 있게 해주실래요? ③ 그것에 대해서는 죄송해요. 저도 여기가 초행이에요. ④ 지금 관광하러 나가는 것은 어때요?

어휘 ancient 옛날의, 고대의 you name it 그 밖에 무엇이든지

02 ④

해석 여 여행 준비는 다 되었나요? 몇 시간 있으면 비행기가 출발할 거예요.
남 예. 그런 것 같아요. 죄송하지만 택시 좀 불러주시겠어요? 가지고 갈 짐이 많네요.
여 그럴 필요 없어요. 공항까지 배웅해 줄게요.
남 고마워요! 당신은 매우 친절하군요.

해설 자신을 공항까지 배웅해 준다는 여자의 말에 대한 남자의 응답으로 고마움을 표시하는 말인 "고마워요! 당신은 매우 친절하군요."가 적절하다. ① 죄송해요. 그것에 대해서는 생각해보지 못했어요. ② 서두르세요. 그가 곧 여기에 도착할 거예요. ③ 좋아요. 지금 당장 택시를 부릅시다. ⑤ 참 멍청하기도 하지! 전 늦을 것 같아요.

어휘 baggage 짐 see ~ off ~를 배웅하다

03 ⑤

해석 여 우리는 고통을 경험하지 않고는 성장할 수 없습니다. 근력 훈련에 대해 생각해 보세요. 여러분은 이두박근과 삼두박근에 지칠 때까지 힘을 가합니다. 그것은 어렵고 단기적으로는 고통스럽기까지 하지만 궁극적인 보상은 여러분이 더 강해진다는 것이고 그것은 만족스러울 것입니다. 그것은 악기를 배우든, 스포츠를 하든, 어려운 개념을 이해하려고 애쓰는 것이든 그 어떤 것을 더 잘하려 할 때 일어나는 똑같은 과정입니다.

해설 무엇인가를 하면서 고통이 따를 때 비로소 성장을 이룰 수 있다는 내용이므로 여자가 하는 말의 주제로는 '고통이 성장에 미치는 영향'이 적절하다.

어휘 go through 경험하다 strength 힘, 근력 bicep 이두근 tricep 삼두근 exhaustion 소모, 고갈 eventual 궁극적인 instrument 악기 struggle 애쓰다 concept 개념

04 ②

해석 남 우리가 매일 8잔의 물을 마셔야 한다는 것을 아니?
여 그래, 알아.
남 그럼 넌 매일 물 8잔을 마시니?
여 아니, 그럴 필요는 없다고 생각해.
남 왜? 건강하게 살려면 물을 많이 마셔야 한다고 하잖아.
여 사실, 그건 우리가 잘못 알고 있는 거야.
남 그게 무슨 말이니?
여 물이 아니더라도 수분을 많이 흡수하면 된다는 거야.
남 그 말은 물이 아니고 음료나 과일을 먹어도 된다는 거니?
여 바로 그거야. 과일과 채소는 90% 이상이 수분이야. 그러니까 네가 하루에 8잔의 물을 마시지 못한다 해도 걱정하지 마.

해설 우리의 몸이 필요로 하는 수분은 단순히 물을 마시는 것 외에도 과일과 채소 같은 음식으로부터도 얻을 수 있기 때문에 하루에 필요한 8잔의 물을 마시지 못했다 하더라도 크게 염려할 필요는 없다는 것이 여자의 주장이다.

어휘 misbelief 잘못된 생각 absorb 흡수하다 moisture 수분, 습기 beverage 음료 concerned 염려하는

05 ①

해석 남 쇼에 오신 것을 환영합니다, Barbara.
여 감사합니다.
남 여기에 당신이 도서관 사서라고 적혀 있네요. 맞아요?
여 예. 저는 공공도서관에서 일해요.
남 책을 많이 읽으시나요?
여 예, 꽤 많이 읽어요.
남 가장 좋아하시는 주제는 무엇인가요?
여 전기를 많이 읽어요. 공상 과학 소설도 좋아하고요.
남 그리고 남편의 성함은 David이군요. 여기에 함께 오셨나요?
여 예, 여기에 왔어요.
남 어디 계신가요? 방청객 속에 David 씨가 계신가요? 오, 저기 계시군요. Barbara와 David 씨에게 큰 박수를 쳐 주세요.

해설 "Welcome to the show, Barbara.", "Is David in the audience?", "Let's give a big hand for Barbara and David!"를 통해 남자는 방송 프로그램의 진행자이고 여자는 출연자임을 알 수 있다.

어휘 librarian 사서 subject 주제 biography 전기 science fiction 공상 과학 소설 audience 관객, 방청객 give one a big hand ~에게 큰 박수를 보내다

06 ②

해석 여 무엇을 하고 있니, Thomas?
남 내 꿈의 집을 그리고 있어. 미술 숙제야.
여 봐도 될까? 오, 거의 다 그린 것 같네.
남 그래. 마당의 왼쪽에 있는 휘어진 나무 한 그루가 마지막 부분인데 그것을 그리던 중이었어.
여 그렇구나. 마당에는 배드민턴 코트가 있네.
남 너도 알다시피, 나는 배드민턴 하는 것을 아주 좋아하잖아. 작은 연못 안에 있는 탑은 어때 보여?
여 에펠탑 같네. 그리고 단풍잎 모양의 연못이 독특해.

남 사실, 난 가을의 단풍잎을 좋아해.

여 성에서 살고 싶니? 집이 성 같아.

남 그래, 나는 가능하다면 성 모양의 집을 짓고 싶어.

해설 연못의 모양은 은행잎 모양이 아니라 단풍잎 모양이라고 했으므로 은행잎 모양의 연못은 일치하지 않는다.

어휘 bent 구부러진 resemble 닮다 maple tree 단풍나무

07 ③

해석 여 오, Bruce! 지금 뭘 하고 있는 중이니?

남 옛 영화 포스터들을 정리하고 있어.

여 와! 상당히 많은 포스터를 모았구나.

남 그래. 영화를 보고 그 포스터를 모으는 것이 내가 가장 좋아하는 취미야.

여 오, 너는 Audrey Hepburn의 팬이구나.

남 그래. '로마의 휴일'을 빼고는 그녀가 주연을 맡은 영화의 모든 포스터를 모았어.

여 그거 아니? 우리 오빠도 한때는 영화광이었고 너처럼 포스터 모으는 것을 좋아했어.

남 그 말은 지금은 영화광이 아니란 말이니?

여 응. 그래서 원하는 사람들에게 포스터를 나눠 주고 있어.

남 그가 내가 원하는 포스터를 가지고 있다면 내게 그것을 줄 것 같니?

여 응.

남 그럼 그 포스터를 가지고 있는지 물어봐 줄래?

여 물론, 할 수 있지. 문제없어. 친구 좋다는 게 뭐니?

해설 여자는 영화 포스터 모으기가 취미인 남자를 위해 포스터를 구해 줄 것이다.

어휘 arrange 정리하다 collect 모으다 star 주연하다 mania ~광 What are friends for? 친구 좋다는 게 뭐야?

08 ③

해석 남 안녕, Dorothy. 여기에 책 사러 왔니?

여 그래. 너는? 오, 책은 이미 산 것처럼 보이는구나.

남 응. 문학 수업 숙제를 위해 필요한 소설책이야.

여 그렇구나. 그럼 필요한 책은 다 산 거니?

남 아니, 아직 새로 나온 과학 잡지도 몇 권 사야 해. 너는 무슨 책을 사려고 하니?

여 사실 난 언니 생일 선물로 책을 주려고 해. 하지만 무슨 책을 사야 할지 아직 결정을 못했어.

남 언니는 어떤 장르 읽기를 좋아하는데?

여 전기 읽기를 좋아하는데 어떤 사람의 것을 사야 할지 생각 중이야.

남 Steve Jobs는 어때? 요즘 매우 인기가 있어.

여 아, 그 책 알았어, 그걸 사는 게 좋겠어. 조언해줘서 고마워.

남 뭘. 그건 그렇고, 책을 산 다음에는 뭘 할 거니? 패스트푸드 식당에서 점심이나 같이 먹자.

여 좋은 생각 같아.

해설 여자는 언니의 생일 선물로 줄 책을 사러 서점에 왔다고 했다.

어휘 novel 소설 literature 문학 genre 장르 biography 전기 Think nothing

of it. 신경 쓰지 마세요.

09 ②

해석 여 우린 아직 살 게 많아요, Tom. 램프를 사는 데 25달러밖에 쓸 수 없어요.

남 알았어요. 그럼 좀 더 싼 것을 삽시다.

여 염두에 두고 있는 거라도 있나요?

남 여기 20달러 하는 것이 있고 더 작은 것은 15달러네요.

여 사각형 모양의 작은 것이 마음에 들어요. 책상에 딱 맞을 거예요.

남 그리고 제일 싸요. 좋아요. 그것을 사요.

여 좋아요, 이제 전화기를 골라요.

남 가지고 다닐 수 있는 전화기가 좋겠어요. 당신도 알다시피 무선 전화기요.

여 좋은 생각인 것 같아요.

남 이것은 어때요? 90달러예요.

여 오, 비싸네요.

남 제일 싼 것 보다 겨우 20달러 더 비싸요.

여 좋아요, 그것으로 합시다.

해설 여자는 램프 값으로 15달러를, 무선 전화기 값으로 90달러를 지불할 것이므로 총 금액은 105달러이다.

어휘 can afford to ~을 감당할 능력이 있다 square (정)사각형의 portable 가지고 다닐 수 있는, 운반할 수 있는 cordless 전화선이 없는

10 ①

해석 남 Jennifer, Smith 씨에게 전화해 줄 수 있어요?

여 그럼요. 그럼 뭐라고 말씀드릴까요?

남 금요일 약속을 취소하고 싶다고 말해주세요.

여 알겠습니다, 사장님. 그런데 왜요?

남 그날 여동생의 결혼식에 가야 해요.

여 아, 그렇군요. 여동생이 런던에 산다고 들었어요. 비행편은 예약하셨나요?

남 아직이요. 혹시 예약해 주실 수 있나요?

여 그럼요. 오, 사인하셔야 할 서류가 몇 개 있어요.

남 좋아요. 가져오세요. 그리고 판매 보고서를 5부 복사해 주셨으면 합니다.

여 알겠습니다, 사장님.

해설 남자가 여동생의 결혼식에 참여해야 하는 것이지 여자가 결혼식장을 예약해야 하는 것은 아니다.

어휘 appointment 약속 book 예약하다 flight 비행(편) signature 사인, 서명

11 ④

해석 여 대나무는 주로 더 따뜻한 지역에 분포되어 있는 빨리 자라는 식물이다. 그것은 중국의 장수의 상징이고 인도에서 그것은 우정에 대한 상징이다. 열대 기후에서는 울타리나, 다리, 또는 지팡이 등뿐 아니라 집을 짓는 재료로도 사용된다. 대나무는 낚싯대를 만드는 데 사용된 전통적인 재료였는데, 1880년대 중반 유리 섬유의 발명 이래로 낚싯대로의 사용이 급격히 줄었다. 대나무 줄기의 빈 구멍은 아시아의 많은 나라에서

음식을 요리하는 데 사용된다.

해설 1880년대 중반 이후, 유리 섬유의 발명 이래로 낚싯대로의 사용이 급격히 줄어들었다고 했다.

어휘 primarily 주로 distribute ~을 분포시키다 element 재료, 요소 construction 건설 fishing rod 낚싯대 fiberglass 유리 섬유 decline 줄다 rapidly 빠르게 hollow 구멍 stalk 줄기

12 ①

해설 남 오늘밤엔 TV를 봐요. 어떤 채널을 보고 싶어요?
여 글쎄요, CSI와 뉴스가 보고 싶어요. 편성표는 어때요?
남 CSI는 3개 채널에서 해요. 당신이 고르세요.
여 지금 몇 시예요?
남 5시 40분이에요.
여 5시 40분이라고요? 그럼 이 채널은 안 되네요.
남 그럼 이 두 채널만 남네요.
여 음. 짧은 뉴스가 좋겠네요. 30분짜리 뉴스가 좋아요. 저는 뉴스보다 먼저가 아니라 나중에 CSI를 보고 싶어요.
남 좋아요! 그럼 이 채널을 봐요.
여 알겠어요. 뉴스를 보기 전에 저녁을 만들 시간이 있겠네요.
남 당신이 저녁을 하겠다는 건가요?
여 알겠어요. 하지만 당신이 설거지를 한다면요.

해설 지금은 5시 40분이므로 그 이전 것은 안 될 것이고 먼저 30분짜리 뉴스를 보고 CSI를 보겠다고 했으므로 두 사람이 볼 채널은 1번이다.

어휘 Take your pick. 고르세요. offer 제공하다 wash up 설거지를 하다

13 ④

해설 (초인종이 울린다.)
여 밖에 누구예요?
남 Karl이야.
여 Karl? (문을 연다.) 무슨 일이니?
남 그냥 생일 축하한다고 말하려고 들렀어.
여 Karl, 너 내 생일이 내일이라는 거 알지, 그렇지?
남 알아. 네 생일 파티에 초대도 받았잖아. 하지만 내일 출장을 가야 해.
여 오, 좋지 않은데. 그럼 파티에 올 수 없다는 거야?
남 응. 그래서 오늘 들른 거야. 선물도 가져왔어. 뭔지 맞춰 봐.
여 모르겠어. 책 아니면 장갑?
남 아니.
여 그러지 말고, 지금 당장 말해 줘.
남 알았어. 이 25송이의 장미는 너를 위한 거야.

해설 생일 선물을 샀다는 남자의 말에 여자는 무슨 선물인지 묻고 있으므로 남자의 응답으로 "알았어. 이 25송이의 장미는 너를 위한 거야."가 가장 적절하다. ① 그것에 대해선 아무것도 모르겠어. ② 책은 늘 좋은 선물이야. ③ 네가 원하는 건 어떤 것이든 빌려줄 수 있어. ⑤ 걱정 마. 이건 너와 나 사이의 비밀이야.

어휘 What's up? 무슨 일이니? go on a business 출장가다 stop by 들르다 drop by 들르다

14 ②

해설 (전화벨이 울린다.)
남 분실물 센터입니다. 무엇을 도와드릴까요?
여 예, 어제 가방을 잃어버려서 전화를 드렸어요.
남 알겠습니다. 그런데 어제 저희에게 들어 온 가방은 모두 38개예요. 무슨 색이고 재질은 어떤가요?
여 검은색이고 가죽으로 만든 것입니다.
남 여기에는 24개의 가죽 가방이 있어요. 정보가 될 만한 것을 더 말해주시겠어요?
여 네. 앞에 지퍼가 달려 있고 긴 끈 하나가 달려 있어요.
남 앞에 주머니가 있나요?
여 아뇨, 하지만 옆에 휴대 전화를 넣을 수 있는 주머니가 하나 있어요.
남 알겠습니다, 얼마나 큰가요?
여 저는 그것을 어깨에 메요.

해설 가방을 잃어버려 분실물 센터에 전화를 건 여자와 직원인 남자의 대화로 남자가 가방의 크기를 물었으므로 "저는 그것을 어깨에 메요."라고 말하면서 가방이 숄더백이라는 것을 알려주는 것이 적절하다. ① 찾아 주셔서 감사합니다. ③ 죄송합니다. 그런 가방은 없어요. ④ 잠깐만요. 확인해 볼게요. ⑤ 주머니가 몇 개 있는 가죽 가방이에요.

어휘 lost and found 분실물 센터 strip 길고 가느다란 조각

15 ③

해설 여 Jenny는 영어 선생님이다. 그녀는 수업 자료를 학생들에게 나누어준다. 그것은 어휘 목록이다. 잠시 후, Tommy가 일어나서 인쇄물이 부족하다고 말한다. Jenny는 인쇄물의 수를 정확히 세었다고 생각한다. 하지만 인쇄물이 부족한 것은 사실이다. Jenny는 Tommy를 보내 그녀의 책상에서 인쇄물 몇 장을 가져오게 해야겠다고 결정을 내린다. 그녀는 Tommy에게 책상에 가서 시험지 몇 장을 가져오라고 부탁한다. 그런데 Tommy는 그녀의 책상이 어디인지 모른다. 이 상황에서 Tommy가 선생님에게 할 말로 가장 적절한 것은 무엇인가?
Tommy 선생님, 선생님의 책상이 어디인지 잘 모르겠어요.

해설 Tommy 선생님의 책상이 어디 있는지 모르는 상황이므로 "선생님의 책상이 어디인지 잘 모르겠어요."라고 말하는 것이 가장 적절하다. ① 우리가 왜 시험을 봐야 해요? ② 시험지가 몇 장 필요하세요? ④ 저희는 시험을 볼 거라는 통보를 받지 못했어요. ⑤ 선생님 책상 위에 충분한 인쇄물이 없어요.

어휘 give out 배포하다 vocabulary 어휘 accurately 정확하게

16-17 ②, ③

해설 여 저희 Lakeview 쇼핑몰을 방문해 주셔서 감사합니다. 저희는 Jacob Burk라는 10살 된 남자아이를 찾고 있습니다. 그의 아버지는 아이가 12시 30분경에 가장 좋아하는 아이스크림 가게인 Ben & Jerry's로 아이스크림을 사러 가는 것을 마지막으로 보았다고 합니다. Jacob을 마지막으로 봤을 때, 그는 자신이 산 물건들이 들어 있는 두 개의 쇼핑 가방을 들고 있었습니다. 그리고 그는 붉은색 티셔츠와 청바지를 입고 있었습니다. Jacob은 키가 큰 편으로 130센티미터 정도 됩니다. 그는 마른 편이고 얼굴은 각이 졌습니다. Jacob에 관한 정보가 있으시거나 그가 있는 곳을 알고 계신다면, 그의 부모에게 속히 연락 주시기 바

랍니다. 언제라도 전화나 문자 메시지를 보내시면 됩니다. 전화번호는 281-455-5964입니다. 감사합니다.

해설 **16** 쇼핑몰에서 사라진 아이를 찾기 위한 안내 방송이다.

17 Jacob은 키가 큰 편으로 130센티미터 정도이며 말랐다고 언급되어 있다.

어휘 **item** 품목 **purchase** 구입하다 **slim** 마른, 홀쭉한 **urgently** 긴급하게

🎯 Dictation

01 two ancient palaces
02 lots of baggage
03 strength training / eventual reward / struggling to understand
04 eight glasses of water / absorb much moisture / don't be concerned
05 a librarian / a lot of biographies / give a big hand
06 almost finished / resembles a maple tree's leaf / a castle-like house
07 collected so many posters / who want them / friends for
08 literature class / her birthday gift / nothing of it
09 have in mind / buy a telephone / cheapest one
10 cancel Friday's appointment / book the flight / make five copies
11 regions of warmer climates / elements of house construction / empty hollow
12 on the schedule / leaves these two channels / offering to cook
13 dropped by / Guess what it is
14 lost my bag / 24 black leather bags
15 enough hand-outs / are not enough / where her desk is
16-17 to buy ice cream / he'd purchased / text at any time

09회 듣기 모의고사

p.54-55

01 ⑤	02 ⑤	03 ③	04 ⑤	05 ①	06 ⑤
07 ③	08 ⑤	09 ④	10 ⑤	11 ④	12 ④
13 ⑤	14 ②	15 ③	16 ⑤	17 ④	

01 ⑤

해석 남 영화 보러 갈래, 아니면 연주회를 보러 갈래?
여 영화 보러 가고 싶어.
남 보고 싶은 영화가 있니?
여 응. 놓치고 싶지 않은 영화가 있어.

해설 보고 싶은 영화가 있냐는 질문에 대해 놓치고 싶지 않은 영화가 있다고 답하는 것이 가장 적절하다. ① 아니, 그건 돈 낭비야. ② 물론, 명심할게. ③ 아니, 나는 액션 영화를 더 좋아해. ④ 응, 그는 내가 제일 좋아하는 영화배우야.

어휘 **waste** 낭비 **keep ~ in mind** ~를 명심하다

02 ⑤

해석 여 가족들은 어떻게 지내요? 오랫동안 못 봤네요.
남 맞아요. 오래 되었네요. 아버지만 빼고 다들 잘 지내요.
여 아버지께 안 좋은 일이 있나요?
남 지난달 내내 아프셨어요.

해설 아버지께 일어날 수 있는 좋지 않은 일로 지난달 내내 아프셨다는 내용이 가장 적절하다. ① 세월이 화살처럼 빠르네요. ② 그는 이 일에서는 잘못한 것이 없어요. ③ 몇 년 동안 같을 거예요. ④ 우리 집에 당신을 초대하고 싶어요.

어휘 **ill** 아픈 **past** 지난 **except** ~을 제외하고는

03 ③

해석 남 시간은 희소한 상품이 되었다. 모든 사람이 더 많은 시간을 원한다. "시간이 조금만 더 있다면"이라는 말이 전 세계의 사무실과 가정에서 메아리 친다. 조급증은 현대 사회의 고질적인 문제가 되고 있다. 사람들은 점점 더 오랜 시간을 일하고 하루 일과에 더 많은 일을 집어넣으려고 애쓰고 있다. 조급증의 증상에는 승강기의 문이 저절로 닫히는 데 걸리는 몇 초를 아끼기 위해 '닫힘' 버튼을 눌러대고 언제 어디서나 전화를 받느라 한 번에 한 가지의 일을 할 수 없는 것이 있다. 점점 더 많은 사람들이 끊임없는 활동으로 계속 돌아가는 기계에 자신을 올려놓고, 더욱 많은 업무량을 떠맡으며, 이유를 묻기 위해 한순간도 멈추지 않고 있다.

해설 조급증이 현대 사회의 고질적인 문제가 되고 있다고 말하고 있다.

어휘 **scarce** 희귀한 **commodity** 상품 **refrain** (시, 노래 등)반복(구) **hastiness** 조급(증) **chronic** 고질의, 만성의 **struggle** 발버둥 치다, 몸부림치다 **symptom** 증상 **jab** 찌르다 **constant** 끊임없는, 변함없는 **workload** 업무량

04 ⑤

해석 여 Peter, 또 직원회의를 놓쳤네요. 오늘 무슨 일이 있었나요?
남 늦어서 죄송해요. 교통 정체에 한 시간 동안 잡혀 있었어요.
여 얼마나 멀리서 다니시나요?
남 이 끔찍한 교통 정체만 없으면 고작 30분 거리예요. 그래서 자전거를 타고 출근하려고 생각 중이에요.
여 하지만 너무 위험하다는 생각이 들어요. 당신 집에서 여기까지 오는 자전거 도로도 없잖아요, 그렇지 않아요?
남 맞아요. 그럼 어떻게 하죠?
여 좀 더 일찍 일어나는 게 어떨까요?
남 그러고 싶어요. 하지만 전 아침형 인간이 아니에요. 아침에 잘 못 일어나겠어요.
여 그렇다면 지하철은 어때요?
남 지하철은 너무 붐비고 지저분해요.
여 하지만 어쨌든 정확하잖아요. 아침에는 시간을 잘 지키는 게 가장 중요

하다고 생각해요.

남 전적으로 동의해요. 다른 선택은 없는 것 같네요. 충고 감사해요.

해설 여자는 아침에는 제 시간에 출근하는 것이 가장 중요하다며 지하철로 출근하는 것이 좋겠다고 말하고 있다.

어휘 traffic jam 교통 정체 risky 위험한 crowded 혼잡한 punctual 시간을 잘 지키는

05 ①

해석 남 엔진을 꺼주세요.

여 네. 왜 제 차를 세우셨는지 말씀해 주시겠어요?

남 당신이 빨간불인데 그냥 지나쳤기 때문이에요.

여 하지만 제가 지나갈 때는 노란불이었어요. 경관님.

남 당신이 지나갈 때 분명히 빨간불이었어요. 사진 증거도 가지고 있어요. 면허증 좀 보여주시겠습니까?

여 죄송해요. 가지고 있지 않아요. 사실은 집에 두고 왔어요. 하지만 보험 증권은 가지고 있어요. 여기 있어요.

남 여기서 기다리세요. 금방 돌아오겠습니다.

해설 빨간불을 그냥 지나쳐서 운전한 여자와 이를 단속하는 경찰 간의 대화이다.

어휘 switch A off A를 끄다 pull over 차를 길 한 쪽에 대다 definitely 명확히 insurance policy 보험 증권

06 ⑤

해석 (전화벨이 울린다.)

남 안녕하세요, Chris예요. 크리스마스 특별 방의 장식이 어떻게 되고 있는지 확인하려고 전화했어요.

여 잘 되고 있어요. 창문 앞에 큰 크리스마스트리를 세웠어요.

남 잘 했어요. 손님들이 좋아할 거예요. 팔걸이의자도 놓았나요?

여 네. 트리 왼쪽에 두었어요.

남 샴페인은 어떻게 했어요?

여 지시하신 대로 샴페인 한 병과 잔 두 개를 둥근 테이블 위에 두었어요.

남 눈사람 인형은 구했나요? 아이들이 아주 좋아할 것 같아요.

여 네. 겨우 하나 구해서 테이블 위에 두었어요.

남 마지막 손질로 덧붙인 것은 없나요?

여 커다란 선물 상자를 하나 트리 아래에 두었어요.

남 훌륭하군요! 하나 더요. 방의 사진을 찍어서 우리 호텔 홈페이지에 올리는 것을 잊지 마세요.

여 걱정 마세요. 이미 그렇게 했어요.

해설 테이블 위에는 강아지 인형이 아니라 눈사람 인형이 놓여 있어야 한다.

어휘 decoration 장식 manage 애를 써서 ~하다

07 ③

해석 남 실례합니다. 콘서트 표를 사려고 줄을 서서 기다리고 있는 건가요?

여 네.

남 부탁 좀 들어주시겠어요?

여 물론이죠. 무엇이죠?

남 제 가방을 맡아주시겠어요? 화장실에 가고 싶어서요.

여 물론이죠. 오래 걸리세요? 줄이 빠르게 줄어들고 있어요.

남 아니에요. 잠깐 화장실에 가려는 것뿐이에요. 음료수를 너무 많이 마신 것 같아요.

여 어서 가세요. 가방은 제가 안전하게 보관하고 있을 게요.

해설 남자는 콘서트 표를 사려고 줄을 서 있는 여자에게 화장실에 다녀오겠다며 가방을 맡아 줄 것을 부탁했다.

어휘 keep an eye on ~를 지켜보다, 감시하다 nature's call 〈구어, 완곡적〉 생리적 요구 (대소변이 마려움)

08 ⑤

해석 남 Mary, 걱정스러워 보여. 무슨 일 있어?

여 생물학 과목에 낙제할 것 같아.

남 왜 그런 말을 하는 거야?

여 그게, 기말고사에서 아주 나쁜 성적을 받았거든.

남 출석은 잘 하고, 과제물도 다 제출했어?

여 응. 출석과 과제물에는 문제가 없어.

남 흠. 실험실은?

여 자주 가지 않아. 요즘 신경 쓰는 일이 많아서.

남 그 과목을 다시 듣는 것은 어때?

여 그럴 수가 없어. 내년에 졸업하려면 이 과목을 꼭 수강해야 하거든. 어쩌면 좋지?

남 교수님께 네 상황을 설명 드려 봐.

해설 여자는 졸업하는 데 필요한 과목인 생물학에 낙제할까 봐 걱정하고 있다.

어휘 fail 낙제하다, 실패하다 grade 성적 regularly 어김없이, 규칙적으로 hand in 제출하다 assignment 과제(물) on one's mind 신경이 쓰여, 마음에 걸려 graduate 졸업하다 take a class 수업을 듣다, 수강하다

09 ④

해석 남 이 소포를 런던에 속달로 보내고 싶어요. 얼마인가요?

여 55달러예요. 손님. 이런, 유감스럽게도 무게가 초과되었네요. 추가 요금을 지불하셔야 해요.

남 문제없어요. 추가 요금은 얼마인가요?

여 15달러예요. 그래서 총 70달러예요.

남 만약에 대비해서 소포에 보험을 들고 싶어요. 보험료는 얼마죠?

여 전체 요금의 20%예요.

남 좋아요. 여기 100달러예요.

여 감사합니다. 여기 잔돈하고 영수증이요.

해설 소포 요금이 70달러, 보험료가 총 비용의 20%로 14달러이므로 84달러를 지불해야 한다. 100달러를 냈으므로 거스름돈은 16달러이다.

어휘 by express 빠른우편으로, 속달로 overweight 중량 초과의 extra charge 추가 요금 insure 보험을 들다 just in case 만일의 경우에 대비해서 insurance 보험료, 보험

10 ⑤

해석 여 그럼, 보통 하루 일과는 어떤가요? 당신은 항상 아주 바빠 보여요.

남 음, 저는 보통 5시쯤에 일어나서 6시까지 컴퓨터로 일을 해요.

여 왜 그렇게 일찍 일어나세요?

남 음, 7시 버스를 타려면 7시 20분 전에 집을 나서야 해요. 집에서 버스 정거장까지 걸어서 20분 정도 걸리거든요.

여 그럼 몇 시에 직장에 도착하세요?

남 버스로 한 시간 정도 걸리지만 사무실 바로 앞에 버스가 정차해요.

여 그거 좋군요. 그럼 퇴근은 언제 하나요?

남 5시쯤이요. 그러고 나서 6시 반쯤에 저녁을 먹고, 아내와 저는 8시까지 아이들과 놀아요.

해설 8시까지 아이들과 놀아준다고 언급한 후 이후 일정에 대한 시간은 언급하지 않았으므로 취침 시간은 알 수 없다.

어휘 work on the computer 컴퓨터로 일하다 get to work 출근하다 get off work 퇴근하다

11 ④

해석 남 시드니 차이나타운의 중심에 우수 식당상을 수상한 바 있는 East Ocean 레스토랑이 있습니다. 중국 전통 요리와 현대 요리를 한 장소에서 즐기십시오. 하루에 두 번 100가지가 넘게 제공되는 저희의 유명한 딤섬을 포함한 군침 도는 독특한 메뉴에서 고르십시오. 각 테이블에는 필요하실 때 언제든 점원을 부르실 수 있도록 호출기가 설치되어 있습니다. 다양한 종류의 와인과 맥주도 드실 수 있습니다. 사업이나 개인적인 모임을 위한 방이 준비되어 있습니다. East Ocean은 19세 이상인 고객만 이용할 수 있습니다. 예약을 하시려면 9212-4189로 전화 주십시오.

해설 술을 판매하고 있으며 19세 이상인 손님만 이용할 수 있다.

어휘 award-winning 수상한, 표창을 받은 cuisine 요리 mouth watering 군침 도는 dim sum 딤섬(고기, 어패류, 야채 등을 만두피에 싸서 굽거나 찐 요리) be equipped with ~을 갖추고 있다 occasion 특별한 행사, 모임 be available to 이용 가능하다

12 ④

해석 여 뭘 보고 있어, Tim?

남 한국으로 갈 여름휴가 여행 상품을 찾고 있어.

여 어디 보자. 어떤 것이 제일 좋은 것 같아?

남 한국의 서쪽 지역과 제주도를 합한 7일짜리 여행이 가장 좋은 것 같아. 한국의 위쪽 끝에서 아래쪽 끝까지 여행할 수 있어.

여 흠. 네 말이 맞겠지만 우리 예산을 훨씬 넘어가잖아. 게다가 그 여행을 선택하면 집에 돌아와서 쉴 시간이 없을 거야.

남 맞아. 그걸 완전히 잊었네. 서울이나 제주도 여행은 어때?

여 휴가를 서울 같은 대도시에서 보내고 싶지는 않아. 틀림없이 붐비고 시끄러울 거야. 그리고 난 전에 제주도에 가본 적이 있어. 이번에는 새로운 곳에 가 보고 싶어.

남 그렇구나. 어쨌든 그것들은 우리 휴가로는 좀 짧기도 하고. 그럼 남은 선택은 하나뿐이네.

여 어째서? 두 가지가 남았잖아.

남 너와 같은 이유야. 한국의 동쪽 지역은 전에 여행한 적이 있거든. 여행 경비가 우리가 정한 범위를 약간 넘지만 문제없을 것 같아.

여 그래, 감당할 수 있겠어. 좋아, 전화해서 좀 더 알아보자.

해설 여행 예산과 두 사람의 선호를 고려하고 이미 여행한 장소를 제외하면 ④번의 Western Korea Tour만 남는다.

어휘 location 장소 duration 기간 way over 훨씬 더 budget 예산 afford ~할 여유가 있다 find out ~을 알아내다

13 ⑤

해석 남 혹시 Amy가 어디 있는지 아세요? 어디에서도 찾을 수가 없어요.

여 전화해서 병가를 냈어요.

남 사실을 말해주세요. 그녀가 직장을 구하고 있다는 것을 알고 있어요.

여 맞아요, 하지만 그녀는 아무도 모르기를 바라요.

남 왜 그만두려는 거예요?

여 제 생각에는 그냥 더 나은 직장을 찾고 있는 것 같아요.

남 남의 떡이 더 커 보일지는 모르지만 그녀는 여기서도 훌륭한 직장에서 일하고 있잖아요.

여 하지만 그녀의 마음은 더 이상 우리 회사에 없어요.

남 **그렇다면, 우리는 그녀를 붙잡아서는 안 되겠네요.**

해설 동료의 마음이 완전히 떠났다는 말에 그렇다면 더는 말릴 수 없다는 말로 대화를 완성할 수 있다. ① 무엇이 그녀가 그렇게 일을 열심히 하게 만들었나요? ② 이 지루한 일이 지긋지긋해요. ③ 그녀가 병에서 회복하기를 바라요. ④ 그녀는 지금 바로 병원에 가야 해요.

어휘 sick and tired of ~에 진절머리가 나는 recover from ~로 부터 회복하다 hold ~ back ~을 저지하다 job-hunt 일자리를 구하다 call in sick 전화를 걸어 병가를 내다 The grass is greener on the other side. 남의 떡이 더 커 보인다.

14 ②

해석 여 걱정이 있는 것처럼 보여. 무슨 일이야?

남 저 학생 회장에 선출되었어요, 엄마.

여 아주 좋은 소식이구나. 뭐가 문제니?

남 제가 그 일을 하기에 충분한 자질이나 경험이 있는지 모르겠어요.

여 너무 자신을 비하하지 않는 것이 좋겠구나.

남 하지만 전 정말 충분치 못하다고 생각해요.

여 만약 학생들이 네가 정말 충분치 못하다고 생각했다면, 너를 선택하지 않았을 거야.

남 정말 그렇게 생각하세요?

여 **그럼, 다 잘 될 거야.**

해설 학생 회장에 선출되었으나 자신이 자질이 없다고 생각하는 아들에게 엄마가 할 수 있는 말은 잘 될 거라는 격려의 말이다. ① 어떻게 생각해야 할지 모르겠구나. ③ 지금 그것을 하지 않아도 돼. ④ 걱정하지 마. 그건 네 잘못이 아니야. ⑤ 아버지에게 물어본 후에 결정하자.

어휘 student council 학생회 qualification 자질, 자격 run somebody down ~를 부당하게 비판하다

15 ③

해석 **여** Jason의 친구인 Brian은 2주 전에 운전 교습을 받기 시작했다. 그는 다른 사람의 도움 없이도 차를 운전할 수 있다고 자신했다. 며칠 전에 그는 어머니의 차를 허락 없이 운전했다. 하지만 차를 주차하다가 뒤쪽 범퍼에 커다랗게 긁힌 자국을 내고 말았다. 그날 밤, 그의 어머니가 긁힌 자국을 발견하고 매우 화가 났다. 그녀는 그에게 뭔가 아는 것이 있는지 물었다. 하지만 Brian은 자신은 아무 관련이 없는 일이라고 대답했다. 죄책감을 느낌과 동시에 어찌할 바를 모르게 된 Brian은 Jason에게 조언을 구한다. 이 상황에서 Jason이 Brian에게 할 말로 가장 적절한 것은 무엇인가?

Jason Brian! 음, 정직이 최선의 방법이야.

해설 허락 없이 차를 운전하다가 차를 크게 긁고 어머니에게 시치미를 뗀 친구에게 솔직히 용서를 구하는 것이 좋겠다는 충고를 하는 것이 가장 적절하다. ① 조심해서 운전해. ② 네가 상관할 바 아니야. ④ 네가 할 수 있는 것은 없어. ⑤ 기운 내! 다음에 더 잘할 수 있을 거야.

어휘 **confident** 자신만만한 **permission** 허락, 허가 **scratch** 긁힌 자국 **rear** 뒤의, 후방의 **notice** 알아채다 **guilty** 죄책감을 느끼는

16–17 ⑤, ④

해석 **남** 소아과 의사들과 영양학자들은 종종 학생들이 제대로 된 아침을 먹는 것이 얼마나 중요한지 강조한다. 하지만 아침 식사의 정확한 이점은 부분적으로는 아침 식사가 언제 제공되는가에 달려 있을지도 모른다. 최근에야 비로소 연구원들은 영양소가 학생들의 기억력과 학습에 어떻게 영향을 미치는지 연구하기 시작했다. 소아과 의사와 심리학자로 구성된 한 연구팀이 발표한 연구에서 학생들은 기억력 검사를 받고, 세 집단으로 나뉘었다. 한 집단의 학생들은 학교에서 매일 콘플레이크와 우유로 아침을 제공 받았으며, 또 다른 집단의 학생들은 아침 식사를 하지 않았으며, 나머지 집단의 학생들은 집에서 아침 식사를 했다. 식이요법을 한지 2주 후에 이 모든 학생들이 재검사를 받았다. 결과는 학교에서 아침을 먹은 아이들이 아침을 거른 학생들 보다 훨씬 더 높은 기억력 수치를 보여주는 것으로 나타났다. 여기까지는 놀라울 것이 없다. 하지만 기억력 검사를 하기 두 시간 전에 집에서 식사를 한 아이들 또한 검사 30분 전에 학교에서 시리얼을 먹은 학생들보다 낮은 점수를 기록했다. 이것은 아이들이 언제 아침 식사를 하는지가 그들이 그날의 수업을 얼마나 잘 기억하는가를 결정한다는 것을 보여준다. 연구팀은 학생들의 시리얼 그릇을 학교 수업이 시작하기 몇 시간 전에 채워주는 것(수업 시작 시간보다 몇 시간 일찍 아침을 주는 것)이 수업이 시작하기 30분 전에 먹는 식사보다 학생들에게 덜 이롭다고 결론지었다.

해설 **16** 기억력 검사 30분 전에 아침 식사를 한 아이들이 2시간 전에 아침을 먹은 학생들보다 훨씬 나은 점수를 받았다고 말하고 있다. 아이들이 아침 식사를 하기에 가장 좋은 시간을 알려 주는 것이 이 글의 목적이다.

17 집에서 먹는 것보다 학교에 와서 아침을 먹는 것이 더 도움이 된다는 말이 있지만 수업 시작 바로 전에 먹는 것이 도움이 되기 때문이지 장소의 문제는 아니다.

어휘 **pediatrician** 소아과의사 **nutritionist** 영양학자 **stress** 강조하다 **benefit** 이익, 이득 **depend on** ~에 의존하다 **in part** 일부분, 어느 정도 **investigate** ~을 조사하다 **nutrition** 영양, 영양소 **consume** 섭취하다 **affect** ~에 영향을 미치다 **psychologist** 심리학자 **divide** ~을 나누다 **skip** 거르다 **significantly** 상당히 **determine** ~을 결정하다 **retain** 유지하다

🎯 Dictation

01 any movies in mind

02 been a long time

03 the chronic trouble / never stopping for a moment

04 without those terrible traffic jams / how about the subway / being on time is the most important thing

05 pulled me over / your driver's license

06 I'm calling to check / put it on the table

07 waiting in line / It'll be safe with me

08 I got a really bad grade / taking the class again

09 by express / this package insured

10 work on the computer / get off work

11 mouth-watering dishes / business and personal occasions

12 looking for tour packages / be crowded and noisy / a little bit over our price limit

13 called in sick / the grass is greener on the other side

14 was elected president / stop running yourself down

15 big scratches on the rear bumper / Feeling guilty

16-17 when breakfast is served / the youngsters who ate at school / how well they retain the day's lessons

🎯 10회 듣기 모의고사
p.60-61

01 ①	02 ②	03 ②	04 ②	05 ⑤	06 ①
07 ⑤	08 ②	09 ④	10 ③	11 ④	12 ④
13 ①	14 ②	15 ⑤	16 ③	17 ④	

01 ①

해석 **여** 안녕, Bill. 뭐 듣고 있어?

남 안녕, Jason Mraz의 'I'm Yours'를 듣고 있어. 그런데, 넌 여기 왜 왔어?

여 나는 선물로 CD 사러 왔어. 도와줄래?

남 물론, 누구에게 선물할 거야?

해설 여자가 선물로 CD를 사려고 하는데 남자에게 고르는 것을 도와달라고 했으므로 남자가 적절한 선물을 추천하기 위해 선물 받을 사람이 누구인지 물어보는 것이 자연스럽다. ② 어서 해. 기다릴게. ③ 왜 안 돼? 같이 듣자. ④ 다음 골목에 있는 카페에 가자. ⑤ 죄송하지만 저희는 Jason Mraz의 CD를 취급하지 않아요.

02 ②

해석 **남** 나 다른 직장으로 옮길까 생각 중이야.

여 왜 그런데? 압박감이 심하니?

남 응. 늘 관리자하고 다툼거리가 많아.

여 그것 참 안됐구나.

해설 관리자와 다툼이 많아 직장을 옮길까 고민하는 남자에게 위로의 말을 하는 것이 가장 적절하다. ① 그건 어디서 들었어? ③ 다행히 나는 내 직업에 만족해. ④ 나는 내 관리자랑 관계가 좋아. ⑤ 왜 안 돼? 내가 이미 관리자에게 그것에 대해 이야기했어.

어휘 **move to** (일자리 등을) ~로 옮기다 **pressure** 압박감 **have disagreement with** 의견이 일치하지 않다.

03 ②

해석 남 신사 숙녀 여러분 안녕하십니까, 저는 기장입니다. 현재 우리가 기계적 결함을 겪고 있다는 사실을 알리게 되어 매우 유감입니다. 비행기에서 내리셔서 터미널에서 기다려 주시기 바랍니다. 탑승구에 있는 저희 Air Asia 직원들이 연결 비행편까지 안내해 드릴 것입니다. 이로 인해 불편을 끼쳐 드려 매우 죄송합니다. 감사합니다. 그리고 좋은 하루 보내십시오.

해설 비행기 기장의 안내 방송으로 현재 기체 고장이 있어 다른 비행기를 갈아타야 한다는 내용이다.

어휘 **captain** 기장 **mechanical problem** 기계적 고장, 결함 **exit** 내리다 **inconvenience** 불편함 **cause** 발생시키다

04 ②

해석 여 우리 대형 유통마트에 갈 건가요?

남 네. 내가 쇼핑 목록을 가지고 있어요.

여 보여 줄래요? 와, 살 게 많네요. 정말 이 물건이 모두 필요해요?

남 다 우리 것은 아니에요. 일부는 내 동생 거예요.

여 오, 당신 동생, Cindy가 물건을 좀 사다 달라고 부탁했군요.

남 그래요. 우리가 대형 유통마트에 갈 거니까 필요한 것이 있는지 물어봤죠.

여 여보, 이 목록을 확인했나요? 제 생각에 빵은 조금만 필요할 것 같은데요. 우리가 빵을 그곳에서 사면, 유통기한 전에 다 먹을 수가 없어요.

남 하지만 거기서 사면 정말 싸잖아요. 소매상에서 빵을 산다고 해도, 훨씬 더 적은 양을 같은 가격에 사잖아요.

여 그렇지만, 그건 음식 낭비라고 생각해요.

남 걱정 말아요. 다 먹을 거예요.

해설 여자는 식품을 대량으로 구매해서 다 먹지 못하는 것이 낭비라고 생각한다.

어휘 **wholesale** 도매(상)의 **expiration date** 유효 기간 **retail** 소매(상)의

05 ⑤

해석 여 와, 여기 정말 좋다!

남 그래, 명동은 서울에서 내가 가장 좋아하는 곳 중 하나야.

여 여기 일본 사람들이 많은 것 좀 봐.

남 그러네. 명동은 외국 관광객들이 꼭 가봐야 할 곳이라고 하더라.

여 그런 것 같아. 여기서 다양하고 맛있는 음식, 쇼핑, 거리 공연을 즐길 수 있잖아. 실은 독일에서 다음 주에 내 친구가 오거든. 추천할 다른 장소가

있니?

남 경복궁은 어때? 수문장 교대식을 볼 수 있어.

여 잘됐다! 내 친구가 한국 역사에 관심이 많거든.

남 내가 한국의 관광 명소에 대한 책 빌려줄게. 살펴봐.

여 고마워.

남 천만에. 친구랑 좋은 시간 보내!

해설 명동, 경복궁 등 외국인 관광객에게 추천할 만한 장소에 대해 이야기를 나누고 있으므로 대화의 주제는 '외국인에게 추천할 만한 관광 명소'이다.

어휘 **must** 꼭 봐야(해야, 사야) 하는 것 **goody** 맛있는 것 **street performing** 거리 공연 **be into** ~에 관심이 많다 **attraction** 관광지 **check out** 살펴보다

06 ①

해석 여 어젯밤에 토크쇼를 봤니?

남 'Hidden Songs' 말하는 거야?

여 응, 맞아. 그래서 봤어?

남 아니, 못 봤어. 자세히 말해 봐. 누가 나왔어?

여 밴드의 이름이 기억이 안나. 남자 세 명과 여자 두 명이었어.

남 어떻게 생겼는데?

여 여자는 둘 다 모자에 흰 양복을 입었어.

남 그리고 다른 남자들은?

여 선글라스를 끼고, 검은 양복을 입었어. 뭐 생각나는 거 있어?

남 남자 중 한 명은 긴 곱슬머리를 하고 있었지?

여 맞아. 그 남자가 드럼을 연주했어. 그리고 여자 둘이 노래를 불렀고, 다른 남자들은 기타를 연주했어.

남 그들이 누군지 알 것 같아. 남자 둘은 머리가 짧고 여자들은 날씬하고 긴 생머리를 하고 있었지, 맞지?

여 맞아, 너는 누군지 아는 것 같구나.

해설 드럼 치는 남자는 짧은 머리를 하고 있으므로 대화의 내용과 일치하지 않는다.

어휘 **in detail** 자세하게 **call up** 생각나다(=remember) **wavy** 웨이브가 있는

07 ⑤

해석 남 안녕하세요. 괜찮으세요? 제가 도와드릴 일은 없나요?

여 네. 경관님. 제 차가 시동이 안 걸려요. 왜 그런지 모르겠어요.

남 글쎄요, 배터리에 문제가 있어서 그럴 수도 있어요.

여 오, 어떻게 해야 하나요?

남 부인, 차량에 보험은 드셨습니까?

여 네, 들었어요.

남 그러면, 보험 회사의 긴급 출동 서비스에 전화하시는 편이 나을 거예요. 30분이면 여기에 도와주러 올 것 같네요.

여 오, 그런 서비스에 대해서는 몰랐어요. 말씀해 주셔서 감사해요.

남 천만에요. 수리원이 당신을 도와주러 올 때까지 순찰차에 있겠습니다. 지금 바로 긴급 출동 서비스에 전화하시고 차에 들어가세요. 바깥이 매우 춥네요.

여 친절하게 해 주셔서 감사드려요.

남 그렇게 고마워하실 필요는 전혀 없어요. 사람을 돕는 것이 제 일이에요.

해설 여자의 차가 시동이 걸리지 않는 상황에서 경찰관이 보험 회사의 긴급 출동 서비스를 요청하라고 조언했으므로 여자는 긴급출동 서비스에 전화를 하여 도움을 구할 것이다.

어휘 **insure** 보험에 들다 **emergency service** 긴급 출동 서비스 **patrol car** 순찰차

08 ②

해석 남 Jenny, 내일이 무슨 날인지 아니?

여 내일은 그냥 수요일인 걸로 알고 있는데. 무슨 특별한 날이야?

남 응. 내일은 '스승의 날'이잖아.

여 오. 시간 정말 빠르구나. 우리가 고등학교 졸업한 지 벌써 3개월도 넘었어.

남 그래, 맞아. 고등학교 때 박 선생님을 정말 뵙고 싶어. 우리 반을 늘 챙겨 주셨잖아. 그래서 내일 꽃을 들고 가서 찾아뵐 거야.

여 그래, 나도 정말 고등학교 시절의 선생님의 도움에 감사드려.

남 당연하지. 그럼, 같이 갈래?

여 그러고 싶지만, 김 교수님과 중요한 선약이 있어.

남 그렇다면, 선생님께 메시지를 보내지 그러니? 아마도 네 메시지를 보면 행복해 하실 거야.

여 오, 그렇지. 메시지를 보내야겠다. 내 안부 좀 전해줘.

해설 스승의 날을 맞이하여 고등학교 시절의 은사님을 찾아뵈려고 하는데 여자가 선약이 있어 같이 갈 수 없다고 하자 대신 문자 메시지를 보내라고 조언했고 여자가 남자의 의견에 동의했다.

어휘 **Teacher's Day** 스승의 날 **prior appointment** 선약 **give sb one's best regards** ~에게 ~의 안부를 전하다

09 ④

해석 남 안녕하세요!

여 안녕하세요. 무엇을 도와 드릴까요?

남 소포 2개를 보내고 싶어요.

여 어디로 보내고 싶으신가요?

남 파리요. 소포 하나를 파리까지 보내는 데 요금이 얼마죠?

여 음, 그건 무게와 서비스에 따라 다르죠. 소포 안에 무엇이 들어 있나요?

남 하나는 음식물이고, 다른 것은 책이에요.

여 각각의 소포 무게를 재 볼게요. 음식물은 6kg이고, 책은 9kg이네요. 각각의 소포가 10kg 이하라서 같은 요금으로 보내실 수 있어요. 각각의 소포에 대해서, 일반 요금은 20달러이고, 급행요금은 50달러입니다.

남 음식물은 급행으로 보내고, 책은 일반으로 보낼게요.

여 네, 알겠습니다.

해설 2개의 소포가 모두 10kg이하라서 같은 무게 범위이지만, 급행요금(50달러)으로 음식물을 보내고, 일반 요금(20달러)으로 책을 보내기 때문에 총 금액은 70달러이다.

어휘 **parcel** 소포 **rate** 요금 **depend on** ~에 따라 다르다 **charge** 요금, 비용 **food stuffs** 음식물 **regular service** 일반 서비스 **express service** 급행 서비스

10 ③

해석 남 안녕하세요, 어떻게 오셨어요?

여 안녕하세요. 등 아래쪽에 심한 통증이 있어서요.

남 등의 통증이 얼마나 오래 됐죠?

여 약 2주 정도 통증이 있었어요.

남 이전에 등에 문제가 있었던 병력이 있으신가요?

여 아뇨, 이번이 처음이에요. 그래서 이유를 모르겠어요.

남 지금 복용하는 약이 있으신가요?

여 아뇨, 통증을 없애기 위해서 가끔씩 아스피린만 복용해요.

남 좋아요, 등을 한번 보도록 하죠. 침대에 엎드려 주세요.

여 알겠습니다. Davis 박사님.

해설 등의 심한 통증, 통증이 지속된 기간, 통증 부위의 병력, 현재 복용하는 약 등에 대한 언급은 있지만 통증 관리법에 대한 언급은 없다.

어휘 **ache** 통증 **back** 등 **history** 병력 **from time to time** 가끔

11 ④

해석 여 요가를 해본 적이 있나요? 요가는 고대 인도에서 유래했습니다. 요가의 목적은 훈련을 통해 자신을 자유롭게 하고 심신을 조절하는 것입니다. 요가를 함으로써 당신은 균형 잡히고, 밝고, 긍정적인 성격을 가질 수 있습니다. 게다가, 근육은 전신 마사지를 통해서 부드러워질 것입니다. 아직도 특별히 하는 일 없이 소파에 앉아 여가를 보내는 사람처럼 집에만 머무르고 계시나요? 일어나서 당장 요가를 시작하세요. 당신이 기억해야 할 한 가지! 요가를 시작할 때 숙련된 강사와 함께 하는 것이 매우 중요합니다. 우리는 숙련된 강사와 요가를 할 수 있는 놀라운 기회를 특별한 가격에 제공하고 있습니다. 관심이 있다면 777-YOGA로 전화 주세요. 당신이 연습하는 동안 그들이 당신의 자세를 바로잡아 줄 수 있습니다.

해설 요가를 통해 근육이 발달하는 것이 아니라 근육이 부드러워 진다.

어휘 **free** 자유롭게 하다 **spirit** 정신 **train** 훈련하다 **practice** 수행하다 **character** 성격 **muscle** 근육 **couch potato** 소파에 앉아 여가를 보내는 사람, 게으르고 비활동적인 사람 **unbelievable** 믿을 수 없는 **skilled** 숙련된

12 ④

해석 남 여보, 타이어를 바꿔야 할 때가 된 것 같아요. 그런 것 같지 않아요?

여 그래요, 타이어 4개가 모두 벌써 닳은 것을 봤어요. 혹시 타이어 가격을 확인해 봤나요?

남 이미 가격을 Tire-Station에서 확인해 봤어요. 이 전단지를 봐요.

여 Hangil과 Komho 타이어 가격이 상당히 좋네요. 두 군데 가격이 모두 개당 120달러에요.

남 그래요, 그 가격이 가장 싸네요. 하지만 운행 시 소음이 있더라고요.

여 그렇다면, Brightstone이나 Panolli 타이어를 사용해 보는 건 어때요? 개당 타이어 가격은 똑같아요. 게다가, 20% 할인도 하고 있어요.

남 그 타이어들은 인도네시아에서 만들어졌어요. 품질에 대해서는 확신할 수가 없어요.

여 그러면, Michilen 타이어를 사용해 보는 건 어때요? 개당 가격은 200달러이지만 4개를 사면 1개를 공짜로 얻을 수가 있고, 게다가 미국에서 만들어졌어요. 좋은 기회 같은데요.

남 좋아요. 그걸로 합시다.

해설 Brightstone과 Panolli의 개당 가격이 같고, 20% 할인을 해주고, 인도네시아에서 만들어졌다고 했으므로 India(인도)로 표기된 Panolli의 타이어 원산지가 잘못 표시되었다.

어휘 **notice** 목격하다, 알아차리다 **wear out** 닳아 없어지게 하다 **by any chance** 혹시 **leaflet** 전단지 **quality** 품질

13 ①

해설 여 드디어 여름휴가예요!
남 네, 그래요. 여름휴가 때 어디에 가나요?
여 네, 뉴질랜드로 여행을 가려고요.
남 정말요? 전에 가본 적이 있나요?
여 네, 이번이 두 번째예요. 작년에 출장 차 다녀왔어요. 당신은 가보셨나요?
남 아뇨, 하지만 언젠가 한번 가고 싶어요.
여 함께 가는 건 어때요?
남 당신도 알다시피 전 여름 강의를 들어야 해요.
여 맞아요. 어쨌든 뉴질랜드의 좋은 것에 대해 아는 거 있나요?
남 '반지의 제왕'이란 영화가 거기서 촬영된 거 알고 있죠, 그렇죠? 그곳의 풍경이 환상적이라고 들었어요.
여 네, 정말 그래요. 같이 갈 수 없어서 아쉬워요.
남 우리에겐 항상 내년이 있잖아요.

해설 여자가 여름휴가 동안 뉴질랜드에 가는데 남자와 함께 갈 수 없어서 아쉬워하고 있으므로 내년에 같이 갔으면 한다는 말을 하는 것이 가장 적절하다. ② 그 영화는 정말 재미있었어요. ③ 뉴질랜드의 음식은 정말 형편없어요. ④ 버스로 약 12시간이 걸릴 거예요. ⑤ 네, 내년에는 정말 미국에 가고 싶어요.

어휘 **business trip** 출장 **film** 촬영하다 **scenery** 풍경

14 ②

해설 여 그만 가봐야겠어. 늦었거든.
남 벌써 가려고? 아직 우리 과학 프로젝트에 대해 할 이야기가 많잖아.
여 나도 더 있고 싶지만, 너무 늦게까지 밖에 있으면 부모님이 걱정하실 거야.
남 부모님께 전화를 하면 되잖아. 조금만 더 이따가 가.
여 내일 수업도 있고, 우리 둘 다 일찍 일어나야 하잖아. 그러니 지금 갈게.
남 알았어. 집까지는 걸어서 30분은 걸리니까 내가 태워 줄게.
여 넌 정말 사려 깊구나. 고마워.
남 내가 태워다 주면 30분은 절약할 수 있어, 그렇지? 30분 더 이따가 가면 안 돼?
여 알았어. 네가 나를 설득했어.

해설 여자가 가려고 하자 남자가 태워다 주면 30분을 절약할 수 있다며 30분 더 머물다가 가라고 했으므로 "알았어. 네가 나를 설득했어."가 응답으로 가장 적절하다. ① 넌 지금 당장 가야 해. ③ 나도 또 다시 이렇게 하고 싶어. ④ 네 부모님은 시간에 관해선 엄격하시구나. ⑤ 나도 운전이 시간을 절약하는 한 가지 방법이라는 것을 알아.

어휘 **give ~ a ride** ~를 태워주다 **on foot** 걸어서 **thoughtful** 사려 깊은

15 ⑤

해설 남 Owen은 공부를 잘 못해서 그의 선생님은 그에 대해서 걱정이 많았다. 선생님은 그의 문제에 대해서 이야기하기 위해 그를 불렀다. 대화 중에 선생님은 Owen이 농구를 잘 한다는 것을 알게 되었다. Owen의 선생님은 그가 학교 농구팀에 들어가도록 도왔다. 그는 연습을 많이 했고 드디어 주전 선수가 되었다. 그는 라이벌 팀과의 경기에서 뛸 수 있는 기회를 잡았다. 4쿼터에, 그는 마지막 순간에 3점 슛을 성공했다. 그것은 버저비터(종이 울림과 동시에 골이 되어 게임을 이기게 하는 슛)였다. 그리고 그의 선생님도 그 자리에 있었다. 경기 후에, Owen의 선생님이 Owen에게 할 말로 가장 적절한 것은 무엇인가?
Owen's teacher Owen, 네 덕분에 게임을 이겼다.

해설 Owen이 버저비터를 던져서 경기에서 이긴 것을 보고 선생님이 Owen에게 할 말은 "네 덕분에 게임을 이겼다."가 가장 적절하다. ① 너는 공부를 더 해야 해. ② 너 좋아 보이지 않는구나. ③ 농구는 너에게 안 맞는구나. ④ 학교에 다시는 늦지 마라.

어휘 **be concerned about** ~에 대해 걱정하다 **key player** 주전 선수 **win at the buzzer** 버저가 울림과 동시에 득점하여 경기에서 이기다

16-17 ③, ④

해설 여 우울증을 심하게 앓아본 적이 있습니까? 우울증을 앓을 때 당신은 슬프거나 걱정스럽거나, 무기력하거나 예민할 수 있습니다. 우울증이 꼭 정신 질환을 의미하는 것은 아닙니다. 정상적인 사람도 우울할 수 있습니다. 하지만, 우울증이 오랜 기간 동안 지속되면, 정신적, 육체적 건강에 부정적인 영향을 미칠 수 있습니다. 정신 건강 측면에서 우울증을 앓는 사람들은 자신이 좋아했던 것에 쉽게 흥미를 잃게 됩니다. 또한 그들은 집중하거나 결정을 내리거나 세세한 사항을 기억하는 데 어려움을 겪습니다. 심한 경우, 자살을 시도할 수도 있습니다. 육체적 건강 측면에서 보면 우울증을 앓는 사람들은 식욕을 잃거나 지나치게 많이 먹습니다. 그들은 또한 잠을 이루기 힘들어하거나 너무 많이 자기도 합니다. 그들은 피로감, 통증, 고통을 느낄 수도 있습니다. 소화 불량은 우울증을 앓는 사람들 사이에서 발생하는 흔한 문제 중 하나입니다.

해설 16 우울증의 여러 정신적, 신체적 증상에 대해 설명하고 있다.

17 우울증의 증상으로 좋아했던 일에 흥미를 잃거나 집중하거나 결정을 내리는 데 어려움을 겪고, 자살을 시도하기도 한다고 언급되어 있다. 사람들을 잘 알아보지 못한다는 내용은 없다.

어휘 **helpless** 무기력한 **irritable** 신경질적인 **mental disorder** 정신 질환 **concentrate** 집중하다 **in terms of** ~면에서 **attempt** 시도하다 **suicide** 자살 **appetite** 식욕 **fatigue** 피곤 **indigestion** 소화 불량

🎯 Dictation

01 By the way

02 have disagreements with

03 some mechanical problems / sorry for any inconvenience

04 going to the wholesale store / before the expiration date / it's a waste of food

05 a must for foreign tourists / the book about tourist attractions

11회 듣기 모의고사
p.66-67

01 ②	02 ④	03 ③	04 ②	05 ⑤	06 ④
07 ②	08 ②	09 ②	10 ③	11 ⑤	12 ⑤
13 ④	14 ②	15 ①	16 ②	17 ④	

01 ②

해석 남 식물을 키우는 것은 제가 생각하던 것만큼 쉽지 않았어요.

여 무슨 말인지 알아요. 식물은 끊임없는 주의와 관심을 필요로 하죠.

남 맞아요. 당신에게도 역시 어려웠나요?

여 **네, 온갖 종류의 문제가 있었죠.**

해설 대화의 흐름으로 보아 두 사람은 모두 식물을 키우는 것이 어렵다는 이야기를 하고 있으므로 남자의 말에 동의하는 대답이 가장 적절하다. ① 너를 위해 내가 돌봐 줄게. ③ 어떤 곤경에 처한다면 나에게 와. ④ 그들이 말하는 걸 알잖아. 쉽게 얻은 것은 쉽게 잃는 법이야. ⑤ 더 나은 미래를 위해 나무와 꽃을 심자.

어휘 take care of ~을 돌보다 plant 심다 constant 끊임없는 attention 관심, 주의

02 ④

해석 여 제 드레스의 이 얼룩을 제거할 수 있나요? 커피를 쏟았어요.

남 흠, 100% 확신할 수는 없지만 최선을 다할게요.

여 언제 찾을 수 있을까요? 이번 일요일에 그 드레스가 필요해요.

남 **준비되면 바로 전화할게요.**

해설 세탁 맡긴 드레스를 언제 찾을 수 있을지 묻는 질문에 세탁이 되면 바로 전화하겠다고 답할 수 있다. ① 저 드레스 색깔이 마음에 들지 않아요. ② 제 생각에 당신은 커피를 너무 많이 마셔요. ③ 정말로 이것은 누구의 잘못도 아니에요. ⑤ 저도 이번 일요일에 약속이 있어요.

어휘 stain 얼룩 spill 흘리다

03 ③

해석 여 안녕하세요, 여러분. 여러분을 위한 좋은 소식이 있습니다. Red Hat Chicken은 이제 두 곳의 편리한 장소에서 여러분을 모실 수 있게 되었습니다. 구 시가지의 손님들께서는 Woodfield Mall 맞은편에 있는 Eastern 대로에 위치한 기존 매장으로 저희를 찾아 주시면 됩니다. 신 시가지의 손님들께서는 Metropolitan 백화점 옆에 있는 Madison 가(街)에 위치한 새로운 매장으로 오시면 됩니다. 하지만 어느 지점을 선택하시든 여러분은 분명 Red Hat Chicken의 가정식 닭튀김, 비스켓, 감자튀김 등을 즐기시게 될 것입니다. 아시다시피 저희는 다른 닭튀김 체인들처럼 배달 서비스를 제공하지는 않습니다. 대신 정말로 맛있는 닭튀김에 관해서라면 신선함이 중요하기에 저희는 신선함을 보장합니다.

해설 새로운 매장의 개점과 그 위치를 알리는 것이 목적이다.

어휘 convenient 편리한 location 위치 original 원래의 delivery 배달 guarantee 보증하다, 보장하다

04 ②

해석 남 정말 멋진 전망이야! 산에 오르니 정말 좋다.

여 그래. 하지만 지금 바로 내려가는 게 좋겠어. 다리가 아파.

남 이거 봐. 정상까지 불과 한 시간 거리야. 산꼭대기까지 가자.

여 날이 어두워지고 있는 걸 모르겠어?

남 문제없어. 손전등이랑 충분한 음식이 있잖아.

여 밤에 등산하는 것은 아주 위험할 수 있어. 응급 구조를 요청해야 할 수도 있어.

남 네 말이 맞아. 우린 이미 많은 힘을 썼어. 그리고 흔히 내려가는 게 오르는 것보다 훨씬 힘들다고들 해.

여 맞아. 거기다 집에 가는 기차 시간표도 고려해야 해.

남 오, 거의 잊고 있었어. 말해 줘서 고마워.

여 천만에. 실망시켜서 미안해.

남 언제든 다음 기회가 있잖아. 서두르자.

해설 여자는 날이 어두워지고 있으므로 바로 산을 내려가야 한다고 말하고 있다.

어휘 peak 정상 emergency rescue 응급 구조 descend 내려가다 ascend 올라가다 take ~ into account ~을 고려하다

05 ⑤

해석 남 Parker 양, 몇 가지만 더 물어 보겠습니다.

여 무엇을 알고 싶으신가요?

남 알다시피 이 일과 관련해서 컴퓨터 작업이 많습니다. 타자는 얼마나 빨리 치십니까?

여 1분에 약 70단어 정도입니다.

남 좋아요. 그럼 이건 필수 사항은 아니지만 우리는 연구를 발표하면 자주 전국 곳곳에서 연구 결과를 발표합니다. 사람들 앞에서 말해 본 경험이 있습니까?

여 음, 네. 작년에 저희 학교 교수님들 앞에서 몇 차례 발표를 했습니다.

남 잘 됐군요. 그리고 물론 당신이 출장을 갈 때는 회사에서 차를 제공합니다.

여 좋네요. 비용을 좀 절약할 수 있겠어요.

남 맞아요. 그럼 더 궁금한 것이 있습니까?

여 네. 해외 출장은 얼마나 있을까요?

남 단지 한 달에 며칠 정도입니다. 하지만 휴일에는 출장이 없을 겁니다.

해설 타자 실력, 사람들 앞에서 말해 본 경험, 해외 출장 등에 대해 묻고 답하는 내용으로 미루어 면접관과 지원자의 대화임을 알 수 있다.

어휘 involved 관련된 requirement 필요조건 publish 발표하다, 출판하다
presentation 발표 throughout 도처에

06 ④

해석 여 안녕, David. 뭘 보고 있어?

남 안녕, Anna. 누나에게서 온 사진엽서야. 사진 속에 있는 아이들이 내 조카들이야.

여 어디 보자. 그들은 미국에 사는 구나, 그렇지?

남 어떻게 알았어? 너에게 그들에 대해 전에 이야기한 기억이 없는데.

여 별거 아냐. 그냥 저쪽 편에 있는 등대 앞의 성조기를 보고 추측했을 뿐이야.

남 그렇구나.

여 나란히 앉아서 물고기가 미끼를 물기를 기다리는 아이들이 너무 귀여워!

남 봐. 개도 앉아서 물고기를 기다리는 것 같아 보여. 정말 그림 같지 않아?

여 응, 맞아. 저곳에 가보고 싶다.

남 갈 수 있어! 다음 달에 거기 방문할 거 거든. 네가 같이 간다면 그들은 틀림없이 널 환영할 거야.

여 정말? 일정을 확인해 보고 알려 줄게.

해설 여자아이는 대화에서 남자아이와 나란히 앉아서 낚시를 하고 있는 것으로 나온다.

어휘 star striped banner 성조기 light house 등대 side by side 나란히 bait 물다 surely 확실히

07 ②

해석 여 언제 집으로 돌아가나요, Ted?

남 이번 토요일에 뉴욕으로 가는 비행기에 좌석을 예약했어요.

여 그럼 여기 런던에서 머물 시간이 딱 이틀 남았네요. 틀림없이 내일 뭔가 하고 싶으실 것 같아요. 박물관은 좀 다녀왔나요?

남 네. 이미 여러 박물관에 다녀왔어요.

여 그럼, 저녁 유람선 관광은 어떠세요?

남 사실 이번 주에 벌써 두 번 다녀왔어요.

여 무엇을 하고 싶어요?

남 음, 극장에 안 간지 오래되었어요.

여 오, 좋아요. Prince Edward 극장에서 훌륭한 뮤지컬을 상연 중이라고 들었어요.

남 잘됐네요! 표는 어떻게 구하죠?

여 표 걱정은 하지 마세요. 제가 구할게요.

남 고마워요. 그럼 제가 저녁을 대접할게요.

해설 남자가 뮤지컬 표를 어떻게 구해야 할지 물어 봤고, 여자는 걱정 말라며 자신이 구하겠다고 말했다.

어휘 reserve a seat 좌석을 예약하다 riverboat tour 유람선 관광 terrific 멋진, 훌륭한 in a long time 오랜만

08 ②

해석 여 왜 그리 심각해 보이나요?

남 아내와 큰 문제가 있어요.

여 무슨 일이에요? 오……. 제발 부인 생일을 또 잊었다고 말하지 마세요.

남 네, 그녀는 크게 상처 받았어요.

여 음. 이 소식이 그녀의 기분을 나아지게 할 수 있다면 좋겠네요.

남 무슨 소식이요?

여 모르세요? 승진하셨어요! 방금 당신의 상사에게 들었어요.

남 정말요? 믿을 수가 없네요. 아내에게 멋진 선물이 될 거예요.

여 비록 조금 늦기는 했지만요.

남 맞아요. 아내에게 관리자가 되었다고 말하고 싶어서 기다릴 수가 없군요.

해설 남자는 여자에게 관리자로 승진을 했다는 소식을 듣고 기뻐하고 있다.

어휘 hurt 다치게 하다 promote 승진시키다 boss 상사, 상관, 고용주, 사장

09 ②

해석 여 안녕하세요, 고객님. 어떤 영화를 보시겠어요?

남 'Toy Story 4'요.

여 몇 장이 필요하세요?

남 어른 두 장, 아동 두 장이요. 얼마인가요?

여 상영 시간대에 따라 다릅니다. 어느 시간대를 원하세요?

남 8시 20분이요.

여 그럼 어른 한 명당 10달러, 아동 한 명당 5달러입니다.

남 알겠습니다. 이 신용 카드로 할인을 받을 수 있습니까?

여 오, 그건 저희 회원 신용 카드네요. 두 명까지 티켓당 2달러 할인을 받을 수 있습니다.

남 그거 잘됐네요. 여기 신용 카드 받으세요.

여 이곳에 서명해 주세요. 영수증 여기 있습니다. 다른 도와드릴 일이 있나요?

남 아뇨, 고맙습니다.

여 'Toy Story 4' 네 장. 어른 두 명, 아동 두 명. 여기 있습니다.

해설 어른 두 명, 아동 두 명이며, 어른은 한 명당 10달러, 아동은 한 명당 5달러이므로 영화표의 총액은 30달러이다. 여기서 두 명까지 2달러 할인이 되므로 총 지불 금액은 26달러가 된다.

어휘 depend on ~에 달려 있다, ~에 따라 다르다 showing 상영 up to ~까지

10 ③

해석 (뉴스 음악)

남 안녕하십니까? Korea Today의 Tom Brown입니다. 오늘의 주요 뉴

스입니다.

- 북미와 서유럽으로의 한국 자동차 수출이 감소하고 있습니다.
- 한국의 평균 출산율이 매년 감소하고 있습니다.
- 한국에서 패스트푸드의 높은 소금 함량이 아동의 건강을 해칠 수 있다고 경고하는 연구 결과가 나왔습니다.
- 한국의 흡연자 수가 지난 5년간 5퍼센트 감소하였습니다.
- 국제 불꽃놀이 축제가 서울에서 열릴 예정입니다.

잠시 후에 다시 찾아뵙겠습니다. 채널 고정하십시오. 여러분은 지금 Korea Today를 시청하고 계십니다.

(뉴스 음악)

해설 패스트푸드에 많이 들어있는 소금이 아동의 건강을 해칠 수 있다는 기사가 소개된 반면 패스트푸드로 인해 비만 인구가 증가했다는 내용은 없다.

어휘 export 수출 decline 감소하다 birthrate 출산율 decrease 감소하다 recent 최근의 content 함유량; 내용물 firework 불꽃놀이

11 ⑤

해석 여 James Cook은 영국의 탐험가이자 천문학자로 태평양, 남극 지방, 북극 지방을 비롯한 전 세계를 여러 차례 탐험하였다. 그의 첫 번째 탐험에서 그는 지구와 태양 사이의 거리를 측정하려는 목적으로 금성이 지구와 태양 사이를 지날 때에 금성을 관찰하기 위해서 타히티로 항해하였다. 이 탐험 기간 동안 그는 호주 북부를 지도에 담기도 하였다. 그는 두 번째로 남극과 이스터 섬을 탐험하였다. 그의 마지막 탐험은 북아메리카와 아시아를 잇는 북서 항로를 찾기 위한 것이었다. Cook은 1779년 2월 14일에 샌드위치 섬에서 폭도들에게 살해당했다. 그는 그때 원주민들이 훔쳐간 범선을 돌려받기 위해서 족장을 인질로 삼으려고 시도하던 중이었다.

해설 Cook은 족장을 인질로 삼아 원주민으로 하여금 그들이 훔쳐간 배를 돌려주도록 하려다 원주민 폭도들에게 살해당했다.

어휘 explorer 탐험가 astronomer 천문학자 expedition 탐험, 탐사 antarctic 남극(지방) arctic 북극(지방) map 지도를 그리다 mob 폭도 hostage 인질

12 ⑤

해석 남 만나서 반갑습니다. 제가 Blue Ocean 수영 학원의 원장입니다. 무슨 일로 오셨나요?
여 신문에 내신 일자리에 지원하려고 합니다. 강사를 몇 명 채용하실 예정이신가요?
남 두 명 내지 세 명입니다. 오전에 초급자와 중급자 반을 가르칠 사람이 필요합니다. 둘 다 가르칠 수 있으세요?
여 아뇨, 전 중급자를 가르치지는 못하고 초급자는 가르칠 수 있습니다.
남 알겠습니다. 수영을 가르친 지는 얼마나 되셨나요?
여 올해로 2년이 됩니다.
남 좋아요. 경험은 충분한 것 같군요. 당신의 첫 수업은 아침 6시에 시작될 것이고 두 번째 수업은……
여 잠깐만요! 아침 6시라고요? 전 여기 8시 반 전에 도착할 수가 없어요. 40킬로미터 떨어진 곳에 살거든요.
남 그러시다면 가르칠 반이 하나밖에 없을 거예요. 괜찮겠습니까?
여 괜찮습니다. 아무 일도 안 하는 것보다는 나을 테니까요.

해설 여자는 중급반은 가르칠 수 없고 멀리 떨어진 곳에 살아서 8시 반 전에는 수업을 시작할 수 없으므로 여자가 맡을 수 있는 반은 10시에 시작하는 반이다.

어휘 director 책임자, 지휘자, 관리자 apply for 지원하다 instructor 교관, 강사 intermediate 중급의

13 ④

해석 (전화벨이 울린다.)
여 안녕, Mike? Anne이야.
남 안녕, Anne. 어떻게 지내?
여 음, 역사 시험공부를 하려는 중이야.
남 집에 있니?
여 응, 보통은 도서관에서 공부를 하지만 집에서 하는 게 공부를 더 많이 할 수 있을 거라고 생각했어.
남 그럼 공부는 열심히 하고 있어?
여 아니, 그렇지 못해. 사실은 지금 야구 경기를 보는 중이야. 넌 어때? 지금 뭐하니?
남 난 종이에 생물학 리포트를 쓰는 중이야.
여 종이에? 집에 컴퓨터가 없니?
남 그게, 있기는 한데 수리 중이야. 그래서 지금은 쓸 수 없어.
여 많은 학생들이 자주 도서관에서 컴퓨터를 사용하잖아. 어째서 넌 그 컴퓨터를 사용하지 않니?
남 **그러고 싶지만 항상 다 사용 중이야.**

해설 남자에게 집에 있는 컴퓨터가 수리 중이어서 리포트를 손으로 쓰고 있다는 말을 듣고 여자는 왜 도서관에 있는 컴퓨터를 사용하지 않는지를 묻고 있다. 이에 대한 응답으로는 "그러고는 싶지만 항상 다 사용 중이야."가 가장 적절하다. ① 생물학은 내가 가장 좋아하는 과목이야. ② 나는 야구를 보는 것이 지루하다고 생각해. ③ 나는 컴퓨터를 수리하는 법을 몰라. ⑤ 내 서재에 있는 책은 무엇이든 마음대로 봐도 좋아.

어휘 get more work done 더 많은 일을 하다 write out 쓰다, 작성하다 repair 고치다, 수리하다 how come ~ 왜, 어째서

14 ②

해석 여 안녕, Ken. 무슨 문제라도 있어?
남 음, 머리가 아파 죽겠어.
여 아스피린은 먹어 봤어?
남 응, 하지만 배만 아프게 해.
여 그럼 더는 아스피린은 안 먹는 것이 좋겠다. 커피는 많이 마시는 편이니?
남 응. 하루에 대여섯 잔 정도.
여 오! 너무 많은 카페인인데! 대신 물을 마시도록 해 봐. 머리는 언제 아프니?
남 대개 사무실에 있을 때 그래.
여 하루에 컴퓨터는 얼마 동안 쓰니?
남 약 여덟 시간에서 열 시간 정도. 컴퓨터 없이는 하루도 살 수 없어.
여 **컴퓨터를 덜 쓰도록 노력해 봐.**

해설 남자는 두통을 호소하며, 하루에 8~10시간 컴퓨터를 사용하고 컴퓨터가 없이는 하루도 살 수 없다고 말하고 있으므로 그에 대한 여자의 응답으로는 컴퓨터 사용을 줄일 것을 권고하는 내용이 적절하다. ① 커피 한 잔 마실래? ③ 나는 컴퓨터

게임에 관심이 없어. ④ 아스피린을 한두 알 먹어 보지 그래? ⑤ 내 사무실에 들르는 게 어때?

어휘 **headache** 두통 **upset** 뒤집힌; 혼란한 **caffeine** 카페인

15 ①

해석 남 Frank는 그의 세 달 전에 은퇴한 할머니에게 전화해서 요즘 어떠신지 여쭤 본다. 할머니는 잘 지내고 있으며 은퇴 후에 아주 바쁘게 지낸다고 말한다. 그녀는 지역 문화 회관에서 상급 컴퓨터 과정을 듣고 있다고 말한다. 그녀는 또한 저녁에는 요가를 배우고 때때로 잠이 오지 않을 때는 늦게까지 자지 않고 인터넷을 한다고 말한다. 그녀의 말을 들으면서 Frank는 비록 할머니가 건강하다고 말씀은 하지만 나이를 고려할 때 너무 많은 일을 하고 있다고 생각한다. 이런 상황에서 Frank가 할머니에게 할 말로 가장 적절한 것은 무엇인가?
Frank 할머니, 휴식을 취하셔야 해요.

해설 Frank는 할머니가 나이에 비해 너무 많은 일을 하는 것이 염려스럽다. 따라서 Frank가 할머니에게 할 말로는 "휴식을 취하셔야 해요."가 가장 적절하다. ② 나이는 마음먹기에 달린 거죠. ③ 그 소식을 들으니 정말 유감이에요. ④ 저축을 좀 하는 게 어때요? ⑤ 컴퓨터처럼 기억력이 좋으시네요.

어휘 **retire** 은퇴하다 **community center** 지역 문화 회관, 마을 회관 **advanced** 고급의 **stay up late** 밤늦게 깨어 있다 **considering** ~를 고려하면

16–17 ②, ④

해석 여 때때로 아이들이 납치됩니다. 가능한 한 빨리 납치된 아이들을 찾아서 집에 돌려보내는 것이 중요합니다. 일반 대중이 납치 사건에 관해 더 빨리 알게 될수록 더 빨리 도움을 줄 수 있습니다. 몇몇 자원봉사자들이 일반 대중에게 납치 사건에 관해 바로 알리는 프로그램을 시작하기로 결심하였습니다. 이 프로그램은 'Care Alert'이라고 합니다. Care Alert 프로그램은 텔레비전과 라디오 방송국에 최근에 납치된 아이에 관한 중요한 정보를 제공합니다. 그러면 방송국들은 누군가 도울 수 있기를 바라면서 대중에게 무슨 일이 일어났는지를 알립니다. 납치 사건에 관해 무언가 목격한 사람이 경찰에 신고할 수 있게 됩니다. 때때로 아이의 부모 중 한 명이 자신의 아이를 납치하곤 합니다. 이러한 납치는 Care Alert 프로그램에서 다루지 않습니다. Care Alert 프로그램은 오직 낯선 사람이 아이를 데려갈 때만 이용됩니다. 납치된 아이는 많은 위험에 처하게 됩니다. 이 새로운 Care Alert 프로그램은 많은 아이들의 생명을 구할 것으로 기대됩니다.

해설 16 몇몇 자원봉사자들이 납치 사건을 바로 알리는 프로그램을 시작하기로 결심했다.
17 Care Alert은 납치 사건 중에서 낯선 사람에 의한 납치 사건만을 다룬다.

어휘 **kidnap** 납치[유괴]하다 **alert** 알리다 **in hopes** 기대하여, 희망을 품고

🎯 Dictation

01 not as easy as / difficult for you

02 remove these stains / get it back

---

03 two convenient locations / no matter which location

04 it is getting dark / descending is much harder

05 involved in this job / I made a few presentations

06 photo postcard from my sister / they are sitting side by side / surely welcome you

07 reserved a seat / we get tickets

08 I'm in big trouble / I can't wait to tell her

09 depends on the showing / get a $2 discount per ticket

10 high salt content in fast food / Stay tuned

11 a British explorer / take the local chief hostage

12 beginner and intermediate level / you have enough experience

13 trying to study / it's being repaired

14 having a lot of bad headaches / without it for a single day

15 entered the community center / doing too many things

16-17 The sooner the public knows / save many children's lives

🎯 12회 듣기 모의고사
p.72-73

01 ①	02 ⑤	03 ②	04 ④	05 ④	06 ②
07 ⑤	08 ④	09 ②	10 ④	11 ③	12 ④
13 ⑤	14 ③	15 ③	16 ⑤	17 ②	

01 ①

해석 여 Jimmy, 오늘 밤에 영화 보러 가지 않을래? 나 영화표가 두 장 있어.
남 미안해. 나는 정말 바빠. 보고서를 써야 하거든.
여 그래? 마감일이 언젠데?
남 이번 금요일까지 끝내야 해.

해설 여자가 마감일이 언제냐고 물었으므로 금요일까지 마쳐야 한다는 응답이 가장 적절하다. ② 그래. 이것을 끝내자마자. ③ 오늘 밤에는 영화를 보고 싶지 않아. ④ 아마 주말에는 가능할 거야. ⑤ 리포트를 끝마치는 것이 현재 나의 가장 우선순위야.

어휘 **priority** 우선, 우선 사항 **due** ~까지 하기로 예정된

02 ⑤

해석 남 실례합니다. 컨벤션 센터로 가는 길을 좀 알려 주시겠어요?
여 오른편에 있는 저 빌딩인데, 제가 알기론 거기에 주차 공간이 없어요.
남 그러면 혹시 제가 몇 시간 동안 차를 둘 만한 곳을 알고 있나요?
여 5번가에 꽤 저렴한 공용 주차장이 있어요.

해설 주차할 만한 곳이 있냐고 물었으므로 "5번가에 꽤 저렴한 공용 주차장이 있어요."라는 응답이 가장 적절하다. ① 주차 요금은 없어요. ② 지하철을 타고 갈 수 있어

요. ③ 컨벤션 센터는 아직 열지 않았어요. ④ 여기에 차를 놔두시면 안 돼요.

어휘 convention center 컨벤션 센터(회의·숙박 시설이 완비된 종합 건물이나 지역) public parking lot 공용 주차장 parking spot 주차 장소

03 ②

해석 남 날씨가 급격하게 변하는 세상에서 자연재해에 대비하는 것은 중요합니다. 특히 장마 기간이 다가옴에 따라 여러분은 갑자기 홍수가 밀려오는 것과 같은 진짜 응급 상황이 닥쳤을 때 어떻게 대처해야 할지 항상 명심해야 합니다. 첫째, 집안에 있을 때 최신 정보를 얻기 위해 라디오와 텔레비전을 켜 두십시오. 비상 용품을 준비하고, 만약 대피하라는 정보를 듣는다면 즉시 그렇게 하십시오. 둘째, 야외에 있다면 높은 언덕이나 빌딩으로 대피하여 침착하게 구조를 기다리십시오. 마지막으로, 차 안에 있는데 차의 시동이 꺼져 버린다면, 즉시 차를 포기하고 높은 언덕으로 올라가십시오. 멈춘 차의 시동을 걸어 보려는 시도에 의해 많은 사상자가 발생하고 있습니다.

해설 자연재해 중 특히 홍수 발생 시 상황별 대처 방법에 대해 소개하고 있다.

어휘 drastic 급격한 essential 필수의 natural disaster 자연재해 monsoon season 장마 기간 keep in mind 명심하다 emergency supply 비상용품 immediately 즉시 patiently 참을성 있게 rescue 구조하다 stall (차의) 시동이 꺼지다 abandon 버리고 떠나다, 포기하다 attempt 시도; ~을 시도하다

04 ④

해석 여 Baker 씨, 말씀 드린 대로 저는 낚시 경험이 없어요.
남 걱정 마세요. 제가 낚시에 관한 모든 것을 알려 드릴게요. 제가 말한 대로만 하세요.
여 그런데, 여긴 다소 조용하네요. 사람들이 대화를 나누지 않아요.
남 그래요. 만약 시끄러우면, 물고기가 누군가 여기 있다는 것을 느끼게 되고 어디론가 가서 숨어버릴 거예요.
여 그렇겠네요.
남 아마도 당신에겐 여기 있는 사람들이 꽤 지루해 보이고, 앉아 있는 것 외엔 아무것도 안 하는 것처럼 보이겠지만, 당신이 물고기를 잡게 되면, 그 순간 얼마나 기쁜지 말로 표현할 수 없을 거예요.
여 오, 아니, 아니에요. 지루해 보이지 않아요. 낚시와 자연을 즐기고 있는 것 같아요. 제 말은 사람들의 얼굴이 매우 평화롭고 행복해 보여요. 사람들의 얼굴을 보니, 물고기를 기다리는 시간을 즐기는 것이 바로 낚시의 진정한 즐거움인 것 같네요.
남 맞아요. 그리고 낚시 후에는 잡은 물고기로 음식을 만들어서 사람들과 나눠 먹을 수도 있어요.
여 낚시는 정말 좋은 여가 활동인 것 같아요.

해설 "I think the real pleasure of fishing is waiting and enjoying the time."에서 여자가 "물고기를 잡는 것보다 그 과정을 즐기는 것이 낚시의 묘미다."라고 생각하고 있음을 알 수 있다.

어휘 hide 숨다 pleasure 기쁨 leisure activity 여가 활동

05 ④

해석 여 다시 사진을 찍기 전에 사진을 좀 봐도 될까요?

남 물론이죠. 여기로 와서 보세요.
여 제 생각엔 이 사진 좋을 것 같아요. 표정이 자연스러워요.
남 그래요, 하지만 이 사진에서는 옷이 선명하게 보이질 않아요. 아마 배경이 너무 어두운 것 같아요.
여 그런 것 같기도 하네요.
남 당신도 알다시피 사진을 선택할 사람은 우리가 아니에요. 우리의 고객이 사진을 선택할 거예요. 그러니까, 사진에서 상품이 선명하게 보여야 해요.
여 그럼, 어떻게 해야 할까요?
남 조명과 반사판을 이용해 봅시다. 광고주들은 대개 밝은 사진을 좋아해요.
여 알겠어요. 이해했어요. 그리고 상품을 가리지 않도록 자세를 취해 볼게요.

해설 사진을 찍는 장면으로 사진사와 모델 간의 대화이다.

어휘 shoot ~의 사진을 찍다 appear 나타나다 vividly 선명하게 reflecting plate 반사판 advertiser 광고주 hide 가리다, 숨기다

06 ②

해석 여 봐, 횡단보도 끝에 공사장이 있어.
남 응, 공사 중 표지판이 보여.
여 도로 포장용 돌도 있네.
남 아마 도로의 보도블록을 바꿀 건가 봐. 하지만 아직 공사를 시작하지는 않았어.
여 맞아. 그곳에 아무도 없어. 그럼, 우린 어떻게 하지? 우리의 목적지는 저 길 끝이잖아.
남 그냥 표시를 무시하고 돌무더기 사이를 지나가자.
여 별로 좋은 생각 같지 않아. 비록 지금은 저기에 일하는 사람이 아무도 없지만, 그래도 위험해 보여.
남 네 말이 맞아. 오, 저기 또 다른 표지판이 있어. "다른 길을 이용하시오." 라고 쓰여 있어.
여 반대편 인도는 걷기에 훨씬 좋아 보여. 길을 따라서 나무들이 늘어서 있어. 가자. 파란불이야.

해설 공사장에는 아무도 없다고 했으므로 사람이 있는 것이 내용과 일치하지 않는다.

어휘 construction 공사 crossing 횡단보도 paving stone 보도블록 ignore ~을 무시하다 along ~을 따라서 get going ~하기 시작하다

07 ⑤

해석 남 Brenda, 지난 금요일 독서 클럽 모임에 왜 오지 않았니?
여 삼촌 집에 가서 사촌 동생들을 돌봤어.
남 왜? 숙모가 바쁘셨어?
여 응, 요즘 숙모가 지역 대학에서 강의 몇 개를 듣고 계셔.
남 그럼 매주 금요일마다 사촌 동생을 돌봐야 하니?
여 아냐. 사실, 그건 교수님이 지난주에 나오지 못해서 보강한 거래.
남 알겠어. 아, 잠깐만! 오늘 목요일이지, 맞지?
여 맞아. 무슨 일 있어?
남 오늘 저녁에 우리 독서 클럽 모임을 갖기로 했어.
여 왜?

남 대부분의 회원들이 금요일에는 파티에 가야 한다고 해서 하루 앞당겼어. 지금 가야겠다. 갈 수 있어?

여 오늘은 빠질 수 없지. 어서 가자!

해설 남자는 금요일마다 있는 독서 클럽 모임이 목요일 저녁으로 앞당겨졌다고 했고 여자에게 갈 의향을 묻자 여자가 서둘러 가자고 대답했으므로 두 사람은 함께 독서 클럽 모임에 갈 것이다.

어휘 look after ~을 돌보다 a sort of 일종의 makeup lesson 보강 수업 move up 날짜를 앞당기다

08 ④

해석 여 Jason, 오랜만이야. 어디 갔었니?

남 여름휴가로 하와이에 다녀왔어.

여 오, 그랬어? 좋은 시간을 보냈겠구나. 근데 Tim이 입원했다는 소식 들었어?

남 아니. 처음 듣는 얘기야. 무슨 일이야?

여 차에 치여서 두 다리에 깁스를 하고 있어. 이번 주 금요일 저녁에 병문안 갈 예정이야. 같이 갈래?

남 가고는 싶지만 금요일 밤에 아빠가 출장에서 돌아오셔. 공항으로 아빠를 태우러 가야 해.

여 엄마한테 부탁해 보지 그러니?

남 엄마 차가 고장 나서 지금 정비소에 있거든.

여 네 형은?

남 다음 주 월요일까지 마쳐야 할 숙제가 있대.

여 알겠어. 그럼 가족들이랑 즐거운 시간 보내.

해설 남자는 같이 병문안에 가고 싶지만 출장에서 돌아오는 아버지를 태우러 공항에 가야 하는 상황이다.

어휘 get hospitalized 입원하다 cast 깁스 repair shop 자동차 정비소

09 ②

해석 여 도와 드릴까요?

남 네, 청바지를 한 벌 사려고요.

여 제 때에 잘 오셨네요. 우리 매장의 청바지 대부분을 20% 할인해 드리고 있어요.

남 잘됐군요. 이것은 얼마인가요?

여 가장 잘 나가는 것 중 하나예요. 정가가 100달러이니까, 90달러에 사실 수 있어요.

남 20% 할인이라고 하지 않으셨어요?

여 네. 하지만 이것은 신제품이라서 10%만 할인 받을 수 있어요.

남 알겠습니다.

여 하지만 두 벌 이상을 사시면 5% 추가로 할인해 드려요.

남 그래요? 그러면, 총액의 15%가 되네요.

여 네, 맞아요.

남 좋습니다. 신제품으로 두 벌을 살게요.

해설 두 벌을 살 경우 15% 할인을 받으므로 200달러의 15%인 30달러가 할인되어 지불할 금액은 170달러이다.

어휘 item 물품, 항목 list price 정가 brand-new 신품의 additional 추가의

10 ④

해석 여 학교 축제는 어땠니?

남 오, 아주 좋았어요. 개인적으로는 아주 바쁜 날이었어요.

여 왜?

남 온갖 종류의 행사에 참여했거든요.

여 무엇을 했는지 말해보렴.

남 우선, 제가 방송제의 사회자라서 무대 장치 설치를 도와줬어요.

여 훌륭하구나. 너는 분명 잘했을 거야.

남 그리고 Jane의 파트너로 댄스 경연 대회에 참여했어요.

여 상을 받았니?

남 안타깝게도, 아뇨. 하지만 좋은 경험이었어요.

여 선생님을 위한 이벤트도 했니? 꽃을 달아드린다든가 말이야.

남 아뇨. 이건 매년 하는 학교 축제예요. 스승의 날 행사가 아니에요.

여 그래. 그 밖에 무엇을 했니?

남 음, 축제가 끝나고 나서 다른 동아리 친구들과 청소를 해야 했어요.

여 와, 정말 바쁜 하루를 보냈구나!

해설 선생님께 꽃을 달아드리는 것은 여자가 행사의 예로 든 것이지 남자가 실제로 한 일은 아니다.

어휘 sort 종류 set the stage 무대 장치를 설치하다 MC(=master of ceremony) 사회자 enter 참가하다

11 ③

해석 남 올리브 나무는 매우 유용하다. 우리는 음식을 만들 때 올리브를 사용하고, 이것에서 기름도 얻는다. 특히, 올리브는 그리스와 이탈리아의 음식에 널리 사용된다. 우리는 기름, 좋은 목재, 월계수 잎(허브), 올리브 열매로 사용하려고 올리브를 심고 재배한다. 올리브 나무는 거의 모든 부분이 사용된다. 올리브 나무는 건조한 지역에서 잘 자라지만, 서리와 오랜 강우에는 약하다. 하지만 올리브 나무에서 수확물을 얻는 것이 어려운 것은 아니다. 때때로 우리는 엄청난 양의 열매를 수확할 수 있지만, 두 해 연속으로 열매를 맺는 경우는 드물다. 올리브는 건강에 좋은 음식으로도 유명하다.

해설 올리브 나무는 건조한 지역에서 잘 자라지만, 서리와 장마에는 약하다고 했으므로 "어떤 기후에서도 잘 자란다."는 것은 일치하지 않는다.

어휘 plant 심다 grow 재배하다 arid 건조한 frost 서리 crop 작물, 수확물 enormous 엄청난, 막대한 gathering 수확물 seldom 좀처럼 ~않는 bear (열매를) 맺다 in succession 잇달아, 계속하여

12 ④

해석 여 이 표를 좀 봐. 이 도표는 일상생활로 인해 소모되는 서로 다른 칼로리 양과 몸의 사용 부분을 보여주는 거야.

남 아, 재미있네. 먼지 털기를 하면 시간당 180킬로 칼로리를 소모할 수 있구나.

여 그래. 먼지 털기가 어깨와 가슴에 작용하기 때문이야. 또한 진공청소기 사용은 등과 팔에 작용하는데, 시간당 240킬로 칼로리를 소모해.

남 옷 쇼핑은 다리, 가슴, 등, 어깨에 작용해서 같은 양의 칼로리를 소모해.

여 맞아. 가장 많은 양의 칼로리를 사용하는 활동이 무엇이지?

남 아이를 그네에 태워 미는 것과 창문 닦기인데, 둘 다 시간당 290킬로

칼로리를 사용해.

여 그렇구나. 나는 아이가 없으니까, 창문 닦기가 가장 많은 칼로리 소모를 위해 선택할 수 있는 것이네.

남 그래. 창문 닦기는 가슴, 어깨, 등, 다리에 효과가 있어.

해설 window washing에 대한 설명이 일치하지 않는다. window washing은 가슴, 어깨, 등, 다리에 효과가 있으며, 시간당 290킬로 칼로리를 소모한다.

어휘 dusting 먼지 털기 work on ~에 효과가 있다, ~에 작용하다 vacuuming 진공 청소하기 swing 그네

13 ⑤

해석 여 음악 치료에 대해 들어본 적이 있니?

남 물론, 들어본 적이 있지. 하지만 정확히 그게 무엇인지는 몰라.

여 음, 그 이름이 내포하는 대로 음악으로 신체 질병을 치료하는 방법이야.

남 어떻게 작용하는데?

여 음악을 듣는 것은 스트레스 호르몬을 낮추고 면역 체계를 향상시켜 줘.

남 재미있네!

여 그래서, 좋은 음악을 들으면 긴장이 풀리고 고통과 긴장에서 벗어날 수 있을 거야.

남 동의해. 음악을 듣는 것은 나의 스트레스를 해소하는 방법 중 하나야.

여 물론. 그런 식으로 음악은 우리가 스스로의 몸을 치료하도록 도와줘.

남 그런데 왜 갑자기 음악 치료 얘기를 꺼냈니?

여 실은, 대학원에서 음악 치료를 공부해 볼까 생각 중이야.

해설 남자가 왜 갑자기 음악 치료에 대한 얘기를 했는지 물어보았으므로 여자는 대학원에서 공부해 볼까 생각 중이어서 얘기를 꺼냈다고 답하는 것이 가장 적절하다. ① 우리는 음악 치료에 대해 더 많이 배워야 해. ② 왜냐하면 치료가 여러 가지 형태로 나누어질 수 있기 때문이야. ③ 음, 나라면 모든 종류의 음악이 다 우리에게 도움이 되는 것은 아니라고 말하겠어. ④ 음악은 오랫동안 의사들 사이에서 인기가 있어.

어휘 music therapy 음악 치료 divide into ~으로 나누다 graduate school 대학원 imply ~을 함축하다 treat 치료하다 drop 감소시키다 get over (병으로부터) 회복되다, 극복하다 suffering 고통 tension 긴장 relieve 덜다, 경감하다 bring up (화제를) 꺼내다

14 ③

해석 남 Julie, 나는 네가 채식주의자인지 몰랐어.

여 나 채식주의자야. 사실 15살 때부터 야채만 먹었어.

남 정말? 무엇 때문에 바뀐 거야?

여 초등학교에 다닐 때 난 운동을 싫어하고 활동을 잘 안하며 사는, 소파에 앉아서 텔레비전만 보는 사람이었거든. 그 결과 살이 많이 쪄서 채식주의자 음식을 고수하기로 결심했어.

남 그래? 채식주의자가 된 후 어떤 종류의 변화를 가장 많이 느꼈니?

여 음, 식습관을 바꾼 후에 거의 20파운드나 빠졌어.

남 정신적인 변화도 있었니?

여 활기가 생겼고 젊어진 것 같고, 무엇보다 나 자신에 대한 자신감이 생겼어.

남 와, 그거 해볼 만한데.

여 맞아. 다시는 고기를 먹지 않을 거야.

남 아마 나도 식단을 바꾸는 것을 고려해 봐야겠어.

해설 마지막 부분에서 남자가 채식주의자가 되는 것이 해볼 만한 가치가 있다고 한 점으로 미루어 보아 자신의 식단을 바꾸어 보는 것을 고려해 볼 것이라는 대답이 가장 적절하다. ① 너도 다이어트를 해야 할 것 같아. ② 왜 채식 위주 식단이 건강하다고 생각해? ④ 있잖아, 비활동적인 생활을 하는 것은 네게 좋지 않아. ⑤ 넌 어렸을 적에 더 많은 고기를 먹었어야 했어.

어휘 vegetarian 채식주의자 inactive 비활동적인 couch potato 움직이지 않고 앉아서 텔레비전만 보는 사람 put on weight 살이 찌다 revitalize 새로운 활력을 주다 rejuvenate 다시 젊은 기분이 들다

15 ③

해석 남 민수는 지역 공동체에서 주최하는 영어 말하기 대회에 참가할 계획이다. 그는 먼저 자신의 원고를 제출해야 한다. 그래서 민수는 며칠 동안 말하기 원고를 썼고 마침내 완성했다. 하지만, 그는 원고에 자신이 없다. 어휘, 문법, 문장 구조에 오류가 있을 지도 모른다. 그는 원고의 실수를 찾기 위해 원고를 읽어 줄 사람이 필요하다고 생각한다. 그래서 그의 영어 선생님인 김 선생님에게 부탁하려고 한다. 이 상황에서, 민수가 김 선생님에게 할 말로 가장 적절한 것은 무엇인가?

Minsu 김 선생님, 제 영어 말하기 원고를 교정해 주시겠어요?

해설 원고 교정을 부탁하는 것이므로 "제 영어 말하기 원고를 교정해 주시겠어요?"라고 묻는 것이 가장 적절하다. ① 저를 위해 말하기 원고를 써 주실 수 있으세요? ② 제 영어 발음 좀 도와주시겠어요? ④ 저는 영어 말하기 대회에 참여하고 싶어요. ⑤ 제 말하기 실력을 향상시키려면 어떻게 해야 할까요?

어휘 participate in ~에 참여하다 proofread 교정을 보다 manuscript 원고 promote 주최하다, 증진시키다 submit 제출하다 confident 자신이 있는 in order to ~하기 위해서

16-17 ⑤, ②

해석 여 대중 연설 수업에 등록한 여러분 모두를 환영합니다. 첫 번째 수업을 시작하기 전에 이 수업에 관해 간략하게 이야기하겠습니다. 우리는 매주 화요일과 목요일 2시부터 4시까지 수업을 할 것입니다. 이 수업에서 여러분은 전반적으로 좋은 연설가가 되기 위한 기본적인 기술과 테크닉을 공부할 것입니다. 평가에 관해 말하자면, 참여도와 출석이 학점의 10퍼센트를, 그리고 기말고사가 전체 학점의 40퍼센트를 차지할 것입니다. 나머지 50퍼센트는 여러분의 대중 연설에 의거하여 평가됩니다. 제 연구실은 이 건물 3층에 있으니, 질문이 있거나 도움이 필요하다면 망설이지 말고 집무 시간 동안 언제든지 찾아오십시오. 좋습니다. 이제 '좋은 연설가들의 특징'에 대한 첫 강의를 시작합시다.

해설 16 첫 수업 시간에 교수님이 수업의 전반적인 사항인 수업 시간, 평가 방법, 면담 요령 등에 관해 공지하고 있는 내용이다.

17 참여도와 출석이 전체 학점의 10퍼센트라고 하였다.

어휘 public speech 대중 연설 sign up for ~에 등록하다 briefly 간략하게 speaking of ~에 관해 말하자면 evaluation 평가 attendance 출석 take up 차지하다 hesitate 망설이다 office hour 집무 시간

🎯 Dictation

01 going out tonight

02 as far as I know

03 it is essential to prepare / all of a sudden / abandon it immediately

04 have no experience in fishing / seem quite bored / make some food with fish

05 before shooting again / Our client will choose / Advertisers usually like

06 a construction site / at the end of that road / looks like much a better place to walk

07 she takes several classes / We were supposed to

08 got hospitalized / go and visit him / now in the repair shop

09 at the right time / get only 10% off

10 all sorts of events / you did a good job / I had to clean up

11 are widely used / in arid areas / get enormous amounts of

12 which consumes the most calories / works on

13 as the name implies / get over your suffering

14 have eaten only vegetables / put on a lot of weight / have a sense of confidence

15 needs to submit / might have errors

16-17 signed up for / takes up 10 percent / the first lesson on

13회 듣기 모의고사

p.78-79

01 ②	02 ⑤	03 ④	04 ④	05 ③	06 ①
07 ③	08 ④	09 ④	10 ④	11 ③	12 ③
13 ⑤	14 ③	15 ④	16 ②	17 ③	

01 ②

해석 여 여보세요, 다음 주 예약 상태를 다시 한 번 확인하고 싶은데요.
남 네, 예약 번호 가지고 계신가요?
여 그럼요, 109453번입니다.
남 **다음 주 금요일 침대가 두 개 있는 방으로 예약되어 있어요.**

해설 여자가 예약 번호를 알려주었으므로 침대가 두 개 있는 방이 예약되었다고 응답하는 것이 가장 적절하다. ① 미안합니다. 전화 잘못 거셨어요. ③ 다음 주말에는 이용 가능한 방이 없습니다. ④ 예약 번호를 잊어버리셨군요. ⑤ 예약 번호가 없으면 도와드릴 수 없습니다.

어휘 book 예약하다 confirmation 확증, 확정 reservation 예약 double check 재확인하다

02 ⑤

해석 남 안녕하세요. 이제 음료를 주문하시겠어요?

여 캐러멜 마키아토에 무엇이 들어있는지 좀 알려 주세요.
남 에스프레소와 우유, 캐러멜 시럽이 들어 있습니다.
여 **맛있을 것 같네요. 두 잔 주세요.**

해설 캐러멜 마키아토에 에스프레소와 우유, 캐러멜 시럽이 들어 있다는 말에 이어질 응답으로는 "맛있을 것 같네요. 두 잔 주세요."가 가장 적절하다. ① 오, 여기서 마실 거예요. ② 아직 주문할 준비가 안됐어요. ③ 괜찮아요. 이미 주문했어요. ④ 와, 캐러멜 마키아토를 만들 수 있어요?

어휘 delicious 맛있는 mix 혼합물

03 ④

해석 남 요즘 들어 피곤하십니까? 매일 잠을 잘 못 자세요? 더 나은 삶을 위해 다음 몇 가지 팁을 고려해 보세요. 첫째, 엄격한 수면 스케줄을 정하십시오. 주말이나 휴일을 포함하여 매일 같은 시간 잠자리에 들고 일어나 보세요. 정해진 수면 스케줄을 고수하는 것은 체내 시계를 형성하여 더 나은 수면을 하도록 이끌어 줍니다. 둘째, 침실 환경을 좀 더 수면 친화적으로 만들어 보십시오. 당신의 수면을 방해하는 모든 방해물을 제거하고 방의 온도는 적당한 통풍과 함께 약간 서늘하게 유지하십시오. 무엇보다도 숙면을 취하는 비결은 올바른 식습관과 규칙적인 운동입니다. 카페인의 섭취를 줄이는 것과 수면 전 술을 피하는 것의 중요성은 아무리 강조해도 지나치지 않습니다.

해설 숙면을 취하기 위해 할 수 있는 세 가지 팁에 대해 소개하는 글이다.

어휘 stick to ~을 고수하다 body clock 체내 시계 disturbance 방해물 interfere with ~을 해치다, 방해하다 adequate 적당한 ventilation 통풍 the key to N/-ing ~의 비결

04 ④

해석 여 다이어트 중이세요?
남 네, 그렇습니다. 제 체중이 너무 걱정돼요.
여 음, 알다시피, 비만은 만병의 원인이죠.
남 동의합니다. 지난 두 달 동안 간신히 10kg를 뺐고, 10kg 더 빼려고 계획 중이에요.
여 와, 힘든 일 같네요. 체중 감량을 위해 어떤 일을 하세요?
남 먼저, 덜 먹으려고 하고 규칙적으로 운동을 해요.
여 아주 좋아요. 건강하게 먹고 운동을 하는 것도 중요해요.
남 네, 하지만 영양 부족이 좀 걱정이에요. 요즘 좀 어지럽거든요.
여 건강을 해치지 않도록 조심하셔야 해요.

해설 여자는 체중을 감량할 때에는 건강하게 먹는 것과 운동을 하는 것이 중요하다고 말했다.

어휘 be on a diet 다이어트를 하다 obesity 비만 barely 간신히, 가까스로 lose weight 체중이 줄다 as well 또한, 역시 a lack of ~이 부족한 nourishment 영양분 dizzy 어지러운

05 ③

해석 남 해외로 가시는 길인가요?
여 실은, 저의 나라로 돌아가는 길이에요.
남 오, 그렇군요. 얼마나 오래 떠나 있으셨나요?

여 3년간이요.

남 참 오랜 시간이군요. 가족들이 보고 싶겠어요.

여 예, 정말 그래요. 가족들을 다시 보게 되어서 무척 기뻐요.

남 다 왔습니다. 여기가 JFK 국제공항입니다.

여 얼마죠?

남 15달러입니다.

여 여기 20달러입니다. 잔돈은 가지세요.

남 오, 너무 많아요.

여 아뇨, 잔돈은 가지세요. 정말입니다.

남 이런, 감사합니다.

해설 택시 안에서 택시 기사와 공항에 가는 승객 간의 대화이다.

어휘 **away** 떨어져 있는, 떠나 있는 **change** 거스름돈

06 ①

해석 여 이곳이 우리가 이사 올 새 아파트예요.

남 와, 이 아파트는 모든 가구가 갖춰져 있군요. 그리고 벽지도 새 것 같아요.

여 가로 줄무늬의 벽지가 맘에 들어요?

남 줄무늬가 없는 것이 더 좋겠지만, 가로 줄무늬도 괜찮아요. 바꿀 필요는 없어요. 그건 그렇고, 둥근 탁자가 마음에 들어요.

여 저도요. 모서리가 없어서 아이들에게도 더 안전하고요. 오, 의자도 딱 맞네요. 4개예요.

남 여보, 텔레비전 세트를 사야 할 것 같지 않아요?

여 텔레비전 없이 딱 좋은 것 같아요. 아이들한테도 좋고요.

남 하지만, 벽 중앙에 텔레비전이 한 대 있다면 완벽할 것 같아요. 소파에 앉아서 텔레비전을 볼 수도 있어요.

여 오, 그 소파는 매우 편안해 보이네요. 새 소파를 사지 않아도 돼서 좋네요.

해설 남자가 벽 중앙에 텔레비전이 걸려 있으면 완벽할 것 같다고 한 것으로 보아 실제로는 텔레비전이 없다.

어휘 **furnished** 가구가 비치된 **horizontal** 수평의, 수평선상의 **comfortable** 편안한

07 ③

해석 남 영화 보러 가자. 'Taken 2'가 상영 중이래.

여 정말 그러고 싶은데 그럴 수 없어.

남 왜 안 되는데?

여 내일 쪽지 시험을 보거든. 네가 들어올 때 막 공부하려던 참이었어.

남 제발! 그냥 쪽지 시험이잖아.

여 안 돼. 학점의 꽤 많은 부분을 차지한단 말이야.

남 나도 내일이 마감인 학기말 과제가 있어. 하지만 이 영화를 보고 싶어서 못 견디겠어. 집에 빨리 돌아올 거야. 가자.

여 미안한데, 이번에는 그럴 수 없을 것 같아. 대신 Steve에게 물어보지 그래?

남 오, 너 그거 몰랐어? 우리 요즘 말 안 해. 지난주에 농구하다가 크게 싸웠거든.

여 그랬어? 네가 먼저 사과하지 그래?

남 어림도 없는 소리! 그냥 DVD나 하나 빌려서 집에서 봐야겠다.

여 좋아. 그렇다면 시간을 좀 내 볼게. DVD 가게에 가자.

해설 극장 대신 DVD나 빌려 보자는 남자의 제안에 여자가 승낙했으므로 두 사람은 DVD가게에 갈 것이다.

어휘 **be about to** 막 ~하려던 참이다 **portion** 부분 **take up** 차지하다 **be on speaking terms** 말을 하다 **Not a chance!** 어림도 없는 소리!

08 ④

해석 남 Kelly, 오늘 밤에 바쁘니?

여 음, 무슨 일인데?

남 에세이 숙제를 끝냈는데 교정을 받을 필요가 있어서.

여 미안해. 오늘 밤에 Linda Baker 교수님을 만나기로 했어.

남 난 정말 너의 도움이 필요해. 교수님과의 약속을 연기할 가능성은 없니?

여 미안해. 다음 학기 장학금을 신청하려면 교수님한테 추천서를 받아야 해.

남 Baker 교수님이 그런 부탁을 할 수 있는 유일한 교수님이야?

여 응. 김 교수님께서는 다음주에 있을 세미나를 준비하느라 바쁘신데. Steve에게 부탁해 보는 게 어때?

남 Steve는 오늘 밤에 가족 모임이 있대.

여 괜찮다면 내가 내일 도와줄 수 있어.

남 오늘 밤 자정까지 선생님께 이 숙제를 이메일로 보내야 해.

해설 에세이 교정을 도와 달라는 남자의 부탁에 여자는 교수님께 추천서를 받으러 가야 하므로 도와 줄 수 없다고 하였다.

어휘 **be supposed to** ~하기로 되어 있다 **put off** 연기하다 **a letter of recommendation** 추천서 **family reunion** 가족 모임

09 ④

해석 남 남동생 생일 선물로 무엇을 살 거야?

여 아직 결정하지 못했어. 네가 하나 추천해 줄래?

남 그래. 가격대는 얼마를 생각해?

여 예상 경비는 대략 50달러야.

남 이 넥타이가 괜찮아 보이고 가격도 적당해. 너는 어때?

여 얼마인데?

남 35달러야.

여 좀 비싼 것 같아. 봐, 이게 아주 좋아 보이는데, 25달러밖에 안 해.

남 좋아. 잘 골랐어. 하지만 네 동생한테 줄 선물로 충분하지는 않은 것 같아. 그러니까 선물로 다른 걸 하나 추가하면 좋겠어. 와이셔츠 같은 거 말이야.

여 와이셔츠?

남 응. 이 와이셔츠는 20달러밖에 안 해.

여 좋아. 그 와이셔츠가 넥타이하고 잘 어울리는 것 같아. 둘 다 살게.

해설 넥타이 25달러, 와이셔츠는 20달러이므로 총 45달러이다.

어휘 **price range** 가격대 **budget** 예산, 예상 경비 **approximately** 대략 **reasonable** (가격이) 적당한 **go with well** ~와 잘 어울리다

10 ④

해석 여 자기소개를 해 주시겠어요?

남 네. 제 이름은 김지호이고 가족과 서울에서 살고 있습니다.

여 중국어를 할 수 있나요?

남 네, 저는 3년 동안 북경에 살았고 대학에서 중국어를 전공했어요.

여 일해 본 적이 있나요?

남 네, 'The China Daily'에서 편집자로 일했습니다. 제 기자로서의 경험이 이 훌륭한 방송국에서 일하는 데 도움이 될 것이라고 믿습니다.

여 물론이죠. 도움이 될 거예요. 마지막으로 하고 싶은 말이 있나요?

남 저를 뽑아주신다면, 후회하지 않으실 거예요. 저는 매우 활발하고 적극적인 사람이기 때문에 기삿거리가 있는 곳이면, 어느 곳이든, 어느 때이든 달려가겠습니다. 대단히 감사합니다.

해설 가족과 산다는 언급은 있지만 가족 관계에 대해서는 언급하지 않았다.

어휘 **introduce oneself** 자기소개를 하다 **major in** ~을 전공하다 **editor** 편집자 **broadcasting** 방송 **regret** ~을 후회하다 **outgoing** 외향적인

11 ③

해석 (뉴스 음악)

남 오늘의 YBC 스포츠 뉴스입니다. 최신 주요 뉴스입니다.

■ Kim은 400m 자유형에서 3분 30초를 기록했는데, 이는 그가 지난해에 수영 챔피언십에서 세운 3분 34초보다 4초 더 빠른 기록입니다. 이것은 또한 세계 신기록입니다. 현재 그는 세계 기록 보유자입니다.

■ 17살인 한국의 Yoon은 토요일에 중국에서 열린 국제 피겨 스케이팅 연맹 그랑프리 3차 대회에서 우승을 차지하였습니다.

■ 남한의 Lee는 일요일 한국 신기록을 세우며 3위를 차지했습니다. 그는 Utah에서 열린 세계 스피드 스케이팅 챔피언십에서 종전에 자신이 갖고 있던 남자 1,000m 1분 7.7초의 기록을 경신했습니다. 이상입니다. 잠시 후에 다시 돌아오겠습니다.

(뉴스 음악)

해설 Yoon은 3위를 한 것이 아니라 3차 대회에서 우승을 한 것이므로 내용과 일치하지 않는다.

어휘 **freestyle** 자유형 **world-record holder** 세계 기록 보유자 **the third round** 3차, 3회전 **national record** 국가 신기록

12 ③

해석 여 이것 보세요, 이것은 아주 유용한 표 같아요.

남 네, 18세 이상이면, 2년마다 혈압을 재야 해요.

여 계속 읽어 주시겠어요?

남 예. 20살이 넘으면, 5년마다 콜레스테롤 검사를 받아야 해요.

여 콜레스테롤이 고혈압의 원인이 될 수 있기 때문일 거예요.

남 그리고 35세가 넘으면, 2년마다 암 검사를 받아야 해요.

여 네. 암은 한국인 사망의 주요 원인 중 하나이죠.

남 또한, 45세 이상이면 3년마다 혈당 수치를 재는 것이 좋아요.

여 맞아요. 당뇨병도 주요 사망 원인 중 하나죠.

남 50세 넘으면, 1, 2년마다 눈 질환이 있는지 점검해 보아야 해요.

여 전부 기억할 수 있어요?

남 아뇨, 하지만 장수를 하려면 많은 노력이 필요하다는 것은 알겠네요.

여 동의해요.

해설 암 검사는 35세가 넘으면 2년에 한 번씩 해야 한다고 했으므로 표와 일치하지 않는다.

어휘 **blood pressure** 혈압 **detect** 탐지하다 **blood sugar** 혈당 **diabetes** 당뇨병

13 ⑤

해석 남 김 선생님, 지난 번 프로젝트에 대한 보수를 받으셨나요?

여 잘 모르겠어요. 은행 계좌를 확인해 보지 않았어요.

남 우리 프로젝트 담당자가 오늘 지불될 거라고 했어요.

여 2, 3일 연기될지도 몰라요. 경영진의 최종 승인을 받지 못했다고 들었거든요.

남 보수가 지급되었는지 확인할 수 있으면 좋을 텐데요.

여 은행에 전화를 해보는 게 어때요? 자동 응답기가 잔고를 알려줄 거예요.

남 그래요? 어떻게 하는 건지 알려 주세요.

여 먼저, 은행에 전화해서 녹음 내용대로 하세요.

남 그게 제가 필요한 정보를 얻기 위해서 해야 할 전부인가요?

여 **계좌 번호, 주민 등록 번호, 비밀번호를 알고 있어야 해요.**

해설 남자가 녹음 내용대로만 하면 되느냐고 물었으므로 응답은 "계좌 번호, 주민 등록 번호, 비밀번호를 알고 있어야 해요."라고 하는 것이 가장 적절하다. ① 물론이죠, 지난 프로젝트에 대한 보수를 지급할 거예요. ② 당신 계좌에 대한 정보는 기밀사항이에요. ③ 아뇨, 당신의 녹음이 만일의 경우에 필요할지도 몰라요. ④ 모르겠어요. 지금 바로 은행에 가 보는 게 어때요?

어휘 **account** 계좌 **confidential** 기밀의 **just in case** ~인 경우에 대비하여 **resident registration** 주민 등록 번호 **approval** 승인 **management** 경영진 **confirm** 확인하다 **balance** 잔고

14 ③

해석 남 왜 이렇게 거울을 오랫동안 쳐다보고 있는 거야?

여 나 쌍꺼풀 수술 받을까 생각 중이야.

남 왜? 네 눈 괜찮아 보이는데.

여 난 항상 좀 더 크고 예쁜 눈을 갖고 싶었어.

남 근데 너 알아? 남자들은 때론 수술해서 고친 것보다 여자들의 자연스러운 얼굴에 더 끌려.

여 그렇게 생각하니?

남 응. 게다가 난 성형 수술에 따른 부작용이 정말 많다고 들었어.

여 알아. 근데 성형 수술로 더 자신감이 생길 거고 스스로에 대해 더 좋게 생각할 거야.

남 네 말이 사실일 수도 있지만 나는 성형 수술의 긍정적 효과보다 부작용이 크다고 굳게 믿어.

여 모르겠다. 어쨌든 매력적인 눈을 갖는 것이 나의 최우선순위야.

남 **음, 그것에 대해 한 번 더 생각해 보는 게 나을 것 같아.**

해설 남자는 시종일관 성형에 부정적인 견해를 보이고 있으므로 쌍꺼풀 수술을 해서 예쁜 눈을 갖는 것이 우선순위라는 여자의 말에 대해 다시 한 번 생각해 보라고 말하는 것이 가장 적절하다. ① 나는 수술이 너에게 자신감을 줄 거라고 믿어. ② 부작용을 걱정할 필요 없어. ④ 음, 나도 쌍꺼풀 수술을 한다면 좋을 텐데. ⑤ 그럼 이왕 하는 김에 코 수술까지 하는 것이 어때?

어휘 **side effect** 부작용 **give a second thought** 다시 생각하다 **double eyelid** surgery 쌍꺼풀 수술 **while you are at it** 내친김에 **appearance** 외모, 모습 **alter** 바꾸다 **plastic surgery** 성형 수술 **confidence** 자신감 **sum** 합계 **attractive** 매력 있는 **top priority** 최우선순위

15 ④

해석 여 Peter는 작년에 대학을 졸업했다. 대학 졸업 후 바로 취업하고 싶었지만, 그러지 못했는데, 취업 전선이 매우 치열했기 때문이다. 그 이후로, 그는 공무원 시험을 준비해 왔다. 하지만 취업 전망은 여전히 희박하다. 경쟁률은 거의 100대1에 달했다. Peter는 매우 낙담해 있다. 그래서 Peter의 어머니는 자신감을 가지라고 Peter를 격려하고 싶다. 이런 상황에서, Peter의 어머니가 Peter에게 할 말로 가장 적절한 것은 무엇인가?

Peter's mother Peter, 절대 포기하지 마. 너는 해낼 거야.

해설 격려의 말이 되어야 하므로, 절대 포기하지 말고 해낼 수 있을 거라는 말이 가장 적절하다. ① 나는 네가 학교 선생님이 되면 좋겠어. ② 잘했어. 축하한다! ③ 나는 네가 공무원이 될 수 있을 거라고 생각하지 않아. ⑤ 너 다시 실패하면 어떻게 할래?

어휘 **civil servant** 공무원 **competitive** 경쟁적인 **civil service exam** 공무원 시험 **job prospect** 취업 전망 **slim** 희박한

16-17 ②, ③

해석 남 Nation 고등학교 캠퍼스 기숙사의 모든 신규 입주자를 환영합니다! 여러분이 여기에서 기숙사 생활을 시작하기 전에, 기숙사 관리 직원은 여러분이 몇 가지 중요한 수칙에 관해 잘 통지 받기를 바랍니다. 첫째, 기숙사 통금 시간은 월요일부터 금요일까지 밤 11시, 그리고 주말에는 낮 12시까지입니다. 이 시간에 현관문은 닫히게 되며 알람이 설정되어 있으므로 제 시간에 기숙사로 들어오기 바랍니다. 둘째로, 기숙사 관리 직원들은 여러분의 개인적인 사생활을 존중하기 위해 최선을 다하겠지만, 청결도와 실내 정비 보수를 위해 학생들의 방에 들어갈 권한을 가지고 있습니다. 마지막으로 알코올 소지나 음주 행위는 어떠한 상황에서도 금지됩니다. 질문이 있다면 기숙사 담당 부서로 연락바랍니다. 감사합니다.

해설 16 새로 입주하는 학생들을 위해 전반적인 기숙사 생활 수칙을 설명하는 글이다.
17 주말에는 낮 12시까지 기숙사에 들어와야 하는 것이지 퇴실해야 한다는 내용은 없다.

어휘 **resident** 거주자 **dormitory** 기숙사 **curfew** 통금 시간 **on time** 시간을 어기지 않고, 시간대로 **maintenance** 유지, 보수 **possession** 소유 **consumption** 섭취 **prohibit** ~을 금하다 **in any circumstances** 어떠한 일이 있어도

🎯 Dictation

01 double check my reservation
02 are you ready to
03 set a strict sleep schedule / Get rid of / cannot be emphasized
04 obesity is the root / a lack of nourishment
05 such a long time / I owe you / Keep the change

06 no lines on the wall / can sit on that couch
07 was about to study / had a huge fight last week / make some time
08 get it proofread / to apply for a scholarship / has a family reunion
09 have in mind / good enough for him
10 majored in Chinese / active and outgoing person
11 a new world record / broke his own record
12 have your blood pressure checked / one of the major reasons / living a long life
13 a couple of days / in order to get the information
14 thinking of getting / side effects in plastic surgery
15 graduated from college / his job prospects / to have confidence
16-17 be well informed / do our best to respect / is prohibited in any circumstances

14회 듣기 모의고사
p.84-85

01 ④	02 ①	03 ③	04 ⑤	05 ④	06 ③
07 ⑤	08 ①	09 ②	10 ②	11 ③	12 ⑤
13 ⑤	14 ①	15 ③	16 ③	17 ④	

01 ④

해석 남 룸메이트와 솔직하게 이야기를 해보는 것이 어때?
여 해봤는데 소용없었어. 그녀는 계속 한밤중에 시끄러운 소리를 내. 정말 그녀 때문에 미칠 것 같아.
남 뭔가 조치를 취해야겠다. 어떻게 할 계획이니?
여 관리인에게 항의해야 할 것 같아.

해설 남자가 이야기를 해도 계속 시끄러운 소음을 내는 룸메이트를 어떻게 할 것이냐고 물었으므로 관리자에게 항의할 것이라고 답하는 것이 가장 적절하다. ① 그녀와 이야기하는 것은 즐거웠어. ② 그녀는 내가 믿을 수 있는 유일한 사람이야. ③ 그녀에게 그렇게 한 이후로 그녀를 대할 수가 없어. ⑤ 그녀가 생각을 바꾸고 그렇게 하지 않겠다고 약속했어.

어휘 **heart to heart** 솔직한 **keep on -ing** 계속 ~하다 **make a noise** 시끄러운 소리를 내다 **drive ~ crazy** ~를 매우 화나게 만들다

02 ①

해석 여 나는 정말 호주에 가고 싶어. 거기에 가본 적이 있니?
남 아니, 아직 없어. 하지만 조만간 그곳에 있는 남동생을 방문하고 싶어.

여 정말? 남동생이 호주의 어느 지역에 사니?

남 지금은 시드니에 살아.

해설 남동생이 호주 어디에 사는지 물었으므로 시드니에 살고 있다고 답하는 것이 가장 적절하다. ② 내가 말할 수 있는 게 없어. ③ 그는 오래된 아파트에 살아. ④ 나는 어떤 장소든 괜찮아. ⑤ 호주는 야생 생물로 유명해.

어휘 be famous for ~로 유명하다 wildlife 야생 생물

03 ③

해설 남 안녕하십니까, 여러분. 올해의 베스트셀러인 'Making People Work for You'의 저자 Brian Berkley 씨를 오늘의 연사로 소개하게 되어 영광입니다. Berkley 씨는 성공한 작가가 되기 전에 월 스트리트에서 BCA Manhattan 은행의 최고 경영자로 15년 이상 일했습니다. 그는 또한 많은 유명 잡지와 전문지에 투자 및 개인 금융에 대한 수십여 개의 사설을 기고한 바 있습니다. 모두 따뜻한 박수로 Brian Berkley 씨를 맞아 주시기 바랍니다.

해설 "It's my honor to introduce today's speaker"와 "Let's all give a warm welcome to Mr. Brian Berkley."를 통해 연설자를 소개하는 것이 목적임을 알 수 있다.

어휘 author 작가 Chief Executive Officer(CEO) 최고 경영자 article 사설, 논설, 기사 invest 투자하다 finance 재무, 금융 journal 정기 간행물 warm welcome 환대

04 ⑤

해설 남 Sally, 해변을 봐! 온통 쓰레기가 널려 있어.

여 맞아. 앉아서 쉴 곳을 찾을 수가 없어.

남 저 플라스틱 컵, 사탕 껍질, 맥주병, 아이스크림 막대기를 봐. 아무도 여기를 청소하지 않는 것 같아.

여 아니야, 네가 잘못 알고 있는 거야. 아침 일찍 해변을 청소하는 수십 명의 청소부들을 봤어.

남 그래? 그럼 문제가 뭐라고 생각해?

여 내 생각에는 쓰레기를 버리는 사람들이 너무 많은 것 같아.

남 쓰레기통을 더 설치하면 어떨까?

여 일시적으로만 효과가 있을 거야. 해변에 너무 많은 행상인들이 돌아다니고 있어. 물을 제외한 다른 음식은 해변에서 먹지 못하게 해야 한다고 생각해.

남 너무 가혹한데. 너는 그것이 가능하다고 생각해?

여 규칙이 시행되고 그것을 따르도록 지키는 고용된 사람들이나 자원봉사자로 구성된 관리 요원들이 있다면 가능할 거라 생각해.

남 그래, 이 상황을 바꾸려면 뭔가 단호한 조치가 이루어져야 해.

해설 여자는 해변의 쓰레기 투기를 근절하기 위해 해변에서 물을 제외한 음식을 허용하지 말아야 한다고 말하고 있다.

어휘 candy wrapper 사탕 껍질 dozens of 수십의, 아주 많은 litterbug (휴지 등을 버려서) 공공장소를 어지르는 사람 install 설치하다 effective 효과적인 temporarily 일시적으로 vendor 행상인 roam 돌아다니다, 배회하다 harsh 가혹한 impose 시행하다 decisively 단호하게

05 ④

해설 남 오늘밤에 도둑이 들었다고 알고 있습니다. 무슨 일이 있었는지 말씀해 주시겠어요?

여 네, 물론이죠. 자고 있었는데 거실에서 큰 소리가 나는 것을 들었어요.

남 그리고 무엇을 하셨죠?

여 일어나서 조용히 아래층으로 갔어요. 그때 한 남자가 창문으로 나가는 것을 보았어요.

남 용의자의 인상착의를 설명해 주시겠어요?

여 네. 갈색 머리에 작은 체격이었어요. 얼굴은 잘 보지 못했지만 하얀 셔츠를 입고 있었어요.

남 그가 뭔가 훔쳐 갔나요?

여 음, 그게 아주 이상했어요.

남 무슨 말씀이죠?

여 그는 냉장고를 넘어뜨리고 음식을 모두 훔쳐갔어요!

해설 용의자의 인상착의, 도난당한 물건 등을 묻고 있으므로 남자는 경찰관이고 여자는 피해자임을 알 수 있다.

어휘 theft 도둑질 downstairs 아래층으로 describe 묘사하다 suspect 용의자 small build 작은 체격 run away with ~와 함께 도망가다 knock down ~을 쓰러뜨리다, 때려눕히다

06 ③

해설 여 여보, 테이블 세팅 끝냈어요? 손님들이 30분쯤 뒤에 올 거예요.

남 알아요. 하지만 제대로 테이블 세팅하는 법을 거의 잊어버렸어요.

여 그렇게 복잡하지 않아요. 접시를 놓는 것부터 시작해요. 그리고 포크들을 접시 바로 왼쪽에 놓아요. 샐러드용 포크, 그러니까 짧은 것이 접시에서 가장 멀리 놓여야 해요.

남 냅킨은 어디에 놓죠?

여 그건 포크 왼편에 두세요.

남 당신이 늘 하던 대로군요. 잔들은 어떻게 할까요?

여 물 잔과 와인 잔을 접시 약간 위 오른쪽에 두세요. 그럼 뭐가 남았죠?

남 음, 나이프와 숟가락들이 남네요.

여 나이프를 접시 바로 오른편에 날이 접시를 향하도록 두세요.

남 나이프 옆에는 뭘 놔야 해요? 짧은 숟가락 아니면 긴 숟가락?

여 짧은 것이 찻숟가락이에요. 나이프 바로 옆에 두세요.

남 알겠어요. 마지막 손질은 나 혼자 할게요.

해설 냅킨은 포크의 좌측에 둔다.

어휘 complicated 복잡한 place 놓다 furthest 가장 멀리 떨어진 slightly 약간 edge 날, 모서리

07 ⑤

해설 남 무슨 일이야? 걱정이 있어 보여.

여 이럴 수가! 가방을 집에 두고 왔어!

남 뭐라고? 농담이겠지!

여 아니야. 그리고 오늘 해야 할 일이 많은데.

남 돌아가서 가져 올 시간은 없니?

여 없어. 20분 후에 수업을 들어가야 해. 내가 쓸 수 있는 펜과 종이가 좀 있니?

남 미안, 없어. 하지만 도서관 자습실에서 구할 수 있을 거야.

여 그거 좋은 생각이다. 오, 여분의 USB 메모리는 있니? 오늘 오후에 생물학 보고서를 써야 해.

남 어디 보자. 그래. 여기 있어.

여 고마워! 넌 내 생명의 은인이야. USB 메모리는 토요일에 돌려줄게.

남 나한테 한 번 신세를 진거야. 또 보고서를 제출하지 않으면 Anderson 선생님께서 몹시 화를 내실 거야.

여 맞아.

해설 남자가 가방을 집에 놓고 온 여자에게 USB 메모리를 빌려주었다.

어휘 extra 여분의 biology 생물학 owe ~을 (…에게) 신세를 지다 submit 제출하다

08 ①

해석 여 안녕, Bill! 늦어서 미안해.

남 왜 늦었어, Maggie? 아니야, 기다려. 말하지 마. 알 거 같아. 알람이 안 울린 거야.

여 아니야. 그런 거 아니야.

남 어디 보자. 그럼 엘리베이터가 고장이 났거나 지난번처럼 헤어드라이어가 고장이 난 거야.

여 제발. 뭐가 문제야? 내가 미안하다고 했잖아.

남 알아. 하지만 이런 일이 항상 생기잖아. 난 항상 너를 기다려야 하잖아.

여 하지만 일부러 늦는 것은 아니야! 항상 이유가 있었다고!

남 알아, 알아. 그럼 이번에는 무슨 이유야?

여 버스가 고장 나서 걸어야 했어.

남 흠……. 더는 절대 늦지 마. 아무튼 점심으로 뭔가 먹자. 배고파 죽겠어.

해설 약속에 늦은 이유가 무엇인지 묻는 남자에게 여자는 버스가 고장이 나서 걸어오느라 늦었다고 대답하고 있다.

어휘 go off (자명종 등) 울리다 out of order 고장난 work 작동하다 mean 의도하다 break down 고장 나다 starve 굶주리다

09 ②

해석 남 안녕하세요. 무엇을 도와드릴까요?

여 자동차를 한 대 빌리려고요.

남 이 목록을 봐 주세요. 저희는 소형, 중형, 대형 자동차를 갖추고 있습니다. 이 소형차는 어때세요?

여 소형차는 저희에게 너무 작은 것 같아요.

남 몇 분이신가요?

여 저를 포함해서 다섯 명이에요.

남 그렇다면 이 대형차를 추천 드릴게요. 하루 이용 요금은 70달러입니다.

여 좀 비싸네요. 중형차가 좋겠어요. 이 파란 차는 어떤가요?

남 왜 차를 고르는 안목이 있으시네요. 하루에 50달러입니다. 얼마 동안 필요하신가요?

여 3일이요. 보험 패키지가 있나요?

남 네, 있어요. 저희 완전 보장 보험 패키지는 3일에 15달러만 추가로 내시면 됩니다.

여 좋네요. 그걸로 할게요. 여기 제 신용카드가 있어요.

해설 하루에 50달러인 자동차를 3일 간 빌리고, 3일 간의 보험료 15달러를 추가로 내야 하므로 여자가 지불할 금액은 165달러이다.

어휘 compact 소형의 full-size car 대형차 recommend 추천하다 rate 요금, 비용 have an eye for ~에 대한 안목이 있다 insurance 보험

10 ②

해석 남 방문 목적이 무엇입니까?

여 먼저 사업상 회의에 참석했다가 서울을 구경할 계획이에요.

남 어디에 머무르실 건가요?

여 시내의 Nexus 호텔에 머무를 거예요.

남 그리고 여행 가방에는 무엇이 들어있습니까?

여 그냥 개인적인 소지품이에요. 옷, 책 몇 권과 노트북 컴퓨터예요.

남 좋습니다. 모든 것이 이상 없습니다. 그런데 이번이 처음 방문이신가요?

여 음, 그렇기도 하고 아니기도 해요. 사실은, 저는 오래 전에 부모님이 서울에서 일하실 때 여기서 태어났지만 그때 이후로 첫 방문이에요.

남 그럼, 즐거운 여행하세요.

여 감사합니다.

해설 체류 기간에 대한 언급은 없다.

어휘 convention 회의, 집회 luggage (여행용) 휴대품, 여행 가방 belongings 소지품

11 ③

해석 여 다가올 여름을 위한 화끈한 액션을 원한다면 'No Escape'가 당신이 볼 영화입니다. Fernando Valenta의 차고, 때리고, 쏘면서 화면을 종횡무진하는 모습이 환상적입니다. 이 영화는 역사에 데이트 영화로 기록될 몇 안 되는 액션 영화 중 하나입니다. 여자들이 멋진 스페인 남자를 보고 한숨짓는 동안 남자들은 Valenta의 혈투에 환호할 수 있습니다. 줄거리는 FBI 요원인 Valenta가 악명 높은 마약단을 소탕하기 위해 벌이는 싸움에 관한 것입니다. 마약단의 아주 악한 두목과 벌이는 화끈한 대결이 있기까지 많은 싸움이 있다는 것을 의미합니다. 'No Escape'는 매일의 일상으로부터의 멋진 탈출구이자 근사한 여름 영화입니다. 놓치지 마세요.

해설 남녀 모두 좋아할 데이트용 영화라는 소개가 있지만 사랑 이야기가 있다는 언급은 없다.

어휘 upcoming 다가오는 blast ~을 격파하다 glory 기뻐하다 rampage 난폭한 행동 gorgeous 화려한 Spaniard 스페인 사람 sigh 한숨 쉬다 bring down ~을 죽이다, 파멸시키다 high-profile 세간의 이목을 끄는 explosive 폭발적인 showdown 대결 grind 힘들고 단조로운 일

12 ⑤

해석 여 박물관 운영 시간에 대해 말씀해 주시겠어요?

남 월요일부터 토요일까지는 오전 9시에서 오후 6시까지 운영합니다. 일요일에는 문을 닫아요.

여 고맙습니다. 박물관 내에서 사진을 찍는 데 플래시를 사용해도 되나요?

남 사진 촬영은 가능하지만 플래시 사용은 금지되어 있습니다. 음식이나 음료수도 안 됩니다.

여 오늘 모든 전시가 일반에 공개되어 있는지 아시나요?

남 동관 건물은 공사 중이지만 나머지 전시실은 개관 중입니다.

여 감사합니다. 입장료는 얼마인가요?

남 성인은 15달러, 아동은 5달러이고 사진이 있는 신분증을 지참한 노인과 학생은 8달러입니다.

여 입장료를 지불한 다음에 나갔다가 다시 들어갈 수 있나요?

남 네. 하지만 티켓을 제시해야 합니다. 또 궁금한 것이 있나요?

여 아뇨. 정말 감사합니다.

해설 신분증이 아니라 티켓을 제시하면 재입장할 수 있다.

어휘 **operation** 운영 **forbid** 금지하다 **prohibit** 금지하다 **exhibit** 전시(품); 전시하다 **under construction** 공사 중인 **gallery** 전시실 **admission** 입장(료) **senior citizen** 노인

13 ⑤

해설 남 그래서 졸업한 다음에는 뭐 할 거야?

여 음, 돈을 좀 저축해 놓았는데 정말 여행을 가고 싶어.

남 잘됐구나. 정말 흥미롭게 들리는 걸!

여 그래. 그리고 직업을 구하고 내 방을 얻을 계획이야.

남 부모님 집에서 살지 않을 거니?

여 응, 일하기 시작한 다음에는 부모님께 의존하고 싶지 않아.

남 무슨 말인지 알겠다. 네가 부러운 걸.

여 넌 어때? 무슨 계획이 있어?

남 나도 직업을 구할 거야. 하지만 부모님과 함께 살 거야.

여 왜 그렇게 하기로 결정했어?

남 난 빈털터리인 데다가 학자금 대출도 갚아야 해.

해설 직업을 구한 다음에도 부모님과 함께 살겠다는 남자의 말에 여자가 이유를 물었으므로 돈도 없고, 대출도 갚아야 한다는 응답이 가장 적절하다. ① 난 경제학에 흥미가 없어. ② 난 일찍 은퇴하고 싶어. ③ 난 부모님과 사이가 몹시 나빠. ④ 난 지난달에 여자 친구랑 헤어졌어.

어휘 **economics** 경제학 **retire** 은퇴하다 **in trouble** 곤경에 빠져서 **break up** 헤어지다 **broke** 돈이 없는 **pay off** (빚 따위를) 다 갚다 **loan** 대출 **get a job** 직장을 구하다 **depend on** ~에 의존하다

14 ①

해설 여 오늘 밤에 뭐하세요? 밖에 나갈래요?

남 오, 미안하지만 안 돼요. 늦게까지 일할 거예요. 이 보고서를 끝내야 하거든요.

여 음, 내일 밤은 어때요? 그때도 뭔가 할 건가요?

남 아뇨. 뭘 할 계획이에요?

여 뮤지컬을 보려고 해요. 제가 뮤지컬을 아주 좋아하는 걸 알잖아요.

남 제목이 뭐죠?

여 세계적으로 유명한 뮤지컬 '캣츠'예요. 보러 갈래요?

남 물론이죠. 가고 싶어요! 하지만 이번에는 제가 표를 사게 해 주세요. 제가 낼 차례예요.

여 그러면 제가 저녁을 살게요.

해설 남자는 함께 보러 갈 뮤지컬 티켓을 자신이 사겠다고 말했으므로 그러면 저녁은 자신이 사겠다는 대답이 가장 적절하다. ② 표는 어디서 구하셨어요? ③ 당신의 보고서를 어디서도 찾을 수가 없어요. ④ 고양이는 정말 놀라운 동물이죠. ⑤ 콘서

트 표가 매진이었어요.

어휘 **treat** 대접하다 **incredible** 놀라운 **sold out** 매진된 **turn** 차례, 순서

15 ③

해설 여 어느 날 Mary는 자명종의 건전지가 다 되는 바람에 7시 30분에 일어났다. 그녀는 1교시 수업에 늦지 않으려고 보통 7시 45분에 버스를 타는데, 그녀가 막 버스 정거장에 도착했을 때 버스가 떠나고 있는 것을 보았다. 다음 버스는 8시까지 오지 않았고 그녀는 1교시 수업에 늦고 말았다. 설상가상으로 선생님께서는 수업 초반에 쪽지 시험을 치르셨고 그녀는 늦는 바람에 시험을 치지 못했다. 선생님은 화가 났고 그녀를 교무실로 불렀다. 교무실에서 그녀는 아침에 있었던 일을 말씀 드리고 정중하게 사과한 후 다음 날 쪽지 시험을 치를 수 있게 해 달라고 부탁했다. 이 상황에서 Mary의 선생님이 Mary에게 할 말로 가장 적절한 것은 무엇인가?

Mary's teacher 미안하지만, 두 번째 기회는 없단다.

해설 Mary는 지각 때문에 놓친 시험을 다음 날 다시 보게 해 줄 것을 부탁하였다. 이에 대해 선생님이 할 수 있는 대답을 고르도록 한다. ① 그렇게 화 낼 필요 없어. ② 충분한 수면을 취하는 것이 중요해. ④ 네 학업이 많은 진전을 보이는구나. ⑤ 너는 선생님께 좀 더 주의를 기울여야겠구나.

어휘 **improvement** 진전, 향상 **pay attention to** ~에게 주의를 기울이다 **in time** 제시간에, 늦지 않고 **get annoyed** 화내다, 골치 아프다 **sincerely** 성실히, 진심으로 **apologize** 사과하다

16-17 ③, ④

해설 여 얼마나 많은 학생들이 빈속으로 학교에 가는지 아십니까? 우리 시에서만 2천 명이 넘는 학생들이 고통을 겪고 있습니다. 배가 고프면 틀림없이 집중해서 공부하기 어려울 것입니다. 다행히 시 정부는 아이들이 잘 먹을 수 있도록 '무료 학교 급식' 프로그램을 시작하였습니다. 18세 미만이면 누구나 무료 아침, 점심을 먹을 수 있습니다. 하지만 이런 무료 식사는 아직 일부 학교에서는 시행되지 않고 있습니다. 학부모들은 학교에 전화를 걸어 자녀가 언제 무료 식사를 할 수 있는지 문의할 수 있습니다. 아이들은 이제 방학에도 아침과 점심을 먹을 수 있습니다. 과거에는 학기 중에만 식사가 제공되었습니다. 많은 가정이 아이들을 위한 이러한 특별한 도움에 매우 기뻐하고 있습니다. 저소득층 가정의 학생이 무료 식사 프로그램에 등록해야만 했으나 이제는 모든 아이들이 참여할 수 있습니다. 시 정부는 이 무료 식사 프로그램에 연간 5백만 달러 이상을 투자합니다. 아이들이 배불리 먹는 것은 매우 중요합니다. 영양이 충분히 공급될 때 육체와 정신이 더 잘 활동합니다. 이 프로그램 덕분에 많은 아이들이 필요한 음식을 일 년 내내 먹을 수 있습니다.

해설 16 무료 급식 프로그램에 대한 전반적인 내용을 소개하고 있다. ⑤의 경우에는 프로그램은 이미 시작된 것이므로 맞지 않다.

17 소득이나 방학 여부에 관계없이 모든 아이들을 대상으로 하는 프로그램이다.

어휘 **concentrate** 집중하다 **make sure** ~을 확실히 하다 **well-fed** 영양이 충분한 **low-income** 저소득 **participate** 참여하다 **nourish** 영양을 주다 **all year long** 일 년 내내

01 have a heart-to-heart chat / drives me crazy

02 would like to visit

03 It's my honor to introduce / Let's all give a warm welcome

04 you got it wrong / I think it is possible

05 Could you tell me / brown hair and a small build / He knocked down

06 how to set the table / sharp edge facing the plate

07 left my bag / time to go back and get it / You owe me

08 I bet I know / I don't mean to be late

09 too small for us / have any insurance packages

10 attend a business convention / is this your first visit

11 upcoming summer / as a date movie / plenty of battles

12 flash photography is forbidden / can I come back in

13 after graduation / stay at your parents' house

14 work late / let me pay for the tickets

15 late for her first class / take the quiz

16-17 not served at some of the schools / all kids can participate

15회 듣기 모의고사
p.90-91

01 ④	02 ①	03 ②	04 ③	05 ⑤	06 ③
07 ②	08 ③	09 ④	10 ⑤	11 ③	12 ⑤
13 ③	14 ③	15 ②	16 ②	17 ④	

01 ④

해석 남 Jenny, 어서! 서둘러! 핼러윈 파티에 늦을 거야.
여 미안. 잠깐만 기다려줘. 옷을 거의 다 입었어.
남 왜 이렇게 오래 걸렸어?
여 핼러윈 의상을 결정할 수가 없었어.

해설 시간이 오래 걸린 것에 대한 이유를 묻고 있으므로 핼러윈 의상을 결정할 수가 없어서 오래 걸렸다고 답하는 것이 가장 적절하다. ① 우리가 늦을 줄 알았어. ② 사탕을 얻으러 가고 싶지 않아. ③ 파티에 가는 데 거의 한 시간이 걸렸어. ⑤ 핼러윈은 미국의 전통 명절이야.

어휘 **trick or treating** 과자 안 주면 장난 칠 테야 (핼러윈 때 아이들이 집집을 다니며 하는 말) **decide on** ~에 대한 결정을 내리다

02 ①

해석 여 Steve, 어디 가니?

남 축구 경기 보러 월드컵 경기장에 가고 있어.
여 오, 오늘 국가 대표팀 예선 경기가 있지, 맞지?
남 응. 호주랑.

해설 국가 대표팀 예선 경기가 있지 않느냐는 질문에 호주를 상대로 한 경기가 있다고 답하는 것이 가장 적절하다. ② 나는 우리 국가 대표팀이 정말 자랑스러워. ③ 월드컵은 4년마다 열려. ④ 맞아. 우리에게 중요한 경기였다고 생각해. ⑤ 맞아. 머리는 축구에서 중요한 신체 부위야.

어휘 **head for** ~를 가다 **national team** 국가 대표팀 **preliminary game** 예선전

03 ②

해석 남 여생을 같이 보내고 싶은 이상형을 찾기를 진심으로 고대하고 있습니까? 여기 당신이 소개팅에서 해야 될 사항과 하지 말아야 할 가장 중요한 사항들이 있습니다. 첫째, 작은 예의가 큰 도움이 될 수 있다는 것을 기억하십시오. 데이트 상대를 위해 문을 잡아 주는 것이나 의자를 꺼내 주는 것은 기본적인 예의입니다. 또한 친근한 제스처나 상대의 질문에 다정한 답변을 함으로써 상대에게 관심이 있다는 것을 보여주세요. 둘째, 소개팅 장소에 늦지 말고 제 시간을 지키세요. 그리고 데이트 상대를 만날 때 끊임없이 자신에 관한 이야기를 함으로써 상대를 지루하게 하지 마세요. 한숨 돌리고 상대에게도 자신에 관해 말할 기회를 주세요.

해설 소개팅에 나가 성공하기 위해 해야 할 일과 하지 말아야 할 일에 관해 조언해 주는 글이다.

어휘 **dreamboat** 이상형 **do's and dont's** 주의사항 **blind dating** 소개팅 **go a long way** 큰 도움이 되다 **date** 데이트 상대 **intimate** 친밀한 **cordial** 다정한 **punctual** 시간을 엄수하는 **come up for air** 한숨 돌리다

04 ③

해석 남 우리 지금 가야 해.
여 너무 일러. 아직 회의까지 두 시간이나 남았어.
남 교통 체증을 고려해야 해. 금요일 밤에는 항상 차가 막혀.
여 알지만 지금 출발하기에는 너무 이른 것 같지 않니?
남 난 그렇게 생각하지 않아.
여 하지만 만약 차가 막히지 않으면, 우리는 거의 한 시간 반을 기다려야 해. 이게 시간 낭비라고 생각하지 않니?
남 전혀 아니야. 만약 일찍 도착하면 기다리면서 서류를 다시 한 번 읽어 볼 수 있어. 우리는 우리의 여유 시간을 매우 효율적으로 사용할 수 있어.
여 하지만, 그곳에 가는 데 보통 30분밖에 걸리지 않아. 30분이면 서류를 다시 읽어 볼 수 있어.
남 그럼, 이렇게 생각해 봐. 교통 체증이 심하면, 우리는 제시간에 도착할 수 없거나 심지어 그들을 오랫동안 기다리게 만들 수도 있어. 회의에 늦는 것은 아주 무례한 일이라는 것을 너도 알잖아.
여 나를 믿어. 안 늦을 거야.

해설 여자는 너무 일찍 약속 장소에 가는 것이 시간 낭비라고 생각해서 조금 더 늦게 떠나기를 바라고 있다.

어휘 **consider** 고려하다, 여기다 **heavy traffic** 교통 체증 **absolutely** 절대적으로 **efficiently** 효율적으로 **get stuck in** ~에 갇히다 **rude** 무례한

05 ⑤

해석 남 실례합니다. 이곳의 담당 직원이신가요?

여 예. 어떻게 오셨나요?

남 음, 어제 이 통지서를 받았어요.

여 무슨 내용인데요?

남 저는 지금 Graduate Tower B에 살고 있는데, 다음주 금요일 전에 거기서 나가야 한다고 해서요.

여 이름이 뭐죠?

남 Kevin Hong이에요.

여 Kevin Hong. 맞네요. 5월 7일 전에 나가야 해요.

남 왜 그런가요?

여 알다시피, 이번 학기가 거의 끝났고, 현재 기숙사 주거 현황을 재조정해야 하거든요.

남 그렇군요. 그러면, 저는 어디로 이사해야 하죠?

여 음, 캠퍼스 밖의 아파트를 얻거나, 우리 기숙사의 다른 방에 지원을 하셔야 해요.

남 흠, 생각할 시간이 좀 필요해요. 언제까지 답변을 드려야 하나요?

여 빠를수록 좋아요.

해설 기숙사 관리사무소에 와서 변동 사항을 문의하는 상황이므로 여자는 기숙사 관리 직원, 남자는 기숙사 입주 학생이다.

어휘 **notice** 통지서 **readjust** 재조정하다 **off-campus** 캠퍼스 밖의 **dormitory** 기숙사

06 ③

해석 여 와, 이 차선은 차가 정말 많네.

남 우리 콘서트에 늦었어. 서둘러서 주차할 곳을 찾아야 해.

여 반대편 차선은 비었어. 저기에 주차하면 되겠다.

남 아니, 그럴 수 없어. 주차 금지 구역이야.

여 그럼 주차장을 찾아보자. 오, 저기 주차장이 있어.

남 저기도 주차할 수 없어. 문 앞에 '만차' 표지판이 있어.

여 하지만 이상하네, 한 군데 빈 곳이 보이는데.

남 맞아. 나도 봤어. 문 옆에 있는 관리인에게 물어보자.

여 저기 주차할 수 있었으면 좋겠다.

해설 관리인이 문 옆에 있다고 했는데 주차장 가운데에 있으므로 대화의 내용과 일치하지 않는다.

어휘 **no-parking zone** 주차 금지 구역 **garage** 차고 **janitor** 관리인, 경비

07 ②

해석 남 Jane, 내가 부탁했던 것을 했어요?

여 예. 성공적으로 했어요.

남 도와줘서 고마워요.

여 오, 별 거 아니에요. 비록 약간 어려움이 있었지만 말이죠.

남 무슨 어려움이었는데요?

여 대학원 지원서에 전공을 표기하지 않으셨더군요.

남 아, 그랬어요? 그래서 어떻게 했어요?

여 대학에서 영문학을 전공하신 것을 알고 있었기 때문에, 지원서에 그것

을 표기했어요.

남 고마워요. 그 사항이 누락된 줄 몰랐어요.

여 그것 말고는 지원서에 문제는 없었어요.

남 잘 했어요. 당신 덕분에 대학원에 지원할 수 있게 되었군요.

여 시험에 합격하시면, 한턱 내셔야 해요.

남 물론이죠, 그럴게요.

해설 남자는 여자 덕분에 대학원에 지원할 수 있었다고 하였고, 여자가 지원서를 접수하는 과정에 있었던 일에 대해 이야기하고 있으므로 여자에게 부탁한 일은 대학원 지원서의 대리 접수임을 알 수 있다.

어휘 **specialty** 전공 **application form** 지원서 **mark** 표기하다 **leave out** 빠뜨리다, 빼놓다 **treat** 대접

08 ③

해석 남 와우, 드디어 중간고사가 끝났어. 시험은 어땠어?

여 괜찮았어. 근데 지금 완전 지쳤어.

남 힘내! James가 오늘 밤 자신의 집에서 파티를 열잖아. 기억 안 나?

여 잠깐, 맞아. 나 완전히 잊고 있었어.

남 어떻게 그걸 잊을 수 있니? 그래서 오늘 밤에 못 온다고?

여 못 갈 것 같아. 식료품을 가져다주러 할머니 댁에 들러야 하거든.

남 너랑 정말 재미있는 시간을 보내고 싶었는데.

여 주로 우리 엄마가 하시는데, 엄마가 오늘 야간 근무라서 나에게 부탁하셨어.

남 오빠한테 대신해 달라고 부탁해 보지 그래?

여 오빠는 내일이 마감인 보고서가 있어서 바쁜대.

남 이런, 그럼 다음에 놀자!

해설 어머니가 야간 근무를 해서 대신 여자가 할머니 댁에 식료품을 가져다주어야 한다.

어휘 **exhausted** 지친, 피곤한 **slip one's mind** 깜빡 잊다 **stop by** 들르다 **night shift** 야간 근무

09 ④

해석 여 김 선생님, 여름 방학은 어떠셨어요?

남 음, 정신없이 바쁜 여름을 보냈어요.

여 오, 왜요?

남 무엇보다도, 3주 동안 하루에 5시간씩 수업을 해야 했어요.

여 3주 간 하루에 5시간이요? 월요일부터 금요일까지였나요?

남 예. 또한, 제 동료 중 한 사람의 요청으로 듣기와 읽기 문제를 만들어야 했어요.

여 얼마나요?

남 처음에는 60문제라고 했는데, 점점 늘어났어요. 70문제, 80문제……. 결국 100문제를 만들었어요.

여 와, 엄청난 양의 작업이네요! 하지만 그 작업에 대한 보수는 물론 받으셨을 거라 생각해요.

남 물론이죠. 보수가 없다면 하지 않았을 거예요.

여 맞아요. 일에 보수가 따르는 것은 당연하죠.

해설 하루 5시간씩 일주일에 5일, 총 25시간을 3주 간 했으므로 총 75시간의 수업을 했고, 출제한 문제의 수는 총 100문제였다.

어휘 **hectic** 정신없이 바쁜 **request** 요구, 요청 **comprehension** 이해력, 파악력 **get paid** 보수, 급여를 받다 **rewarding** 보상이 따르는

10 ⑤

해석 남 엄마, 내년도 학교생활에 변화가 있어 걱정이에요.
여 어떤 변화인지 말해보렴.
남 우선, 1교시를 7시 반에 시작할 예정이래요.
여 너한테 너무 이른 것 같구나.
남 네. 저는 그렇게 일찍 학교에 갈 자신이 없어요. 또 내년에 교복이 바뀔 거래요.
여 정말?
남 네. 이미 학생과 선생님의 설문 조사를 바탕으로 새 교복을 결정했어요.
여 그럼, 나는 새 교복 비용을 걱정해야 하는구나. 그리고 다른 것은?
남 학생회실을 지하로 옮길 거예요.
여 너는 지하가 마음에 들지 않는구나?
남 물론 마음에 들지 않아요. 더 나쁜 건, 내년에 학생회 예산이 삭감된다는 거예요.
여 저런. 설상가상이구나.

해설 등록금 인상에 대한 언급은 없다.

어휘 **period** 교시 **survey** 설문 조사 **expense** 비용 **student union** 학생회 **basement** 지하 **what's worse** 한 술 더 떠서, 더 나쁜 것은 **reduce** ~을 줄이다 **When it rains, it pours.** 안 좋은 일은 한꺼번에 일어난다. 설상가상

11 ③

해석 여 감기를 예방하는 가장 좋은 방법은 이미 감기에 걸린 사람들과 가까운 접촉을 피하고, 손을 철저하게 규칙적으로 씻고, 입과 얼굴을 만지지 않도록 하는 것입니다. 항균성 비누는 감기 바이러스에 아무 효과가 없으며, 바이러스 입자를 제거해 주는 것은 손을 씻는 기계적인 행위입니다. 일반 감기는 아주 다양한 종류의 바이러스에 의해 생기게 되며, 이는 재생산을 하는 와중에 그 구조를 꽤 빈번하게 변형시켜서 끊임없이 변화하는 바이러스 형태를 낳게 됩니다. 그래서 성공적인 면역은 불가능합니다.

해설 항균성 비누는 감기 바이러스에 아무 효과가 없다고 언급하고 있다.

어휘 **existing** 기존의 **thoroughly** 철저하게 **anti-bacterial** 항균성의 **particle** 입자 **alter** 바꾸다 **immunization** 면역

12 ⑤

해석 여 Ryan, 당신 도움이 필요해요.
남 뭐죠?
여 저에게 이 상용 기호들을 설명해 주시겠어요?
남 그러죠. 첫 번째 부호는 'at'이라고 읽어요. 이것은 상업적으로 '~의 비율로'라는 구문의 약자로 이용돼요.
여 그렇군요. 두 번째 표기 '%'는 저도 익숙하네요. 백분율을 나타내요, 그렇죠?

남 물론이죠. 흔한 기호예요. 그리고 세 번째는 '번호'를 나타낼 때 사용되는 것이죠.
여 오, 이건 '번호'를 나타내는군요. 알겠어요. 그리고 네 번째 것은 교재에서 많이 봤어요. '저작권'을 나타내죠.
남 맞아요. 저작권 기호예요.
여 하지만 마지막 것은 잘 모르겠어요. 'R'은 무슨 의미인가요?
남 음. 미국에서 17세 미만의 아이들이 영화를 볼 때는 어른이 함께 동반해야 한다는 것을 나타낸 'R'등급이 매겨진 몇몇 영화들이 있어요.
여 도와주셔서 고마워요.

해설 대화의 'R'은 미국의 영화 상영 등급 'R'에 관한 것이므로 표의 내용과 일치하지 않는다.

어휘 **commercial mark** 상용 부호 **abbreviation** 약자, 축약 **copyright** 저작권

13 ③

해석 여 실례합니다. 제 남편이 어제 이 상의를 드라이클리닝했는데요.
남 예, 그 재킷 기억나요. 무슨 문제가 있나요?
여 남편 말이 아직 안 좋은 냄새가 난대요.
남 그럴 리가요. 분명히 드라이클리닝을 했는데요.
여 당신이 직접 하셨나요?
남 아뇨. 실은 제 조수가 했어요.
여 그러면 어떻게 그렇게 확신할 수 있죠? 남편이 하루 종일 냄새가 나서 견딜 수 없었대요.
남 상의를 옷장 같은 곳에 오랫동안 넣어 두셨다면, 드라이클리닝을 해도 냄새는 잘 사라지지 않는다는 것을 이해하셔야 해요.
여 그러면, 냄새를 없애려면 어떻게 해야 하나요?
남 **몇 시간 동안 밖에 걸어 놓으세요. 하루면 충분할 겁니다.**

해설 여자가 냄새를 없애기 위한 방법을 물었으므로, 남자는 그 방법을 제시하는 것이 가장 적절하다. ① 드라이클리닝이 그것을 할 수 있는 유일한 방법인 것 같아요. ② 창문을 열고 탁한 공기를 좀 내보내요. ④ 죄송합니다. 제가 코가 막혀서 냄새를 맡을 수 없어요. ⑤ 가능한 한 빨리 몇몇 세탁물을 드라이클리닝 맡기는 것이 좋겠어요.

어휘 **dry-clean** 드라이클리닝을 하다 **assistant** 조수 **wardrobe** 옷장 **remove** 제거하다

14 ③

해석 여 아빠, 제가 심은 이 꽃 좀 봐주시겠어요?
남 오, 별로 좋아 보이지 않는구나. 무슨 일이니?
여 전혀 모르겠어요. 전 이걸 정말 정성 들여 돌봤어요. 심지어 영양제도 줬고요.
남 그러면 물을 주는 것에 문제가 있었던 것이 틀림없구나. 얼마나 자주 물을 줬니?
여 삼사일에 한 번이요.
남 음, 그게 문제였구나. 이런 종류는 기껏해야 한 달에 한 번 물을 주면 된단다.
여 정말요? 왜요?
남 왜냐하면 이것은 척박한 토양에서 잘 자라는 내건성 식물이거든. 만약 물을 너무 많이 주면 토양이 너무 비옥해져서 살 수가 없단다.

여 아, 이해했어요. 그럼 물을 덜 주면 살 수 있을까요?

남 아마도 지켜봐야겠는걸.

여 **아, 때론 지나침이 나쁜 것이군요.**

해설 너무 물을 많이 줘서 식물의 상태가 좋지 않게 된 경우이므로 너무 지나친 것이 때론 좋지 않다는 말을 하는 것이 이어질 딸의 말로 가장 적절하다. ① 걱정 마세요, 아빠. 그것은 살 거예요. ② 그것이 곧 죽는다니 믿을 수 없어요. ④ 비옥한 토양이 식물에게 더 좋다고 생각해요. ⑤ 아빠가 좀 더 주의를 기울여야 했어요.

어휘 **rich soil** 비옥한 토양 **have no clue** 전혀 모르다 **nutritional supplement** 영양제 **water** 물주다 **drought-tolerant plant** 내건성 식물 **thrive** 잘 자라다 **condition** 상태, 조건 **poor soil** 척박한 토양

15 ②

해석 남 Brady와 Sarah는 같은 고등학교의 동료 교사이다. 사실 그들은 가까운 친구이자 이웃이기도 하다. 대개 Brady는 아침 일찍 학교에 온다. 그는 부지런한 사람이다. 하지만 Brady는 Sarah가 훨씬 더 부지런하다는 사실을 알고 깜짝 놀란다. Sarah는 아침 6시 반에 학교에 오는 것이 자신의 습관이라고 말한다. 맙소사! 아침 6시 반이라니! Brady는 마음속으로 "도대체 그녀는 몇 시에 일어나는 거지?", "도대체 그녀는 아침 6시 반에 학교에 와서 무엇을 하는 걸까?"라고 생각한다. 지금, Brady는 Sarah에게 왜 그렇게 아침 일찍 학교에 오는지 물어본다. 이 상황에서, Sarah가 Brady에게 할 말로 가장 적절한 것은 무엇인가?

Sarah **Brady, 일찍 일어나는 새가 벌레를 잡는 법이에요.**

해설 왜 그렇게 아침 일찍 학교에 오냐고 물었으므로 아침 일찍 오는 것과 관련된 일찍 일어나는 새가 벌레를 잡는다는 말이 가장 적절한 답변이 된다. ① 지렁이도 밟으면 꿈틀거려요. ③ 유유상종이죠.(같은 깃털을 가진 새들이 함께 모인다.) ④ 산 넘어 산이죠. ⑤ 솜씨 없는 일꾼이 연장 탓하죠.

어휘 **coworker** 동료 **close** 친밀한, 가까운 **diligent** 근면한, 성실한 **think to oneself** 마음속으로 생각하다 **in the world** 도대체 **on earth** 도대체

16–17 ②, ④

해석 여 승객 여러분, 주목해 주십시오! 저는 수석 승무원입니다. 뉴욕에서 인천 국제공항으로 가는 저희 Boeing 747기는 현재 디트로이트 시 상공 35,000피트를 비행 중입니다. 하지만 심한 폭풍우와 거센 바람 때문에 더 이상 앞으로 나아갈 수 없으며 저희는 비행을 중단하고 디트로이트 메트로폴리탄 공항에 비상 착륙할 수밖에 없습니다. 착륙을 하는 동안 안전벨트를 단단히 매시고, 모든 짐은 앞 사람의 좌석 밑에 놓아주시기 바랍니다. 디트로이트의 현지 시간은 오후 3시 30분이며 기온은 화씨 70도입니다. 추후 공지가 있을 때까지 모든 승객은 디트로이트 메트로폴리탄 공항 내에서 대기해 주시기 바랍니다. 날씨가 호전되자마자 다시 이륙할 것입니다. 승객 여러분의 불편을 최소화하기 위해 최선을 다하겠습니다. 감사합니다.

해설 16 기상 악화로 인해 비상 착륙하게 되었음을 승객들에게 공지하는 내용이다.
17 모든 짐은 앞 사람의 좌석 밑에 넣으라고 했다.

어휘 **altitude** 고도 **have no choice** 선택의 여지가 없다 **temporarily** 임시로 **land** 착륙(하다) **luggage** 짐, 수화물 **underneath** ~의 밑에 **take off** 이륙하다 **do one's best** 최선을 다하다 **minimize** 최소화하다

◎ Dictation

01 give me a minute

02 heading for

03 to finding your dreamboat / drawing a chair / Come up for air

04 consider traffic jams / can have a chance / really rude to be late

05 got this notice / to readjust our current housing / time to consider

06 look for a garage / ask the janitor

07 didn't mark your specialty / give me a treat

08 feel exhausted / should stop by / be busy working on

09 five class hours a day / as a request / got paid for the work

10 too early for you / got to worry / will be reduced

11 to prevent a cold / have no effect / during reproduction

12 these commercial marks / it indicates / only allowed to see them

13 still smells bad / put it in a wardrobe

14 have no clue / only once a month / if I water it less

15 a diligent person / When in the world / comes to school so early

16-17 at an altitude of / but to temporarily land / as soon as the weather improves

◎ 16회 듣기 모의고사
p.96-97

01 ③	02 ④	03 ③	04 ④	05 ③	06 ⑤
07 ②	08 ①	09 ③	10 ⑤	11 ⑤	12 ④
13 ⑤	14 ③	15 ③	16 ①	17 ⑤	

01 ③

해석 남 오, John Grisham의 새 소설을 읽고 있군요. 어떤가요?

여 지금까지는 아주 훌륭해요. 눈을 뗄 수 없어요. 읽어 보셨어요?

남 예. 사실은 얼마 전에 다 읽었어요. 결말이 완벽해요.

여 **말하지 마세요! 저도 거의 다 읽어가요.**

해설 남자가 여자에게 소설의 결말에 대해 말하려고 하는 상황이므로 여자의 대답으로 ③이 가장 적절하다. ① 물론이죠! 당신에게 그것을 빌려 줄 수 있어요. ② 그것이 그렇게 빨리 끝나는지 몰랐어요. ④ 언젠가 저 스스로 그에게 말하고 싶어요. ⑤ 제발 그 소설의 제목을 말해주세요.

02 ④

해석 여 Annie 이야기 들었니? 아주 끔찍해.

남 아니, 못 들었어. 그녀에게 무슨 일이 있었니?

여 그녀의 아버지께서 어젯밤에 돌아가셨어. 분명히 Annie는 얼이 빠져 있을 거야.

남 오, 저런! Gordon 씨가 돌아가셨단 말이야?

해설 친구의 아버지가 돌아가셨다는 말을 듣고 놀라면서 다시 확인하는 말을 하는 것이 가장 적절하다. ① 그녀의 아버지가 곧 나아지기를 바라. ② 너 그가 언제 돌아올지 아니? ③ 난 왜 그가 그녀에게 그랬는지 이해가 안 돼. ⑤ 물론이지. 이번 달에 세 번째야.

어휘 **you bet** 물론 **pass away** 죽다, 돌아가시다 **devastated** 엄청난 충격을 받은

03 ③

해석 남 7월 한 달 동안 우리는 헌혈 운동을 벌일 것입니다. 시의 헌혈 차량이 다음 장소들을 방문할 것입니다. 7월 첫째 주에는 Hill Top 쇼핑센터에 헌혈 차량이 있을 것입니다. 7월 12일부터 22일까지는 Metropolitan Cineplex 앞에서 헌혈을 할 수 있습니다. 7월 마지막 주에는 헌혈 차량이 State가에 있는 Civic Center Plaza 앞에 위치할 것입니다. 시간은 오전 10시부터 오후 5시까지입니다. 모든 참가자에게 주스와 쿠키가 제공됩니다. 아시다시피 여름에는 헌혈이 감소합니다. 여러분들의 지원에 진심으로 감사드립니다.

해설 헌혈 차량이 위치할 예정인 장소들을 알려주면서 많은 사람들이 헌혈에 참여해줄 것을 부탁하는 내용이다.

어휘 **drive** 추진, (조직적인) 운동 **donate** 기부하다 **station** 배치하다

04 ④

해석 남 여보, 당신은 이 일을 믿을 수 없을 거예요!

여 뭔데요? 무슨 일이에요?

남 복권에 당첨됐어요!

여 정말이에요? 믿을 수가 없군요!

남 그래요! 당첨된 건 이번이 처음이에요.

여 그런데, 당첨금이 얼마인가요?

남 100달러에 당첨되었어요!

여 100달러라고요? 지금까지 당신이 복권에 쓴 돈이 얼마인지 알아요?

남 확실하지는 않지만 아마 2000달러 정도일 거예요.

여 수지가 너무 맞지 않는다고 생각하지 않아요? 나라면 복권 사는 것을 그만두겠어요.

해설 복권에 당첨이 되었지만 복권 구입에 쓴 돈에 비해 당첨금이 너무 작아 손해라고 했으므로 ④가 여자의 의견으로 가장 적절하다.

어휘 **lottery** 복권 **incredible** 믿을 수 없는, 놀라운 **unprofitable** 이익이 없는, 수지가 맞지 않는

05 ③

해석 여 무엇을 도와드릴까요?

남 통장 잔액을 확인하고 싶어요.

여 예. 계좌 번호를 알려 주시겠어요?

남 381335예요.

여 잔액은 201달러예요.

남 알겠어요. 아버지에게 좀 돈을 부쳐달라고 했는데, 그 돈이 들어 왔는지 알고 싶어요.

여 죄송하지만 최근에 손님 계좌에 입금된 돈은 없어요.

남 오, 이런. 내일 집세를 내야 하는데. 어떻게 해야 하죠?

여 글쎄요. 오늘 저희 컴퓨터에 문제가 좀 있어서요. 그러니까 나중에 전화해서 다시 확인하시는 것이 어때요? 아니면 다시 오세요. 5시까지 영업을 해요.

남 알겠어요, 감사합니다.

여 천만에요.

해설 통장의 잔액을 확인하고, 송금된 돈의 입금을 확인하는 것으로 보아 은행원과 고객 사이의 대화임을 알 수 있다.

어휘 **balance** (통장의) 잔액 **wire** 송금하다 **deposit** 예금, 입금

06 ⑤

해석 남 우리 가족사진을 좀 가지고 왔어. 너한테 보여 주고 싶어서.

여 어디 볼까. 오, 정말 멋진 가족이구나!

남 이분들이 나의 조부모야. 지난달에 할아버지 생신 파티를 했어.

여 초를 보니 할아버지께서 70세이신 것을 알 수 있겠다. 하지만 연세에 비해 아주 젊어 보이셔.

남 맞아. 가운데 있는 이 여자 아이가 내 여동생 Carol이야.

여 이 개가 골든 레트리버 맞니?

남 응, 이름은 Clarence야. 우리가 사진을 찍을 때 항상 앞에 앉아.

여 아주 귀엽네. 이 다른 사진 속의 이분들이 부모님이시니?

남 그래, 그리고 이게 나야. 머리를 짧게 자르기 전이지. 알프스로 스키 여행을 갔었어.

여 네가 스노보드를 탈 줄 아는지 몰랐는데.

남 그때 처음으로 스노보드를 타봤어. 그래서 엄청나게 넘어지고 굴렀지.

해설 머리를 짧게 자르기 전에 찍은 사진이라고 했으므로 머리카락이 길어야 한다.

어휘 **for one's age** ~의 나이에 비해서 **golden retriever** 골든 레트리버(영국 원산의 조류 사냥개) **tumble** 넘어지다

07 ②

해석 남 Melissa, 무슨 일이야? 아주 초조해 보이는구나. 잠깐 가만히 좀 있을래?

여 아니, 안 돼. 어떤 사람의 자동응답기에 메시지를 남기기 위해 용기를 내려고 노력하는 중이야.

남 자동응답기가 무섭니?

여 응. 나는 몸이 얼어붙고 혀가 굳어버려. 그런데 왜 그런지 정말 모르겠어. 나는 그냥 기계에 대고 이야기하는 것이 싫어.

남 내가 대신 해줄까?

여 고맙지만 이건 내가 스스로 해야 할 것 같아.

남 할 말을 써서 읽는 것이 어때?

여 그거 좋은 생각인데. 좋아. "안녕하세요, 저는 Melissa입니다. 세놓은 아파트 때문에 전화했습니다……."

남 전화하는 동안 나는 나가 있을까?

여 말도 안 되는 소리하지 마. 그냥 앉아서 행운이나 빌어줘! 좋아, 이제 준비됐어. 시작한다!

해설 자동응답기에 메시지 남기는 것을 어려워하는 여자에게 남자는 미리 메시지를 적어두었다가 읽으라고 충고한다. 여자가 메시지를 다 적은 상황이므로 이제 전화를 걸 것이다.

어휘 stand still 가만히 있다 get up the nerve 용기를 내다 freeze up 얼다, 얼어붙다 tongue-tied 말을 못하는 on one's own 스스로

08 ①

해석 (전화벨이 울린다.)

남 911 구조대입니다.

여 도와주세요! 제발, 도와주세요!

남 진정하시고 정확히 무슨 문제인지 말씀해 주세요.

여 15층과 16층 사이에 다섯 명과 개 한 마리가 갇혀 있어요.

남 건물의 이름을 아십니까?

여 예, East가에 있는 Glass Tower에서 전화하는 겁니다.

남 비상 단추를 누르셨습니까?

여 예, 하지만 작동이 되지 않았어요. 그리고 저는 개 알레르기가 정말 심해요. 호흡하는 데 많은 어려움을 겪을 수도 있어요.

남 걱정 마세요. 개로부터 가능한 한 멀리 떨어져 있도록 하세요.

여 지금 우리를 이곳에서 꺼내주셔야 해요!

남 이미 구조대와 구급차를 보냈습니다. 잘 들으세요. 문을 열려고 하지 마세요.

여 알겠어요. 오, 제발 서둘러주세요.

해설 층과 층 사이에 갇혀 있어서 꺼내달라고 부탁하고 있으며, 문을 열지 마라는 지시를 하는 것으로 보아 엘리베이터 안에 갇혀 있는 상황임을 알 수 있다.

어휘 emergency 비상사태, 위급 calm down 진정하다, 차분해지다 stuck 움직일 수 없는, 꽉 끼인 allergic to ~에 알레르기가 있는 rescue team 구조대

09 ③

해석 남 제가 도와 드릴까요?

여 예, 롤러블레이드를 찾고 있어요.

남 찾으시는 특별한 스타일이 있나요?

여 틀이 쇠로 되어있는 것을 사고 싶어요. 그리고 좀 짙은 색이 좋겠어요.

남 이 짙은 감색은 어떠세요? 한번 신어 보세요.

여 아주 딱 맞습니다. 얼마인가요? 할인 판매 중이라는 것을 보았습니다.

남 맞습니다. 원래 80달러였지만 20퍼센트 할인해서 64달러입니다.

여 가격이 아주 적당하군요.

남 이것은 두 개를 사면 하나는 20%가 아니라 50%를 할인해 드려요.

여 그거 좋군요! 두 켤레를 사겠습니다.

해설 80달러인데 20퍼센트 할인해서 64달러이지만, 두 켤레를 살 경우 하나는 절반 가격인 40달러에 살 수 있으므로 64달러에 40달러를 더한 104달러를 지불해야 한다.

어휘 rollerblade 롤러블레이드 particular 특별한, 특정한 try on ~을 입어 보다, 신어 보다 reasonable (가격이) 적당한, 비싸지 않은

10 ⑤

해석 여 Jeff, 콘서트는 어땠니?

남 입장하지 못했어.

여 설마! 오랫동안 줄을 선 줄 알았는데.

남 그랬지, 내 차례가 오기 전에 표가 매진되었어. 아주 끔찍했지. 줄을 선 채 10시간을 허비했어.

여 서 있었다고?

남 실은, 잠깐씩 앉아있기도 했지. 음악을 듣고 자고 하면서 시간을 보냈어.

여 잤다고? 침낭을 가지고 있었니?

남 그래. 다행스럽게도 35달러에 할인 판매하는 정말 좋은 침낭을 바로 얼마 전에 샀거든.

여 다음 콘서트에 가려고 하지는 않겠구나.

남 물론, 갈 거야! 토요일 오전 10시에 입장권 판매를 할 거야. 그래서 금요일 아침부터 그곳에 있을 계획이야.

여 너 제정신이 아니구나! 너를 이해할 수가 없어.

해설 표를 사기 위해 줄을 서서 10시간 이상을 기다렸다고 했다.

어휘 stand in line 줄을 서다 be sold out 매진되다 kill time 시간을 보내다 go on 계속되다 figure out 이해하다

11 ⑤

해석 여 Steve! 있잖아, 오늘 저녁에 우리 오페라 보기로 했었지?

남 못 간다고 말하려는 것은 아니겠지, 그렇지? 벌써 자리를 예약해 놓았단 말이야.

여 음, 할 일이 너무 많아서 8시까지 일을 해야 해.

남 오, Susie! 내가 이 오페라를 얼마나 많이 기대했는지 알잖아.

여 미안해, 하지만 어쩔 수가 없어. 다른 날 저녁은 어때?

남 정말? 언제가 편하겠니?

여 다음 목요일로 해볼까? 그게 더 좋을 것 같아.

남 좋아. 틀림없이 표가 남아 있을 거야. 지금 바로 확인해 볼게.

여 미안해. 대신 오늘 간식은 내가 살게. 뭘 먹고 싶니?

남 도넛을 먹고 싶어. 고마워.

해설 여자는 오늘 남자에게 간식을 사주기로 한 것이지 오페라를 보는 날 저녁을 대접하는 것은 아니다.

어휘 arrange 정하다, 조정하다 make up to ~ ~에게 보상[변상]하다

12 ④

남 가 볼만한 문화행사가 있어?

여 응. 그 중에서 한군데 가볼까 생각 중이었어.

남 특별히 하나 추천해 줄래?

여 3월 1일에 마술쇼가 있을 거야.

남 흥미롭구나. 어디에서 해?

여 Berkeley 극장. Golden Gate 공원에서 첫째 토요일에 벼룩시장도 열려.

남 그림 전시회나 영화는 어때?

여 응, 6일에 현대미술관에서 일본 판화 전시회가 열려. 또, 그 다음 날에

는 Fort Mason센터에서 독립영화제가 있어.

남 나는 일본 미술은 잘 몰라.

여 이것이 마음에 들지는 모르겠지만, Lincoln 극장에서 9일, 금요일에 '로미오와 줄리엣'을 해.

남 그거 좋은데. 함께 갈래?

여 물론.

해설 일본 판화 전시회가 6일에 있고 그 다음 날 독립영화제를 한다고 했는데 8일로 표시되어 있으므로 대화의 내용과 일치하지 않는다.

어휘 **recommend** 추천하다. 권하다 **in particular** 특히, 특별히 **flea market** 벼룩시장 **exhibit** 전시(회); 전시하다 **be familiar with** ~에 익숙하다. ~을 잘 알다

13 ⑤

해석 (전화벨이 울린다.)

남 Steven's Shoes입니다. 무엇을 도와드릴까요?

여 안녕하세요. 웹 사이트를 통해서 신발을 한 켤레 구입했는데 문제를 발견했습니다.

남 무엇이 문제인가요?

여 신발을 신자마자 신발 한 짝에 달린 리본이 떨어졌습니다.

남 오, 접착이 잘 되지 않았던 모양이군요. 죄송합니다. 다른 걸로 교환해 드리겠습니다.

여 사실은 전액 환불을 원합니다.

남 다시 한 번 생각해 보시겠어요? 그 신발은 정말 저렴한 상품입니다.

여 아뇨, 환불해 주세요.

남 좋습니다. 즉시 신용카드 결제를 취소해 드리겠습니다.

여 감사합니다. 그럼 신발은 어떻게 돌려드리지요?

남 신발을 가지러 배달원을 보내겠습니다.

해설 신발을 판매자에게 되돌려줄 방법을 묻고 있으므로 ⑤가 가장 적절한 응답이다. ① 걱정 마세요. 제가 당신을 집까지 태워다 드릴게요. ② 왜냐하면 지금 당신이 영수증을 가지고 있지 않기 때문입니다. ③ 상품에 큰 결함이 있을 때만 가능합니다. ④ 시내에서 버스나 지하철을 탈 수 있습니다.

어휘 **defect** 결함 **come off** 떨어지다. 빠지다 **attach** ~을 붙이다 **reconsider** 재고(再考)하다.

14 ③

해석 남 짐 정리는 다 되었니, Tracy?

여 거의. 물어봐 줘서 고마워.

남 그래서, 어떤 아파트야?

여 부엌이 따로 있는 원룸 형 아파트야.

남 위치가 어딘데?

여 Riverside 지역의, 직장 근처야.

남 오, 잘 됐네. 아파트의 어떤 점이 마음에 들어?

여 실내 디자인이 잘 되어 있고 아주 아늑해. 그리고 큰 수영장이 있어.

남 너한테 딱 맞는 것 같구나. 한번 볼 수 있도록 언제 초대해.

여 물론이지. 곧 집들이 파티를 할 거야.

해설 새 아파트로 이사를 한 여자에게 자신을 초대해줄 것을 부탁했으므로 ③이 가장 적절한 응답이다. ① 고마워. 내일 그것을 한 번 볼게 ② 그럴 필요 없어. 내가 이미 점검했어. ④ 너를 포함해서 네다섯 명쯤 있을 거야. ⑤ 다음 주까지 이 아파트로

이사 오고 싶어.

어휘 **settle in** 이사하다 **studio** 침실, 부엌, 욕실이 하나인 아파트 **separate** 분리된 **cozy** 아늑한, 포근한

15 ③

해석 남 토요일 저녁인데 부모님이 주말 동안 오빠 집을 방문 중이어서 Susan은 집에 혼자 있다. 침대에서 책을 읽다가 Susan은 방금 잠이 들었다. 12시가 조금 지났는데 아래층의 갑작스런 소음에 그녀는 잠이 깬다. 누군가 조용히 걸어 다니는 소리가 들린다. 그녀는 경찰에 전화를 걸고 싶지만 너무 무서워서 소리를 내지 못한다. 어떻게 해야 할까 생각하는데 그녀는 계단의 발자국 소리를 듣는다. 그 다음 그녀의 침실 문이 천천히 열린다. 그녀의 아버지와 어머니이다. 그들은 예정보다 더 일찍 돌아온 것이다. 이 상황에서 Susan이 부모님에게 할 말로 가장 적절한 것은 무엇인가?

Susan 무서워 죽을 뻔했어요. 왜 전화하지 않았어요?

해설 집에 혼자 있는데 한밤중에 이상한 소리가 들려서 겁에 질려 있다가 결국 부모님이 일찍 돌아오셨다는 것을 알게 되었다. 따라서 무서웠다는 이야기와 함께 왜 미리 전화를 하지 않았느냐고 묻는 것이 가장 자연스럽다. ① 엄마, 저 왔어요. 뭔가 먹고 싶어요. ② 저 소리 들으셨어요. 경찰에 신고해요. ④ 오빠는 어디 있어요? 저도 오빠가 정말 보고 싶어요. ⑤ 왜 저를 안 깨우셨어요? 저 학교에 늦었어요.

어휘 **scared** 깜짝 놀란, 겁먹은 **downstairs** 아래층으로 **frightened** 무서워하는, 겁먹은 **footstep** 발자국, 발소리 **ahead of** ~보다 앞서서

16–17 ①, ⑤

해석 여 문자 채팅과 메신저 서비스가 온라인상으로 다른 사람들과 소통을 하는 방법으로 빠르게 선호 받고 있다. 이런 형태의 의사소통은 사람들이 정보를 공유하고 외국어와 세계 문화를 거의 실시간으로 배우게 해준다. 게다가 그것은 다른 나라의 사람들과 우정을 쌓는 것을 도와줄 수 있다. 하지만 반대편에 있는 사람이 어떤 사람인지 정말로 모르기 때문에 인터넷으로 친구를 찾을 때 조심하고 숙고해야 한다. 온라인 채팅을 할 때는 언제나 별명을 사용하고 나이, 주소, 실명, 다니는 학교의 이름과 같은 개인 정보를 절대로 밝히지 마라. 또한, 온라인으로 아는 사람을 직접 만나는 것은 위험할 수 있다. 하지만 만나고 싶으면 반드시 공공장소에서 만나고 친구나 가족과 함께 가도록 하라. 끝으로, 자신이 위험하다고 느껴지면 경찰에 연락을 하라. 다른 사람들과 채팅하는 것은 당신이 조심한다면 재미있고 교육적인 활동이 될 수 있다.

해설 **16** However 이하에 이 글의 목적이 나온다. 인터넷을 통해서 친구를 사귀는 경우 주의해야 할 점에 대해서 이야기하고 있다. ① 온라인으로 친구를 사귀는 것에 대해 충고하려고 ② 온라인 어학 교육을 홍보하려고 ③ 개인 정보 유출에 대해 경고하려고 ④ 새로운 소셜 네트워크 서비스를 광고하려고 ⑤ 보이스 피싱을 처리하는 방법을 교육하려고

17 컴퓨터 통신을 통해 접촉하는 사람에게 자신이 다니는 학교를 밝히지 말라고 했지 재학 중인 학교를 확인하라고 한 것은 아니다.

어휘 **instant messaging** 네트워크 상에서 실시간으로 메시지나 파일을 주고받는 것 **real time** 실시간으로 **give out** 공개하다, 발표하다, 말해버리다 **acquaintance** 아는 사람 **in person** 직접, 몸소

01 How do you like it / take my eyes off

02 It's terrible / passed away

03 visit the following locations / The last week of the month / will be served to

04 I won the lottery / how much you have spent on / if I were you

05 check my balance / wire me some money / call us later to check again

06 I want to show them / looks quite young for his age / in the other picture / stood on a snowboard

07 You look so nervous / afraid of answering machines / writing your message down / wish me luck

08 five people and a dog stuck here / push the emergency button / sent a rescue team

09 I prefer rather dark colors / That's quite reasonable

10 wasted ten hours standing in line / try to get into the next concert / I can't figure you out

11 arranged to see an opera / How about another night / To make it up to you

12 any cultural events worth going to / Where is that taking place / I'm not familiar with

13 I found something wrong with them / must have been poorly attached / cancel your credit card payment

14 Are you all settled in / what do you like about your apartment / Invite me over sometime

15 her parents are visiting her brother / after hearing a sudden noise downstairs / Wondering what to do

16-17 favored ways of communicating with others online / they can help people establish friendships / never give out personal information / It can be very dangerous to meet online acquaintances in person

17회 듣기 모의고사
p.102-103

01 ④	02 ①	03 ④	04 ②	05 ④	06 ③
07 ①	08 ③	09 ③	10 ③	11 ④	12 ⑤
13 ④	14 ③	15 ⑤	16 ③	17 ④	

01 ④

해석 남 와! 아주 건강해 보이는군요. 어디에서 그렇게 선탠을 했어요?
여 플로리다에서 휴가를 보내고 막 돌아왔습니다. 일광욕을 하면서 그냥 쉬는 것이 정말 좋았어요.

남 누구와 함께 갔나요?
여 **남편과 시댁 식구하고 갔어요.**

해설 휴가를 보내고 온 사람에게 누구와 함께 갔는지 물었으므로 응답으로 ④가 가장 적절하다. ① 소설을 몇 권 가지고 갔어요. ② 저는 그곳에 사는 친구가 없어요. ③ 그건 가족 휴가로 완벽해요. ⑤ 천둥 번개가 치면서 비가 왔어요.

어휘 **in-law** 인척(姻戚, 혼인에 의하여 맺어진 친척) **lightning** 번개 **suntan** 볕에 그을음, 선탠

02 ①

해석 여 Daniel! Lisa 좀 봐. 그녀의 드레스가 매우 이상해.
남 그렇지 않은 것 같은데. 내가 보기에는 그냥 괜찮은 것 같아.
여 농담하는 거야? 유행에 뒤쳐진 것 같지 않니? 저 스타일은 몇 년 전에 지나갔어.
남 **왜 그래. 그녀에게 잘 어울리는데.**

해설 괜찮아 보이는 옷을 유행이 지났다고 비판하고 있으므로 응답으로 ①이 가장 적절하다. ② 그녀가 언제 돌아왔는지 모르겠어요. ③ 그러면 그것을 그녀에게 빌려주는 게 어때? ④ 이제 네가 왜 그것을 사고 싶어 하는지 알겠어. ⑤ 응, 그녀는 옷에 너무 많은 돈을 소비해.

어휘 **behind the times** 유행에[시대에] 뒤져서 **go out** 사라지다. 쇠퇴하다

03 ④

해석 여 안녕하세요, 여러분. 저는 운동 프로그램 책임자 Jenny Stewart입니다. 이 대학교에는 모든 운동 시설이 캠퍼스의 동북쪽에 있습니다. 미식축구, 축구, 럭비 또는 야구에 사용되는 여섯 개의 다목적 운동장이 있습니다. 또한 네 개의 농구 코트와 실내 하나, 실외 하나, 두 개의 수영장이 있습니다. 또한 건강한 몸을 갖고 유지하는 데 필요한 모든 운동 설비를 갖춘 최신 피트니스 센터가 있습니다. 우리는 여러분이 강한 뼈와 근육을 발달시키는 것을 돕고 싶습니다. 이제 여러분의 질문에 기꺼이 답을 해드리겠습니다.

해설 대학교에 있는 운동장, 농구장, 수영장, 헬스장 등의 체육 시설을 소개하기 위한 담화이다.

어휘 **coordinator** 조정자, 책임자 **facility** 시설 **multipurpose** 다목적의 **athletic** 운동의, 체육의 **get in shape** 좋은 몸 상태(몸매)를 유지하다

04 ②

해석 남 긴급사태는 어디서나 언제나 일어날 수 있습니다. 모든 사람이 긴급사태에 대비하는 것이 중요합니다. 위급 상황의 신고 전화번호는 911입니다. 하지만 당신은 도움을 청하기 위해 그 전화를 걸 준비가 되어 있습니까? 911에 전화를 걸 때는 말을 명확하게 해야 합니다. 겁먹지 않도록 하십시오. 첫째, 문제가 무엇인지 설명하십시오. 그 다음, 문제가 어디에서 발생했는지 당신이 누구인지 말하십시오. 주소를 잘못 말하면 긴급구조대가 그곳에 도착하는 데 더 오랜 시간이 걸린다는 것을 의미합니다. 긴급구조를 필요로 하는 사람의 이름을 알려주십시오. 그밖에 다른 질문에 대답을 하십시오. 모든 정보를 알려주었다는 확신이 들 때까지 전화를 끊지 마십시오.

해설 비상전화에 전화를 할 때 효과적인 구조가 이루어질 수 있도록 통화하는 방법을 알려주고 있다.

어휘 **panic** 공황을 일으키다. 겁에 질리다 **stay on the line** 계속 통화하다

05 ④

해석 남 이봐, Carol, 저 남자 좀 봐요.

여 가득 찬 바구니를 들고 있는 남자 말인가요? 저 사람은 자신이 무슨 짓을 한다고 생각하는 걸까요?

남 모르겠어요. 하지만 누군가 뭐라고 말해 줘야겠어요.

여 조심해야 해요. 소량 계산대 줄에서 나오라고 하자 싸움을 건 사람에 대한 이야기를 들었어요.

남 하지만 저 줄은 5개 이하의 물건을 산 사람만을 위한 것이잖아요.

여 예, 맞아요. 하지만 낯선 사람을 대할 때에는 조심해야 해요. 화를 낼지도 몰라요.

남 저 표지판을 보지 못했을지도 몰라요. 우리가 저 사람에게 가서 좋게 이야기할 수도 있을 것 같은데요.

여 관리자를 부르는 것은 어떨까요?

남 관리자가 오기 전에 저 사람 계산이 끝날 거예요.

여 음, 그럼, 저 남자 차례가 되었을 때 계산원이 어떻게 하는지 봅시다.

남 저 사람이 표지판을 보지 못한 거라면 저 사람을 다른 줄 뒤로 가서 기다리게 하는 것은 정말 공평하지 못해요. 가서 이야기할래요.

해설 남자는 많은 물건을 구입한 사람이 소량 전용 계산대 줄에 서 있는 것을 보고 가서 말해 주겠다고 했다.

어휘 **watch out** 조심하다 **express line** 빠른 줄, (슈퍼마켓의) 소량 구매자용 계산대 **deal with** 다루다, 대하다 **cashier** 출납원, 회계원

06 ③

해석 여 자, 만찬용 접시의 가운데에 냅킨을 올려놓는 것부터 시작하겠어요. 더 큰 접시를 말하는 겁니다.

남 좋아요. 이제 뭘 하나요?

여 물 컵을 놓아야 합니다. 접시 위, 약간 오른쪽에 놓으세요.

남 이렇게 말인가요?

여 맞습니다. 이제, 여기 이 작은 접시는 빵을 놓기 위한 것입니다. 만찬용 접시 위 왼쪽에 놓으세요.

남 알겠습니다. 다음은 뭔가요?

여 은식기입니다. 이 칼을 만찬용 접시 오른쪽에 놓으세요. 그 다음 숟가락을 칼 오른쪽에 놓으세요.

남 이렇게 말인가요?

여 잘 했어요. 이제 접시 왼쪽에 먼저 이 큰 포크를 놓으세요. 그건 만찬용 포크입니다. 그리고 그 왼쪽에 이 더 작은 포크를 놓으세요. 그건 샐러드용입니다. 아주 잘했어요!

남 고마워요, Riley 부인. 아주 큰 도움이 되었어요!

해설 작은 포크가 왼쪽, 큰 포크가 오른쪽에 놓여야 한다.

어휘 **silverware** 은그릇, 은식기류

07 ①

해석 (전화벨이 울린다.)

남 여보세요, Benson Software 소비자 상담실입니다.

여 안녕하세요, 저는 Lakeside 슈퍼마켓의 Judy Williams입니다. 지난 주에 보내신 CD-Rom 때문에 전화 드렸습니다.

남 오, Williams 씨. 그 제품에 무슨 문제가 있습니까?

여 충분한 수량을 보내지 않은 것 같습니다.

남 오, 저런. 죄송합니다. 몇 개를 받으셨나요?

여 50개를 받았는데, 저희는 150개를 주문했습니다.

남 잠깐만요, 주문을 확인해보겠습니다. 저, 우리 기록에 의하면 50개를 주문하신 것 같은데요.

여 오, 정말인가요? 아마 착오가 있는 것 같군요. 틀림없이 150개를 주문했는데요.

남 Williams 씨, 착오가 있었던 점 사과드립니다. 가능한 한 빨리 100개를 추가로 보내드리겠습니다.

여 대단히 감사합니다. 불편을 끼쳐드려서 죄송합니다.

남 별 말씀을요.

해설 주문한 수량의 상품이 배달되지 않아서 여자는 확인을 하기 위해 전화를 했고 남자는 모자라는 수만큼의 상품을 다시 보내기로 했다.

08 ③

해석 여 안녕, Robert! 대본은 어떻게 되어가니?

남 오, Laura, 안녕. 그게 문제가 좀 있어. 우리 연극의 결말을 어떻게 할 것인지 결정을 못하겠어.

여 반전이 필요하다고 생각하지 않아? 그것이 없으면 좀 따분할 것 같아.

남 그래, 하지만 그럴듯한 반전을 만들어내기에는 시간이 충분하지 않아.

여 제출 마감 날짜가 언제인데?

남 수요일이야. 참가 신청서와 대본을 Crawford 선생님에게 제출해야 해.

여 어쩔 수 없을 것 같은데. 너 문자 왔네. 누가 보낸 거야?

남 Crawford 선생님이야. 봬! 우리 운 좋다.

여 어디 보자. 신청 마감 날짜가 금요일로 연기되었네. 이제 이틀이 더 생겼어.

남 연극 대회에서 우승할 좋은 징조인 것 같아.

여 나도 그러면 좋겠어.

해설 연극대회에 참가하기 위한 연극대본 제출 마감 날짜가 얼마 남지 않아 걱정을 하다가 마감 날짜가 연기되어서 기뻐하는 상황이다.

어휘 **surprise ending** 반전(反轉) **dull** 따분한 **deadline** 기한, 마감 시간 **turn in** 제출하다 **entry** 참가, 출전, 출품물

09 ③

해석 남 안녕하세요. 도와드릴까요?

여 디지털 캠코더를 사려고 합니다.

남 잘 오셨습니다. 저희는 다양한 디지털 캠코더를 판매하는데 사실 지금 20퍼센트 할인 판매를 하고 있습니다.

여 잘됐군요. 망원 렌즈가 좋은 캠코더를 찾고 있습니다.

남 이건 어떻습니까?

여 음, 이것도 좋지만 화면이 더 큰 것을 원합니다.

남 그럼 이건 어떤가요?

여 500달러군요. 이 가격이 할인 전 가격인가요, 네?

남 예, 하지만 그 모델은 10퍼센트밖에 할인이 안 됩니다. 최신 모델 가운데 하나거든요.

여 좀 비싸지만 마음에 듭니다. 좋아요, 이걸로 하겠습니다.

해설 원래 가격이 500달러인데 최신 모델이기 때문에 20퍼센트가 아닌 10퍼센트 할인이 적용된다. 따라서 450달러를 지불해야 한다.

어휘 **quality** 질좋은, 고급의 **latest** 최신의, 최근의

10 ③

해석 여 이봐, Nick! 자동차를 사는 데 너의 충고가 필요해.

남 좋아. 어떤 종류의 차를 사고 싶은데?

여 아마도 중형 승용차 아니면 SUV야. 결정을 못하겠어.

남 SUV가 더 실용적이기 때문에 나는 SUV를 권하겠어. 내 말은 이동할 때 많은 것을 실을 수 있다는 거야.

여 SUV의 연료 효율이 승용차에 비해 아주 낮다고 하던데.

남 그건 사실이지만, SUV가 더 강력하기 때문이야. 그리고 안전 요인들도 고려해야 해.

여 SUV가 승용차보다 더 안전하다는 말이니?

남 그래. SUV가 보통 차체가 더 튼튼하고 안전장치가 더 많아.

여 하지만 SUV는 승용차보다 더 비싸. 나는 예산이 빠듯하단 말이야.

남 그렇다면 중고차를 사는 건 어때? 내 친구 중 하나가 중고차 거래를 해. 그가 좋은 가격에 해줄 거야.

여 오, 정말? 그거 좋겠는데!

남 그에게 너한테 연락을 하라고 말할게.

해설 가격(more expensive), 안전성(safer), 연료 효율(fuel efficiency), 적재 능력 (carry a lot of stuff)은 언급되었지만 '승차 인원'은 언급되지 않았다.

어휘 **SUV** 스포츠용 자동차(Sport Utility Vehicle) **make up one's mind** 결정하다 **practical** 실용적인, 실질적인 **travel** 이동하다 **budget** 예산(안), 가계 **feature** 특징 **get in touch with** ~와 연락하다

11 ④

해석 남 안녕하세요. 와주셔서 감사합니다. 오늘 저녁 저는 아프리카 대륙의 음악을 간단히 소개해 드리려고 합니다. 아프리카 서부에서 기원한 다양한 양식의 음악이 있습니다. 여러분이 들으셨으면 하면 한 가지 예가 juju입니다. Juju는 나이지리아 전통 음악에 바탕을 두고 있지만, 북으로만 연주되지 않고 기타와 건반 악기도 사용됩니다. Juju는 1920년대에 시작되어, King Sunny Adé와 같은 국제적으로 유명한 연주자들 덕분에 지금도 인기가 있습니다. Juju는 '던지기'또는 '던진 물건'을 뜻하는 Yoruba어 단어이고, 연주할 때 청중은 보통 juju 음악가들에게 지폐 세례를 퍼붓습니다.

해설 국제적으로 유명한 연주자들 덕분에 지금도 인기가 있다.

어휘 **continent** 대륙 **originate from** ~에서 생기다, 시작되다 **Nigerian** 나이지리아의 **renowned** 유명한 **shower ~ with ...** ~에게 … 세례를 퍼붓다

12 ⑤

해석 남 안녕하세요, 주차 허가증을 받고 싶습니다. 9번 주차구역이 이용 가능한가요?

여 예, 그렇습니다. 성함이 어떻게 되시나요?

남 Steve Carlson입니다.

여 그리고 주소와 전화번호는요?

남 Washington가 3251번지이고 555-0103입니다.

여 좋아요. 자동차 연식과 제조사가 어디인가요?

남 2003년 형 Ford사의 Explorer입니다.

여 그리고 번호판은 어떻게 됩니까?

남 AWJ 130입니다.

여 됐습니다. 한 학기에 210달러이고 1년은 420달러입니다.

남 가을 학기 동안만 필요합니다.

여 좋아요. 요금을 보내 주시면 허가증을 보내 드리겠습니다.

남 좋아요. 대단히 감사합니다.

해설 남자가 필요한 기간은 가을 학기 동안이라고 했는데 '1년'에 체크 되어 있는 것이 대화 내용과 다른 것이다.

어휘 **permit** 허가(증), 면허 **parking lot** 주차 공간 **license plate** 자동차 번호판

13 ④

해석 여 안녕, Frank. 어떻게 지내니?

남 잘 지내, 하지만 바빠.

여 오늘 오후에 영화 보러 갈 시간을 낼 수 있겠니?

남 그럴 수 있으면 좋겠지만 숙제가 많아.

여 그러지 말고 좀 쉬면서 해. 너는 항상 공부만 하는구나! 너도 모르는 사이에 로봇으로 변할 거야.

남 글쎄, 나는 할 일이 많아. 너는 할 일이 없니?

여 있었지만 끝냈어. 사실 오늘이 내 생일이야.

남 정말? 몰랐어! 생일 축하해!

여 고마워. 너와 함께 축하를 하고 싶었어.

남 그럼, 그렇게 이야기하는데 내가 어떻게 거절할 수 있겠니? 너한테 설득 당했어.

여 **네가 마음을 바꿔서 기뻐.**

해설 영화를 보러 가자는 여자의 제안을 처음에는 거절했지만 여자의 생일이라는 말을 듣고 결국 받아들였으므로 가장 적절한 응답은 ④이다. ① 지금은 뭘 하고 싶니? ② 미안하지만 일부러 그런 건 아니야. ③ 그럼 이번 토요일로 하자. ⑤ 대신 비디오 게임을 하는 건 어때?

어휘 **take off** ~을 쉬다 **get over with** ~을 끝내다 **refuse** 거절하다 **talk ~ into ...** ~을 …하도록 설득하다

14 ③

해석 여 잠깐, Dave! 너 도대체 뭘 하고 있는 거니?

남 무슨 말이야?

여 너는 재활용 하지 않니? 어떻게 유리를 버릴 수 있니?

남 진정해, Cathy. 우리 동네에는 병을 재활용할 수 있는 장소가 없어.

여 미안해. 오염에 대한 조사를 좀 했는데 쓰레기를 버릴 장소가 없다는

것을 알게 되어서 그랬던 거야.

남 나도 정말 환경을 걱정해. 나는 그냥 청소를 하고 싶었어.

여 이봐, 우리 봉투를 살펴보고 병을 꺼내는 것이 어때? 내가 집에 가지고 가서 재활용할게.

남 그래도 괜찮겠니?

여 전혀 문제없어. 우리는 좋은 재활용 프로그램을 가지고 있어. 우리 동네에서는 신문, 병, 그리고 캔을 일주일에 한 번씩 수거해 가.

남 <u>그래, 소매를 걷고 일을 해 보자.</u>

해설 병을 그냥 버리려고 하는 남자에게 여자는 병을 자신의 집으로 가지고 가서 재활용 하겠다고 제안을 했고 남자가 이를 받아들였으므로 가장 적절한 응답은 ③이다. ① 우리는 또한 비닐봉투를 사용하지 않도록 노력해야 해. ② 그거 좋구나. 그리고 교통은 어때? ④ 이 병들을 전부 어떻게 하지? ⑤ 모든 쓰레기를 처리하기에 그것은 충분하지 않아.

어휘 plastic bag 비닐봉지 roll up ~을 감아올리다 in the world 도대체 dispose of ~을 처리하다 run out of ~가 바닥나다 go through 살펴보다, 조사하다

15 ⑤

해석 여 Peter와 Betty는 거의 10년 동안 친한 친구로 지냈다. 지난달 Betty는 새 아파트로 이사를 했고 오늘 집들이를 하고 있다. Peter는 그 파티에 참석하고 있는데, 지금 거실에서 몇 사람과 이야기를 나누고 있다. 하지만 그는 다소 불편해 보이고 자신의 시계를 자주 본다. Peter는 굉장한 야구팬인데, 오늘 그가 가장 좋아하는 팀의 중요한 경기가 있다. 그 경기는 지금 중계되고 있지만, TV는 꺼져 있다. Peter는 점수를 알고 싶어 한다. 이런 상황에서 Peter가 Betty에게 할 말로 가장 적절한 것은 무엇인가?

Peter <u>내가 TV를 켜도 되겠니?</u>

해설 친한 친구의 집이지만 TV를 켜도 되는지 물어보는 것이 가장 적절할 것이다. ① 내가 뛰어난 TV 수리기사 한 사람을 알아. ② 언제 야구장에 한번 가자. ③ 나를 저 여자에게 소개시켜 줄 수 있니? ④ 시간 좀 알려 줄래?

어휘 uncomfortable 불편한 broadcast 방송하다 ball park 야구장

16-17 ③, ④

해석 여 신사 숙녀 여러분. 국회에 나갈 여러분의 대표로 저를 뽑아 주신다면 매일 여러분의 요구가 충족되도록 하기 위해 제가 할 일이 몇 가지 있습니다. 우선, 학교에 더 많은 세금이 투자되도록 새로운 법의 발의를 계획하고 있습니다. 훌륭한 교사를 채용하고 공립학교를 새로 짓기 위해 새로운 자금이 사용될 것입니다. 둘째, 저는 도심 부활 프로젝트를 제안합니다. 이 프로젝트는 우리의 도심으로 사람들이 다시 돌아오도록 새로운 사업장, 새로운 택지, 그리고 새로운 녹지를 조성할 것입니다. 그리고 셋째, 우리 시민들의 늘어나는 요구를 충족시키기 위해 경전철 시스템을 다음 10년 동안 건설할 것을 제안합니다. 저는 일상적인 요구와 염려를 모르는 직업 정치인이 아닙니다. 저는 기업체 소유주로 일을 했기 때문에 여러분이 겪는 노고와 어려움에 대해 독특한 시각을 가지고 있습니다. 제가 선출된다면 여러분의 문제와 걱정거리가 지역적인 그리고 국가적인 차원에서 다루어지도록 할 것을 약속드립니다. 감사합니다.

해설 16 공약을 제시하며 자신을 국회의원으로 선출해 줄 것을 당부하는 내용이다. ① 새 공립학교를 선전하려고 ② 새 사업에 투자자를 끌어들이려고 ③ 유권자의 지지를 호소하려고 ④ 어떤 정치인의 업적을 칭찬하려고 ⑤ 정부의 정책을 비판하려고

17 사람들을 다시 도심으로 돌아오게 하기 위한 정책들을 제시하고 있다.

어휘 congress 의회, 국회 ensure 보장하다, 확실하게 하다 funding 자금 조달 meet 충족시키다 revitalization 생기 회복, 소생, 부활 residential 주거의, 거주용의 light rail train 경전철 unique 독특한 lose touch with ~에 뒤처지다, ~와의 접촉[연락]이 끊어지다 perspective 전망, 시각, 견해 address 접근하다, (문제를) 다루다

🎯 Dictation

01 sit in the sun and just relax

02 Her dress looks very funny / That style went out years ago

03 the coordinator of our sports program / you need to get in good shape

04 Emergencies can happen anywhere and at any time / When you call 911 / speak clearly / Stay on the line

05 somebody should say something / to leave the express line / How about calling the manager / wait in another line

06 putting the napkin in the center of the dinner / above the dinner plate to the left / put this smaller fork to the left of that

07 you don't seem to have sent us enough / I'm sorry about the misunderstanding

08 I can't decide how to end our play / turn in the entry form / The application due date has been extended

09 sell a variety of digital camcorders / something with a wider screen

10 I need your advice on buying a car / carry a lot of stuff / more powerful / more safety features / buying a used one

11 originating from / is based on a traditional form of Nigerian music / thanks to internationally renowned performers

12 I want to get a parking permit / And your license plate / for the fall semester

13 take some time off / when you put it that way

14 There's no place to recycle bottles / we're running out of / got a good recycling program

15 close friends / he appears rather uncomfortable / Peter wants to know the score

16-17 if you elect me to be your representative / build new public schools / bring people back to the heart of our city / with your everyday needs and concerns

18^회 듣기 모의고사

01 ②	02 ②	03 ⑤	04 ②	05 ②	06 ⑤
07 ③	08 ③	09 ①	10 ④	11 ⑤	12 ③
13 ④	14 ①	15 ④	16 ④	17 ④	

01 ②

해석 남 Cindy! 네 사무실은 냉장고 같아!

여 아니, 그렇지 않아! 나한테는 딱 맞아. 쾌적해.

남 맞아, 네가 북극곰이라면. 나를 좀 봐. 소름이 이층으로 돋았어!

여 **너는 과장하는 거 같아.**

해설 여자는 별로 춥지 않다고 생각하므로 소름에 소름이 돋았다고 과장하는 남자에 대한 응답으로 ②가 가장 적절하다. ① 너 자신에게 너무 가혹하게 굴지 마. ③ 나는 오리와 거위를 구분할 수 없어. ④ 너는 차가운 것을 마셔야 해 ⑤ 북극곰의 수가 감소하고 있어.

어휘 **exaggerate** 과장하다 **tell ~ from ...** ~과 …을 구별하다 **goose pimple** 소름, 닭살 (=goose bumps = gooseflesh)

02 ②

해석 여 사고 싶은 것이 더 있습니까?

남 아뇨, 됐습니다. 이게 다입니다.

여 알겠습니다. 여기 있어요. 그리고 교환이나 환불을 원하시면, 일주일 안에 가져오셔야 해요. 영수증 가져오는 것 잊지 마세요.

남 **고맙습니다. 기억하고 있을게요.**

해설 영수증을 가져와야 환불이나 교환이 가능하다고 했으므로 ②가 가장 적절하다. ① 그럼 두 개 다 살게요. ③ 잘됐네요. 영수증을 가져왔어요. ④ 정말이요? 더 생각해 볼게요. ⑤ 당신이 왜 그것을 했는지 이해할 수 없어요.

03 ⑤

해석 여 Catherine의 예절 시간입니다. 저는 Catherine Jones이고 오늘 밤에는 데이트 예절에 관해서 말씀 드리겠습니다. 말하기와 듣기를 번갈아 가며 해야 합니다. 데이트 상대가 뭔가 흥미로운 이야기를 하면 응답을 하세요. "오, 정말인가요?" 또는 그냥 "그래요"라고 말하면 됩니다만 어쨌든 뭔지 말하세요. 자신에 대해서 이야기하는 데 약간의 시간을 보내세요. 데이트 상대가 당신을 알고 싶어 할 것입니다. 하지만 당신의 생활의 모든 세세한 부분까지 말해 주지는 마세요. 전 남자 친구나 여자 친구에 대해서는 절대로 이야기하지 마세요. 그리고 종교와 정치 같은 논란이 있을 수 있는 주제는 조심하세요. 음악과 영화에 대한 이야기로 시작해도 좋습니다. 그렇게 하면 공통된 가치관을 알 수 있게 될 것입니다.

해설 데이트할 때 지켜야 할 예절 가운데 대화를 올바로 이끌어가는 방법을 설명하는 내용이다.

어휘 **take turns** 교대로 ~하다 **detail** 세부, 상세 **definitely** 분명히, 확실히 **controversial** 논란을 일으키는 **religion** 종교 **politics** 정치(학)

04 ②

해석 여 자, 뭐가 문제인 것 같나요?

남 Max가 밤새 잠을 자지 못했어요. 그리고 오늘 아침에는 아무 것도 먹지 않으려고 했어요. 그리고 보세요, 오른쪽 귀를 계속 잡아당깁니다.

여 뭔가 잘못된 것 같군요. 체온을 재 보게 Max를 잡아주시겠습니까? 예, 열이 있군요.

남 Max가 불쌍해요. 저 슬픈 눈을 보세요.

여 내일이면 나아질 겁니다. 이 약을 먹으면 염증이 빨리 낫는 데 도움이 될 겁니다.

남 무슨 염증인가요?

여 귀에 염증이 있습니다. 내일 데려가시면 됩니다.

남 무슨 말씀이세요?

여 제가 밤새 이곳에 데리고 있으면 좋겠다는 뜻입니다.

남 하지만 저는 혼자 살아요. 저는 친구로 그가 필요해요.

여 겨우 하루 밤이에요.

남 하루 밤은 긴 시간이에요. 그가 저와 함께 집으로 갈 수 있기를 바라요.

해설 여자는 강아지의 염증 치료를 위해 강아지를 하루 동안 병원에 데리고 있는 것이 좋겠다고 했다.

어휘 **take one's temperature** ~의 체온을 재다 **fever** 열 **pill** 알약 **get over** 이겨내다, 극복하다 **infection** 전염, 감염 **overnight** 밤새, 하룻밤 동안

05 ②

해석 (전화벨이 울린다.)

남 여보세요?

여 Smith 씨인가요?

남 예, 접니다.

여 안녕하세요, Smith 씨. 저는 2B호에 사는 Janet Anderson입니다.

남 안녕하세요, Anderson 부인. 무슨 일입니까?

여 난방 장치가 작동하지 않아서 전화 드렸습니다. 오늘 아침에 일어나보니 집이 아주 추웠어요. 제 남편과 저는 지금 아주 심한 감기에 걸렸습니다.

남 오, 그러시다니 죄송합니다. 수리공을 보내겠습니다.

여 오늘 보내실 건가요?

남 예, 물론이지요. 12시 이전이 될 겁니다.

여 좋습니다. 대단히 감사합니다. 안녕히 계세요.

해설 여자가 자신의 집의 난방 장치가 고장이 났다는 사실을 알려 주자 남자는 수리공을 보내겠다고 말한다. 따라서 집주인과 세입자 사이의 대화임을 알 수 있다.

06 ⑤

해석 여 James! 책 표지를 디자인하는 데 충고가 좀 필요해요.

남 이것이 책의 제목인가요? 우주의 신비?

여 예, 이 책은 우주에 관한 거예요. 행성을 하나 가운데 넣을 생각이에요. 둘레에 고리가 있는 둥근 행성이요.

남 토성처럼 생긴 행성 말인가요?

여 예. 그리고 로켓 하나가 그 행성을 향해 나아갈 거예요, 이처럼요.

남 내 생각에는 로켓이 그 행성을 떠나는 것이 더 좋을 것 같군요.

여 음……. 당신말이맞네요. 행성 너머에 밝은 별을 몇 개 넣는 것이 어떨까요?

남 아니면 은하가 더 매력적일지도 모르겠군요. 신비로운 색깔의 셀 수 없이 많은 별과 행성 말이에요.

여 나는 그렇게 생각하지 않아요. 그렇게 하면 디자인이 너무 복잡해질 거예요. 그냥 멀리 있는 별 몇 개로 할게요.

남 제목은 어디에 넣은 건가요? 배경 그림 위에 놓으면 좋을 것 같은데.

여 내 생각도 그래요. 그럼, 다 됐네요. 큰 도움이 되었어요. 고마워요.

해설 남자가 은하를 넣는 것을 제안했지만 여자는 디자인이 너무 복잡해질 것을 우려해 별만 몇 개 넣겠다고 했다.

어휘 planet 행성 Saturn 토성 galaxy 은하, 은하계 attractive 매력적인 numerous 매우 많은, 무수한 complicated 복잡한 distant 먼, 떨어진

07 ③

해석 (전화벨이 울린다.)

남 여보세요?

여 안녕, Bruce. 나 Pam이야.

남 오, Pam! 지금 어디 있니?

여 아직 Detroit에 있어. 비행기 출발이 지연되었어.

남 비행기가 언제 출발하는지 아니?

여 적어도 1시간 이내에는 출발할 것 같지 않아.

남 그럼 자정까지 이곳에 도착하지 못하겠네.

여 그래. 그래서 전화한 거야. 네가 공항에 나오는 것이 많이 번거로울까?

남 물론 아니야. 이륙하기 직전에 나한테 전화만 해.

여 고마워, 그렇게 할게. 그리고 너한테 줄 좋은 선물을 하나 샀어. 그건⋯⋯.

남 말하지 마. 내가 직접 알아낼 거야.

여 좋아. 나중에 만나.

해설 비행기 출발 지연으로 도착이 늦어질 것을 예상한 여자가 남자에게 공항으로 마중 나와 줄 것을 부탁하고 있다.

08 ③

해석 남 안녕하세요, 저는 Sam Brown이라고 합니다. 저는 여기서 거의 10년간 살았어요. 우리 부모님은 제 옆집에 사시고요.

여 만나서 반가워요. 저는 Rachel Johnson예요.

남 이 집의 새 주인이신가요?

여 예. 저의 첫 집이에요. 아주 신이 나요.

남 축하해요! 저 TV를 들려고 애쓰시는 것을 보았어요. 도와드리려고 왔어요.

여 오, 감사합니다. 아주 친절하시군요.

남 별거 아니에요. 제가 이쪽 끝을 잡을까요?

여 예. 셋에 들어요. 하나, 둘, 셋.

남 우⋯⋯. 무거운데요. 가지고 계신 TV가 이것 하나뿐이길 바랄게요.

여 예, 맞아요. 좋아요. 바로 여기에 놓아요.

남 다른 것도 가지고 들어올까요?

여 아뇨, 제가 마무리할 수 있어요. 저 TV가 가장 힘든 것이었어요. 정말 고마워요.

해설 옆집에 이사 온 여자가 TV를 옮기는 데 고생하는 것을 보고 도와주는 상황이다.

어휘 set down 내려놓다 deal with 다루다, 처리하다

09 ①

해석 (전화벨이 울린다.)

여 안녕하세요, 저는 Sherry라고 합니다. 도와드릴까요?

남 예, 8월 4일 공연 표 두 장을 사고 싶습니다.

여 잠깐만 기다려주세요. 예, 1장에 15달러짜리 표가 있습니다.

남 학생 특별요금이 있습니까?

여 예, 학생 표는 10달러입니다.

남 알겠어요. 그거 좋네요.

여 좋아요, 1장에 10달러짜리 학생 표 2장입니다. 1장 당 1달러씩 수수료도 있습니다. 요금을 어떻게 지불하시겠습니까?

남 10분 동안 표를 보관해 주실 수 있습니까? 제가 한 블록밖에 떨어지지 않은 곳에 있거든요.

여 그렇게 해드리죠. 그리고 매표소에서 표를 찾으시면 수수료는 없습니다. 성함과 전화번호를 알려 주시겠습니까?

남 예. Travis Johnson이고, 310-555-0176입니다.

여 좋아요. 학생 가격으로 적용 받으려면 잊지 말고 학생증을 가지고 오세요.

남 대단히 고맙습니다. 안녕히 계세요.

해설 원래 1장 당 1달러씩의 수수료가 있으나 표를 매표소에서 직접 찾을 경우에는 수수료가 없다. 따라서 1장에 10달러인 학생 표 2장 값만 지불하면 되므로 20달러를 지불해야 한다.

어휘 service charge 봉사료, 수수료 pick up (표, 세탁물 등을) 찾다 box office (극장 등의) 매표소

10 ④

해석 여 Johnny, 오늘 오후에 어디 갈 일 있니?

남 왜요? 사다 드릴 거라도 있나요, 엄마?

여 아니. 그냥 마당 치우는 것을 네가 도와줄 수 있는지 알고 싶어서.

남 그럴 수 있으면 좋겠지만 야구 연습하러 가야 해요. 간다고 말했거든요. 내일 하는 건 어때요?

여 좋아. 그런데 돌아와서 세차는 할 수 있니?

남 내일 하루 종일 비가 올 거라는 이야기를 들었어요. 이번 주말에 하기로 약속할게요.

여 너는 항상 약속을 하지만 한 번도 지키지는 않는구나.

남 엄마, 그런 게 아니에요. 저는 그저 제가 한 말을 잊을 뿐이에요.

여 알았어, 알았어. 나가는 길에 쓰레기는 버려줄 수 있겠지, 그렇지?

남 그럼요, 문제없어요. 제가 또 해드릴 일은 없나요, 엄마?

여 옷이나 더럽히지 않도록 조심해라. 그리고 저녁 식사 시간에 늦어서는 안돼.

남 노력할게요. 이따가 봐요.

해설 야구를 하면서 옷이 더럽혀지지 않도록 조심하라는 당부는 있었지만 옷을 세탁하라는 말은 없었다.

어휘 be supposed to ~ ～하기로 되어 있다 take out 내놓다, 꺼내다

11 ⑤

해석 여 태양곰은 동남아시아의 열대우림에서 주로 발견되는 곰이다. 태양곰은 섰을 때 길이가 약 4피트로 곰과에서 가장 작은 동물이다. 보통 수

컷이 암컷보다 약간 더 크다. 다른 곰들과 달리 태양곰의 털은 짧고 부드럽다. 이것은 아마 이 동물이 서식하는 저지대 기후 때문일 것이다. 연한 노란색의 편자 모양 표시가 있는 가슴을 제외하고 검은 색 털이 몸의 대부분을 덮고 있다. 이 독특한 표시 때문에 태양곰이라는 이름이 생겼다. 비슷한 색깔의 털이 입과 눈 주위에서도 발견된다.

해설 입과 눈 주위에도 가슴의 노란색 털과 비슷한 색깔의 털이 있다고 했으므로 ⑤가 일치하지 않는다.

어휘 *primarily* 주로, 첫째로 *tropical* 열대의 *slightly* 약간, 조금 *lowland* 저지대 *inhabit* 거주하다, 서식하다 *horseshoe* 편자 *distinct* 다른, 독특한

12 ③

해석 여 여름 방학 중 일자리를 구하고 있습니다.
남 전일 근무에 관심이 있나요?
여 예.
남 주말에도 일할 수 있습니까?
여 아뇨. 일요일마다 교회에 가야 하고 주말에는 공부도 해야 합니다.
남 알겠어요. 어느 학교를 다닙니까?
여 George Washington 대학에 다닙니다.
남 언제 졸업할 예정인가요?
여 다음 6월에요.
남 특별한 기술이나 관심 있는 분야가 있습니까?
여 음, 다른 사람들과 함께 일하는 것을 좋아하고, 스페인어를 할 줄 압니다.
남 알겠습니다. 좋아요, Nelson양. 최대한 빨리 연락을 드리겠습니다.

해설 대학 졸업 예정인데 대학교 졸업을 한 것으로 잘못 표시되어 있다.

어휘 graduate school 대학원 get in touch with ~와 연락하다

13 ④

해석 여 봐요! 저기 야영장이 있어요. Simpson 부인이 야영지 번호를 종이에 적어 주었어요. 그것이 어디 있는데. 오! 여기 있네요.
남 흠……. Simpson 부부가 텐트에서 잔다는 것을 상상할 수 있나요? 분명히 70살은 되었을 텐데!
여 오, 아니에요! Simpson 부부는 사실 야영을 하는 것이 아니에요. 그들은 텐트에서 자지 않아요. 그들은 자신들의 침대에서 자요.
남 자신들의 침대에서요? 어떻게 그럴 수가 있나요?
여 Simpson 부부는 이동 주택으로 여행을 해요. RV라고 부르지요.
남 레크리에이션용 차량 말인가요?
여 예. 아마 침실, 욕실, 부엌, 세탁기, 건조기 등이 있을 거예요.
남 상상하기가 힘들어요. 나는 RV를 타본 적이 없어요.
여 나도 없어요.
남 잠시 후면 실물을 보게 되겠군요.

해설 두 사람 모두 이동 주택을 직접 본 적이 없으므로 응답으로 ④가 가장 적절하다. ① 그에게 여기가 어딘지 물어봅시다. ② 텐트에서 자는 것도 재미있겠군요. ③ 그렇다면 RV를 사지 않는 것이 더 좋겠군요. ⑤ 이 날씨에 야영을 한 것이 후회가 돼요.

어휘 camp out 야영하다 campground 야영지, 캠프장(campsite) motor home 이동 주택 recreational vehicle 레저용 차량

14 ①

해석 남 무슨 일이 일어났습니까? 방금 가게에 다녀오는 길입니다.
여 오, 이렇게 보게 되니 정말 다행이에요. 아파트 안에 갇힌 것이 아닌가 걱정했어요. 아이들은 어디 있나요?
남 아내와 함께 동물원에 갔습니다.
여 아, 잘됐어요. 다 안전하시군요!
남 불이 언제부터 시작되었나요?
여 11시 30분쯤 화재경보기가 울렸어요. 건물 관리인이 건물 밖으로 대피하라고 알려주었죠.
남 화재가 어떻게 시작되었는지 아시나요?
여 아니오. 어떤 사람들은 Harrison 씨 집에서 시작되었다고 생각해요. 그 사람들은 휴가 중이거든요.
남 끔찍하군요! 어떻게 해야 하나요?
여 지금 우리가 할 수 있는 일은 지켜보는 것밖에 없어요.

해설 불이 난 상황에서 어떻게 해야 하는지 묻는 말에 대한 응답으로 가장 적절한 것은 ①이다. ② 빨리 다른 일자리를 찾는 것이 좋겠어요. ③ 우리 함께 휴가를 가는 것이 어때요? ④ 문 자물쇠를 바꿀 때가 된 것 같아요. ⑤ 과식을 하지 않도록 더 조심해야 해요.

어휘 be trapped in ~ ~에 갇히다 go off (화재경보나 자명종, 사이렌 등이) 울리다

15 ④

해석 남 금요일 저녁인데 Steve는 식료품 가게에서 쇼핑을 하고 있다. 그는 내일 있을 소풍을 위해 식료품을 사고 있다. 아내가 준 쇼핑 목록을 들고, 그는 통로 사이를 왔다 갔다 하고 있다. 필요한 물건들을 찾는 것이 그에게는 좀 힘든 일이다. 그는 아내가 지금 같이 있으면 좋겠다고 생각을 한다. 그때 사과를 고르다가 스피커를 통해서 10분 후에 매장 문을 닫는다는 안내를 듣는다. 쇼핑 목록을 살펴본 후, 그는 최소한 20분이 더 필요하다고 짐작한다. Steve가 점원이 지나가는 것을 보고 점원에게 할 말로 가장 적절한 것은 무엇인가?
Steve 실례합니다. 쇼핑을 10분 더 할 수 있을까요?

해설 식료품 가게가 문 닫을 시간이 다 되었는데 쇼핑을 끝내지 못했다면 ④라고 하는 게 자연스럽다. ① 안녕하세요, 제 아내가 이곳에서 쇼핑을 하는 것을 본 적이 있나요? ② 안녕하세요. 사과 고르는 것을 좀 도와주실 수 있습니까? ③ 미안합니다만, 어디서 손을 씻을 수 있는지 아세요? ⑤ 안내방송이 무슨 내용이었는지 알려주시겠습니까?

어휘 announcement 알림, 공고 back and forth 앞뒤로, 이리저리 aisle 통로, 복도 estimate ~을 어림하다, 추정하다

16-17 ④, ④

해석 남 오늘날에는 전 세계적으로 미국의 패스트푸드 식당이 없는 나라는 거의 없습니다. 맥도날드가 특히 성공했습니다. 100여 개국에 8,000개가 넘는 맥도날드가 있습니다. 사실 맥도날드의 수익 가운데 59퍼센트가 자국 외의 점포에서 나오고 있습니다. 그리고 이 액수는 증가할 것으로 보입니다. 각 나라는 자국의 음식을 가지고 있습니다. 이 음식이 사라져 가고 있으며 우리의 식단이 미국화 되고 있습니다. 저는 맥도날드 같은 미국의 기업이 우리의 문화를 파괴하고 있다고 생각합니다. 우리는 이제 그들을 저지해야 합니다!

여 맥도날드 같은 패스트푸드 체인이 성공한 데에는 많은 이유가 있습니다. 우선, 그들은 외국인의 기호에 맞춰 변화했습니다. 예를 들면, 맥도날드는 프랑스에서는 포도주, 인도에서는 채식주의자용 햄버거, 그리고 노르웨이에서는 연어 샌드위치를 팝니다. 해외에서 패스트푸드의 성공에 기여한 다른 요인들은 청결, 가족적인 분위기, 그리고 효율적인 서비스 등입니다. 미국의 패스트푸드가 다른 나라의 문화를 파괴하고 있다고 말하는 것은 터무니없는 것입니다. 아무도 햄버거를 사도록 시키지는 않습니다. 사람들이 패스트푸드 먹기를 거부한다면, 모든 패스트푸드 식당은 문을 닫을 것입니다.

해설 **16** 남자는 패스트푸드에 의해 음식의 미국화가 이루어져서 각국의 문화가 파괴되고 있다고 주장하고 있다. ① 패스트푸드가 건강에 미치는 영향 ② 패스트푸드가 인기 있는 이유 ③ 외식 산업의 전망 ④ 미국의 패스트푸드의 악영향 ⑤ 다국적 기업의 기원

17 "사람들이 패스트푸드 먹기를 거부하면 패스트푸드 식당은 문을 닫을 것이다."라는 말은 "패스트푸드 식당이 결국 모두 문을 닫을 것으로 판단한다."는 것과는 다른 의미이다.

어휘 **influence** 영향 **prospect** 전망, 예상 **multinational corporation** 회사, 기업 **adapt to ~** ~에 적응하다 **salmon** 연어 **contribute to ~** ~에 기여하다 **efficient** 능률적인, 효율적인

🎯 Dictation

01 I feel comfortable / my goose pimples have goose pimples

02 I guess that's all / you should bring them back

03 take turns talking and listening / Spend some time talking / be careful with / start out by

04 stop pulling on / help him get over / to keep me company

05 the house was freezing / send the repair person over

06 advice on designing / a circle with a ring around it / be more attractive / You've been a great help

07 The flight's been delayed / to come out to the airport / find it out myself

08 I've been living here / That's very kind of you / Let's set it down

09 we have tickets for $15 each / How would you like to / there's no service charge

10 clean up the yard / when you get back / can take out the garbage

11 about four feet in length / due to the lowland climates / in the shape of

12 Are you interested in / When will you graduate / We'll get in touch with

13 on a piece of paper / are not really camping out / Recreational Vehicle / It's hard to imagine

14 What happened / The fire alarm went off / They're on vacation

15 walks back and forth / the store closes in ten minutes / a clerk passing by

16-17 come from restaurants / We have to stop them now / have adapted to foreign tastes / It's ridiculous to say

🎯 **19**회 **듣기 모의고사**

p.114-115

01 ②	02 ①	03 ②	04 ③	05 ⑤	06 ③
07 ①	08 ③	09 ①	10 ⑤	11 ④	12 ④
13 ⑤	14 ⑤	15 ⑤	16 ⑤	17 ②	

01 ②

해석 남 안녕하세요? 도와드릴까요?
여 어머니의 날을 위해 꽃을 좀 사고 싶습니다.
남 봄꽃다발을 예쁜 꽃병에 넣어드리는 건 어떨까요?
여 그거 좋겠습니다. 어머니가 좋아하실 거예요.

해설 꽃가게 주인이 어머니날 선물로 꽃다발을 제안했으므로 대답으로는 ②가 가장 적절하다. ① 그러면 아버지를 위해서는 무엇을 살까요? ③ 전 이미 그녀를 위한 꽃을 샀어요. ④ 당신 이렇게 비싼 선물을 살 수 있나요? ⑤ 예뻐 보이네요. 그런데 그녀의 치수를 모르겠어요.

02 ①

해석 여 나는 사상 최고의 싼 것만 찾아다니는 사람이야.
남 오, 이런. 또 무슨 일이야. 이번에는 뭘 샀는데?
여 길을 걷다가 어떤 남자가 유명 상표 핸드백을 100달러에 팔고 있는 걸 봤지. 그 사람과 흥정을 해서 반값에 하나를 샀어.
남 잠깐! 그거 틀림없이 가짜일 거야.

해설 유명 상표의 핸드백을 길거리에서 반값에 샀다는 말을 들었으므로 대답으로는 ①이 가장 적절하다. ② 이제 너는 온라인으로 쇼핑하는 법을 아는구나. ③ 미안하지만 내 예산을 벗어났어. ④ 고마워. 내가 딱 원하던 거야. ⑤ 이게 제 마지막 제안이에요. 사거나 그냥 가세요.

어휘 **Give me a break!** 믿을 수 없어!, 잠깬! **fake** 가짜의, 위조의 **out of budget** 돈이 없는 **Take it or leave it.** 사든지 말든지 마음대로 하세요. **bargain hunter** 싼 것만 찾아다니는 사람

03 ②

해석 남 안녕하세요. 저는 Mike Brown 경관입니다. 시의 다른 지역과 비교할 때 강력 범죄가 거의 없는 것은 사실이지만 차량 절도의 수가 거의 두 배로 증가했습니다. 여러분을 겁주려고 제가 여기 나온 것은 아닙니다. 여러분의 자동차를 더 안전하게 만들어 줄 몇 가지 간단한 조언을 하려는 것입니다. 우선, 차고가 있으시면 그 차고를 당구대가 아니라 자동차를 위해 사용하십시오. 가장 중요한 것은 차안에 귀중품이 있다면 트렁크에 감추십시오. 단 1분 동안이라도 귀중품을 좌석에 놔두지 마십시오.

해설 자동차를 차고 안에 보관하거나 자동차 좌석 위에 귀중품을 놓아두지 않는 것이 차량 절도 예방 방법이라는 것을 설명하는 담화이다.

어휘 **violent** 격렬한, 폭력적인 **compare** 비교하다 **theft** 절도, 도둑질 **scare** 위협하다, 겁나게 하다 **valuables** 귀중품 **billiard table** 당구대

04 ③

해석 남 이봐, Amy. 너 애완견 있지, 그렇지?

여 그래. 왜?

남 네 조언이 필요해.

여 무슨 일인데?

남 어머니께서 나에게 애완동물을 사주겠다고 약속하셨어. 그런데 개와 고양이 중에서 결정을 못하겠어.

여 내가 너라면 난 개를 사겠어. 개가 고양이보다 붙임성이 더 좋잖아.

남 알아, 하지만 개는 고양이보다 더 시끄럽잖아, 특히 어린 강아지는 말이야.

여 그건 네가 그들을 어떻게 돌보느냐에 달려있어. 그리고 어디를 가든지 개를 데리고 다닐 수도 있고.

남 좋아. 알겠어. 그럼 좋은 개를 살 수 있는 곳을 아니?

여 물론이지. 네가 원한다면 언제든지 너와 함께 갈 수도 있어.

남 정말이니? 도와줘서 고마워. 지금 바로 가자.

해설 붙임성이 더 좋고 어디든지 데리고 갈 수 있다는 이유로 개를 기를 것을 권하고 있으므로 ③이 여자의 의견이다.

어휘 depend on ~ ~에 달려 있다 convinced 확신을 가진

05 ⑤

해석 남 잠깐, 기다려요! 그건 제 차입니다.

여 오, 그래요? 그렇다면 견인차는 필요 없겠군요.

남 예! 지금 바로 옮기겠습니다!

여 좋아요. 소화전 옆에 주차하는 것은 불법입니다.

남 압니다. 하지만 주차할 곳이 없어서요. 잠깐 다녀온 겁니다.

여 알겠습니다. 딱지 여기 있습니다.

남 저에게 딱지를 떼시려고요?

여 맞습니다. 법을 어겼으니까요.

남 하지만 아주 잠깐 주차한 건데요.

여 소방관들이 물을 필요로 할 때는 매 1분이 중요합니다.

남 네. 알겠습니다.

해설 남자가 소화전 옆에 차를 주차해 놓아서 여자가 주차위반 딱지를 발급하는 상황이다. 따라서 남자는 운전자이고 여자는 경찰관임을 알 수 있다.

어휘 defendant 피고인 inhabitant 거주자 janitor 관리인, 수위 tow truck 견인트럭 illegal 불법의 fire hydrant 소화전

06 ③

해석 남 Linda, 우리 결혼식 케이크를 결정했나요?

여 아뇨, 아직 안했어요. 마음을 정하기 어려워요. 함께 의논하는 것이 어때요?

남 좋아요. 모든 하객들이 볼 수 있도록 꽤 높아야 할 것 같아요. 3단 케이크가 어때요?

여 David, 우리 식탁은 연단 위에 있을 거니까 2단이면 충분할 거예요.

남 아, 맞아요. 초는 몇 개나 꽂을 건가요?

여 두 개로 하죠. 하나는 당신 거, 하나는 내 거.

남 이제 우리는 남편과 아내로 하나가 되었으니까 내 생각에는 하나가 더 좋을 것 같아요.

여 그거 좋네요. 함께 하나의 초를 불어서 끄면 멋진 장면이 될 거예요. 장식은 어떻게 할까요?

남 장미가 있는 하트 장식이 예쁠 거예요. 당신 생각은 어때요?

여 그건 너무 평범해요. 나는 더 독특한 걸로 하고 싶어요. 하트 장식과 신랑 신부 모형이 더 좋아 보일 거예요.

남 좋아요. 그리고 케이크 옆면에 뭐라고 쓰고 싶어요?

여 간단한 걸로 해요. '영원히 사랑해'는 어때요?

남 그거 좋군요. 멋진 웨딩 케이크가 될 거예요. 빨리 보고 싶어요.

해설 남자는 하트 모양과 장미꽃이 있는 장식을 제안했지만 여자는 장미보다 신랑 신부 모형이 더 좋겠다고 했으므로 ③은 대화의 내용과 일치하지 않는다.

어휘 layer 층, 단 podium 연단, 지휘대 bride and groom 신랑 신부

07 ①

해석 남 저 좀 도와주시겠습니까? 저는 John Davis라고 합니다. 이 학교의 학생이었습니다.

여 오, 안녕하세요. 기억납니다. 어떻게 지내요?

남 잘 지냅니다, 감사합니다.

여 무엇을 도와드릴까요?

남 토플 시험 신청서를 얻고 싶습니다.

여 국제 토플 IBT 말인가요? 봅시다. 여기 이 선반 위에 있었는데. 전부 다 가져간 모양입니다.

남 정말인가요? 하나도 없나요?

여 미안하지만 다음 주에 신청서가 올 때까지 기다려야 합니다.

남 신청서가 오면 저에게 하나 보내주시는 건 어떨까요?

여 그러죠. 주소가 어떻게 되나요?

남 East Park Avenue 1223번지에 삽니다. 고맙습니다.

해설 남자가 여자에게 신청서를 보내달라고 하고 주소를 알려줬으므로 정답은 ①이다.

08 ③

해석 남 Julie, 나 정말 걱정이 돼.

여 뭔데?

남 글쎄, 어젯밤에 내가 갔던 파티 알지?

여 그래. 너는 회의에 가야 했지만 대신 그 파티에 갔어, 맞지?

남 그래. 어쨌든, Nick과 함께 차를 타고 집으로 돌아왔어. Nick은 차를 상당히 빨리 몰았지. 그는 트럭 한 대를 추월하다가 교통 표지판을 들이받았어.

여 너희들 멈추었니?

남 음, 멈췄어야 한다는 걸 알지만 Nick은 괜찮다고 말했어.

여 오, 큰일 났네! 사고를 낸 후 멈추지 않는 것은 법을 어기는 것이야.

남 그래. 알아.

여 지금 경찰에 전화하는 게 어때?

남 하지만 그렇게 하면 Nick이 곤란해질 텐데. 난 어떻게 해야 할지 모르겠어.

해설 친구가 운전하는 차를 타고 파티에서 돌아오는 길에 교통사고가 났지만 그냥 온 것을 걱정하고 있으므로 남자가 걱정하는 이유로 ③이 가장 적절하다.

어휘 street sign 도로 (교통) 표지판 break the law 법을 어기다

09 ①

해석 남 도와드릴까요?

여 예, 베개를 좀 보고 싶습니다.

남 많은 다양한 종류가 있습니다. 둘러보세요.

여 꽃무늬로 된 거위 솜털 베개 있습니까?

남 예, 있습니다. 이것들은 어떻습니까?

여 오, 예쁘군요. 이것들을 사겠습니다. 얼마인가요?

남 가격표에는 하나에 50달러라고 되어 있지만, 지금 할인 판매 중입니다. 그래서 20퍼센트 할인됩니다.

여 오, 아주 좋은 가격이군요. 그럼 그것으로 4개 주세요.

남 손님, 운이 좋으시군요. 우리는 3 플러스 1 판매도 하고 있습니다. 세 개를 사시면 하나를 공짜로 받을 수 있습니다.

여 오늘 이곳에 들르기를 잘 했군요.

해설 원래 하나에 50달러인데 20퍼센트 할인이 되어 40달러이다. 4개가 필요한데 3 개를 사면 하나를 공짜로 주는 행사도 하고 있으므로 3개 값 즉, 120달러만 지불 하면 된다.

어휘 pillow 베개 down (새의) 솜털 on sale 할인 판매 중인 stop in 들르다

10 ⑤

해석 여 시드니에 오시면 정말 즐거우실 겁니다. 시드니 항구는 매우 아름답고 세계에서 가장 큽니다. 다양한 유람선 관광을 선택할 수 있습니다. 정 말로 토착 동물을 보고 싶다면 타롱가 동물원으로 가야 합니다. 캥거루 와 코알라를 포함한 호주의 특이한 동물들이 모두 그곳에 있습니다. 시 드니 수족관에는 150미터가 넘는 투명 터널이 수중을 관통해 있습니 다. 여러분 주변과 머리 위로 헤엄치는 물고기와 상어를 볼 수 있습니 다. Sydney 수산 시장은 아주 저렴한 가격으로 고급 지역 해산물을 즐 길 수 있는 정말로 좋은 곳입니다. 시장 직원들은 방문객에 익숙해서 친절하고 협조적입니다.

해설 Sydney Harbor, Taronga Zoo, Sydney Aquarium, Sydney Fish Market는 언급되었지만 '오페라 하우스'에 대한 내용은 없다.

어휘 exhibit 전시품 reasonable 적당한, 비싸지 않은

11 ④

해석 남 당신에게 힘과 인내심이 있다면 Tough Guy & Girl Challenge는 바 로 당신을 위한 대회입니다. 8월 14일에 개최되는 이 독특한 비포장 도로 달리기 행사는 13세 이상의 남녀 모두 참가할 수 있습니다. 늪 건 너기, 거미줄 그물 오르기, 진흙 미끄럼, 그리고 밧줄 다리가 포함된 코 스에서 자신에게 도전해 보세요. 다양한 천연 장애물과 인공 장애물들 을 통과해 달리고 걷고 기어오를 수 있습니다. 12킬로미터 풀코스와 6 킬로미터 하프코스로 두 가지 코스가 있습니다. 개인 참가비는 10달러 이며, 20인 이상의 단체에게는 10퍼센트 할인됩니다. 모든 참가자에 게는 운동모자가 무료로 제공됩니다. 가족 또는 친구와 아주 놀라운 경 험을 함께 하시기 바랍니다.

해설 20인 이상의 단체에게는 참가비가 10퍼센트 할인된다고 했으므로 "10명 이상의 단체에게는 참가비가 할인된다."는 내용과는 일치하지 않는다.

어휘 endurance 인내, 인내력 off-road 포장도로를 벗어난 competitor 경쟁자, 선

12 ④

해석 여 실례합니다. 이 노선을 전에 이용한 적이 없어서요. 이 버스가 얼마나 자주 여기 오는지 알려 주시겠어요?

남 봅시다. 평일 낮 시간에는 약 10분마다 운행됩니다.

여 혹시 러시아워에는 얼마나 자주 운행되는지 아세요? 이 버스를 타고 출근하기 시작할 거예요.

남 잘 생각하셨네요! 죄송하지만 그때는 얼마나 자주 운행하는지 모르겠습 니다.

여 낮 시간보다는 더 자주 오겠죠.

남 아마 그럴 겁니다.

여 그리고 주말은 어때요?

남 토요일과 일요일은 운행 간격이 같고, 밤에는 15분마다 운행합니다. 시내에 있는 버스 정류장에 가면 시간표를 구할 수 있습니다.

여 아, 잘됐군요. 그렇게 하겠습니다. 도와주셔서 감사합니다.

남 천만에요.

해설 토요일과 일요일의 운행 간격 시간이 같고, 낮에는 10분, 밤에는 15분 간격으로 운행되는 버스는 ④이다.

13 ⑤

해석 남 여기 출신입니까?

여 아뇨. 저는 한국의 서울에서 왔어요.

남 그러세요? 그거 흥미롭군요. 서울은 한국의 수도 맞지요?

여 예, 맞습니다.

남 새해를 맞아서 집에 갈 계획인가요?

여 농담하세요? 서울은 이곳에서 아주 멀어요!

남 그건 아무런 문제가 되지 않아요. 이 도시에서 서울로 가는 항공편이 많 아요.

여 예, 하지만 당신은 한 가지 중요한 사실을 빠뜨렸어요.

남 그게 뭔가요?

여 비행기 요금이지요! 저는 학생이고 이곳에서 아르바이트로 일을 할 뿐이 에요.

남 그럼, 서울까지 얼마인가요?

여 **확실히는 모르지만 저에게는 너무 많은 돈이에요.**

해설 서울까지 비행기 요금이 얼마인가를 묻는 것이기 때문에 ⑤라고 답하는 것이 가 장 자연스럽다. ① 850달러입니다! 어떻게 지불하시겠습니까? ② 약 12시간 걸 립니다. 아주 지루하죠. ③ 저는 식당에서 일하면서 시간당 5달러를 받습니다. ④ 예, 대부분의 물건들이 그곳에서는 꽤 비쌉니다.

어휘 pretty 꽤, 아주 flight 비행(편) airfare 항공 운임

14 ⑤

여 하루 저녁에 몇 시간을 자니?

남 보통 9시간 아니면 10시간.

여 와! 많이 자는구나!

남 나는 그렇게 생각하지 않아. 사람마다 필요한 수면의 양이 다르다고 생

각해.

여 네 말이 맞을지도 몰라. 하지만 대부분의 사람들에게는 8시간이 보통이라고 읽었어.

남 아마 그것이 평균이겠지. 하지만 모든 사람은 다르다고 생각하지 않니?

여 잘 모르겠어. 나는 8시간은 많은 것 같아.

남 너는 몇 시간 자는데?

여 보통 5시간 아니면 6시간.

남 **그러니 9시간이 너무 많다고 생각하는 것이 당연하지.**

해설 5~6시간 자는 여자가 보기에는 남자의 수면 시간인 9~10시간이 많다고 생각되는 것이므로 ⑤가 가장 적절한 응답이다. ① 그건 너무 많다고 생각하지 않아? ② 그렇게 늦은 시간에 뭘 하니? ③ 난 아침 일찍 공부하는 쪽이 더 좋아. ④ 난 한 시간 이상 집중할 수 없어.

어휘 no wonder ~ ~하는 것도 놀랄 일이 아니다 plenty 충분한 양

15 ⑤

해석 남 Susan은 얼마 전에 한 회사에서 근무하기 시작했다. 하루는 동료 한 명이 그녀에게 다가와서 함께 오페라 구경을 가자고 청했다. Susan은 오페라를 본 적이 없었고 오페라를 좋아하지도 않았다. 하지만 그녀는 무례하게 보이는 것이 싫었다. 그래서 그녀는 오페라를 보러 갔지만, 전부 이탈리아어로 되어 있었고 정말 지루했다. 그 후, Susan은 사무실에서 그를 피하려고 했다. 하지만 며칠 후 그녀는 그와 마주치게 되었고, 그가 다른 오페라를 보러 가자고 초대했다. 이런 상황에서 그녀가 할 말로 가장 적절한 것은 무엇인가?

Susan **그날 다른 약속이 있어요.**

해설 좋아하지 않는 오페라 구경을 가자고 하는 남자에게 할 말로 가장 적절한 것은 ⑤이다. ① 전 아직 이탈리아어를 잘 못해요. ② 전 그저 다른 날까지 기다릴 수 없어요. ③ 이번엔 제가 표를 살게요. ④ 대신에 오페라를 보러 가고 싶어요.

어휘 engagement 약속, 약혼 co-worker 같이 일하는 사람, 동료 come up to ~에게 다가가다 run into 우연히 만나다, 마주치다

16-17 ⑤, ②

해석 여 오늘은 MP3 플레이어에 관해 이야기하겠습니다. 이런 미디어 플레이어는 사용자로 하여금 언제 어디서든 MP3 오디오 파일과 다른 형식의 파일을 들을 수 있게 합니다. 그렇다면 이것은 여러분과 같은 외국어 학습자에게 무엇을 의미할까요? 첫째, 교재의 읽기 자료를 오디오 CD로부터 디지털화해서 MP3 오디오 파일로 변환한 후 미디어 플레이어에 업로드할 수 있습니다. 그러면, 학습자는 해당 수업 교재를 보면서 미디어 파일을 들을 수 있게 됩니다. 게다가, 많은 MP3 오디오 플레이어는 자신의 목소리를 녹음할 수 있는 녹음 기능을 가지고 있습니다. 이 기능의 한 가지 실용적인 용도는 디지털 음성 일기를 쓰는 것입니다. 즉, 전통적인 일기와 아주 비슷하게 일상 생활사를 매주 기록할 수 있는 것입니다. 이런 일기를 계속 씀으로써 학습자는 몇 주, 몇 달, 몇 년이 지난 후에 시간을 거슬러 올라가 언어 학습에 있어서의 진전의 증거를 들을 수 있습니다.

해설 16 외국어 학습에 MP3 플레이어를 활용할 수 있다는 사실을 알려주고 있다. ① 특별한 MP3 플레이어를 선전하려고 ② 듣기의 중요성을 강조하려고 ③ 불

법적인 MP3 파일 사용에 대해 경고하려고 ④ 미디어 플레이어의 개선을 요청하려고 ⑤ 외국어 학습 방법을 한 가지 알려주려고

17 자신의 목소리를 녹음했다가 나중에 들을 경우 외국어 실력이 얼마나 늘었는지 확인할 수 있다고 했으므로 MP3 플레이어의 '음성 녹음' 기능이 언급된 것이다.

어휘 format 틀, 형식 digitalize 디지털화하다 convert 전환하다, 변화시키다 corresponding 상응하는, 대응하는 journal 신문, 일지, 일기 evidence 증거

Dictation

01 a bouquet of spring flowers

02 the greatest bargain hunter / for half price

03 has almost doubled / use it for your car / not even for a minute

04 I need your advice / It depends on / I'm ready to go there with you

05 to park beside a fire hydrant / You broke the law

06 make up my mind / one would be better / What do you think / I can't wait to see it

07 I used to be a student / get an application / How about sending me

08 I got a ride back / we should have stopped / get into trouble then

09 Take a look / they are on sale now / you can get one free

10 a variety of different tours / clear tunnels pass through / at very reasonable prices

11 is open to both male and female / get a 10% discount

12 every ten minutes or so / under the regular daytime schedule / Don't mention it

13 pretty far from here / I only work part-time

14 different amounts of sleep / seems like plenty to me

15 a co-worker came up to her / tried to avoid him / she ran into him

16-17 what does this mean / look over the corresponding material / By maintaining such a journal

20회 듣기 모의고사

p.120-121

01 ④	02 ③	03 ②	04 ③	05 ②	06 ③
07 ⑤	08 ⑤	09 ④	10 ①	11 ④	12 ②
13 ④	14 ②	15 ④	16 ④	17 ③	

01 ④

해석 여 어젯밤에 농구 경기 봤니?

남 아니. 보고 싶었지만 공부를 해야 했어. 누가 이겼니?

여 Chicago Bulls가 이겼어. 3초가 남았을 때 2점 차로 지고 있었는데 Jordan이 종료벨과 동시에 3점 슛을 넣어서 이겼지.

남 내가 좋은 경기를 놓친 것 같구나.

해설 마지막 순간에 역전이 된 경기를 남자가 보지 못한 것이므로 응답은 ④가 가장 적절하다. ① 난 공부를 더 열심히 해야 했는데. ② Bulls 팬에게는 참 안됐네. ③ 그가 심하게 다친 것이 아니길 바라. ⑤ 너와 함께 경기를 봐서 좋았어.

어휘 **buzzer beater** 경기 종료벨과 동시에 이루어지는 득점

02 ③

해석 (전화벨이 울린다.)

남 Urban Outfitters입니다. 무엇을 도와드릴까요?

여 안녕하세요! 며칠 전에 온라인으로 셔츠를 하나 샀어요. 근데 문제가 있어요.

남 뭐가 문제인지 말씀해 주시겠습니까?

여 치수가 맞지 않습니다. 교환해 주실 수 있나요?

해설 온라인으로 구입한 옷에 문제가 있다고 했고, 무엇이 문제인지 물었으므로 ③이 가장 적절한 응답이다. ① 당신의 가게에 제 지갑을 놓고 온 것 같아요. ② 모르겠어요. 찾으면 당신에게 말해 줄게요. ④ 내가 사고 싶었던 셔츠를 찾을 수가 없어요. ⑤ 이 CD가 읽혀지지 않아요. 환불 받을 수 있을까요?

03 ②

해석 남 저는 얼마 전에 Detroit에서 이곳으로 이사를 왔습니다. 아직 이 도시에 아는 사람이 아무도 없지만, 직장 사람들은 아주 친절합니다. 저는 중심가에서 일을 하는데 아직 차가 없습니다. 그래서 중심가까지 직통으로 가는 버스 노선이 있는 집을 찾고 싶습니다. 저는 미혼이지만 침실이 두 개 있는 집을 원합니다. 하지만 한 달에 600달러밖에 낼 수 없습니다. 이 도시에 새로 왔기 때문에 가구가 하나도 없어서 가구를 갖춘 집이 필요합니다. 저는 요리하는 것을 정말 좋아하는 것은 아니기 때문에 아주 큰 부엌이 필요하지는 않습니다. 하지만 욕조는 있어야 합니다.

해설 위치, 침실의 수, 임대료 등의 조건을 설명하는 것으로 보아 자신이 얻고자 하는 아파트를 설명하기 위한 담화임을 알 수 있다.

어휘 **furnished** 가구가 비치된 **bathtub** 욕조

04 ③

해석 여 오늘 저녁 퇴근 후에 한 잔할 거야. 함께 갈래?

남 고마워, Mary. 나도 가고 싶어. 하지만 허리가 정말 아파!

여 왜? 무슨 일이 있었어?

남 그러니까, 어제 체육관에서 운동을 했는데 무리한 것 같아.

여 오, 가엾어라. 그럼, 어떻게 할 생각이니?

남 아무 것도 안 할 거야.

여 있잖아, 네가 다니는 체육관에 사우나가 있는지 알아봐.

남 글쎄, 그래, 있는 것 같아. 하지만 이용해 본 적이 없어.

여 한번 해봐.

남 그건 살을 빼기 위한 것 아냐? 그리고 나는 그 안의 열기가 좋지 않을 것 같아.

여 다소 뜨겁지만 쑤시는 근육을 정말로 풀어줄 거야.

해설 운동을 심하게 해서 허리가 아픈 남자에게 사우나에서 근육을 풀어보라고 충고하는 내용이다.

어휘 **gym** 체육관(gymnasium) **overdo** 지나치게 하다, 무리하다 **sauna** 사우나, 증기탕 **sore** 아픈, 쑤시는

05 ②

해석 여 이것이 내가 대도시에서 일하는 것을 싫어하는 이유들 가운데 하나야.

남 나도 알아. 매일 똑같아.

여 아주 끔찍해! 밤새 이곳에 있을지도 몰라! 휘발유가 떨어지지 않으면 좋겠는데.

남 그건 걱정하지 마. 충분할 거야.

여 라디오를 켜보자. 좋은 음악이라도 나올지 알아.

남 미안하지만 라디오가 고장이야.

여 내일은 지하철을 타야겠어. 집까지 계속 서있을지도 모르지만 시간은 훨씬 덜 걸릴 거야.

남 네가 부럽다. 우리 집 근처에는 지하철역이 없어. 그래서 지하철을 타고난 후에 버스로 갈아타야해.

여 오, 신호가 녹색으로 바뀌었다. 하지만 보라고! 아무도 움직이질 않아!

남 진정해! 앞에 큰 사고라도 없기를 바랄 뿐이야.

해설 신호가 바뀌었는데도 움직이지 않는다고 말하는 것으로 보아 두 사람은 자동차 안에서 교통 체증에 관해 대화를 나누고 있음을 알 수 있다.

어휘 **run out of ~** ~이 바닥나다, ~이 다 떨어지다 **envy** 부러워하다

06 ③

해석 여 서둘러요! 늦었어요!

남 잠깐만요. 열쇠가 없어요.

여 항상 탁자 위에 놓아두잖아요, 그렇죠?

남 네. 하지만 지금은 거기 없어요.

여 소파 밑을 보셨나요? 발로 차버렸을지도 모르잖아요.

남 아마도요. 아니요. 보이지 않아요.

여 책상 위에는 없어요. 서랍 속에도 없고요.

남 아, 이제 기억났다. 문을 연 후에 주머니 속에 집어넣었어요. 내 비옷이 어디 있는지 알아요?

여 예. 옷장 속에 있는 것을 봤어요.

남 알았어요. 잠깐만요. 찾았어요. 갑시다.

해설 열쇠를 주머니 속에 넣었다고 하면서 비옷이 어디 있는지 물었으므로 옷장 안에서 열쇠를 찾았을 것이다.

어휘 **coffee table** (소파 앞에 놓는) 탁자 **nope** 아니(= no)

07 ⑤

해석 여 Peter, 오늘 시내에 갈 거니?

남 응, 왜?

여 나 좀 태워 줄 수 있니? 심부름일 해야 해서.

남 정확히 어디를 가야 하는데?

여 은행에 가야 해. King대로와 2번가 모퉁이에 나를 내려줄 수 있겠니?

남 King대로와 2번가라고? 물론이지. 거기가 어딘지 알아. 하지만 왜 은행에 가려고 하니? 교내에 있는 현금인출기를 사용하지 않고?

여 내 현금 인출 카드가 안 되기 때문이야. 새 카드를 발급 받아야 해. 그런데, 너는 시내에서 뭘 할 거니?

남 나는 법원에 갈 거야. 과태료를 내야 해.

여 설마! 나도 과태료를 내야 하는데. 지난주에 위반딱지를 받았어.

남 하지만 너는 운전을 하지 않잖아.

여 알아. 무단횡단으로 딱지를 받았어. 나는 교내에서 조차 길 한 가운데로 건너는 것이 불법이라는 것을 몰랐어!

해설 현금 인출 카드에 문제가 있어서 새 카드를 발급 받기 위해 은행에 가려고 한다.

어휘 **run errands** 심부름가다 **drop off** ~를 (차에서) 내려주다 **ATM** 자동 현금 인출기 (Automated Teller Machine) **courthouse** 법원 **jaywalk** 무단횡단하다 **illegal** 불법의

08 ⑤

해석 남 금연하기로 결심했어요.

여 오, Jerry, 정말 기뻐요. 흡연이 당신 건강에 아주 해롭다는 것을 당신도 알잖아요. 금연하고 몇 주만 있으면 큰 차이를 느낄 거예요.

남 하지만 살이 많이 찔까봐 좀 겁이 나요. 담배를 끊으면 초조해서 훨씬 더 많이 먹는다고들 하잖아요.

여 그건 걱정하지 말아요. 그건 그냥 사람들이 하는 말이에요.

남 확실해요?

여 들어봐요. 운동 프로그램에 참여해요. 그러면 마음이 편안해질 거예요. 나는 담배를 끊었을 때 전혀 살이 찌지 않았어요.

남 맞아요. 당신은 전혀 문제가 많은 것 같지 않았어요.

여 쉽지는 않았지만 건강을 유지해서 손자들이 자라는 것을 볼 정도로 오래 살고 싶어서 담배를 끊었어요.

남 사실, 나는 내 건강에 대해서는 조금도 걱정하지 않아요. 나는 아주 건강해요.

여 그럼 왜 금연을 결심하게 되었나요?

남 담배를 피우지 않는 사람들이 방에서 나가달라고 요청하는 것을 참을 수가 없어요.

해설 다른 사람들이 밖으로 나가서 담배를 피우라고 하는 것을 참을 수 없다고 했다.

어휘 **nerves** 신경과민 **get involved in ~** ~에 참여하다

09 ④

해석 남 원래 항상 조깅을 했나요?

여 오, 아뇨. 전에는 아무 운동도 하지 않았어요.

남 정말이요? 언제 조깅을 시작했습니까?

여 약 다섯 달 전에요. 하루에 1마일씩 달리기 시작했죠. 처음에는 달리는 것이 싫었어요. 하지만 몇 주가 지난 후부터 기분이 좋아지기 시작했어요. 지금은 2마일을 더 달립니다.

남 얼마나 자주 달리나요?

여 매일이요. 당신은 어때요? 운동을 하세요?

남 전에는 했었죠. 하지만 지금은 시간을 낼 수가 없어요. 그런데, 얼마나 빨리 달리나요?

여 처음에는 아주 느렸어요. 1마일을 달리는 데 14분이나 걸렸으니까요.

남 지금은 어때요?

여 2배 빠르고 하루에 3마일을 달려요. 하지만 언젠가 3마일을 18분 이내에 뛰고 싶어요.

해설 하루에 달리는 거리는 3마일이고, 소요 시간은 처음에는 1마일에 14분이 걸렸지만 지금은 2배 빠르다고 했으므로 현재는 1마일에 7분, 즉 3마일에 21분이 걸리는 것을 추측할 수 있다.

10 ①

해석 여 당신은 시장인 Anderson에게 다시 투표하실 건가요?

남 정말로 아직 결정을 하지 못했어요. Anderson이 해온 직무에 완전히 만족하지는 않아요.

여 그가 당선되기 전보다 거리가 정말로 훨씬 더 깨끗하다는 것은 사실이에요.

남 알아요. 도시의 모습에 있어서는 훨씬 더 만족스럽다는 것을 인정합니다. 하지만 도시를 깨끗하게 하는 데 도움을 준 것이 세금 인상이었다는 것을 잊지 마세요.

여 범죄는 어때요? 범죄율이 전보다 낮아요.

남 그래요, 그것은 그의 공으로 인정해야 해요.

여 그리고 노숙자 캠페인으로 인상적인 일을 해냈어요.

남 그의 재개발 프로젝트로 노숙자의 수가 줄었다는 것은 사실이에요.

여 그리고 실업자의 수도 역시 줄었어요.

남 그것이 그에게 다시 투표하게 만드는 가장 큰 요인입니다. 하지만 확실히 마음을 정하기 전에 다음 일요일 토론까지 기다릴 겁니다.

해설 don't forget that it was the tax increase that helped to clean the city라고 했으므로 세금이 인상되었다고 판단해야 한다.

어휘 **admit** 인정하다 **credit** 공적, 업적 **impressive** 인상적인 **unemployed** 직업이 없는, 실직한 **tempt** 유혹하다 **debate** 토론, 논쟁

11 ④

해석 여 이상한 작은 애완동물들이 많이 있지만 Mexican walking fish보다 더 특이한 동물은 거의 없다. 이 동물의 자연 서식지는 멕시코시티 근처의 호수이다. 이 동물은 물속에서 살지만 사실은 물고기가 아니다. 개구리처럼 이 동물은 양서류이다. 이 동물은 최고 30센티미터까지 자라는 길고 끈적거리는 몸, 그리고 네 개의 다리를 가지고 있다. 하지만 이 동물의 호기심을 유발하는 외모가 유일한 색다른 특징은 아니다. 이 동물은 독을 만드는데 그 독은 이 동물을 맛이 없게 만들어서 포식자가 되려고 하는 어떤 동물에게나 달갑지 않은 식사가 된다. 이 동물은 또한 놀라운 재생 능력을 가지고 있다. 이 동물은 잘려나가거나 손상을 입은 다리를 약 8주 내에 다시 자라게 할 수 있고, 새 다리는 전의 다리처럼 기능한다.

해설 독을 만들어 먹이를 잡는 것이 아니라 다른 동물의 먹이가 되지 않는다고 했으므로 ④는 담화의 내용과 일치하지 않는다.

어휘 **peculiar** 독특한, 색다른 **native** 원산의 **habitat** 서식지, 거주지 **amphibian**

양서류 **slimy** 끈적끈적한, 진흙의 **distasteful** 맛없는 **predator** 포식자, 육식 동물 **regeneration** 재생

12 ②

해석 (전화벨이 울린다.)
여 Carter 박사 병원입니다.
남 안녕하세요, Carter 박사님에게 진찰 예약을 하고 싶습니다.
여 처음 진찰 받으시는 건가요?
남 예, 그렇습니다. 저의 이름은 Jack Wagner입니다.
여 좋습니다. Wagner 씨. 내일 오후는 어떠십니까?
남 수요일 오후까지는 이곳을 떠나 있을 겁니다.
여 그럼 목요일 4시는 어떠세요?
남 음……. 오전에 빈 시간은 없습니까?
여 있습니다. 하지만 금요일과 토요일뿐입니다.
남 그렇게 오래 기다릴 수는 없습니다. 저녁 몇 시까지 문을 엽니까?
여 7시 이전에 오시면 Carter 박사님의 진료를 받으실 수 있을 것입니다.
남 여행에서 돌아오는 날 7시까지 올 수 있을 거예요.
여 좋아요. 그때 기다리겠습니다. 안녕히 계세요.

해설 여행을 갔다가 수요일 오후에 돌아올 예정이어서 처음에는 수요일 이후를 생각했지만 저녁 7시까지 진료가 가능하다는 말을 듣고 수요일로 예약을 했다.

어휘 **opening** 빈 시간, 빈자리 **make it by** ~까지 도착하다

13 ④

해석 남 안녕하세요. Walt Disney World에 가고 싶어서 Florida 항공편에 관한 정보가 필요합니다.
여 알겠습니다. Orlando까지 좋은 요금을 제시해 드릴 수 있을 겁니다. 1등석, 2등석, 아니면 일반석 중 어떤 좌석으로 가시겠습니까?
남 물론 일반석이죠. 가장 싼 요금을 원합니다.
여 좋습니다. 그리고 편도인가요, 왕복인가요?
남 왕복입니다. 12일 일요일에 출발해서 18일 토요일에 돌아오고 싶습니다.
여 일요일 오전에 아주 저렴한 요금이 있습니다. 145달러밖에 되지 않지만 직항편이 아닙니다. Atlanta에서 비행기를 갈아타셔야 합니다. 직항편이 있지만 그 요금은 680달러입니다.
남 좋습니다. Atlanta에서 갈아타겠습니다.
여 알겠습니다. 12일 일요일 아침 8시 15분에 출발해서 12시 15분에 Orlando에 도착합니다.
남 좋습니다.
여 그리고 한 가지 더 있습니다. 그 요금은 특별 할인 요금이기 때문에 환불이 되지 않습니다.
남 괜찮습니다. 저는 계획을 바꾸지 않을 겁니다.

해설 요금이 아주 싸지만 환불할 수 없는 비행기 표라는 말을 들었으므로 응답으로 ④가 가장 적절하다. ① 문제없습니다. 시간이 많아요. ② 대단히 감사합니다. 그 말을 들으니 마음이 놓이는군요. ③ 그렇다면 목적지를 바꾸고 싶군요. ⑤ 그건 말이 안 됩니다. 여기 영수증이 있잖아요.

어휘 **destination** 목적지 **make sense** 이치에 맞다. 말이 되다 **one-way** 편도 **round-trip** 왕복 **refundable** 환불 가능한

14 ②

해석 여 너는 왜 컴퓨터에다 대고 말을 하니?
남 말을 하는 게 아냐. 명령을 내리는 거야.
여 무슨 말이니?
남 이 훌륭한 소프트웨어 프로그램 때문이야. 내가 하는 말을 알아듣고 그 말을 받아 적는 거야.
여 와. 그럼 전혀 타이핑을 할 필요가 없는 거야?
남 그래. 그게 바로 핵심이야. 나는 타이핑이 느리기 때문에 이 프로그램이 나를 살려주는 거야.
여 나도 한번 해볼 수 있을까?
남 응, 먼저 컴퓨터가 너의 목소리를 인식할 수 있도록 훈련을 시켜야 해.
여 오. 왜?
남 모든 사람들의 발음이 다르기 때문이야. 컴퓨터가 너의 목소리를 모르면 실수를 해.
여 내 컴퓨터에도 이걸 설치해야겠다.

해설 사람의 말을 인식해서 글자로 입력시키는 컴퓨터 프로그램을 보고 편리함을 깨닫게 된 여자의 응답으로 ②가 가장 적절하다. ① 누구나 가끔씩 실수를 할 수 있어. ③ 네가 말하는 것은 마치 원어민처럼 들린다. ④ 내일까지 내 컴퓨터를 수리하고 싶어. ⑤ 미안하지만 나는 그것을 완벽하게 하려고 최선을 다했어.

어휘 **dictation** 명령, 구술 **lifesaver** 생명의 은인. 곤경에서 구해주는 물건 **recognize** 알아보다. 인식하다

15 ④

해석 남 금요일 저녁에 Jane은 혼자 슈퍼마켓에서 쇼핑을 하고 있다. 여느 때처럼 슈퍼마켓은 사람들로 붐비고 그녀의 쇼핑 카트는 식료품으로 가득 차 있다. 이제 Jane은 쇼핑을 거의 끝내고 계산대의 긴 줄에서 기다리고 있다. 그러다가 그녀는 뭔가를 사는 것을 잊어버렸다는 사실을 갑자기 깨닫게 된다. 그녀는 내일 맛있는 스테이크를 만들어 주겠다고 남편과 아이들에게 약속을 했다. 그녀는 돌아가서 고기를 사려고 결심을 하지만 긴 줄의 끝으로 다시 돌아가고 싶지는 않다. 이런 상황에서 Jane이 자기 뒤에 있는 사람에게 할 말로 가장 적절한 것은 무엇인가?
Jane 죄송한데, 제 자리를 좀 맡아 주시겠습니까?

해설 긴 줄 끝에 다시 서서 기다리고 싶지 않을 때 뒤에 있는 사람에게 할 말로 가장 적절한 것은 ④이다. ① 이곳은 카드 소지자만을 위한 계산대예요. ② 먼저 하세요. 저는 남편을 기다리고 있는 중이에요. ③ 실례합니다. 이 근처에서 저의 아이들을 보셨어요? ⑤ 스테이크 양념 만드는 법을 알려 주셔서 감사해요.

어휘 **holder** 소지인. 보유자 **as usual** 여느 때처럼 **be crowded with** ~로 붐비다 **checkout counter** 계산대

16-17 ②, ③

해석 여 이메일 계정은 거의 모두 무료이기 때문에 국제 통신용으로 인기를 얻었습니다. 하지만 최고의 이메일 계정을 어떻게 찾을 수 있을까요? 첫째, 회사가 얼마나 오래 존재할지를 고려하세요. 회사가 여러 해 동안 존재했다면 앞으로도 오랫동안 존재할 가능성이 더 많습니다. 아무도 내일 서비스가 끊길지도 모르는 이메일 계정을 개설하기 원하지 않습니다. 둘째, 무제한이나 큰 이메일 저장 용량을 제공하는 회사를 선택하세요. 과거에 회사들은 몇 백 메가바이트의 메일함을 제공했지만 지

금은 사진이나 영상을 전송하기 위해 꽤 큰 용량이 필요하기 때문에 그 용량을 무제한으로 늘리고 있습니다. 끝으로 스팸, 즉 정크 메일을 걸러내기 위해 어떤 기능을 이용할 수 있는지 살펴보세요. 스팸은 바이러스를 퍼뜨릴 뿐만 아니라 생산성을 떨어뜨리는 심각한 문제가 되고 있는데, 원치 않는 메시지를 검토하고 삭제하는 데 많은 시간이 걸리기 때문입니다. 이런 절차를 수행하는 것은 당신이 가능한 최고의 이메일 계정을 얻도록 해줄 것입니다.

해설 **16** 이메일 계정을 선택할 때 고려해야 할 사항들을 알려주고 있다. ① 이메일을 사용해서 의사소통하는 것을 장려하려고 ② 이메일 계정을 선택하는 방법을 가르쳐 주려고 ③ 최신 인터넷 기술을 공표하려고 ④ 이메일을 효율적으로 쓰는 방법에 관한 정보를 주려고 ⑤ 정크 메일에 의해서 생기는 피해에 대해 경고하려고

17 불필요한 이메일을 삭제하는 데 시간을 소모하게 되면 생산성이 떨어지므로 스팸 메일을 걸러내는 기능을 확인하라고 했다.

어휘 **account** 계정, 계좌 **storage** 저장, 보관 **filter** 거르다 **productivity** 생산성 **delete** 삭제하다

🎯 Dictation

01 hit a three-point buzzer beater

02 there's a problem

03 I've just moved here / goes directly downtown / I'll need a furnished place

04 my back is killing me / I overdid it / relax your sore muscles

05 run out of gas / I might stand / change to a bus after the subway

06 always put them on / Not in the drawers / I've found them

07 I have to run some errands / Why don't you use / I just got a ticket / cross in the middle of the street

08 gain a lot of weight / stay healthy / what made you decide to

09 How often do you run / It took me as many as / I'm twice as fast

10 before he was elected / give him some credit / I make up my mind

11 growing up to / it makes them distasteful / as functional as

12 make an appointment / I'll be out of town until / I can make it by 7

13 I can get a good fare / it's not direct / the ticket is not refundable

14 doing dictation on it / that's the point / it makes mistakes

15 is almost done with her shopping / She decides to go back

16-17 almost all of them are free / around for years to come / what features are available for / it takes much time to

---

21회 🎯 듣기 모의고사
p.126-127

01 ②	02 ⑤	03 ④	04 ②	05 ⑤	06 ④
07 ②	08 ②	09 ②	10 ③	11 ①	12 ④
13 ③	14 ②	15 ③	16 ④	17 ②	

01 ②
해석 남 실례합니다. Royal Sports Center로 가는 길을 알려 주시겠어요?
여 Royal Sports Center요? 모퉁이에서 좌회전을 해서 두 블록 직진하세요.
남 좌회전해서 두 블록 직진하라. 좋아요, 알겠습니다. 그 다음은요?
여 그게 다예요. 오른쪽에 스포츠 센터가 보일 거예요.

해설 남자가 여자에게 Royal Sports Center로 가는 길을 물었고 여자의 응답에 이어 그 다음에 가야 할 길을 묻고 있으므로 가장 적절한 대답은 ②번이다. ① 걱정 마세요. 당신은 그 센터에서 일할 수 있어요. ③ 거기까지 지하철로 5분밖에 안 걸려요. ④ 그러면 회원 카드를 제출해야 해요. ⑤ 미안해요, 난 그 센터에 가는 데 관심이 없어요.

02 ⑤
해석 여 미안해요, 이 DVD를 3일 늦게 반납합니다.
남 그럼, 죄송하지만 연체료를 내야 해요.
여 저, 연체료가 얼마죠?
남 하루에 1달러입니다. 모두 3달러를 내셔야 해요.

해설 DVD 연체료가 얼마인지 묻는 여자의 물음에 대한 남자의 응답으로 가장 적절한 것은 ⑤이다. ① 미안합니다. 연체료가 무엇이죠? ② 그는 연체료를 낼 필요가 없었어요. ③ 맞아요. 이 가게 회원이에요. ④ DVD를 얼마에 샀나요?

03 ④
해석 남 모든 부모는 자녀가 신체적으로뿐만 아니라 지적으로도 발달하기를 원한다. 좋은 영양분은 자녀가 신체적으로 발달하는 것을 도와줄 것이다. 그러나 자녀의 지적 능력은 어떻게 발달시켜 줄 수 있는가? 마음을 달래는 음악과 마사지가 정신적 발달을 촉진시킴으로써 자녀에게 유익할 수 있다. 자녀에게 책을 읽어 주는 것도 자녀의 정신적 발전을 촉진시킨다. 사실, 사랑스럽고 애정 어린 그 어떤 상호 접촉이라도 자녀가 지적으로 발달할 수 있도록 도움을 줄 것이다.

해설 '유아의 지적 능력을 어떻게 발달시킬 수 있는가?'라고 물어 본 다음, 이에 대한 답으로 '마음을 달래는 음악, 마사지, 책 읽어 주기, 애정 어린 상호 접촉'등을 제시했다.

어휘 **intellectually** 지적으로 **nutrient** 영양분 **intellectual ability** 지적 능력 **soothing** 달래는, 진정시키는 **benefit** 유익하다, ~에게 이익을 주다 **foster** 육성하다, 촉진하다 **affectionate** 애정 어린, 정감 있는

04 ②
해석 남 안녕, Jane. 너 괜찮아? 너 어젯밤에 시간 외 근무를 했잖아. 거의 11

시까지 말이야.

여 물론, 문제없어. 언제나처럼 건강해.

남 와, 대단하다! 넌 정말로 건강한 것 같아. 네 건강에 무슨 비결이라도 있니?

여 그럼, 있지. 내 건강 비결은 아침에 과일을 먹는 거야.

남 음, 과일이 우리 몸에 좋다고는 들었어.

여 있잖아, 과일을 먹으면 비타민 C를 많이 섭취할 수 있고 면역 체계를 강화할 수 있어.

남 면역 체계가 강화된다고? 그건 몰랐어.

여 더 좋은 건 과일에 식이섬유가 많이 들어 있다는 거야. 식이섬유가 콜레스테롤 수치를 낮추어 준다는 것은 알고 있지, 그렇지?

남 그래, 알고 있어. 네가 왜 네 건강 비결이 과일이라고 말했는지 알겠어.

여 아침에 과일을 많이 먹으면 먹을수록 더 건강해진다는 사실을 명심해.

해설 여자는 자신의 건강 비결이 아침에 과일을 먹는 것이라고 하면서 과일이 건강에 미치는 긍정적인 영향을 말하고 있다.

어휘 **work overtime** 시간 외로 일하다. 잔업하다 **fit** 건강한 **stay healthy** 건강을 유지하다 **strengthen** 강화하다 **immune system** 면역 체계 **dietary fiber** 식이 섬유

05 ⑤

해석 여 축하하네. 드디어 자네가 아빠가 되었네.

남 예, 너무 행복해요.

여 여기 아기 기저귀랑 젖병 일세.

남 고맙습니다. 아기를 보셨어요?

여 아직 못 봤네. 오, 손자가 정말로 보고 싶어.

남 정말 귀여워요.

여 누굴 닮았나? 자넨가, 아니면 Angela인가?

남 Angela는 아기가 저를 꼭 닮았다고 하더라고요.

여 그럼, 매우 똑똑한 아기겠구나.

남 저도 그러면 좋겠어요.

여 그런데, Angela는 어떤가? 내 딸은 괜찮은가?

남 예, 이제 괜찮아요. 장모님을 기다리고 있어요. Angela를 보러 가요.

해설 "축하하네. 드디어 자네가 아빠가 되었네. 손자가 정말로 보고 싶어."라고 말한 여자의 말을 토대로, 여자는 할머니이고 대화를 나누는 상대방은 여자의 사위임을 추론할 수 있다.

어휘 **diaper** 기저귀 **milk bottle** 젖병 **I'm dying to** 정말로 ~하고 싶다 **look like** ~을 닮다(=resemble)

06 ④

해석 남 여보, Sally가 학교에서 그린 그림 봤어요?

여 아뇨, 아직 못 봤어요. 어디 우리 사랑스러운 딸이 그린 그림을 한번 볼까요.

남 여기 있어요. Sally가 풍경화를 그린 것 같아요.

여 그래요, 오른쪽에 있는 해바라기와 하늘 위를 날고 있는 새를 보세요. 정말 잘 그렸어요.

남 맞아요. 이 구름은 어때요? 꼭 하트 모양 같아요.

여 정말로 귀여워요. 정말 영리한 아이예요!

남 가운데 있는 이 사과나무도 상당히 잘 그린 것 같아요.

여 맞아요. 당신이 선생님이라면, 그녀의 그림에 몇 점을 주겠어요?

남 100점이요! 정말로 좋아요. 당신은요, 여보?

여 음, 90점 정도요. Sally가 하늘 위에 무지개를 그렸다면, 나도 100점을 주었을 거예요.

남 음, 난 무지개가 없는 지금 그대로의 그림이 완벽한 것 같아요.

해설 하늘에 무지개를 그렸다면 100점을 주겠다는 말을 통해 무지개가 없음을 알 수 있다.

어휘 **draw** 그리다 **landscape picture** 풍경화 **quite** 상당히

07 ②

해석 여 우리 어머니의 생신이 내일인 거 잊지 마세요!

남 걱정 마요! White 가(街)에 있는 해산물 식당을 벌써 예약해 놨어요.

여 잘했어요. 고마워요, 여보.

남 생일 선물은요? 뭐라도 샀어요?

여 예, 샀어요. 이 브로치 세트를 샀어요. 어때요?

남 오, 아름다운데요. 장모님께서 분명히 좋아하실 거예요.

여 그랬으면 좋겠어요.

남 그런데, 선물용 포장을 하면 브로치가 더 좋아 보일 거예요.

여 그렇게 생각해요? 하지만, 포장지가 남은 게 없어요.

남 걱정 말아요. 지금 가서 괜찮은 포장지를 좀 사 올게요.

여 고마워요. Anderson Mart로 가세요. 거기가 가장 가까우니까.

해설 남자가 지금 가서 포장지를 사 온다고 했다.

어휘 **reserve** 예약하다 **brooch** 브로치 **be sure to** 반드시 ~하다 **gift-wrap** 선물용으로 포장하다 **wrapping paper** 포장지

08 ②

해석 (전화벨이 울린다.)

여 Green 쇼핑 몰, 고객 서비스부입니다. 무엇을 도와드릴까요?

남 10일 전에 이 웹 사이트에서 캠코더를 주문했어요.

여 주문에 무슨 문제라도 있나요?

남 큰 문제가 있죠. 아직까지 캠코더를 받지 못했어요.

여 정말요? 확인해 볼게요. 이름을 알려 주시겠습니까?

남 제 이름은 Daniel Redford예요.

여 잠시만 기다려주세요. Sudder Street에 있는 Pacific 아파트에 살고 계시네요, 맞나요?

남 예, 맞아요.

여 죄송합니다. 저희가 고객님의 주문 내역을 배송 부서에 전하지 못했어요. 컴퓨터 상에 에러가 있었음이 틀림없습니다.

남 뭐라고요? 이해할 수가 없군요.

여 정말로 죄송합니다.

해설 남자는 10일 전 Green 쇼핑 몰의 웹 사이트를 통해 캠코더를 주문했지만 아직까지 제품을 받지 못해서 문의하려고 전화를 했다.

어휘 **transfer** 옮기다, 이전하다 **malfunction** 에러, 오작동

09 ②

해석 여 안녕하세요, 도와드릴까요?

남 예. 7살짜리 딸에게 줄 생일 선물을 찾고 있어요.

여 그럼, 이 공주 인형은 어때요? 아주 인기 있답니다.

남 오, 귀여운데요. 얼마죠?

여 30달러입니다. 하지만, 오늘은 20% 할인 행사를 하고 있어요.

남 좋은데요. 알았어요. 이것을 살게요.

여 고맙습니다.

남 선물용으로 포장해 주세요?

여 알겠습니다. 아, 그리고 이 옷 세트도 구입하면 따님이 더욱 기뻐할 거예요. 5달러밖에 안 해요.

남 좋아요. 그것도 주세요.

해설 남자는 30달러짜리 인형을 20% 할인된 가격으로 구입하고 5달러의 의상 세트도 추가로 구입했으므로 남자가 지불해야 할 전체 금액은 29달러이다.

10 ③

해석 남 Jennifer, 오늘 오후에 새 아파트에 필요한 가구를 사는 게 어때요?

여 내 마음을 읽었군요. Star 가구점에 가요. 그곳에서 좋은 가구를 좋은 가격에 팔아요.

남 그래요. 가기 전에 무엇을 살지 생각해 봅시다.

여 좋아요. 무엇보다도 침대와 소파를 사야 해요.

남 맞아요. 식탁과 의자도 사야 할 것 같아요.

여 우리 언니가 이미 우리를 위해 대리석 식탁을 샀다고 말 안 했나요? 식탁은 살 필요가 없어요.

남 잘됐어요. 그럼 의자만 사면 돼요.

여 맞아요. 아, 옷장도 사야 해요. 지금 가지고 있는 것은 너무 구식이에요. 좀 더 현대적이고 독특한 스타일의 옷장을 사고 싶어요.

남 알았어요. 오, 우리가 사야할 것들이 많군요.

해설 여자는 자신의 언니가 대리석 식탁을 주기로 했으므로 식탁을 살 필요가 없다고 말했다.

어휘 most of all 무엇보다도 marble 대리석 old-fashioned 구식의

11 ②

해석 남 가장 권위 있는 학교 행사 중의 하나인 자원봉사 에세이 대회에 대해 말해 줄게요. 이 대회는 제 20회 개교기념일을 기념해서 열려요. 개교기념일 1주일 전인 10월 1일에 대회가 개최될 거예요. 자원 봉사활동 경험이 있는 학생들만 이 대회에 참가할 수 있어요. 1등 수상자는 최신 디지털 카메라를 받게 될 거예요. 에세이는 1,500단어에서 2,000단어 사이여야 하고 언제나처럼 문학 선생님들이 참가자들의 글을 읽고 평가할 거예요. 많은 학생들이 대회에 참가해서 글쓰기 실력을 뽐내길 바라요.

해설 "It will be held on October first, which is just a week before the anniversary day."를 통해 정답이 ②임을 알 수 있다.

어휘 prestigious 권위 있는 in celebration of ~을 기념해서 foundation 설립 participate in ~에 참가하다 evaluate 평가하다

12 ④

해석 여 George King이 우리 도시에서 콘서트 연다는 거 알아?

남 George King이라고? 오, 그는 내가 가장 좋아하는 재즈 음악가야. 언제? 어디서?

여 Music Center에서 10월 13일부터 20일까지.

남 Music Center 회원 카드가 있어서, 어떤 공연도 30% 할인 받을 수 있어.

여 좋은데. 그러면 입장료가 20달러니까 6달러를 절약할 수 있어.

남 예약을 해야겠다. 온라인으로 예약할 수 있니?

여 당연하지!

남 공연 보면서 George 사진을 많이 찍을 거야.

여 내 생각에는 그렇게 할 수 없을 것 같아.

남 왜?

여 공연 중에는 사진 촬영이 금지된다고 포스터에 나와 있거든.

해설 온라인으로도 예매를 할 수 있다고 했으므로 ④가 적절치 못하다.

어휘 admission 입장료 be allowed to ~해도 괜찮다

13 ③

해석 남 실례합니다. 들어가도 될까요?

여 예. 들어오세요. 문은 열려 있어요.

남 안녕하세요, Brown 씨. 잠시 대화를 나눌 수 있을까요?

여 그럼요, 무슨 일이죠, Jack?

남 내일 하루 휴가를 낼 수 있을까요?

여 왜요? 무슨 특별한 일이 있나요?

남 Denver에 계시는 할아버지, 할머니께서 내일 저를 보러 오시거든요. 지하철을 타시겠다고 하셨지만 제 생각엔 공항으로 마중 나가는 게 좋을 것 같아서요.

여 알았어요. 이해해요. 그분들이 이곳에 몇 시에 도착하실 예정이죠?

남 2시에 도착하세요.

여 그렇군요. 내일 휴가를 내도록 하세요.

해설 남자 직원이 조부모님께서 내일 올 예정이어서 공항으로 마중 나갈 수 있게 휴가를 얻고 싶다고 말을 한다. 이어질 말로 가장 적절한 것은 ③이다. ① 정말이요? 당신은 정말로 운이 좋군요. 부러워요. ② 고마워요. 그러면 다음주에 만나요. ④ 물론이죠! 그 경우에는 당신 잘못이 아니에요. ⑤ 당신이 할아버지, 할머니를 좋아하는 이유를 알겠어요.

어휘 have the day off 휴가를 내다 pick ~ up ~을 마중 나가다. 데리러 가다 be supposed to ~하기로 되어 있다

14 ②

해석 남 Lucy, 아빠가 할머니 집에 가 있는 동안 네가 무엇을 해야 하는지 기억하고 있지?

여 그럼요, 아빠.

남 좋아, 한 번 더 확인해 보자. 동생이 울면 무엇을 해야 하지?

여 기저귀를 갈아주거나 우유를 주면 돼요.

남 그래. 그래도 계속해서 울면?

여 안아 주면 돼요.

남 좋아. 그리고 거실에 있는 식물에 물주는 것 잊지 마라.

여 걱정 마세요. 잊지 않을 게요.

남 네 숙제는? 숙제는 벌써 다 했니?

여 그럼요, 이미 다 했어요.

남 알았다. 아빠는 이제 가마. 동생 잘 돌봐라.

해설 집을 떠나기 전에 마지막으로 아빠가 할 수 있는 말로 ②가 가장 적절하다. ① 응, 아기들을 돌본 경험이 있어. ③ 미안. 오늘밤에 할머니를 방문할 거야. ④ 정말? 그럼 너는 분명 숙제를 잘못 이해했음이 틀림없어. ⑤ 천만에. 너의 도움이 없었다면, 해내지 못했을 거야.

어휘 go on ~ing 계속해서 ~하다 water 물을 주다

15 ③

해석 여 실외 활동을 좋아하는 Andrew는 친구 Kate와 함께 Rainier 산을 오르고 있다. 지금까지, 그들은 9시간도 넘게 등산을 했고 정상에 거의 다 왔다. Kate는 피곤함을 느껴서 휴식을 취하기를 원한다. Kate가 지쳐있음을 눈치 챈 Andrew는 짧은 휴식을 취할 것을 제안한다. 두 사람은 앉아서 물을 마시고 간식을 약간 먹는다. 약 20분 후, Andrew는 해가 지기 전에 정상에 도착하기 위해서는 다시 등반을 시작해야 한다고 생각한다. 이 상황에서, Andrew가 Kate에게 할 말로 가장 적절한 것은 무엇인가?

Andrew 가자. 정상이 바로 저기에 있어.

해설 Andrew는 해가 지기 전에 정상에 도달하기 위해서는 이제 다시 등반을 시작해야 한다고 생각하므로 ③이 할 말로 가장 적절하다. ① 마음껏 먹어. 저녁은 내가 사는 거야. ② 미안, 나는 등산에 관심이 없어. ④ 난 너무 지쳤어. 더는 갈 수 없어. ⑤ 걱정 마. 물과 과자는 내게 충분히 있어.

어휘 outdoor activity 야외 활동, 실외 활동 take a break 휴식하다, 쉬다 notice 알아차리다 exhausted 지친 summit 정상

16-17 ④, ②

해석 여 안녕하세요, 오늘 여러분 앞에서 말을 하게 되어서 영광입니다. 저는 Gina Jackson이고, 경제학을 전공하는 2학년 학생입니다. 저는 학생회관 옆에 있는 빈 터의 활용 방안에 대해 말씀드리고자 여기 나왔습니다. 학교에서 이곳에 주차장을 지을 계획이라는 소식을 들었습니다. 이 결정은 정말로 말이 안 됩니다. 이곳은 농구장을 세움으로써 학생들의 학교생활 개선을 위해 개발되어 져야 합니다. 많은 학생들은 운동을 할 공간이 충분하지 않다고 불평합니다. 만약 학교가 농구장을 짓는다면, 이 문제에 대한 해결책의 역할을 할 것입니다. 학교가 작년에 헬스클럽 대신에 교수 식당을 지었던 사실을 기억하시나요? 올해에도 똑같은 일이 일어날까 걱정입니다. 학교 측에 요청하고 싶습니다. 학교는 왜 학생들의 의견을 듣지 않나요? 학생회관 옆의 빈 터는 학생들을 위해 개발되어야 한다고 다시 한 번 강하게 주장합니다.

해설 16 "The area should be developed for the improvement of students' school life by building a basketball court."라는 말에서 여자가 하는 말의 목적을 알 수 있다. ① 주차장의 재건축을 요구하려고 ② 학생들의 자가용 등교를 막으려고 ③ 학생들을 농구 대회에 초대하려고 ④ 농구장 건설을 요청하려고 ⑤ 주차장을 지으려는 학교의 결정을 칭찬하려고

17 "I heard that the school is planning to build a parking lot on this area."를 통해 정답이 ②임을 알 수 있다.

어휘 major in ~을 전공하다 vacant 비어있는 student union 학생회관, 학생 자치회 complain 항의하다, 불평하다 serve 기여하다 insist 주장하다

🎯 Dictation

01 tell me the way to / I got it

02 I'm three days late / how much is the late fee

03 develop your child's intellectual abilities / any loving and affectionate interactions

04 any secret to your health / Strengthen the immune system

05 dying to see my grandson / Is my daughter OK

06 drew a landscape picture / the shape of a heart / had drawn a rainbow over the sky

07 reserved a table / buy some nice wrapping paper

08 How may I help you / Let me check / didn't transfer your order

09 I'm looking for / Could you gift wrap it

10 You read my mind / Didn't I tell you that / we have now is too old-fashioned

11 Let me tell you / in celebration of / participate in the contest / show off your writing skills

12 I can get a 30% discount / I should make reservations / not be allowed to take pictures

13 Could I have the day off / they supposed to get here

14 let me check again / she goes on crying / water the plants

15 So far / taking a short break / to reach the summit

16-17 it's an honor to speak to you / makes absolutely no sense / it would serve as / I strongly insist once more

🎯 22회 듣기 모의고사

p.132-133

01 ①	02 ⑤	03 ②	04 ④	05 ③	06 ④
07 ④	08 ⑤	09 ③	10 ③	11 ⑤	12 ④
13 ④	14 ③	15 ④	16 ②	17 ②

01 ①

해석 남 엄마, 다음 주 금요일이 제 생일인 것 잊지 마세요.

여 당연하지! 어떻게 엄마가 우리 사랑스러운 아들의 생일을 잊을 수 있겠니? 생일 선물로 받고 싶은 것이 있니?

남 디지털 카메라요. 디지털 카메라를 받고 싶어요.

여 알았다. 최신 카메라로 사줄게.

해설 생일 선물로 디지털카메라를 받고 싶다는 남자의 말에 대한 여자의 응답으로 가장 적절한 것은 ①이다. ② 도와줘. 디지털 카메라를 잃어버린 것 같아. ③ 걱정 마. 친구에게 빌릴게. ④ 이 디지털 카메라 사용법을 모르겠어. ⑤ 축하해! 이건 네 생일 선물이야.

02 ⑤

해석 여 안녕하세요, 이번 주 수요일 Seattle 행 비행기 표를 사고 싶어요.
남 잠시만 기다려 주세요. 죄송합니다만 모든 표가 매진되었어요.
여 유감이네요. 금요일은요?
남 <u>그날은 표가 있습니다. 몇 시에 출발하실 건가요?</u>

해설 금요일에 출발하는 Seattle 행 비행기 표가 있냐는 여자의 물음에 대한 남자의 응답으로 가장 적절한 것은 ⑤이다. ① 내가 당신이라면, 비행기를 타고 시애틀에 갈 거예요. ② 물론이죠! 시애틀은 방문하기 좋은 곳이에요. ③ 금요일이요? 좋아요, 그날 함께 영화를 봐요. ④ 멋지게 들리는데요. 언제 여행에서 돌아왔어요?

03 ②

해석 여 많은 사람들이 건강, 행복 그리고 삶의 다른 영역에 영향을 끼치게 되는 과다한 스트레스를 경험하고 있습니다. 사실, 사람들을 병원으로 이끄는 건강 문제의 90% 이상이 스트레스와 관련이 있다고 추정됩니다. 하지만, 생활 습관을 조금만 바꾼다면 당신이 느끼는 스트레스가 상당히 줄어듭니다. Rey 박사님께서 오늘밤 이 자리에서 우리에게 일상생활의 스트레스를 줄이는 방법을 알려줄 것입니다. Rey 박사님은 심리학 교수이자 베스트셀러인 '여러분 모두에게 행복한 바이러스를' 이란 책의 저자이기도 합니다. 커다란 박수로 Rey 박사님을 맞이해 주십시오.

해설 스트레스를 줄여 주는 방법에 대해 강의를 할 예정인 Rey 박사를 소개하는 내용의 담화이다.

어휘 excess 과다한 affect 영향을 끼치다 estimate 추정하다 stress-related 스트레스와 연관이 있는 considerably 상당히 psychology 심리학 applause 박수

04 ④

해석 남 봐! 나 새 MP3 플레이어 샀어.
여 언제 샀는데? 디자인이 너무 멋지다.
남 메모리칩이 16기가바이트야. 너도 한 개 사는 게 어때?
여 얼마 주고 샀는데?
남 놀라지 마. 겨우 50달러 주고 샀어.
여 겨우 50달러? 정말? 어디서 샀는데?
남 www.everything.com에서. 그 쇼핑 사이트 접속해 봤어?
여 아니. 거기서 MP3 플레이어를 저렴하게 파니?
남 그래. 다른 곳에 비해 MP3 플레이어, 디지털 카메라, 그리고 휴대 전화 같은 모든 종류의 전자 제품을 상당히 저렴한 가격에 판매하거든.
여 정말? 좋아, 나도 그 웹 사이트에 방문해 봐야겠다.
남 네가 후회하지 않을 거라고 확신해. 정말로 좋은 사이트거든.

해설 남자는 www.everything.com이란 쇼핑사이트가 정말로 좋은 사이트라고 말했으므로 정답은 ④이다.

어휘 electronics 전자 제품, 전자 기기 at a low price 저렴하게, 염가로 compare 비교하다 regret 후회하다

05 ③

해석 남 괜찮아? 안 좋아 보이네.

여 치통이 있어요.
남 정말? 규칙적으로 양치질을 하지 않아서 그런 것 같은데.
여 아마도요. 이제부터는 밥 먹은 후에 양치하는 것을 잊지 않을 게요.
남 그리고 초콜릿이랑 사탕 먹는 것도 그만 두고. 넌 그런 건강에 안 좋은 것을 너무나 많이 먹어.
여 알았어요. 노력할게요.
남 엄마가 오면 네 엄마나 내가 너를 치과에 데리고 갈게.
여 엄마가 언제 오시는데요?
남 방금 30분 있으면 온다고 전화가 왔어.
여 치아가 그다지 많이 상하지 않으면 좋으련만.

해설 초콜릿이나 사탕 같은 단 음식을 많이 먹고 제대로 양치를 안 해서 치통을 느끼고 있는 딸과 아빠 사이에 이루어지는 대화이다.

어휘 regularly 규칙적으로 from now on 이제부터 junk 몸에 안 좋은 음식

06 ④

해석 여 Peter, 이리 와라. 너와 이야기할 것이 있단다.
남 알았어요. 그게 뭐죠?
여 네 담임 선생님께서 네게 성적표를 주셨다고 말씀하셨어.
남 그랬어요? 죄송해요, 엄마. 엄마를 실망시켜 드리고 싶지 않았어요.
여 그래 네 성적표는 어디에 있니? 여전히 네 가방에 있니?
남 아니요, 제 방에 숨겼어요.
여 그래? 어디에? 실은 책상 서랍과 옷장을 확인해 봤단다.
남 저, 베게 아래에 놓았어요.
여 정말? 그곳을 확인했어야 했는데, 침대 아래만 찾아 봤구나.
남 엄마, 정말로 죄송해요. 다음에는 더 열심히 공부할게요.
여 알았다. 어쨌든 지금 바로 성적표를 가지고 오너라.
남 알았어요, 엄마. 잠시만 기다려 주세요.

해설 남자가 언급한 "I put it under the pillow."를 통해 성적표가 베개 아래 있음을 알 수 있다.

어휘 disappoint 실망시키다 hide 숨기다 search 수색하다, 찾다

07 ④

해석 여 David, 인도 여행 준비는 어떻게 돼 가고 있어?
남 지금까지는 좋아. 어제, 비행기표를 구했어.
여 루피화로 환전은 했니?
남 아니. 인도에서 환전하는 것이 더 좋다고 들어서 말이야.
여 응, 그 말이 맞아. 지난달에 인도를 방문한 내 친구도 같은 말을 했어.
남 네가 함께 가면 여행이 더욱 재미있을 텐데 말이야.
여 너도 알잖아. 나는 일을 해야 해. 어쨌든, 기념품 사 오는 것 잊지 마.
남 알았어. 그런데, 너 겨울용 침낭 있니?
여 응.
남 그럼, 나 좀 빌려 줄래? 나는 여름용 침낭밖에 없어서 말이야.
여 알았어, 내일 가져다줄게.

해설 인도로 여행을 떠날 예정인 남자는 겨울철 침낭이 없어서 여자에게 이를 빌려달라고 부탁하였다.

08 ⑤

해석 (전화벨이 울린다.)

남 여보세요?

여 Robert Kim이랑 통화를 하고 싶은데요.

남 접니다.

여 안녕하세요, 저는 Cathy Johnson이에요. 아파트를 세놓는다는 광고를 봤습니다. 아직 가능한가요?

남 그럼요. 학생인가요 아니면 직장인인가요?

여 지역 방송국에서 일하고 있습니다.

남 알겠어요. 애완동물이 있나요? 사실, 저희 아파트에서는 애완동물을 기를 수가 없거든요.

여 그건 걱정 마세요. 애완동물은 없어요.

남 좋아요. 결정하기 전에 와서 아파트를 한번 둘러보는 것이 어때요?

여 알았습니다. 오늘 저녁 퇴근 후에 찾아봬도 될까요? 7시쯤일 거예요.

해설 "I saw your ad about renting an apartment. Is it still available?"을 통해 정답이 ⑤임을 알 수 있다.

어휘 **rent** 임대하다, 빌려주다 **have a look at** 한번 보다

09 ③

해석 (전화벨이 울린다.)

남 Little King 식품입니다. 무엇을 도와드릴까요?

여 채소를 좀 사고 싶은데요. 집으로 배송해 줄 수 있나요?

남 그럼요. 어떤 채소가 필요하신가요?

여 양배추, 당근 그리고 토마토요. 양배추랑 당근은 얼마인가요?

남 양배추는 한 통에 2달러이고, 당근은 킬로그램당 1달러입니다.

여 그럼, 양배추 다섯 통이랑 당근 3킬로그램 주세요.

남 알겠습니다. 그리고 토마토는 얼마나 필요하신가요? 토마토는 킬로그램당 3달러입니다.

여 5킬로그램 주세요. 그게 다예요.

남 알겠습니다. 주소를 말씀해 주시겠어요?

여 Green Street 14번지에 살고 있어요.

남 알겠습니다. 30분 후에 배송해 드리겠습니다.

해설 여자는 한 개에 2달러 하는 양배추를 다섯 통, kg당 1달러하는 당근을 3kg, kg당 3달러인 토마토를 5kg 주문했으므로 여자가 지불해야 할 총 금액은 $28이다.

10 ③

해석 남 Sally의 집에서 Potluck dinner가 있을 거라는 소식 들었어요?

여 Potluck dinner요? 그게 무엇이죠?

남 그게, 초대 받은 모든 사람들이 먹을 것을 가지고 오는 식사예요.

여 좋은데요! 그럼 우리는 무엇을 가지고 가죠?

남 Sally가 칠면조를 요리할 것이라고 했고, Jane은 피자를 구울 거라고 했어요.

여 그럼, 우리는 쿠키를 좀 가지고 가는 게 어때요?

남 Chris가 초콜릿 케이크를 가지고 올 거라고 했으니까, 쿠키는 좋은 생각이 아닌 것 같아요.

여 좋아요, 샐러드를 만들어요. 샐러드를 가지고 가면, 저녁이 완벽해 질 거예요.

남 당신 말에 전적으로 동의해요. 여보, 샐러드에 과일을 좀 넣는 것은 어때요?

여 좋은 생각이에요. 샐러드에 충분한 과일을 넣을 게요.

해설 쿠키를 가지고 가는 것이 어떤가라는 여자의 물음에 남자는 좋은 생각이 아니라고 하였으므로 정답은 ③이다.

어휘 **potluck dinner** (여러 사람들이) 각자 음식을 조금씩 가져 와서 나눠 먹는 식사 **turkey** 칠면조 **totally** 완전히, 전적으로 **add** 더하다, 첨가하다 **make sure** 반드시 ~을 하다

11 ⑤

해석 남 안녕하세요, 학생 여러분. 해마다 개최하는 단편 영화제에 대해 말해 줄게요. 언제나처럼, 이 대회는 학교 축제의 일부로 열릴 거예요. 우리 학교에 다니는 학생이면 누구나 이 대회에 참가할 수 있고요. 단편 영화의 내용은 예를 들어 클럽 활동 같은 여러분의 학교생활에 관한 것이어야 해요. 단편 영화의 길이는 5분에서 7분 사이여야 해요. 심사위원이 영화 동아리 가입 학생이었던 작년과는 달리, 올해에는 영화를 사랑하는 12명의 선생님들이 여러분의 단편 영화를 심사할 거예요. 1등상은 최신 비디오카메라예요. 더 많은 정보를 원하면, 학교 웹 사이트를 방문하세요.

해설 "Unlike last year, when the judges were movie club students, this year 12 teachers who love movies will judge your movie clip."라고 했으므로 정답은 ⑤이다.

어휘 **annual** 해마다 일어나는, 해마다의 **hold** 개최하다, 열다 **attend** 참석하다, 출석하다 **participate in** ~에 참가하다 **content** 내용

12 ④

해석 여 Sam, 신혼여행 동안 어느 호텔에 머무를지 결정했나요?

남 Hillside 호텔 어때요? 별 다섯 개짜리 특급 호텔이에요.

여 좋아요. 그러면, 지금 바로 방을 예약해요.

남 하지만, 문제는 가격이에요. 바다 전망을 가진 가장 싼 방 가격이 하루에 110달러거든요.

여 그건 너무 비싸요. 우린 하루에 100달러 이상은 쓸 수 없어요.

남 그럼, 바다 전망은 포기해야 해요.

여 괜찮아요. 하지만, 인터넷을 접속할 수 있는 방에 머물고 싶어요.

남 그럼 두 개 중에서 고르면 되겠네요. 어느 것이 더 마음에 들어요?

여 글쎄요, 디럭스방이 더 좋은 것 같아요.

남 좋아요. 그 방을 지금 예약할게요.

해설 디럭스방 중 하루에 100달러를 넘지 않으며, 인터넷을 사용할 수 있는 방은 ④이다.

어휘 **reserve** 예약하다 **ocean view** 바다가 보이는 전망 **access** 접근, 출입

13 ④

해석 남 실례합니다.

여 무엇을 도와드릴까요?

남 어젯밤에 인터넷으로 차를 예약했거든요.

여 성함과 주소를 알려 주시겠습니까?

남 제 이름은 Allen Kim이고요 Oxford가 87번지에 살고 있습니다.

여 잠시만 기다려 주세요. 아, 하루 동안 오픈카를 예약하셨군요. 맞습니까?

남 예, 맞아요.

여 보험을 포함해서 하루 비용이 80달러입니다. 어떻게 지불하기를 원하십니까?

남 현금으로 할게요. 80달러 여기 있습니다.

여 감사합니다. 고객님의 차는 앞문 옆에 있습니다.

해설 남자가 금액을 지불하고 거래가 성사되었으므로 여자 직원이 할 수 있는 말로 가장 적절한 것은 ④이다. ① 어디 봅시다. 이 오픈카로 할게요. ② 유감스럽게도 아직 운전면허가 없어요. ③ 내가 당신이라면, 주유소에 들르겠어요. ⑤ 정말요? 저도 Oxford가의 아파트에 살아요.

어휘 **convertible car** 오픈카 **insurance** 보험 **pay in cash** 현금으로 지불하다

14 ③

해설 여 실례합니다. 지하철에다 제 핸드백을 놓고 내렸어요. 핸드백 찾는 것을 도와줄래요?

남 언제 잃어버리셨는지 말씀해 주시겠어요?

여 오늘 오후, 약 3시경이요.

남 타고 계셨던 열차의 번호를 아시나요?

여 아니요, 몰라요. 하지만 지하철은 Milford행이었어요. 저는 시청역에서 내렸고요.

남 알겠습니다. 가방의 모양을 말씀해 주시겠어요?

여 네모난 모양이고 흰색이고 꽃무늬가 그려진 가방이에요.

남 신분증이나 운전 면허증 같은 것이 가방 안에 있나요?

여 아니요. 휴대 전화랑 책 몇 권이 있어요.

남 알았습니다. 잠시만 기다려 보세요. 가서 확인해 볼게요.

해설 지하철에서 핸드백을 놓고 내린 여자가 지하철 분실물 센터에 가서 직원에게 찾아 줄 것을 부탁했으므로 직원의 대답으로 적절한 것은 ③이다. ① 실례지만, 분실물 보관소가 어디인가요? ② 언제 당신의 지갑을 잃어버린 것 같나요? ④ 두 번째 선반에 있는 핸드백은 얼마인가요? ⑤ 감사합니다. 당신 덕분에 제 핸드백을 찾았어요.

어휘 **get off** 내리다, 하차하다 **describe** 묘사하다 **square-shaped** 사각형 모양의 **driver's license** 운전 면허증

15 ④

해설 여 Ron은 학교 선생님이고, 여자 친구가 있다. 그의 여자 친구인 Andrea는 론과 같은 학교에서 근무한다. Ron은 내일이 Andrea의 생일이기 때문에 그녀의 선물을 사려고 액세서리 가게에 있다. 그는 Andrea에게 목걸이를 사 주려고 생각하고 있다. 그는 점원이 추천해 주는 것이 마음에 들지 않는다. 그래서 점원이 그에게 또 다른 목걸이를 보여 준다. 이번에 Ron은 목걸이가 마음에 든다. 그 목걸이는 그가 사기를 원했던 것과 똑같다. 이 상황에서 Ron이 점원에게 할 말로 가장 적절한 것은 무엇인가?

Ron 이것이 좋네요. 이것을 살게요. 얼마죠?

해설 점원이 자신이 사려고 하는 것을 보여주었을 때 할 말로 ④가 가장 적절하다. ① 좀 더 싼 것을 보여 줄래요? ② 제가 찾는 것은 목걸이가 아니라 귀걸이에요. ③

여기요. 액세서리 가게는 어디에 있죠? ⑤ 이 목걸이를 환불할게요. 여기 영수증이요.

어휘 **recommend** 추천하다 **appeal** 호소하다

16-17 ②, ②

해석 여 잘 알다시피, 마늘은 강한 맛과 냄새로 유명합니다. 마늘은 전 세계적으로 요리를 할 때 광범위하게 사용되며, 우리는 마늘이 들어있는 음식은 건강에 좋다고 믿습니다. 하지만 "동전에 양면이 있다"라는 속담처럼, 마늘 또한 신체에 부정적인 영향을 끼칩니다. 마늘은 매우 강해서 마늘을 너무 많이 먹으면 소화기관에 염증 또는 심지어 상처가 생길 수도 있습니다. 또한 마늘에 알레르기가 있는 사람들도 있습니다. 만약 이 사람들이 마늘을 먹으면 피부 발진이나 두통과 같은 증세에 시달릴 수 있습니다. 마늘은 잠재적으로 혈액을 묽게 만들 수 있어서 수술 전에는 먹지 않는 것이 가장 좋습니다. 이러한 내용을 염두에 두십시오. 좋습니다. 다 됐습니다. 휴식 시간 후에, Orange Hall에서 여러분 스스로 마늘빵을 만드는 시간을 가질 것입니다. 요리 기구부터 밀가루까지 모든 것이 완벽하게 준비되어 있습니다. 약간의 휴식 시간을 가진 후에 Orange Hall로 가십시오.

해설 16 동전에 양면이 있는 것처럼 마늘도 신체에 부정적인 영향을 미친다고 하면서 이에 대한 구체적인 내용을 말하고 있으므로 정답은 ②이다. ① 사람들은 어떻게 마늘을 처음으로 먹게 되었나 ② 마늘 섭취의 부작용 ③ 생마늘의 영양적 가치 ④ 생마늘을 사용하는 다양한 방법 ⑤ 마늘이 그렇게 강한 맛과 냄새를 가지는 이유

17 "After the break, you'll have time to make garlic bread on your own at the Orange Hall."을 통해 정답이 ②임을 알 수 있다.

어휘 **proverb** 속담 **irritation** 염증; 초조 **suffer from** ~로 고통 받다 **skin rash** 피부 발진 **potentially** 잠재적으로 **flour** 밀가루

◎ Dictation

01 How could I forget

02 book an airline ticket / all the tickets are sold

03 bring people into doctors' offices / how to reduce / with a big round of applause

04 How much did you pay for it / at low prices / compared to other sites

05 You don't look well / From now on / take you to the dentist / in 30

06 I have to discuss with you / where is your report card / I should have checked there

07 So far so good / it's better to exchange money / bring back a souvenir

08 Is it still available / no pets are allowed / have a look at

09 have them delivered to my place / I have five cabbage heads / Could you tell me your address

10 what are we going to bring / I don't think cookies are a good idea / I totally agree with you

11 I'm going to tell you about / will judge your movie clip

23회 듣기 모의고사

p.138-139

01 ①	02 ⑤	03 ④	04 ③	05 ③	06 ⑤
07 ④	08 ①	09 ⑤	10 ②	11 ④	12 ④
13 ③	14 ①	15 ④	16 ⑤	17 ③	

01 ①

해석 남 이번 주 금요일이 아내 생일이에요. 어떤 선물이 좋을까요?

여 보석은 어때요? 금 목걸이가 괜찮을 거예요.

남 금 목걸이요? 아내가 정말로 좋아할 거라고 생각해요?

여 그럼요! 모든 여성은 보석을 좋아해요.

해설 생일 선물로 금 목걸이를 해주면 아내가 좋아하지 묻는 물음에 대한 응답으로 가장 적절한 것은 ①이다. ② 이 금 목걸이를 환불해 주시겠어요? ③ 미안해요, 생일 파티에 참석할 수 없어요. ④ 당신의 아내가 당신과 함께 일을 했어야 했어요. ⑤ 좋아요, 이 목걸이를 살게요. 얼마죠?

02 ⑤

해석 여 드디어 브라질과 영국의 월드컵 결승전이 오늘 저녁에 열려.

남 그래, 어느 팀이 우승할 것 같아?

여 당연히 브라질이지. 브라질을 이길 수 있는 나라는 없어. 넌 어떻게 생각하니?

남 나도 그렇게 생각해. 브라질이 반드시 이길 거야!

해설 브라질이 우승할 것 같다는 여자는 남자에게 의견을 물어본다. 이에 대한 남자의 응답으로 가장 적절한 것은 ⑤이다. ① 난 축구에 관심이 없어. ② 그래, 브라질을 방문하고 싶어. ③ 너랑 같이 갈 수 없을 것 같아. ④ 물론이지! 영국이 브라질보다 잘 살아.

03 ④

해석 남 안녕하세요! 잠시만 주목해 주세요. 여러분에게 새로운 사물함 세트가 오늘 오후에 배송된다는 소식을 알려드립니다. 내일 학교에 와서 낡은 사물함을 가져가고 새로운 것을 설치할 것입니다. 따라서 학생 여러분

은 오늘 학교를 떠나기 전에 사물함을 비워 주십시오. 교과서나 교복 같은 개인 물품은 학생 건물의 메인 홀에 놔 둘 수 있어요. 하지만 각각의 품목에 자신의 이름을 쓰는 것을 잊지 마세요. 협조해 주셔서 감사합니다.

해설 'I want all students to clear out their locker'라고 말했으므로 정답은 ④이다.

어휘 inform 알려 주다 take away 제거하다, 치우다 belonging 소지품, 소유물 cooperation 협조

04 ③

해석 남 내 새 아파트에 대해서 어떻게 생각해?

여 상당히 좋은데. 거실 전망이 멋져.

남 그게 내가 이 집을 임대하기로 결심한 이유야.

여 하지만 실내 공기가 별로 신선하지 않은 것 같지 않아?

남 새로 지었기 때문이야. 시간이 흐르면서 괜찮아질 거야.

여 거실에 식물을 좀 두는 게 어때? 실내 공기의 질을 개선하는 데 도움이 될 거야.

남 좋은 생각이야.

여 하루에 두 번 적어도 30분씩 모든 창문을 열어 두는 것도 효과적이야.

남 그래, 알고 있어.

여 전자 공기 청정기 또는 정화기를 설치하면, 금상첨화일 거야.

해설 거실에 식물을 두거나 창문을 모두 열어 두거나 공기 청정기 등을 설치하면 실내 공기가 좋아진다는 내용이 언급되고 있으므로 정답은 ③이다.

어휘 newly-built 새로 지은 improve 나아지다 effective 효과적인 purifier 정화기 the icing on the cake 금상첨화

05 ③

해석 (문을 두드린다.)

남 들어와요.

여 안녕하세요, 여기 말씀하신 비디오테이프예요.

남 좋아. 이제부터 우리는 이 테이프를 보고 또 봐야 해. 선수들도 마찬가지고 말이야.

여 알겠어요. Dega 감독님.

남 그래, Laura가 결승전에 뛸 수 있을 것 같아?

여 그런 것 같아요. 무릎에 더는 통증이 없다고 말했거든요.

남 좋아! Jessica는 어때? Jessica가 슬럼프를 극복해야 하는데 말이야.

여 글쎄요. 제가 그 점에 대해서 Jessica와 대화를 나누려고 노력하고 있어요.

남 자넬 믿네. Jessica가 결승전에 뛸지 안 뛸지는 자네에게 달려 있어.

여 그런데, 결승전 전략은 어떻게 되나요?

남 최선의 방어가 최선의 공격이라는 말 알지. 그게 내 전략일세.

해설 남자와 여자가 선수들에 관해 이야기 하고 있다. 여자는 선수들을 관리하고 남자는 경기 전략을 짜는 것으로 보아 감독과 트레이너의 관계임을 알 수 있다.

어휘 mention 언급하다 over and over 반복해서 get over 극복하다 strategy 전략, 전술 defense 방어 offense 공격

06 ⑤

해석 여 Patrick, 이 사진을 봐. 5년 전의 우리의 모습이야.

남 맞아. 그때 우리는 정말로 젊어 보인다.

여 사진 속의 네 곱슬머리를 봐. 정말 우스워.

남 하지만 그때에는 그 헤어스타일이 매우 인기 있었어. 네 큰 안경은 어떻고? 정말로 너랑 안 어울려.

여 네 말에 동의해. 오, 너 그때는 안경을 안 꼈구나.

남 맞아. 그 당시에는 안경을 낄 정도로 시력이 나쁘지 않았거든.

여 하지만 알지, 너는 안경을 안 끼던 전보다 안경을 끼는 지금이 더 멋있어 보여.

남 고마워. Lucy, 이 사진에서 네가 하고 있는 이 머리띠는 생일 선물로 내가 사 준 것이지, 그렇지?

여 맞아. 이 하트 모양의 귀걸이도 네가 준 선물이야.

남 그래, 내 선물을 받고서 정말로 좋아했던 것이 기억나.

해설 "My eyesight was not bad enough to wear glasses then."라는 말을 통해 사진 속의 남자는 안경을 쓰지 않았음을 추론할 수 있다.

어휘 curly 곱슬곱슬한 suit 어울리다 eyesight 시력

07 ④

해석 (전화벨이 울린다.)

여 여보세요? May입니다.

남 안녕, May. 나야, Ralph. 잘 지내?

여 안녕, Ralph! 나야 잘 지내지. 넌 어때? 서울로 출장 간다는 소식을 들었는데.

남 응. 그래서 너한테 전화 한 거야. May, 부탁 하나만 해도 될까?

여 당연하지. 서울에 있는 동안 네 애완견을 돌봐 주길 원하니?

남 아니. 그 일은 내 사촌이 해줄 거야. May, 네 휴대용 컴퓨터 좀 빌려 줄 수 있어?

여 네 것은 어쩌고? 한 달 전에 새로 샀잖아.

남 지금 모니터가 깨져 있어서 가져갈 수가 없어.

여 아, 알았어. 좋아. 내일 사무실로 가져다줄게.

남 고마워, May. 너는 항상 나에게 큰 도움이 되는구나.

해설 서울로 출장 가는 남자는 여자에게 휴대용 컴퓨터를 빌려 달라고 부탁하였다.

08 ①

해석 (전화벨이 울린다.)

여 안녕하세요, Sun&Moon 쇼핑입니다. 무엇을 도와드릴까요?

남 예. 지난주에 웹 사이트를 통해서 가죽 재킷을 주문했거든요.

여 주문하신 내역에 무슨 문제가 있나요?

남 그게, 주문을 취소하고 싶어서요.

여 왜 취소를 원하시나요?

남 아내가 어제 똑같은 것을 사가지고 왔거든요.

여 알겠습니다. 이름이랑 주소를 알려 주시겠어요?

남 제 이름은 Lee Thomson이고요. 주소는 Wellington가 Victoria 아파트 708호입니다.

여 잠시만 기다려 주세요. 됐습니다. 고객님의 주문이 취소되었습니다.

남 감사합니다.

해설 웹 사이트를 통해 가죽 재킷을 주문한 남자는 아내가 자신이 주문한 재킷과 똑같은 것을 사 오자, 자신이 주문할 것을 취소하기 위해 전화를 한 것이다.

09 ⑤

해석 남 실례합니다만, 한국어 문법 코스를 수강하고 싶은데요. 전 초보자예요.

여 두 개의 코스가 있어요. 하나는 일반 코스로 수강료가 70달러이고요, 다른 하나는 집중 코스로 수강료가 120달러예요.

남 두 코스의 차이가 뭐죠?

여 일반 코스는 일주일에 3번 수업이 있고 집중 코스는 매일 있어요. 제 생각에 집중 코스가 더 좋을 것 같네요.

남 좋아요, 집중 코스를 수강할게요. 교재도 구입해야 하나요?

여 예. 교재 가격은 15달러입니다.

남 알았어요. 교재도 주세요. 신용카드로 지불해도 되나요?

여 그럼요. 카드를 주시겠습니까?

남 여기 있습니다.

여 고맙습니다. 여기에 서명을 해 주시겠습니까?

해설 한 달에 120달러하는 집중반을 수강하기로 한 남자는 교재를 15달러 주고 추가로 구입하였으므로 남자가 지불해야 할 총 금액은 135달러이다.

어휘 take a course 강의를 듣다 intensive 집중적인, 철저한 difference 차이

10 ②

해석 남 너무 배가 불러요. 저녁이 정말로 맛있었어요.

여 나도 배가 불러요. 하지만 디저트를 좀 먹고 싶네요. 당신은요?

남 나도요. 수박과 바나나를 먹읍시다. 수박과 바나나를 좋아하죠, 그렇죠?

여 그래요, 과즙이 많고 달콤해서 좋아해요. 알겠지만, 내가 어렸을 때 엄마가 나를 '과일 킬러'라고 부르곤 했어요.

남 과일 킬러라고요? 재미있네요. 수박과 바나나를 제외하고 또 무슨 과일을 좋아해요?

여 딸기와 사과요. 딸기 주스 마시는 걸 정말로 좋아하고 아침에 사과를 먹곤 했어요.

남 당신이 거의 모든 종류의 과일을 좋아한다는 것을 알고 있어요. 하지만 당신이 포도를 먹는 것을 지금까지 본 적이 없어요.

여 맞아요. 지난여름에 포도를 먹고 식중독에 걸렸었거든요. 그 이후로 포도를 안 먹어요.

남 오, 정말이요? 몰랐어요.

여 음, 특히 여름철에는 음식을 먹을 때 조심해야 해요.

해설 "Last summer, I got food poisoning after eating some grapes. After that, I don't eat them any more."를 통해 정답이 포도임을 추론할 수 있다.

어휘 juicy 즙이 많은 food poisoning 식중독

11 ④

해석 여 좋습니다. 플로리다에서 가장 인기 있는 축제 중 하나인 딸기 축제에 대해 말씀드리겠습니다. 축제는 3월 1일에 시작해서 3월 10일에 끝납니다. 축제는 Rainbow Green 공원에서 열립니다. 500명이 넘는 딸기 재배 농부들이 축제에 참석할 것이고 축제 기간 동안에 자신들이 재

배한 맛있는 딸기를 선보일 것입니다. 나이에 관계없이 입장료는 무료이고, 방문객들은 시중의 절반 가격인 단 돈 5달러에 1kg의 딸기를 살 수 있습니다. 방문객은 또한 가장 맛있는 딸기를 의미하는 '올해의 딸기'를 고를 기회를 가지게 됩니다. '올해의 딸기'를 재배한 농부는 현금으로 1,000달러의 상금을 받게 됩니다.

해설 입장료는 무료이다.

어휘 entrance fee 입장료 regardless of ~에 관계없이 receive 받다

12 ④

해석 남 Ann, 뭘 보고 있니?
여 음, 내비게이션을 하나 사고 싶어서. 하지만, 좋은 것을 고르기가 쉽지 않네.
남 내 생각엔 적어도 7인치 모니터는 필요할 것 같은데.
여 맞아.
남 FreeRoad를 사지 그래?
여 FreeRoad는 평판이 그다지 좋지 않아. 그리고, 난 DMB 기능이 있는 내비게이션을 사고 싶어.
남 구입비용으로 최대 얼마를 생각하고 있는데?
여 300달러.
남 그러면, Cambridge사에서 나온 이것은 어때?
여 그래, 그것이 좋은 선택인 것 같다. 좋았어, 그것을 주문할게.

해설 '최소한 7인치의 모니터', '300달러 이하', 'DMB 기능이 있는', 위의 조건에 모두 부합하는 것은 Wide Tank이다.

어휘 reputation 평판 be willing to 기꺼이 ~하다

13 ③

해석 남 드디어, LA Lakers랑 Chicago Bulls의 결승전이 오늘 밤에 열려.
여 그래. 시합이 정말 흥미진진할 거야.
남 올해에는 어느 팀이 우승할 것 같아?
여 당연히 LA Lakers지.
남 하지만, Chicago Bulls도 이기기에 쉬운 팀은 아니야. 수비력은 리그에서 가장 강하니까 말이야.
여 알아. 하지만 Lakers에는 Koby Bryant가 있어. 그는 내가 지금껏 본 최고의 슈터야.
남 Koby도 경기에 나갈까? 내가 아는 한, 그는 발목 부상에서 완전히 회복되지 않았어.
여 그것은 사실이 아니야. 그는 완전히 회복해서 경기에 나갈 것이라고 감독이 말했어.
남 그 말이 사실이라면, Lakers가 이길 가능성이 더 크겠는 걸.
여 당연하지! 이 경기가 정말로 기대돼.

해설 남자가 LA Lakers가 이길 확률이 크다고 말했을 때, 여자의 응답으로 가장 적절한 것은 ③일 것이다. ① 걱정하지 마. 내 발목은 괜찮아. ② 맞아. Lakers가 가장 유명한 팀이야. ④ 하지만 내가 응원하는 팀은 LA Lakers야. ⑤ 맞아. 더 일찍 예약 했어야 했어.

어휘 root for 응원하다, 힘을 북돋아주다 hold 개최하다 defeat 쳐부수다

14 ①

해석 여 오, 벌써 5시예요. 서둘러요. 사람들이 곧 도착할 거예요.
남 걱정 말아요, 집들이 파티를 위한 모든 것이 거의 준비되었어요.
여 뒷마당은 청소했나요?
남 예, 했어요. 식탁도 정리했고, 바비큐도 불 피울 준비가 다 되었어요.
여 좋아요, 전 이제 막 집안 청소를 끝냈어요.
남 음식은요?
여 어제 고기와 채소를 좀 샀어요.
남 그럼, 고기와 채소를 뒷마당에 가져다 놓을게요. 그러면, 요리할 준비가 다 된 것이니까요.
여 정말요? 고마워요, 여보. 당신은 참 자상한 남편이에요.
남 **천만에요. 내가 할 일이 또 있나요?**

해설 식탁 정리, 바비큐 준비 등 여러 가지 일을 한 남편에게 아내가 고맙다고 하면서 정말 자상한 남편이라고 했으므로 응답으로 가장 적절한 것은 ①이다. ② 서둘러요. 그렇지 않으면 우린 콘서트를 놓칠 거예요. ③ 음, 난 파티에 가는 것엔 관심이 없어요. ④ 그건 중요하지 않아요. 만약 당신이 좋다면 나도 괜찮아요. ⑤ 고기나 해산물 중에 저녁으로 뭘 먹고 싶어요?

15 ④

해석 남 Robert는 작은 포도밭을 가지고 있어서 그것으로부터 생계를 유지하고 있다. Robert는 아내 Jessica와 함께 포도를 재배한다. 그들은 일년 내내 열심히 일한다. 마침내, 포도를 수확할 시기가 되었다. 잘 익은 포도를 보면서, Robert는 올해 많은 이익을 낼 것으로 확신한다. Robert는 매우 기쁘다. Robert는 이 모두가 아내 Jessica가 열심히 일한 덕분이라고 생각한다. Robert는 Jessica에게 무언가를 말하고 싶다. 이 상황에서, Robert가 Jessica에게 할 말로 가장 적절한 것은 무엇인가?
Robert **당신 덕분에 올해 좋은 포도를 수확하게 됐어요.**

해설 고생한 아내에게 무언가 말을 하고 싶은 Robert가 할 수 있는 말로 가장 적절한 것은 ④이다. ① 배고파요. 먹을 것이 있나요? ② 포도가 좋아 보이네요. 5킬로그램을 살게요. ③ 난 포도밭을 팔고 싶어요. 당신은 어때요? ⑤ 사실, 전 다른 어떤 잼보다도 포도 잼을 좋아해요.

어휘 vineyard 포도밭 well-ripened 잘 익은 profit 이익 be sure 확신하다

16-17 ⑤, ③

해석 여 마지막 질문을 할게요. 인생에서 성공하고 싶나요? 당연히 그렇겠죠! 인생에서 성공하기를 원하지 않는 사람은 없지만, 사실 정말로 성공하는 사람은 겨우 몇 명일뿐이에요. 왜 이럴까요? 이것은 많은 사람들이 오늘 해야 할 일을 내일로 미루기 때문이에요. 한 때, 저는 월요일에 월말 시험 준비를 시작하겠다고 결심했어요. 하지만 월요일이 왔을 때, 화요일에 시작하겠다고 결심했어요. 화요일에는 수요일까지 기다리기로 결심했죠. 결국 준비를 하지 않았고 시험에 떨어졌어요. 그때부터 저는 중요한 것은 어떤 것도 다음 날로 미루지 않아요. 좋아요, 이게 다예요. 점심시간 후에, 여러분은 2층의 Rainbow 홀에 가서 올해 여러분이 이루기를 바라는 목표를 적는 시간을 가질 거예요. 들어 주셔서 감사합니다. 점심 식사 맛있게 하세요.

해설 16 "I would never put off anything important until the next day."를 통해 정

답이 ⑤임을 추론할 수 있다. ① 티끌 모아 태산이다. ② 겉만 보고 판단하지 마라. ③ 서툰 일꾼이 연장을 탓한다. ④ 김칫국부터 마시지 마라. ⑤ 오늘 할 일을 내일로 미루지 마라.

17 "you'll have some time to write down some goals that you want to accomplish this year."를 통해 정답이 ③임을 추론할 수 있다.

어휘 **in practice** 사실, 실제로 **put off** 미루다 **accomplish** 이루다. 성취하다

Dictation

01 What do you think
02 is taking place
03 I would like to inform you / to clear out their lockers / Thank you for your cooperation
04 It's quite good / As time goes by / the icing on the cake
05 From now on / has to get over / the best defense is a good offense
06 They really don't suit you / you look better now
07 That's why I'm calling you / The monitor is broken / a great help to me
08 I'd like to cancel it / Could I have your name
09 I'm a beginner / is held three times a week / Can I pay with my credit card
10 my mom used to call me / I got food poisoning / be careful of eating food
11 It will take place in / regardless of age / have a chance to choose
12 what are you looking at / you're willing to spend / that's a good choice
13 not be easy to defeat / I've ever seen / he has made a full recovery
14 clean the backyard / everything will be ready to cook
15 makes a living from it / well-ripened grapes / He wants to say something
16-17 Let me ask you / put off the things / From then on / Thank you for listening

24회 듣기 모의고사

p.144-145

01 ③	02 ③	03 ①	04 ①	05 ②	06 ③
07 ④	08 ②	09 ⑤	10 ⑤	11 ⑤	12 ⑤
13 ①	14 ③	15 ④	16 ②	17 ③

01 ③

해석 여 이 핑크 샌들이 나에게 어울리는 것 같아요.
남 저도 그렇게 생각합니다. 이것을 구입하면, 후회는 하지 않을 거예요.
여 좋아요, 이것을 살게요. 얼마죠?
남 30달러입니다. 정말로 좋은 거래에요.

해설 핑크 샌들을 구입하기로 결심한 여자가 가격이 얼마인지 물었으므로 응답으로 가장 적절한 것은 ③이다. ① 어제 샌들을 잃어버렸어요. ② 정말이요? 정말로 고마워요. ④ 2달러를 지불하면, 샌들을 고쳐 드릴게요. ⑤ 좋아요, 이 핑크 샌들을 살게요.

02 ③

해석 남 안녕하세요, 어떻게 도와드릴까요?
여 노트북 컴퓨터가 갑자기 작동을 멈추었어요.
남 알았습니다. 컴퓨터에 무슨 일이 있었나요?
여 음, 키보드에 커피를 쏟았어요.

해설 고장이 난 노트북 컴퓨터에 무슨 일이 있었느냐는 남자의 물음에 대한 여자의 응답으로 가장 적절한 것은 ③이다. ① 좋아요. 이 프로그램을 설치할게요. ② 알았어요. 이 노트북 컴퓨터를 살게요. ④ 그럼요. 내 노트북 컴퓨터를 쓸 수 있어요. ⑤ 노트북 컴퓨터가 훨씬 사용하기 편해요.

03 ①

해석 여 신사 숙녀 여러분, 현재 시장에서 가장 효과가 있는 차량 광택제를 소개해 드리겠습니다. 저는 Car Protector를 말씀드리는 것입니다. 여러분의 차를 빛나게 할 뿐만 아니라 먼지까지 제거해 주는 Car Protector를 말씀드리는 것입니다. 지금 Car Protector 패키지를 구매하십시오. 그러면 청소 솔 세트를 완전히 무료로 얻을 수 있습니다! 서두르십시오! 이 행사는 10월 31일까지만 지속됩니다. 당신의 Car Protector를 지금 가지십시오!

해설 "서두르십시오! 이 행사는 10월 31일까지만 지속됩니다. 당신의 Car Protector를 지금 가지십시오!"를 통해서, 상품을 광고하는 내용임을 추론할 수 있을 것이다.

어휘 **efficient** 효과적인 **remove** 제거하다 **dirt** 먼지 **promotion** 판매 촉진 행사

04 ①

해석 여 네 구직 인터뷰가 이번 주 금요일이지, 그렇지 않니?
남 그래, 맞아. 약간 긴장 돼. 알다시피, 이번이 처음으로 하는 구직 인터뷰 잖아.
여 음, 인터뷰에 정시에 도착해야 해. 그렇지 않으면, 면접관들이 너에 대해 나쁜 인상을 가질 거야.
남 당연히, 그래야지.
여 네 옷도 중요한 역할을 할 거야. 회색 계열의 정장이 다른 색깔보다는 괜찮을 것 같아.
남 알았어, 충고 고마워.
여 아, 네가 명심해야 할 것이 한 가지 더 있어.
남 그게 무엇인데? 말해 봐.
여 질문에 대한 네 대답에 관한 것이야. 만약 면접관들이 네가 대답하기에

너무나 어려운 질문을 하면, 너는 "죄송합니다. 그 점에 대해서는 잘 모르겠습니다."라고 말하는 게 나아.

남 네 말은 정직이 최선의 방책이다 이 말이지, 맞지?

여 그래, 맞아.

해설 인터뷰 시간에 늦지 말고, 회색 계열의 정장을 입고, 모르는 질문에 대해서는 솔직히 모른다고 말하라고 조언해 주고 있다.

어휘 **have a bad impression of ~** ~에게 나쁜 인상을 가지다 **play an important role** 중요한 역할을 하다 **gray-colored suit** 회색 계열의 양복

05 ②

해석 남 안녕하세요, 무엇을 도와드릴까요?

여 저, 휴대 전화를 사러 두 시간 전에 여기에 왔거든요.

남 그래서요...

여 집에 도착하자마자, 지갑을 잃어버린 것을 알았어요.

남 여기서 지갑을 잃어버린 것 같으세요?

여 예, 그런 것 같아요. 제가 들렀던 가게 중의 한 곳에다 지갑을 놔두고 온 것 같아요. 이곳에 오기 전에 휴대 전화 가게에 갔었어요. 그 직원이 분실물센터에 가서 물어보는 게 나을 거라고 말했어요.

남 네, 알겠어요. 오늘 여성용 지갑이 몇 개 들어왔어요. 지갑의 모양을 말씀해 주시겠어요?

여 하트무늬가 그려진 사각형의 지갑이에요.

남 손님께서 말씀하신 것과 같은 것이 있는 것 같아요.

여 정말이요?

남 잠시만 기다려 주세요. 안에 가서 확인해 볼게요.

해설 쇼핑몰에 왔던 여자가 지갑이 없어진 것을 발견하고 찾으려고 분실물 센터에 가서 대화를 나누고 있으므로 분실물 센터 직원과 지갑 분실자의 관계이다.

어휘 **as soon as** ~하자마자 **realize** 깨닫다, 알아차리다 **Lost and Found** 분실물 센터, 분실물보관소 **describe** 묘사하다, 설명하다

06 ③

해석 여 Oh, Eric! 와 줘서 고마워.

남 내가 어떻게 네 생일 파티에 빠지겠니, Sally?

여 음, 내 생각에는 네가 여기 온 것은 내 생일 파티 때문이 아니라 네 소개팅 때문인 것 같은데.

남 하하. 그래, 누가 Gina니?

여 창문 옆에 서 있는 여자 세 명 보여?

남 응. 긴 머리를 하고 있는 여자가 Gina니?

여 아니, 그 아이는 Anica야. Gina는 파마머리에 짧은 치마를 입고 있어.

남 커다란 귀걸이를 한 여자애 말이니?

여 그래, 맞아. 어때?

남 오, 매우 귀여운 것 같은데. 맘에 들어.

해설 Eric이 소개받게 될 Gina는 창문 옆에 서 있으면서, 파마머리에 짧은 치마를 입고 있고, 커다란 귀걸이를 하고 있는 여성이다.

어휘 **not because of A but because of B** A 때문이 아니라 B 때문에 **blind date** 소개팅

07 ④

해석 여 Albert, 우리는 매우 어려운 경제 상황에 처해 있어요. 절약을 시작해야 해요.

남 그런 것 같아요. 일부 직원을 해고하는 것은 어떨까요?

여 좋은 생각이 아닌 것 같아요.

남 그러면, 공장을 시골 지역으로 이전하는 것은 어떨까요?

여 내 생각도 그래요. 그렇게 되면, 정부로부터 지원을 받을 수도 있으니까요.

남 맞아요.

여 우리가 은행에서 대출을 받을 수 있을까요?

남 글쎄요, 잘 모르겠네요.

여 Albert, ABC 은행에 가서 대출에 대해 문의를 해 볼래요?

남 알겠습니다. 지금 바로 갈게요.

여 아, 그런데, 신상품은 언제 출시되죠?

남 이번 달 말에요.

해설 지금 사정이 어려운 여자는 남자에게 "Albert, can you go to ABC bank to inquire about it?"라고 부탁하였다.

어휘 **financial** 재정의, 금융의 **lay off** 해고하다 **rural** 시골의 **inquire** 문의하다

08 ②

해석 남 Jenny, 뉴욕에 도착하려면 얼마나 더 가야하죠?

여 두 시간이요. 먼 길이라는 것을 알잖아요.

남 그래요. 하지만, 비행기를 탔다면 벌써 도착했을 거예요.

여 맞아요. 하지만 이미 엎질러진 물인 걸요.

남 어쨌든, 다음 휴게소를 들릅시다.

여 왜요?

남 배가 고파요. 1시 이후에 아무 것도 먹지 않았어요.

여 알았어요. 샌드위치랑 음료수를 좀 살게요.

남 고마워요. 봐요! 다음 휴게소가 10km 떨어져 있다는 표지판이에요.

여 그래요. 기름은 어때요? 지금 기름을 넣어야 하나요?

남 아니요. 기름은 지금 충분해요.

해설 휴게소를 왜 들르려고 하느냐는 여자의 물음에 남자는 "I'm hungry. You know, I haven't eaten anything since one o'clock."라고 했다.

어휘 **reach** 도착하다 **It's no use crying over spilt milk.** 엎질러진 우유에 대해 울어 봐야 소용이 없다. **service area** 휴게소

09 ⑤

해석 여 안녕하세요, 테니스 라켓을 구입하고 싶은데요.

남 마음에 두고 계신 특별한 라켓이 있나요?

여 Teran사에서 나온 라켓이 있나요?

남 예, 있습니다. Teran사에서 나온 라켓은 두 종류가 있습니다. 하나는 50달러이고요, 다른 하나는 70달러입니다.

여 어느 것이 더 가볍죠?

남 두 번째 것이 더 가볍습니다. 일반적으로, 더 비싼 것이 더 가볍거든요.

여 알았어요. 더 가벼운 것을 살게요. 그리고 헤어밴드와 손목 밴드도 있나요?

남 예. 헤어밴드는 10달러이고, 손목 밴드는 5달러예요. 이 제품도 역시

Teran사에서 나온 것입니다.

여 그럼, 헤어밴드 한 개하고, 손목 밴드 두 개 주세요. 모두 다 해서 얼마인가 요?

남 잠시만요. 계산해 드리겠습니다.

해설 여자는 70달러짜리 테니스 라켓과 10달러짜리 헤어밴드를 한 개, 5달러짜리 손 목 밴드를 두 개 사기로 했으므로 총 지불할 금액은 90달러이다.

어휘 have ~ in mind ~을 염두에 두고 있다 wristband 손목 밴드 add up 더하다

10 ⑤

해석 남 Sara, 나 드디어 다음 주 금요일에 한국에 가.

여 와, 부럽다. 한국에서 어떤 도시를 제일 먼저 가니?

남 부산! 거기서 1주일간 머물러서 해변을 즐길 거야.

여 나도 일전에 부산을 방문한 적이 있어. 정말로 아름다운 도시야. 다음 목적지는 어디야?

남 부산 근처에 있는 마산과 울산을 방문할거야.

여 마산과 울산? 음, 그 도시들에 대해서는 들어본 적이 없어.

남 아마 그 도시들이 부산만큼 크지 않아서 일거야. 이 도시들을 방문한 후에, 광주에 갈 거야.

여 대전 또는 한국의 수도인 서울은 어때?

남 서울은 나의 최종 목적지야. 하지만 대전을 방문할 어떤 계획도 갖고 있지 않아.

여 왜? 대전 또한 여행하기 좋은 도시라고 들었는데 말이야.

남 알아, 하지만 지금까지 벌써 대전을 두 번이나 방문했거든.

해설 남자는 대전을 이미 두 번이나 방문했기 때문에 이번에는 방문할 계획이 없다고 말했다.

11 ⑤

해석 여 1945년 1월 26일에 태어난 Tom Jones는 주로 단편 소설을 쓴 미국 의 작가이다. Jones는 Illinois주의 Aurora에서 자랐고 하와이 대학을 다녔으며 그곳에서 야구팀의 포수로 활약했다. Jones는 대학을 졸업 한 후에 군대에 가서 베트남전에 참전했다. 그의 전쟁 경험은 글쓰기에 영향을 끼쳤다. 1993년에 출간된 그의 첫 번째 책은 단편 소설 모음집 이었다. 이 이야기들은 고통과 죽음의 주제를 다루었다. 최근에 Jones 는 영화를 위한 시나리오를 쓰기도 했다.

해설 현재 남자는 영화배우로 활동 중인 것이 아니라, 영화 시나리오를 작성 중이다.

어휘 primarily 주로 short story 단편 소설 raise 기르다. 재배하다 influence ~에 영향을 끼치다

12 ⑤

해석 여 Ken, 이리 와 봐. 게시판에 새로운 직업이 올라왔어.

남 어디? 오, Little Indian Pizza에서 배달 직원을 구하고 있네.

여 너 오토바이 면허증 가지고 있지, 그렇지?

남 응, 작년에 취득했어.

여 그럼, 이 일자리에 지원하는 게 어때? 21살도 넘었잖아.

남 하지만, 임금이 좋은 것 같지 않아.

여 수습 기간에 시간당 8달러면 다른 아르바이트에 비하면 좋은 거야.

남 하지만 정직원 임금은 그다지 높지 않잖아. 시간당 10달러밖에 안 한 다고.

여 살면서 모든 것을 다 가질 수는 없다는 점을 명심해.

남 네가 무슨 말 하는지 알아. 하지만, 이 일에 지원하고 싶지는 않아.

해설 정직원 임금은 12달러가 아니라 10달러라고 했다.

어휘 delivery person 배달 직원 apply for ~에 지원하다 training period 수습 기 간 feel like ~ing ~하고 싶은 기분이 들다

13 ①

해석 여 Kevin, 학교 게시판에서 오페라 'My Life' 포스터 봤어?

남 아니. 말해봐.

여 다음달 1일부터 말일까지 로얄 문화 센터에서 그 오페라가 공연될 거 래.

남 입장권은 얼마인데?

여 20달러인데 학생한테는 50% 할인해 준대.

남 오. 우리는 10달러만 내면 되네. 좋아. 같이 가자.

여 나야 좋지. 하지만, 표를 예매해야 할 걸. 이 오페라 매우 인기 있거든.

남 인터넷을 통해 예매할 수 있니?

여 그럼, 할 수 있지.

남 그럼, 표를 예매할 수 있는 인터넷 사이트도 알아?

여 www.ticketforyou.com이야.

남 **좋아. 그럼, 내가 표 두 장을 예매할게.**

해설 오페라 'My Life'를 볼 예정인 여자와 남자가 나오고, 남자가 여자에게 입장권을 예약할 수 있는 웹 사이트를 물어보자 여자는 www.ticketforyou.com이라고 대 답한다. 이 말을 들은 남자가 할 수 있는 말은 ①일 것이다. ② 나도. 내가 예상했던 것 보다 더 별로였어. ③ 뮤지컬 보는 것 대신에 오페라 보자. ④ 신분증을 가진 학 생은 50% 할인받을 수 있어. ⑤ 죄송하지만 이 티켓들을 환불하고 싶습니다.

어휘 school board 학교 게시판 perform 상연하다 reserve 예매하다. 예약하다 through ~을 통해

14 ③

해석 여 안녕하세요, 무엇을 도와드릴까요?

남 예. 중국어 회화 수업을 들으려고 하는데요.

여 예전에 중국어 회화는 수강한 적이 있었나요?

남 아니요, 이번이 처음이에요.

여 그럼, 초급반에 들어가시면 되겠네요. 수강료는 두 권의 교재를 포함해 서 70달러입니다.

남 학생들은 20% 할인이 있다고 들었는데요. 저는 대학생이거든요.

여 미안해요. 그 할인은 여름방학과 겨울방학에만 적용됩니다.

남 정말요? 몰랐어요.

여 하지만, 그것이 우리 학원의 방침입니다.

남 알았어요. 여기 70달러.

여 **고맙습니다. 이 양식을 작성해 주시겠어요?**

해설 수강 신청에 필요한 여러 질문이 끝난 후에 남자가 자신이 수강할 수업을 결정을 하고 수강료를 지불하였을 때, 여자 직원이 할 수 있는 말로 가장 적절한 것은 ③ 이다. ① 전혀요. 도와주셔서 감사합니다. ② 하지만 전 중국어를 유창하게 하지 못해요. ④ 거스름돈 여기 있습니다. 수업 잘 들으세요. ⑤ 그럼, 저는 여름 코스를

듣고 싶어요.

어휘 **policy** 방침, 정책 **fill out** 작성하다, (서류 등을) 메꾸다

15 ④

해설 여 Cindy는 세탁소에 있다. Cindy는 세탁해야 할 옷이 블라우스가 세 장, 정장이 두 벌 있다. Cindy는 점원에게 세탁비용이 얼마나 되는 지 그리고 얼마나 오래 걸리는지 물어본다. 점원은 블라우스는 한 장 당 3달러, 정장은 한 벌당 5달러이고, 세탁하는 데 걸리는 기간은 이틀 이라고 말한다. Cindy는 오늘 저녁에 찾을 수 있는지 궁금하다. 점원 은 추가 요금을 지불하면, 옷을 오늘 저녁에 찾아갈 수 있다고 대답한 다. Cindy는 옷이 가능한 한 빨리 세탁되기를 원한다. 이런 상황에서, Cindy가 점원에게 할 말로 가장 적절한 것은 무엇인가?

Cindy 알았어요. 제가 얼마나 더 지불해야 되죠?

해설 Cindy가 점원에게 옷을 오늘 저녁에 찾을 수 있느냐고 물어보자 점원은 추가 요 금을 내면 가능하다고 대답한다. 옷을 빨리 찾기를 원하는 Cindy가 할 수 있는 말 로 가장 적절한 것은 ④일 것이다. ① 당신의 영수증을 볼 수 있을까요? ② 오, 이 블라우스 당신한테 정말 잘 어울려요. ③ 내일 휴가를 쓸 수 있을까요? ⑤ 이 세탁 소를 언제 열었는지 물어봐도 될까요?

16-17 ②, ③

해설 남 와, 바람이 너무 시원해!

여 그래, 맞아. 두통은 어때? 전보다 좋아졌니?

남 그런 것 같아. 멋진 바람 덕분에 더 나아졌어.

여 천만다행이다! 사실 걱정을 많이 했거든.

남 더는 걱정 안 해도 돼. 이제 괜찮으니까. 봐! 저 위에서 갈매기가 날고 있어.

여 오, 정말로 아름답다. 갈매기들을 사진 찍고 싶어.

남 그럼 내가 선실에 가서 카메라를 가지고 올게. 여기서 잠깐만 기다려.

여 그럴래? 고마워. 아, 지금 배고프지 않니?

남 음…… 약간. 알다시피, 두통 때문에 오늘 아침부터 아무 것도 못 먹었 잖아.

여 맞아. 네가 선실에 가는 동안 내가 아래층에 있는 매점에 가서 샌드위 치를 살게.

남 좋아. 오렌지 주스도 사다 줘.

해설 **16** 여자가 하늘을 나는 갈매기의 사진을 찍고 싶다고 하자 남자가 선실에 가서 카메라를 가지고 오겠다고 했으므로 정답은 '배'이다.

17 "Then let me go fetch the camera from the cabin."을 통해 정답이 ③임 을 파악할 수 있다.

어휘 **thanks to** ~덕분에 **seagull** 갈매기 **fetch** 가지고 오다 **cabin** 선실 **downstairs** 아래층에서

◉ Dictation

01 looks good on me / I'll take it

02 stopped working

03 makes your car shine / This promotion runs

---

04 you should be on time / you should keep in mind / honesty is the best policy

05 As soon as / at the Lost and Found department / Let me check inside

06 Thanks for coming / because of your blind date / has her hair permed

07 laying off some workers / get a loan from a bank / At the end of this month

08 it's no use crying over spilt milk / fill up on gas

09 any special brand in mind / the lighter it is / I have to pay all together

10 I'll stay for a week / I've already visited

11 primarily of short stories / graduating from the university / dealt with the themes

12 There is a new job on the board / apply for the job / I know what you mean

13 get a 50% discount / Fine with me / where we can book tickets

14 I'd like to take / I'll put you in the beginners' class

15 at the dry cleaner's / how long it will take / pays an additional fee

16-17 What a relief / go and fetch the camera / while you go to the cabin

01 ②	02 ②	03 ④	04 ①	05 ③	06 ②
07 ③	08 ①	09 ④	10 ⑤	11 ④	12 ③
13 ①	14 ②	15 ①	16 ⑤	17 ①	

01 ②

해설 여 이 노트북 컴퓨터와 저 데스크톱 컴퓨터 중에서 어느 것이 더 좋은 것 같 니?

남 내가 너라면 노트북 컴퓨터를 살 거야.

여 그래? 노트북 컴퓨터를 선호하는 무슨 이유가 있어?

남 사용하기에 더 편리한 것 같아.

해설 노트북 컴퓨터를 데스크톱 컴퓨터보다 선호하는 이유가 있느냐는 여자의 물음에 대한 남자의 응답으로 가장 적절한 것은 ②이다. ① 나는 이 컴퓨터를 살 수 있다 고 확신해요. ③ 물론 내 공책을 빌릴 수 있어요. ④ 노트북 컴퓨터는 쉽게 고장이 나요. ⑤ 저는 노트북 컴퓨터를 매우 선호해요.

어휘 **convenient** 편리한 **prefer** 선호하다

02 ②

해석 남 실례합니다, 영화 'Silent King' 표 세 장 살 수 있을까요?
여 네. 영화를 몇 시에 보고 싶으시죠?
남 저녁 7시요.
여 모두 해서 24달러입니다. 영화 재미있게 보세요.

해설 저녁 7시에 상영하는 영화를 보겠다는 남자의 말에 대한 여자의 응답으로 가장 적절한 것은 ②이다. ① 당신의 영화는 정말 좋아요. ③ 미안해요, 오늘 저녁에 당신을 만날 수 없어요. ④ 나머지 돈을 빌려 줄게요. ⑤ 이 영화에 나를 초대해 주어서 고마워요.

03 ④

해석 여 이번 주말을 위한 흥미진진한 일을 찾고 계십니까? Wild World 동물원으로 오십시오. 드디어 저희 Wild World 동물원이 개장합니다! 200종이 넘는 동물이 여러분을 기다리고 있습니다. 코알라나 캥거루 같은 야생동물을 만지고 껴안아 보십시오. 여러분에게 결코 잊을 수 없는 경험을 선사할 것입니다. 동물을 보는 것 또한 여러분들에게 흥미진진한 순간이 될 것입니다. 다양한 종류의 해양 동물을 볼 수 있는 수족관이 있습니다. 동물원에 와서 주말을 즐기십시오.

해설 "At last, we, Wild World Zoo, have opened our doors!"와 "Come and enjoy your weekend at the zoo."라는 문장을 통해 개장한 동물원을 홍보하고 있음을 추론할 수 있다.

어휘 such as ~같은 unforgettable 잊을 수 없는 various 다양한

04 ①

해석 남 나에게 자전거 타기는 직장에 가는 가장 기분 좋은 방법 중 하나이다. 운전할 때처럼 스트레스를 만들기는커녕, 자전거 타기는 내 스트레스를 줄여준다. 자전거를 타고 출근하면 대기 오염이 줄어든다. 또한 연료비와 차량 수리비를 절약할 수 있다. 무엇보다도, 나에게 가장 큰 혜택은 자전거를 타면 시간을 효율적으로 이용할 수 있다는 것이다. 출근길에 차가 막혀서 꼼짝 못하는 경험을 한 적이 결코 없다.

해설 자전거를 타면 출근길 스트레스가 줄어들고, 공기 오염도 줄어들고, 기름 값이 절약된다는 내용이다.

어휘 commute 통근하다, 통학하다 relieve 완화시키다, 줄어들게 하다 enable 가능하게 하다 above all 무엇보다도 efficiently 효율적으로

05 ③

해석 여 Bill, 무슨 생각해요?
남 이 집에 대해서요.
여 이 집이라고요? 왜요?
남 음, 알겠지만, 이 집에 5년도 넘게 살았잖아요.
여 예, 시간이 정말 빨리 가네요. 아이들이 벌써 초등학교에 다니고 있어요.
남 그래서 좀 더 넓은 집으로 이사를 갈까 생각 중이에요.
여 정말요? 그러면, 아이들이 매우 좋아할 거예요.
남 저도 그렇게 생각해요. 어디로 이사하고 싶어요?
여 Laymond 지역이 좋을 것 같아요. 좋은 공공 도서관도 있고 대중교통

도 편리하니까요.
남 알았어요. 내일 Laymond 지역의 부동산에 가볼게요.

해설 집을 옮긴다는 남자의 말을 들은 여자는 '그러면 아이들이 무척 좋아할 것이다'라고 대답한다. 이런 내용을 근거로, 남편과 아내 사이에 이루어지는 대화임을 추론할 수 있다.

어휘 spacious 넓은 public transportation 대중교통 convenient 편리한

06 ②

해석 남 봐! 경주가 곧 시작될 거야.
여 그래. 10분 후면 누가 세상에서 가장 빠른지 알 수 있어.
남 그래. 누가 우승할 것 같니?
여 당연히, Tyson Guy지.
남 Tyson Guy? 그 사람이 누구야?
여 양 손을 위로 들고 있는 선수가 보이니?
남 목걸이를 하고 있는 사람 말하는 거야?
여 아니, 그 사람은 Gerry Cooper야. 나는 바로 그 옆 사람 말하는 거야.
남 오, 원피스 유니폼을 입고 있네. 유니폼이 매우 독특하다.
여 그가 우승할 거라고 확신해.

해설 여자가 말하고 있는 Tyson Guy 선수는 양손을 위로 올리고 있고 Gerry Cooper 옆에 있으면서, 원피스 유니폼을 입고 있는 사람이다.

어휘 raise 올리다 unique 독특한

07 ③

해석 여 Charles, 마라톤을 한다고 이야기를 들었어.
남 그래. 살을 빼려면 운동을 해야 할 거 같아서.
여 생각 잘 했어. 마라톤이 살 빼는 데는 분명히 좋은 방법이니까.
남 마라톤에 대해 뭐 좀 아니?
여 고등학교 시절 내가 육상부 소속이었다는 거 몰랐어?
남 정말? 그럼, 오늘 오후에 나랑 같이 쇼핑몰에 갈래?
여 쇼핑몰에는 왜 가려고 하는데?
남 마라톤 신발이 필요해서 말이야. 어떤 신발을 사야할지 모르겠어.
여 좋아. 도서관 앞에서 4시에 만나자.
남 알았어, 도와줘서 고마워. 내가 맛있는 저녁 살게.

해설 살을 빼기 위해 마라톤을 시작한 남자는 마라톤 신발을 사러 함께 쇼핑몰에 가 줄 것을 여자에게 부탁하였다.

어휘 lose weight 살을 빼다 belong to ~에 속하다

08 ①

해석 남 오, 최신형 스마트폰이구나. 언제 샀어?
여 지난 주말에. 매우 싼 가격에 샀어.
남 정말? 어떻게?
여 공동 구매란 말 들어 봤어?
남 응, 들어 봤어. 그럼, 얼마나 싸게 샀니?
여 거의 반값에 샀어.
남 굉장한데! 공동 구매를 통해서 물건을 사는 게 어렵지 않니?

여 아니. 그냥 웹 사이트에 가입해서 거기서 하라는 대로 하기만 하면 돼. 그게 다야. 정말로 간단해.

남 그 웹 사이트 주소를 좀 알려 줄래? 사실, 나도 전화를 바꾸려고 생각하고 있었거든.

여 www.buytogether.com이야.

남 알았어, 지금 바로 그 웹 사이트에 가입해야겠어. 이제부터 나도 돈을 좀 절약할 수 있겠구나.

해설 여자가 웹 사이트를 알려주자, 남자는 그 사이트에 바로 가입하겠다고 하면서 "I'll be able to save some money from now on."이라고 말하였으므로 웹 사이트를 통해 싼 가격으로 공동구매할 것임을 추론 할 수 있다.

어휘 **brand-new** 최신형의 **cooperative buying** 공동 구매

09 ④

해석 여 아들에게 줄 선물을 찾고 있어요. 좋은 것을 추천해 주시겠어요?

남 이 게임이 어때요?

여 오, 이 게임은 정말로 흥미진진해 보여요.

남 맞아요. 지금 이 게임이 10대들 사이에서 가장 인기 있답니다.

여 좋아요, 이것을 살게요. 얼마죠?

남 14달러입니다. 아드님이 매우 좋아할 거예요.

여 그러길 바라요. 아, 5달러 할인 쿠폰이 있는데. 사용할 수 있나요?

남 보여주시겠어요? 죄송하지만 사용할 수 없어요. 이 쿠폰은 예전 게임 상품들을 위한 것입니다. 고객님께서 구입한 게임은 가장 최신 게임이거든요.

여 음, 알았어요. 20달러 여기 있어요.

남 고맙습니다. 잔돈 여기 있습니다.

여 아, 마우스 패드 있나요? 마우스 패드가 한 개 필요해요.

남 음, 제가 무료로 한 개를 드릴게요. 잠시만 기다리세요.

해설 14달러 최신 게임 CD를 구입하기로 한 여자는 20달러를 지불했으므로 거스름 돈으로 받게 될 금액은 6달러이다.

어휘 **at the moment** 현재, 지금 **for free** 무료로, 공짜로

10 ⑤

해석 남 Stella, 네가 학교 배구부에 가입했다고 들었어.

여 그래. 배구는 내가 좋아하는 운동이거든.

남 야구는 어때? 야구의 광팬이라고 말하지 않았어?

여 그래, 맞아. 야구는 내가 좋아하는 또 다른 운동 중 하나야.

남 다른 여학생들과는 달리 넌 정말로 운동을 좋아하는 것 같아.

여 그래, 맞아.

남 겨울 스포츠도 좋아하니?

여 그럼, 스케이트와 스키를 정말 좋아해. 정말로 흥미진진한 스포츠잖아.

남 와, 넌 정말 스포츠를 사랑하는 사람이 틀림없어. 수상 스포츠는?

여 음, 그게 내가 유일하게 언급하고 싶지 않은 부분이야. 사실 수영을 하는 법을 모르거든.

남 정말? 오, 너 같은 스포츠팬이 수영을 못한다니 이해가 안 된다.

해설 수상 스포츠를 좋아하느냐는 남자의 물음에 여자는 자신이 언급하기 싫은 것이 수상 스포츠라고 하면서 수영을 못한다고 대답했으므로 정답은 수영이다.

어휘 **volleyball** 배구 **mention** 언급하다, 말하다

11 ④

해석 남 Paralympics에 대해 들어 본 적이 있나요? Paralympics는 장애인을 위한 올림픽입니다. 최초의 Paralympics는 1960년 이탈리아의 로마에서 개최되었고, 그때부터 4년마다 올림픽 경기가 열리는 해에 같이 열립니다. 1960년 로마대회에서 23개국 약 400명의 선수로부터 2004년 아테네 대회에서는 136개국의 약 3,800여명의 선수가 참가하는 등, 하계 Paralympics에 참가하는 선수들의 수가 증가하고 있습니다. 러시아의 소치에서 2014년 동계 Paralympics가 개최될 것이고, 반면에 2016년 하계 Paralympics는 브라질의 리우 데 자네이로에서 개최될 것입니다.

해설 'The number of athletes participating in the Summer Paralympics has increased"라고 했으므로 '출전 선수가 해마다 줄고 있다'는 일치하지 않는다.

어휘 **disabled** 신체장애의 **athlete** 운동선수 **host** 개최하다, 주최하다

12 ③

해석 여 실례지만, 캠핑 장비랑 침낭을 빌리고 싶어요.

남 얼마 동안이나 필요하시죠?

여 10일간이요.

남 침낭의 대여료는 하루에 2달러이고요. 다른 캠핑 장비의 대여 가격은 용품마다 다릅니다.

여 알겠습니다. 배낭은 어때요? 하루에 얼마죠?

남 크기에 따라 다른데요. 25리터짜리 배낭은 하루에 3달러이고, 45리터짜리 배낭은 그 가격의 두 배예요.

여 그럼, 25리터짜리 배낭을 빌릴게요.

남 다른 것은요?

여 텐트도 필요해요.

남 하루에 10달러이지만, 1주일 이상 빌리시는 분들께는 30% 할인해 드려요.

여 좋군요.

해설 45리터짜리 배낭의 대여료는 하루에 3달러인 25리터짜리 배낭의 두 배라고 했으므로 6달러이다.

어휘 **equipment** 장비 **rental fee** 대여료 **depend on** ~에 달려 있다

13 ①

해석 여 여보, 크리스마스 휴가 때 아이들이랑 여행을 가는 것이 어때요?

남 제가 생각하고 있던 것도 바로 그거예요.

여 어디 마음에 둔 곳이라도 있어요?

남 괌은 어때요? 아이들이 수영하는 것을 좋아하잖아요.

여 하지만, 작년에 갔다 왔잖아요. 전 좀 새로운 곳에 가고 싶어요.

남 그러면, 시드니는 어때요? 시드니는 아름다운 해변으로 유명한 곳이에요.

여 좋아요. 하지만, 비용이 많이 들지 않을까요?

남 그렇지 않아요. 시드니에 갔다 온 제 친구 말에 따르면, 시드니 여행 비용이 괌 여행 비용보다 약간 더 비싸대요.

여 정말이요? 그렇다면, 시드니로 가요. 아이들한테 그것을 말해 줄게요.

남 알았어요. 아이들이 매우 좋아할 거예요.

해설 크리스마스 휴가 기간에 자녀들과 함께 해외여행을 계획하고 있는 여자와 남자는 시드니로 가기로 결정을 한다. 여자가 아이들에게 이 사실을 알리겠다고 말을 하였을 때 남자가 응답할 말로 가장 적절한 것은 ①이다. ② 하지만, 정말로 시드니에 가고 싶어요. ③ 미안해요, 여행을 갈 여유가 없어요. ④ 전에 시드니에 가 본 적이 있나요? ⑤ 여행 비용이 얼마나 들었나요?

14 ②

해석 남 Jenny, 내일이 학교 개교기념일이야. 좋은 계획 있니?

여 글쎄, 오후에 시청 근처에 있는 미술관에 갈 계획이야.

남 미술관에 간다고?

여 응, 피카소 그림 전시회가 있거든. 나는 피카소를 매우 좋아해.

남 그럼, 저녁에는 시간 있어?

여 응, 그때는 시간 있어. 왜? 뭐 좋은 계획이라도 있어?

남 괜찮으면, 내가 짐 싸는 것 좀 도와줄래?

여 아, 너 일요일에 새 아파트로 이사하기로 되어 있지.

남 맞아. 그래서 도움이 좀 필요해.

여 **그럼, 내가 도와줘야지. 친구 좋다는 게 뭐야.**

해설 이사를 갈 예정인 남자가 여자에게 도움을 청했으므로 여자의 응답으로 가장 적절한 것은 ②이다. ① 이 아파트가 상당히 맘에 들어요. 좋아요, 이 아파트를 구입할게요. ③ 저는 그것을 원해요, 하지만 그 그림은 제게는 너무 비싸요. ④ 미안, 내일 저녁에는 미술관에 가야 해. ⑤ 네가 미술관을 방문했었다면, 너도 만족했을 텐데.

어휘 exhibition 전시, 전시회 pack (짐을) 꾸리다

15 ①

해석 여 Derrick은 엄마 Juliet이 백화점에서 일을 하기 때문에 집안일 하는 것을 종종 도와준다. 오늘, 학교가 끝나고 Derrick이 집에 왔을 때, 그는 거실이 매우 어수선하고 정돈되지 않았음을 알아차린다. 그래서 그는 거실을 청소하기로 마음먹는다. 그는 진공청소기를 이용하여 카펫을 청소한다. Juliet이 일을 끝내고 집에 와서 깨끗한 거실을 보고 깜짝 놀란다. Juliet이 Derrick에게 거실을 청소했는지를 물어보자, Derrick은 그렇다고 대답을 한다. 이 상황에서 Juliet이 Derrick에게 할 가장 적절한 말은 무엇인가?

Juliet **고맙다. Derrick. 넌 정말 착한 아들이야!**

해설 직장에 다니는 엄마를 돕기 위해 Derrick이 청소를 했다는 사실을 알게 된 엄마가 할 말로 가장 적절한 것은 ①이다. ② 그것을 하는 것을 잊었어. 지금 바로 집을 청소하게. ③ 오, 네가 다른 일자리 구하는 것을 도와주었어야 했는데 말이야. ④ 너랑 같이 그 백화점에서 일해도 괜찮니? ⑤ 설거지를 끝냈어. 다른 할일이 있니?

어휘 realize 알아차리다 messy 지저분한 vacuum cleaner 진공청소기

16-17 ⑤, ①

해석 남 실례합니다, 질문 하나 해도 될까요?

여 예, 그럼요, 무엇을 도와드릴까요?

남 사실, 오늘이 제 아내 생일이라서 생일 케이크를 사고 싶어요. 빵집이 어디에 있나요?

여 아래층 에스컬레이터 바로 옆에 있습니다. 그런데, 우리 호텔 회원 카드를 가지고 있으신가요?

남 예, 다이아몬드 클럽 회원이에요.

여 잘 됐네요. 다이아몬드 클럽 회원에게는 생일 케이크를 무료로 주거든요.

남 정말이요? 좋네요. 그럼 전 꽃을 사기만 하면 되겠군요. 꽃가게도 있나요?

여 그럼요, 빵집 바로 옆에 있어요.

남 알았어요, 지금 바로 가서 꽃을 사야겠어요.

여 가시기 전에 객실 번호와 케이크를 받고 싶은 시간을 말씀해 주세요. 그 시간에 객실로 케이크를 보내드릴게요.

남 좋아요. 저는 1004호에 머물고 있어요. 저녁 7시까지 케이크를 보내 주세요.

여 알겠습니다. 저희 호텔에서 좋은 시간 보내세요.

해설 16 객실 번호를 알려 주면 생일 케이크를 객실로 보내 주겠다는 여자의 말을 통해 호텔 리셉션 데스크 앞에 있음을 추론할 수 있다.

17 "I'll go and buy some flowers right away."를 통해 남자가 꽃을 사러 갈 것임을 알 수 있다.

어휘 be located 위치하다 receive 받다, 수령하다

⦿ Dictation

01 Is there any reason

02 What time do you want to

03 Are you looking for / It will be an unforgettable experience

04 commute to work / enables me to save / above all / getting stuck in traffic

05 what are you thinking about / time really flies / I'll go to a real estate agency

06 In ten minutes / raising both his hands / It looks very unique

07 a good way to lose weight / I have no idea / thank you for helping me

08 at a very low price / Isn't it difficult to buy goods / Could you tell me / from now on

09 recommend a good one / At the moment / Can I use it now / Here is your change

10 you're a great fan of / you must be a sports lover / how to swim

11 Olympics for disabled people / has been held the same year

12 I'd like to rent / It depends on the size / for more than a week

13 going on a trip / any places in mind / is famous for its beautiful beaches

14 I'm planning to / I'm a great fan of / If you don't mind

15 do the housework / clean the place / comes home from work

16-17 may I ask you something / we give a birthday cake for free / please let me know / enjoy your stay

01 ②	02 ④	03 ①	04 ③	05 ④	06 ③
07 ④	08 ⑤	09 ③	10 ⑤	11 ⑤	12 ③
13 ⑤	14 ②	15 ①	16 ⑤	17 ①	

01 ②

해석 여 따님인 Kristi가 학교에서 좀 우울해 보입니다. 집에서는 어떤지요?
남 사실, 집에서는 어떤 이야기도 하지 않으려 합니다. 오직 하루 종일 스마트폰으로 친구들하고만 이야기를 나눕니다.
여 그녀에게 어떤 문제가 있는 것이 틀림없습니다. 따님과 함께 학교 상담사를 만나 보는 것이 어때요?
남 글쎄요. 그녀에게 적절하다고 생각되지 않습니다. 조금 기다려 봅시다.

해설 학교와 집에서 모두 문제가 있어 보이는 딸 Kristi와 함께 학교 상담사를 만나보도록 권했으므로 가장 적절한 답은 ②이다. ① 그녀가 좀 아파요. 부탁 하나만 들어주시겠어요? ③ 그녀는 친구와 말하는 것을 피하고 있어요. 그녀가 너무 걱정돼요. ④ 아뇨. 걱정하지 마세요. 제가 그녀를 잘 돌볼게요. ⑤ 그녀에게 학교에서 스마트폰을 쓰는 것은 금지되어 있다고 말하세요.

어휘 all day long 하루 종일 avoid ~을 피하다 forbid ~을 금하다

02 ④

해석 남 무슨 일이 생겼나요? 당신이 저에게 제출할 보고서를 거의 30분 동안 기다리고 있어요.
여 미안해요, 하지만 지금 컴퓨터가 작동을 하지 않아요. 고치려고 해 보았지만, 실패했어요.
남 바이러스 검사를 했나요? 컴퓨터가 바이러스에 감염되었을 수도 있어요.
여 물론이죠. 하지만 다른 문제가 있는 것 같아요.

해설 남자가 바이러스 검사는 했냐고 물었으므로 가장 적절한 대답은 ④이다. ① 저는 이것을 친구 중 한 명에게 빌려줬어요. ② 당신은 지금 서비스 센터에 전화할 수 있어요. ③ 마지막으로 바이러스 검사를 하세요. 감염되었을 수도 있어요. ⑤ 아뇨, 전 영어 수업 보고서만 끝냈어요.

어휘 work 작동하다 fix 고치다, 수리하다 infect 감염시키다

03 ①

해석 여 사람들은 칼슘을 생각하면, 대개 우유를 떠올린다. 하지만 항상 그래야만 하는가? 사실 우유가 유일한 칼슘의 공급원은 아니다. 칼슘의 수많은 공급원 중 하나일 뿐이다. 물론 우유와 유제품이 대부분의 사람들에게 있어 칼슘의 가장 편리한 공급원인 것은 사실이지만, 검푸른 잎채소 또한 칼슘을 공급한다. 게다가 비타민 D는 우리 몸의 칼슘 흡수를 돕는다. 우리 몸이 칼슘을 얻는 또 다른 방법은 뼈로부터 칼슘을 빼내는 것이다. 혈액 내 칼슘이 지나치게 적어지면, 몸은 뼈로부터 칼슘을 뽑아낸다. 단순히 더 많은 칼슘을 섭취한다고 해서 빌려온 칼슘을 갚을 수 있는 것은 아니기 때문에 이러한 현상이 자주 일어나지 않도록 주의해

야 한다.

해설 우리 몸이 칼슘을 얻는 방법으로 우유와 유제품, 검푸른 잎채소, 뼈로부터의 칼슘 흡수를 제시하고 있다.

어휘 Calcium 칼슘 dairy product 유제품 convenient 편리한 leafy 잎이 많은 supply 공급하다 absorb ~을 흡수하다

04 ③

해석 여 기아로 고통 받는 어린이를 위한 마라톤 경기에 참여할 거야.
남 6월에 하는 것 말이야?
여 그래. 대략 6시간 안에 완주할 수 있을 거야.
남 시도하지 않는 것이 좋을 것 같아. 너무 힘들 것 같아.
여 아니, 힘들지 않아. 달리는 것은 쉬워. 나는 매일 아침마다 조깅도 한단 말이야.
남 이봐! 조깅은 마라톤과는 달라. 너는 훈련이 필요해.
여 그렇지만 나는 이미 참가 선수로 등록이 되어 있어. 나는 완주할 거야.
남 오, 맙소사! 그러면 너는 당장 훈련을 시작해야만 해.
여 매일 한 시간 정도씩 달려야 할까?
남 이런, 너 마라톤에 대해 아무것도 모르는구나. 지금부터 만나서 함께 연습하자.
여 고마워. 나는 네가 그렇게 이야기할 줄 알았어.
남 저녁 식사 전인 6시에 만날까?
여 좋아. 그때 보자.

해설 'Come on! Jogging is different from marathons. You need training.'이라는 남자의 말을 통해 마라톤을 완주하기 위해서는 훈련이 필요하다는 남자의 의견을 알 수 있다.

어휘 starve 굶주리다 register 등록하다 entrant 참가 선수

05 ④

해석 남 그녀의 상처가 완전히 치료되었습니다. 그렇지만 그녀의 망각 증세는 더 나빠지고 있어요.
여 알아요. 하지만 돌봐 줄 사람이 없어요.
남 그것이 큰 문제군요. 그녀가 길을 잃으면, 그녀의 망각 증세 때문에 그녀를 찾기가 어렵습니다.
여 어떻게 해야 할까요? 저는 그녀를 돌볼 시간이 거의 없어요. 일을 해야 해요.
남 입주 근무하는 간호사를 고용하는 것이 어떨까요?
여 고용했지요. 하지만 그녀는 엄마를 제대로 돌보지를 못했고 떠나버렸어요.
남 그럼 우리 병원에 있는 노인을 위한 요양소를 이용하실 수가 있어요. 당신이 원한다면 추천서를 드릴 수 있습니다.
여 정말인가요? 오, 잘됐군요. 제 어머니가 그 곳에서 얼마나 오래 계실 수 있나요?
남 그녀의 경우에, 대략 6개월 정도 머무를 수 있습니다.
여 어머니의 상태가 더 좋아질 수 있는지 이야기해 주실 수 있나요?
남 제가 아는 한, 그녀의 상태가 긍정적이라고 생각합니다.
여 고맙습니다. 약간 안심이 되는군요.

해설 환자의 망각 증세에 대한 의견을 제시하고 요양소에 머무를 것을 권유하는 의사

와 환자의 보호자와의 관계이다.

어휘 **forgetfulness** 망각 증세 **hire** 고용하다 **live-in** 입주 근무하는 **senior citizen** 노인 **ward** 요양소 **recommendation** 추천서 **outlook** 예상, 장래성

06 ③

해석 여 우리 집 좀 봐. 정말 지저분하다.
남 엄마랑 아빠가 곧 오실거야. 우리 집을 좀 치워야 할 것 같아.
여 전적으로 동감이야. 부모님이 이걸 보면 우리에게 화 내실거야.
남 응. 우리가 해놓은 걸 봐. 내 검은 양말이 소파 위에 있어.
여 넌 심지어 어젯밤에 저녁을 먹고 피자 박스와 콜라 캔을 테이블 위에 남겨 두었잖아.
남 집을 어질러 놓은 것이 나 혼자라고 생각하지 않아. 너의 바지와 티셔츠를 봐. 바닥에 있잖아. 옷걸이에 거는 게 어때?
여 알겠어. 지금 바로 할게. 넌?
남 난 진공청소기로 카펫을 청소할게. 청소에 집중할 수 있게 TV를 꺼줄래?
여 좋은 생각이야. 좋은 점이 뭔지 알아? 적어도 우리 양말을 물어뜯을 고양이가 없다는 거야.

해설 'we don't have a kitten that bites our socks.'라는 문구를 통해 고양이가 없다는 것을 알 수 있다.

어휘 **clean up** 청소하다 **couch** 소파 **mess up** 어지럽히다 **slacks** 바지 **hang ~** 을 걸다 **hanger** 옷걸이 **vacuum** 진공청소기로 청소하다 **kitten** 고양이

07 ④

해석 남 안녕, Cindy. 나 Vincent야.
여 안녕, Vincent. 무슨 일이야?
남 Angela가 어제 나에게 왜 소리를 질렀는지 말해 줄 수 있어?
여 오, Vincent. Angela가 너를 오해했을 지도 몰라.
남 하지만 그녀는 나에게 이유를 이야기해 주지 않았어. 내가 그녀에게 잘못했다면, 나는 그녀에게 사과할거야.
여 아니, 너의 잘못이 아니야. 그녀의 잘못이지.
남 정말 그렇게 생각해? 오, 나는 그녀를 이해할 수가 없어.
여 마음 편히 가져. 아마 그녀가 너에게 이야기하기 두려웠나봐.
남 왜? 그녀가 사과한다면, 나는 받아들일 수 있을 텐데.
여 정말이니? 사실, 그녀는 자신의 행동에 대해 정말 후회했고 너에게 편지를 전해달라고 부탁했거든.
남 내가 지금 그 편지를 읽어 봤으면 좋겠어.
여 네가 원한다면, 너에게 지금 그 편지를 가져다줄 수 있어.
남 그러면, 한 시간 뒤에 Mac's cafe에서 만날까?
여 좋아. 그때 보자.

해설 사과 편지를 Vincent에게 전해 달라는 부탁을 받은 Cindy가 할 일은 ④이다.

어휘 **apologize** 사과하다 **regret** 후회하다 **behavior** 행동 **deliver** 전달하다

08 ⑤

해석 남 안녕, Ann. 네가 승진했다고 들었어. 축하해!
여 고마워.

남 그런데, 무슨 일 있어? 기뻐 보이지 않네.
여 아, 아무것도 아니야. 그냥……. 갑자기 내가 이 회사에서 일하는 게 나에게 안 맞는 것처럼 느껴져. 내 직업을 바꾸고 싶어.
남 정말? 왜? 너 네가 하는 일을 좋아했잖아. 승진한 후에 너무 많은 일이 주어졌나 보구나.
여 아니야, 할 일이 너무 많다면 상사와 이야기해서 일정을 변경하거나 다른 일을 할 수 있어. 게다가 내 동료들은 늘 나를 도와줄 거야.
남 그러면 나한테 너의 문제를 말해줄 수 있을까? 아마 우리는 문제를 함께 해결할 수 있을 거야.
여 사실, 나는 매주 월요일에 모든 임원진 앞에서 프레젠테이션을 해야 해. 내가 수줍음을 많이 타는 편이라는 거 알잖아. 나도 극복해야 하는 걸 알지만, 지금은 너무 일러. 난 아직 준비가 안됐어.

해설 여자의 마지막 말에서 매주 월요일에 하는 발표를 힘들어 한다는 것을 알 수 있다.

어휘 **get a promotion** 승진하다 **suddenly** 갑자기 **coworker** 직장 동료 **executive** 임원진 **overcome** 극복하다

09 ③

해석 남 저는 아이들에게 줄 선물을 찾고 있어요.
여 곰 인형은 어때요? 한 개에 30달러예요. 그런데, 하나를 사면 하나는 공짜로 드려요.
남 와, 좋군요. 하지만 제 아이들에게는 곰 인형이 너무 많아요.
여 모두 딸인가요?
남 네. 8살과 10살이에요.
여 그러면, 이 인형은 어때요? 면으로 만들어졌어요.
남 얼마예요?
여 조금 비쌉니다. 각각 50달러예요.
남 너무 비싸군요. 이 꼭두각시는 얼마죠?
여 오, 꼭두각시 한 개는 40달러고 두 개를 사시면 총액에서 20퍼센트 할인해 드릴게요.
남 좋아요. 두 개 살게요. 아이들이 좋아하겠군요.
여 저도 그렇게 생각해요. 포장해 드릴게요.

해설 남자 손님은 결국 한 개에 40달러인 꼭두각시를 샀고 두 개를 사면 20퍼센트 할인되므로, 64달러를 지불하게 된다.

어휘 **cotton** 면 **puppet** 꼭두각시

10 ⑤

해석 남 커피 좀 드시겠어요?
여 감사하지만 됐어요. 방금 한 잔을 마셨어요. 그럼 무용 수업에 대해 설명을 해주시겠어요?
남 알겠어요. 라틴 댄스, 탭 댄스, 살사 댄스, 벨리 댄스 수업이 있어요.
여 왜 많은 종류의 무용 수업이 있네요. 하나를 선택하기가 어려워요.
남 당신이 관심 있는 것이 무엇이든 골라보는 것이 어때요? 마음에 두고 있는 게 있나요?
여 사실 전 탭 댄스에 관심이 있어요. 이것이 살 빼는 데 도움이 될까요?
남 물론이죠, 당연히. 춤을 배우려고 하는 이유가 그것인가요?
여 사실, 맞아요. 시간표를 보여주시겠어요?
남 여기 있어요. 평일에는 오후와 저녁 수업이 있고 토요일에는 오전 수업

이 있어요. 일요일에는 수업이 없어요.

여 보통 한 수업 당 사람이 몇 명이나 있나요?

남 음, 수업 시간에 따라 다른데, 대개 열 명 정도예요. 어떻게 이곳을 알게 되었는지 물어봐도 될까요?

여 신문 광고에서 봤어요. 그런데 수업료는 얼마인가요? 너무 비싸지 않았으면 좋겠네요.

해설 무용 강사에 대한 언급은 하지 않았다.

어휘 give an explanation 설명하다 as a matter of fact 사실은

11 ⑤

해설 여 가장 매력적인 아이스 링크가 Kew Gardens에 개장되었으며, 그곳은 실외 스케이트의 재미를 경험할 수 있는 이상적인 장소입니다. 멋진 풍경과 매혹적인 분위기와 더불어, Kew에서 스케이트를 타는 것은 모든 사람에게 반드시 해야만 하는 성탄절의 특별한 경험거리가 되었습니다. 핫초코와 같은 뜨거운 음료수를 제공하는 카페가 있어서, 모든 연령대의 스케이트를 즐기는 사람들은 얼음 위에서 한 두 바퀴를 돌고 난 뒤 몸을 따뜻하게 할 수 있습니다. 그리고 여러분은 기념품 가게에서 친구와 가족을 위해 특별한 것을 살 수도 있습니다. 이곳은 오전 10시에 문을 열고 오후 10시에 문을 닫습니다. 18세 이하의 모든 사람은 무료입니다. 게다가 성인들은 일인당 5달러라는 가장 싼 가격으로 이용할 수 있습니다. 자, 이번 겨울 Kew Gardens에서 가장 신나는 경험을 해보십시오!

해설 18세 이하의 사람들은 무료로 이용할 수 있으나, 그 이상의 성인들은 5달러의 입장료를 내야 한다.

어휘 enchanting 매혹적인 spectacular 멋진 magical 매혹적인 must do 해야만 하는, 필수의 treat 예기치 않은 멋진 경험 warm up 몸을 따뜻하게 하다

12 ③

해설 남 와, 우리는 여기서 많은 것들을 즐길 수 있겠다.

여 지금 피곤하지 않아? 나 너무 피곤해서 어떤 것도 할 수가 없어.

남 이봐! 우리가 지금 잘 즐기지 못하면 나중에 후회하게 될 거야.

여 알겠어. 사우나에 가는 건 어때?

남 그렇지만 사우나는 겨울에만 이용할 수 있어.

여 안타깝다. 어쨌든, Peter, 나는 여기서 쉬는 것이 좋겠어.

남 그러면 저녁 식사 후에 Barbecue & Beer에 가자.

여 그래. 그런데, 만약 네가 원한다면 너 혼자 뭐든지 할 수 있어. 아직 3시거든.

남 너는 괜찮아?

여 걱정하지 마. 난 그냥 피곤할 뿐이야.

남 알았어. 그러면, 해변을 따라 뛰고 난 뒤에 너와 함께 저녁을 먹어야겠어.

여 좋은 생각이야. 어서 가.

해설 남자는 여자가 쉬고 싶다는 말에 저녁을 먹을 때까지는 아무것도 하지 않을 생각이었으나, 여자의 권유에 해변을 달리고 오겠다고 했다.

어휘 sauna 사우나 on one's own 혼자서

13 ⑤

해설 남 새로운 학기의 시작이구나.

여 그래. 할 일이 너무 많아.

남 맞아. 그런데, 너 Dave를 본 적 있니?

여 아니. 오랫동안 Dave를 보지 못했어. 걱정이 되기 시작해.

남 그러면 너도 그에 대해 듣지 못했구나. 사실, 지난 학기에 Dave가 나에게 전공을 바꿀 거라고 이야기를 했지만 진짜 그럴 거라고 생각하지는 않았거든.

여 정말? Dave는 나에게 어떤 말도 하지 않았는데.

남 글쎄, Dave는 아버지가 자신이 변호사가 되기를 원해서 전공을 선택한 거였거든.

여 알고 있어. 그럼 그는 어떤 전공에 관심이 있었어?

남 그는 항상 수학을 공부하길 원했어.

여 오, 이런. 친구로서 그에게 조언해 주는 건 어떨까?

남 좋은 생각이야. 하지만 지금 그를 어떻게 찾을 수 있을까?

여 **그의 집에 먼저 전화해 보는 건 어떨까?**

해설 Dave와 이야기를 나눌 것을 결심하고, 그를 어떻게 찾을지 물어보았으므로 ⑤가 적절하다. ① 좋아. 우리는 그의 가장 좋은 친구이야. ② 나는 그것이 그의 평생 꿈이라는 것을 알아. ③ 그가 그것을 하는 것은 어려울 거야. ④ 나도 수학을 공부하는 것을 좋아해.

어휘 term 학기 semester 학기 mathematics 수학

14 ②

해설 남 너의 휴가는 어땠어?

여 굉장했어! 가족과 함께 해변에서 마음껏 즐겼어.

남 너는 제주도에 갔었지, 그렇지?

여 아니, 휴가가 3일 뿐이어서 속초에 갔어.

남 너의 막내딸인 Cindy도 데리고 갔어?

여 물론이야. 그 아이는 그곳에서 노는 것을 좋아했어. 바닷가에서 모래성을 만들면서 즐거워했어.

남 너와 가족은 그 곳에서 멋진 시간을 보낸 것 같구나.

여 그래. 그리고 하루 종일 가족과 함께 있으니까 행복했어.

남 맞아! 휴가 떠나기 전에 너는 일 때문에 너무 바빴어. 지금 네가 느끼는 감정을 알 수 있어.

여 그래. 가족과 더 많은 시간을 보낼 수 있다면 좋으련만.

남 **오, 너는 이번 겨울에 또 다른 휴가를 즐길 수 있어.**

해설 휴가를 갔다 와서 가족과 즐겁게 보낸 시간을 그리워하고 있는 여자에게 남자가 할 수 있는 말로 가장 적절한 것은 ②이다. ① 안됐구나. 네가 너의 직업을 좋아하면 좋으련만. ③ 나는 출장 때문에 지금 나가야 해. ④ 끔찍했었어. 제주도에 갈 걸 그랬나봐. ⑤ 너는 다음 달까지 휴가를 연기할 수 있어.

15 ①

해설 남 Edner는 생물 수업 보고서를 작성하고 있었다. 그렇지만 그의 인터넷 접속이 좋지 못했고 적절한 책도 가지고 있지 않아서 보고서를 끝낼 수 없었다. 그래서 그는 친구인 Peter에게 도움을 요청하기 위해 전화를 했다. 하지만 Peter도 충분한 책을 갖고 있지 않았고, 또한 인터넷에서 적절한 논문을 찾을 수 없었다. 그도 그의 보고서에 대해 걱정을

하고 있었다. 그때, Peter는 Louise가 생물학에 관심이 많으며 그 주제에 관한 많은 책을 갖고 있다는 것이 생각났다. 그래서 Peter는 그와 Edner 둘 다 Louise에게서 어떤 도움을 얻을 수 있겠다는 생각이 들었다. 이러한 상황에서, Peter가 Edner에게 할 말로 가장 적절한 것은 무엇인가?

Peter Edner, Louise에게 물어보자. 그녀는 아마 우리를 도와줄 거야.

해설 Louise가 생물 과목에 관심이 많고 그녀가 생물에 관한 많은 책을 갖고 있어서 도움을 줄 수 있을 것이라는 대화이다. ② 너의 보고서를 벌써 끝냈니? ③ 괜찮아. 할 수 있는 것이 아무것도 없어. ④ Louise는 나에게 우리를 도와줄 수 없다고 이야기를 했어. ⑤ 그것을 끝내기 위해서 함께 공부하는 것이 어떨까?

어휘 **access** 접속, 접근 **article** 논설, 기사 **occur to** ~에게 생각나다

16-17 ⑤, ①

해석 남 우리 학교는 Griffin 선생님의 학생들에게 쏟은 노력과 헌신과 더불어 SAT 점수에서 엄청난 향상을 하였습니다. Griffin 선생님은 그녀의 노력과 열심히 일한 덕분으로 2천 달러뿐 아니라 Los Angeles 고등학교 동창회에서 수여한 표창장을 받았습니다. 그녀는 그 상금을 주저하지 않고 장학 기금으로 기부해 주셨습니다. 그래서 저희 학교 위원회는 이번 달에 자격이 되는 학생에게 그 특별 장학금을 수여하기로 결정을 내렸습니다. 우선, 부모의 수입이 가장 중요합니다. 수입이 낮을수록 장학금을 받을 가능성이 더 높아집니다. 두 번째이자 마지막으로, 여러분의 학교 성적이 적어도 평균 B이상이어야 합니다. 지금 그 장학금을 받을 후보자가 되고 싶다면 교실에 있는 지원서를 써야만 합니다. 더 많은 정보를 얻고자 원한다면 학생회실에 방문하시면 됩니다. 들어주셔서 감사합니다.

해설 16 Griffin 선생님이 받은 상금이 장학 기금으로 기부되어 이번 달에 자격이 되는 학생에게 장학금을 수여할 예정임을 알려주는 내용이다.

17 글의 초반에 Griffin 선생님의 노력으로 학생들의 SAT성적이 향상되었음이 언급된다.

어휘 **dramatic** 극적인, 인상적인 **improvement** 향상 **perseverance** 인내, 노력 **alumni** 동창회 **association** 협회 **hesitation** 주저함 **eligible** 자격이 되는 **candidate** 후보 **application** 지원

🎯 Dictation

01 looks a little depressed / all day long

02 for almost half an hour

03 should always this be / pulling it from bones / by eating more calcium

04 You'd better not try / registered as an entrant / From now on

05 to take care of her / As far as I understand it

06 I totally agree with you / I don't think it is only me / I'll do it right now

07 I will apologize / Take it easy / I wish I could read the letter

08 got a promotion / I don't feel like / In addition / make a presentation

09 that sounds good / they're a little expensive / I'll wrap them up

10 give me an explanation / It's hard to / As a matter of fact / I saw newspaper ads

11 it is an ideal place / serving drinks / get something special / at the cheapest price

12 we'll regret it later / I'd rather rest here / on your own / I'll have dinner

13 quite a long time / change his major / That's a good idea

14 How was your vacation / happy to play there / I wish I could

15 to ask for help / At that time / get some help

16-17 received an award / without hesitation / The lower it is / fill out an application form

27회 | 듣기 모의고사
p.162-163

01 ④	02 ①	03 ④	04 ①	05 ②	06 ①
07 ③	08 ②	09 ④	10 ②	11 ③	12 ④
13 ①	14 ①	15 ④	16 ②	17 ⑤	

01 ④

해석 남 Smith 교수님이 처음으로 나에게 독자적인 과제를 주셨어.
여 축하해! 교수님이 네가 그것을 할 자격이 있다고 생각하시는 거야.
남 글쎄, 나는 내가 혼자 힘으로 그것을 할 만한 충분한 자격이 있는지 잘 모르겠어.
여 용기를 내! 넌 내가 아는 학생 중에서 가장 훌륭한 학생이야.

해설 교수가 준 독립 과제로 인해 부담스러워하는 친구에게 용기를 북돋아 주는 상황이다. ① 겨우 서문 쓰기를 끝냈어. ② 멋지다! 너의 과제를 끝냈구나! ③ 어느 것을 의미하는 건지 모르겠어. 확인해볼게. ⑤ 좋은 것 같아! 그것에 대해 쓸 아이디어가 있니?

어휘 **independent** 독립적인 **qualification** 자격 **introduction** 서문; 소개

02 ①

해석 여 다음 달에 1000m 수영 경기에 참가하기로 했어.
남 농담 하지 마! 넌 본격적으로 훈련을 받지도 않았잖아. 난 네가 완주하지 못할까봐 걱정이 되는데.
여 넌 내가 그 경기를 어떻게 마치는가를 보기만 하면 돼. 난 이미 훈련을 시작했어.
남 좋아. 네가 경기에 이기면 저녁을 살게.

해설 1000m 수영 경기에 참여하겠다는 친구와 이야기를 나누는 상황이다. 여자가 경기하는 것을 지켜보라고 했으므로 남자가 할 말로 적절한 것은 ① 이다. ② 네가 자랑스러워. 경주를 마쳤구나! ③ 내가 그것을 하기에 충분한 경험이 있는지 모르겠어. ④ 경기를 위해 행운을 빌어줘. 난 최선을 다

할 거야. ⑤ 나에게 끔찍한 경험일 것 같아서 두려워.

어휘 take part in ~에 참가하다 seriously 진지하게 treat ~에게 한턱내다 wish A luck A를 위해 행운을 빌다 awful 무서운, 끔찍한

03 ④

해석 여 이달 초, 나는 집에서 가스 냄새를 맡았다고 생각했지만, 남편은 그렇지 않았기 때문에 별 일이 아니라고 생각했다. 하지만 지난주에 거실에서 혼자 텔레비전을 시청하고 있는데 또 가스 냄새를 맡았다. 나는 가스가 새고 있다고 확신할 수는 없었지만 머리도 약간 아팠다. 나는 즉시 집의 모든 문과 창문을 열고 가스 회사에 전화를 했다. 기술자가 20분쯤 후에 도착했고 파이프에서 가스가 새고 있다고 확인해 주었다. 그때, 나는 가스 누출이 의심되면 즉시 가스 회사에 전화해야 한다는 것을 깨달았다. 왜냐하면 후회하는 것보다는 안전한 것이 항상 더 낫기 때문이다.

해설 가스가 누출되었음을 직감하자마자 신속한 대처가 필요하다는 내용이다.

어휘 leak 누출 slight 경미한 confirm ~을 확인하다 right away 즉시 suspect 의심하다

04 ①

해석 (전화벨이 울린다.)
남 여보세요, Mike Collins입니다.
여 여보세요, 저는 Lila의 엄마입니다. Lila는 당신 딸의 친구인데, 아실지 모르겠네요.
남 오, Lila요. 압니다. 지금 Jenny가 당신의 집에서 그녀와 놀고 있죠, 그렇지 않나요?
여 네, 맞아요. 그런데, 저의 딸인 Lila가 Jenny의 휴대폰을 실수로 수영장에 빠뜨렸어요. 아이들이 그것을 건져서 말렸지만, 휴대폰이 작동을 멈추었습니다.
남 오, 지금도 여전히 작동하지 않나요?
여 작동하지 않아요. 정말 죄송합니다. 그래서 망가진 휴대폰에 대해 보상을 해 드리고 싶어요.
남 그렇게 말해 주셔서 고맙지만, 이 일이 저에게는 너무 갑작스럽네요.
여 알아요. 하지만, 딸의 실수 때문에 제 마음이 너무 안 좋아서요. 제 딸이 한 일은 제 책임이니까요. 실수든 아니든 상관없이 말이죠.
남 알겠어요. 생각할 시간을 좀 주시겠어요?
여 물론이죠. 결정하시면 전화주세요. 다시 한 번 죄송해요.

해설 여자는 Lila의 엄마로서 자신의 딸이 실수로 친구의 휴대폰을 고장 냈기 때문에 변상을 해 주겠다고 말하고 있다.

어휘 by mistake 실수로 fish A out (물 속에서) A를 찾아내다 compensate ~에게 보상하다

05 ②

해석 여 오랜만이구나, Peter.
남 오, 정말 많이 보고 싶었어요, Jane.
여 드디어 대학을 졸업했구나. 축하한다!
남 감사합니다. 하지만 미래가 약간 두려워요.

여 왜? 너는 로스쿨에 갈 거잖아, 그렇지 않니?
남 맞아요. 하지만 솔직히 말하면, 제가 정말로 하고 싶은 일인지 확신이 서지 않아요.
여 그러니? 내가 아는 한 너는 모든 것을 잘 했지. 너는 영리한 소년이었고 훌륭한 사람이 될 거야.
남 저에게 용기를 주는 말이에요. 제가 당신의 수업을 가장 좋아했다는 것을 알고 계세요?
여 정말? 너는 종종 나에게 장난을 치려고 했지만 나는 너의 장난을 좋아했단다.
남 오, 그 시절이 그리워요.
여 네가 자랑스럽다. 내가 너와 같은 훌륭한 학생을 가르쳤다는 것은 행운이었어.
남 고맙습니다. 열심히 공부해서 훌륭한 변호사가 될게요.

해설 Peter가 Jane의 수업을 가장 좋아했다고 말하는 것으로 보아, 교사와 제자의 관계다.

어휘 Long time no see. 오랜만이야. graduate from ~을 졸업하다 to tell the truth 솔직히 말하면 as far as I know 내가 아는 한 encouraging 용기를 북돋워 주는 play tricks on A A에게 장난을 치다 brilliant 훌륭한

06 ①

해석 여 오, 이거 전부 좋아 보인다.
남 맞아, 여기 있는 가구들 전부를 살 수 있었으면.
여 이해해, 하지만 우리는 우선 책상, 의자, 침대가 제일 필요해.
남 왼쪽에 책장이 달린 책상은 어때? 아주 실용적인 것 같은데.
여 그래, 그런데 우리 방엔 이미 책장이 충분히 있어. 또 다른 책장은 필요 없을 것 같아.
남 그럼, 큰 서랍이 달린 앤틱 스타일 책상은 어때?
여 저 책상은 우리 방에는 너무 큰 것 같지 않아? 난 더 작고 단순한 것이었으면 좋겠어.
남 오, 저기 봐. 우리 방에 딱 맞을 것 같아. 단순하고, 작고, 서랍도 많이 있어.
여 어디? 찾았다. 창문 옆에 있는 책상 말하는 거 맞지? 좋아. 저것으로 하나 사자. 그 다음은 뭐지? 의자야, 맞지?
남 계단 옆에 있는 저 흰색 의자는 어때? 우리 책상과 잘 어울릴 것 같아.
여 응, 나도 그렇게 생각해. 마지막으로 침대를 사야해.
남 위를 봐. "침대는 위층에 있습니다."라는 표지판이 있어.

해설 창문 옆에 있는 책상은 작고 서랍이 많다고 했으므로 일치하지 않는 것은 ①이다.

어휘 bookshelf 책장 practical 실용적인 drawer 서랍 prefer ~을 선호하다

07 ③

해석 여 저, 도쿄에 대한 정보를 얻고 싶어요.
남 휴가에 그 곳에 갈 계획이세요?
여 네. 하지만 확실하지는 않아요.
남 만약 가신다면, 언제 가고 싶으십니까?
여 아마도 8월쯤이 될 거예요. 대개 저는 8월에 휴가를 가거든요.
남 8월에는 보통 여행객이 아주 많지만, 지하철 여행을 권해드릴게요.
여 왜 그런지 말씀해 주시겠어요?

남 도쿄는 지하철 시스템이 잘 되어 있어요. 관광객이 돌아다니기 쉬워요. 게다가 버스 여행보다는 비용이 덜 들어가요.

여 저는 단체 여행을 싫어해요.

남 물론, 혼자서 여행하실 수 있어요. 원하신다면 여행을 위한 안내 책자를 드릴 수 있어요.

여 제가 그것을 지금 당장 얻을 수 있을까요? 정말 보고 싶군요.

남 알겠습니다. 잠깐 기다리십시오.

해설 남자는 여자에게 도쿄 여행을 위한 안내 책자를 찾아 주게 될 것이다.

08 ②

해석 남 지금 서점에 가도 되요?

여 너무 늦은 시간이야, David. 서점이 언제 문을 닫지?

남 10시에 닫아요. 걱정 마세요, 엄마. Mike와 함께 갈 거예요.

여 지금 9시구나. 좋아. 가려무나. 그런데, Mike는 오는 중이니?

남 사실 Mike는 이미 여기에 와 있어요. 현관에서 저를 기다리고 있어요.

여 오, Mike의 어머니에게 이 스카프를 보내 줘야 하는 것이 지금 막 기억이 났구나.

남 제가 Mike에게 지금 들어오라고 할까요?

여 잠깐만 기다려라. 그럴 필요가 없구나.

남 왜요? Mike가 자기 엄마에게 가져다줄 수 있어요.

여 아직 포장을 하지 않았단다. David, 이것을 담을 작은 상자를 사다줄 수 있겠니?

남 책을 좀 사고 나서 사도 될까요?

여 그래, 물론이지. 아! 그리고 리본도 좀 사다 주렴.

남 알겠어요. 상자와 리본 사는 것을 잊지 않을게요.

해설 David가 어머니에게 서점에 가도 되냐고 물은 후 Mike와 함께 간다고 했으므로 두 사람은 함께 서점에 갈 것이다.

어휘 porch 현관 wrap ~ up 포장하다

09 ④

해석 남 도와드릴까요?

여 네. 제 딸을 위한 수영복을 찾고 있어요.

남 아이가 몇 살인가요?

여 9살이에요. 그 애는 분홍색을 좋아해요.

남 이것은 어떤가요? 이것은 비키니 타입입니다.

여 좋아 보이네요. 얼마인가요?

남 40달러입니다만, 30퍼센트 할인해서 사실 수 있습니다.

여 괜찮군요. 한 가지 더요. 물안경을 볼 수 있을까요? 제 걸로요.

남 어떤 색깔을 원하시나요? 하얀색, 검은색, 그리고 파란색이 있습니다.

여 하얀 것이 좋겠군요.

남 그러면, 이것은 어떻습니까? 지금 25달러인데, 할인은 안 됩니다.

여 좋아요. 수영복과 수경 둘 다 사겠어요. 포장해 주시겠어요?

해설 딸 수영복은 40달러에서 30퍼센트 할인했으므로 28달러가 되고, 수경은 할인 없이 25달러이므로 둘을 합치면 53달러가 된다.

10 ②

해석 여 Josh, Ashley Jude를 알고 있니?

남 응원단장 말이지? 그래, 알고 있어.

여 음, 사실대로 말하면, 그녀가 너에게 관심이 있어.

남 뭐라고? 그녀가 나를 어떻게 알아?

여 작년에 배드민턴 경기에서 너를 봤대.

남 오, 그때, 내가 단식 경기에서 우승을 했지.

여 그래. 네가 운동을 너무 잘해서 Ashley가 너에게 관심을 가지게 됐어.

남 와! 굉장한데! 그녀는 우리 학교에서 가장 예쁜 여학생이잖아. 모든 남자 아이들이 그녀를 좋아하지.

여 맞아. 자, 네가 원한다면, 너는 그녀를 만날 수 있어. 그녀가 너를 만나고 싶어 해.

남 그렇지만 나는 키도 크지 않고 영리하지도 않고 그리고 나는……

여 부끄러워 마. 너는 분명 멋진 남학생이니까.

남 그렇지만, 생각할 시간이 좀 필요해. 어쨌든 고마워.

해설 Ashley는 배드민턴 경기에 참가하지 않았다. ① 그녀가 학교에서 하는 일 ② 그녀가 배드민턴 경기에 참가한 이유 ③ 다른 남학생들이 그녀에 대해 생각하는 것 ④ 그녀가 Josh를 인식하게 된 때 ⑤ 그녀가 관심 있어 하는 사람

어휘 notice 주시하다 singles match 단식 경기 think over ~를 생각하다, 심사숙고하다

11 ③

해석 남 마우스는 사람의 손 안에 쥐어지는 장치이다. 그것은 상자처럼 생긴 물체 안에 있는 볼과 접촉하는 두 개의 롤러로 구성되어 있다. 사용자는 그것을 평평한 표면 위에서 굴릴 수가 있다. 만약 표현이 평평하지 않으면 때때로 작동하지 않을 수도 있다. 그것이 평면을 따라 굴려지게 되면, 커서가 화면상에서 대응하는 방향으로 움직인다. 원래 이것은 많은 스위치를 가지고 있는 입력 판자의 일부분이었다. 사람들은 컴퓨터와의 의사소통을 보다 쉽게 하려고 노력했고, 결국 15년간의 연구 끝에 이것이 만들어졌다. 이것은 상업적으로 성공적이고, 기술적으로 영향력이 있는 Macintosh 디자인 덕분에 인기를 얻게 되었다. 이 장치는 꼬리 같은 줄이 달려 있는 작은 상자의 모습 때문에 이런 이름으로 불렸다.

해설 원래의 것은 많은 스위치를 가지고 있는 입력 판자의 일부분이었으므로 단독 입력 장치로 버튼 없이 사용된 것이 아니다.

어휘 hand-held 손 안에 드는 크기의 device 장치 consist of ~로 구성되다 surface 표면 corresponding 상응하는, 대응하는 simplify 단순화하다 commercially 상업적으로 influential 영향력이 큰 tail-like 꼬리 같은

12 ④

해석 여 음, 우리 다음 달에 도쿄로 출장을 가야 해.

남 비행기 표를 미리 예약하자.

여 봐. 이 사이트에서 비행기 표를 예약할 수 있어.

남 정말? 좋은데. 여행사에 가서 하는 것보다 더 쉬울 거야.

여 회의가 금요일에 있지만, 좀 더 일찍 도착한다면, 준비할 시간을 충분히 가질 수 있을 거야.

남 그러면, 수요일 아침에 떠나는 이 비행기는 어때?

여 그렇지만 김포 공항은 집에서 너무 멀어. 나는 인천 공항이 좋아. 너는 어때?

남 나는 둘 다 좋지만, 김포 공항이 불편하다면 인천 공항으로 하자. 어디보자. 매주 수요일 오후에는 어머니를 병원에 모셔다 드리니까, 수요일 저녁 이후는 괜찮아.

여 그러면, 우리가 선택할 수 있는 건 하나 남는군.

남 좋아, 그걸로 하자. 좋은 점은 그래도 회의 준비를 할 시간이 하루는 있다는 거야.

해설 두 사람은 금요일에 있는 회의를 위해 우선 수요일에 출발하려고 했으나, 김포 공항은 여자 집에서 멀고, 수요일 오후에는 남자가 어머니를 병원이 모셔다 드려야 해서 목요일 아침 비행기로 가기로 했다.

어휘 on business 사업차 beforehand 미리 prepare for ~을 준비하다

13 ①

해석 남 도와드릴까요?

여 네. 제 가방 끈이 심하게 찢어졌어요.

남 한번 볼게요. 오, 들기엔 너무 무겁군요.

여 맞아요. 저는 항상 가방에 너무 많은 것을 넣고 다녀요.

남 더 튼튼한 것으로 교체하는 것이 낫겠어요.

여 이것보다 더 튼튼한 끈이 있나요?

남 네, 그리고 색깔이나 재질에 대해서는 걱정 마세요. 이것들은 어때요? 이것들 중에 선택할 수 있어요.

여 몇 가지 다른 종류의 끈이 있지만, 내 가방과 어울릴 것 같지 않아요. 오, 이건 원래 끈과 같아 보이네요.

남 맞아요. 같은 거예요. 다른 것들이 마음에 들지 않는다면, 두 개의 끈을 사용하는 건 어때요? 그것이 더 튼튼할 거예요.

여 좋은 생각이네요. 제 직업 때문에 항상 가방에 많은 종이와 책을 넣거든요.

남 자, 2시간 후에 가방을 가지러 오거나, 원한다면 여기서 기다릴 수 있어요.

여 그럼 6시에 돌아오는 게 좋겠어요.

해설 기다렸다가 수선된 가방을 가져갈 수 있고, 또는 2시간 후에 찾으러 올 수 있다는 말에 대한 적절한 응답은 ①이다. ② 굉장해! 여기 얼마나 머무를 거야? ③ 택배로 그것을 보낼게요. ④ 오, 오래 걸리지 않았군요. 멋져 보여요. ⑤ 내일 아침 그것을 가져가는 것이 어때요?

어휘 tear 찢어지다 overload ~에 너무 많이 싣다 replace 교체하다 quality 재질

14 ①

해석 여 어젯밤 TV에서 Hymann 쇼를 봤니?

남 아니, 나는 Peter와 함께 농구 경기를 하러 갔었어. 그리고 나는 TV 보는 것을 좋아하지 않아.

여 음, 너는 꽤 큰 사건을 놓쳤어.

남 무엇인데? 특별한 것이야?

여 물론, 그래. 진행자인 Hymann이 Bill Jones에게 몇 가지 사적인 질문을 했어.

남 유명한 가수 Bill말이야? Bill이 어떤 여배우와 한 사건에 관련되어 있지?

여 그래. Bill은 그 질문에 대답하기를 거절했고, Hymann에게 화를 냈어.

남 TV에서? 정말 무례하군!

여 그것이 다가 아니야. 그가 욕을 했어.

남 아마도, 그가 그 당시에는 자신의 진실한 감정을 속일 수가 없었나 봐. 그도 우리와 같은 사람이거든.

여 맞아. 나도 그렇게 생각해. 그렇지만 그는 그런 행동을 하지 말았어야 했어.

남 유명한 사람이 된다는 것은 너무 어려워.

해설 유명한 가수가 TV에서 욕을 하게 된 경우에 대해 이야기를 나누면서 그래도 유명인은 그렇게 행동하면 안 된다는 말을 했으므로 그에 대한 응답으로 가장 적절한 것은 ①이다. ② 나는 TV보는 것보다는 농구 경기하는 것을 더 좋아해. ③ 너는 어젯밤 그 쇼를 봤음이 틀림없어. ④ 미안하지만, 그는 그것에 대해 어떤 것도 이야기하지 않았어. ⑤ 오, 너는 나의 연기를 봤어야 했는데.

어휘 affair 사건, 일 call one names ~의 욕을 하다

15 ④

해석 여 Ralph는 오늘 밤 Susan과 데이트를 할 예정이다. 그는 그녀에게 뭔가 특별한 것을 선물하기로 결정하고, 백화점에 갔다. 하지만 그는 무엇을 사야할 지 결정할 수 없었고, 그녀에게 적당한 선물을 고를 수 없었다. 게다가, 그의 눈에 들어온 것들은 너무 비쌌다. 결국, 그는 포기하고 백화점을 막 떠나려고 했다. 그때, 친구인 Albert를 만났고, Albert가 선물을 자신보다 더 잘 고를 수 있을 수도 있겠다는 생각이 들었다. 그래서 그는 Albert에게 도움을 청하기로 결정했다. 이 상황에서, Ralph가 Albert에게 할 말로 가장 적절한 것은 무엇인가?

Ralph 어떤 종류의 선물이 여자에게 좋을지 아니?

해설 Albert가 자신보다는 여자 친구를 위한 선물을 더 잘 고를 수 있을 거라고 생각하고 도움을 요청하기로 마음을 먹었으므로 ④가 가장 적절하다. ① 네가 데이트를 못했다는 말을 들으니 유감이구나. ② 너는 그녀를 위해 향수를 샀어야 했어. ③ 너의 충고 고마워. 그녀를 위해서 꽃을 살 거야. ⑤ 데이트를 위해 어떤 옷을 입어야 할지 말해 줄래?

16-17 ②, ⑤

해석 여 안녕하십니까, 여러분. 전에 공지해 드렸던 것처럼 여름 학교가 6월 11일부터 7월 6일까지 개최됩니다. 현재 우리는 스포츠 캠프도 포함하기로 결정을 내렸습니다. 그 캠프는 기술 향상과 체력 단련을 위한 것입니다. 그래서 그 새 프로그램과 함께 여름 학교에 대해 여러분께 보다 정확하게 알려드리겠습니다. 학습 프로그램은 오직 8학년 학생을 위한 것이며 오전 8시 15분부터 오후 3시 30분까지로 예정되어 있습니다. 학생들은 수학, 독서, 그리고 언어 분야에서 그들의 학습 능력 수준에 따라 그룹 별로 나누어지게 됩니다. 이 프로그램에서의 강조점은 이 세 가지 학습 영역 각각에서의 복습과 능력 강화에 관한 것입니다. 여름 체육 프로그램들은 6학년부터 12학년까지의 학생들을 위한 것입니다. 이 프로그램들은 배구, 농구, 그리고 체력 단련 캠프를 포함하고 있습니다. 더 많은 정보를 원하시면 학교 홈페이지에 접속해 주시기 바랍니다. 감사합니다.

해설 16 여름 학교에 대한 전반적인 설명을 해주는 내용이다.

17 학습 프로그램은 학습 능력에 따라 그룹으로 나누어진다고 했다.

어휘 notice 공지하다 physical fitness 체력 단련 precisely 정확하게 emphasis 강조 volleyball 배구

01 got enough qualifications

02 decided to take part in

03 it was not a big deal / had a slight headache / showed up in about 20 minutes / to be safe than sorry

04 by mistake / I want to compensate / to think it over

05 to tell the truth / play tricks on me / I'm proud of you

06 I wish I could buy / with a large drawer / by the window

07 get some information / for travelers to go around / I really want to check it

08 He is waiting for me / wrapped it up / I won't forget

09 How about this one / They would be for me / Could you wrap them up

10 to tell the truth / How amazing / time to think this over

11 in contact with a ball / it can fail to work / tried to simplify

12 on business / time to prepare for it / there's only one choice left

13 Let's have a look / several different kinds of straps / pick up your bag

14 you missed quite an event / refused to answer the questions

15 as a suitable present / was about to leave / ask for his help

16-17 according to their academic skill level / For more information

28회 듣기 모의고사

p.168-169

01 ③	02 ⑤	03 ⑤	04 ②	05 ②	06 ⑤
07 ④	08 ④	09 ⑤	10 ②	11 ①	12 ⑤
13 ③	14 ④	15 ⑤	16 ⑤	17 ⑤	

01 ③

해석 여 David, 무척 심각해 보이는구나. 시험 결과에 무슨 문제가 있니?
남 아니요, 그런 것이 아니에요. 그냥 더 이상 학교에 가고 싶지 않아요.
여 오, 이런. 학교에서 너에게 무슨 일이 있었는지 말해보렴.
남 Mike가 저의 나쁜 시력을 가지고 놀려요.

해설 학교에 가기 싫다면서 엄마에게 그 이유를 말하는 상황이다. ① 지금 그에게 맞는 것 같지 않아요. ② 당신은 지금 스마트폰을 사용할 수 없어요. ④ 걱정하지 마세요. 제가 그를 잘 보살필게요. ⑤ 제가 그에게 당신과 무슨 일이 있었냐고 물어볼게요.

02 ⑤

해석 남 Sue, 교복이 너에게 짧아 보이는구나.
여 사실, 교복을 입을 때마다 불편해요.
남 너 많이 자랐구나. 교복을 살 때는 네가 그렇게 크지 않았는데.
여 교복을 하나 더 사주시는 것이 어때요, 아빠?

해설 교복이 작아서 불편한 딸이 아빠에게 할 말로 가장 적절한 것은 ⑤이다. ① 제 바지의 길이가 더 짧았으면 좋겠어요. ② 전 교복을 딱 맞게 입는 것이 더 좋아요. ③ 걱정하지 마세요. 저는 몇 달 후에는 더 클 거예요. ④ 당신의 몸에 딱 맞게 교복을 수선합시다.

어휘 **uncomfortable** 불편한 **reform** 고쳐 만들다

03 ⑤

해석 여 안녕하세요, 여러분. 저는 여러분의 사장인 Jessica입니다. 저는 여러분에게 기분 좋고 신나는 소식을 알리고자 여기에 있습니다. 여러분은 판매 부서의 Jack London을 알 것입니다. 최근에 그는 위험한 병에 걸려서 병원에 입원했습니다. 그리고 여러분은 그가 그 고통스러운 수술을 어떻게 감당해 냈는지 잘 알고 있습니다. 이제 그가 돌아왔습니다! 그는 건강하고, 우리와 함께 다시 일할 수 있습니다. 여러분의 지지와 기도가 없었더라면, 우리는 그를 다시 볼 수 없었을지도 모릅니다. 저는 그가 자랑스럽고 그와 함께 있게 되어 매우 행복합니다. 여러분도 저와 같으리라 믿습니다. 그래서 우리는 오늘밤 7시에 파티를 열 것입니다. 와서 그의 회복을 축하해 줍시다. 오늘밤에 여러분 모두를 보게 되기를 바랍니다. 들어주셔서 감사합니다.

해설 복귀 직원을 위한 파티를 개최할 것임을 알려주는 내용의 글이다.

어휘 **sales department** 판매 부서 **endure** 견디어 내다 **surgery** 외과 수술 **prayer** 기도 **hold a party** 파티를 열다 **recovery** 회복

04 ②

해석 여 아빠, 할아버지가 생일 선물로 저에게 돈을 주셨어요.
남 좋겠구나! 무엇을 살 계획이니?
여 전 새 스마트폰을 사고 싶어요. 제가 이미 가지고 있는 돈과 이 돈을 더하면, 제 생각에 새 스마트폰을 살 수 있을 것 같아요. 그래도 될까요?
남 좋은 생각인 것 같지 않구나. 너의 휴대 전화는 오래 되지 않았어. 너는 일 년 반 전에 휴대 전화를 샀어.
여 하지만, 아빠. 저는 정말 스마트폰을 갖고 싶어요. 제 친구들은 모두 스마트폰을 가지고 있는 걸요.
남 하지만, 너의 돈을 사용하는 가장 좋은 방법은 아니란다.
여 일 년 동안 스마트폰을 사려고 돈을 모았어요. 제가 엄격하게 계획을 세워서 돈을 쓴다는 걸 아빠도 아시잖아요.
남 안단다. 하지만 내 생각에 너의 휴대 전화는 쓸 만하단다. 네 돈을 쓰는 데 좀 더 주의하는 편이 좋겠구나.
여 아빠, 이것은 충동구매가 아니고 돈 낭비도 아니에요. 일 년 동안 계획했던 거예요. 그러니 이번 한 번만 봐 주세요.
남 알았다. 나는 네가 낭비하는 사람이 아니라는 것을 확신한다. 네가 그것을 계획한 것이 아니라면 허락하지 않겠지만, 네가 그것을 꽤 오랫동안 계획했다고 말하니 사도록 허락해 줄게.

해설 여자는 아빠에게 자신이 일 년 전부터 휴대 전화를 사기 위해 계획을 하고 돈을 모았으므로 휴대 전화를 사는 것이 낭비가 아니라고 말하고 있다.

어휘 impulsive buying 충동구매 give A a break A를 봐주다 wasteful 낭비하는

05 ②

해석 남 한번 타 봐도 될까요?
여 물론입니다. 여기 있는 것은 어느 것이든 다 시승해 보실 수 있어요.
남 오, 매우 좋군요. 그런데, 이것들은 인터넷에서 본 것하고는 조금 달라 보이는데요.
여 다르다고요? 당신도 알다시피, 모든 것이 중고예요.
남 그렇지만 약간 긁힌 자국이 있어요. 이것을 보세요. 이것은 약간 패이기도 했고요. 홈페이지에서 보았을 때는 완벽해 보였거든요.
여 네, 맞아요. 사진이 모든 것을 말해줄 수는 없어요. 하지만 그래도 연비는 매우 훌륭해요. 엔진도 잘 작동되고요.
남 얼마인가요?
여 1000달러입니다. 차를 운전할 때마다, 좋은 승차감을 즐기실 수 있어요.
남 음, 제겐 너무 비싼 것 같아요. 할인해 줄 수 있나요?
여 그러면 900달러는 어때요? 더 이상은 싸게 해드릴 수 없어요.
남 좋아요. 살게요. 신용카드를 사용할 수 있나요?
여 물론입니다. 여기서 가장 좋은 차를 고르셨어요.

해설 used(중고의)라는 표현으로 보아 중고 자동차를 판매하는 곳에서 중고차를 사고 있으므로 ②번이 가장 적절하다.

어휘 dented 움푹 들어간 fuel efficiency 연비 quality 질 ride 승차

06 ⑤

해석 남 분실물 센터입니다. 무엇을 도와 드릴까요?
여 오늘 아침 9시쯤 가방을 잃어버렸어요. 여기에 있는지 찾아봐 주시겠어요?
남 알겠습니다. 오늘 사람들이 가방 몇 개를 가지고 왔어요.
여 좋네요. 제 가방은 검은 색이에요.
남 검은 색 가방이라고요? 선반에 있는 검은 색 가방이 보이세요?
여 아니요. 전자제품만 몇 개 보이는데요. 첫 번째 칸에 전화기하고 두 번째 칸에 카메라요.
남 위에서부터 세 번째 칸을 자세히 보세요. 검은 색 가방 몇 개가 보일 거예요. 검은 사각형 가방이 당신 것인가요?
여 아니요. 제 것은 그렇게 크지 않아요. 오, 네 번째 칸에 검은 것이 있네요. 봐도 될까요?
남 물론 되지만, 제 생각에 당신 가방은 아닌 것 같네요. 이건 검은 색의 둥근 모자예요. 당신의 가방에 대해 좀 더 자세히 설명해 보실래요?
여 알겠어요. 가죽 끈이 달린 작고 동그란 가방이에요.
남 그럼, 당신의 설명하고 들어맞는 건 여기 없는 것 같네요. 비슷한 것이 들어오면 바로 전화할게요. 도와주지 못해서 유감이네요.
여 어쨌든 고맙습니다.

해설 네 번째 칸에 있는 것은 검은색 둥근 모자이지 가죽 끈이 달린 작고 동그란 검은 가방이 아니다.

어휘 Lost and found 분실물 센터 turn in ~을 제출하다 electronics 전자제품 in detail 자세히 leather 가죽 description 설명

07 ④

해석 여 좋은 아침이야. 이번 주 금요일 시험은 준비됐니?
남 충분하지는 않아. 어젯밤에 잠이 들어 버렸어.
여 그렇지만 열심히 공부했잖아. 걱정하지 마. 좋은 점수를 받을 거야.
남 아니. 이번에는 달라. 머리가 아프고 요즈음엔 공부에 집중할 수가 없어.
여 시험을 볼 때 너무 긴장을 하는 걸지도 모르겠다.
남 맞아. 내 생각에 나는 시험 공포증 같은 것이 있나봐.
여 시험 공포증? 증상이 어떤데? 머리가 아프다고 했고, 다른 증상은?
남 열도 있는 것 같아.
여 내 생각에 너는 감기에 걸린 것 같아. 시험 공포증 때문이 아니라. 약을 먹고 좀 쉬는 게 좋겠어.
남 알겠어. 약국에 들러서 약을 좀 사야겠다.
여 그리고 공부하는 데 도움이 필요하면, 나에게 말해. 너와 함께 공부를 하거나 공책을 빌려 줄 수 있어.
남 잘 됐다. 내가 약을 먹고 잠이 들 경우에 대비해서 옆에서 나를 깨워줄 누군가가 있었으면 좋겠어. 그렇게 해줄래?
여 물론이지.

해설 남자는 약을 먹고 쉬는 것이 좋겠다고 하며 약을 먹고 잠이 들었을 때 옆에서 깨워줄 사람이 필요하다고 했으므로 ④번이 가장 적절하다.

어휘 fall asleep 잠이 들다 concentrate on ~에 집중하다 phobia 공포증 symptom 증상 come down with ~의 병에 걸리다 take a pill 약을 먹다 drop by 들르다 drugstore 약국

08 ④

해석 여 우리의 테니스 시합이 몇 시에 시작하지?
남 11시. 시합 준비를 해야 해. 기분은 어때?
여 나쁘지 않지만, 긴장 돼.
남 테니스 라켓은 가져왔어?
여 오, 이런. 라켓을 가져오지 않았어. 어쩌면 좋아! 우리 학교에 테니스 라켓이 있니?
남 남아 있는 것이 없어. 어제 다른 팀에서 라켓을 모두 빌려갔다고 들었거든.
여 그러면, 서둘러 집에 가서 내 라켓을 가져와야겠구나.
남 진정해. 내 생각에 Harry는 항상 학교에 테니스 라켓을 가지고 와. 매일 오후에 수학 선생님하고 테니스를 치거든.
여 나는 Harry를 잘 몰라. 그래서 네가 그를 찾아서 나에게 테니스 라켓을 빌려 줄 수 있는지 물어봐 줄래?
남 오, 저쪽을 봐! 그가 걸어가고 있어. 여기서 기다려. 내가 가서 말해 볼게.
여 그가 여기에 있으니까 같이 갈게. 나를 그에게 소개만 시켜줘. 결국, 내 일이잖아.

해설 테니스 시합이 있는데 라켓을 두고 와서 Harry에게 라켓을 빌리려고 하는 상황이다. ① 그와 테니스를 치기 위해 ② 그가 라켓 구하는 것을 돕기 위해 ③ 그에게 그녀의 라켓을 가져다주기 위해 ④ 그에게 라켓을 빌리기 위해 ⑤ 그의 라켓을 친구

에게 빌려 주기 위해

어휘 **nervous** 긴장한 **overall** 결국

09 ⑤

해석 여 지금이 몇 시예요?

남 12시 30분이에요. 미안해요. 또 늦었어요.

여 집에 일찍 온다고 약속했잖아요, 그렇지 않아요?

남 그랬지요. 하지만 중요한 회의가 있었어요.

여 그렇지만 그 회의가 8시에 끝날 거라고 말했잖아요.

남 맞아요. 하지만 예정된 시간에 회의를 끝낼 수가 없었어요.

여 나는 당신의 건강이 너무 걱정이 돼요. 요즘 너무 피곤해 보여요.

남 걱정하지 말아요. 몸조심하려고 노력 중이에요. 게다가 나는 나의 일이 좋아요.

여 알아요. 하지만 십대가 아니잖아요. 그건 그렇고, 회의는 언제 끝났어요?

남 10시에 끝났지만 집으로 오는 길에 사고가 있었어요.

여 자동차 사고요? 괜찮아요?

남 내 차가 약간 들어갔지만, 괜찮아요.

여 오, 정말 다행이에요! 항상 조심해요.

해설 남자가 집에 도착한 것은 12시 30분이고, 회의가 끝난 시간은 10시였다. 따라서 회의를 끝낸 후 집에 도착하는 데 걸린 시간은 2시간 30분이다.

어휘 **on one's way home** 집으로 오는 도중에

10 ②

해석 남 매우 안 좋아 보이는구나.

여 네, 아주 피곤해요. 오늘 가게에 사람들이 아주 많았거든요. 바쁜 날이었어요.

남 정말 많은 일을 했겠구나. 따뜻한 차 한 잔 마시면서 이야기를 좀 하는 건 어떠니?

여 좋은 생각이에요! 오늘 재고 정리 세일이 있었고, 평상시보다 한 시간 일찍 문을 열었어요.

남 그렇게 일찍? 보통 10시에 시작하잖아. 내 생각에 손님들이 오기엔 너무 이른 시간 같구나.

여 저도 그렇게 생각했어요. 하지만, 제가 완전히 틀렸다는 게 입증됐죠. 아마 지난 한 달 내내 텔레비전에 광고를 한 덕분인 것 같아요.

남 그래, 아마도.

여 너무 바빠서 앉아 있을 시간이 1분도 없었어요. 점심 식사 전에 거의 백 명의 사람들이 옷을 입어보는 것을 도와줘야 했거든요.

남 와, 정말 많구나.

여 점심 식사 이후엔 심지어 더 많은 사람들이 왔어요. 오늘 얼마나 많은 손님들이 방문했는지, 얼마나 많이 벌었는지 계산했어요.

남 내일이 토요일이니 더 많은 사람들이 올 거라고 예상하겠구나, 그렇지?

여 물론이죠. 오늘의 두 배를 예상하고 있어요. 오늘의 고객 수가 300명이었고, 수입은 평상시의 약 두 배였어요.

해설 가게의 하루 운영 시간에 대한 언급은 없다.

어휘 **awful** 끔찍한 **hectic** 매우 바쁜 **clearance sale** 재고 정리 세일

11 ①

해석 여 저는 지체가 부자유한 여성이며, 이쪽은 봉사견인 Buddy입니다. Buddy는 저를 돕고 어디든 저와 함께 가기 위해서 특별히 훈련받았습니다. 지금 저는 몇 가지 제안을 하고자 합니다. Buddy에게 말을 걸거나 쓰다듬기 전에 그러한 행동이 괜찮은지 저에게 물어봐 주세요. 저의 개는 저의 안전을 위해서 일하고 있는 것이지 저와 함께 노는 것이 아닙니다. 개에게 있어서 한순간의 부주의함이 저에게 심각한 상해를 가져올 수 있습니다. 저의 개가 방해받지 않고 일할 수 있게 해 주세요. 그리고 Buddy에게 재주를 부릴 것을 요구하지 마십시오. 앞에서 말했다시피, 그는 저를 돕기 위해서 있는 것이지 여러분을 즐겁게 해 주기 위해서 있는 것이 아닙니다. Buddy에게 먹이를 주지 마세요. 이것 또한 그가 저에게 집중하는 것을 방해할 수 있습니다. 그리고 마지막으로 저희가 안전하게 계단, 승강기, 복도 등을 다닐 수 있도록 우리가 필요로 하는 공간을 확보해 주시기 바랍니다. 감사합니다.

해설 Buddy를 쓰다듬기 전에 허락을 구해줄 것을 요청했으므로 쓰다듬지 말라는 것은 아니다.

어휘 **pet** ~을 쓰다듬다 **inattention** 부주의 **interrupt** 방해하다 **demonstrate** ~을 보여주다 **mention** ~을 언급하다 **prevent A from B** A가 B하는 것을 방해하다 **negotiate** 통과하다

12 ⑤

해석 남 Susan, 영화 보러 가자. 여기 영화 상영표야.

여 그래, 어디 보자. 난 공포 영화를 안 좋아해. 이 중에 공포 영화가 있니?

남 NEXT는 꽤 무섭다고 들었어. 그럼 10시에 오만과 편견을 보는 건 어때?

여 오전에는 여동생이 숙제하는 것을 돌봐 줘야 해. 오후 시간은 어때?

남 안 돼. 내일 3시에 피아노 수업이 있고, 5시에는 치과에 가야해.

여 그래도, 저녁에 영화 보러 갈 수 있어.

남 맞아. 근데, 사실 난 로맨틱 영화를 정말 좋아하지는 않아.

여 알았어. 그럼 오만과 편견은 사랑 이야기이고, Queen Victoria도 그러니까, 우리가 선택할 수 있는 건 한 가지 남았네.

남 좋아. 그 영화 보러 가자.

해설 저녁 시간에 상영하면서 공포 영화와 로맨틱 영화가 아닌 것은 ⑤이다.

13 ③

해석 남 엄마, 제가 설거지 하는 것을 도와드릴까요?

여 오, 고맙다, Dave. 숙제는 다 했니?

남 물론, 다 했어요. 그리고 기말고사를 위해서 수학을 공부했어요.

여 잘했다! 엄청난 변화구나!

남 저는 더 나은 행동을 하고 더 열심히 공부하기로 마음먹었어요.

여 네가 이상하구나. 나에게 무슨 할 말이 있니?

남 아니요, 없어요. 저는 단지 엄마를 위해 좋은 사람이 되고 싶었을 뿐이에요.

여 나에게 정말 많은 감동을 주는구나. 고맙다.

남 그런데, Scott의 엄마는 Scott에게 새 게임을 사주셨어요. 그것은 교육적이에요.

여 아냐, 그렇지 않아. 단지 게임일 뿐이란다.

남 하지만 그것은 나의 지능 수준을 향상시킬 수 있다고 말하는데요.
여 그래서 내가 그것을 네게 사주기를 바라는 거지, 그렇지?

해설 Dave가 엄마를 도와드리고 공부를 하면서 엄마의 환심을 산 후 게임을 사달라는 본심을 드러낸 상황이므로 엄마의 응답으로 가장 적절한 것은 ③이다. ① 네, 저는 그를 좋아해요. 그는 멋진 녀석이에요. ② 어서 말해봐. 바로 그것이 엄마가 존재하는 이유란다. ④ 글쎄, 저녁 식사 후에 설거지를 할 수 있겠구나. ⑤ 그런 말을 들으니 유감이구나. 너는 친구를 도와주어야 한다.

어휘 behave oneself 잘 행동하다 touch 감동시키다

14 ④

해석 여 안녕, David. 어떻게 지냈니?
남 잘 지냈어. 너는 더 좋아 보이는구나, Jane. 넌 어때? 가족들은?
여 물론, 우리 잘 지내. 때때로 아빠는 네가 얼마나 영리하고 멋졌는지 말씀하셔. 그리고 Philip은 항상 네가 얼마나 훌륭한 테니스 선수였는지 이야기하고 있어.
남 Ben 삼촌이랑 Martha 이모, Philip이 많이 보고 싶었어.
여 그들도 널 그리워 해. 엄마는 너를 몹시 기다리고 계셔.
남 그래? 지금 당장 그녀를 만나 뵈러 가자.
여 천천히 해. Philip을 만나야지. 그는 지금 밖에 차에서 기다리고 있어.
남 오, Philip이 여기 있어? 왜 안으로 들어오지 않았어?
여 그와 나 중에 한 명은 차에 있어야 해. 주차 공간이 없어서. 가자.
남 오, 그를 빨리 만났으면 좋겠어.

해설 공항에 마중 나온 사촌인 Philip이 차에서 기다리고 있다고 했으므로 가장 적절한 응답은 ④이다. ① 안됐구나. 나도 정말 그가 보고 싶어. ② 지금 Philip을 만날 수 없다는 것이 유감이야. ③ 이제 Martha 이모와 점심을 먹자. ⑤ Ben 삼촌과 나는 정원을 거닐곤 했어.

어휘 fabulous 아주 멋진

15 ⑤

해석 여 Super Racers는 이번 주말에 콘서트를 열 계획이다. Mary는 이 그룹을 정말 좋아하고 아버지도 좋아하셔서, 아버지와 함께 콘서트에 가기로 결심했다. 그래서 그녀는 아버지에게 이번 주 토요일에 그녀와 함께 콘서트에 갈 수 있는지를 물어본다. 아버지는 그 말을 듣고 기뻐하지만, 이번 주말에 출장 때문에 갈 수 없다고 말한다. 그는 그녀가 얼마나 가고 싶어 하는지 알고, 그래서 그녀를 실망시키고 싶지 않다. 그는 Super Racers의 다음 공연 일정을 확인했고, 다음 달에 또 다른 공연이 있다는 것을 알아냈다. 이 상황에서, Mary에게 그의 아버지가 할 말로 가장 적절한 것은 무엇인가?
Mary's father 우리는 다음 달 콘서트에 갈 수 있어. 어떻게 생각하니?

해설 Mary의 아버지가 다음 달 공연 일정을 알아냈기 때문에 Mary에게 할 수 있는 이야기로 가장 적절한 것은 ⑤이다. ① 미안하지만, 다른 사람을 찾는 것이 좋겠다. ② 내 생각에 다음 공연 일정을 확인하는 것이 좋을 것 같구나. ③ 미안하구나. 출장 때문에 갈 수가 없구나. ④ 너를 실망시켜서 미안하지만 난 갈 수 없어.

16–17 ⑤, ⑤

해석 여 9학년 학생으로서, 여러분의 자녀는 지금 자신의 학업에서 가장 중요한 국면에 들어서고 있습니다. 부모로서 여러분은 자녀가 앞으로의 4

년에 걸쳐서 졸업까지 계속해 나가도록 용기를 북돋아 주는 것이 중요합니다. 통계에 따르면, 고등학교를 졸업한 학생 중 겨우 32 퍼센트가 고등학교에서 대학 교육을 이해하고 이어갈 수 있는 지식을 얻었습니다. 여러분의 도움으로, 여러분의 자녀가 9학년에서 탁월해질 수 있으며 졸업까지 계속 학업을 이어나갈 수 있습니다. 학생에게 보탬이 되는 가정 환경은 여러분 자녀의 고등학교에서의 성공이라는 면에서 엄청난 차이점을 만들어낼 수 있습니다. 여러분은 학업에 대한 관심을 기울이면서, 주의 깊게 여러분의 자녀가 가정에서 학업에 집중할 수 있도록 해야 합니다. 사실 많은 고등학교 중퇴자들은 그들 부모가 그들에게 좀 더 많은 것을 기대했더라면 더 열심히 공부했을 거라고 말을 했습니다. 지금 우리는 절실하게 여러분의 자녀를 위한 여러분의 도움을 기대하고 있습니다. 들어주셔서 감사합니다.

해설 16 9학년 학생의 학부모에게 부모가 가정에서 자녀의 학업에 관심을 가지고, 공부할 수 있는 분위기를 조성해 주는 것이 중요하다는 것을 말해주고 있다.
17 언급된 통계는 고등학교를 졸업한 학생 중 고등학교 시절에 대학 학업에 필요한 지식을 습득한 학생들의 비율이다.

어휘 phase 국면 ensure ~을 확실하게 하다 statistics 통계, 통계 자료 excel 뛰어나다 supportive 지지하는 tremendous 거대한 dropout 탈락자

◎ Dictation

01 you look so serious
02 whenever I wear it
03 I'm here to announce / how he endured / we will hold a party
04 I don't think it's a good idea / That's not the best way / in my opinion
05 all of them are used / The engine works well / It's my last offer
06 if it is here / the third shelf from the top / As soon as I get a similar one
07 Are you ready for / concentrate on my studies / drop by the drugstore / In case I fall asleep
08 We must prepare for it / There are none left / He's walking over there / it's my business
09 you look exhausted / there was a car accident / how fortunate
10 It was a hectic day / I was totally wrong / how much we earned / almost double the usual
11 As I mentioned before / prevent him from focusing on me
12 let's have a look / help my sister with her homework / Frankly speaking
13 help you wash the dishes / What a change / That touches me
14 How have you been / waiting for you eagerly / There's no parking space
15 will give concerts / because of a business trip
16-17 one of the most important phases / According to statistics / make your child focus on studying / we are looking forward to

자극하다, 강화하다 blood circulation 혈액 순환 astronaut 우주 비행사

29^회 듣기 모의고사

p.174-175

01 ⑤	02 ③	03 ③	04 ⑤	05 ①	06 ⑤
07 ②	08 ③	09 ①	10 ③	11 ③	12 ③
13 ④	14 ①	15 ②	16 ⑤	17 ④	

01 ⑤

해석 여 Andy, 여름휴가를 위한 계획이 있어?
남 차를 타고 전국을 여행할거야. 이미 부모님의 허락을 받았어.
여 부러운데. 그러면, 얼마나 걸릴 것 같아?
남 **정확한 계획을 세우지는 않았지만 아마 2주 정도.**

해설 전국일주 여행이 얼마나 걸릴지 물어보는 질문에 대한 적절한 대답은 ⑤이다. ① 2주 걸렸어. 아주 멋진 경험이었어. ② 몇 가지 특별한 계획을 제외하면, 평소와 비슷해. ③ 모두가 여름 방학 동안에는 기분이 들떠. ④ 2주. 하지만 엄마는 허락하지 않을 거야.

어휘 permission 허락

02 ③

해석 남 커피 한 잔 마시러 가자. 지금 매우 피곤한 걸.
여 그런데 너 오늘 커피를 많이 마신 것 같은데. 오늘 몇 잔이나 마신거야?
남 네 잔 내지 다섯 잔 정도. 사실, 커피가 없으면 난 하루도 살 수 없을 거야.
여 **이런, 커피 마시는 양을 줄이는 것이 좋겠는데.**

해설 하루에 커피를 4, 5잔을 마시는 친구에게 할 수 있는 말로는 ③이 적절하다. ① 내가 커피를 좋아하지 않는 걸 알잖아. 난 콜라가 더 좋아. ② 네 말에 동의해. 나도 카페인을 많이 섭취해. ④ 네 건강은 걱정하지 마. 카페인이 없는 음료야. ⑤ 잠깐 쉬는 건 어때? 내가 커피를 대접할게.

어휘 cut down 줄이다 free ~이 없는 treat ~을 대접하다

03 ③

해석 여 안녕하세요, 여러분. 저는 Susan Johnson입니다. 저는 어떤 특별한 기회를 알려드리고자 여기에 와 있습니다. 자, 여러분 모두 그것이 어떤 기회인지 궁금하실 겁니다. 그것은 피부 관리에서 가장 훌륭한 전문가를 만나 보는 기회입니다. 그렇지만, 이것은 사람이 아니라 일종의 음식입니다. 저는 여러분이 이 소식에 놀랄 것이라는 것을 압니다. 그리고 실망하지 마십시오. 그 음식은 더 젊어 보이도록 여러분의 얼굴에서 주름을 제거해 줄 것이고 혈액 순환을 자극하는 데 도움을 줄 것입니다. 이 음식을 보십시오. 이것은 알약처럼 보입니다만, 우주에서 우주 비행사가 먹는 음식의 종류입니다. 자, 여기로 와서 한번 드셔 보십시오. 주저하지 마세요.

해설 피부 미용에 도움을 주는 음식을 선전하고 있는 내용이다.

어휘 opportunity 기회 rid A of B A에게서 B를 제거하다 wrinkle 주름 stimulate

04 ⑤

해석 남 여러분은 어떻게 건물이 아플 수 있는가에 대해 들어본 적이 있습니까? 가끔 같은 건물에서 일하거나 사는 많은 사람들이 두통, 인후통, 기침 그리고 특정한 병명이 없는 다른 증상들을 가지게 됩니다. 또한 그들은 그 질병을 어디에서 얻었는지 알지 못합니다. 그러나 일반적으로 그들이 건물 밖으로 나가게 되면 증상이 완화됨을 느낍니다. 이것은 아픈 건물 증후군의 전형적인 경우입니다. 보통 그 문제는 건물 내에 있는 공기 순환과 관련이 있습니다. 오래된 공기가 적절한 시기에 건물에서 빠져나가지 못하거나 새로운 공기가 오염이 되는 경우입니다. 또한, 흔한 화학적인 공기 청정제가 외부에서 유입되는 오염원일 수도 있는데, 그것은 이 상황을 더 악화시킬 수 있습니다. 마지막으로, 인간 또는 동물의 바이러스가 빌딩 안에 갇혀서 증식될 수도 있습니다. 그 결과 사람들은 기분이 안 좋아집니다.

해설 공기 순환이 잘 안 되거나 오염이 되거나, 바이러스 등이 건물 안에 쌓이게 되면 건물 자체도 고통의 병을 앓게 될 수 있다는 내용이다. ① 인간의 바이러스가 증식될 수 있는 이유 ② 인간에게 병을 일으키는 고층 건물들 ③ 오염원이 될 수 있는 화학 청결제들 ④ 안녕(安寧)을 위한 공기 순환의 중요성 ⑤ 빌딩 자체가 병으로 고통 받는 경우

어휘 headache 두통 cough 기침 symptom 증상 circulation 순환 pollutant 오염원 worsen 악화시키다

05 ①

해석 여 배수구에 무슨 문제가 있나요?
남 머리카락으로 막혀서 물이 넘쳤어요.
여 끔찍해요! 제가 여기 이사 온지 이틀밖에 안됐어요.
남 이 문제를 빨리 찾아내서 운이 좋은 겁니다.
여 하지만 이것은 내 잘못일 리가 없어요. 전에 여기에 살았던 사람들이 욕조를 청소하지 않았던 것 같아요.
남 나도 그렇게 생각해요. 어쨌든, 이 경우는 쉽게 해결될 수 있어요. 이 산성의 성분의 액체가 저기 아래에 있는 머리카락을 녹일 수 있을 거예요.
여 오, 냄새가 매우 심하군요.
남 그래서 욕조를 사용한 뒤에는 항상 청소해야 해요.
여 알겠어요. 비용은 얼마인가요?
남 음, 출장비로 25달러만 지불하면 됩니다.
여 너무 비싸지만 돈을 드릴게요. 여기 있어요.
남 감사합니다. 배수구에 문제가 있으면 언제든 전화 주세요.

해설 욕조의 막힌 배수구 때문에 수리하러 온 사람이므로 배관공과 세입자 관계에 해당된다.

어휘 drain 배수구 clog ~을 방해하다, 막다 overflow 넘쳐흐르다 acid 산성의 dissolve 녹이다

06 ⑤

해석 남 나 셔츠를 사고 싶어. 봐! 저기 쇼윈도에 셔츠가 좀 있어. 확인해 볼 수 있을까? 만약 좋은 것이 있으면 가서 살 수 있어.
여 좋아. 어떤 종류의 셔츠를 사고 싶어? 왼쪽에서 첫 번째 셔츠는 어때?

남 글쎄. 너무 꽃무늬가 많아. 보는 것만으로도 머리를 아프게 하는 걸.

여 너는 단정하고 무늬가 별로 없는 셔츠를 좋아해. 맞지?

남 응. 그러면, 두 번째는 어때? 이 셔츠는 하얀색이고 체크무늬야.

여 괜찮아 보이는데, 오른쪽에서 첫 번째 셔츠는 어떻게 생각해?

남 내가 깔끔한 것을 좋아한다고 해도, 저건 너무 단순하다고 생각하지 않니? 심지어 점 하나도 없어.

여 까다롭긴! 단순하지만 너무 단순하면 안 된다니. 내 생각엔 세 번째 셔츠가 너에게 딱 맞을 것 같아.

남 파란 줄무늬가 좋아 보여. 저 옷을 사고 싶어.

여 이런! 간판을 봐. 문을 닫았어. 다음에 다시 오자.

해설 오른쪽에서 첫 번째 셔츠는 아무 무늬도 없는 셔츠라고 했으나 그림에서는 도트 무늬이므로 ⑤번이 정답이다.

어휘 **tidy** 단정한 **striped** 줄무늬가 있는

07 ②

해석 여 우리 집들이가 내일이에요.

남 준비는 됐어요? 내 생각에 우리가 많이 준비한 것 같지 않아요.

여 걱정 마요. 거의 끝나가요. 당신은 그냥 집을 청소해 주세요. 제가 모든 음식과 음료를 준비할게요.

남 알았어요. 내일 아침에 집을 청소할게요. 그런데 집 전체를 청소해야 하나요? 그러니까, 집안뿐만 아니라 차고를 포함해서 바깥쪽도 말이에요.

여 아이들이 이미 차고와 앞, 뒷마당을 청소했으니까 당신은 집안만 청소하면 돼요.

남 훌륭해요. 청소를 제외하고 내가 도울 수 있는 게 있을까요?

여 아뇨, 없어요. 아이들과 내가 오늘 아침에 가게에 가서 음식을 위한 재료를 샀어요. 또 요리법을 출력해서 냉장고에 붙여놨어요.

남 완벽한 것 같네요. 그럼 내가 해야 할 일을 할게요.

여 고마워요, 여보. 큰 도움이 될 거예요. 우리 파티는 훌륭할 거예요.

해설 여자는 남자에게 집안을 청소해 주기를 부탁했다.

어휘 **housewarming party** 집들이 **except for** ~을 제외하고는 **ingredient** 재료, 성분 **recipe** 요리법 **refrigerator** 냉장고

08 ③

해석 남 왜 자동판매기를 치고 있어?

여 오, Robert. 이 기계에서 또 50센트를 잃었어. 정말 멍청한 기계라니까!

남 놀랍지도 않은 걸. 그게 항상 고장 난다는 걸 몰랐니?

여 알고 있었지만, 오늘은 괜찮을 거라고 생각했어.

남 그건 내 돈도 삼켰어. 하지만, 자동판매기를 치는 것은 전혀 효과가 없어.

여 난 화가 났었어. 어쨌든, 자동판매기에 '고장' 표지판을 붙이는 건 어떨까?

남 좋은 생각이야. 그렇지 않으면 같은 일이 다른 사람에게도 일어날 거야.

여 그러면 표지판을 만들어 줄 수 있니? 나는 자동판매기 회사에 전화를 걸게.

남 좋아, 그런데 전화번호를 알아?

여 그럼, 기계 앞 쪽에서 찾을 수 있어. 난 내 돈을 돌려받아야 해.

남 오, 잊어버려. 아무것도 아니잖아.

여 아니, 이건 중요한 거야. 어쨌든, 난 여기서 너를 기다릴게.

남 알았어. 곧 돌아올게.

해설 여자는 기계에 들어가 있는 돈을 돌려받기 위해서 자동판매기 회사에 전화를 하려는 것이다. ① 기계를 수리하려고 ② 기계를 교환하려고 ③ 잃어버린 돈을 되돌려 받으려고 ④ 경고 표지판을 만들려고 ⑤ 커피를 또 한 잔 사려고

어휘 **vending machine** 자동판매기 **out of order** 고장 난 **work** 효과가 있다 **get ~ back** 돌려받다

09 ①

해석 남 도와드릴까요?

여 네. 만 원짜리 지폐를 잔돈으로 바꾸고 싶어요.

남 죄송하지만 여기는 은행이 아니에요.

여 은행이 아닌 것은 알아요. 하지만 저는 잔돈이 필요해요. 도와주세요.

남 알았어요. 하지만 딱 한 번 만이에요, 알겠죠?

여 알겠어요. 5천 원짜리 지폐 한 장과 나머지는 천 원짜리로 주세요.

남 그렇지만 천 원짜리가 그렇게 많지 않아요.

여 그러면, 동전도 괜찮아요.

남 좋아요. 5천 원 짜리 한 장하고, 천 원짜리 지폐 4장, 백 원짜리 동전으로 나머지를 받는 건요?

여 글쎄요, 너무 많은 동전은 원하지 않아요. 백 원짜리 대신에 5백 원짜리 동전은 어떤가요?

남 좋아요. 그럼 여기 있어요. 세어보세요.

여 됐네요. 매우 고맙습니다.

해설 만 원을 5천 원짜리 지폐 한 장과 천 원짜리 지폐 4장 그리고 나머지는 동전으로 바꾸는데, 100원짜리 대신에 500원짜리로 교환했으므로, 500원짜리 2개를 얻게 될 것이다.

어휘 **note** 지폐 **change** 잔돈, 거스름돈 **count** ~을 세다

10 ③

해석 남 그럼, Somalia에 얼마나 오랫동안 머무르고 있나요?

여 대략 일 년 동안이요. 전 여기서 불쌍한 사람들을 돕기 위해 살고 있어요.

남 전쟁 때문에 이 나라에서 많은 사람들이 부상을 입고 죽어가고 있어요.

여 맞아요. 전 의사는 아니지만 다친 사람들을 돌보고 있어요.

남 오, 어렵지 않나요?

여 어렵지만 매력이 있어요.

남 그것에 대해 이야기해 줄 수 있나요?

여 음……. 사람들이요. 그들은 너무 순수하고 선량해요. 저는 매일 그들로 부터 많은 것을 배워요.

남 그렇지만 그들은 음식 부족과 질병으로 고통 받고 있어요.

여 맞아요. 하지만 그들은 대부분의 어려움을 잘 극복하고 있어요.

남 정말 대단하군요! 당신에게 가장 보람을 주는 것은 무엇인가요?

여 음, 사랑의 중요성을 배우는 것이요.

해설 의료진이 증원되어야 할 필요성에 대한 언급은 전혀 없었다.

어휘 **conflict** 전쟁, 싸움 **injured** 부상을 입은 **attraction** 매력, 사람의 마음을 끌어당기는 힘 **suffer from** ~로 고통 받다 **shortage** 부족 **rewarding** 보람 있는

11 ③

해석 남 국제적인 피아노 경연대회인 "The Muse"가 그리스의 가장 아름다운 섬 중 하나인 Santorini에서 열릴 것입니다. 2013년 9월 1일부터 8일까지 여행객들과 섬의 주민들 모두가 젊은 피아니스트들의 연주를 듣는 멋진 기회를 갖게 될 연중행사입니다. 이 경연대회의 주목적은 앞으로 새로운 인재를 발굴하고 소개하려는 것입니다. 경연대회는 15세에서 30세의 피아니스트들에게 열려 있습니다. 일등상을 받은 사람은 1000달러를 받게 될 것입니다. 참가자든 심사위원, 조직위원, 청중이든지 간에 이 대회에 관련이 있는 모든 사람들은 경쟁적이지만 정감 있는 분위기를 즐기게 될 것입니다.

해설 관광객과 섬의 주민들 모두가 참여할 수 있는 행사이다.

어휘 **resident** 거주자 **competition** 경연대회 **jury** 심사위원단 **competitive** 경쟁의

12 ③

해석 남 Alice. 너의 휴가는 언제야?
여 다음달 16일부터 23일까지야.
남 내 휴가가 네 휴가보다 좀 더 기네. 15일에서 25일까지야.
여 그럼 우리 여행안내 책자를 보자.
남 음, 우리는 호주에는 갈 수가 없어.
여 맞아. 정말 가고 싶었지만 이번에는 갈 수 없어.
남 그럼 언젠가 갈 수 있어. 중국은 어때?
여 Derrick, 나의 휴가에 대해서 너에게 이야기하지 않았니? 우리는 갈 수 없어.
남 오, 잊었어. 필리핀은 어때? 거기서 스쿠버 다이빙과 골프를 즐길 수 있어.
여 그렇지만, 기간이 너무 짧아. 조금 비싸지만, 난 발리에 가고 싶어.
남 좋아. 그곳에 가자.
여 오, 휴가가 정말 기다려지는데.

해설 여자가 발리에 가고 싶다고 하자 남자가 동의했고, 그 중 여자와 남자의 휴가 기간과 일치하는 것은 ③이다.

어휘 **brochure** 안내 책자 **look forward to** ~을 기대하다

13 ④

해석 남 왜 방학이 시작됐어요.
여 신나 보이는구나. 방학 계획은 세웠니?
남 글쎄요, 우선 공부해야 하고, 그리고 놀고……
여 Tom, 너의 방학 계획표를 한번 보자.
남 엄마. 계획표는 중요한 것이 아니에요. 나는 기계가 아니에요.
여 알아, Tom. 하지만 훌륭한 삶은 계획과 함께 시작한단다.
남 엄마, 제발요. Bill과 Peter가 밖에서 저를 기다리고 있어요.
여 난 널 이해해. 하지만……
남 엄마가 무슨 이야기를 할지 알아요. 시작이 반이다.

여 똑똑하구나! 좋아. 친구들과 놀고 난 뒤에 방학 계획표를 만들어 보자.
남 좋아요, 엄마. 그리고 오늘 밤 Bill의 집에서 자도 돼요?
여 **안 돼. 나와의 약속을 잊지 마.**

해설 오늘 밤 Bill의 집에서 머물러도 되냐고 엄마에게 허락을 구하고 있으므로, 그에 어울리는 응답이 필요하다. ① 미안해. 다신 이런 일이 일어나지 않을 거야. ② 아무 문제없어. 이미 엄마에게 부탁했어. ③ 오, 대단하군. 6시에 널 만날 것을 기대하고 있을게. ⑤ 너의 방학 계획표를 보는 게 어때?

어휘 **Well-planned is half of well-done.** 시작이 반이다.(=A good beginning is half done. Starting is half-done.) **stay over** (남의 집에서 하룻밤) 자다

14 ①

해석 여 연말 파티에 참석할거지?
남 물론이지. 이번 주 토요일이라고 들었는데.
여 맞아. 드디어 한 해가 가는구나.
남 맞아, 세월이 참 빠르지. 그런데 너도 갈 거니?
여 너 내가 그 파티 조직위원인 걸 몰랐어?
남 굉장하다! 네가 준비한다면 파티는 멋질 거야.
여 그런 말을 들으니 기뻐. 최선을 다할게.
남 그건 그렇고, 어떤 특별한 것을 준비했니?
여 사실 노래 경연대회를 할 거야.
남 정말? 하지만 사람들을 노래 부르게 하려면 꽤 어려울 텐데. 사람들은 많은 사람들 앞에서 노래하기를 좋아하지 않을 거야.
여 걱정하지 마. 우리는 멋진 해결책을 가지고 있어. 하지만 그건 비밀이야.
남 **그래? 아주 기대되는데.**

해설 남자는 호기심을 갖고 어떤 것인지를 물었고, 여자는 그것이 비밀이라고 말했다. 이것에 대한 남자의 응답으로는 ①이 가장 적절하다. ② 굉장하군! 하지만 난 너에게 어떤 것도 이야기해 줄 수 없어. ③ 알겠어. 너와 함께 갈 수 없다는 것이 유감이야. ④ 하지만 그게 얼마나 오래 걸릴지 모르겠어. ⑤ 그러면, 다음 주 토요일에 만나는 것이 어때?

어휘 **organizer** 조직위원 **do one's best** 최선을 다하다 **have difficulty -ing** ~하는 데 어려움을 겪다

15 ②

해석 여 Christine은 아시아와 아시아 문화에 대해 호기심을 약간 가지고 있었다. 특히 그녀는 부탄 같은 나라에 가고 싶어 했다. 하지만 그녀는 그 나라에 대해 전혀 몰랐다. 그래서 그녀는 부탄 여행에 대한 정보를 얻고자 여행사를 방문했다. 여행사 직원은 배낭여행은 추천하지 않는다고 말하며 단체 여행을 가야하며 방을 나눠 쓰거나 추가 요금을 내고 혼자 방을 쓸 수 있다고 권했다. 그녀는 추가 요금을 내고 싶지는 않지만 혼자 방을 쓰는 것을 원했다. 그래서 그녀는 방을 혼자 쓰기로 결정했다. 이 상황에서, Christine이 직원에게 할 말로 가장 적절한 것은 무엇인가?
Christine 좀 비싸지만 혼자서 머무는 것이 더 낫겠어요.

해설 추가 비용을 내고 혼자 방을 쓰기로 결정한 Christine이 할 말로 가장 적절한 것은 ②이다. ① 이 여행을 포기하는 것이 좋겠어요. 어쨌든, 감사합니다. ③ 그것은 당신이 굉장한 경험을 할 수 있는 가장 좋은 기회입니다. ④ 부탄을 여행하는 것에 대해 조언을 해 주실 수 있나요? ⑤ 티베트에 가는 건 어떻습니까?

그곳은 배낭여행을 하기에 좋습니다.

어휘 **curiosity** 호기심 **agent** 직원 **backpacking tour** 배낭여행

16–17 ⑤, ④

해석 여 우선, 저를 도와준 Alice에게 감사를 드립니다. 저의 편지에 대한 그녀의 신속하고 예의바른 답장이 없었다면, 저는 이 나라에 오기로 결정하지 못했을 것입니다. 그리고 제가 Nairobi 공항에 도착했을 때 저를 기다려준 사람도 바로 Alice였습니다. 그녀는 항상 어떤 걱정이나 문제들에 답해주기 위해 자원봉사자 숙소 근처에 있었습니다. 사실, 저는 특히 제 나이가 17살로 어리고 여자 혼자서 여행한다는 점 때문에 이곳에 오기 전에 아주 걱정했습니다. 하지만 저는 제 인생에서 가장 멋진 5주를 보냈습니다! 저는 이 고아원에서 일하는 것이 정말 좋고 저의 자원봉사에 자부심을 느낍니다. 아이들과 이야기하고 함께 놀면서 지내는 것은 정말 근사합니다. 저는 이 프로그램을 꼭 다른 사람들에게 추천할 것입니다. 지금 저는 내일 이 나라를 떠나야 한다는 것이 아주 유감입니다. 저는 여러분과 여러분의 친절을 영원히 기억할 것입니다. 이 깜짝 파티를 준비해 주셔서 정말 감사합니다. 또, 모든 멋진 친구들에게 작별인사를 하게 되어 슬픕니다.

해설 16 자원봉사를 하러 왔다가 다시 돌아가는 사람을 위한 파티이다.

17 해외로 나와 고아원에서 자원봉사를 하고 있다.

어휘 **decent** 예의바른, 알맞은 **orphanage** 고아원 **definitely** 꼭

◎ Dictation

01 any plans for summer vacation

02 get some coffee

03 I'm here to announce / rid your face of wrinkles / come up here

04 sore throats / the problem is related to / can worsen this situation

05 What's wrong with / can be fixed easily / How much would it cost

06 Can we just check / with checkered patterns / How picky you are

07 It's almost done / Is there anything I can do / It'd be a big help

08 it's always out of order / can you make it / get my money back

09 just this once / some coins would be fine / Count them

10 how long have you been / I'm caring for / they are suffering from

11 It's an annual event / The competition is open to / competitive but friendly atmosphere

12 It runs from / but not this time / looking forward to our holiday

13 let me take a look at / Well-planned is half of well-done / stay over at

14 time flies / I'll do my best / have some difficulty

15 had some curiosity / to get some information / with an extra charge

---

16-17 around the volunteer house / I was so nervous / take pride in / I'm sad to say goodbye

30회 듣기 모의고사
p.180-181

01 ①	02 ①	03 ①	04 ③	05 ⑤	06 ②
07 ④	08 ②	09 ①	10 ②	11 ①	12 ⑤
13 ③	14 ②	15 ④	16 ②	17 ④	

01 ①

해석 남 엄마, 더 이상 학교로 휴대폰을 가져가지 않을 거예요.
여 무슨 일이 있었니? 넌 휴대폰 없이 살 수 있는 사람이 아니잖아.
남 사실은, 벌을 받았어요. 수업 중에 제 휴대폰이 울렸거든요.
여 네가 아주 좋은 선택을 했다고 생각한다.

해설 수업 중에 휴대폰이 울려서 벌을 받았고 그 때문에 휴대폰을 학교에 가져가지 않겠다는 아들에게 엄마가 할 말로 가장 적절한 것은 ①이다. ② 그는 너에게 벌점을 주면 안 돼. ③ 스마트폰을 어떻게 쓰는지 나에게 말해 줄래? ④ 난 수업 중에 내 휴대폰을 꺼놓을 거야. ⑤ 분실물 보관소를 확인해보는 건 어때?

어휘 **penality** 벌점, 벌 **to tell the truth** 사실은 **turn off** ~을 끄다

02 ①

해석 여 아주 긴장한 것처럼 보이는구나. 힘내! 넌 잘할 수 있어.
남 고마워요, 엄마. 하지만 가사를 잊어버릴까봐 너무 두려워요.
여 걱정하지 마, David. 대기만성이란 말이 있어. 이건 너의 첫 번째 오디션일 뿐이야.
남 저의 꿈을 이루기 위해서 최선을 다할게요.

해설 오디션에 처음 참가해서 긴장한 자신을 격려하는 엄마에게 아들이 할 말로 가장 적절한 것은 ①이다. ② 당신은 할 수 있어요. 이제 숨을 깊게 쉬어 보세요. ③ 다행히 난 아무 실수도 하지 않았어요. ④ 걱정하지 마세요. 그 실패가 저를 낙담시키지 않았어요. ⑤ 이 수업이 끝난 후에 당신은 가사 쓰기를 시작할 수 있어요.

어휘 **nervous** 긴장한 **Late fruit keeps well.** 대기만성 **breathe** 숨 쉬다 **to one's relief** 다행히 **discourage** 낙담시키다 **lyrics** 가사

03 ①

해석 여 당신의 나라의 국기가 무엇을 의미하는지 알고 있습니까? 동호회와 조직들 또한 자신을 나타내는 깃발을 가지고 있습니다. 예를 들어, 올림픽기는 경기를 위해 다섯 대륙에서 온 모든 사람들이 함께 함을 의미하는 다섯 개의 올림픽 고리를 특징으로 삼고 있습니다. 각각의 깃발은 독특한 목적과 의미를 지니고 있습니다. 이제 우리 클럽에서 여러분은 다양한 깃발의 독특한 의미를 배울 수 있으며 자신만의 깃발을 만들 수 있습니다. 여러분이 자신과 가족을 위한 깃발을 만든다고 상상해 보세

요. 신나지 않습니까? 물론, 아이들도 함께 할 수 있습니다. 서둘러서 가입하세요!

해설 깃발 제작 동호회의 참여를 권유하는 내용이다.

어휘 flag 깃발 represent 나타내다 feature ~을 특징으로 하다 continent 대륙

04 ③

해석 여 오, 너무 더워. 에어컨을 켜야겠어.
남 하지만 아직 섭씨 28도도 안 됐어. 우리가 기계의 도움을 받을 필요는 없어 보여.
여 그렇지 않아. 너무 습하고 덥다고. 난 이런 날씨를 견딜 수가 없어.
남 찬 음료를 마시는 건 어때? 그리고 내가 창문을 열어 놓을게. 그것이 너의 기분을 더 나아지게 할 거야.
여 널 이해할 수가 없어. 일하는 동안의 이런 날씨 같은 더위는 우릴 비효율적으로 만들어.
남 하지만 너의 건강을 위해서 자연스러운 방법으로 공기를 순환시키는 것이 더 좋아.
여 좋아. 받아들이겠어. 하지만 더 이상 견딜 수 없을 때는 에어컨을 켤 거야.
남 나의 의견을 받아줘서 고마워.
여 넌 약간 구두쇠 같아.
남 아냐. 그렇지 않아. 사실 난 절약 같은 것이 아니라 너의 건강에 대해 염려할 뿐이야.
여 알겠어. 고마워.

해설 건강을 위해서는 에어컨을 켜는 것 보다 자연스럽게 공기를 순환시키는 것이 좋다고 말하고 있다.

어휘 Celsius 섭씨 mechanical 기계의 humid 습기 찬 stand 견디다 ineffective 비효율적인 circulate 순환시키다 stingy 인색한

05 ⑤

해석 여 Andrew, 피곤해 보이네요. 어젯밤 잠을 잘 못 잤나요?
남 네. 어제 Peter가 밤새 저를 깨웠어요.
여 안됐군요. 그가 많이 울었나요?
남 네. 계속 울었고, 달래고 쓰다듬으며 그 아이 옆에 있어야 했어요.
여 오, 이런. 하지만 다행히도 이제 아파 보이지는 않군요.
남 정말요? 그가 너무 많이 우는 것 같아서 어젯밤에 아주 걱정했어요. 이제는 자는군요. 정말 귀여워요!
여 그래요. 그런데, 당신의 아내는 언제 돌아오나요?
남 다음 주 화요일이요. 그녀가 돌아오면 마음이 놓일 거예요.
여 이해해요. 서둘러요. 그렇지 않으면 또 지각할 거예요.
남 벌써 8시군요. Peter를 잘 돌봐주세요.
여 걱정 마세요. 그는 좋은 아이이고 나를 좋아하는 것 같아요.
남 고맙습니다. 당신을 보면 저희 할머니가 생각나요. 그녀는 저를 늘 돌봐주셨죠. 이것은 이번 주 당신의 보수예요. 잊을 뻔 했네요.
여 고마워요.

해설 Peter 때문에 잠을 못 잔 아버지와 아이를 돌봐 주는 사람의 대화다. 따라서 ⑤가 가장 적절하다.

어휘 awake 잠이 깬 soothe 달래주다, 진정시키다 pat ~을 가볍게 두드리다 remind A of B A에게 B를 생각나게 하다 look after ~을 돌보다 nearly 거의

06 ②

해석 여 이것들을 어떻게 생각해?
남 이 방에 있는 모든 그림들을 네가 그렸니?
여 응, 물론이지. 나는 그림 그리는 것을 좋아해.
남 멋지다! 이것이 무엇을 나타내는지 설명해 줄래?
여 컵은 우리의 마음을 뜻해. 그것은 많은 것들과 생각을 담을 수 있어.
남 그렇구나. 난 큰 창문 옆에 있는 저 그림이 좋아. 아주 흥미로운 해바라기야.
여 그렇게 생각해? 나는 고흐를 존경해. 그래서 그의 그림을 모방했어.
남 그의 것과 비슷하기는 한데 약간 다르구나. 딱 하나의 해바라기만 있어서 너의 독창성을 잘 표현해주고 있어.
여 고마워. 이 그림은 어때?
남 나를 안정시켜 줘. 빗속에서 우산을 들고 있는 여인이 나의 흥미를 끌어.
여 그리고 이 그림을 봐. 설악산의 풍경을 그렸어. 나는 이것을 가장 좋아해.
남 매우 좋은 풍경화네.

해설 해바라기 그림에서 해바라기는 오직 한 송이만 있다고 했지만 그림에는 여러 송이의 해바라기가 있으므로 ②번이 정답이다.

어휘 respect 존경하다 imitate 모방하다 originality 독창성 attract ~을 매혹하다 scenery 풍경

07 ④

해석 남 안녕, Monica.
여 안녕, Ted. 단정하고 기분 좋아 보이는데. 좋은 일 있니? 어디에 가니?
남 숨길 수가 없군. 나 오늘 Susan과 만날 거야.
여 축하해! 결국 성공했구나!
남 응, 하지만 조금 힘들었어.
여 어디서 그녀를 만날 거야?
남 Tasha's Garden에서. 그곳은 아주 아름답고 낭만적인 장소라고 들었어.
여 나도 그곳을 알아. 거기에 가본 적이 있어. 정말 멋져.
남 Susan과의 데이트가 정말 걱정스러워.
여 걱정하지 마. 너의 특별함으로 잘해낼 거야. 그런데 그 식당 옆에 있는 서점으로 나를 데려다 줄 수 있니?
남 물론이야. 차에 타.
여 정말 고마워. 널 여기서 만나다니 운이 좋구나.

해설 여자는 남자에게 Susan과의 데이트 장소인 식당으로 가면서 그 옆의 서점에 데려다 줄 것을 부탁했다.

어휘 uniqueness 유일함, 비길 데 없음 give A a ride A를 태워주다 hop in 자동차에 타다

08 ②

해석 남 Gena, 이번 주 수요일에 회의에 참석할 수 없어요.

여 할 수 없다고요? 왜요? 당신 없이 회의를 하고 싶지 않아요.

남 어머니가 너무 아프셔서 병원에 그녀를 모셔가야 해요. 그녀 혼자 가게 할 수는 없어.

여 맞아요. 하지만 그날 있는 출장은 어떻게 되는 거예요? 수요일 저녁에 San Diego로 갈 예정이잖아요.

남 제 출장에 대해서 알고 있었어요? 사실 어머니의 병 때문에 출장을 포기할까 해요.

여 하지만 그것은 당신의 경력에서 매우 중요한 일이에요. 그렇죠?

남 맞아요. 이 회사에서 승진을 할 좋은 기회예요. 나도 알아요.

여 비행기 시간 바꾸는 건 어떨까요?

남 글쎄요. 그러기엔 너무 늦은 것 같지만, 지금 당장 공항에 전화해 볼게요. 걱정해줘서 고마워요.

여 천만에요. 그리고 만약 표를 바꿀 수 없다면 이 문제에 대한 다른 해결책을 생각해 봐요.

해설 남자는 비행기 표를 바꾸려고 전화를 할 것이다.

어휘 promotion 승진

09 ①

해석 여 퀸즈 피자에 전화해 주셔서 감사합니다. 무엇을 도와드릴까요?

남 네. 포테이토 피자를 주문하려고요.

여 어떤 사이즈를 원하시나요?

남 라지 사이즈는 얼마인가요?

여 17달러입니다. 그렇지만, 하나를 주문하면 미디엄 사이즈를 공짜로 얻을 수 있어요.

남 음. 미디엄 사이즈는 어때요?

여 그 경우에는 스파게티를 공짜로 얻을 수 있어요. 그리고 가격은 13달러입니다.

남 그러면 미디엄 사이즈의 포테이토 피자를 주문할게요.

여 콜라는요? 큰 콜라는 2달러에요.

남 오, 전 콜라 할인 쿠폰이 있어요.

여 쿠폰이 있으면, 당신은 50퍼센트 할인해서 큰 콜라를 가질 수 있어요.

남 알겠습니다. 큰 콜라로 할게요. 저는 New York 거리의 137번지에 살고 있어요.

여 고맙습니다. 20분 후에 배달될 거예요.

해설 미디엄 사이즈의 피자를 선택했으므로 13달러이고, 콜라는 쿠폰을 사용해서 1달러에 사게 된다. 따라서 총 액수는 14달러가 될 것이다.

어휘 order 주문하다 additional 부가적인 absolutely 완전히

10 ②

해석 여 드디어 도착했구나. Bill. 오랫동안 너를 기다렸어.

남 늦어서 미안해. 세미나가 막 끝났어.

여 어쨌든 너를 다시 봐서 반가워.

남 넌 오늘 더 좋아 보이는데. 그게 뭐야? 만화책?

여 응. Polly 이모가 그것을 가져다 주셨어. 아주 재미있어.

남 왜! Alice가 만화책을 보다니! 아주 놀라운데.

여 이 책들이 없다면, 나는 여기에서의 이 지겨운 생활을 견딜 수 없었을 거야.

남 그 말을 들으니 안됐구나. 밖으로 나가는 게 어때? 내가 도와줄게.

여 좋아. 하지만 다른 사람들을 조심해야 해. 그들은 시끄러운 것을 싫어해.

남 저 여자는 매우 아파 보여. 정말 불쌍하다!

여 맞아. 나에게 저기 있는 휠체어를 갖다 줄 수 있니?

남 그래.

해설 주변에 아픈 사람들이 있고, 여자가 이동할 때 휠체어가 필요한 것으로 보아 병원이다.

11 ①

해석 여 Holland Flowers Festival에 오신 것을 환영합니다. 올해의 Festival은 세계에서 가장 큰 실내 꽃 정원에 차려져 있습니다. 여러분은 아름다운 봄 정원에서 다채로운 꽃들 사이로 끝없이 걸어 다닐 수 있으며, 박람회에 대한 모든 정보를 얻을 수 있습니다. 우리는 올해 "TOP SPORT"라는 주제를 선택했는데, 꽃을 경작하는 것은 높은 수준의 운동 경기를 치르는 것과 같은 성취를 얻기 때문입니다. 매일 오후 1시에 열어서 오후 9시에 문을 닫습니다. 표는 인터넷이나 전화로 구입하실 수 있습니다. 2월 20일에서 24일까지 열리는 Holland Flowers Festival은 여러 가지 생각, 영감 그리고 창조성으로 차고 넘칠 것입니다. 놓치지 마세요!

해설 세계에서 가장 큰 실내 정원에서 행사가 열린다고 했으므로 야외 정원에서 행해지는 행사가 아니다.

어휘 endlessly 끝없이 cultivate 경작하다 brim ~으로 넘치다(with) inspiration 영감

12 ⑤

해석 남 피트니스 센터 프로그램이구나. 무언가를 배울 시간은 있어?

여 응, 하지만 오직 수요일과 금요일에만 가능해.

남 그러면 수영은 어때? 넌 수영을 잘 하잖아.

여 나는 내가 할 수 없는 것을 배우고 싶어.

남 요가는 어때? 요가가 너의 건강에 좋을 것 같아.

여 그러고 싶지만, 금요일 아침에는 별로 시간이 없어.

남 그러면 수요일이나 금요일에 재즈 댄스를 배울 수 있겠다.

여 하지만 나는 춤추는 것을 좋아하지 않아. 스쿼시를 배울 수 있을까? 웨이트 트레이닝을 통해서는 내가 배울 것이 없는 것 같아.

남 물론이지. Jane도 스쿼시를 배우고 있는걸.

여 정말이야? 그러면, 나도 그것을 해야겠다.

남 그런데 너는 수요일 저녁에는 불어 수업이 있잖아. 그렇지 않니?

여 맞아. 하지만 하나가 남았으니 그것을 선택할 수 있어.

해설 여자는 금요일 오후에 하는 스쿼시를 선택하게 될 것이다.

13 ③

해석 남 드라이브하기에 멋진 날씨에요, 그렇지 않나요?

여 그렇구나. 날 불러줘서 고마워, Mike.

남 엄마. 이건 아무것도 아니에요. 저는 정말 엄마와 함께 드라이브를 하고 싶었어요.

여 왜! 아들과의 데이트라.

남 엄마, 저는 엄마가 무엇을 생각하는지 알아요. Andrew에 대해서는 걱정하지 마세요.

여 오, 내가 걱정하는 것을 알고 있었니?

남 네, 물론이에요. Andrew가 자신의 문제들을 이야기해줬어요. 게다가 그도 엄마를 걱정하고 있어요.

여 그가 나를 걱정해? 하지만 나에 대한 그의 행동은 여전히 나쁜데.

남 엄마, Andrew는 자신의 문제들을 알고 있고 그것을 고치려고 노력해요.

여 그는 어렸을 때 멋진 아이였단다. 난 너만큼 그 아이를 아주 사랑해. 그렇지만 그 아이는 내가 항상 너와 비교한다고 이야기를 해.

남 마음 편히 하세요, 엄마. Andrew가 저에게 엄마를 위해 좋은 아들이 되겠다고 말했어요.

여 그가 그랬어? 그 말을 들으니 정말 기쁘구나.

해설 Andrew가 엄마를 속하게 한 후 Mike가 엄마를 위로하며 나누는 대화이다. 여기서 엄마가 할 수 있는 말로는 ③이 가장 적절하다. ① 글쎄, 너는 나에게 좀 더 친절해야 해. ② 나는 네가 그녀를 이해해야 한다고 생각해. ④ 오, 맙소사. 그가 직장을 잃었다는 것을 알지 못했어. ⑤ 어쨌든, 멋진 식사를 대접해 줘서 고마워.

어휘 **correct** 고치다 **compare** 비교하다

14 ②

해석 여 오늘이 이 사무실에서의 마지막 날이에요.

남 무슨 말 하는 거예요? 농담이죠?

여 아뇨, 정말이에요. 전 이 직장을 그만둬요.

남 왜요? 당신은 사장이 굳건하게 믿고 있는 실무진 중 한 명이에요.

여 알아요, 하지만 전 그래야만 했어요. 다른 선택권이 없거든요.

남 남편인 Philip 때문에 그래요?

여 맞아요. Philip이 Boston으로 전근을 가게 되었고, 전 그곳으로 함께 가기로 결정했어요.

남 그러면 Boston에서 다른 직장을 얻었어요?

여 네, 하지만 중간 관리자로 시작해야 해요.

남 그 말을 들으니 유감이네요.

여 하지만 남편과 함께 행복한 삶을 사는 것이 저에겐 가장 중요한 것이에요.

남 하지만 당신의 선택을 후회하지 않길 바랄게요.

해설 여자가 Boston에서 중간 관리자직을 얻어 떠나게 된다는 사실에 남자는 매우 아쉬워하고 있다. ① 걱정하지 마세요. 그것은 한 시간이면 끝날 거예요. ③ 당신은 정말 친절하군요! 지금 당신의 제안을 받아들일게요. ④ 오, 이런. 당신이 New York에 갈 수 없다니 유감이에요. ⑤ 아뇨, 안 할 거예요. 전 부인과 함께 있는 것이 행복해요.

어휘 **executives** 관리직, 경영진 **firmly** 굳건히, 확고하게 **transfer** 옮기다, 이동하다

15 ④

해석 남 Derreck은 자동차 판매원으로서의 그의 직업을 그만 두고 싶었다. 그는 그 직업에 실증을 느꼈다. 사실, 그는 가르치는 것에 관심이 있었고, 그의 전공은 수학 교육이었다. 그래서 그는 새로운 직업을 찾기 시작했다. 하지만 새로운 직업을 찾는 것은 쉽지 않았고, 그는 다시 자동차 판매원으로 돌아가기로 결심했다. 실망한 상태에서 그는 누나인 Patty에게 전화를 걸었다. 전화를 끊고 난 뒤, Patty는 그를 도와줄 방법을 찾기로 결심했다. Patty는 남편에게 Derreck이 가르치는 것과 관련된 직업을 찾을 수 있는지 물어보았다. Patty의 남편은 영어 선생님이었고, 그는 그녀에게 자신의 학교에서 수학 선생님을 구하고 있다고 말했다. 지금, 희망으로 가득 차서 그녀는 남동생인 Derreck에게 전화를 걸었다. 이 상황에서, Patty가 Derreck에게 할 말로 가장 적절한 것은 무엇인가?

Patty 서둘러, 너의 소망을 위한 또 다른 기회가 있어.

해설 Derreck은 직업을 바꾸려 하고, Patty는 마침 적당한 자리가 있다는 것을 알게 된다. 이럴 때 Patty가 할 수 있는 말은 ④이다. ① 힘내. 너의 직장으로 다시 돌아갈 시간이야. ② 잠깐 휴식을 위해 여행을 떠나는 것이 어떨까? ③ 네가 어려움을 극복했다고 하니 매우 기쁘다. ⑤ 내가 장담하건데, 자동차 판매원이 너에게 가장 적절한 직업이야.

어휘 **hang up** 전화를 걸다 **related to** ~와 관련된 **take a rest** 휴식을 취하다 **overcome** 극복하다 **bet** 확신하다 **suitable** 적절한

16–17 ②, ④

해석 여 제가 이렇게 아름다운 장소에 있다는 것을 믿을 수가 없어요. 멋지네요!

남 이 해변은 아름답고 깨끗하기로 매우 유명해요.

여 맞아요. 우리의 휴가를 완전히 즐길 수 있겠군요. 세상에! 저 남자를 보세요.

남 오, 이런. 저 젊은이가 모래사장에 불붙은 담배꽁초를 버렸어요. 정말 수치스러운 일이네요!

여 그가 왜 그런 행동을 하지요? 그 사람 뒤에 걸어오는 누군가가 이 지역을 청소할 거라고 생각하는가 보죠?

남 그는 세상이 재떨이라고 생각하는 것 같아요.

여 당신도 알다시피, 저는 결코 담배를 피울 권리를 부정하는 사람은 아니에요. 그렇지만 저런 행동은 참을 수가 없네요. 우리는 무언가를 해야 해요.

남 맞아요. 그리고 담배꽁초는 분해되는 것도 아니지요.

여 저는 가서 자신이 버린 담배꽁초를 당장 주우라고 말하겠어요.

남 잠깐만요! 그가 당신에게 화를 낼 수도 있어요. 사실 그가 훌륭한 청년이라면 그는 다시는 그런 행동을 하지 않을 거예요.

여 그렇지만 저는 그에게 그렇게 하도록 하는 것이 저의 의무라고 생각해요. 나와 같이 가든지 여기서 기다리세요.

해설 16 담배꽁초를 버린 남성에게 직접 가서 자신이 버린 것을 도로 주우라는 말을 해야 하는 것이 자신의 의무라고 말하고 있다.

17 남자에게 가서 자신이 버린 담배꽁초를 주우라고 할 것이다. ① 그녀를 따라오지 않게 그를 설득하기 ② 그녀가 앉았던 자리를 청소하기 ③ 환경을 위한 캠페인 준비하기 ④ 남자에게 자신이 버린 것을 주우라고 요청하기 ⑤ 젊은이에게 가서 담배를 피우지 말라고 요청하기

어휘 **cleanness** 깨끗함 **ashtray** 재떨이 **deny** 부정하다 **butt** 담배꽁초 **biodegradable** 생물분해성의

01 I've got some penalties
02 Late fruit keeps well
03 to represent them / make your own flag / Hurry up and join
04 It's too humid / in a natural manner / to be a little stingy
05 kept me awake / How cute he is / take good care of / looked after me
06 I like to draw paintings / It's similar to his / It calms me
07 can't hide anything / have been there / Just hop in
08 business trip on that day / to get a promotion / Thank you for your concern
09 What size do you want / I have a discount coupon / in 20 minutes
10 for a long time / What are those / Sorry to hear that
11 You can walk around / get all kinds of information / at a high level
12 I have little time / there's one spot left
13 Thank you for inviting me / he worries about you / Take it easy
14 Are you joking / There's no other choice / I'm really sorry to hear that
15 was tired of / it wasn't easy to find / related to teaching
16-17 such a beautiful place / What a shame / Either come with me or stay here

---

31회 듣기 모의고사
p.186-187

01 ⑤	02 ②	03 ⑤	04 ③	05 ⑤	06 ③
07 ④	08 ⑤	09 ③	10 ②	11 ②	12 ③
13 ③	14 ⑤	15 ③	16 ⑤	17 ④	

01 ⑤

해석 여 도와드릴까요?
남 예. 제 저축 예금 통장에 돈을 좀 입금하고 싶어요.
여 얼마나 입금하려고 하나요?
남 이 돼지 저금통에 있는 금액 모두요.

해설 통장에 입금하고자 하는 금액을 묻고 있으므로 대답으로 가장 적절한 것은 ⑤이다. ① 500달러를 대출 받고 싶어요. ② 제 추측에 그렇게 오래 걸리지는 않을 거예요. ③ 문제될 것 없습니다. 이 저울 위에 올려놓으세요. ④ 당신이 원하시면 좀 빌려드릴 수 있어요.

어휘 deposit 입금하다 savings account 저축 예금 scale 저울 piggy bank 돼지 저금통

02 ②

해석 남 이 풍경을 보세요! 대단하지 않나요?
여 그래요. 이것은 제가 지금껏 본 중 가장 멋진 야경이네요.
남 이곳에 전에 와 본 적이 있죠, 그렇지 않나요?
여 예, 하지만 그 때는 제가 너무 어렸어요.

해설 멋진 야경을 볼 수 있는 이곳에 전에 와 본 적이 있는지를 묻고 있으므로 대답으로 가장 적절한 것은 ②이다. ① 아뇨, 그에 관해서 들어 본 적이 없어요. ③ 걱정하지 말아요. 저는 밤에 운전하는 것에 익숙해요. ④ 남산의 야경이 훨씬 더 근사해요. ⑤ 초대해주셔서 감사하지만 갈 수 없을 것 같아요.

어휘 something 대단한 것 be used to ~ing ~에 익숙하다

03 ⑤

해석 여 The Young Persons News Award는 12세와 15세 사이의 모든 학생에게 열려 있습니다. 우리는 모든 뉴스 방송에 대한 여러분의 논평, 제안, 분석, 비평을 찾고 있습니다. 이 대회를 통해, 우리는 어떻게 하면 뉴스 방송을 젊은 사람들에게 더 흥미롭게 만들 수 있을지를 알고 싶습니다. 여러분의 아이디어를 대회의 출품작으로 보내 주세요. 상의 일부로 여러분은 뉴스 방송을 직접 만들어 볼 기회와 뉴스 담당 기자들과 하루를 보낼 기회를 부여받을 것입니다. 출품 마감일은 12월 20일입니다. 저희에게 출품작을 보내 주세요.

해설 경연대회를 통해 뉴스 방송에 대한 십대들의 견해를 파악하려는 목적으로 경연대회에 참가할 것을 권유하는 내용이다.

어휘 suggestion 제안 criticism 비평 entry 출품작

04 ③

해석 여 미안해요, 하지만 이것을 할 수 없을 것 같아요.
남 Rachel. 그것에 관해 이미 여러 차례 이야기했잖아요.
여 그래요, 그래요. 하지만 주사를 맞아야 한다는 생각에 견딜 수가 없어요.
남 오래 걸리지 않을 거예요. 게다가, 내가 당신 곁에 있어 줄 것이고요.
여 혈액 검사를 해야 했던 고등학교 시절에 거의 기절했던 것 당신도 알잖아요.
남 그것은 오래 전 이야기예요.
여 알아요, 하지만 마치 어제 일 같아요. 아직도 저를 많이 괴롭히고 있어요.
남 그것은 단지 두려움일 뿐이며 두려움을 극복해야 해요.
여 그것은 당신 말처럼 그리 쉽지 않아요.
남 적어도 시도는 해 봐야죠. 모든 사람은 자신만의 두려움을 갖고 살지만 그들은 그것들을 극복해요.
여 알았어요, 하지만 모든 과정이 진행되는 동안 제 옆에 있겠다고 약속해 줘요.
남 약속할게요. 장담하건대, 당신은 할 수 있을 거예요.

해설 남자는 두려움은 극복되어야 하며 그것을 극복할 수 있음을 확신한다고 여자에게 말해 주고 있다.

어휘 needle injection 주사 faint 기절하다 bother 괴롭히다 overcome 극복하다 get over ~을 극복하다 procedure 절차, 과정

05 ⑤

해석 여 기다리게 해서 죄송합니다.

남 괜찮아요. 적어도 이제 나오기는 했잖아요.

여 금요일 저녁은 아주 바쁩니다.

남 이해해요. 방금 당신에게 벌어진 일을 보았어요. 괜찮아요? 접시를 거의 떨어뜨릴 뻔 했잖아요.

여 괜찮아요. 감사합니다.

남 모든 부모들이 아이들을 잘 통제하는 것이 아니라서 당신의 일은 아이들에게 세심한 주의를 기울여야 할 필요가 있는 것 같아 보이네요.

여 좀 그렇기는 하지만 그것이 일의 일부라고 생각해요.

남 글쎄요. 전 아이들이 그런 행동하는 것을 용납하지 않아요. 영화관, 백화점, 병원과 같은 공공장소에서는 특히 그래요.

여 잘 아시네요. 사실, 아이들은 어떻게 행동해야 하는지를 배울 필요가 있어요. 죄송하지만, 식사 맛있게 하세요. 주문들이 많아서요.

남 오, 미안해요. 제가 붙들고 있었군요.

해설 여자가 기다리게 한 것에 대해 사과하였고, 식사를 잘 드시라며 처리해야 할 주문이 있다고 말한 것으로 비추어 볼 때 식당에서 종업원과 손님 사이에 일어날 수 있는 대화이다.

어휘 tray 접시 keep ~ under control 통제하다. 관리하다 put up with 참다 attendant 종업원

06 ③

해석 여 이 사진이 회사 체육대회에서 찍은 사진이야?

남 응. 잘 나왔지. 그렇지 않니?

여 잘 나왔네. 뒤쪽에서 손에 수건을 들고 있는 사람이 너니?

남 응. 줄다리기가 끝난 후에 찍은 거였는데, 땀을 많이 흘렸어.

여 오, 그렇구나. Sammy는 누구야? 아직도 뛰어서 출근하니?

남 응. 그는 스포츠머리를 하고 있어. 첫 줄에 앉아 있고, 오른손에 손목 밴드를 하고 있어.

여 몸이 좋네. 사무실에서 네 옆에 앉는 여자는 누구야? 근무 중에 남자친구에게 늘 전화한다고 네가 말했잖아.

남 그녀는 Grace야. 커다란 정사각형 귀걸이를 하고 첫 줄에 앉아 있어.

여 와우! 세련되어 보이는데. 네 테니스 파트너인 Tina는 누구야?

남 그녀는 내 옆에 서 있어. 그녀는 늘 머리띠를 하고 다녀.

여 안경을 쓰고 첫 줄 중간에 앉아 있는 사람이 너의 상사이겠구나.

남 맞아.

해설 Sammy는 손목 밴드를 왼손이 아니라 오른손에 차고 있다고 했다.

어휘 field day 체육대회 in good shape 체격이 좋은 gorgeous 멋진. 화려한

07 ④

해석 여 안녕하세요, 아빠. 다녀왔습니다. 엄마 집에 계세요?

남 아니, 운동하러 가셨어.

여 휴! 생일 축하 메시지는 녹화하셨어요?

남 아직 못 했어. 그건 그렇고 케이크하고 초 사왔니?

여 아빠, 저 믿어도 되는 것 아시잖아요. 42개의 초와 이 케이크 보세요.

남 잘했어! 여기 비디오카메라가 있어. 위층에서 비디오 삼각대를 가져 올래?

여 알았어요, 아빠. (잠시) 여기 있어요. 비디오카메라는 어떻게 작동하죠?

남 이 버튼을 누르고 카세트를 안으로 밀어 넣으럼. 비디오테이프를 처음으로 돌리는 것을 명심하고.

여 되감기 버튼이 어디 있죠? 오, 여기 있네요.

남 녹화를 시작하고 싶을 때 녹화 버튼을 눌러. 그렇지만 지금 하지는 마. 먼저 삼각대에 카메라를 설치해야 하니까. 잠시만 기다려.

해설 생일을 맞이한 엄마에게 축하 메시지를 녹화하기 위해 아빠가 삼각대에 카메라를 고정시키려고 하고 있다. 따라서 "비디오 삼각대 설치하기"가 가장 적절하다.

어휘 tripod 삼각대 upstairs 위층에 rewind 되감다

08 ⑤

해석 (전화벨이 울린다.)

여 여보세요. First Bank입니다. 무엇을 도와드릴까요?

남 안녕하세요. Susan과 통화할 수 있을까요?

여 잠시만 기다리세요. 죄송합니다만 그녀가 통화중이네요. 잠시 기다리시겠습니까 아니면 그녀에게 전화를 드리라고 할까요?

남 전화를 해 달라고 해 주세요. 제 전화번호는 734-9925입니다.

여 알겠습니다. 그런데, 송금에 문제가 있었나요?

남 아뇨. 전 귀하의 은행에 계좌를 개설하지 않았습니다.

여 그러면 그녀가 상담할 때 친절하게 굴지 않았습니까?

남 아뇨, 전혀요. 사실, 전 Susan에 대해 아는 것도 없고요, 어떻게 생겼는지도 기억이 안 나요. 전 그녀가 거기 근무하는지도 몰랐어요.

여 오, 그렇군요. 그럼 무엇 때문인지 여쭈어 봐도 될까요?

남 물론이죠. 전 택시 운전사예요. 그녀가 제 택시에 휴대 전화를 두고 내렸고 제가 그것을 발견했어요.

여 오, 친절도 하셔라. 가능한 한 빨리 당신에게 전화를 드리도록 조치할게요.

해설 남자는 택시 운전사로 승객이 놓고 내린 휴대 전화를 돌려주려고 승객의 직장으로 전화를 건 상황이다.

어휘 transfer 송금. 계좌 이체 checking account 당좌 예금 계좌

09 ③

해석 (전화벨이 울린다.)

남 여보세요.

여 안녕, Tobi. 나야, Sara. 오늘 저녁에 우리 집에 올래? 컴퓨터를 새로 샀어.

남 정말? 마침내 구입했구나.

여 응. 가능한 한 빨리 와. 너와 정말로 컴퓨터 게임을 하고 싶어.

남 알았어. 30분 후에 출발할 수 있을 거야.

여 잘 됐네! 오는 길에 Tim을 데려올래? 그는 집에 있어.

남 Tim을 데려오라고? 왜?

여 목발을 하고 있는데 컴퓨터 게임을 하고 싶어 미치겠대.

남 알았어.

여 얼마나 걸릴까?

남 여기서 Tim의 집까지 자전거로 30분 정도 걸려. 거기서 네 집까지 30분 정도 걸리고.

여 그렇다면 여기에 6시 경에 도착하겠구나. 저녁 내내 즐길 수 있도록 내가 저녁을 준비할게.

남 좋은 생각이네. 그때 보자.

해설 30분 후에 출발 가능하고, Tim의 집까지 30분, 거기서부터 30분 더 걸리므로 총 1시간 30분 후에 만나게 된다. 그 시간을 여자는 6시 경이라고 하고 있으므로 현재 시각은 4시 30분경이다.

어휘 on crutches 목발을 하고 있는 itch to~ ~하고 싶어 좀이 쑤시다

10 ②

해석 남 실례합니다. 도와주실 수 있나요?

여 물론이죠.

남 등 통증에 효과가 있는 것이 있을까요?

여 이 연고가 아주 좋습니다.

남 그것은 사용해 보았습니다. 사실 도움이 되지 않았어요. 전 하루에 10시간 정도 컴퓨터 앞에 앉아 있어요. 제 생각엔 그게 문제인 것 같아요.

여 이 등받이 쿠션을 사용해 보는 건 어때요? 아마 도움이 될 거예요.

남 알겠습니다. 한 번 써 보죠. 그리고 특별히 알아야 할 사항이 있을까요?

여 예, 있습니다. 컴퓨터로 일하실 때 앞으로 기대지 않도록 하세요. 그리고 자주 쉬시면서 근육을 풀어주세요.

남 알겠습니다. 말씀대로 하죠. 감사합니다.

해설 마사지를 받아보라는 내용은 여자의 조언에 없다.

어휘 backache 등 통증 ointment 연고 instruction 지시 사항 frequent 빈번한

11 ②

해석 여 어제 River Place 쇼핑몰에서 달걀 먹기 대회가 열렸습니다. 약사인 Sharon Rose는 우승을 하기는 했지만 최고의 달걀 먹기 선수가 되고자 하는 시도는 실패하고 말았습니다. 이것은 세계 기록을 깨뜨리려는 그녀의 두 번째 시도였습니다. 두 달 전의 대회에서 그녀는 한 시간에 51개의 달걀을 먹는 데 성공했습니다. 이번에는 53개의 삶은 달걀을 먹었습니다. 그러나 그것은 Sam Wilson의 세계 기록을 깨뜨리기에 3개의 달걀이 부족한 것입니다. 2년 전, Sam은 대회에서 55개의 달걀을 먹어 치웠습니다. Sharon은 실망한 표정이 역력하였습니다. 하지만 그녀는 두 달 후 또 다른 대회에서 세계 기록에 도전하겠다고 말했습니다.

해설 첫 번째 대회에서 51개의 달걀을 먹었고 이번에는 53개를 먹었으므로 이전 기록을 경신하였다는 ②번이 일치한다.

어휘 pharmacist 약사 hard-boiled (달걀을) 완숙으로 삶은 obviously 명백하게

12 ③

해석 남 비디오를 아직 결정하지 못했니? 그러면 Bed of Roses와 One Fine Day 두 가지 중 하나는 어때?

여 싫어, 그것들은 오래된 영화이고 Brad Pitt도 안 나오잖아. 게다가, 난 이미 결정했어.

남 어디 보자. Spy Game이라고? Brad Pitt영화여야 하는 거야?

여 넌 내가 선택해도 좋다고 했고 난 Brad Pitt 영화를 보고 싶어.

남 Brad Pitt를 꺼리는 것은 아니지만 그 영화는 약간 지루하다고 들었어.

여 Fight Club은 어때?

남 절대 안 돼! 그것은 액션 영화잖아. 너도 알다시피 난 액션 영화를 싫어해. 잠깐만. 여기 내가 못 본 Brad Pitt영화가 있어. Meet Joe Black이라고.

여 나는 그 영화에 대해 정확하게는 잘 모르지만 꽤 길다는 얘기는 들었어. 봐봐! 2시간 30분짜리야.

남 그래? 그렇다면 전체 내용을 다 볼 수는 없잖아. 첫 번째 것으로 결정하자. 너무 지루하지 않기를 바라.

여 그렇게 지루하지는 않아. Brad Pitt는 내가 알아. 그것을 대여하자.

해설 여자가 맨 처음 결정한 영화는 Spy Game이다.

어휘 decide on 결정하다 check out 대여하다

13 ③

해석 여 도와드릴까요, 손님?

남 예, 지난주에 여기서 이 시계를 구입했는데 문제가 좀 있어서요.

여 무엇이 문제인 것 같으세요?

남 저기, 판매원이 방수가 된다고 했지만 수영장에서 차고 있으니까 물이 가득 차버렸어요.

여 어디 봅시다. 아, 예, 이 브랜드에 문제가 좀 있습니다. 비슷한 모델로 바꾸어드릴까요?

남 사실, 환불 받고 싶어요.

여 물론 그러시겠지요. 환불해 드릴 수 있어요. 영수증은 가지고 계신가요?

남 예, 여기 있습니다.

여 감사합니다.

남 아시겠지만 판매하는 물건을 좀 더 세심하게 확인해야 할 것 같아요.

여 염두에 두겠습니다. 대단히 감사합니다.

해설 하자가 있는 시계를 환불 받으면서 손님이 파는 물건에 대해 신중을 기해줄 것을 당부하고 있으므로 ③이 응답으로 가장 적절하다. ① 기다리시게 해서 죄송합니다. ② 영수증 가지고 오는 것을 잊지 마세요. ④ 뭐라고요? 제 잘못이 아니라고 말했잖아요. ⑤ 디자인이 기능만큼 중요하다고 생각해요.

14 ⑤

해석 여 오늘 밤 정말 춥네요.

남 네, 그러네요. 하지만 사실 전 추운 날씨를 좋아해요.

여 그러세요? 하지만 저는 별로 안 좋아하거든요. 그런데, 오늘밤 이런 날씨에도 정말 많은 사람들이 콘서트에 왔네요.

남 네, 주말에는 꽤 붐벼요.

여 여기에 자주 오세요?

남 네, 전 사실 자주 와요.

여 그러면 열렬한 힙합 팬이신가 봐요?

남 네, 그래요. 당신은요?

여 사실 전 아니에요. 하지만 오늘 밤엔 오빠가 밴드의 단원으로 나와서요. 저를 콘서트에 초대했어요.

남 정말요? 정말 멋지네요! 오빠 이름이 뭐예요?

해설 남자는 열렬한 힙합 팬이고, 여자의 마지막 말에서 오빠가 오늘 콘서트에 나온다고 했으므로 ⑤가 응답으로 가장 적절하다. ① 물론이죠. 정말로 추운 날씨가 좋아요. ② 와우, 정말로 환상적인 연주회였어요. ③ 제가 열렬한 힙합 팬인 것을 모르나요? ④ 먼저 주말 일정을 확인해 볼게요.

어휘 **freezing** 몹시 추운, 어는 **crowded** 붐비는, 혼잡한

15 ③

해석 남 식당에서 나가는 길에 Peter는 옛 친구 Sally를 우연히 만났다. 그들은 같은 고등학교를 졸업했으며 Peter가 결혼해서 마을을 떠날 때까지 이웃으로 살았다. Peter는 그녀를 한동안 만나지 못해서 서로의 근황을 알아둘 필요가 있다고 생각했다. 그는 그녀가 여전히 모든 종류의 애완동물을 기르는지, 그녀의 남편은 여전히 해외에 근무하는지 궁금했다. 그래서 그는 그녀에게 근처 카페에 가서 커피를 마시며 서로에 관해 대화를 더 나누자고 말하기로 결심했다. 이 상황에서 Peter가 Sally에게 할 말로 가장 적절한 것은 무엇인가?
Peter 근처에 아는 카페가 있어. 가서 대화를 나누자.

해설 오랜만에 만난 친구와 카페에 가서 이야기를 더 하고자 하는 상황이므로 ③이 가장 적절하다. ① 미안하지만 충분히 먹었어. ② 마지막으로 본 지 몇 년 되었어. ④ 네가 여전히 애완동물을 집에 두고 있는지 궁금해. 개와 고양이들 말이야. ⑤ 애완동물을 다 집에 두는 것이 어렵지 않아?

어휘 **run into** 우연히 마주치다 **in ages** 오랫동안 **catch up on** 따라잡다, 미룬 것을 한꺼번에 하다

16-17 ⑤, ④

해석 남 오늘은 우리 지역의 박물관의 상황에 대해 이야기해 보겠습니다. 우리는 특별 전시회, 보수 관리, 직원 월급 등의 비용으로 박물관을 운영하는 데 돈이 많이 든다는 것을 압니다. 이 모든 비용에도 불구하고, 박물관은 예술적, 사회적, 과학적, 정치적 유산을 보존하고 전시하기 때문에 대중에게 개방되어야 합니다. 박물관은 또한 모든 연령대의 사람들에게 교육의 기회를 제공합니다. 만약 박물관이 정부로부터 충분한 재정적 지원을 받지 못한다면, 박물관은 입장료를 부과할 수밖에 없을 것이며, 이것은 부득이하게 많은 잠재적인 방문자의 접근을 제한하게 될 것이고, 특히 가난한 사람들과 교육과 문화적 기회가 이미 제한된 사람들로부터 학습의 권리가 빼앗게 될 것입니다. 완전한 접근(무료 입장)은 문화적, 교육적 기회를 제공하는 데 필수적입니다. 정부는 박물관 입장료를 징수하기 시작한 이후로 Seattle에 있는 박물관들의 관람객 수가 15퍼센트 감소했다는 것을 명심해야 합니다.

해설 16 시민들의 기본권인 문화적, 교육적 권리를 위해 정부가 박물관에 지원을 아끼지 말아야 한다는 내용이므로 정답은 ⑤이다.

17 박물관에 정부 지원이 풍족하지 않을 경우, 입장료를 부과하게 되고, 그러면 교육적, 문화적 기회가 이미 제한되어 있는 사람들에게 또 다른 교육적, 문화적 기회 박탈이 될 것이라고 주장하고 있다. 따라서 정답은 ④이다.

어휘 **run** 운영하다 **maintenance** 유지(관리) **preserve** 보존하다 **heritage** 유산, 전통 **fund** 자금을 제공하다 **sufficiently** 충분히 **charge** 부과하다 **inevitably** 불가피하게 **deprive** ~을 빼앗다

Dictation

01 deposit some money

02 Isn't it something

03 Through this competition / send your ideas / The closing date for entries

04 I am afraid I can't do / I'm going to be with you / people get over

05 what just happened to you / under control / how to behave

06 sweat a lot / He is in good shape / She looks gorgeous

07 you can count on me / Make sure / Just wait a second

08 she's on another line / have checking account / how kind of you

09 as soon as possible / on your way here / How long will it take

10 Why don't you use / take frequent breaks / I'll do what you say

11 to break the world record / short of breaking

12 I've already decided / I don't mind

13 it was filled with water / Do you have your receipt

14 It's freezing / it gets pretty crowded / He invited me

15 ran into his old friend / catch up on each other's news / decided to ask

16-17 open to the public / will be forced to / will be deprived of / keep in mind

32회 듣기 모의고사
p.192-193

01 ⑤	02 ④	03 ⑤	04 ③	05 ⑤	06 ①
07 ⑤	08 ⑤	09 ②	10 ⑤	11 ④	12 ④
13 ③	14 ⑤	15 ②	16 ④	17 ⑦		

01 ⑤

해석 여 이 드레스 어때?
남 와우, 대단한데! 너에게 완벽하게 어울려!
여 그러지 말고, 말로만 그러는 것 알아.
남 아니야, 진짜야. 그 드레스를 입으니까 정말 아름다워.

해설 남자가 여자가 입은 드레스가 잘 어울린다고 말하자 여자는 재차 진심을 말해달라고 하고 있으므로 ⑤가 남자의 응답으로 가장 적절하다. ① 기분이 좋네. 어쨌든, 고마워. ② 내가 그 드레스를 입어볼게. ③ 저기에 탈의실이 있어. ④ 말보다 행동이라는 것을 알지?

어휘 **fit** 어울리다 **flattered** 기쁜 **fitting room** 탈의실 **Actions speak louder than words.** 말보다 행동이 중요하다

02 ④

해석 남 곧 엄마가 되는군요. 축하해요!
여 고마워요. 전 제가 엄마가 될 것이라는 것이 아직도 실감이 나지 않아요.
남 그렇게 될 거예요. 아들과 딸 중 어느 쪽을 더 선호하세요?
여 사실, 건강하기만 하면 개의치 않아요(아들이든 딸이든 상관없어요).

해설 출산을 앞두고 있는 여자에게 태어날 아기가 아들과 딸 중에서 어느 쪽을 원하는지를 남자가 묻고 있으므로, ④가 여자의 응답으로 가장 적절하다. ① 걱정 마세요. 전 좋은 엄마가 될 거예요. ② 저는 임신한지 8개월하고 보름 됐어요. ③ 글쎄요, 미리 알아보고 싶지 않았어요. ⑤ 끔찍했어요. 매일 아침 구역질이 났어요.

어휘 pregnant 임신한 beforehand 미리 feel nauseous 구역질이 나다

03 ⑤

해석 남 시 창립 200주년을 축하하는 배너에 후원할 수 있는 마지막 기회를 공고합니다. 시의 도처에 설치된 배너가 185개인 가운데, 어떤 분들은 아직도 배너를 주문할 수 있는지에 대해 계속 문의하고 있습니다. 네, 설치할 수 있는 배너가 15개 있습니다. 12월 31일까지 신청하셔야 합니다. 그 배너들은 내년 12월 31일까지 유지될 것입니다. 후원금은 250달러이고, 거리에 설치되는 배너의 양면에는 사업이나 가족의 정보를 실을 수 있습니다. 신청은 Pazda에게 pazda@banner.com으로 메일을 보내시면 됩니다. 더 많은 정보를 얻으려면 759-6188로 전화하여 Sharon Barker를 찾으면 됩니다.

해설 도입부에서 시 창립 200주년을 기념하기 위하여 배너에 후원할 수 있는 마지막 기회를 공고한다고 하였으므로 답은 ⑤가 가장 적절하다.

어휘 install 설치하다, 비치하다 throughout 도처에

04 ③

해석 여 아주 흥미로운 기사인데!
남 무슨 기사인데?
여 고등학교 여학생과 남학생, 그리고 그들의 성적에 관한 거야.
남 내용이 뭔데?
여 여학생이 남학생보다 좋은 성적을 받고 있대. 그리고 남학생과 여학생의 성적 차가 점점 더 벌어지고 있고.
남 현재 상황이 약간 걱정되기는 하지만, 놀랄 일도 아니네. 성적에 관한 한 내가 너를 한 번도 이겨본 적이 없잖아. 그건 그렇고, 분명 이유가 있을 텐데.
여 어떤 사람들은 남학생들이 스포츠 활동에 더 관심이 많아서래.
남 일리 있는 말이네. 알다시피, 나는 주말마다 미식축구를 하잖아.
여 그리고 교사들이 여학생들에게 호의를 베푼다고 말하는 사람들도 있어.
남 글쎄, 믿을 수가 없군. 너는 그렇게 생각 안 하지, 그렇지?

해설 흥미 있는 기사에 관한 내용은 'grade gap between boys and girls'이므로 두 사람의 대화 주제는 ③이다.

어휘 article 기사 come as no surprise 놀랄 일도 아니다 when it comes to ~에 관한 한 make sense 이치에 맞다 favor 호의를 베풀다

05 ⑤

해석 남 돌아온 것을 환영합니다. 여기서 기다리신 분들을 위해 한 말씀해 주시죠.
여 감사합니다. 이 일을 해내서 정말 기쁩니다.
남 대단하십니다. 미국 전역을 자전거로 일주하는 것은 어땠습니까?
여 글쎄요, 기분이 좋을 때도 좀 있었고, 그저 힘든 일이라는 생각만 들 때도 있었고, 어떤 때는 아주 무섭기도 했어요.
남 아프리카 식량 원조 캠페인에 돈을 얼마나 모으셨는지 아세요?
여 확실히는 몰라요. 대략 백만 달러 정도라고 생각합니다. 자전거로 여행하며 돈을 모으기로 결심할 때 기대했던 것보다는 많은 금액이에요.
남 놀랍군요. 축하합니다! 이제 뭘 하실 건가요?
여 Chuck은 당장 머리를 자를 것이고요. 저는 적어도 이틀은 잘 겁니다.
남 매우 피곤하신가 보군요. TV를 시청하고 계신 분들에게 한 말씀해 주세요.
여 격려와 지속적인 성원에 감사드립니다.

해설 남자는 질문을, 여자는 답변을 하는 것으로 보아 두 사람의 관계를 추측할 수 있고, 마지막 말미에 시청자에게 한 마디 해달라는 남자의 말이 결정적 힌트가 된다. 남자는 기자이고 여자는 자선기금 모금자이다.

어휘 make it 달성하다, 해 내다, 도착하다 incredible 놀라운 immediately 즉시

06 ①

해석 남 공원을 산책하기에 정말 멋진 날씨야!
여 그래, 주변을 둘러봐. 정말 평화로워.
남 저기 벤치의 노부부는 정말 편안해 보여.
여 그래, 행복해 보여. 나무 옆에서 두 명의 아이들이 야구를 하네.
남 부럽다. 동생과 프리스비 놀이를 했던 기억이 나. 정말 재미있었어.
여 저기 나무의 또 다른 쪽에는 강아지와 놀고 있는 소년이 보이니?
남 응, 그들은 정말 행복한 시간을 보내는 것처럼 보여.
여 노부부 커플 뒤에 세 명의 소녀들도 행복해 보여. 그들은 즐겁게 줄넘기를 하고 있어.
남 오, 그러네. 나무 앞쪽에서 걸으려고 하는 아기를 봐. 아주 사랑스러워.
여 정말 귀여운 아기구나!
남 나는 이곳이 정말 좋아. 자주 여기에 오자.
여 좋아. 나도 이렇게 아름다운 공원 옆에 살게 되어서 기뻐.

해설 프리스비는 남자가 어려서 동생과 했던 놀이이고, 야구를 하는 아이들을 보며 생각한 장면이다. 따라서 두 소년이 프리스비 던지기를 하는 것이 대화 내용과 일치하지 않는다.

어휘 elderly 연세가 드신 skip 줄넘기를 하다

07 ⑤

해석 여 어떻게 지내니, Richard?
남 안녕, Lynn. 아주 좋아!
여 척 보면 알겠어. 얼굴에 나와 있어.
남 나는 행복할 이유가 충분해.
여 그래? 무슨 일이 있었는데?
남 참가한 대회에서 상을 받은 것을 막 알게 되었어.
여 그래? 멋지다. 그래 뭘 받았니?

남 아직 몰라. 이 번호로 전화해서 내가 뭘 받았는지 알아봐야 해.

여 당장 전화를 해보지 그래? 궁금하잖아. 하와이로 휴가 가게 될지 누가 알아.

남 음, 네가 보시다시피, 난 너무 떨려서 전화를 할 수가 없어.

여 그렇다면, 내가 네 대신 해줄게. 별 것도 아닌데.

남 고마워.

해설 남자는 떨리는 마음에 부상으로 받게 될 상품을 확인하기 위한 전화를 할 수 없을 것 같다고 하자 여자가 대신 해 주겠노라고 나서고 있다.

어휘 have every reason to ~하는 것도 당연하다 no big deal 별것이 아니다

08 ⑤

해석 남 이봐요! 여기에요!

여 안녕하세요! 다 왔어요. 기다리게 해서 미안해요.

남 괜찮아요.

여 실은, 고속도로 반대 차선에서 연쇄 추돌사고가 발생했어요. 견인차, 구급차, 경찰차가 오고 난리였어요. 정말 볼 만 했어요.

남 자동차와 버스가 무슨 일인지 보느라 속도를 늦추었겠네요.

여 맞아요. 사람들은 늘 호기심이 많잖아요.

남 그렇지요. 내가 짐을 들게요. 와우! 보기보다 무겁네요.

여 그래서 데리러 나와 달라고 부탁한 거예요. 그런데 고마워해야 할 이유가 하나 더 생겼어요.

남 무슨 이유인지 궁금하네요.

여 나와 주지 않았으면 택시를 타야 했을 거예요. 알다시피, 지하철은 자정이 넘으면 운행을 중단하잖아요.

남 난 또 뭐라고요. 그만 하세요. 피곤하겠어요. 여기서 나갑시다.

여 알았어요. 차는 어디 있어요?

남 주차장에서 주인을 기다리고 있지요.

해설 여자가 늦은 이유는 고속도로 반대 차선에 연쇄 추돌사고가 있었고, 이를 구경하느라 차량들이 서행해서이다.

어휘 pile up 연쇄 추돌사고 expressway 고속도로

09 ②

해석 남 내일 영화를 보고 싶어. 볼래?

여 그래. 사실, Tom Cruise가 나오는 새 영화가 보고 싶었어.

남 나도. 잠시만. 언제 하는지 알아볼게. 미안, 연결 속도가 좀 늦어.

여 괜찮아. 천천히 해.

남 여기 있네. 하루에 6차례 상영을 한다고 나와 있어. 첫 상영은 11시이고 마지막 상영은 8시야. 8시 상영 영화가 좋을 것 같은데. 너는 어때?

여 여동생하고 저녁을 먹기로 되어 있는데 7시까지는 집에 올 수 있을 거야.

남 잘 됐네. 7시 30분에 데리러 갈게. 이런, 잠깐만. 8시 상영 영화가 매진이네.

여 글쎄, 우리의 운이 거기까지인가 봐.

남 이봐, 11시 상영 영화는 어때? 끝나고 근사한 점심을 먹을 수도 있어.

여 괜찮을 것 같은데.

남 그러면 영화 시간 30분 전에 내가 데리러 가면 어때? 너희 집에서 영화관까지 20분 정도 걸릴 거야.

여 알았어. 그때 봐.

해설 11시 상영 영화를 보고자 하며 끝나고 점심을 먹을 수 있다는 말에서 오전임을 알 수 있으며, 영화 시작 30분 전에 데리러 가겠다는 의견을 내고 있으므로 만나기로 한 시각은 오전 10시 30분이다.

어휘 feel like ~하고 싶다 connection 연결 be sold out 매진되다

10 ⑤

해석 여 무슨 일을 하세요?

남 출판업을 합니다.

여 그래요? 출판업은 아주 재미있을 것 같은데요.

남 사실, 어찌 보면 그럴 수 있지만 아주 힘든 일이랍니다. 그러니까 부지런해야 한단 말이죠.

여 그렇군요. 좋은 출판업자가 되기 위해서는 달리 뭐가 필요할까요?

남 사람들과 잘 어울려야 해요.

여 그리고 제 생각에는 팀에서 일을 잘 해야겠군요.

남 아, 예. 그것은 틀림없는 사실입니다. 그리고 또한 참을성이 있어야 합니다.

여 저는 참을성을 유지하는 데 약해요. 문제점을 다루고 있을 때 특히 그래요!

남 직장에서 문제점을 다루는 법을 배우는 데에는 시간이 좀 걸려요. 그리고 무엇보다도, 장시간 동안 집중할 수 있어야 합니다.

여 오, 전 끔찍할 정도로 집중을 못해요. 저는 전혀 집중을 할 수가 없어요.

해설 좋은 출판업자가 되기 위한 조건으로 남자는 근면성, 참을성, 친화력, 집중력을 꼽고 있다.

어휘 involve ~을 필요로 하다 get along with ~와 어울리다 patient 참을성있는 deal with 다루다 above all 무엇보다도

11 ④

해석 여 천식은 숨을 쉬는 통로를 좁게 만드는 장애입니다. 이것은 폐로 들어오고 나가는 공기의 양을 감소시켜 숨을 쉬는 것을 어렵게 합니다. 세계보건기구는 천식이 전 세계 약 2억 명의 사람들에게 영향을 끼친다고 말합니다. 천식은 아이들에게 가장 흔한 만성적인 질병입니다. 전 세계 모든 나라 사람들에게 영향을 끼치며 사회적, 경제적 신분을 구별하지 않습니다. 천식은 수백만 명의 개인뿐만 아니라, 가족과 경제 상황 등에도 똑같이 영향을 미칩니다. 이 병으로 인한 경제적 비용은 매년 2백억 달러에 이른다고 합니다. 세계보건기구는 전 세계적으로 천식의 비율이 10년마다 평균적으로 50% 증가한다고 경고하고 있습니다.

해설 경제적, 사회적 신분에 의해 구분되지 않는다고 하였으므로 ④가 담화의 내용과 일치하지 않는다.

어휘 asthma 천식 breathing passage 공기 통로 chronic 만성의 discriminate 구별하다, 차별하다.

12 ④

해석 여 Rich, 어디 있었어?

남 무슨 말이야?

여 이틀 동안 연락하려고 했었는데, 전화를 안 받았잖아.

남 오, 휴대 전화 수리를 하고 오늘 찾았어. 그런데, 무슨 일이야?

여 역사 과목 조별 보고서에 관해 이야기 좀 해야지. 오늘 모일 수 있을까?

남 오늘은 안 돼. 사실 누나와 내가 부모님 20주년 결혼기념일을 준비하느라 꽤 바빴거든.

여 오, 정말? 뭘 했는데?

남 부모님 선물을 구입했고 집 청소를 했어. 오늘은 장을 봐서 부모님께 멋진 저녁을 대접해 드려야 해.

여 그럼, 내일이나 모레는 어때?

남 내일은 삼촌을 모시러 가야 하는데, 그렇게 오래 걸리지는 않을 거야. 모레는 아르바이트가 있어.

여 그러면, 내일이 너에게 더 편리해 보이네.

해설 역사 과목의 조별 보고서를 위해 내일 만나는 것이 편리하다고 생각하고 있고 삼촌을 모시러 가는 날이기도 하므로 목요일이 내일에 해당된다.

어휘 anniversary 기념일 grocery 식료품 take long 오래 걸리다

13 ③

해석 남 엄마, 웹 사이트 콘테스트에서 이집트 행 비행기 표 두 장을 땄는데요, 어떤 친구를 데리고 갈지 정할 수가 없어요.

여 Morris를 데리고 가지 그래? 너의 가장 친한 친구잖아.

남 그러면 되지만 문제는 표가 다음 달에만 유효하다는 거예요. 그는 다음 달에 법학 학위 최종 시험을 보게 되어서 갈 수가 없어요.

여 그러면, 늘 Kevin이 있잖아. 너는 그랑 어울려 노는 것을 좋아하고.

남 그는 이집트에 이미 두 번이나 갔다 왔어요. 그래서 다시 가는 것에 관심이 없을 것 같아요.

여 Sam을 데려가지 그래? 그는 늘 네가 문제가 있을 때마다 너를 위해 있어 주잖니.

남 그러고 싶지만 그는 새 직장을 얻어서 며칠 휴가를 내는 것이 가능하지 않아요.

여 그럼, 표를 어떡할 건데?

남 제 생각에는 엄마와 아빠가 거기서 즐거운 시간을 보낼 것 같은데요.

해설 이집트에 함께 갈 친구가 없어서 표를 부모님께 드리고 싶다는 내용을 간접적으로 표현한 ③이 남자의 응답으로 가장 적절하다. ① 사장님께 며칠 휴가를 요청할 생각이에요. ② 다른 대회에 참가할 거예요. ④ 묻지 마세요. 그곳에 가고 싶어 한 것은 당신이었잖아요. ⑤ 그가 이집트에 갈 수 있도록 그를 위해 일을 할 거예요.

어휘 degree 학위 final 최종 시험 day off 휴일

14 ⑤

해석 남 그래서 희생자가 언제 죽었다고 생각해요?

여 여자의 체온으로 보건대, 자정 무렵에 살해된 것 같아요.

남 이 방이 살인이 일어난 곳이라고 생각하세요?

여 그녀가 부엌에서 살해된 다음 침실로 옮겨진 것 같아요.

남 사망 원인을 아직 단정 지을 수 없나요?

여 무거운 물체로 머리를 맞은 것 같아요. 야구 방망이를 발견해서 그것이 살해에 사용되었는지를 알아보기 위해 연구소에 보냈어요.

남 좋아요. 그리고 살인 사건 신고는 누가 했지요?

여 아침 8시에 출근한 가정부에 의해서 접수되었어요.

남 용의자는 있어요?

여 네. 그녀가 간밤에 이웃사람과 다투는 모습이 목격되었어요.

해설 살인사건에 대한 용의자가 있는지를 묻고 있으므로 ⑤가 여자의 응답으로 가장 적절하다. ① 유감이군요. 사람을 잘 못 보셨어요. ② 예, 그녀는 돈을 훔쳤다는 혐의를 받았어요. ③ 전 그렇게 생각하지 않아요. 그녀는 자살을 하지 않았을 거예요. ④ 물론이죠. 긴장감과 짜릿함으로 가득했어요.

어휘 victim 피해자 judging by ~으로 판단해 볼 때 body temperature 체온 murder ~을 죽이다 take place 발생하다 drag ~을 질질 끌고 가다 maid 하녀 suspect 용의자 commit suicide 자살하다 suspense 긴장감, 서스펜스 thrill 전율, 스릴 argue with somebody ~와 다투다

15 ②

해석 남 Dave는 출장으로 멀리 와 있다. 그가 집을 떠난 지 벌써 일주일이다. 일주일간의 회의를 마치고 내일 오후 Dave는 아내와 딸 Sue가 살고 있는 캘리포니아 행 비행기에 몸을 실을 것이다. Sue가 선물로 무엇을 갖고 싶은지를 묻기 위해서 Dave가 전화를 한다. 그리고 아내가 전화를 받는다. 잠시 그녀와 이야기를 한 후, 그는 Sue와 통화할 수 있는지를 묻는다. 그러나 아내는 Sue가 곤히 잠들어있다고 말한다. Dave는 Sue가 무엇을 갖고 싶어 하는지 아내에게 묻기로 결심한다. 이 상황에서 Dave가 아내에게 할 말로 가장 적절한 것은 무엇이겠는가?

Dave 여보, Sue에게 어떤 종류의 선물을 줘야 할까?

해설 출장에서 돌아가기 전에 딸이 원하는 선물이 무엇인지를 아내에게 묻고자하는 상황이므로 ②가 남자가 할 말로 가장 적절하다. ① 놀라지 마세요. 내일 그곳에 갈 거예요. ③ 우리가 여기에 온지 벌써 일주일이 되었네요. ④ 그녀가 일어나면 제게 전화해 달라고 말씀해 주세요. ⑤ 회의는 어떻게 되어 가고 있나요? 거의 다 끝났죠, 그렇지 않나요?

어휘 business trip 출장 conference 회의 flight 비행(기) give a call 전화하다

16-17 ④, ⑤

해석 여 여러분, 안녕하십니까? 저희 한국 항공을 이용해 주셔서 감사합니다. 저희 비행기는 런던행 KE 070편입니다. 저는 이 항공기의 객실 승무원 매니저인 Ann Jackson입니다. London까지의 비행시간은 이륙 후 10시간 30분으로 예상하고 있습니다. 모든 개인적인 전자 제품은 이륙을 위하여 전원을 꺼주시기 바랍니다. 만약 비행 안전 모드가 있는 장치를 사용하고자 하신다면, 출발을 위해 끄기 전에 가능한지 확인하여 주시기 바랍니다. 안전벨트 사인에 불이 꺼지면 여러분은 그 전자 제품을 사용하실 수 있습니다. 이륙 전에 안전을 위해 좌석 벨트를 착용해 주시고 좌석 등받이는 똑바로 좌석 테이블은 제자리로 해 주십시오. 휴대용 전화기와 전자기기는 비행시간 내내 사용이 금지되어 있습니다. 여러분의 많은 협조에 감사드립니다. 도움이 필요하시면 저나 저희 승무원을 불러 주시기 바랍니다. 편안한 여행되시기 바랍니다. 감사합니다.

해설 16 비행 이륙 전의 안내방송이다. ① 비행 중 안내 ② 착륙 전 안내 ③ 착륙 후 안내 ④ 이륙 전 안내 ⑤ 이륙 후 안내

17 휴대 전화는 비행 내내 사용이 불가능하므로 일치하지 않는 것은 ⑤이다.

어휘 business trip 출장 conference 회의 flight 비행(기) give a call 전화하다

어휘 take-off 이륙 stow away 집어넣다, 치우다 at all times 항상 cooperation 협조

Dictation

01 It fits you perfectly

02 Which one do you prefer

03 throughout the town / apply for it / Applications are available

04 What does it say / When it comes to / That makes sense / You don't think so

05 Welcome back / We're not sure / his hair cut / viewers in front of their TV sets

06 look around / having a good time / What a cute baby he is

07 Your face shows it / I won a prize / It's no big deal

08 kept you waiting / That was something / Let's get out of here

09 Just give me a second / I'll pick you up / it might work

10 What do you do for a living / get along well with people / how to deal with

11 reduces the amount of air / in all countries around the world / rates are increasing

12 for a couple of days / What have you done / that won't take long

13 hanging out with him / what are you going to

14 where the murder took place / determine the cause of death / reported the murder

15 is away on a business trip / gives a call / decides to ask

16-17 bound for London / before turning it off / fasten your seat belt / the other flight attendants know

33회 듣기 모의고사
p.198-199

01 ④	02 ④	03 ①	04 ⑤	05 ②	06 ④
07 ①	08 ③	09 ④	10 ④	11 ④	12 ②
13 ③	14 ③	15 ④	16 ②	17 ④	

01 ④

해석 여 해커가 내 컴퓨터 파일에 침입한 것 같아!
남 무슨 종류의 비밀번호를 사용하니?
여 비밀번호는 짧고 기억하기 쉽게 해 두고 있어.
남 **약간 길고 특이한 것으로 만들어야 해.**

해설 컴퓨터 파일을 해킹당한 여자가 비밀번호를 기억하기 쉬운 것을 사용한다고 하였으므로 ④가 남자의 응답으로 가장 적절하다. ① 이제 어디다 두었는지 기억이 나네. ② 서로 연락을 주고받자. ③ 와, 그 비밀번호는 너무 복잡해. ⑤ 이건 너와 나 사이의 비밀로 하자.

어휘 get into ~에 들어가다 keep in touch with ~와 연락하고 지내다 complicated 복잡한

02 ④

해석 남 여기 햇볕에 탄 부분을 위한 무언가가 필요해요.
여 이 로션을 발라보세요. 아픔을 덜어 줄 거예요.
남 얼마나 자주 바르죠?
여 **아픔이 멈출 때까지 세 시간마다 발라주세요.**

해설 햇볕에 탄 곳에 바를 연고를 얼마나 자주 바르는지를 묻고 있으므로 ④가 응답으로 가장 적절하다. ① 일주일이면 통증이 없어질 거예요. ② 가끔 당신이 내게 준 셔츠를 입어요. ③ 그것은 어떤 부작용도 없을 것이라고 확신해요. ⑤ 사용할 준비가 되어 있지 않으면 개봉하지 마세요.

어휘 sunburn 볕에 탐 apply 바르다 relieve 덜어주다 put on 바르다 side effect 부작용

03 ①

해석 여 운동과 수업 이외의 다른 활동이 학교에서 줄어들고 있는 시점에서 단순히 청량음료를 없애는 것은 일시적인 조치에 불과합니다. 청량음료가 비만과 당뇨병의 문제를 악화시키는 데 기여하고 있음을 알고 있습니다. 하지만 비만과 당뇨병을 예방해 주는 체육 교육과 운동 프로그램이 매년 학교 예산에서 줄어들고 있다는 것을 잊어서는 안 됩니다. 자동판매기를 학교 밖으로 몰아내는 모든 노력을 고맙게 생각합니다. 그리고 그러한 노력들이 건강에 필수적인 프로그램의 중요성을 부각하는 것까지 확대되기를 제안하는 바입니다.

해설 단순히 자판기를 학교에서 없애는 것에 그치지 말고 건강 관련 프로그램의 중요성을 부각시켜 달라고 제안하고 있다. 따라서 건강 관련 프로그램을 장려하기 위해 한 말이다. ① 건강 관련 프로그램을 장려하려고 ② 자동판매기의 설치를 요구하려고 ③ 학교 프로그램을 늘린 것에 감사하려고 ④ 학교의 운동 프로그램의 축소를 칭찬하려고 ⑤ 더 많은 환대를 제공하지 못한 것에 대해 사과하려고

어휘 extracurricular activities 정규 수업 외의 활동 nothing but 단지 ~일 따름인 (=only) temporary 일시적인, 임시의 obesity 비만 diabetes 당뇨병 trim 삭감하다 vending machine 자동판매기 highlight 부각하다

04 ⑤

해석 여 안녕, Jonathan. 너희 집은 괜찮아?
남 우리 집? 무슨 말이야?
여 너 그 소식 못 들었구나? 최근에 우리 동네가 빈집 털이범 때문에 골치래.
남 정말이야? 조심해야겠구나. 어, 나 친구들이랑 이번 금요일에 여행을 가서 일주일 동안 집을 비울 거야.
여 일주일이나? 너무 길다. 너 분명히 신문 배달을 중지시켜야 해.
남 조언 고마워.
여 너 우유 같은 것을 배달시키지 않니?
남 응. 우유를 이틀에 한 번 배달시켜.
여 그것도 반드시 중지시키고.
남 알았어. 우체국에 전화해서 모든 우편물을 일주일 동안 중지시켜 달라고 부탁해야 겠네.

여 아주 중요한 지적이야. 어떤 것이든 현관에 오랫동안 방치되어 있으면 너희 집은 빈집 털이범의 범행 대상이 되거든.

남 그런 정보를 줘서 정말 고마워.

해설 빈집 털이가 기승인 가운데, 여자는 뭐든 오랫동안 손대지 않은 채로 있으면 그 집이 범행 대상이 된다며, 집에 배달되는 것을 중지시킬 것을 조언하고 있으므로 ⑤가 정답이다.

어휘 **sneak thief** 빈집 털이범 **go on a trip** 여행을 가다 **every other day** 이틀마다 **hold** 멈추게 하다 **doorstep** (현관 등의) 문 앞의 계단

05 ②

해석 남 Sydney. 배우 세 명이 필요해요.

여 당신이 필요로 하는 배우가 이 도시에 있다면 즉시 데려다 줄게요.

남 거물을 찾는 것은 아니고 특정 외모를 갖춘 일반 배우 셋을 찾고 있어요.

여 일반 배우 셋이라고요? 알았어요. 필요한 사항을 말해 보세요.

남 우선 두 명의 남자가 필요해요. 첫 번째 남자는 젊어야 되고 두 번째는 중년이어야 해요.

여 젊은 배우와 중년 배우. 알았어요. 좀 더 자세하게 말해 주세요.

남 첫 번째 배우는 갈색 머리를 가진 보통 키에 보통 체격의 사람이에요.

여 그리고 두 번째 배우는요?

남 갈색 머리에 키가 작고 체격이 커야 해요.

여 알았어요. 세 번째는 여자이겠군요?

남 네. 금발에 젊은 편이고 키가 크고 말라야 해요.

여 알았어요. 당장 찾아볼게요.

해설 남자는 여자에게 자신의 영화에 출연할 배우를 구해달라고 하고 있고, 여자는 배우를 찾아서 공급해주는 역할을 하는 사람이므로 중개인이다.

어휘 **regular** 일반적인 **description** 묘사, 특징 열거 **build** 체격 **heavyset** 체격이 큰

06 ④

해석 남 우리 늦을 거 같아. 탑승할 시간이야. Jackson 선생님은 어디 계시니?

여 모르겠어. 오, 잠시만, 저기 탑승게이트 옆에서 보안요원이랑 이야기하고 계시네.

남 무슨 말씀을 하시는 걸까.

여 Jack과 Jill은 어디 있어?

남 한참동안 못 봤는데. Jack이 비행기 멀미약이 필요하다고 말하지 않았어?

여 그랬어? 오, 그들이 약국에 있네.

남 우린 시간이 얼마 없고, 지금 벌써 많은 사람들이 줄을 서 있어. 우리도 줄을 서야 해.

여 잠깐만, Margaret은 어디 있니?

남 오, 그녀를 잊고 있었네. 그녀는 부모님께 이메일을 보내야 한다고 했어. 저쪽에서 Michael이랑 컴퓨터를 사용하고 있어.

여 모두 모아서 빨리 비행기에 탑승하자.

해설 Michael은 컴퓨터 옆에서 휴대 전화를 사용하고 있으므로 대화 내용과 일치하지 않는다.

어휘 **board** 탑승하다 **motion sickness** 멀미

07 ①

해석 여 안녕, Eric.

남 안녕, Cindy. 여기는 어쩐 일이야?

여 너를 만나러 왔어. 땀 좀 봐.

남 응. 액자 몇 개를 못으로 박았거든. 무척 힘이 드네!

여 그랬구나. 저기 있잖아. 부탁 하나 들어줄 수 있을까?

남 일단 들어나 보자고. 뭔데?

여 내가 네 차를 좀 쓸 수 있을지 궁금해서.

남 내 차를 쓰겠다고? 지금 말이야?

여 응. 할머니를 모시러 공항에 가야 하거든. 3시 30분에 도착하실 예정이셔서.

남 그럼 5시 반까지 돌려줄 수 있니? 어머니를 쇼핑몰에 태워드려야 하거든.

여 물론이지. 공항까지 30분밖에 안 걸려.

해설 여자는 할머니를 모시러 갈 수 있도록 차를 빌려달라고 부탁하고 있다. ① 그녀에게 그의 차를 사용하도록 해 주기 ② 액자에 못을 박아주기 ③ 그녀와 시간을 좀 보내주기 ④ 그녀를 공항까지 태워다 주기 ⑤ 쇼핑몰에서 그녀를 데리고 오기

어휘 **sweat** 땀을 흘리다 **nail** 못질하다 **picture frame** 액자

08 ③

해석 (전화벨이 울린다.)

여 안녕하세요? Flower Station입니다. 무엇을 도와드릴까요?

남 어제 제가 꽃다발을 주문했는데, 아직도 도착하지 않았어요.

여 확인해 볼게요. 주문번호를 알고 계신가요?

남 예, 주문번호는 FS2315G입니다.

여 아, Smith씨. 배달원에게 확인해 볼게요. 잠시만 기다려 주실래요?

남 그러죠. (잠시)

여 배달원과 이야기했는데, 그가 그 주소로 배달하러 갔는데 아무도 안 계셨다고 하네요.

남 제 주소를 정확하게 적은건가요?

여 아마 올바른 주소가 아닐 수도 있어요. 어제 전화의 연결 상태가 매우 안 좋았던 걸로 기억해요. 주소를 한번 확인해 주시겠어요?

남 New York 22번가 43번지입니다.

여 실수가 있었네요. 우리 시스템에는 23번가로 입력되어 있어요.

남 그건 받아들일 수가 없네요. 당신들은 배달 주소를 정확하게 확인했어야만 했어요. 이제 어떻게 하실 건가요?

여 정말 죄송해요. 그건 모두 우리 잘못이에요. 당장 꽃을 배달하도록 하겠습니다.

해설 남자는 자신의 집으로 꽃이 배달되지 않아서 이를 확인하기 위해 전화를 걸었다.

어휘 **a bouquet of** 한 다발의 **connection** 연결, 통화상태

09 ④

해석 여 일을 아주 잘 하셨네요.

남 제가 한 일이 마음에 든다니 기쁘군요.

여 여기 100달러짜리 지폐입니다. 잔돈은 가지세요. 훌륭하게 일해 주신 것에 대한 보답입니다.

남 죄송합니다, 사모님.

여 예? 뭐가 잘못됐나요?

남 받아야 할 금액을 받지 못한 것 같아서요.

여 무슨 말씀이세요? 도배하는 데 50달러, 페인트칠 하는 데 40달러이지 않나요?

남 그래요, 맞습니다. 그렇지만 벽지 값은 잊으셨군요.

여 아, 미안합니다. 제가 요즘 건망증이 이렇게 심하다니까요! 얼마죠?

남 30달러입니다.

여 알겠습니다. 잠시만 기다리세요! 여기 30달러입니다.

해설 처음 지불한 100달러는 도배비용 50달러, 페인트 칠 비용 40달러, 수고비 10달러였고 여기에 추가로 도배지 비용 30달러를 지불하므로 총 130달러를 지불하였다.

어휘 change 잔돈 deserve 받을 자격이 있다 wallpaper 도배지, 도배하다

10 ④

해석 여 안녕, 여보.

남 그래, 오늘 하루 어땠어요? 좀 피곤해 보이네요.

여 네. 오늘 바빠서 점심 먹을 시간도 없었어요. 그건 그렇고 식료품점에 들렀어요?

남 네, 들렀어요. 목록에 있는 것을 모두 샀어.

여 오, 고마워요. 오늘 학교에 Ben을 데리러 가서 선생님과 대화를 좀 했어요?

남 선생님께서 Ben이 아주 잘 하고 있다고 말씀하셨어요.

여 그리고 오늘 세탁소에 양복 맡기는 것 잊지 않고 했어요? 당신도 알다시피 여동생 결혼이 이번 토요일이잖아요.

남 네, 여보. 기억해서 했어요.

여 그리고 세탁기 고쳐달라고 수리공에게 전화는 했어요?

남 했어요. 내일 아침 10시에 여기로 올 거예요.

여 아무 것도 잊지 않았네요! 당신 없으면 난 뭘 할 수 있을까요?

해설 여자 여동생의 결혼식은 이번 토요일에 열리므로 결혼식 참석은 오늘 남자가 하기로 한 것이 아니다.

어휘 stop by 들르다 grocery store 식료품점 washer 세탁기

11 ④

해석 여 Teddy Bear 박물관에 오신 것을 환영합니다. 이곳에는 Teddy Bear에 관해 여러분이 알고 싶어 하는 모든 것이 있습니다. Teddy Bear 박물관은 2001년 4월 24일에 개관했습니다. 이곳에는 역사관과 예술관이 있으며, 선물의 집도 있습니다. 박물관은 매일 오전 9시에서 오후 7시까지 연중무휴로 개관합니다. 음식과 음료는 박물관 안으로 가지고 들어갈 수 없습니다. 박물관의 선물의 집인 Teddy Bear Republic은 800개 이상의 제품을 구비하고 있습니다. 거기서 여러분들은 Teddy Bear 인형, 장신구, 티셔츠, 컵 등 그밖에 많은 것을 구입하실 수 있습니다. Teddy Bear 박물관은 전에는 없었던 Teddy Bear 엔터테인먼트로 그 어느 때보다 더 많이 흥미로울 것입니다.

해설 박물관은 국경일과는 상관없이 매일 오전 9시에서 오후 7시까지 연중무휴로 개관한다고 했다.

어휘 contain 내포하다, 포함하다 gallery 화랑, 미술관 entertainment 오락, 연예, 여흥

12 ②

해석 여 자 이제 뭘 하고 싶니?

남 Fashion Show를 보러 가자.

여 그럴 수 없어. 그 쇼는 이미 10분 전에 시작했어. 게다가 우리는 예매도 하지 않았어.

남 아, 정말 그 쇼 보고 싶은데.

여 걱정 마. 세 시간 후에 볼 수 있어.

남 좋았어. Snow Festival은 몇 시에 시작하지?

여 4시 30분에 시작해.

남 오, 그것을 보려면 4시간 이상을 기다려야만 하네.

여 그래. 그럼 지금 우리가 볼 수 있는 것은 하나 밖에 없네.

남 맞아. 거기로 가자. 그 전에, Fashion Show를 예약하자.

해설 Fashion Show가 10분 전에 시작되었으므로 현재 시각은 12시 10분. 따라서 현재 볼 수 있는 것은 12시 30분에 시작되는 Bird Show이다.

13 ③

해석 (전화벨이 울린다.)

여 전화를 주어서 정말 고마워요.

남 미안해요, 여보. 메시지를 이제 막 확인했어요. 아주 힘든 날이었어. 내가 이 많은 회의를 담당하고 있다는 것 당신도 알지요? 불은 여전히 나갔나요?

여 네. 그리고 불만이 아니에요. 모든 것이 나갔어요. 이 정전의 규모가 얼마나 큰지 혹시 알아요?

남 아니오, 하지만 지금 온라인에 접속해서 알아볼게요. Carla, 약 다섯 개 주가 정전인 것 같아요!

여 언제 다시 들어올 것이라고 나와 있어요?

남 어디 봅시다. 내일이 지나야 들어올 것이라고 여기 나와 있네요.

여 오, 안 돼요.

남 당신과 함께 있어주지 못해 미안해요.

여 저도요. 촛불을 켜고 일하고 있는데 아주 낭만적이에요.

남 일을 한다고요? 전기도 안 들어오는데요?

여 **네. 노트북 컴퓨터가 아직은 충전되어 있어요.**

해설 정전이 됐는데 일을 한다는 것에 대해 놀라움을 표현했으므로 ③이 여자의 응답으로 가장 적절하다. ① 잠깐만요! 그렇게 오래 가지 않을 거예요. ② 문제될 것 없어요. 곧 할게요. ④ 아니오. 전기 없이 사는 것은 매우 불편해요. ⑤ 네, 동의해요. 촛불은 낭만적인 분위기를 조성할 수 있어요.

어휘 in charge of ~을 담당하고 있는 blackout 정전 last 지속하다 in no time 즉시(=at once) charge 충전하다

14 ③

해석 남 Sonia? 안녕, 오래간만이야.

여 Greg? 와우! 만나서 정말 반가워.

남 얼마나 됐지?

여 3년쯤 됐어.

남 음, 시간 빠르군! 그래 말해 봐. 무슨 일을 하고 지냈어?

여 똑같은 일이지. 같은 고등학교에서 여전히 스페인어를 가르치고 있어.

남 그리고 해변 가에 있는 그 대저택에서 여전히 살고 있고?

여 변변치도 않은 것인데. 그래, 너는 새로운 일이 뭐가 있어?

남 오, 그냥, 이것, 저것.

여 클럽에서 여전히 수영도 하고 운동도 하는지 궁금해.

남 나는 지금 라틴 댄스에 푹 빠져 있어.

해설 예전처럼 여전히 수영과 운동에 빠져 있는지를 묻고 있으므로 ③이 남자의 응답으로 가장 적절하다. ① 응, 나는 밖에서 서성이곤 했어. ② 오래전에 직장을 옮겼어. ④ 물론이지. 애완동물을 산책시키는 것은 정말 재미있어. ⑤ 아직도 가지고 있어. 아주 아름다운 집이야.

어휘 **nothing to speak of** 대단하지 않은 것

15 ④

해석 여 Pena 부인은 남편의 행방불명을 신고했다. 그녀의 남편은 공항에서 짐을 기다리고 있는 동안 사라졌다. 지금 Pena 부인은 경찰서에 있다. 한 경찰관이 그녀에게 남편의 인상착의와 옷, 직업을 묻는다. 남편의 직업이 은행장임을 들은 경찰관은 돈이 인출된 흔적이나 계좌 이체된 흔적이 있는지를 묻는다. 그와 자신의 계좌를 확인한 후 그녀는 어떤 거래도 없음을 알게 된다. 이 상황에서 Pena 부인이 경찰관에게 할 말로 가장 적절한 것은 무엇이겠는가?

Ms.Pena 아뇨, 돈의 인출이나 이체 기록은 없었어요.

해설 경찰관이 Pena 부인에게 돈의 인출 기록 여부를 물었으며, 확인한 결과 인출 기록이 없으므로 ④가 가장 적절하다. ① 여기에서 계좌를 개설한 것 같지는 않아요. ② 공항에 있은 후로 그를 보지 못했어요. ③ 미안합니다만 지금은 드릴 말씀이 없습니다. ⑤ 제가 뭘 잘못했나요? 저는 과속하지 않았어요, 그렇죠?

어휘 **luggage** 짐, 수화물 **transfer** (돈의) 이체, 송금 **transaction** 거래 **open an account** 계좌를 개설하다 **withdrawal** 인출 **speed** 과속하다

16-17 ②, ④

해석 (전화벨이 울린다.)

남 여보세요?

여 여보세요. Jackson 씨이신가요?

남 네, 제가 Peter Jackson입니다.

여 안녕하세요. TV29에서 전화 드렸습니다. 저희는 당신이 사시는 지역에서의 TV시청 습관에 대한 조사를 시행하고 있습니다. 몇 가지 여쭤봐도 될까요? 잠깐이면 될 거예요.

남 그러시죠, 어떻게 도와드릴까요?

여 음, 우선 저희 시청자들의 평균 연령을 알고자 합니다. 당신과 부인의 나이가 어떻게 되시나요?

남 우리는 둘 다 45세입니다.

여 좋습니다. 직장에 다니시나요?

남 네, 저는 중학교 교사이고 아내는 기자입니다.

여 자녀는 있으신가요?

남 네, 셋이 있습니다. 하지만 저희는 아이들에게 TV를 보게 하지 않아요.

여 네, 그럼 다음 질문으로 넘어가겠습니다. 대략 하루에 몇 시간 정도 가족이 TV를 시청하시나요?

남 별로 많이 보지는 않아요, 한 시간 반 정도네요. 아내와 저는 저녁에 뉴

스를 보는 것을 좋아한답니다.

여 네, Jackson씨, 시간 내주셔서 대단히 감사합니다.

해설 16 시청자들의 TV를 시청 습관에 대해 조사하려고 전화하였음을 여자의 두 번째 말에서 밝히고 있다.

17 선호하는 프로그램에 대한 언급은 남자가 추가로 말한 내용으로 여자가 질문한 사항은 아니다.

어휘 **conduct a survey** 조사하다 **find out** 알아내다 **employ** 고용하다

⊙ Dictation

01 got into / easy to remember

02 Apply this lotion

03 getting rid of soda / appreciate all those efforts

04 I go on a trip / Make sure to hold it / Thanks again for all the tips

05 fit a particular description / few more details / I'll find them

06 It's time to board / what he's talking about / board the flight

07 You are sweating / Can you do me a favor / takes half an hour

08 Let me check for you / we made a mistake / It was our fault

09 Keep the change / What do you mean / How forgetful these days

10 stop by the grocery store / to leave your suit / You forgot nothing

11 everything you want to know / is open daily / as never before

12 didn't make a reservation / we have to wait for / Let's go there

13 checked my messages / to find out / not come back on

14 How long has it been / how time flies / nothing to speak of

15 waiting for his luggage / there aren't any transactions

16-17 May I ask a few questions / Are you employed / Not too much really

34회 | 듣기 모의고사
p.204-205

01 ①	02 ④	03 ①	04 ②	05 ③	06 ③
07 ③	08 ①	09 ③	10 ④	11 ②	12 ⑤
13 ④	14 ③	15 ①	16 ③	17 ③	

01 ①

해석 여 여보, 집안일을 도와줄 수 있어요?
남 물론이죠. 난 늘 함께 할 준비가 되어 있어요. 내가 뭘 해야 하지요?
여 당신이 부엌 싱크대를 청소해요. 청소하는 동안 나는 세탁을 할게요.
남 **문제될 것 없어요.**

해설 집안일을 함께 하기로 한 가운데, 여자는 남자에게 싱크대 청소를 부탁하고 있으므로 ①이 남자의 응답으로 가장 적절하다. ② 세탁소가 어디 있는지 알아요. ③ 물이 새어나와요. 배관공에게 전화해 줄래요? ④ 조심해요. 보기보다 무거워요. ⑤ 그러면 세탁기를 새로 삽시다.

어휘 house chore 집안 허드렛일 do the laundry 세탁을 하다

02 ④

해석 남 여기요, 아주머니. 여기 제 자리에 앉으시지 그래요?
여 오, 괜찮아요.
남 아뇨, 진짜로요. 저는 곧 내리거든요.
여 **오, 감사합니다. 친절도 하셔라.**

해설 자리 양보를 하는 남자에게 여자가 할 수 있는 말이므로 ④가 여자의 응답으로 가장 적절하다. ① 당신이 그곳에서 내리는 것을 보았어요. ② 그러면 제가 가방을 들어드릴게요. ③ 휴대폰 챙기는 것을 잊으셨네요. ⑤ 오해하지 마세요. 지금 좀 피곤할 뿐이에요.

어휘 get off 내리다

03 ①

해석 남 엄마. 잠시 시간 있으세요?
여 물론이지. 무슨 일이니?
남 그게, 저 용돈이 좀 더 많아야 할 것 같아요.
여 왜? 충분히 받고 있다고 생각하지 않니?
남 그렇다고 생각했었는데요. 이제 고등학생이니까 친구들과 더 많이 어울려야 하는데, 돈이 추가로 들어.
여 그게 유일한 이유니?
남 그것은 아주 합당한 이유이고요. 또 하나의 이유가 있어요. 제가 요즈음 집안일을 더 많이 거들고 있어요.
여 예를 들자면?
남 아버지 구두를 일주일에 한 번씩 닦아 드리고 있고요, 매주 일요일에 쓰레기를 분리해서 내다 놓고 있고요, 가끔씩 어머니 설거지도 도와드리고 있어요.
여 듣고 보니 타당한 이유가 있어 보이는 구나. 아버지가 집에 오시면 의논해 보도록 하마.

해설 용돈을 올려 달라는 요구에 엄마가 그 이유를 듣고 용돈 인상을 요구할 만하다고 말하고 있는 것으로 보아 두 사람이 나누는 대화의 주제는 '용돈 인상의 타당성'이라고 볼 수 있다.

어휘 allowance 용돈 hang around with ~와 어울리다 separate 분리하다

04 ②

해석 남 안녕하세요, Linda.
여 안녕하세요, Henry. 저기요, 이런 말씀 드려서 죄송하지만, 오……. 신경 쓰지 마세요.
남 Linda, 뭔데요? 뭔가 당신의 신경을 거슬리는 것이 있군요.
여 글쎄, 그렇게 심각한 것은 아니에요. 강아지의 배설물 때문에요. Jack을 배웅할 때 그것을 꽤 자주 보게 되요.
남 오, 미안해요. 개를 묶어 놓도록 할게요. 알려주셔서 고마워요. 오, 그러니까 생각이 나는 데요, 차고 세일 때 구입하신 그 새 스테레오 시스템 기억나시죠?
여 그런데요?
남 지난밤에 아주 늦은 시간에 틀어놓고 계시던데, 그것 때문에 두세 시간 정도 잠을 못 잤어요.
여 그래요? 미안해요. 그게 그렇게 시끄러운지 몰랐어요.
남 다소 좀 크긴 했어요. 그런 적이 한 번에 불과하지만 그래도 말씀드리는 것이 좋을 것 같아서요.
여 물론이죠. 우리가 서로 불편해하는 점들을 다 내놓고 이야기해서 좋네요.
남 저도 그래요. 문제점이 생길 때마다 해결할 필요가 있어요.

해설 두 사람은 이웃 관계로 서로 불편을 끼치는 일이 있으면 이야기해서 풀어야 한다는 생각에 동의하고 있다.

어휘 see off 배웅하다 keep ~ on a leash 줄로 묶어두다 come to think of it 생각해보니, 그러고 보니 garage sale 차고 세일(집 차고에서 하는 염가판매) straighten out 해결하다 work it out 해결하다 come up (뜻밖의 일 따위가) 생기다

05 ③

해석 여 당신이 전자공학전문가인가요?
남 전문가라고 할 정도까지는 아니고요.
여 질문을 다시 해보죠. 전자공학분야에 오랫동안 몸담고 계셨나요?
남 예. 20년 동안요.
여 소형 마이크로폰을 설치할 수 있나요?
남 글쎄요, 어떤 마이크로폰이냐에 따라 다릅니다.
여 할 수 있는지 없는지만 말하세요.
남 예, 할 수 있습니다.
여 Daily News의 편집장인 Bob Gibson을 만난 적이 있죠?
남 그에 관해 들어본 적도 없는 것 같은데요.
여 그렇다면 시내 바에서 당신과 Bob이 술을 마시고 있는 이 사진을 설명해 주시겠습니까?
남 글쎄, 전 그가 Bob Gibson인지 몰랐습니다.
여 더 이상 질문 없습니다, 판사님.

해설 여자가 다그치듯 질문을 하고 남자는 피해가듯 애매하게 답변을 하고 있으며 질문 말미에 여자는 제 삼자인 판사(Your Honor)에게 더 이상 질문이 없음을 말하고 있는 것으로 보아 검사와 증인의 관계이다.

어휘 electronics 전자공학 rephrase 바꾸어 말하다 miniature 소형의, 모형의 editor 편집장 prosecutor 검사 witness 증인

06 ③

해석 여 Jimmy, 축하한다! 마침내 아버지가 되었구나.
남 어서 오세요, 어머니. 시간 맞추어 도착하셨네요. 아기를 막 보려던 참

이에요. 이쪽으로 오세요.

여 마침내 내가 첫 손자를 보게 되는 구나. 누가 내 손자인지 말하지 마렴.

남 알았어요, 어머니. 여기에요. 아기들을 보세요.

여 어디 보자. 오, 다들 똑같이 보이는구나. 양쪽 끝에서 자고 있는 두 아기
는 내 손자가 아닌 것 같고.

남 할머니가 와 계시는데 감히 어떻게 잠을 잘 수 있겠어요?

여 이 울음 소리가 손자에게서 나오는 거니?

남 아뇨. 그는 천장만 쳐다보고 있어요.

여 오, 천장을 쳐다보고 있는 아기가 둘 있구나. 한 아기는 손으로 뭔가를
잡으려는 듯 하고, 다른 아기는……. 찾은 것 같구나. 발 하나가 담요 밖
으로 나와 있지, 그렇지?

남 와우! 어떻게 아셨어요, 어머니?

여 실은, 네가 아기였을 때 그랬단다.

해설 천장을 쳐다보고 있는 아기 중 하나가 두 손으로 뭔가를 잡으려고 해야 하므로 ③
번 아기가 그림과 일치하지 않는다.

어휘 **make it in time** 시간에 맞추어 도착하다 **be about to** 막 ~하려는 참이다 **alike**
비슷한 **in the presence of** ~가 있는 데서

07 ③

해석 여 하늘을 봐.

남 엄청난 눈보라가 오는 것 같은데. 밖이 꽤 어두워지고 있어!

여 지난밤에 일기예보를 봤어. 이번 주말에 눈보라 주의보가 내렸어.

남 그래? 얼마나 많은 눈이 내릴 것이라고 말했어?

여 20센티미터. 그들이 그렇게 말했어.

남 듣고 보니 작년의 그 거대한 눈보라와 비슷할 것 같은데. 기억나? 아무
도 출근할 수 없었어. 사실상, 거의 도시 전체가 폐쇄되었지.

여 기억하고 있어. 남편은 차를 눈 속에서 파낸 후 허리에 문제가 생겼어.

남 봐! 이미 눈이 내리기 시작하고 있어.

여 이봐, 사장님께 조금 일찍 퇴근할 수 있도록 해 달라고 부탁하는 것은 어
때?

남 좋은 생각이야. 아마 사장님도 그렇게 생각하고 있을지도 몰라. 가 보
자.

해설 눈이 오기 때문에 조금 일찍 퇴근하게 해 달라고 사장님께 건의하기로 했다.

어휘 **weather forecast** 일기예보 **be supposed to** ~할 것이다 **practically** 실
제로, 거의 **dig ~ out** ~을 파내다

08 ①

해석 여 이거 믿을 수가 없군. Jim 아니니?

남 Margo? 얼굴에 여드름투성이이던 소녀?

여 응, 나야. 너 경찰관이구나.

남 응, 지금 그게 나의 직업이야.

여 고등학교 시절에 넌 항상 변호사가 되고 싶어 한 것으로 기억하는데.

남 응. 그 당시의 온통 변호사에 관한 TV프로그램 때문이었던 것 같아. 법
학과에 들어갔지만 그것이 나를 위한 직업이 아님을 깨달았어.

여 위험하지는 않니? 총을 가진 그 모든 범죄자들…….

남 가끔씩은 더 위험했으면 하는 바람이야. 지금은, 네가 보다시피, 하는
일이라곤 교통 위반 딱지를 발부하는 것뿐이야. 사실, 좀 따분하지. 그
건 그렇고, 이게 네 차니?

여 아니. 내가 차를 불법으로 도로에 주차할 사람이 아닌 것 알잖아.

해설 도로에 불법 주차된 차가 여자의 차인지를 묻는 남자의 말에 이어지는 '도로에 불
법 주차하는 사람은 아니야.'라는 말에서 대화가 도로에서 이루어짐을 알 수 있다.

어휘 **pimple** 여드름 **career** 직업 **criminal** 범죄자 **illegally** 불법으로
courtroom 법정

09 ③

해석 남 도와드릴까요?

여 예. 진열되어 있는 스웨터를 보고 있었어요.

남 핑크에 회색이 가미된 것 말씀인가요?

여 아뇨. 전 파란색 스웨터를 말씀드리는 겁니다.

남 오, 그건 남성용 스웨터인데요.

여 맞아요. 남편에게 주려고요. 어떤 색깔이 있나요?

남 짙은 녹색과 연한 청색이 있습니다.

여 둘 다 남편이 좋아하는 색상이네요. 가격은 얼마죠?

남 원래는 100달러이지만 20% 할인된 가격으로 살 수 있어요.

여 두 벌을 살게요. 각각의 색깔로.

남 그래요? 그렇다면 두 벌 째는 추가로 10달러를 깎아드릴게요.

여 좋아요!

해설 한 벌에 100달러이지만 20% 할인 중이므로 한 벌 가격은 80달러. 여자가 두 벌
을 산다고 하자 남자는 두 번째 것에 한해 10달러를 더 할인해 줄 수 있다고 하므
로 70달러가 된다. 따라서 총합은 150달러이다.

어휘 **pale** 연한 **a couple of** 두 개의 **additional** 추가의

10 ④

해석 여 아, Stewart 씨. 새 일자리를 찾고 계시죠. 본인 소개 좀 해 주시겠어
요?

남 아, 저는 어렸을 때 조종사가 되는 꿈을 꾸곤 했어요. 공항에 가서 비행
기를 지켜보는 것을 좋아했어요.

여 그렇지만 현재 조종사는 아니시죠? 왜 조종사가 되지 않았어요?

남 보다시피, 저는 안경을 써요. 14세부터 안경을 쓰기 시작했어요. 저는
심한 근시랍니다.

여 그럼 당신의 전공은 무엇인가요?

남 전기 공학을 전공했습니다.

여 좋아요, 그러면 당신의 직업 경력에 대해 말해줄 수 있나요?

남 저는 정비공입니다. 사실, 저는 라디오의 부품을 만드는 작은 회사에서
일했지만 급여가 너무 낮았어요. 그것으로 가족을 부양할 수 없었습니
다.

여 알겠습니다. 당신의 의료 기록에 대해서 물어볼 수 있을까요?

남 물론입니다. 저는 어떤 심각한 질병도 앓지 않았습니다.

여 좋습니다. 그러면 당신을 위한 적당한 일이 있습니다. 엘리베이터 수리
공입니다. 어떠세요?

남 좋아 보이는군요. 대단히 감사합니다.

해설 보수에 관해 여자가 질문한 내용은 없고 남자가 기술공 일을 그만둔 이유로 보수
가 가족을 부양하기에 충분하지 않아서라고 답하고 있다.

어휘 **nearsighted** 근시의 **mechanic** 기술자, 정비사 **support** 부양하다 **medical
history** 의료 기록

11 ②

해석 여 〈Lifestyle〉지에서는 여론조사를 통해 18세에서 44세 사이의 100명의 사람들에게 그들의 "주말"과 "휴가"에 대한 선호를 물었습니다. 조사 결과는 우리가 나이를 먹어감에 따라 "재미있게 보내는 것"에 대한 우리의 생각도 나이를 먹는다는 것을 보여 주었습니다. 18~24세의 사람들은 최고의 주말 활동으로 "파티를 여는 것"을 꼽은 반면, 25~34세의 사람들은 주말을 보내는 방법으로 하이킹이나 스키가 최고라고 말했습니다. 35~44세의 사람들은 "가족과 함께 쉬는 것"이 주말을 보내는 가장 좋은 방법이라고 답했습니다. "휴가" 항목에서는 18~24세의 사람들은 "해변으로 가는 것"이 휴가를 보내는 최고의 방법이라고 답한 반면, 25~34세의 사람들은 그보다 해외여행을 더 선호합니다. 35~44세 그룹은 지역 관광지를 차로 잠깐 둘러본다고 응답했습니다.

해설 "가족과 함께 쉬는 것"이 주말을 가장 잘 보내는 것이라고 답한 연령대는 35~44세이다.

어휘 conduct 실시하다 preference 선호 have fun 재미있게 보내다

12 ⑤

해석 여 Del, 잘 지냈어?
남 안녕, Marcia. 난 잘 지냈어. 지난밤에 음악 시상식을 봤어?
여 아니. 난 너무 바빴어. 시상식은 어땠어?
남 좋았지만 B3이 올해의 노래로 선정되었다는 것을 믿을 수 있니? 난 그 그룹을 이해할 수가 없어.
여 흠. 난 B3은 훌륭한 그룹이라고 생각해.
남 글쎄, Candy Warner는 어떻게 생각해? 그녀가 최고 신인 가수상을 수상했어.
여 당연히 받아야 할 상을 받은 것이라고 생각해.
남 나는 동의할 수 없어. 또 뭐가 있었더라? 오, 최우수 록밴드는 Horn of Plenty에게 돌아갔어.
여 대단하군. 난 그 그룹이 정말 좋아.
남 정말? 글쎄. 난 그 그룹 좋아하지 않아.
여 최우수 댄스 앨범 상은 Tessa Traynor에게 돌아갔을 거라고 확신하는데.
남 제대로 맞추었어. 하지만 난 그 상을 Jimmy Rollins가 수상했어야 했다고 생각해. 오, 최고 팝 앨범상은 The Castaways에게 돌아갔어.
여 농담하는 거지! 그들은 상을 받을 자격이 없는데.
남 전적으로 동감이야.

해설 The Castaways가 최고 팝 앨범 상을 받을 만한 자격이 없다는 것에 두 사람이 동의하고 있다.

13 ④

해석 (전화벨이 울린다.)
여 여보세요?
남 여보세요, Jessica? 나야 Rob.
여 안녕, Rob. 전에는 미안했어. 급한 일이 생겨서 약속을 지킬 수 없었어.
남 괜찮아. 적어도 전화를 해서 내가 추위에서 기다리는 것을 막아 주었잖아.
여 그나마 위안이 되네! 그건 그렇고, 무슨 일이야?
남 그게. 이번 주말에 뭘 할 건지 알아보려고 전화한 거야.
여 사실, 아무 계획이 없어. Glory Hounds의 콘서트에 가고 싶었는데 표를 구할 수가 없었어.
남 그렇다면 너의 기도가 이뤄졌네.
여 무슨 말이야?
남 **토요일 공연 표를 두 장 구했어.**

해설 가고 싶었던 콘서트의 표를 구하지 못했다는 여자의 말에 남자는 너의 기도가 이루어졌다고 언급하고 있고 여자가 그 의미를 묻고 있으므로 ④가 남자의 응답으로 가장 적절하다. ① 우리 교회에 목사님이 새로 오셨어. ② 내 말은 네가 교회에 다닌다는 거야. 그렇지 않니? ③ 그렇다고 단언해도 돼! 난 그 쇼를 보고 싶어 죽겠거든. ⑤ 무슨 의미인지 알지. 약속은 지켜져야 해.

어휘 urgent 급박한 keep one's promise 약속을 지키다 prayer 기도

14 ③

해석 여 안녕, Tom. 뭐 하고 있니?
남 안녕, Lin. 내일 경기의 일정을 적고 있어. 16세 미만인 팀간의 배구 경기가 있어.
여 선수가 누구니?
남 여기 목록이 있어. 봐봐.
여 Steve, Otis, Ali, Tom. 왜! 너도 뛰는구나. Nick? Nick은 16세 미만이 아닌데! 지난 토요일에 그의 생일 파티에 갔어. 지난 토요일에 16세가 되었어.
남 그래서 뭐? 16세 하고도 3일일 뿐인데.
여 안 돼, Tom. 그가 16세면 16세 미만은 아니야.
남 이봐, Lin. Nick은 경기를 뛰어야 해. 그가 경기를 하지 않으면 누구도 경기를 할 수 없어. 그가 없으면 팀을 구성할 만한 충분한 선수가 없어.
여 **그것은 변명이 될 수 없어. 공평하지 않은 일이야.**

해설 16세 미만의 경기에 16세가 넘은 친구가 참가하는 것에 대해 부당성을 여자가 지적하고 있는 상황이므로 ③이 응답으로 가장 적절하다. ① 난 네가 훌륭한 선수라는 것을 알고 있어. ② 미안하지만 이번에는 나를 빼 줘. ④ 그러니까 이겼는지 졌는지 말해 봐. ⑤ 나도 거기에 가면 좋겠는데 난 그때 바빠.

15 ①

해석 여 Angela는 기자이다. 그녀는 현지의 유력 신문사에서 일한다. 요즈음 그녀는 노숙자에 관한 연재 기사를 쓰고 있다. 오늘 그녀는 거리에서 사는 한 노숙자와 인터뷰를 했다. 인터뷰에서 그녀는 그 노숙자의 과거에 관해 많이 알게 되었다. 놀랍게도, 그녀는 그가 대학 학위를 가지고 있으며 한때 대기업에서 일한 적이 있다는 것을 알았다. 호기심이 발동한 그녀는 그가 어떻게 해서 거리에서 구걸하여, 그날 벌어서 그날 먹고 사는 신세가 되었는지를 알고 싶었다. 이런 상황에서 그녀가 노숙자에게 할 말로 가장 적절한 것은 무엇인가?
Angela **그래서, 그 후에 어떻게 되었는지 말씀해 주세요.**

해설 인터뷰를 하던 노숙자가 대학을 졸업하고 대기업에 다닌 적이 있다는 것을 알고 호기심이 발동하여 그 경위를 알고자 하는 상황이므로 ①이 가장 적절하다. ② 그날 벌어 그날 살아가는 삶이 어떤가요? ③ 부모님들은 당신이 무슨 일을 하는지 아세요? ④ 설마 당신의 인생에 만족하신다는 것은 아니겠죠. ⑤ 인터뷰 감사합

니다. 큰 도움이 되었습니다.

어휘 **article** 기사 **degree** 학위 **end up -ing** 결국 ~하게 되다 **live from hand to mouth** 하루 벌어 하루 살다

16–17 ③, ③

해석 여 안녕하세요. 많은 분들이 이곳에 와주신 것을 보니 기쁩니다. 오늘 시간을 내주셔서 감사합니다. 오늘 이렇게 뵙고자 한 것은 아주 중요한 한 가지 사안에 대해 여러분들의 협조를 요청하고 싶어서입니다. 최근에 몇몇 학부모님이 학생들을 승용차로 등교시키고 있는 데 그것과 관련하여 몇 가지 문제점들이 대두되고 있습니다. 첫째로, 매우 위험합니다. 여러분이 자제분을 내려주는 곳은 많은 학생들이 바쁘게 등교하는 곳입니다. 사고가 날 수도 있습니다. 둘째, 이것이 교통의 흐름을 막기 때문에 인근 주민으로부터 많은 민원이 야기됩니다. 셋째, 부모님이 차를 가지고 있지 않거나 태워 줄 수 없는 학생들의 마음을 상하게 할 수 있습니다. 마지막으로 못지않게 중요한 것은 부모님에게 의존하여 등교하는 아이들은 밖에 많이 나갈 필요가 없기 때문에 신발 및 교복에 관한 학교 규정을 어기는 경향이 있습니다. 학교의 모든 일을 책임지고 있는 사람으로서, 여러분이 협조해 주시면 정말로 감사하겠습니다.

해설 16 여자는 학교의 모든 일을 책임지는 사람이므로 교장이고, 듣는 사람은 학생들을 승용차로 등하교 시키는 사람, 즉 학부모이다.

17 승용차 등교의 문제점에 대한 언급 가운데 주변 환경오염에 관한 내용은 제시되지 않았다.

어휘 **involved in** ~가 관련된 **vehicle** 차량 **give ~ a ride** 차로 태워다 주다 **last but not least** 마지막으로 **turn to** 의존하다

🎯 Dictation

01 with some house chores / do the laundry

02 I'm getting off soon

03 I need a bigger allowance / I have one more reason / I sometimes help you

04 keep him on a leash / we've straightened everything out

05 Let me rephrase my question / I've heard of him / No further questions

06 Two babies sleeping at both ends / looking at the ceiling / One of his legs is sticking out

07 snowstorm warning for this weekend / the whole city was shut down / ask the boss to allow us to go home

08 You're a police officer / All those criminals out there / who parks her car illegally on the road

09 What colors does it come in / one of each in both colors

10 looking for a new job / I used to love going / tell me about your job history / ask for your medical history

11 describe their preferences / having fun / having a party / relaxing with the family / going to the beach

12 How was the show / she got what she deserves / can't agree with you more

13 I couldn't keep my promise / your prayers are answered

14 Who is on the team / He turned 16 / nobody can play

15 works for a leading local newspaper / Surprisingly enough / how he ended up begging on the street

16-17 I need your cooperation / Where you drop them off / tend to break the school rules

35회 듣기 모의고사

p.210-211

01 ②	02 ⑤	03 ②	04 ①	05 ③	06 ③
07 ④	08 ①	09 ①	10 ⑤	11 ⑤	12 ③
13 ②	14 ②	15 ④	16 ①	17 ④	

01 ②

해석 남 제 손에 뭐가 있는지 보세요.
여 와우! 근사해 보이네요. 그게 뭐예요?
남 제가 뒷마당의 과일 나무에서 땄어요. 맛을 보시고 의견을 말해 주세요.
여 흠, 약간 쓴 것 같네요.

해설 남자는 여자에게 자신이 뒷마당에서 딴 과일을 맛보고 의견을 말해 달라고 했으므로 ②가 여자의 응답으로 가장 적절하다. ① 당신은 남을 잘 배려해요. ③ 이것은 당신을 위한 것이에요. 생일 축하해요. ④ 이것이 제가 찾고 있던 것이 아니에요. ⑤ 잘 차려 입으셨지만 제 취향은 아니네요.

어휘 **taste** 취향, 기호; 맛보다 **considerate** 사려 깊은 **rather** 약간, 꽤

02 ⑤

해석 여 안녕, Ben. 어떻게 지냈어?
남 잘 지냈어. 학교로 돌아갈까 생각중이야.
여 그것 잘 됐네! 뭐 때문에 그런 결심을 한 거야?
남 뭐, 좀 더 도전적인 일을 하고 싶어서.

해설 여자가 학교로 돌아가서 다시 공부하기로 결심하게 된 계기를 묻고 있으므로 ⑤가 남자의 응답으로 가장 적절하다. ① 빠를수록 좋아. ② 네 조언을 따를게. ③ 내 결정이 옳은 것으로 밝혀졌어. ④ 그래? 너는 무엇을 전공하기로 결심했니?

어휘 **what made you ~** 무엇 때문에[왜] ~ 했니? **follow** ~을 따르다 **turn out** ~임이 밝혀지다 **challenging** 도전 의식을 북돋우는

03 ②

해석 (전화벨이 울린다.)
남 Cornerstone Properties에 전화 주셔서 감사합니다. 여기 이번 주 새로운 부동산 목록을 살펴보시죠. 이번 주 가장 좋은 상품은

Lakeshore가에 있는 멋진 해안가 아파트입니다. 이 꼭대기 층 아파트는 각각 화장실이 딸려 있는 세 개의 커다란 침실을 갖추고 있습니다. 또한 개별 화장실 하나와 거실 바깥쪽으로 커다란 발코니가 있습니다. 부엌은 작지만 모든 최신 가전제품을 다 갖추고 있습니다. 이 아파트는 반드시 한번 보셔야 합니다. 서두르세요! 아주 빨리 팔릴 겁니다. 이 부동산에 관해 교환원과 통화하고 싶으시면 1번을 누르시고 등록 번호 7-4-1을 말씀하세요.

해설 금주의 최고 아파트를 소개하며 반드시 한번 보라고 권하고 그 방법을 알려주고 있다. 따라서 부동산 물건을 광고하는 것이 목적이다.

어휘 property 부동산 look 봄, 보기 stunning 굉장히 멋진 separate 별개의 appliance 가전제품 must-see 꼭 보아야 할 것

04 ①

해석 남 와 주셔서 감사합니다.
여 천만에요. Jimmy에게 무슨 문제가 있어 보이나요?
남 글쎄, 그가 집중을 잘하지 못 하는 것 같아요. 학습 능력에 대해서도 다소 우려되는 바가 있고요.
여 예를 들어주실 수 있을까요?
남 수학 능력이 조금 약해요.
여 수학이 그의 장점 중의 하나는 아니라는 것을 알고 있어요.
남 그리고 맞춤법도 다소 부족합니다.
여 그렇군요. 가정교사를 붙여야 할까요?
남 그게 나쁜 생각은 아니지만 아무래도 돈이 좀 들지요. 그가 숙제를 할 때 옆에서 앉아 있는 것으로 충분할 것 같아요.
여 감사합니다. 염두에 두겠습니다.
남 Jimmy는 잠재력이 뛰어나기 때문에 그가 나아지는 모습을 보고 싶어요.
여 그렇게 말씀해 주시니 너무 감사합니다.

해설 학생의 학습 능력을 키우는 문제로 교사와 학부모가 대화를 나누고 있으므로 학습 능력 개발이 대화의 주제로 가장 적절하다.

어휘 ability 능력 spelling 맞춤법 tutor 가정교사 keep A in mind A를 잊지 않고 있다 potential 잠재력

05 ③

해석 여 여기, 제가 문을 잡아드릴게요.
남 고마워요.
여 가지고 계신 서류들이 다 뭐에요?
남 회사 연간 보고서를 작업하고 있어요. 시간이 많이 걸리네요. 그래서 집에 일을 좀 가져가는 중이에요.
여 정말 피곤해 보이네요. 잠도 안 주무시나 봐요.
남 사실, 잘 못 자요. 할 일이 많아요. Bob이 병원에 입원 중이어서 그의 일까지 해야 해요.
여 오, 다른 분들 중에 도와주실 분이 없나요?
남 부탁을 해 봤는데, 모두들 너무 바쁜데요.
여 그것 참 안 됐군요. 그건 그렇고, 차는 지하에 주차되어 있나요?
남 예. 지하까지 타고 내려갈 거예요.
여 알았어요. 저는 여기서 내려야 해요. 제가 도울 일이 있으면 알려주세요.

남 그렇게 말해주어서 고마워요. 내일 뵐게요.

해설 문을 잡아주겠다는 여자의 첫 말과 지하에 차가 주차되어 있어서 지하까지 내려간다는 남자의 말, 여자는 여기서 내린다는 말 등을 종합하면 승강기 안에서 이루어지는 대화임을 알 수 있다.

어휘 hold ~을 붙들다, 잡다 annual 연간의 basement 지하

06 ③

해석 여 할아버지, 이 흑백 사진은 뭐죠?
남 그건 할아버지가 군대에 있을 때 찍은 사진이란다. 누가 할아버지인지 맞추어 보렴.
여 글쎄, 모든 군인들이 똑같은 모자를 쓰고 있어요. 그래서 할아버지를 알아보기가 더 어렵네요.
남 잘 살펴보렴. 모자에 선이 보이지 않니?
여 오, 그렇군요. 할아버지 모자에 줄이 몇 개 있었죠?
남 난 병장이었어. 그러니까 네 줄이 있는 모자를 쓰고 있었어.
여 잠시 보고요. 네 줄 모자를 쓰고 있는 군인이 세 명이 있는데, 할아버지는 다소 큰 편이니까. 가장 작은 군인은 아니겠군요.
남 그래.
여 그리고 할아버지는 안경을 쓰고 있고. 그렇다면 우측에서 두 번째 남자이겠군요.
남 사실 그 때는 시력이 아주 좋아서 안경을 쓰지 않았어.

해설 병장(네 줄 계급 모자)이고 키가 가장 작은 사람은 아닌 가운데, 손녀딸은 할아버지의 현재 안경을 쓴 모습을 보고 안경 쓴 병장이 할아버지라고 생각하지만 할아버지는 당시에는 시력이 좋아 안경을 쓸 필요가 없었다고 말하고 있으므로 안경을 안 쓴 병장임을 알 수 있다.

어휘 black-and white 흑백 recognize 알아보다 sergeant 병장 eyesight 시력

07 ④

해석 남 Melissa, 아직도 그 남자를 사귀고 있니? 그 남자 이름이 뭐였지?
여 Roger. 응. 사실, 다음 달에 결혼할 예정이야.
남 그래? 서로 사귀기 시작한지 석 달 쯤 되지 않니?
여 응. 정확히 하자면 3개월하고 5일이야.
남 와우! 너희 둘 정말 좋아하는 구나. 준비는 어떻게 되어가니?
여 아주 순조롭게 되어가고 있어. 우리가 직접 계획하고 있지만 부모님들이 재정적으로 많이 도와주고 계셔.
남 일이 많을 거야. 이봐, 어디 가서 이야기 좀 하는 게 어때?
여 나도 그랬으면 좋겠지만 웨딩드레스를 맞추러 가는 중이야.
남 멋지겠다.
여 웨딩드레스를 입었을 때 멋지게 보이려고 지금 살을 빼고 있어.
남 행운을 빌어. 그럼 나중에 보자.

해설 결혼식에 입을 웨딩드레스를 맞추러 가고 있음을 여자의 말을 통해서 알 수 있다.

어휘 go out with A A와 사귀다 get married 결혼하다 see 교제하다 to be exact 정확히 finance 재정 get fitted for ~에 맞추다

08 ①

해석 (전화가 울린다.)

여 여보세요?

남 네, 엄마.

여 그래, Paul. 공부는 잘 되니?

남 그래서 전화를 거는 거예요. 집에 손님들이 아직 계세요?

여 응, 계셔. 그것은 왜 묻니?

남 글쎄, 여기서 집중이 잘 안 되어서요. 너무 시끄러워요.

여 무슨 말이요? 도서관에 있는 것 아니니?

남 예, 맞아요. 그렇지만 누군가의 핸드폰이 늘 울리는 것 같아요.

여 그 도서관에는 핸드폰에 관한 방침이 없니?

남 있어요. 핸드폰을 끄거나 진동으로 해 놓으라는 표시가 사방에 있어요. 그렇지만 대부분 신경을 쓰지 않는 분위기 같아요.

여 사서에게 이야기하지 그래? 그들이 틀림없이 뭔가 조치를 취할 거야.

남 알았어요. 아무래도 그렇게 해야겠어요.

해설 도서관에서 휴대 전화가 자꾸 울려서 공부에 집중이 안 되어 집에서 공부가 가능한지 알아보려고 전화를 했다.

어휘 concentrate 집중하다 policy 정책, 방침 all over the place 사방에 vibrate mode 진동 모드 care 관심을 가지다 librarian 사서

09 ①

해석 남 안녕하세요. 뭘 도와드릴까요?

여 안녕하세요. 이 사진들이 아주 잘 나와서요. 액자에 넣고 싶어요.

남 알겠습니다. 어떤 액자를 하고 싶으세요?

여 글쎄, 저기 있는 하트 모양의 액자로 하면 가격이 얼마나 될까요?

남 원래는 액자 한 개 당 10달러이지만 10%를 할인해 드릴 게요.

여 조금 더 깎아 줄 수 없어요? 제가 최근에 필름을 다섯 통이나 현상한 것 아시잖아요.

남 사실, 그래서 10%를 깎아드리는 겁니다. 사진을 몇 장이나 액자에 넣을 건가요?

여 모두 합해서 10장이요.

남 그렇다면 추가로 1달러 더 깎아드리죠. 물론 사진 한 장당 말입니다.

여 이제 적당한 가격이네요.

해설 10달러에서 10%(1달러)를 깎아 주었고, 후에 추가로 1달러씩 더 깎아 주었으므로 80달러가 정답이다.

어휘 frame 액자에 넣다 develop 현상하다 reasonable (가격이) 적당한

10 ⑤

해석 여 여보세요. Central Hospital에서 전화 드립니다. 전화 드린 이유는 화요일 오전 10시 30분에 따님의 진료 예약이 되어 있다는 것을 확인하기 위해서입니다. 따님은 Jennings 박사의 진찰을 받도록 되어 있습니다. 박사님의 진료실은 병원 10층에 있습니다. 10분 일찍 오셔서 접수원에게 도착 사실을 알려주시기 바랍니다. 혹시 예약을 취소하려거든, 적어도 한 시간 전에는 알려주시기 바랍니다. 735-9116으로 전화를 하시면 됩니다. 즐거운 하루 보내시고, 내일 뵙겠습니다.

해설 진료 과목에 대한 언급은 없다.

어휘 make sure ~을 분명히 하다 receptionist 접수원

11 ⑤

해석 여 George, 너 야구 하지, 그렇지 않니?

남 예, 그래요. 기회가 날 때마다 하고 있어요.

여 야구 장비는 어디서 구입하니?

남 시내에 Mickey's Sports라는 좋은 스포츠 용품점이 있어요. 온갖 종류의 운동 장비를 갖추고 있고 가격도 괜찮아요.

여 잘 됐네. 내 딸이 야구를 막 시작했거든. 그녀가 뭐가 필요할까?

남 글러브 있나요?

여 아니, 유니폼만 받았어. 이제 7살이거든. 야구 모자는 있지만 그게 다야.

남 그렇다면 좋은 글러브가 필요할 거예요. 배트와 공도 있어야지요. 아, 분명히 좋은 야구화가 필요할 거예요. 그러면 충분할 것 같은데요.

여 아주 도움이 많이 되었어. 고맙다, George!

해설 야구복은 동네 야구팀에서 받은 것이지 남자가 구매를 추천한 제품이 아니다.

어휘 equipment 장비 sporting goods 스포츠 용품 athletic 운동의 definitely 분명히

12 ③

해석 남 안녕하세요. 오늘의 전국 일기 예보입니다. 북서부지역은 현재 낮은 온도를 보이고 있으며 약간의 비와 함께 시원하고 구름이 끼겠습니다. 우산 잊지 마세요. 남동부지역은 날씨가 매우 좋을 것입니다. 일반적으로 따뜻하고 해가 나겠으며 때때로 가벼운 바람이 불겠습니다. 중남부지역은 종일 비가 내리겠으며 오후부터는 강한 바람도 불 것입니다. 기온은 15도 정도로 떨어질 것으로 보입니다. 동북부지역에 계실 거라면 따뜻하게 입으시기 바랍니다. 날씨가 차고 바람이 심할 것이며 눈이 계속 내릴 것입니다. 남서부지역은 기온이 높고 곳곳에 회오리바람의 가능성이 있습니다. 이상이 지금 시간의 예보입니다. 즐거운 하루 보내세요.

해설 중남부지역의 온도는 약 15도로 떨어질 것이라고 했다.

어휘 pleasant (날씨가) 좋은, 상쾌한 occasional 가끔의, 때때로의 throughout ~ 동안, 내내 degree (온도계 등의) 도 Celsius 섭씨 steady 끊임없는

13 ②

해석 여 Jake, Juan의 생일 파티에 초대 받았지?

남 응. 하지만 가야 할지 모르겠어. 넌 갈 거니?

여 물론이지! 근사할 거야. Juan은 금년에 멕시코식 생일 파티를 열거야. 피나타를 할거야. 근사하지 않니?

남 그게 뭔데?

여 그것은 종이로 만든 동물인데 캔디로 가득 차 있어. 그런 다음, 나뭇가지처럼 높은 곳에 매달아. 우선, 생일을 맞은 소년의 눈을 가려.

남 재미있겠다. 그런 다음에는 뭘 하지?

여 그런 다음 그가 피나타를 막대기로 쳐. 그러고 나서 우리가 순서대로 피나타를 치는 거야.

남 알겠어. 그게 열리자마자 모든 캔디가 쏟아져 나오는 거지?

여 맞아. 재미있을 거야. 새로운 사람들을 만날 좋은 기회일 거야. 게다가 Juan의 어머니가 요리를 기가 막히게 잘 하신다고 들었어!

남 **그 모든 것을 놓칠 수 없지. 알았어, 갈게!**

해설 생일파티에 초대 받고도 망설이는 남자가 생일파티의 근사한 내용과 뛰어난 요리

솜씨에 대해 듣고 나서 하는 말이므로 ②가 가장 적절하다. ① 미안하지만 난 요리를 못 해. ③ 오, 그에게 초대장을 보내는 것을 잊었어. ④ 어머니가 아주 자랑스럽겠구나. ⑤ 내가 그의 파티에 초대받으면 좋으련만.

어휘 **fabulous** 근사한 **blindfold** 눈가리개를 하다 **take turns -ing** 번갈아 ~하다 **crack open** 부서져서 열리다 **awesome** 최고의

14 ②

해석 여 핼리혜성에 대해 들어본 적 있어? Edmund Halley의 이름을 딴 혜성이야.
남 그것에 관한 뭐 말이야?
여 그것이 75년마다 온다는 것을 알고 있니?
남 아니. 마지막으로 온 게 언제야?
여 1986년이야. 내가 태어나기도 전이었어!
남 그러니까 그것은 2061년에나 돌아오겠네, 그렇지?
여 응. 혜성 얘기를 하다 보니, 저 위에 하나 있네. 봐봐!
남 어디? 오, 저건 혜성이 아냐. 저건 유성이야. 유성을 보면 소원을 빌어야 해!
여 그래, 넌 뭘 빌었니?
남 그것은 비밀이야. 내 입은 봉해졌어. 너는 뭘 빌었어?
여 <u>나는 그런 것들을 안 믿어.</u>

해설 유성을 보고 소원을 비는 관행을 알고 있는 남자가 여자에게 뭘 빌었는지를 묻고 있으므로 ②가 여자의 응답으로 가장 적절하다. ① 아마 내가 죽은 다음에 올 거야. ③ 정말로 그것을 보고 싶었으니까. ④ 사실, 난 천문학을 전공하고 싶어. ⑤ 어렸을 때 유성을 쫓곤 했었지.

어휘 **comet** 혜성 **name after** ~의 이름을 따서 짓다 **shooting star** 유성 **make a wish** 소원을 빌다 **seal** 봉하다 **astronomy** 천문학 **chase** ~을 뒤쫓다

15 ④

해석 여 Andrew는 작은 회사에서 일한다. 그는 첫 직장인데다가 자신의 상사와 동료가 마음에 들어서 자신의 일을 좋아한다. Andrew는 어머니에게서 전화를 받는다. 어머니에 따르면 식당을 40년 동안 경영해 오시던 아버지가 갑자기 쓰러지셨으며 위독하다고 한다. Andrew는 서둘러 뉴욕행 비행기를 예약하고 공항으로 향한다. 공항으로 가던 도중 그는 어린 시절 아버지가 손님을 맞이하고 테이블을 차리는 법을 가르쳐 주시던 때를 되돌아본다. 그러다가 그는 사장에게 전화를 해서 며칠 휴가를 요청해야 함을 깨닫는다. 그가 전화를 하고 사장이 받는다. 몇 마디 주고받은 후 그는 이제 전화를 건 이유를 말씀드려야 한다고 생각한다. 이 상황에서 Andrew가 사장에게 할 말로 가장 적절한 것은?
Andrew <u>며칠 휴가를 낼 수 있을까요? 아버님이 상태가 안 좋으세요.</u>

해설 아버지가 위독하다는 말을 듣고 공항으로 이동하던 중 사장에게 전화를 걸어 휴가를 요청해야 하는 상황이므로 ④가 남자가 할 말로 가장 적절하다. ① 아버지는 어떠세요? 상태가 좋아 지시나요? ② 아버님의 식당으로 초대하고 싶어요. ③ 저희 아버지의 식당을 인수하시는 것이 어때요? ⑤ 그만 두어야 할 것 같아요. 제가 아버지의 식당을 물려받아야 해요.

어휘 **co-worker** 동료 **own** ~을 소유하다 **collapse** 쓰러지다 **critically ill** 심각할 정도로 아픈 **hurriedly** 서둘러, 황급히 **look back on** ~을 회상하다 **set the table** 상을 차리다 **take over** 인수하다

16–17 ①, ④

해석 남 안녕하세요. 6시 뉴스, Ted Parker입니다. 한때 미국에서 두 번째로 큰 서점이었던 Borders가 이제 역사 속으로 사라진다는 소식을 전하게 되어 유감입니다. Borders가 어제 파산을 선언했습니다. Borders는 1971년, 미시간 대학의 캠퍼스에 처음으로 서점을 열었습니다. 결국 세계적으로 1,200개 이상의 서점을 갖춘 회사로 성장하였습니다. 미국에서 두 번째로 큰 서점이 되었습니다. 하지만, 서툰 경영, 온라인 시장에 대한 잘못된 판단, 불안정한 경제 사정이 Borders를 괴롭혔습니다. 오늘 Borders는 남아 있는 399개의 서점을 폐업하고 11,000여 명에 달하는 종업원을 해고한다고 선언하였습니다. Borders의 실패를 바라보는 서점 업계는 앞으로 어떤 형태로든 책을 파는 것에 대해 비관적 입장입니다. 전문가 Michael Norris의 말입니다. "책을 사는 사람들이 점점 더 줄어들 거예요. Borders에서 책을 구입하던 사람들이 전자책으로 돌아설 것이라고 믿는다면 그들은 이빨의 요정을 믿는 것이랍니다." 출판 업계가 큰 위기에 빠져 있는 것 같습니다.

해설 16 Borders의 파산을 계기로 위기에 빠진 출판 업계에 대해 보도하고 있다.
17 Borders의 설립자에 대한 언급은 없다.

어휘 **declare** ~을 선언하다 **bankruptcy** 파산 **misreading** 잘못 읽음 **rocky** 불안정한 **lay off** 해고하다 **pessimistic** 비관적인 **analyst** 분석가 **turn into** ~으로 변하다 **crisis** 위기

🎯 Dictation

01 in my hand / tell me what you think

02 going back to school

03 Our best buy this week / all the latest appliances

04 he is failing to concentrate / Should I get him a tutor / keep that in mind

05 hold the door for you / You look really tired / ride this to the basement

06 I was in the army / I wore the hat with four lines / I had such a good eyesight

07 getting married next month / to be exact / with the finances / to get fitted for my wedding dress

08 still over at our place / It's too noisy / all over the place / what I should do

09 These pictures came out really well / Can you come down a little bit more / quite reasonable

10 you have made a reservation for / on the tenth floor / If you have to cancel your reservation

11 I play every chance I get / Does she have a glove

12 with some light rain / calls for rain throughout the day / with a steady snowfall

13 if I should go / we blindfold the birthday boy / it cracks open

14 it comes around / you should make a wish

15 suddenly collapsed and is critically ill / ask for a few days off

16-17 declared bankruptcy / a misreading of the online market / pessimistic about selling books / seems to be in deep crisis

만점 적중

수능 듣기 모의고사 35회

수능 영어영역 듣기평가 대비

수능 듣기 만점을 위한 최적의 학습서

➔ **실제 수능 형식**을 가장 잘 반영한 문제 구성

➔ 오답과 문제 함정을 **정확하고 완벽하게 분석한 해설**

➔ 들고 다니며 손쉽게 암기하는 **휴대용 어휘 리스트 제공**

듣기 MP3 & 휴대용 어휘 암기 리스트
www.nexusbook.com에서 무료 다운로드

◀ 🎧 **MP3 바로 듣기**

LISTENING

핵심구문 204개로 직독직해 완전정복!

구문독해
204

★★★★★
**강남인강
선정 교재**
★★★★★

- **독해와 어법을** 한번에 끝내는 효과적인 학습서
- 핵심 구문 204개로 막힘 없이 **직독직해 완성**
- 2000개의 문제를 통한 **핵심 구문 반복학습 효과**
- 혼동하기 쉬운 구문의 비교 학습을 통한 이해력 향상
- 실제 시험 유형의 장문 **어법 문제 수록**

| **구문독해 204** | BOOK 1 ǀ 김상근 지음 ǀ 205×265 ǀ 320쪽(정답 및 해설 포함) ǀ 각 권 15,000원 |
| | BOOK 2 ǀ 김상근 지음 ǀ 205×265 ǀ 340쪽(정답 및 해설 포함) ǀ 각 권 15,000원 |

NEXUS makes your next day

www.nexusEDU.kr
t.02-330-5500 f.02-330-5555
NEXUS Edu

THIS IS

전면 개정판

READING

중등부터 고등까지 모든 독해의 확실한 해결책!

▶ 실생활부터 전문적인 학술 분야까지 다양한 소재의 지문 수록
▶ 서술형 내신 대비까지 제대로 준비하는 문법 포인트 정리
▶ 지문 이해 확인 또 확인, 본문 연습 문제 + Review Test
▶ 원어민의 발음으로 듣는 전체 지문 MP3 (QR 코드 & www.nexusbook.com)
▶ 확실한 마무리 3단 콤보 WORKBOOK

강남인강
선정 교재

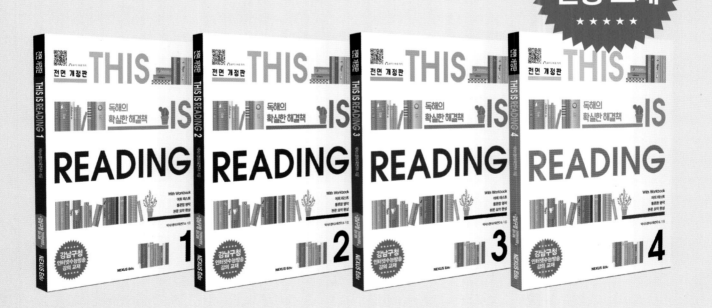

THIS IS READING

THIS IS READING 전면 개정판 1	넥서스영어교육연구소 지음 I 205×265 I 118쪽 I 10,000원
THIS IS READING 전면 개정판 2	넥서스영어교육연구소 지음 I 205×265 I 122쪽 I 10,000원
THIS IS READING 전면 개정판 3	넥서스영어교육연구소 지음 I 205×265 I 122쪽 I 10,000원
THIS IS READING 전면 개정판 4	넥서스영어교육연구소 지음 I 205×265 I 122쪽 I 10,000원